FAIRBAIRN AND THE OBJECT RELATIONS TRADITION

LINES OF DEVELOPMENT
Evolution of Theory and Practice over the Decades

Series Editors: Norka T. Malberg and Joan Raphael-Leff

Other titles in the series:

The Anna Freud Tradition: Lines of Development—Evolution of Theory and Practice over the Decades
    edited by Norka T. Malberg and Joan Raphael-Leff

FAIRBAIRN AND THE OBJECT RELATIONS TRADITION

Edited by
Graham S. Clarke and David E. Scharff

KARNAC

First published in 2014 by
Karnac Books Ltd
118 Finchley Road
London NW3 5HT

Copyright © 2014 to Graham S. Clarke and David E. Scharff for the edited collection, and to the individual authors for their contributions.

The rights of the contributors to be identified as the authors of this work have been asserted in accordance with §§ 77 and 78 of the Copyright Design and Patents Act 1988.

All rights reserved. No part of this publication may be reproduced, stored in a retrieval system, or transmitted, in any form or by any means, electronic, mechanical, photocopying, recording, or otherwise, without the prior written permission of the publisher.

British Library Cataloguing in Publication Data

A C.I.P. for this book is available from the British Library

ISBN-13: 978-1-78049-082-3

Typeset by V Publishing Solutions Pvt Ltd., Chennai, India

Printed in Great Britain

www.karnacbooks.com

CONTENTS

ACKNOWLEDGEMENTS — xi

ABOUT THE EDITORS AND CONTRIBUTORS — xiii

SERIES EDITORS' FOREWORD — xix

INTRODUCTION — xxi
by James S. Grotstein

INTRODUCTION — xxiii
by Graham S. Clarke and David E. Scharff

PROLOGUE — xxxi
Fairbairn the writer
by Maurice Whelan

PART I: HISTORICAL

INTRODUCTION TO PART I — 3
Graham S. Clarke and David E. Scharff

CHAPTER ONE
From instinct to self: the evolution and implications of W. R. D. Fairbairn's theory of object relations — 5
David E. Scharff and Ellinor Fairbairn Birtles

CHAPTER TWO
From Oedipus to Antigone: Hegelian themes in Fairbairn 27
Gal Gerson

CHAPTER THREE
Making Fairbairn's psychoanalysis thinkable: Henry Drummond's natural laws of the spiritual world 41
Gavin Miller

CHAPTER FOUR
Splitting in the history of psychoanalysis: from Janet and Freud to Fairbairn, passing through Ferenczi and Suttie 49
Gabriele Cassullo

CHAPTER FIVE
Fairbairn, Suttie, and Macmurray—an essay 59
Neville Symington

CHAPTER SIX
Religion in the life and work of W. R. D. Fairbairn 69
Marie T. Hoffman and Lowell W. Hoffman

CHAPTER SEVEN
Fairbairn and homosexuality: sex *versus* conscience 87
Hilary J. Beattie

CHAPTER EIGHT
Fairbairn in Argentina: the "Fairbairn Space" in the Argentine Psychoanalytic Association (APA) 101
Mercedes Campi, Adrián Besuschio, Luis Oswald, Isabel Sharpin de Basili, and Rubén M. Basili

CHAPTER NINE
Some comments about Ronald Fairbairn's impact today 115
Otto F. Kernberg

PART II: CLINICAL

INTRODUCTION TO PART II 127
Graham S. Clarke and David E. Scharff

CHAPTER TEN
Why read Fairbairn? 131
Thomas H. Ogden

CHAPTER ELEVEN
On the origin of internal objects in the works of Fairbairn and Klein
and the possible therapeutic consequences 147
Bernhard F. Hensel

CHAPTER TWELVE
Fairbairn: Oedipus reconfigured by trauma 161
Eleanore M. Armstrong-Perlman

CHAPTER THIRTEEN
Sitting with marital tensions: the work of Henry Dicks in
applying Fairbairn's ideas to couple relationships 175
Molly Ludlam

CHAPTER FOURTEEN
W. R. D. Fairbairn's contribution to the study of personality disorders 185
Carlos Rodríguez-Sutil

CHAPTER FIFTEEN
Fairbairn: abuse, trauma, and multiplicity 197
Valerie Sinason

CHAPTER SIXTEEN
Fairbairn and multiple personality 209
Paul Finnegan and Graham S. Clarke

CHAPTER SEVENTEEN
Fairbairn and "emptiness pathology" 223
Rubén M. Basili, Isabel Sharpin de Basili, Adrián Besuschio, Mercedes Campi,
and Luis Oswald

CHAPTER EIGHTEEN
Fairbairn's unique contributions to dream interpretation 237
Joshua Levy

CHAPTER NINETEEN
The analyst as good object: a Fairbairnian perspective 249
Neil J. Skolnick

CHAPTER TWENTY
Expanding Fairbairn's reach 263
David E. Scharff

PART III: THEORETICAL

INTRODUCTION TO PART III 277
Graham S. Clarke and David E. Scharff

CHAPTER TWENTY-ONE
The contribution of W. R. D. Fairbairn (1889–1965) to psychoanalytic theory and practice 281
John Padel

CHAPTER TWENTY-TWO
John Padel's contribution to an understanding of Fairbairn's object relations theory 295
Graham S. Clarke

CHAPTER TWENTY-THREE
Fairbairn elaborated: Guntrip and the psychoanalytic romantic model 309
Michael Stadter

CHAPTER TWENTY-FOUR
From Fairbairn to Winnicott 323
Henri Vermorel

CHAPTER TWENTY-FIVE
Fairbairn and Ferenczi 333
Graham S. Clarke

CHAPTER TWENTY-SIX
Mitchell reading Fairbairn 343
Ariel Liberman

CHAPTER TWENTY-SEVEN
Fairbairn's influence on Stephen Mitchell's theoretical and clinical work 355
Aleksandar Dimitrijevic

CHAPTER TWENTY-EIGHT
Self and society, trauma and the link 365
Jill Savege Scharff

CHAPTER TWENTY-NINE
Fairbairn and Pichon-Rivière: object relations, link, and group 379
Lea S. de Setton

CHAPTER THIRTY
The "intuitive position" and its relationship to creativity, science, and art in Fairbairn's work 391
Ricardo Juan Rey

CHAPTER THIRTY-ONE
Revising Fairbairn's structural theory 397
David P. Celani

CHAPTER THIRTY-TWO
Fairbairn's accomplishment is good science 411
Joseph Schwartz

CHAPTER THIRTY-THREE
Fairbairn and partitive conceptions of mind 417
Tamas Pataki

CHAPTER THIRTY-FOUR
Fairbairn and the philosophy of intersubjectivity 431
James L. Poulton

PART IV: APPLICATIONS

INTRODUCTION TO PART IV 445
Graham S. Clarke and David E. Scharff

CHAPTER THIRTY-FIVE
Fair play: a restitution of Fairbairn's forgotten role in the historical drama of art and psychoanalysis 447
Steven Z. Levine

CHAPTER THIRTY-SIX
Viewing Camus's *The Stranger* from the perspective of W. R. D. Fairbairn's object relations 461
Rainer Rehberger

CHAPTER THIRTY-SEVEN
The family is the first social group, followed by the clan, tribe, and nation 471
Ron B. Aviram

CHAPTER THIRTY-EIGHT
Fairbairn's object relations theory and social work in child welfare 483
James C. Raines

ENVOI 497

INDEX 499

ACKNOWLEDGEMENTS

We would like to thank the *International Journal of Psychoanalysis* for permission to reprint David E. Scharff and Ellinor Fairbairn Birtles's "From Instinct to Self: The Evolution and Implications of W. R. D. Fairbairn's Theory of Object Relations" (1997) and Thomas Ogden's "Why Read Fairbairn?" (2010).

We would also like to thank the European Psychoanalytical Federation for permission to reprint John Padel's "The Contribution of W. R. D. Fairbairn (1889–1965) to Psychoanalytic Theory and Practice" (1973).

Hilary Beattie would like to thank Caro Birtles and the Trustees of the National Library of Scotland for permission to reproduce the drawing on p. 95

Paul Finnegan and Graham S. Clarke would like to thank the Group D'Artagnan—Eugenio Canesin Dal Molin, Julia Catani, Davi Berciano Flores, Isabella S. Borghesi—for translating their chapter 'Fairbairn and multiplicity' into Portuguese. And the editors of *Revista Brasileira de Psicanalise* for publishing it in Volume 47, no. 2, 2013.

Jill Savege Scharff's chapter, "Self and society, trauma and the link", previously published as a feature, "Object relations" in *New Therapist*, May/June 2012, The Trauma Edition 79: 5–14, appears by permission of the publisher Lee Domoney.

We are most grateful to Caro Birtles and the Fairbairn family for allowing us to reproduce photographs of W. R. D. Fairbairn on the cover of the book.

ABOUT THE EDITORS AND CONTRIBUTORS

Eleanore M. Armstrong-Perlman, MA, in philosophy of mind; Tavistock qualification, psychoanalytic psychotherapy and family therapy. Thirty years' clinical practice with serious mental illness; former chair, Psychoanalytic Psychotherapy Training, Guild of Psychotherapists, London; former theoretical concepts editor, *British Journal of Psychotherapy*.

Ron B. Aviram, PhD, is an instructor in clinical psychology (psychiatry), Columbia University College of Physicians and Surgeons; clinical supervisor, New York Presbyterian Hospital's doctoral internship and completed psychoanalytic training at William Alanson White Institute. He is author of *The Relational Origins of Prejudice: A Convergence of Psychoanalytic and Social Cognitive Perspectives*, and writes on psychoanalytic aspects of problems in society.

Rubén Mario Basili, MD, in psychiatry (University of Buenos Aires, honours degree), is a full member of the Argentine Psychoanalytic Association (APA), professor at APA seminars, training analyst and training supervisor, and author of several books and papers published in Argentina and abroad. He is a founding member and coordinator, Espacio Fairbairn, APA.

Hilary J. Beattie, PhD, is a psychologist and psychoanalyst in private practice in New York City. She is assistant clinical professor of medical psychology, Columbia University Department of Psychiatry, and also a faculty member at the Columbia Psychoanalytic Center. Her research interests are in psychoanalytic approaches to literature (notably the work of R. L. Stevenson) and the Scottish contribution to psychoanalysis, on which she has published numerous articles.

Adrián César Besuschio, MD, University of Buenos Aires, is a psychiatrist with the Health Ministry of Buenos Aires. He is an associate member of the Argentine Psychoanalytical Association and of the International Psychoanalytical Association, and a member, Espacio Fairbairn (APA). His specialties are in forensic and occupational medicine. He is on the board of "El Borda", the leading psychiatric hospital in Argentina.

Mercedes Campi, MD, in psychiatry (University of Buenos Aires), is a member of the Argentine Psychoanalytic Association (APA), professor at the APA's Psychoanalysis Institute and Espacio Fairbairn at APA. She is the author of several works on psychoanalysis.

David Celani, PhD, is a clinical psychologist. A former adjunct professor, St Michael's College, Colchester, Vermont, he is retired from private practice in Burlington, Vermont. He has published *The Treatment of the Borderline Patient: Applying Fairbairn's Object Relations Theory in the Clinical Setting*, followed by *The Illusion of Love: Why the Battered Woman Returns to her Abuser*; *Leaving Home: How to Separate from Your Difficult Family*, and *Fairbairn's Object Relations Theory in the Clinical Setting* (2010).

Gabriele Cassullo is a clinical psychologist and holder of a research doctorate in human sciences; and professor, clinical psychology, University of Turin (Italy). He is currently researching and publishing on the history of clinical psychology and psychoanalysis.

Graham S. Clarke, PhD, is visiting fellow, Centre for Psychoanalytic Studies, University of Essex, UK. He is author of *Personal Relations Theory: Fairbairn, Macmurray and Suttie*.

Aleksandar Dimitrijevic, PhD, clinical psychology, is assistant professor of psychology, Belgrade University, Serbia. He is a member, Belgrade Psychoanalytical Society.

Paul Finnegan, MD, is a psychoanalyst in private practice in Toronto, Canada.

Gal Gerson, DPhil, is a senior lecturer, University of Haifa's School of Political Sciences. His publications cover the history of liberalism, gender in political theory, and the interface between political thought and psychoanalytic theory.

Bernhard Hensel, MD, is a psychiatrist and psychoanalyst, and a training analyst, German Psychoanalytical Society (DPV), IPA, and the Giessen Institute of Psychoanalysis and Psychotherapy. He was senior co-editor, *W. R. D. Fairbairn's Bedeutung für die Moderne Objektbeziehungstheorie* and contributor to the German edition of Fairbairn and Sutherland with Rainer Rehberger and others.

Lowell W. Hoffman, PhD, is co-director of the Society for Exploration of Psychoanalytic Therapies and Theology; co-director, the Brookhaven Institute for Psychoanalysis and Christian Theology; co-director and practising psychoanalyst and clinical psychologist, the Brookhaven Center, Allentown, PA, and a graduate of the New York University Postdoctoral Program in Psychotherapy and Psychoanalysis.

Marie T. Hoffman, PhD, is adjunct clinical assistant professor of psychology, New York University Postdoctoral Program in Psychotherapy and Psychoanalysis; co-director, the Society for Exploration of Psychoanalytic Therapies and Theology; director, the Brookhaven Institute for Psychoanalysis and Christian Theology; and co-director and psychoanalyst and clinical psychologist, the Brookhaven Center in Allentown, PA.

Otto F. Kernberg, MD, FAPA, is director, Personality Disorders Institute, New York Presbyterian Hospital, Westchester Division; professor of psychiatry, Weill Medical College of Cornell University; past president, International Psychoanalytical Association; training and supervising analyst, Columbia University Center for Psychoanalytic Training and Research; author of thirteen books and co-author of twelve others. His latest book is *The Inseparable Nature of Love and Aggression*.

Steven Z. Levine, Leslie Clark Professor in the Humanities, Department of History of Art, Bryn Mawr College. He is the author of *Monet, Narcissus, and Self-Reflection: The Modernist Myth of the Self* and *Lacan Reframed: A Guide for the Arts Student*.

Joshua Levy, PhD, is a training analyst and supervisor, Toronto Psychoanalytic Institute; a faculty member, Toronto Institute of Contemporary Psychoanalysis; and associate professor of psychiatry, Toronto University.

Ariel Liberman is a psychoanalyst in private practice in Madrid. He is a member of the Argentinian Psychoanalytic Society and of the Madrid Psychoanalytic Association, both of the International Psychoanalytical Association, and the Institute of Relational Psychoanalysis in Madrid. He is a member of the board of the Spain-Chapter of the International Association of Relational Psychoanalysis and Psychotherapy and of the editorial board of CeIR. He is the co-author of two books on Winnicott.

Molly Ludlam, a psychoanalytic psychotherapist, formerly practised with couples, individuals, and parents at the Scottish Institute of Human Relations. A British Society of Couple Psychotherapists and Counsellors full member, she is now editor of its journal *Couple and Family Psychoanalysis*. She co-edited, with V. Nyberg, *Couple Attachments: Theoretical and Clinical Studies*.

Gavin Miller is senior lecturer in English literature and medical humanities in the School of Critical Studies, and co-director, Medical Humanities Research Centre, University of Glasgow. He has been published widely in literary studies and the history of the psy-disciplines, more recently on the overlap between theology, spirituality, and psychotherapy. He is currently working on a monograph, *Science Fiction and Psychology*.

Luis Oswald is a long-serving member, Asociación Psicoanalítica Argentina; coordinator, Research Group: Psychoanalysis and Community (APA); chapter member, Psychoanalysis, Subjectivity and Community of APSA-APA; and secretary, Fairbairn Space (APA). He is professor of clinical psychoanalysis in CIPEA. He has contributed articles to the journals of the APA and the National Academy of Sciences of Buenos Aires.

Tamas Pataki is an honorary senior fellow, University of Melbourne (School of Historical and Philosophical Studies). He studied philosophy at the University of Melbourne and psychoanalysis at University College, London. He co-edited, with Michael Levine, Racism in Mind and wrote Against Religion. Forthcoming is his book, Wish-fulfillment in Psychoanalysis and Philosophy: The Tyranny of Desire.

James L. Poulton, PhD, is a psychologist in private practice in Salt Lake City. He is adjunct professor in psychology, University of Utah, and a member of the faculty, International Psychotherapy Institute, Washington, DC. He is the author of *Object Relations and Relationality in Couple Therapy*.

James C. Raines, PhD, is department chair of health, human services and public policy at California State University, Monterey Bay. He is past president of the Illinois Association of School Social Workers, and of the Midwest Council of School Social Workers. He has had three books published by Oxford University Press.

Rainer Rehberger is a doctor in psychotherapy and internal medicine, and a psychoanalyst and group analyst, in Frankfurt am Main, Germany. He is the author of numerous publications and presentations on psychosomatics, second generation victims and culprits of the Shoah, Fairbain's object relations, psychoanalysis of compulsive disorders, abandonment panic, separation anxieties, grieving, and hoarders.

Ricardo Juan Rey, MD, is assistant professor in psychiatry, Ramos Mejía Hospital, University of Buenos Aires School of Medicine, Argentina. He is a member of the Argentine Psychoanalytic Association (APA); a senior researcher in psychiatry, Barceló Foundation, School of Medicine, Buenos Aires, and a member, International Association for Psychoanalysis in Couples and Family.

Carlos Rodríguez-Sutil gained his PhD in psychology from the Universidad Complutense, Madrid (1990) with a thesis on the philosophy of psychology of Wittgenstein. He is president of the IPR (Relational Psychotherapy Institute) and a member of the board of IARPP-Spain. He has published more than eighty articles and books. He is in private practice.

David E. Scharff is chair and former director, the International Psychotherapy Institute, Washington, DC; member and chair, Work Group on Family and Couple Psychoanalysis of the International Psychoanalytical Association; author and editor of thirty books and many articles, including (with Ellinor Fairbairn Birtles) *From Instinct to Self: Selected Writings of W. R. D. Fairbairn*, and most recently (with Jill Savege Scharff) *The Interpersonal Unconscious*.

Jill Savege Scharff, MD, is co-founder, International Psychotherapy Institute (IPI); founding chair and supervising analyst, International Institute for Psychoanalytic Training at IPI; clinical professor of psychiatry, Georgetown University; teaching analyst, Washington Psychoanalytic

Institute; and psychoanalyst and couple and family therapist, Chevy Chase, Maryland. She is author and editor of twenty-five books, including *The Autonomous Self: The Work of John D. Sutherland*, *The Psychodynamic Image: The Work of John D. Sutherland on Self and Society*, and *The Legacy of Fairbairn and Sutherland*.

Joseph Schwartz, PhD, is a training therapist and supervisor at the Bowlby Centre, London. His books include *Cassandra's Daughter: A History of Psychoanalysis in Europe and America* (Penguin & Karnac), and *Ritual Abuse and Mind Control: The Manipulation of Attachment Needs* (Karnac).

Lea S. de Setton, PhD, is a member, the International Psychoanalytical Association; faculty member, International Psychotherapy Institute and International Institute for Psychoanalytic Training, Chevy Chase, Maryland; former chair of IPI-Panamá; and faculty member, Doctorate Program, Catholic University (USMA), Panama. She is a psychologist, psychoanalyst, and psychotherapist in private practice with individuals, couples, and families in Panama.

Isabel Sharpin de Basili is a clinical psychologist and full teaching member, Argentine Psychoanalytical Association (APA). She is the author of papers and books in Argentina and abroad, and has presented at national and international congresses.

Valerie Sinason, PhD, is director of the Clinic for Dissociative Studies, London, and president, the Institute of Psychotherapy and Disability, Harlow, UK. She is a poet, writer, child and adult psychotherapist and adult psychoanalyst, and former consultant psychotherapist, the Tavistock Clinic and St George's Hospital, London. She edited *Trauma, Dissociation and Multiplicity*.

Neil J. Skolnick, PhD, is a faculty member and supervisor, NYU Postdoctoral Program in Psychoanalysis, and faculty member and supervisor at the National Institute for the Psychotherapies (NIP) where he sits on the board of directors. He edited, with Susan Warshaw, *Relational Perspectives in Psychoanalysis*, and with David E. Scharff, *Fairbairn, Then and Now*. He maintains a private practice in psychoanalysis and supervision in Manhattan.

Michael Stadter, PhD, is a clinical psychologist in private practice, in Bethesda, MD. He is a founding faculty member, the International Psychotherapy Institute; and a facultymember, the Washington School of Psychiatry. His most recent publications are *Presence and the Present: Relationship and Time in Contemporary Psychodynamic Therapy*, and "Pleasure and Pain in the Contemporary Practice of Psychodynamic Therapy" in the journal, *Psychodynamic Practice*.

Neville Symington is former chairman, Sydney Institute for Psychoanalysis; former president, Australian Psychoanalytical Society; and fellow, British Psychoanalytical Society. He is author of many books including *Emotion and Spirit, Narcissism: A New Theory, The Making of a Psychotherapist, A Pattern of Madness, Becoming a Person through Psycho-Analysis*, and *The Psychology of the Person*.

Henri Vermorel, MD, is a training psychoanalyst, Société Psychanalytique de Paris; a teacher, University of Savoie, Chambery, France; former president, Groupe Lyonnais de Psychanalyse, and former editor, *Revue Francaise de Psychanalyse*. He was the editor, *Sigmund Freud et Romain Rolland: Correspondance 1923–1936*, and a volume in F of Fairbairn's papers.

Maurice Whelan is a psychoanalyst and writer in Sydney, Australia; a fellow of the British Psychoanalytic Association and British Psychoanalytical Society; and a member, Australian Psychoanalytical Society. He has published three non-fiction books on education, psychoanalysis, and literature, and three works of fiction, a novel and two books of poetry.

SERIES EDITORS' FOREWORD

Norka Malberg and Joan Raphael-Leff

This book celebrates the man who un-split the psychic atom. It articulates the momentous and often underestimated revolution instigated by Fairbairn's work, away from replacing solipsism with the fundamental need for human connectedness, vital throughout our lives.

Throughout its many chapters, *Fairbairn and the Object Relations Tradition* manages to convey the enormity of this paradigm shift—away from the fractured Freudian mind formed in isolation, a cohering body ego within a somatic predisposition and biological instinct (drive theory), to an *object relations* focus—the pristine ego self-recognised through the minds of others, becoming both structured and fragmented by their attunement and misrecognition.

With increased sophistication of research tools, Fairbairn's 'libido-as-object-seeking' challenge to Freud has now been confirmed by myriad neonatal studies, demonstrating even a newborn's innate desire to relate. And, building on Fairbairnian thinking, there has been a further postmodern shift towards what might be called a *'subject relations'* theory—the dialogical latticework of nonconscious self/other configurations that each partner brings to an intersubjective dyad.

These and many other themes are reflected in this book's rich offerings. To their great credit, Graham S. Clarke and David E. Scharff have generated a cross-continental multidisciplinary gathering of contributors, from Australia, Latin and North America, Europe and Asia. Accessibility is ensured by the format common to all our volumes: four overlapping categories—Historical, Clinical, Theoretical, and Application, each with a scholarly introduction by the co-editors.

The purpose of this series which Oliver Rathbone entrusted to us as series co-editors, is to honour a spectrum of psychoanalytic pioneers. By definition, these thinkers, like Fairbairn, have ventured into unknown or unclaimed territories—opening up new areas of theoretical enquiry and/or therapeutic work. Each volume explores the context in which a particular pioneer's ideas arose, inspiring a tradition that expanded the original thinking through research, clinical developments, or practical applications across international borders and generations.

We trust that this fine collection of essays portraying Fairbairn's legacy will provide a welcome resource for professionals, students, candidates, and interested lay readers, stimulating new work in the field.

Joan Raphael-Leff and Norka Malberg
London

INTRODUCTION

James S. Grotstein

This is an extraordinary work: extraordinary in many ways. The choice of the subject, Fairbairn; the unusually well-crafted editing; the number of Fairbairn scholars who made contributions (thirty-nine); and the editorial choreography of the contributions. By editorial choreography I mean, while I was reading the book, I began to wonder if it had been written by a single author, partially because the flow of the chapters appeared seamlessly connected, and yet in its vastness the work was virtually all inclusive in dealing with Fairbairn's works—to say nothing of being inclusive of many of his unpublished works, which the Fairbairn family put at the editors' disposal.

Fairbairn had been a virtual Cassandra until recent times when his then futuristic, revolutionary ideas have become regarded as being of unusual value. Though formal in manner, writing style, and psychoanalytic technique, he was extraordinarily humanistic in his outlook, as is clearly seen in his concept of the primacy of importance of infantile dependency and of object relations and their ramifications. He was a keen analytic explorer, much like Ferenczi and especially Bion (whom he knew). He was the only analyst, to my knowledge, to create an anatomic scaffolding for the unconscious (endopsychic structure). The structure clearly anticipated the Kleinian concept of the pathological structure or psychic retreat. His work with trauma and religion was, along with so many other fields of study, seminal. If, for instance, we reunite the "exciting object" with the "rejecting object", we create the diabolical tantaliser who rejects and torments after he seduces.

It was unfortunate that Winnicott and Klein marginalised him. He had so much in common with them. His work, in my opinion, neatly complements Klein's and anticipates Winnicott's.

This is a gem of a book. I do so much want it to be successful: it is much needed.

INTRODUCTION

Graham S. Clarke and David E. Scharff

In the view of the two of us who have had the privilege of editing this volume, Fairbairn has been the unifying theoretician behind the British object relations tradition by which we mean the Independent or Middle group of the British Psychoanalytic Society represented most notably in the mid twentieth century by Fairbairn, Guntrip, Winnicott, and Balint, as opposed to object relations thinking within Britain which would include Melanie Klein and her followers (Bacal, 1987; Clarke, 2011; Sutherland, 1980). Fairbairn's object relations theory provided the foundation for the wholesale shift within psychoanalysis to relational ideas that occurred in the last generation all over the world. He was a close student and great admirer of Freud, and knew Melanie Klein's work intimately. Drawing on his study of modern philosophy both for a new vision and for the critical thinking that marked his writing from the outset, he could see both the strengths and the weaknesses of their ideas. Reading through his lecture notes for his teaching of medical and psychology students at the University of Edinburgh in the 1930s, it has been possible to trace his close study of Freud and his critical thinking which resulted in the formulation of a new paradigm for psychoanalysis that burst on the scene in his writings of the 1940s, most of them published in the *International Journal of Psychoanalysis*, the *British Medical Journal*, and the *British Journal of Medical Psychology*, and then collected together and published in his landmark book, *Psychoanalytic Studies of the Personality* (Birtles & Scharff, 1994).

We have put together this book with the intention of showing Fairbairn's accomplishment, his central role in the redefinition of psychoanalysis in the second half of the twentieth century, and of exploring the array of ideas that have built on his work. We invited authors who we thought could update his ideas by considering them critically with the same fine grain that he examined the ideas of Freud, Klein, and other forebears and contemporaries. Undoubtedly, he got some things wrong. Modern developments have affected what we can make of some of his original propositions. No science or art is or should be immune to revision. Newton's ideas hold up, but they take a different place in physics in the light of Einstein, quantum mechanics, and chaos theory. Just so, Freud, Klein, and Fairbairn need continual re-examination for their relevance, and for the current place of their ideas in our theoretical and clinical thinking. Through his career, Fairbairn applied his new point of view broadly beyond analysis, to applications to medical, educational, and sociological fields, and, importantly, to developing a highly original psychology of art. Melanie Klein was influenced strongly by Fairbairn's papers as they were published in the *IJPA* during the early 1940s, which led to her rethinking her own work and renaming the "paranoid" position as the "paranoid-schizoid" position (Klein, 1946). We should also note that Fairbairn's model of the mind was one basis for the theoretical work of John Bowlby in the development of attachment theory, which is not explored in this volume (Bowlby, personal communication, 1973).

We are aware that over the years one of the obstacles to people coming to grips with Fairbairn's revolutionary ideas is the condensed and, to many, difficult style of his philosophically trained mind. Our prologue by Maurice Whelan mounts a trenchant defence of Fairbairn as a powerful and engaging writer which, we hope, will do much to dispel such concerns. We also hope that the contributions to this volume, while still as serious as ever about communicating the heart and soul of Fairbairn's vision, will be readily accessible to the general reader.

The focus of this volume spans past, present, and future. It begins with a summary and re-evaluation of Fairbairn's ideas from the position of nearly twenty years ago when his less known selected papers were first collected together and published. It documents the spread and influence of his ideas worldwide. And most of all, it showcases new ideas that have sprung from the platform his work provided, looking forward to the continuing evolution of ideas built both on those of his formulations that have stood the test of time, and on modifications and corrections that modern contributors offer. Inviting and gathering these has been an exciting task for us, and we hope that you, the reader, will share in the excitement of discovery that is here presented.

What is the object relations tradition that Fairbairn originated?

Fairbairn offered a fundamentally new way of seeing people psychoanalytically. In a Copernican revision of classical theory Fairbairn declared that Freud's pleasure principle could no longer be seen as the centre of the psychological universe, and that his structural model also needed recasting so that the individual's world was not begun with a formless id out of which an ego grew, but began with an active, energetic, ego structure that was fundamentally object seeking and object relating. Crucially, we need to remember that this also led him to reformulate the focus of the therapeutic process—the engine of change. No longer could he hold with the idea that it was genetic reconstruction, the abreaction of memories, or transference interpretation, but fundamentally it was the relationship between patient and therapist, that determined the outcome of therapy. As he wrote,

> I am convinced that it is the patient's relationship to the analyst that mediates the "curing" or "saving" effect of psychotherapy. Where long-term psychoanalytical treatment is concerned, what *mediates* the "curing" or "saving" process more specifically is the development of the

patient's relationship to the analyst, through a phase in which earlier pathogenic relationships are repeated under the influence of transference, into a new kind of relationship which is at once satisfying and adapted to the circumstances of outer reality. (quoted in Birtles & Scharff, 1994, p. 128)

This central point was also summed up by John Macmurray, a fellow Scot and contemporary, from whom Fairbairn drew, and who we quote to make the point that Fairbairn was not "an isolated self" alone in his thinking.

We need one another to be ourselves. This complete and unlimited dependence of each of us upon the others is the central and crucial fact of personal existence. Individual independence is an illusion; and the independent individual, the isolated self, is a nonentity. (*Persons in Relation*, 1961, p. 211)

Fairbairn revolutionised what Freud had offered by writing that the child and growing person was not primarily motivated by pleasure seeking, but by the need for relationship. He described the origins of this process in the following terms:

The process of differentiation of the object derives particular significance from the fact that infantile dependence is characterized not only by identification, but also by an oral attitude of incorporation. In virtue of this fact the object with which the individual is identified becomes equivalent to an incorporated object, or, to put the matter in a more arresting fashion, the object in which the individual is incorporated is incorporated in the individual. This strange psychological anomaly may well prove the key to many metaphysical puzzles. (*Psychoanalytic Studies of the Personality*, 1952, p. 42)

The baby, from the beginning, is actively looking for a person with whom to relate, who will not just suckle him or her but will offer warmth and shelter and protection and, above all, love. Newborns are primarily motivated to relate deeply and lovingly to another person, and do everything in their power to maintain that relationship even to their own detriment. Indeed, one of Fairbairn's discoveries was the child's need to dedicate herself even to a bad object because of this fundamental need for relationship.

Fairbairn formulated his approach—the "object seeking" and "object relating" understanding of persons—in contrast to the classical Freudian instinctual approach in the series of papers written or published in the early Forties during World War II, although many of these ideas are already present in his earliest clinical papers printed, some for the first time, in his only book, *Psychoanalytic Studies of the Personality* (1952). For Fairbairn it is the earliest relationship with others that establishes a way of being and relating that is the foundation that will strongly influence who the person will become as an adult. This is not deterministic. It is a general hypothesis about the relational attributes and personal qualities that an adult has, and their origins in early relations with mother, father, siblings, and extended family. Fairbairn did not thoroughly explore the situation of historical specificity in which different child-rearing practices within different social systems produce different persons, different personalities, different psychopathologies; and individual circumstances and constitutional factors will influence the degree to which such experiences are manifest. But he did explore the situation of socialisation in communism, and was indeed interested in this question (1935).

While Fairbairn acknowledged, as did Freud before him, that there are constitutional factors involved, his theory is firmly based upon the view that we come to be the people we are through our relations with our fellows. In that sense we could say it is existentialist: we are what we make of what we are made of. It is thus a wider view than just the psychoanalytic, and more than just a theory of psychopathology—although that is what it has sometimes been called. It is this investigation of the wider personal, psychological, social, spiritual, and political ramifications of Fairbairn's theory that we seek to explore in this book.

When we first conceived of the book we wanted to keep its remit as open as possible so that the variety of approaches and the range of interests would become manifest, and the synergy between the different aspects of this tradition would prompt further discussion beyond these pages, leading to renewed recognition and acknowledgment of Fairbairn's contribution, and therefore to its wider exploration and application. We approached people from a range of different backgrounds and a worldwide geographic distribution, whose previous work was related to furthering an understanding of Fairbairn's theory and practice in a wide variety of directions. We were gratified to receive an overwhelmingly positive response. We thank the many contributors to the book for their vital participation in this process, which we hope has been a learning experience for all concerned.

During the early development of the book, and, in some respect triggered by it, a further collection of Fairbairn's papers was donated to the manuscript collection of the National Library of Scotland in Edinburgh by the Fairbairn family. These have been used to great effect in a number of chapters, resulting in new and illuminating research both into Fairbairn's ideas and into his personal history. We believe these to have been the last remaining papers of Fairbairn held in private hands, so the collection in the National Library of Scotland, and the repository of Fairbairn's own library, now held by the University of Edinburgh, represent all the extant works owned or written by Fairbairn, and comprise an invaluable source of material for further research and investigation.

We would like to extend our deepest gratitude to the indefatigable work of Ellinor Fairbairn Birtles in keeping her father's ideas alive and available to the public and to Caro Birtles and the Fairbairn family for their generous donation of Fairbairn's papers to the National Library of Scotland.

Structure of the book

In keeping with the series we have divided the contents of the book into four general categories—Historical, Clinical, Theoretical and Applications—though it would be fair to say that many of the contributions straddle several of these topics and different orderings of the contributions would have been possible. At the head of each part we have added a brief introduction to outline how each part holds together.

All the chapters in this book bar three were written specifically for this publication. The three previously published papers reprinted here might be called "anchoring points" for the first three parts. The initial paper by David E. Scharff and Ellinor Fairbairn Birtles, who did so much to develop her father's ideas, puts Fairbairn in a psychoanalytic context at the end of the twentieth century, and shows the degree to which his ideas have become a commonplace of the assumptions of the profession, a foundation that is all too often unrecognised. In the second part, we reprint Thomas Ogden's masterful reminder of the importance of reading Fairbairn—a paper that has already found a wide resonance within the profession. In the third part, the reprinted paper is a model of clarity by John Padel. It is an excellent early review of Fairbairn's theory as a whole. Padel, Sutherland, and Guntrip represented the backbone of the sympathetic independent British support for Fairbairn's work from the publication of *Psychoanalytic Studies of the Personality* in 1952 to his wider recognition in the 1980s.

If you review the content of these three reprinted papers, it is clear that each has a different focus. Through the reprinted papers we can trace the actual history of psychoanalytic theory and practice along with the effects that Fairbairn's theory has had on the development of psychoanalysis. In the Historical part we see where Fairbairn's ideas might have come from, and the sort of social and historical settings in which they flourished. Here the question becomes, "To what extent did Fairbairn originate this tradition and where else did it come from?" It becomes clear that these ideas come out of a complex cultural milieu long in the making. The influence of Aristotle, Hegel, the Scottish Enlightenment and nineteenth-century Scottish interpreters of the Enlightenment, and the Presbyterian Church all play a part in the formation of Fairbairn's character and the evolution of his theory. Fairbairn's complex involvement with religion and his psychosexual development through his own upbringing and experience as reflected in his self-analytic notes are implicated in this process: witness the two contributions to this book that have benefited most from the recent additions to the manuscript collection at the National Library of Scotland. Fairbairn's relationship with Scottish contemporaries Suttie and Macmurray, whose ideas he shared to varying degrees, are also considered in detail.

Fairbairn's work has taken a long time to become known internationally. His influence has been greatest in the UK, Canada, and the USA. As his work has been influential within Europe as a whole, we have commissioned contributions from Scotland, France, Germany, Italy, Israel, Serbia, and Spain in the book. There are also contributions from Australia, Panama, and Argentina where there has been a well established long-term interest in Fairbairn's ideas. This is represented, in the Historical part, by an account of the development of a "Fairbairn Space" within the Argentinian Psychoanalytic Association—what in the UK might be called a "Fairbairn Special Interest Group". The "Fairbairn Space" has carried out a detailed study of Fairbairn's work and overseen its active application to a wide range of psychiatric and psychoanalytic contexts. The Latin American dimension to the development of Fairbairn's ideas is reflected in the fact that we have four other contributions to the book with strong Argentinian links.

In the Clinical part, beginning with Thomas Ogden's encouragement to read and reread Fairbairn, we have a number of clinically related investigations into key areas of theory. The origin and nature of internal objects and the differences between Fairbairn and Klein is a motif that runs throughout the book, as the differences between Fairbairn—representing British object relations theory—and the object relations theory of Klein are explored by different authors. In general, unless explicitly stated, all subsequent references to object relations thinking will be to the British object relations thinking initiated by Fairbairn. The place of the "Oedipus situation" is illustrated clinically with examination of significant differences between Fairbairn and Freud.

The extension from individual to couple therapy noted by Kernberg in the Historical part is later investigated in greater depth through attention to the importance allocated to Henry Dicks, and David and Jill Scharff's clinical use of Fairbairn's theory for therapy of couples and families. Fairbairn's contribution to the study of personality disorders, to the abuse, trauma, and the specifically "schizoid" nature of the multiplicity of dissociative identity disorder (D.I.D.) that can follow severe trauma, are all looked at from a clinical point of view. From Argentina comes a comprehensive attempt to classify a wide-ranging group of psychopathologies and to identify an underlying mechanism based in the idea of "schizoid conflict" that is so intrinsic to Fairbairn's theory. Fairbairn's own theory of dreams and dreaming as "state of affairs" or short "films" of inner reality is discussed both in relation to Winnicott's approach to dreams, and the importance of the countertransference. The place of the therapist as a "good object" is discussed and illustrated with clinical examples, using a relational view of the interaction between analyst and analysand, and based upon key ideas from Fairbairn's account of the pitfalls in the development of ontological security. Finally, the relationship between Fairbairn's theory and the future co-development of psychoanalysis, developmental psychology, attachment theory, and neuro-psychoanalysis is investigated.

In the Theoretical part we look at the ways that Fairbairn's theory has been understood and developed by a number of different theorists and at the wider problems which that theory has influenced. Our first contribution is by one of the less well known but most astute commentators on Fairbairn—psychoanalyst and Shakespearean scholar John Padel. This is followed by an appreciation of Padel's contribution to the understanding of Fairbairn over a number of years through his publications on object relations and presentations to the British Psychoanalytical Society. In other papers, Fairbairn's relationship to Guntrip and Winnicott is investigated in detail, followed by similarities between aspects of Ferenczi's work on trauma and Fairbairn's theory. There are then two papers considering Stephen Mitchell involvement with Fairbairn's ideas, followed by two papers exploring Pichon-Rivière's concept of the Link that partly derives from Fairbairn, and its resonance with Fairbairn's work. Another Argentinian analyst puts forward a view on the earliest position that the baby starts from, one he first proposed at the 2005 Scottish conference on Sutherland and Fairbairn. He relates this to creativity and art in Fairbairn's thinking.

Fairbairn's structural theory has always been a matter of controversy, but here we have a critical look at the theory from the point of view of a therapist trying hard to apply Fairbairn's theory but finding that aspects of the theory, as he understands it, will not work without revision. In a similar vein, we explore the standing of the scientific status of Fairbairn's theory. Finally in this part we also have two detailed philosophical investigations of Fairbairn's theory: one, of the idea of sub-egos and objects as a concept of mind, considering the arguments against such a view and then developing a novel and coherent way of understanding Fairbairn's theory; the second article places Fairbairn's thinking squarely in a European intersubjectivist tradition, represented by Merleau-Ponty, pointing to subtle differences in the ways that Fairbairn formulated his theory at different times in order to underline the importance of particular ways of describing the development of the endopsychic structure.

It has been gratifying that a number of contributions to the book make use of papers not normally considered when Fairbairn is being discussed, not just the papers in the second and third parts of *Psychoanalytic Studies of the Personality* but also his two papers on art, which have long been ignored as were a number of other papers that were made more easily available with the collection *From Instinct to Self* (1994). In particular the importance of Fairbairn's thinking on sociological and group matters is raised by some of the contributors. This promises to be an exciting new extension of his ideas. Finally, in the Applications parts of the book we see how Fairbairn's ideas might be extended, and thus influence the realms of art and creativity, literature and film, sociology, group activities, social work, and child care practices.

We hope that this volume, bringing together as it does contributions from a wide range of backgrounds by those who find common ground in their interest in Fairbairn, will find echoes in the wider culture of psychoanalysis and beyond. We hope that it will go a considerable way towards enabling us to clarify much that remains unsettled in the theory of object relations developed by Fairbairn. We believe that a fully extended theory of object relations is essential to further progress of psychoanalysis, and to its wider acceptance in concert with developmental psychology, attachment theory, neuroscience, and the social sciences as a whole.

We would like to thank all our contributors for their dedication and hard work and for their stimulating contributions to the continuing understanding of Fairbairn and the object relations tradition.

We would also like to thank the series editors Joan Raphael-Leff and Norka Mahlberg for giving us this exciting opportunity and Oliver Rathbone and Karnac for their generous support.

Graham Clarke has enjoyed the process greatly and benefited much from his productive collaboration with David Scharff. Graham would also like to thank his colleague Paul Finnegan for his friendship and their joint work over a number of years and his wife Sandra for her sensitive support and help during the process of editing this book and beyond.

David Scharff has enjoyed this fruitful and collegial collaboration so generously offered by Graham Clarke, and is grateful to all our contributors who generously and enthusiastically offered reviews and new ideas to enliven and mine the rich vein that Fairbairn first discovered. As so many times before, his wife Jill has supported the work, and contributed far more than her own specific contribution.

References

Bacal, H. A. (1987). British object-relations theorists and self-psychology: some critical reflections. *International Journal of Psychoanalysis, 68*: 81–98.

Birtles, E. F. & Scharff, D. E. (Eds.). (1994). *From Instinct to Self: Selected Papers of W. R. D. Fairbairn, Volume II: Applications and Early Contributions*. Northvale, NJ: Jason Aronson.

Clarke, G. S. (2011). On: The narcissism of minor differences. *International Journal of Psychoanalysis, 92*: 231–233.

Fairbairn, W. R. D. (1935). The sociological significance of communism considered in the light of psychoanalysis. *British Journal of Medical Psychology, 15*(3): 218–229. In: *Psychoanalytic Studies of the Personality* (pp. 233–246). London: Tavistock, 1952.

Fairbairn, W. R. D. (1952). *Psychoanalytic Studies of the Personality*. London: Tavistock.

Fairbairn, W. R. D. (1955). Observations in defence of the object-relations theory of the personality. *British Journal of Medical Psychology, 28*(2, 3): 144–156. In: E. F. Birtles & D. E. Scharff (Eds.), *From*

Instinct to Self: Selected Papers of W. R. D. Fairbairn, Volume II: Applications and Early Contributions (pp. 111–128). Northvale, NJ: Jason Aronson, 1994.

Klein, M. (1946). Notes on some schizoid mechanisms. *International Journal of Psychoanalysis, 27*: 99–110.

Macmurray, J. (1961). *Persons in Relation, Volume II of The Form of the Personal.* London: Faber & Faber.

Sutherland, J. D. (1980). The British object relations theorists: Balint, Winnicott, Fairbairn, Guntrip. *Journal of the American Psychoanalytic Association, 28*: 829–860.

PROLOGUE

Fairbairn the writer

Maurice Whelan

Some say Fairbairn is hard to read; he is too dense, too theoretical. He hasn't the writing flair of Freud and unlike Klein and Winnicott doesn't take you inside his consulting room to immerse you in the immediacy of the contact with a patient. I have always been intrigued by these comments because my own experience reading him is quite the opposite. So when asked to be part of this project I welcomed the opportunity to clarify my ideas, and hopefully to convey that clarity and make it possible for others to reap the full rewards of reading Fairbairn.

I began by posing some questions. Does it matter how people write? Is style significant? In psychoanalytical writing is content all important? Does it matter how we arrive at our understanding of the human mind as long as that understanding assists our patient? To provide some answers I sought the assistance of a few writing heavyweights, Sigmund Freud, Marcel Proust, and the English essayist William Hazlitt.

Good writing was important to Freud. (He was awarded the 1930 Goethe Prize for Literature.) In May 1922 Freud wrote to the writer Arthur Schnitzler (1862–1931). Schnitzler had trained as a doctor and a neurologist but turned from medicine to literature. Referring to Schnitzler's writing Freud said, "Whenever I get deeply interested in your beautiful creations I always seem to find behind their poetic sheen the same pre-suppositions, interests and conclusions as those familiar to me as my own" (Jones, 1957, p. 474).

Freud compliments Schnitzler on his "artistic gifts", his "mastery of language", his "creativeness". Freud deserves our compliments for exhibiting similar qualities, his papers being a supreme example of his capacities as a writer.

In *Remembrance of Things Past* Marcel Proust wrote:

> Style for the writer, no less than colour for the painter, is a question not of technique but of vision: it is the revelation, which by direct and conscious methods would be impossible, of the

qualitative difference, the uniqueness of the fashion in which the world appears to each one of us ... And it is perhaps as much by the quality of his language as by the species of ... theory which he advances that one may judge of the level to which a writer has attained in the moral and intellectual part of his work. Quality of language, however, is something that theorists think they can do without, and those who admire them are easily persuaded that it is no proof of intellectual merit. (1913–1927, 3, p. 916)

Proust states that style and vision and quality of language are interwoven threads that combine to determine the value of a text. To know the particularities of the individual writer is the key to reaping our just rewards from the labour we extend in reading them.

I have taught Fairbairn for twenty years. Though I consider him among the most important figures in psychoanalysis, I do not start with his ideas. I begin by attending to him as a writer and the piece of writing I start with is his 1954 paper, "Observations on the Nature of Hysterical States". This is the first page.

In addition to such intrinsic interest as hysterical states may be expected to possess for the psychopathologist, they must always assume a quite special significance for him owing to the fact that it was upon the intensive investigation of these states that modern psychopathology was founded. It was, of course, at the Salpetriere in Paris that this investigation was originally set in motion by Charcot; but it is to Janet, his pupil and successor in research, that we owe the formulation of the concept of hysteria as a recognizable clinical state. Janet's achievement was not confined, however, to a classification and description of hysterical symptomatology. It included an attempt to provide a scientific explanation of the genesis of the phenomena displayed by the hysteric; and the explanatory concept which Janet formulated was, of course, the classic concept of "dissociation". In terms of this concept the hysterical state is essentially due to inability on the part of the ego to hold all the functions of the personality together, with the result that certain of these functions become dissociated from, and lost to, the rest of the personality and, having passed out of the control of the ego, operate independently. The extent of the dissociated elements was described by Janet as varying within wide limits, so that sometimes what was dissociated was an isolated function such as the use of a limb, and sometimes a large area or areas of the psyche (as in cases of dual and multiple personality); and the occurrence of such dissociations was attributed to the presence of a certain weakness of the ego—a weakness partly inherent, and partly induced by circumstances such as illness, trauma or situations imposing a strain upon the individual's capacity for adaptation.

Dissociation as described by Janet is, of course, essentially a passive process—a process of disintegration due to a failure on the part of the cohesive function normally exercised by the ego. The concept of "dissociation" thus stands in marked contrast to the concept of "repression" formulated somewhat later by Freud in an attempt to provide a more adequate explanation of hysterical phenomena. Freud was familiar with the investigations conducted at the Salpetriere, to which he himself paid an extensive visit; but his researches into the nature of hysteria were preponderantly of an independent character. Thus his explanatory concept of repression was based essentially upon his own experience of the reactions of hysterical patients in his practice in Vienna. (pp. 105–106)

Fairbairn begins by drawing attention to the place of hysteria in the history of dynamic psychiatry, psychology, and psychoanalysis. He mentions Charcot and Janet and presents Janet's achievements, describing his interest in both description and explanation. Fairbairn takes us through stages of knowing: observation, description, classification, preliminary attempt at a scientific explanation, and formulation of an explanatory concept. With Janet he goes through all these stages and having done so proceeds to examine and critique them. Where weaknesses are found, Fairbairn points out the need to strengthen the existing order or develop a whole new understanding. He singles out Janet's understanding of dissociation. In Janet's concept of dissociation the ego cannot hold all the functions of the personality together. The cause is a certain weakness of the ego. Fairbairn points out a shortcoming of such a view, namely that a passive process is inferred. He moves on to Freud's concept of repression. Because Freud sees repression as an active process, great opportunities for a dynamic psychology are opened up.

The points I have drawn attention to are but a few of the many in this packed first page, which even today I take delight in reading. This page of writing illustrates the core idea I wish to communicate. To prepare the ground I turn to my final heavyweight, the great English essayist, William Hazlitt, and in particular to a piece Hazlitt wrote about his friend Joseph Fawcett:

> I have heard [Fawcett] explain "That is the most delicious feeling of all, to like what is excellent, no matter whose it is". In this respect he practised what he preached ... There was no flaw or mist in the clear mirror of his mind. He was as open to impressions as he was strenuous in maintaining them. He did not care a rush whether a writer was old or new, in prose or in verse—"what he wanted" he said "was something to make him think" ... He gave a cordial welcome to all sorts, provided they were the best in their kind. He was not fond of counterfeits or duplicates. His own style was laboured and artificial to a fault, while his character was frank and ingenuous in the extreme ... Men who have fewer native resources, and are obliged to apply oftener to the general stock, acquire by habit a greater aptitude in appreciating what they owe to others. Their taste is not made a sacrifice to their egotism and vanity, and they enrich the soil of their minds with continual accessions of borrowed strength and beauty. (pp. 224–225)

* * *

I have allowed my heavyweights to do a significant amount of punching for me as I advance my case and argue for greater attention to Fairbairn as a writer. Proust's contribution articulates the belief that the quality of writing reflects the quality of thought. The theorists think the quality of language is something we can do without, Proust tells us. Freud is firmly on Proust's side in that argument.

A writer's style is like a writer's fingerprint. It is a fingerprint of his mind and his—to use an old-fashioned word—sensibilities. If we return and read again the Fairbairn piece I have reprinted, we find not only a short history of psychological thought on hysteria but we are told a story, a story about Charcot who had an original idea and how that idea, like a baton, is taken up and passed by others who followed. The story is part of Fairbairn's vision. And he tells the story on his own unique way.

Now an opposing argument can claim that everyone is entitled to their own style and all styles should be treated equally. Not so, I would assert and the reasons I would advance at this juncture are contained in the piece from Hazlitt.

The portrait Hazlitt paints of Joseph Fawcett is an image befitting Ronald Fairbairn. It is delicious to like what is excellent no matter whose it is. Fairbairn moves from Charcot to Janet to Freud. He describes the progress of thought without diminishing or extolling any single person. He has acquainted himself with the particular contribution each man has made and presents it to us for our admiration. Fairbairn wrote his MD thesis on "Dissociation and Repression". He admired Freud's advancements. That he points to areas of criticism where further thought or alteration was desired in no way detracted from his respect. Allied to his criticism was a keen sense of gratitude. He could, like Fawcett enrich the soil of his mind with accessions of borrowed strength and beauty.

The penultimate comparison I will make between Fairbairn and Fawcett relates to the latter not being fond of counterfeits and duplicates. Counterfeits are false: false ideas, false styles. Duplicates duplicate; they fail to develop their own mind and style.

And now I can summarise this chapter. From my first reading of Fairbairn I was aware of being in the presence of a man who knew his own mind, and who, through his particular style, was introducing me to the workings of that mind. He invites you to sit alongside him, and attend to the workings of your mind. When I am in his company I imagine him as a very patient teacher and colleague, keen to know how I am attending to the evidence on hand, what concepts I am using, what language I employ to express my thoughts. He encourages a deep and honest interest in human beings and their sufferings. He invites us to be respectful, endlessly curious, and ever intent on broadening our understanding of humanity. This is Fairbairn's contribution and challenge when we read him: to think for ourselves; to satisfy our own minds; to welcome good knowledge regardless of where it originates; to express ourselves in a voice that is uniquely ours. The voice in question is free from narcissistic self-aggrandisement—in Hazlitt's terms, devoid of vanity and affectation. The person with such a voice has one priority: to speak in a way that helps others to think.

I leave the content of his ideas in the safe hands of all the other contributors to this book. If I have made it possible for the reader to reap greater rewards from reading Ronald Fairbairn I will have succeeded in my task.

References

Fairbairn, W. R. D. (1954b). Observations on the nature of hysterical states. *British Journal of Medical Psychology, 27*: 105–125. In: D. E. Scharff & E. F. Birtles (Eds.), *From Instinct to Self: Selected Papers of W. R. D. Fairbairn, Volume I: Clinical and Theoretical Papers* (pp. 13–40). Northvale, NJ: Jason Aronson, 1994.

Hazlitt, W. (1822). On criticism. In: P. P. Howe (Ed.), *Complete Works of William Hazlitt (1930–1934) Vol. 8* (pp. 224–225). London: Dent.

Jones, E. (1957). *The Life and Work of Sigmund Freud. Vol. 3, The Last Phase 1919–1939* (p. 474). New York: Basic.

Proust, M. (1913–1927). *Remembrance of Things Past. Vol. 3* (p. 916). C. K. Scott Moncrieff, T. Kilmartin, & A. Mayor (Trans.). London: Penguin, 1981.

PART I

HISTORICAL

INTRODUCTION TO PART I

Graham S. Clarke and David E. Scharff

We begin with assessment of Fairbairn's background, origins, and theory, many themes from which are taken up throughout the book. Written by David E. Scharff and Ellinor Fairbairn Birtles, Fairbairn's daughter, who worked tirelessly to keep Fairbairn's ideas alive, their joint editorship of the two-volume *From Instinct to Self* (1994), published twenty years ago, documents Fairbairn's magnificent contribution to psychoanalytic thinking. David E. Scharff's and Ellinor Fairbairn Birtles's 1997 paper locates Fairbairn's work philosophically within the history of psychoanalysis, and points to his widespread but under-acknowledged influence. Intrinsic to their argument is a thorough summary of Fairbairn's theory.

The next four contributions, exploring the connection with and influence between Suttie and Fairbairn, point to work that has gone on, subsequent to the original publication in 1997 of the paper (reprinted here), researching the historical and social context in which Fairbairn was developing his revolutionary theory. Gal Gerson identifies Hegelian themes in Fairbairn's work and argues that he follows a different path from other contemporary object relations theorists like Suttie, Bowlby, and Winnicott. Based upon the often-overlooked sections and chapters in *Psychoanalytic Studies of the Personality* that concern social issues, Gerson argues that Fairbairn's idea of mature dependence is based upon finding a balance between family and state in which the state is the higher order institution, which is why the instance of Sophocles's *Antigone* is material. This might also reflect the influence of Aristotle on Fairbairn's thinking since, "For Aristotle, political activity is not merely a way to pursue our interests, but an essential part of the good life" (Michael Sandel, 2011). Consequently, mature dependence must involve playing a full role in the social world. (Ron Aviram, in the Applications part, also takes up this theme with an investigation into Fairbairn's social thinking.)

Gavin Miller draws attention to the many religious and scientific influences in the late Victorian and Edwardian Scottish cultural context "in which love itself was dignified as a scientific reality worthy of methodical investigation" (Miller, this volume, p. 47). This helped to make possible the thinking of both Fairbairn and Suttie. Gabriele Cassullo addresses the project of integrating Janet's and Freud's model of mind with reference to the work of Ferenczi, Suttie, and Fairbairn.

Neville Symington looks at the relationship between Scottish contemporaries Fairbairn, Suttie, and Macmurray and the roots of their theories. He thinks that both Fairbairn and Suttie, while they tried to transcend Freud's theory, failed to go far enough in their advocacy of relationship in human communication. He argues that only John Macmurray's "natural theology" is an adequate grounding for the sort of "reciprocal relations" that psychoanalysis aspires to.

Thanks to a recent donation of Fairbairn's personal papers by the Fairbairn family to the National Library of Scotland, who hold all of Fairbairn's other manuscripts, it is now possible to investigate aspects of Fairbairn's personal life more thoroughly than even the excellent biography of Fairbairn by "Jock" Sutherland. Marie and Lowell Hoffman have used the newly available manuscript material to look in detail at Fairbairn's lifelong involvement with the church and religion and to suggest deep resonances between Fairbairn's views and Calvinism. Hilary Beattie has used Fairbairn's less well known papers and his newly available self-analytic notes to go more deeply into his personal struggles over his own sexuality.

Fairbairn's work has been influential in Argentina for a long time. A number of contributions throughout the book illustrate that connection. Mercedes Campi and her co-authors' introduction to the "Fairbairn Space" in Argentina gives a history of Fairbairn's influence in that country along with the current concerns of the group which are developed further in the Clinical part.

Returning to the present status of Fairbairn's thinking within contemporary psychoanalysis, Otto Kernberg, who, as much as anyone, has kept the ideas of Fairbairn relevant, reinforces the conclusions that Ellinor and David drew in 1997. Kernberg notes the degree to which different traditions within psychoanalysis have run in parallel without converging even though they represent similar approaches. In particular he notes the similarities between Fairbairn and Edith Jacobson. Kernberg also points to ways in which Fairbairn's model has been expanded by people like Henry Dicks who applied it to couple therapy, a topic considered by Molly Ludlam in the Clinical part.

References

Birtles, E. F., & Scharff, D. E. (Eds.) (1994). *From Instinct to Self: Selected Papers of W. R. D. Fairbairn, Volume II: Applications and Early Contributions*. Northvale, NJ: Jason Aronson.

Sandel, M. (2011). *Aristotle, The Politics: A short overview of the reading*. http://www.justiceharvard.org/resources/aristotle-the-politics/ last accessed 1 December 2012.

Scharff, D. E., & Birtles, E. F. (Eds.) (1994). *From Instinct to Self: Selected Papers of W. R. D. Fairbairn, Volume I: Clinical and Theoretical Papers*. Northvale, NJ: Jason Aronson.

CHAPTER ONE

From instinct to self: the evolution and implications of W. R. D. Fairbairn's theory of object relations*

David E. Scharff and Ellinor Fairbairn Birtles

In 1952 Ernest Jones wrote in his introduction to Fairbairn's *Psychoanalytic Studies of the Personality*:

> Instead of starting, as Freud did, from stimulation of the nervous system proceeding from excitation of various erotogenous zones and internal tension arising from gonadic activity, Dr. Fairbairn starts at the centre of the personality, the ego, and depicts its strivings and difficulties in its endeavour to reach an object where it may find support ... All this constitutes a fresh approach in psycho-analysis which should lead to much fruitful discussion. (p. v)

W. R. D. Fairbairn brought an original voice and formulation to psychoanalysis. Without general awareness among analysts, his theoretical contributions have guided the revolution in psychoanalysis during the past twenty-five years (Greenberg & Mitchell, 1983; Sutherland, 1989), and his formulations have contributed to the widespread application of analysis to other areas—to the study of trauma and multiple personality, infant development, marriage and the family, religion and pastoral care, to the understanding of groups, institutions, and society, to psychology of the arts, and to an evolution in the philosophical understanding of human experience. Nevertheless, his ideas passed from being little known to being general assumptions without ever being widely and distinctly acknowledged. In this paper we begin by discussing Fairbairn's background and the philosophical and psychoanalytic origins of his thought; we then outline

---

*Reprinted from *International Journal of Psychoanalysis* (1997), 78: 1085–1103, with kind permission.

the central tenets of his object relations theory of the personality, and finally we briefly consider its wider implications. It has been suggested that the extent of Fairbairn's contribution has been largely unrecognised because he worked in relative isolation in Edinburgh, Scotland from the 1920s until his death in 1964. Close study of the context in which he developed his innovative ideas shows that the seeds of his mature ideas were present from his first records of his thinking in the middle 1920s, when he was writing and teaching graduate and postgraduate students in philosophy, psychology, and medicine. Despite his distance from London, Fairbairn kept well informed about psychoanalytic developments in London, and especially the new work of Melanie Klein, but it is true that he was unable to respond in person to the issues taken up in the "Controversial Discussions" undertaken in London during the war, although he did submit one brief contribution that was read for him (King & Steiner, 1991). He also had frequent if periodic contact with many of the important British analysts during the 1940s and 1950s. The geographical separation from major analytic societies may even have helped preserve Fairbairn's independence of mind, but it may also have kept his ideas from receiving the understanding and recognition they deserved. For instance, critical commentary written in response to Fairbairn's articles and his book within British psychoanalysis in the 1940s and 1950s failed to appreciate the magnitude of Fairbairn's move from a biological instinct theory to a psychological theory of a self chiefly motivated by the need for relationships throughout life. Although Fairbairn provided a new paradigm for the twentieth century (Sutherland, 1989), one which ultimately organised the ensuing development of psychoanalysis, only a few analysts recognised this at the time he was writing.

Soon, however, the heart of Fairbairn's work became an intrinsic, accepted core of the thinking of the Independent Group of British analysts, whose prominent members included Balint, Winnicott, Sutherland, and Bowlby. His work was always of immediate interest to Melanie Klein and her followers, as was hers to him (Klein, 1946; Scharff, 1996). However, because Klein remained dedicated to Freud's drive theory even while stressing the importance of object relationships from the beginning, we will see later how her theory, like Freud's, remained grounded in the mould of nineteenth-century mechanical physics, in the need of the child to rid himself of excessive increments of the drive derivatives. Since instinct theory retains a somatic rather than psychological basis for mental function, Klein's theory works best for those conditions in which the model of early infantile dependence based on somatic need offers a useful metaphor. It is more problematic as an account of mature adult responsibility and interdependence.

Fairbairn altered his orientation fundamentally, shifting from Freud's topographical, impulse, and structural models to a psychology based on the need for and internalisation of relationships. His theoretical shift was based on the alternative motivation of a dynamic self seeking an object from whom it gained recognition and security. This shift also provided the theoretical basis for the centrality of the therapeutic relationship, and therefore presaged the clinical shift in the writing of the Kleinians and others to the use of countertransference and of the therapist's subjective experience (Heimann, 1950; Klein, 1952; Winnicott, 1949). His understanding of the importance of the relationship with the mother and family in infant and child development came fifteen years before Winnicott's and Bowlby's published accounts and expansion of ideas in this realm, and were an important part of the climate in which they later developed their contributions. His theory still remains fundamental to a rigorous underpinning of their work.

Fairbairn's training and experience

On 16 November 1916, while on active duty in the Royal Artillery in Scotland and shortly before his posting to the Middle East, Fairbairn visited the "Craiglockart Hosp. (for nerve-shaken officers)", where he met "the Cambridge psychologist Capt. [W. H. R.] Rivers" (Fairbairn's diary, 1916). The hysterical injuries, or war neuroses, that he saw there made an indelible impression on him and he decided to undertake medical training in order to become a psychotherapist. His study of Freud began in 1919 with *The Interpretation of Dreams* and continued until his death in 1964. In 1921, while still a medical student, he began analysis with Dr Ernest Connell three to five times per week from July of that year probably until the end of December 1922. Connell was an Australian, who came to Edinburgh in 1920 and practised psychoanalysis there from 1921. From Fairbairn's diaries, it *appears* that Connell held an appointment at Craighouse Mental Hospital during the 1920s. It has not been possible to establish when his analysis with Connell ended as the diaries for 1923, 1924, and 1925 are the only ones missing in a series that goes from 1910–1964. However, Fairbairn started private psychoanalytic practice in 1923, when he qualified in medicine. From that date until 1935 he held a variety of appointments at mental hospitals in and around Edinburgh, which ran concurrently with his lectureships in psychology in the discipline of mental philosophy from 1927–1935, and in psychiatry from 1931–1932. His special subject was adolescence, and he also taught philosophy. He used psychoanalytic techniques in his clinical work at the University Psychological Clinic, and, from 1933, at the Child and Juvenile Clinic. In 1929, while acting as an expert witness, he was the first person to introduce the concept of "diminished responsibility" in a court of law.

From 1929, when Fairbairn attended the International Psychoanalytical Congress in Oxford, he was internationally acknowledged in psychoanalysis. He was elected as an associate member of the British Psychoanalytical Society in 1931 and a full member in 1939. His experience of the dissociative symptomatology of sexually and physically abused children, and of adults suffering from war neurosis, began with his clinical work in 1923 and continued to the end of his life. In spite of his personal reservations as to its validity (1932, unpublished) Fairbairn followed Freud's example and undertook self-analysis (Sutherland, 1989, pp. 65–82).

The philosophical origins of Fairbairn's thought

Fairbairn brought to his own writing a careful study of Freud's major contributions and a dedication to logical thought derived from his training in philosophy. For this reason it is relevant to review the philosophical origins of his point of view. There are two distinct philosophical traditions within European thought. The first, Platonic tradition, is dissociative in that it examines discrete parts of functions in isolation from the whole. The second, derived from Aristotle, is integrative, relating parts to each other within a whole. Freud's view of human nature assumed a Platonic division between mind and body, a dualism that was enshrined in the Christian intellectual tradition and which was consistent with the nineteenth-century scientific tradition. In this view, mind and body are concrete entities whose mode of connection is conflictual opposition, leading by analogy to Freud's ideas of conflict between life and death instincts or between sex and aggression, id and ego, and the individual and society. In Freud's view of mental health, conflictual dualism is expressed in the form of what Isaiah Berlin (1949) called "negative freedom", that is, freedom "from" interference from internal or external forces. In this way a fundamentally exclusive and defensive psychology was incorporated into psychoanalytic theory.

In contrast, Fairbairn's critical reorientation of psychoanalysis assumes a dialectical idea of human nature, an Aristotelian view expanded in the nineteenth century by Kant and Hegel, who defined human nature as integral and participatory: each individual strives for integration and reciprocity. Mind and body have equal status, and conflict is accommodated through the medium of change and mutually influencing reciprocity between differing elements.

Fairbairn's philosophical roots sprang from his extensive studies in the Department of Mental Philosophy, undertaken as his first degree at Edinburgh University before his medical studies. There the focus was on the psychology of man and the products of his mind, undertaken in such studies as logic, ethics, and the philosophies of law and education. The metaphysical content of the syllabus was influenced by the interest of Professor Andrew Seth, later called Pringle-Pattison (1882) and that of his contemporaries, in the philosophical development of Kantian and Hegelian ideas. Fairbairn supplemented this background with postgraduate studies in Greek philosophy and the German language, undertaken in Germany. This course of study gave him a thorough knowledge of the philosophical accounts of the subjective experience of that which is "other", a sensibility that includes the subject's capacity for self-reflection. We will see shortly that this background eventually crystallised as a mainstay of Fairbairn's own theory of internalised object relations.

In the Hegelian philosophical account, the innate capacities for language, symbolisation, and rational thought are understood to be dependent for their development on an adequate environment. The dialectic exchange between subject and object (the "other") results in a new relationship or synthesis. The relationships between subject and object provide the progressive epistemological element necessary for the growth of language and thought. Fairbairn's understanding of this philosophical point of view enabled him to place relational meaning and value, rather than gratification, at the motivational centre.

In order to discuss Fairbairn's intellectual shift in more detail, let us review the Aristotelian and Hegelian origins of his thinking in more detail. Aristotle was the first Western philosopher to develop a holistic psychology based on his observations of the effects that one object had on another, and the extent to which the one was active in response to the other. Using this methodology, Aristotle moved from Platonic psychology in which the *form* of the human being—the body—was devalued and the power of reason exalted, to one in which the *experience* of existing in a world of phenomena is contained with the form of the person. Mind and body thus have equal status. Aristotle wrote, "Man is an animal naturally formed for society." The major consequence of a shift from a discrete entity in which development is preprogrammed to one in which "Man" is defined as a "social animal" is to highlight the role of physical and emotional dependence. It is for this reason that infantile dependence and its vicissitudes play such a significant role in Fairbairn's psychoanalytic account.

In 1807 Hegel wrote that the dissatisfactions of unsatisfied desire are allied to each person's need to possess that which is "other". This notion of the unsatisfactory nature of encounters motivated by desire became, in Fairbairn's theory, the root motivation for splitting of the ego, and thus for the construction of endopsychic structure, personality development, and psychopathology. Through these routes, Fairbairn developed a psychology of individuation and of the identity of the self essentially based on the meaning of relationships rather than on instinctual gratification.

Hegel drew on three major factors described by Aristotle (Schacht, 1972, pp. 292–293). In the first, "essence" is defined as "your very nature", what we now recognise as genetic inheritance, within which rationality is a defining characteristic of the human species. The second factor is "coming-to-be"—the change from potentiality to actuality that can be seen in the case of the infants who have the unactualised potentiality to become fully rational beings. The third is the "originative source of change … in one thing in relation to another". Many changes in living creatures appear at first to be of their own doing, but on closer inspection can be seen to be responses reactive to their experience in the environment. The changes involved in physical maturation originate within the child himself "coming-to-be", while the child's adaptive response to his parents and to external reality would fit in the category of reactive change. When the environment is satisfactory, "self-realisation" occurs—that is to say, optimal actualisation of potential.

For Hegel, rational decisions have to be self-conscious. Being human involves the capacity for rational thought and self-reflection. Perhaps it was in following Hegel's lead in this area that Fairbairn posited an early capacity for mental sorting as the basis for splitting and repression, which he thought begins so early in life. It has been argued that Fairbairn assumed too great a capacity for cognition in infants. One of his arguments against Freud's theory of the unconscious was that there is no reason for infantile affective experience to be repressed if it is the result of instinctual stimulation alone. Experience must first reach some level of cognition or recognised experience before repression is required. Modern infant research as reported by Stern (1985) has confirmed the early functioning of cognition in infants. Fairbairn, following Stout (1927), had already argued that "[A]lthough the mental life of the infant belongs characteristically to the perceptual level, it is not altogether devoid of ideational, and even conceptual, elements" 1943b, p. 293).

Now let us listen to Hegel:

> It is the facts or the contents in our consciousness, of whatever kind they are, that give character or determination to our feelings, perceptions, fancies and figurative conceptions; to our aims and duties; and to our thoughts and notions. From this point of view, feeling, perception, etc. are the forms assumed by these contents. The contents remain one and the same, whether they are merely felt, or felt with an admixture of thoughts, or merely and simply thought. In any one of these forms, or in the admixture of several, the contents confront the consciousness, or are its object. But when they are thus objects of consciousness, the modes of the several forms ally themselves with the contents, and each form of them appears in consequence to give rise to a special object. (1817, p. 243)

Here Hegel can be seen to be describing an unconscious process through which affect is associated with "facts" or "contents" in the mind. It is this association, which may be a complex of affects connected with the "fact" or mental image, that is the "special object". Thus inner objects are composed of "fact"—the image of the object—and the affects attached to it. In Fairbairn, the mother as the "fact" or "content" is seen in three affective modes: alluring, rejecting, and acceptable or "good". These are the *"forms assumed by* contents". Each form, in conjunction with the "fact"—the mother—then gives rise to the objects which Fairbairn described as "exciting", "rejecting", or "ideal" respectively. We will discuss the details of this idea later, but the point here is that because the mother is defined by three separate affective experiences, she becomes three separate mothers, each of whom embodies a separate relationship with the child. This view of the child as experiencing separate mothers is consistent with Fairbairn's postulation of splitting of the object.

For Hegel, self-consciousness "requires an object from which to differentiate itself". Such an object has to be recognised as alien and a "form of opposition to it". The Hegelian scholar, Singer, writes:

> There is therefore a peculiar kind of love-hate relationship between self-consciousness and the external object. The relationship, in the best tradition of love-hate relationships, comes to the surface in the form of desire. To desire something is to wish to possess it … to transform it into something that is yours and thus to strip it of its foreignness. (1983, p. 57)

Singer notes that such desire arises from the need for self-consciousness to find an external object but "yet finds itself limited by anything that is outside itself" (p. 58). To "desire something is … an unsatisfactory state for self-consciousness". In this dilemma, Singer notes that Hegel makes "the object of self-consciousness another self-consciousness". This implies that the object is returned to the external world, and has its own autonomy—no longer controlled by the subject. In Fairbairn's model, splitting of the object into three parts occurs in order that the individual should retain limited control over unsatisfactory aspects of the object, leaving the ideal or satisfactory object free for interaction and connection with the external world. This is Fairbairn's way of representing the infant's recognition of another independent "self-consciousness". Because the central ego is associated with the ideal object in the inner world, external reality always plays an important role in relationships of the inner world.

The acknowledgement by the infant that the mother is separate also carries the implication that the infant himself is perceived by the mother as separate, and that the infant understands this mental separateness. Self-consciousness includes recognition that the self is an object both to the mother and to himself. That is to say, the condition of self-consciousness is one of fundamental splits in the ego, fitting Fairbairn's contention that splitting of the ego is universal.

We saw that Hegel made "the object of self-consciousness another self-consciousness". For Hegel this took the form of God or the Absolute Spirit. In secular form, the state is a representation of the absolute. The important point here is complex: that which is other is also that within which the self is incorporated. Fairbairn also drew attention to this phenomenon:

> The process of differentiation of the object derives particular significance from the fact that infantile dependence is characterised not only by identification, but also by an oral attitude of incorporation. In virtue of this fact the object with which the individual is identified becomes equivalent to an incorporated object, or, to put the matter in a more arresting fashion,

the object in which the individual is incorporated is incorporated in the individual. (1941, pp. 42–43)

We have stressed the Hegelian origins of Fairbairn's philosophical position because it serves to clarify the distinction between his view of human nature and that of Freud. Although Hegelian ideas provided the underpinning from German philosophy in Freud's student days, it was Schopenhauer's ideas that provided the cultural milieu within which he was educated. Discussing Freud's philosophical background, Ellenberger (1970, pp. 541–542) and Anzieu (1986, p. 32) record his attendance at Brentano's lectures. Brentano's (1973) main contribution to philosophy was a theory in which it is "the intentionality or directedness of mental states that marks off the mental from the physical" (Blackburn, 1994, p. 49). Here we can see a possible connection with Freud's early notions of wish fulfilment, but the notion of intentionality also fits well with Schopenhauer's (1886) contention of will as the driving force of human motivation.

Additionally, Schopenhauer suggested that drives and desires can become psychically suppressed and distorted. Ellenberger wrote that Thomas Mann "felt that Freud's description of the id and ego was 'to a hair' Schopenhauer's description of the will and the intellect, translated from philosophy to metaphysics" (1970, p. 209). While the accuracy of this comment can be questioned, another aspect of Schopenhauer relevant to Freud is his contention that it is only when the individual achieves a state of dissociation from drives and desires that peace or "Nirvana" can be attained. While Nirvana is an Eastern concept, it is compatible with the Freudian idea that the psyche seeks a condition of stasis. It is also compatible with the theory of inertia of Helmholtz (1847), to whom Freud was connected by Brücke, a teaching colleague of both Helmholtz and Freud. In summary, we can say that the view of human nature assumed by Brentano, Schopenhauer, Brücke, and Freud is that of an atomistic individual *acted upon* by both internal (instinctual) and external (environmental) forces. In contrast, for Hegel and Fairbairn the individual person is *acting within* specific relationships, initially within the family and then within increasingly larger units of human society, which are themselves in an active dialectic with the environment. Thus for Hegel and Fairbairn the person seeks the optimum development of potential in common and in concert with others, rather than in spite of them.

Fairbairn and the philosophy of science

A fuller understanding of the philosophical origin of Fairbairn's contribution allows us to locate psychoanalysis as an integrated discipline within the mainstream of twentieth-century thought. When we turn to the contrasting scientific frameworks that Freud and Fairbairn used to develop their metapsychology, we can see a difference that parallels the contrast between Freud's Platonic dualism and Fairbairn's Aristotelian integration. It was Fairbairn's revised view of the scientific assumptions underpinning psychoanalysis that gave his theory an essential philosophical and scientific coherence that cannot be separated from his clinical insights.

Freud's ideas relied upon the nineteenth-century mechanical view of physics dominated by Helmholtz's (1847) conception of energy as divorced from structure, that is to say that a body is essentially inert until there is an outside application of a "quantum" of energy. When the energy source is withdrawn, the body's energy is determined by the laws of inertia, and because of resistance, tends to return to rest. Freud viewed mental energy as if it were an external source of energy applied to the mind, which he viewed almost as if it were made up of contents analogous to things with a measurable mass. Energy, therefore, came to bear on opposing forces that took the form of opposing instincts with conflicting aims. When Freud applied this model to mental structure, the conflicting aims of the ego and id instincts—and later the life and death instincts—had to be resolved. He perceived that a state of inertness would take over if the energy was suppressed or neutralised. Freud's theory of repression fitted both his clinical observations and his view of the mind as conforming to the laws of Newtonian physics. In this model, repression acts as a de-energising force, producing a steady state of the mind at rest, and thus a stable mental structure.

Freud's (1923b) structural model also postulates the apparently evolutionary development of the ego out of the id, and of the superego out of the ego. This use of phylogenic ideas in association with evolutionary ones can be traced to Freud's friendship with Stanley Hall. Hall (1904) thought that just as the foetus passes through the full evolutionary process (ontogeny recapitulates phylogeny), so the individual psyche's development recapitulates the evolution of mind. Hall's postulation of this process during adolescence led him to suggest that phylogenic development was responsible for disruptive social and pathological behaviour. Freud followed the implications of this evolutionary model of mind in *Civilization and Its Discontents* (1930a), where he depicted the individual in direct conflict with society throughout the life cycle. Hence, Freud extended the conflictual and dualistic mode to the entire realm of discourse between the individual and the external world. The individual, divided against his instincts internally, was also beset beyond himself by being inherently in conflict with society.

In contrast, the twentieth-century view of science is interactive and interdependent. It originated with Einstein, Planck, and Heisenberg among others. The shift in scientific model came directly as a result of the implications of Einstein's 1901 theory of relativity in which $E = mc^2$. In this formula, energy and mass are interchangeable and interrelated. From this discovery, a new model of physics conceptualised physical bodies as composite entities that contain an inherent potential that is actualised by means of active interactions with the external environment. Moreover, the idea of "opposing forces" was reformulated into a theory of mutual attraction and synthesis. An example from physics occurs when atoms combine to form molecular structures with different and distinct characteristics unlike the elements that make up the new molecule. The qualities of the new molecules cannot be predicted by knowledge of the component elements nor of the energy involved in the transformation. In the modern scientific view, all substances have spatial relationships within their environment that are determined both by physical and energic factors. Thus energy and structure are inseparable.

From his first study of *The Ego and the Id* (1923b), Fairbairn found Freud's use of energy problematic without knowing exactly how to resolve his sense of the incongruity in Freud's argument (Scharff & Birtles, 1994). He already understood that energy and structure could not be divorced in the way that Freud's mind/body dualism implied. Eventually, he was able to formulate a psychology in which mental structure and content are interrelated. In his new object relations theory of the personality, he replaced Freud's idea of mental energy with the postulation that mental structure and content are joined by an affective charge that gives meaning and that is the hallmark of the relationship between the two.

The early studies

Fairbairn's early writing and teaching were unpublished until 1994 (ibid.). In the years from 1928 to 1930, he concentrated on understanding three aspects of Freud's contribution: psychic structure, instinct theory, and the nature of repression. He seemed to have intended to write a book-length explication and critique of Freud. The early seminar notes and papers are extremely thorough, but his ambition to write a book on Freud was apparently given up in the mid-1930s when he moved from his academic post at Edinburgh University to full-time private practice.

Initially, Fairbairn focused his attention on psychic structure. In lecture notes for classes he taught at Edinburgh University (1928), he identified logical inconsistencies in Freud that he felt were associated with Freud's postulates concerning the topography of mental structure. It was logically inconsistent, Fairbairn wrote, to say that the ego grew out of the id but was in fundamental opposition to it, as it was to assert a similar opposition of the superego to the ego. In his papers on the superego written in the next year, Fairbairn explored Freud's account of the relationship between the three structures (1929a). His arguments hinge on the primitive nature of the Freudian superego and its functioning as both a conscious and an unconscious phenomenon, and as both agent and subject of repression. He thought his own clinical experience demonstrated that Freud mistook psychic functions and phenomena for structures. While he had no doubt about the reality of the observable *phenomena* of superego *functioning*, he concluded that its *operation* within the psyche does not signify a separate structure opposed to the ego and imposed upon it. Instead, he followed Freud's account of the development of the superego *function* as analogous to a process of object identification, but he added that this development is associated with "sentiment formation", a first step along the path of locating the central role of affects in object relations. He wrote, "If the superego is usually more organised than a complex and less organised than a secondary personality, it would yet appear to be a psychical organisation of a similar order" (ibid., p. 101).

These early papers and seminar notes follow Freud in viewing the id as the home of instinctive impulses, but the questions Fairbairn raised in writing them mark the beginning of his theoretical reorientation from instinct theory to a theory of personality based on the relationship of the ego to its objects. Already in 1929 Fairbairn asked, "How is the super-ego repressed if it is itself the structural agent of repression?" He concluded that *the ego is a dynamic entity* and *the superego a mental function designed to promote progressive adaptation to the environment*. The superego function can then be undertaken *by any relationship* into which the ego, "or part of the ego", enters with an object.

In this early attitude of questioning, he took a first step to his later position, based on the inseparability of matter and energy, in which superego functions are matters of internal relations of mutual influence between ego and object, that is, towards his later description of superego functions carried out by internalised ego structures derived from the early mother–child relationship and from the reorganisation of these in the Oedipal period (Fairbairn, 1954b, 1963a). It is of more than incidental interest that it is in these lectures that Fairbairn first used the term "organised self" instead of the term "ego", a first step on the road to personalising endopsychic structure. Although he never fully delineated this shift himself, it remains an assumption within his theory that was later elaborated by his students Guntrip (1969) and Sutherland (1994) with Fairbairn's approval.

Fairbairn's study of Freud's structural theory was followed by a study of libido theory and of the life and death instincts (1930). He related Helmholtz's influence to Freud's use of the idea of "opposing forces". Much later, Fairbairn summarised this early work when he wrote,

> … although Freud's whole system of thought was concerned with object-relationships, he adhered theoretically to the principle that libido is primarily pleasure seeking, i.e. that it is directionless. By contrast, I adhere to the principle that libido is primarily object-seeking, i.e. that it has direction … Thus Freud's view that libido is primarily pleasure-seeking follows directly from his divorce of energy from structure; for, once energy is divorced from structure, the only psychical change which can be envisaged as other than disturbing, i.e. as pleasant, is one which makes for the establishment of an equilibrium of forces, i.e. a directionless change. By contrast, if we conceive of energy as inseparable from structure, then the only changes which are intelligible are changes in structural relationships and in relationships between structures, and such changes are essentially directional. (1944, p. 126)

Fairbairn's doctoral thesis (1929b), written at about the same time as the early papers on the superego, was titled "Dissociation and Repression". In it, he traced contributions from Freud, Janet, Rivers, and McDougall, among others. He was still bound by Freud's use of the pleasure principle when he concluded that dissociation is a general capacity of man, while repression is a specific instance of the operation of dissociation in relation to that which is "unpleasant". But he continued his early move beyond the pleasure principle when he wrote, "[I]n the case of repression the dissociated elements consist essentially in tendencies belonging to mental structure" (p. 79). If we widen the notion of that which is "unpleasant" beyond the notion of simple gratification and take note of the affective component in its meaning, we move towards Fairbairn's later contention that what is repressed is the experience of failures of loving care that are most perceived as "unpleasant" by the infant. This study of the relationship of dissociation and repression formed the background for Fairbairn's later idea of splitting of the personality under the impact of extreme experience of the "unpleasant", as illustrated in his later formulation that splitting and repression of the personality occur under the impact of a person's "frustration of his desire to be loved as a person and to have his love accepted" (1941, pp. 39–40).

Fairbairn's object relations theory

Between 1940 and 1944, Fairbairn wrote the series of papers which constitute the heart of his contribution and which were published as the first four papers of *Psychoanalytic Studies of the Personality* (1952). In the first of the papers, "Schizoid Factors in the Personality" (1940a), he described the ubiquitous quality of splitting in the personality.

This was followed by "A Revised Psychopathology of the Psychoses and Psychoneuroses" (1941), in which he based the framework of psychopathology on the vicissitudes of dependence. Aristotelian psychology holds that dependency is necessary for development, as we have noted. Fairbairn wrote in this paper that the total dependence of the newborn takes a gradual developmental path to the mature dependence of the adult personality. Neither physical nor psychic development is attainable in isolation, so the individual is necessarily dependent upon relationships with other individuals in the external world. The child's initial dependence on parents is gradually transformed to adult dependence on other adults, and on culture, education, political order, law, and nature. Fairbairn described mature dependence as "a capacity on the part of the differentiated individual for cooperative relationships with differentiated objects" (1941, p. 145). In mature dependence, individuals are able to accept and relate to the integrity of other selves. In this paper, Fairbairn goes on to describe phobic, obsessional, hysterical, and paranoid syndromes as varying "transitional techniques" for handling internal object relationships during the transition from infantile dependence to mature dependence, rather than seeing these symptoms as deriving from failures at specific psychosexual stages to which the individual later regresses.

The third paper of the collection, "The Repression and the Return of Bad Objects (with Special Reference to the 'War Neuroses')" (1943a), described the dedication of the ego to painful object relationships lest it lose part of itself. Here Fairbairn must also have been drawing on his considerable experience with psychic trauma, obtained as a combat officer in World War I, and from seeing abused children clinically in the 1930s (Birtles & Scharff, 1994; Sutherland, 1989). In trauma and rejection, painful part-object relations are split off and repressed, but they continue to press for expression and recognition—for a return to consciousness. Here Fairbairn was able to explain why children tend so persistently to blame themselves for bad experiences even in the face of abuse. They are, he said, trying to maintain the object as good in order to maximise the chance of being loved. If the object is seen as bad, then nothing the child can do, not even atonement for badness, will secure love—a condition he termed "unconditional badness", while if the child sees itself as bad and the object as good but treating the child badly because of the child's own badness, there is a chance of being loved if only the child can right things himself ("conditional badness") (1943a, pp. 65–72).

By 1944, Fairbairn could make a formulation of object relations theory which was essentially complete. In "Endopsychic Structure Considered in Terms of Object-relationships" (1944) he wrote that the infant is born with an ego that is initially whole but undifferentiated. In the face of inevitable dissatisfactions in handling by the mother, the infant first incorporates the object to deal with the pain of the frustration. However, now faced with the problem of having a painfully rejecting object inside, the central part of the ego—or central ego—splits off and represses those aspects of the object still felt to be intolerably painful. He added that a part of the ego itself is always split off in conjunction with these part-objects, and that this constellation of ego and object is characterised by the affective tone of the problematic relationship which cannot be borne in consciousness. He described the fate of ego and object constellations organised around persecution and rejection, which he termed a relationship between the internal saboteur (the ego component) and the rejecting object. (He later called these the anti-libidinal ego and rejecting object.) The other class of painful object relationship is that between the libidinal ego and libidinal object (later termed the exciting object), described as a relationship built around the excessive excitement of need—that is, the relationship with part of the mother who is felt to overfeed, hover anxiously, or act seductively. The central ego itself acts to repress both the rejecting object constellation and the libidinal object constellation, the motive being that they are too painful to be borne in consciousness.

Some years later, Fairbairn added that there was a parallel relationship between central ego and its object, which he called the ideal object—that aspect of the object not subject to repression. In the case of the hysteric, the ideal object is shorn of sexuality and aggression, leaving it a neutralised object (Fairbairn, 1954b). The complete endopsychic structure is therefore made up of six subparts, which are in dynamic relation to each other through repression and mutual influence. He further noted that even the object parts of the self are actually ego structures, and therefore capable of initiating psychic action (1944, p. 132), a situation illustrated by the possibility of the patient acting in a way that can be seen as being in identification with the way the patient felt previously treated by a parent.

The following diagram provides a synopsis of Fairbairn's six-part structure of the personality.

Finally, Fairbairn described the way the internal ego and object structures exert dynamic influence on each other. The situation he described specifically involved what he called secondary repression of libidinal ego and libidinal object by the anti-libidinal ego. (This situation is indicated by an arrow in Figure 1.) Clinically we see patients who use anger to cover up

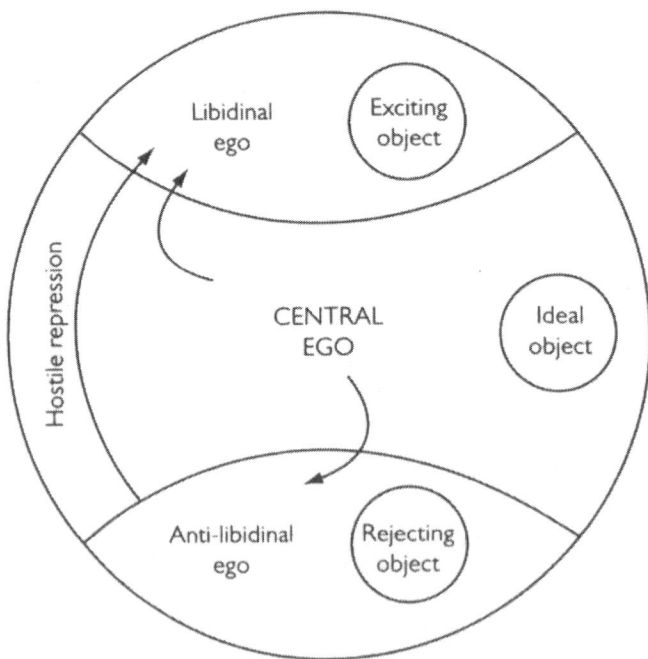

Figure 1. Fairbairn's model of psychic organisation. The central ego in relation to the ideal object is in conscious interaction with the caregiver. The central ego represses the split-off libidinal and anti-libidinal aspects of its experience along with corresponding parts of the ego that remain unconscious. The libidinal system is further repressed by the anti-libidinal system. (From D. E. Scharff, 1982. By permission, Routledge.)

the affect of unrequited longing stemming from their libidinal object constellation. They are more comfortable with an angry stance towards objects than with painfully unsatisfied longing. Although Fairbairn did not describe the parallel situation, once he pointed the way to the internal dynamic relationship between object relations sets, we can see that the libidinal ego can also secondarily repress the anti-libidinal relationship, as represented in patients who show an exaggerated sense of love and hope—a too-good-to-be-true personality—in order to mask resentful anger that is even more painful to them. The point that emerges is that all internal structures are in constant dynamic interaction with each other. This dynamic is more fluid and changeable in health than in pathology, where it tends to become fixed or frozen in one or another pattern.

In "Endopsychic Structure" (1944) and later in his paper "Observations on the Nature of Hysterical States" (1954b), Fairbairn also discussed the Oedipus situation in revolutionary terms, writing that it was not dependent upon a castration complex or on the possession or lack of a penis, or even on active and passive sexual characteristics. The beginning of the Oedipal problem, he noted, was based upon the original deprivation of the abandoned baby on the hillside (ibid., pp. 27–29), associated with the capacity of the parents to thwart, frustrate, and reject the child. The development of sexuality depends not on ideas phantasised by the child, but upon the living reality of the dependence relationship as understood by the child to involve sexual relatedness, and exciting and rejecting objects projected into sexual parts of the body. Gender and sexual orientation are dependent upon a blend of identification and object-seeking. Maturity for Fairbairn is no longer a matter of a genitality which sexually infuses the personality, but of a mature individual with a capacity to relate to a whole other person when both of them are understood to have genitals. In consequence, it is the parent's own mature responsiveness to the child's needs which predisposes that child to future mental health and well-being, rather than a relatively isolated aspect of sexual development.

Fairbairn did not overlook the way psychic development depended upon and interacted with inherent genetic and constitutional capacities as embodied in Freud's concept of drives. His own view of drives requires some clarification. The view of "instincts" (1930), which orchestrates his work, involved two main types of tendencies. Those that could be properly defined as drives are concerned with the preservation of the body. These respond to internal states such as hunger, object need, and sexual desire. The second group of tendencies are "reactive" and respond to experience in the external world. Frustration and consequent anger and aggression come into this category, and he clearly believed that aggression, while of fundamental importance, was a secondary, reactive tendency (1952, 1963). However, object relationships can incorporate any affect that has arisen as a response to either internal or external tendencies. In such situations, reactive tendencies operate in a manner analogous to "drives". An example of this would be violent behaviour that had originated as anger due to infantile frustration incorporated affectively within an internalised relationship.

Fairbairn thought that potential in each individual is dependent upon genetic predisposition. The internal structures and genetic capacities of the individual confer a flexibility for development in the same way that the structure of the carbon atom defines its capacities for molecular relationships. This much derives from Freud's discussion of the drives and inherited basis of personality. But for Fairbairn, such development is always in concert with actual experience, and the drives achieve meaning only within the structure of relational experience (1956b).

Inner reality, and therefore personality, are the outcome of continuous series of a dialectic of encounters between endowment and external reality.

Fairbairn took as his beginning point an integral ego that intrinsically seeks relationships with important sustaining figures. This picture of the ego we might now call an unformed inherent potential to become a self (Sutherland, 1994). Within the sustenance of these relationships, the infant and growing child takes into his psyche both experiences that are painfully frustrating and those that are satisfying. As the child does this, his psyche is organised by this introjection of objects and by a splitting of the ego (or self) into units of relational structures. In the process the child constructs an internal reality that is derived from experience with external reality. The mind is thus made up of structures that contain prior relational experience, although these structures are heavily modified by the intrinsic process of the structuring itself—by the limitations of the child's capacity to understand at the time experience is taken in, and by the distortions and modifications introduced by developmental issues and the biases of the child's prior experience. Once inner reality is thus established, it monitors and influences external reality and relationships in a never-ending cycle, in which it also continues to be modified by these external relationships.

Although Fairbairn's model was built largely out of the study of pathological development, he always intended that it should explain normal development and thus form the framework for a general psychology. We can amend Fairbairn's theory in order to bridge the gap to a general psychology in the following ways, which we believe to be consistent with his actual use of his concepts. In the normal personality, the central self contains tendencies of need for objects, and of need for separation from objects within the context of relationships. Both the desire for objects (the libidinal tendency that includes sexual longing), and the need for separation from objects (the anti-libidinal tendency that includes limit setting) are normal ways of relating. It is only when these are excessive that they become pathological. Internal objects are embedded in the self structures of which they are a part, but we can also see that the needy exciting object and the rejecting object are in part associated with central self and the object of the central self as objects of libidinal attachment and limit-setting objects respectively. All the elements of internal object relations are in constant dynamic relation to each other. The situation can be summarised in the following diagram.

The fixity that occurs when patients attempt to maintain patterns as defensive closed systems, attempting to bar continual interaction with and feedback from others, tends to make the inner world resemble a closed system. This is the situation of resistance, which in Fairbairn's view emanated not solely from internal conflict between mental structures, or from reluctance to making the unconscious conscious. He thought that patients' resistance in psychotherapy stemmed from a reluctance to exposing parts of the patients' internal reality to therapists, to an unwillingness to give up parts of their internally organised self:

> I have now come to regard ... the greatest of all sources of resistance [to be] the maintenance of the patient's internal world as a closed system ... [I]t becomes still another aim of psychoanalytical treatment to effect breaches of the closed system which constitutes the patient's inner world, and thus to make this world accessible to the influence of outer reality. (1958, p. 84)

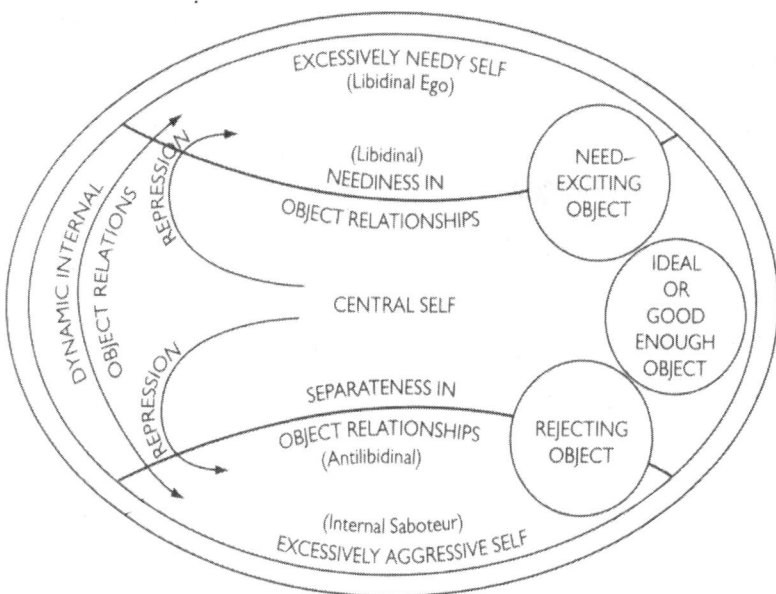

Figure 2. Revision of object relations theory. Neediness and separateness are aspects of the Central Self. Exciting and Rejecting Objects partly communicate with the Ideal Object and are partly repressed. All aspects of self and object are in dynamic relation. (From D. E. Scharff, 1992. By permission, Jason Aronson.)

Under these circumstances, the patient feels that psychoanalysis is an assault on the inner world as a closed system, and trains his resistance on the person of the analyst, who he comes to feel is responsible for the assault.

A fundamental contribution of object relations theory comes from the principle inherent in the formulation of the complex relationship between the infant and the mother. It is the notion that one must understand the subjective experience of the child to understand the meaning of the object relationships involved. Nevertheless, while the child-centred view that Fairbairn maintained in developing his notions of endopsychic structure gave him a new and powerful perspective, it also limited his ultimate reach. We can now see how the mother–child paradigm can be enriched by the newer analogies of current scientific understanding, by a view derived from field theory of the inextricability of objects from their context, a view that was adumbrated when Fairbairn wrote, "[T]he object in which the individual is incorporated is incorporated in the individual" (1941, p. 43). His description of "exciting" and "rejecting" objects also contains within it the potential for a more subtle appreciation than the original formulation. In a broader perspective, acceptance and rejection are experienced by the mother as well as the child. In order to experience a satisfying relationship, both mother and child have to be able to give and to receive: the experience must by definition be interdependent and interactive, what has now been called "intersubjective" (Stern, 1985).

When Fairbairn modified psychoanalytic theory, he replaced Freud's model based on a differentiation between conscious and unconscious structure with a focus on the differentiation between inner and outer realities. Freud's structural model was concerned with the progressive taming of the drives. Fairbairn replaced this with an open systems, information-processing model able to take advantage of the cybernetic principles of the newer models made available through modern physics, chemistry, and mathematics. This shift made it possible for analytic theory to move beyond a two-dimensional theory in which the individual only moves in a linear direction, growing by moving forward and retreating through regression to fixation at prior positions as a result of trauma or overwhelming stress. In Fairbairn's model, the individual structures internal reality out of accumulated experience, but does so in order to understand current external reality at each successive phase. The storage of prior history allows the individual to make sense of current experience, and the internal reality that conserves structure while, at the same time, it continues to be susceptible to modification throughout life. In psychoanalysis, current experience with the analyst gives information about internal object relations because these are what the patient is using, as he or she does in every interpersonal encounter, to make sense of the therapeutic experience.

As he described his object relations theory of the personality, Fairbairn came to realise that it is the relationship between patient and therapist that is the crucial factor for growth and change, not, as others had considered, the single factors of exact interpretation, genetic reconstruction, transference interpretation, or any particular technical recommendations isolated from the personal factor. Rather, it is the use of technique within the growth-promoting relationship that is the fundamental agent of change:

> In my own opinion, the really decisive factor is the relationship of the patient to the analyst, and it is upon this relationship that the other factors … depend not only for their effectiveness, but for their very existence, since in the absence of a therapeutic relationship with the analyst they simply do not occur … [W]hat I understand by "the relationship between the individual and his analyst" is not just the relationship involved in the transference, but the total relationship existing between the patient and analyst as persons. (1958, pp. 82–83)

This shift of emphasis stemmed directly from his proposal for a new theoretical basis for psychoanalysis. It is a shift that has been sustained in contemporary analysis, which has now moved even further to emphasise the person of the analyst and the use of the analyst's subjective experience as a fundamental therapeutic tool (Gill, 1984; Hoffman, 1991, 1996; Jacobs, 1991; Spillius & Feldman, 1989). In this practical way, object relations theory also laid the ground for further developments of analytic theory itself, and for its application to many other fields in new and interesting ways: to research in the mother–infant relationship and in infant development, to group and institutional applications, to the use of psychoanalytic theory and technique with families and couples, and to new developments in social theory, theology, and group relations.

Fairbairn began to apply object relations theory to social policy, social issues, philosophy of science, child development, education, and the psychology of art. His first steps in these directions went far enough for us to see the potential range and usefulness of his ideas (Fairbairn, 1952; Scharff & Birtles, 1994). Later writers have enlarged on the many implications of Fairbairn's work. The first to do so were Guntrip and Sutherland, both of whom were analysand, student, and colleague to Fairbairn. Guntrip began by summarising Fairbairn's work (Guntrip, 1961). He suggested to Fairbairn that the term "self" more accurately described the issues Fairbairn had been discussing while using the term "ego" (1969). Fairbairn expressed agreement with him (Sutherland, 1989). Guntrip followed the theme of the self's search for an elusive sustaining object, which he summarised in his work on the "regressed libidinal ego"—that part of the ego which becomes deeply repressed in consequence of the failure to find a sustaining relationship with an object (Guntrip, 1969). Some have felt that Guntrip's specific theoretical elaboration distorted the symmetry of Fairbairn's theory, but it is clear that Guntrip extended the reach of Fairbairn's contribution towards a theory of the self. The concept of the regressed libidinal ego is an extrapolation from Fairbairn's theory, which describes a mental state rather than a structure, depicting the unconscious but subjective experience of the failure of the mother to perceive and communicate to the infant her acceptance of the infant's selfhood. The failure of experience of self-development seems to represent a combination of the effect of aggression redirected, turned from the object to the libidinal self, and of subjective experience of the failure of the self in the face of experience with a mother who is unavailable because of preoccupation or depression. The result is that the child incorporates a non-responding and non-affirming aspect of the object as central to its primary relationship.

Sutherland began by spreading the word. In a landmark paper given at the Menninger Clinic (Sutherland, 1963), he outlined the scientific basis for Fairbairn's work and made it available to a wider audience in America, which included Kernberg, who discussed Sutherland's paper (Kernberg, 1963), and made a great deal of use of Fairbairn's contribution in his own subsequent work (1976, 1980). Sutherland's encyclopaedic grasp facilitated the growth of psychoanalytic theory and application partly through his own writing, but principally through his editorship of the central international vehicles of psychoanalysis—the *British Journal of Medical Psychology*, the *International Journal of Psychoanalysis*, and the *International Psychoanalytical Library*, and through his stewardship of the Tavistock Clinic as its medical director for twenty-one years. In these ways he kept Fairbairn's ideas alive and well as a quiet but strong undercurrent in the development of psychoanalysis.

It was not until the publication of Sutherland's biography of Fairbairn in 1989, and the gathering of Sutherland's own papers, published as *The Autonomous Self* (1994), that we could see how his own interest in the evolution of the self moved the theoretical work forward, especially in the realm of investigation of the self as an overarching entity throughout life which bridges from the individual's internal object relations to relations with other individuals and with the wider society.

Of the other writers who applied Fairbairn's work in important ways, perhaps the best known is John Bowlby (1969, 1973, 1980). Bowlby specifically acknowledged his Fairbairnian orientation in the development of attachment theory and the ethological approach to infant development (personal communication), which have spurred the enormous increase in our understanding of the mother–infant relationship during the last twenty-five years while also leading to other research which has enhanced our understanding of the biology of mind (Schore, 1994). Henry Dicks (1967) blended Fairbairn's contribution with Klein's work on projective identification in applying object relations theory to marital work and to a psychology of interaction. This in turn allowed Shapiro and Zinner (collected in J. Scharff, 1989) and Scharff and Scharff

(1987, 1992) in the USA to continue the application to families as well. Kernberg (1963, 1976, 1980) made Fairbairn's work known in the USA and gave object relations new impetus worldwide. This was consolidated by Grotstein's work, *Splitting and Projective Identification* (1981), which furthered the idea of the centrality of splitting in development and psychopathology. Sutherland (1989) has made the point that there is more than an echo of Fairbairn's writing about the self in the language of Kohut's contributions (1971, 1977), giving confirmation about the way Fairbairn's new orientation for analytic theory had become so much a common property that others thought they had discovered the paths he had pioneered. More recently, Rayner (1991), Padel (1972, 1991), Ogden (1986), and Grotstein and Rinsley (1994) explored the ramifications of Fairbairn's work further. Mitchell (1988) has placed it at the centre of his relational theory, and Scharff and Scharff have continued to foster the application of Fairbairn's concepts to family and marital therapy, trauma, and to an integrated view of psychotherapy and psychoanalysis based on self and object relations (D. Scharff, 1992, 1996; J. Scharff, 1992; J. & D. Scharff, 1994).

Fairbairn's ideas are now so central to the vision of psychoanalysis that they often pass for truisms, making it hard to remember a time when the need for relationships was not seen as the central fact of development and of therapy, when splitting and its vicissitudes were not understood to be important from the beginning of life. Before Fairbairn, the analyst was held to be an impersonal projection screen, striving to be technically correct and uninvolved. The focus on relatedness that originated with his vision has fundamentally reordered psychoanalysis. It has also shaped the contributions of analysis to philosophy, science, the humanities, and social understanding. Fairbairn taught us that relationships are at the centre of psychoanalytic theory and practice. But, more important, he led us to see that personal relationships form the essence of our human experience.

References

Anzieu, D. (1986). *Freud's Self-Analysis* (P. Graham, Trans.). Preface by M. M. R. Khan. London: Hogarth.
Berlin, I. (1949). Two concepts of liberty. In: *Four Essays on Liberty*. Oxford: Oxford University Press, 1969.
Birtles, E. F., & Scharff, D. E. (Eds.) (1994). *From Instinct to Self: Selected Papers of W. R. D. Fairbairn, Volume II: Applications and Early Contributions*. Northvale, NJ: Jason Aronson.
Blackburn, S. (1994). *Oxford Dictionary of Philosophy*. Oxford: Oxford University Press.
Bowlby, J. (1969, 1973, 1980). *Attachment and Loss, Volumes I, II, and III*. London: Hogarth.
Brentano, F. (1973). *Psychology from an Empirical Standpoint* (A. C. Rancurello, Trans.). London: Routledge, 1995.
Dicks, H. V. (1967). *Marital Tensions*. London: Routledge.
Ellenberger, H. F. (1970). *The Discovery of the Unconscious*. London: Fontana, 1994.
Fairbairn, W. R. D. (1928). The ego and the id. In: E. F. Birtles & D. E. Scharff (Eds.), *From Instinct to Self: Selected Papers of W. R. D. Fairbairn, Volume II: Applications and Early Contributions* (pp. 4–5). Northvale, NJ: Jason Aronson, 1994.
Fairbairn, W. R. D. (1929a). The superego. In: E. F. Birtles & D. E. Scharff (Eds.), *From Instinct to Self: Selected Papers of W. R. D. Fairbairn, Volume II: Applications and Early Contributions* (pp. 80–114). Northvale, NJ: Jason Aronson, 1994.

Fairbairn, W. R. D. (1929b). Dissociation and repression. In: E. F. Birtles & D. E. Scharff (Eds.), *From Instinct to Self: Selected Papers of W. R. D. Fairbairn, Volume II: Applications and Early Contributions* (pp. 13–79). Northvale, NJ: Jason Aronson, 1994.

Fairbairn, W. R. D. (1930). Libido theory re-evaluated. In: E. F. Birtles & D. E. Scharff (Eds.), *From Instinct to Self: Selected Papers of W. R. D. Fairbairn, Volume II: Applications and Early Contributions* (pp. 115–156). Northvale, NJ: Jason Aronson, 1994.

Fairbairn, W. R. D. (1940a). Schizoid factors in the personality. In: *Psychoanalytic Studies of the Personality* (pp. 3–27). London: Tavistock, 1952.

Fairbairn, W. R. D. (1941). A revised psychopathology of the psychoses and the neuroses. In: *Psychoanalytic Studies of the Personality* (pp. 28–58). London: Routledge, 1952.

Fairbairn, W. R. D. (1943a). The repression and the return of bad objects (with special reference to the "war neuroses"). *British Journal of Medical Psychology, 19*: 327–341. In: *Psychoanalytic Studies of the Personality* (pp. 59–81). London: Tavistock, 1952.

Fairbairn, W. R. D. (1943b). Untitled contribution to the "Controversial Discussions". Read by Dr Edward Glover at the British Psychoanalytical Society on 17 February 1943. In: E. F. Birtles & D. E. Scharff (Eds.), *From Instinct to Self: Selected Papers of W. R. D. Fairbairn, Volume II: Applications and Early Contributions* (pp. 293–294). Northvale, NJ: Jason Aronson, 1994.

Fairbairn, W. R. D. (1944). Endopsychic structure considered in terms of object-relationships. *International Journal of Psychoanalysis, 25*: 70–92. In: *Psychoanalytic Studies of the Personality* (pp. 82–136). London: Tavistock, 1952.

Fairbairn, W. R. D. (1952). *Psychoanalytic Studies of the Personality*. London: Tavistock.

Fairbairn, W. R. D. (1954b). Observations on the nature of hysterical states. In: D. E. Scharff & E. F. Birtles (Eds.), *From Instinct to Self: Selected Papers of W. R. D. Fairbairn, Volume I: Clinical and Theoretical Papers* (pp. 13–40). Northvale, NJ: Jason Aronson, 1994.

Fairbairn, W. R. D. (1956b). Re-evaluating some basic concepts. In: D. E. Scharff & E. F. Birtles (Eds.), *From Instinct to Self: Selected Papers of W. R. D. Fairbairn, Volume I: Clinical and Theoretical Papers* (pp. 129–138). Northvale, NJ: Jason Aronson, 1994.

Fairbairn, W. R. D. (1958a). On the nature and aims of psycho-analytical treatment. *International Journal of Psychoanalysis, 39*(5): 374–385. In: D. E. Scharff & E. F. Birtles (Eds.), *From Instinct to Self: Selected Papers of W. R. D. Fairbairn, Volume I: Clinical and Theoretical Papers* (pp. 74–92). Northvale, NJ: Jason Aronson, 1994.

Fairbairn, W. R. D. (1963a). Synopsis of an object-relations theory of the personality. *International Journal of Psychoanalysis, 44*: 224–225. In: D. E. Scharff & E. F. Birtles (Eds.), *From Instinct to Self: Selected Papers of W. R. D. Fairbairn, Volume I: Clinical and Theoretical Papers* (pp. 155–156). Northvale, NJ: Jason Aronson, 1994.

Freud, S. (1923b). *The Ego and the Id. S. E., 19*. London: Hogarth.

Freud, S. (1930a). *Civilization and its Discontents. S. E., 21*. London: Hogarth.

Gill, M. M. (1984). Psychoanalysis and psychotherapy: a revision. *International Journal of Psychoanalysis, 11*: 161–179.

Greenberg, J. R., & Mitchell, S. A. (1983). *Object Relations in Psychoanalytic Theory*. Cambridge, MA: Harvard University Press.

Grotstein, J. S. (1981). *Splitting and Projective Identification*. New York: Jason Aronson.

Grotstein, J. S., & Rinsley, D. B. (Eds.) (1994). *Fairbairn and the Origins of Object Relations*. London: Free Association.

Guntrip, H. (1961). *Personality Structure and Human Interaction*. London: Hogarth.

Guntrip, H. (1969). *Schizoid Phenomena, Object Relations and the Self*. New York: International Universities Press.

Hall, G. S. (1904). *Adolescence: Volumes 1 & 2*. New York: Appleton.
Hegel, G. W. F. (1807). *The Phenomenology of Spirit*. Oxford: Oxford University Press, 1979.
Hegel, G. W. F. (1817). The logic of Hegel. In: *The Encyclopaedia of the Philosophical Sciences* (W. Wallace, Trans.). Oxford: Clarendon Press, 1874.
Heimann, P. (1950). On countertransference. *International Journal of Psychoanalysis, 31*: 81–84.
Helmholtz, H. von (1847). Uber die Erhaltung der Kraft. In: Energy conservation as an example of simultaneous discovery by T. S. Kuhn (1957). In: M. Clagett (Ed.), *Critical Problems in the History of Science* (pp. 321–356). Madison, CT: Wisconsin University Press, 1959.
Hoffman, I. Z. (1991). Discussion: Toward a social-constructivist view of the psychoanalytic situation. *Psychoanalytic Dialogues, 1*: 74–105.
Hoffman, I. Z. (1996). Merton M. Gill: A study in theory development. *Psychoanalytic Dialogues, 6*: 5–53.
Jacobs, T. J. (1991). *The Use of the Self: Countertransference and Communication in the Analytic Situation*. Madison, CT: International Universities Press.
Kernberg, O. F. (1963). Discussion of Sutherland's "Object relations and the conceptual model of psychoanalysis". *British Journal of Medical Psychology, 36*: 121–124.
Kernberg, O. F. (1976). *Object Relations and Clinical Psychoanalysis*. New York: Jason Aronson.
Kernberg, O. F. (1980). *Internal World and External Reality: Object-Relations Theory Applied*. New York: Jason Aronson.
King, P., & Steiner, R. (Eds.) (1991). *The Freud-Klein Controversies: 1941–1945*. London: Routledge.
Klein, M. (1946). Notes on some schizoid mechanisms. *International Journal of Psychoanalysis, 27*: 99–110.
Klein, M. (1952). The origins of transference. *International Journal of Psychoanalysis, 33*: 433–438.
Kohut, H. (1971). *The Analysis of the Self*. New York: International Universities Press.
Kohut, H. (1977). *The Restoration of the Self*. New York: International Universities Press.
Mitchell, S. (1988). *Relational Concepts in Psychoanalysis*. Cambridge, MA: Harvard University Press.
Ogden, T. H. (1986). *The Matrix of the Mind*. Northvale, NJ: Jason Aronson.
Padel, J. (1972). The contribution of W. R. D. Fairbairn. *Bulletin of the European Psychoanalytical Federation, 2*: 13–26.
Padel, J. (1991). Fairbairn's thought on the relationship between inner and outer worlds. *Free Associations, 24*: 589–615.
Pringle-Pattison, A. S. (1882). *The Development from Kant to Hegel*. London: Williams & Norgate.
Rayner, E. (1991). *The Independent Mind in British Psychoanalysis*. Northvale, NJ: Jason Aronson.
Schacht, R. L. (1972). Hegel on freedom. In: A. MacIntyre (Ed.), *Hegel: A Collection of Critical Essays* (pp. 289–328). London: University of Notre Dame Press.
Scharff, D. E. (1982). *The Sexual Relationship*. London: Routledge.
Scharff, D. E. (1992). *Refinding the Object and Reclaiming the Self*. Northvale, NJ: Jason Aronson.
Scharff, D. E. (Ed.) (1996). *Object Relations Theory and Practice: An Introduction*. Northvale, NJ: Jason Aronson.
Scharff, D. E., & Birtles, E. F. (Eds.) (1994). *From Instinct to Self: Selected Papers of W. R. D. Fairbairn, Volume I: Clinical and Theoretical Papers*. Northvale, NJ: Jason Aronson.
Scharff, D. E., & Scharff, J. S. (1987). *Object Relations Family Therapy*. Northvale, NJ: Jason Aronson.
Scharff, D. E., & Scharff, J. S. (1991). *Object Relations Couple Therapy*. Northvale, NJ: Jason Aronson.
Scharff, J. S. (Ed.) (1989). *Foundations of Object Relations Family Therapy*. Northvale, NJ: Jason Aronson.

Scharff, J. S. (1992). *Projective and Introjective Identification and the Use of the Therapist's Self*. Northvale, NJ: Jason Aronson.

Scharff, J. S., & Scharff, D. E. (1994). *Object Relations Therapy of Physical and Sexual Trauma*. Northvale, NJ: Jason Aronson.

Schopenhauer, A. (1886). *The World as Will and Idea*. London: J. M. Dent—Everyman, 1997.

Schore, A. N. (1994). *Affect Regulation and the Origin of the Self*. Hillsdale, NJ: Lawrence Erlbaum.

Singer, P. (1983). *Hegel*. Oxford: Oxford University Press.

Spillius, E. B., & Feldman, M. (Eds.) (1989). *Psychic Equilibrium and Psychic Change: Selected Papers of Betty Joseph*. London: Routledge.

Stern, D. (1985). *The Interpersonal World of the Infant*. New York: Basic.

Stout, G. F. (1927). *The Groundwork of Psychology*. London: W. B. Clive.

Sutherland, J. D. (1963). Object relations and the conceptual model of psychoanalysis. *British Journal of Medical Psychology, 36*: 109–124.

Sutherland, J. D. (1989). *Fairbairn's Journey to the Interior*. London: Free Associations.

Sutherland, J. D. (1994). *The Autonomous Self* (J. S. Scharff, Ed.). Northvale, NJ: Jason Aronson.

Winnicott, D. W. (1949). Hate in the countertransference. In: *Collected Papers: From Paediatrics to Psychoanalysis* (pp. 194–203). London: Hogarth, 1958.

CHAPTER TWO

From Oedipus to Antigone: Hegelian themes in Fairbairn

Gal Gerson

Within the history of psychoanalytic theory, the shift from drive to relation is so dramatic that the undercurrents within it might be overlooked. The mid-century British theorists who transformed psychoanalysis are often perceived as a single front, with each of its constituents offering a unique contribution: Suttie initiating the move by openly challenging Freud, Balint and Winnicott providing clinical observations and innovative concepts, Bowlby linking the new theory to broader scientific concerns, and Fairbairn constructing the explanatory model. Second-generation authors like Ainsworth and Khan are seen as further elaborating this complex but distinct approach to psychology (Gomez, 1997; Holmes, 1993; Schwartz, 1999).

Object relations theorists have similarly been described as sharing a single ideology that was aligned with the comprehensive post-war social settlement. This worldview has been described by both admirers and critics as having at its heart a perception of the family typical of mid-century thinking. Continuous parental care was assumed to be the core factor in individual and social health. The conditions for enabling such care within the modular two-generations household and instructing the individuals charged with it were perceived as the basic social entitlements (Gerson, 2004; Mayhew, 2006; Riley, 1983; van der Horst, & van der Veer, 2010).

A further look would hint at nuances within this picture. Fairbairn's position would begin to stand out. Here, I point to some attributes that make his views distinct. I want to suggest that Fairbairn's perspective, and the underlying character that makes for its differences from much of the other object relations school, have to do with Fairbairn's affinity with Hegel and the way that Hegel was interpreted in Britain.

Fairbairn's link to Hegel is known and has been established by Birtles (2002, 2005; see also Scharff & Pereira, 2002), who focuses on the contribution of the dialectic idea to clinical theory and practice. Here, I add an investigation of what Hegel implies for Fairbairn's attitude to society and politics. Fairbairn's developing ideas and the shifts of emphasis within his work have been described by Kernberg (2002), Mitchell (2000), and Scharff (2005). His historical and textual links to like-minded psychologists, as well as his intellectual roots in social Christianity and in the Scottish Enlightenment have similarly been uncovered (Clarke, 2006; Miller, 2008). I largely take these complexities for granted. I examine Fairbairn's work as a single oeuvre. I particularly concentrate on a string of essays that appear as the later chapters of *Psychoanalytic Studies of the Personality* (1952) and address subjects that go beyond the clinic.

The next part is a short exposition of Hegel's social ideas and the ways in which these ideas were adapted in the public context of early twentieth-century Britain. This is followed by comments on the relationship between this social theory and mid-century British psychoanalysis. Fairbairn's perception of the mind as both unified and divided is accounted for next. Then, the discussion proceeds to Fairbairn's views on the encounter between the family and the state, and on the issue of formal exclusion and boundaries in society.

Dialectic and society

Hegel views reality as mediated through the mind. Essentially unified, mind always divides against itself, as it grasps every concept partially, which invites the discomfort involved in the parts not grasped. These "enlightened" and "dark" sides are usually referred to as thesis and antithesis. Propelled by the need for recognition, mind expands its range of contacts and experiences. In the process, mind encounters challenges that cannot be absorbed into its current perceptions, and is therefore compelled to reorganise itself into a new synthesis that encompasses both thesis and antithesis. Every element in this picture derives its meaning from its place in the current phase: what is objective and external now may become internal and subjective later, when a new external instance is met with. The self defines itself by an always-unstable relation to others, thus initiating the dialectic, creating in the process a civilisation which is itself governed by the dynamics of mind (Brooks, 2007).

Hegel (1851) rules out revolutionary enthusiasm, as dialectic process implies that change cannot be anticipated or actively pursued. He recommends that individuals be geared to the fullest participation in their current social system, which incorporates previous theses and antitheses, thus presenting the highest level of integration available. As it contains all these ingredients, society is multilevelled. Its units range from the smallest and most physically intuitive—the family—to the broadest and ethically most fulfilling—the state. The apparently contradictory demands that family and state make on the citizen should be arbitrated by placing them in a hierarchy. Hegel uses the eponymous character of Antigone in Sophocles's play as an illustrative device. Having attempted to assert the demands of kinship by burying her renegade brother in contravention of governmental edict, Antigone is buried alive. Neither denied nor elevated, kinship lies subdued beneath the more advanced structures of politics and law. The state's harshness is itself testimony to its significance. Citizens would kill and die for it in war, thus making the state more than a contractual relationship where individuals seek to maximise their private gain. The state is the site where individuals acknowledge, through risk and death, that they are obliged to the world around them.

In Britain, Edwardian reformers turned to Hegel to explain how society could be understood as more than the sum of private interests (Den Otter, 1996; Nicholson, 1990). Hegelian social thought helped its adherents to conceptualise the relationship between home and town square, and between citizens and dropouts.

Authors like Bernard Bosanquet equated personal fulfilment with visible participation in society as it currently stands. Its fundamental unit is the family. While the couple are attracted sexually, sexuality derives its significance from "a need for union, and an attraction outside the immediate self" (Bosanquet, 1899, p. 101). The family has itself to be acknowledged by the external world. It generates objects for the world to see, such as offspring and property. Preoccupation with these objects urges breadwinners on. The household's significance renders it a subject of special recognition by the state (ibid., pp. 171, 187). The state's own significance as the synthesis of all other associations is similarly affirmed. Those who concentrate on "exclusive objects" such as the family or the church, Bosanquet writes, are "prey to stagnation" (p. 103). While patriotism may appear to conflict with loyalty to one's household, allegiance to one's country is a commitment to what binds together all households (p. 176). Citizenship is active productivity and independence rather than a passive and unconditional right. Advice may be offered to the needy so as to give them means with which to tackle their difficulties, but they are expected to strive on their own (Bosanquet, 1910). People who lack the will to make good use of this counsel and seek direct relief instead, exclude themselves from full citizenship. The population is accordingly split in two—the citizens, and the intentional paupers, who are placed beyond the pale of participation.

Hegel and object relations

A Hegelian strand crosses the entire object relations concept. People are made who they are by relating, and relationship is dynamic, thereby creating new personal identities that move from one contradiction or paradox to the next, with objectivity and subjectivity changing places rather than representing fixed positions. Infantile omnipotence and parental compliance give rise to mature recognition of dependence, while at the same time and on a different plain the infant is dependent and the adult gives sustenance. Maturity neither disowns the childlike fantasy of omnipotence, nor seeks to fulfill it. Adult personality is a synthesis that incorporates earliest holding as well as its loss (Ogden, 1992).

These parallels between Hegelian and object relations thought work well on the individual level. They strain, however, when reaching generalisation about society and its ends. In Hegelian thought, the state and its use of force are essential. By contrast, Suttie and Winnicott dislike the notion that the appeal to force may be unavoidable and that, accordingly, the social unit that can deploy it is central to public life. For them, society may in principle be structured throughout by the benevolent character of the first relationships. The move from one social plain to the next is smooth rather than dialectic. In Suttie (1952), appropriate maternal care has the power to delete the traces of any frustration its gradual withdrawal arouses. Where the mother is confident enough, she is capable of gently distancing herself from the child by turning his attention to shared pursuits. She is freed from the need to cater minutely. Children do not grow up with pent-up anger. In a society based on such families, aggression is marginal. It asserts itself only where women are weakened by a culture that perceives them as inferior, and where, as a result, mothers find it difficult to wean their children from direct care. In such a culture, children view the mother as both weak and frustrating. The result is that any deep bond is a source of shame, as it points back to dependence on feeble woman. Despising tenderness, such a society would put a premium on aggression.

Suttie's world is binary. On its one side, he places a peaceful matriarchy where mothers are strong and adults both self-confident and capable of caring relationships. On its other side, he places a warlike society of aggressive males and subjugated females, with both genders tormented by the sediments of infantile dependence. Suttie is openly pessimistic about the encounter between these two civilisations: the sick warriors will win in a direct confrontation with the peaceful matriarchy. Cycles are either benevolent or malevolent, and the contact between the good and the bad cycles has the one result of contaminating the good and destroying it (Gerson, 2009).

Similarly, in Winnicott (1971, 1986) health depends on a sense of creativity, which in turn hinges on the infant's realization that he can share an interest with the mother instead of focusing on her directly. This opens up possibilities of shared pursuits that can extend to the peer group and to the rest of society. Making a difference to the world by staking out one's notions in shared space, one grows out of illusory omnipotence, connects to others, and develops a sense of autonomy. One is therefore expectant rather than suspicious about others' differences from one's self. Health is favourable to democracy, as it allows for tolerance of diverging opinion and for enthusiasm about social exchange. However, when the process fails because of environmental factors, neglect, or otherwise insufficient holding, the individual perceives life as futile, and would therefore resent the creativity of others. From this derives a need to limit and dominate others, which "eventually could build up into a dictatorship" (Winnicott, 1986, p. 232). Such pathologies may arise from disruptions such as war, in which families are separated and homes broken.

Like Suttie's, Winnicott's world divides between the poles of peace and democracy on the one hand, and war and tyranny on the other. As the dynamic of attachment is basically identical within the family and outside it, care transcends any specific location: it extends from the home to the state. Winnicott advocates the same pattern of close and persistent holding for principals of reformatory schools as for mothers and their children, or therapists and their patients (ibid., pp. 96–97). Such recommendations land Winnicott and Suttie at some distance from the social notions espoused by Hegel and his British interpreters, for whom the personality is measured by its ability to participate in the power-wielding state which is valued precisely because of its difference from the home, and for whom full citizenship merits a formal distinction to mark it off from the dropouts who do not make the effort.

Wholes and splits

All this holds for most of the mid-century theoretical object relations work. Fairbairn is a different case, as his social outlook as well as nuances within his stand on therapy approach Hegel closely. I first want to point out that the fundamental assumptions of Fairbairn's outlook are Hegelian. Fairbairn views mind as essentially unified, but at the same time as universally divided against itself and seeking reintegration through engagement with the external world.

Fairbairn's theory hinges on early-life experiences: the splitting of the self into three self parts and three corresponding objects. However, in spite of the significance of infant life, Fairbairn rarely describes childcare in detail. Uniquely among contemporary male analysts, Fairbairn was an active parent who cared directly for his own children (N. Fairbairn, 1987, pp. 21–22). This may go some way towards accounting for his avoidance of such idealising passages about parenting as occasionally characterise Suttie and Winnicott, but it makes the paucity of nursery concretisation in his work even more outstanding. His treatment of what happens in early life is technical. It proceeds along formal axes of splits and phases that he presents in diagrammatic form.

One reason for this may be that splitting is, for Fairbairn, largely independent of context. When conceptualising it, one may neglect local detail. As Grotstein (1994b) writes, Fairbairn insists on the initial wholeness and innocence of the child's personality. The depth of this perception may be illustrated by examining the concept of what Fairbairn calls the exciting object and its corresponding libidinal self. Why should excitement, in the sense Fairbairn ascribes to it, generate a split? Libido is the self's quest for an object, so that perceived neglect or censure are experienced as acute distress that results in internal restructuring. However, excitement is a surplus, not a deficit, of relating: it is "overdoing a good thing" (Scharff, 2005, p. 8). What in such an experience of the object invites a crisis which is equivalent to the frustration of the ego's drive towards relationship while actually deriving from the undue satisfaction of that drive?

One possible answer is that the object's presence challenges the self's original unity. When the infant is not organised to accept it, maternal attention overwhelms the system with inputs from an otherwise valued source. Unlike the introjection that follows rejection by the object, this distress does not derive from a threat to the self's value. It derives from a threat to the self's structure: to its internal contiguity. The self organises against this threat by relegating the task of meeting it to a specialised portion. Original wholeness has therefore to occupy an axiomatic status within the model similar to the ego's being relation-seeking. Fairbairn has to assume an original and therefore essentially integrated whole, for which excitement is a threat.

However, universal wholeness is immediately succeeded by equally universal division. "This would not hold true," Fairbairn (1952) explains, "… in the case of a theoretically perfect person … but then there is really nobody who enjoys such a happy lot" (p. 8). As Mitchell (2000) points out, the deprivation that leads to splitting is anchored in the move from animal to human. It is the price of the species' adapting to changing circumstances (pp. 77–78). The schizoid personality is not an incidental disturbance, but an unavoidable condition of existence. Both the original integrity of the subject and its splintering are given. What Fairbairn describes is not a plot or a journey, but the essential condition of the psyche.

The global nature of splitting and the personality organisation based on it distinguish Fairbairn from Suttie. In Suttie (1935, p. 29), the child begins from a solipsistic illusion in which he is not distinct from the objects around him. This is transformed by the experience of the mother's relative distance. The potential frustration that follows is alleviated by proper maternal response. There is no corresponding experience of overstimulation, unless the relationship is pathological, as happens when the mother is weak and clings to the child for her own self-esteem. Under what Suttie describes as healthy circumstances, the gradual loosening of holding is the single axis of development. Its ample management paves the road for a personality which is at once autonomous and caring. There is no question of disintegration from original wholeness, and there is no issue with the reintegration of split parts. When pathogenic reaction to excitement does appear, it manifests in the personality's content rather than in its structure, and its occurrence depends on local culture rather than on the universal architecture of the self.

This disparity between Suttie and Fairbairn has implications for their attitude to the possibility of social perfectibility. In Suttie, infantile solipsism is replaced by healthy relating to the mother, and then to society. As repression leaves no traces, it makes possible a non-violent civilisation. Fairbairn, by contrast, views ego-splitting as universal. Accordingly, he cannot envisage a culture that does not extract emotional prices. Human life is always incomplete.

Health consists in the ability to advance beyond the preoccupation with the internal objects and their corresponding egos (Ogden, 2010). This ability shows in the individual's engagement with real-life objects: with imperfect other people and the various imperfect fora in which they interact. Integration is gained by gearing the entire personality with its various parts for an encounter with the outside. But the pull of the internal world always remains. Illness is defined by succumbing to it. "My life," Fairbairn quotes a patient, "is interfering with my neurosis" (quoted in Scharff & Birtles, 1994, p. 91). Fairbairn comments that this attests to a "tendency on the part of the individual to keep his aggression localized within the confines of the inner world as a closed system" (p. 92). The analytic project is one in which life takes precedence over neurosis.

Fairbairn's worldview therefore encompasses both the prevalence of split wholes, and the imperative to transcend them and engage with external objects, which are themselves impacted by splits. This engagement cannot be easy. It necessarily involves an element of resistance. The mature dependence, which is its end, is an always-incomplete process of integration from internal constituents.

Family and polity

But what would a healthy engagement with the external world look like? Fairbairn implies that it should take place on several distinct levels. Chief among them are the home and the national society. People react primarily to their internal balances rather than to material circumstances (Fairbairn, 1952, p. 234). Psychology rather than economy is the key to social analysis. Units based on psychological essence survive radical upheavals. The family is such a unit.

Through the trope of Oedipus, psychology exposes the conflicted character of human life. For Fairbairn, the Oedipal situation means not only the frustration of the son by the will of the father, but all patterns and difficulties of early attachment. As they can only be raised by caregivers, all individuals are shaped by these patterns. In their minds, people always live within family households, where they relate to attachment figures. This remains true under all circumstances: "Even if the epoch envisaged in Aldous Huxley's ... *Brave New World* ever dawns and the babies of the future are conceived in bottles, it by no means follows that the Oedipus situation will be ... abolished" (ibid., p. 244). Citing Freud and contemporary anthropological study, Fairbairn writes that the family is the "foundation upon which the higher forms of social organization and culture rest" (p. 236). Family is therefore an essential constituent of a broader hierarchy. Associations based on the extension of family ties to a larger scale, such as the clan, may disappear, but the family itself cannot disappear, as it is internalised in each person's mind.

For all its flaws, the home is indispensable. Libido seeks an object rather than climactic gratification, and the home provides the setting for this quest. The household-based "bourgeoisie" discipline, though occasionally constricting, is a reasonable settlement that allows infants to grow. Accordingly, Fairbairn rejects Marxism as an attempt to resolve the internal division involved in early nurture by replacing the family with a communist collective (ibid., p. 242). The fact that this cannot really be done, he points out, is revealed by the Soviet leadership cult: a regime that declared the cessation of family attachments could not survive unless it presented itself as a type of family, with a father-figure at its head (p. 244).

However, while the home creates the potential for individual separation and autonomy, that potential is fully realised elsewhere. The close attachment to parents and then to spouses retains traces of infantile dependence. These recede where individuals share an interest outside themselves: not in, but with each other. Maturity, for Fairbairn, *"involves an abandonment of relationships based upon primary identification in favour of relationships with differentiated objects"* (ibid., p. 42, emphasis in original).

For Fairbairn (ibid., p. 34), mature dependence means that individuals are able to see each other as both separate and connected. This move away from "primary identification" entails an arena where individuals can manifest their reliability as adults and exercise some detachment from their narrowest interests. It requires organised and collective risk-taking and the social unit that can engage in such pursuits. Civil life and the organisational unit that holds it together are the site for this achievement: with the demise of intermediate units such as the clan, the national society alone is left as a counterpart to the family (pp. 237–238).

However, the family and the state have to coexist:

> The survival of the family as a social institution shows that the nation has failed to eradicate the family group as it eradicated the clan and the tribe, and has been compelled to make terms with the family by incorporating it into the national organization. (p. 238)

As all people in civilisation find it difficult to leave their internal world behind, the society based on healthily differentiated individuals has to contend with a constant traction back from civil life into the more intimate experience of the household. Fairbairn warns that "[A]n intense conflict still persists between the family and the state. The extent of this conflict is liable to be obscured by the fact that it is so largely a hidden or, more strictly speaking, *repressed* conflict" (p. 238).

The polarity of family and state emerges in crises such as war, when the ability to commit oneself impersonally demands what might be experienced as a renunciation of one's internal world and its attachments. Such conditions expose the fragility of the loyalty to the collective. Citizens might subsequently withdraw their attachment from society as a whole and fall back on the world of the family, with its patterns of close holding. The home is favourably contrasted with the harsh environment of the organisations in which the citizens have to function and with the public arena generally. This condition, Fairbairn (ibid., p. 281) writes, is referred to in public debate as the decline of morale. It was evident in Britain during the interwar period. When totalitarian apologists mentioned the "degeneracy of the democracies", they pointed to a real occurrence, a "lack of public spirit", which "manifested itself in an obvious reluctance on the part of the individual to make personal sacrifices in the interests of the national group", and in a corresponding emphasis on "personal … and familial interests" (p. 283).

This accounts for the phenomenon of shell shock, which has, Fairbairn (ibid.) contends, more to do with internal make-up than with actual fighting. Otherwise, he argues, one would not be able to explain dysfunction in conscripts who had never participated in combat. Their illness stems directly from preferring the attachments of private life—ultimately that of child to caregiver—to the mature dependence expected of citizens:

> An unmistakable disturbance of the personality is … involved in the development of a war neurosis. This disturbance is part and parcel of the regression involved in that revival of a hidden state of infantile dependence. (p. 286)

For the military patient, the early household is not properly placed beneath the outer layers of civic obligations. It disrupts the patient's ability to perform on such obligations. The neurotic soldier "has remained … so closely identified with his original love-objects that he is incapable of establishing any stable emotional relationship with the military group" (p. 281).

However, ignoring early attachments, even within the context of war, is as detrimental as unduly emphasising them. Fairbairn's comments on wartime neuroses focus on the regressive streak in those soldiers who are made ill by their service. But the same text describes militarism as similarly pathological: not as the opposite pole of evading military service through symptoms, but as another form of the same phenomenon. A conscript who identifies with the army to the point of denying all other associations merely transfers infantile dependence to another object. Instead of submerging himself in the parent, he does so with the institution. In both cases, one observes a lack of differentiation and a failure of mature dependence. Like the casualties of homesickness, the militarists are harmful for the purposes of the army itself. Externally conveying the impression of being "as keen as mustard", these individuals "are intolerant of such delays as are involved in training, become irritated by routine duties and soon begin to smart under the imagined failure of the military authorities to reward their devotion" (ibid., p. 278). This frustration betrays an illness as acute as that of the service-evader.

What society requires, then, is a multilevelled personality that can acknowledge its internal divisions without being overwhelmed by them. Attachment to both home and civil community is essential. This preference for complexity underpins Fairbairn's support for democracy. As earlier mentioned, Fairbairn argues that in the interwar period, Western nations suffered from a regressive mood. However, totalitarian regimes are even more vulnerable to such regression. While they seem better mobilised, this appearance is achieved at the price of turning the state itself into an early attachment figure. Citizens are not allowed to hold loyalties that differ from the collective will, which is tellingly presented to them as a close family member, usually a father character. In terms of individual health, dictatorships are flawed, because they do not provide their subjects with locations which can draw them out of their internally split world and offer them a remedial experience.

This spells dictatorship's demise. If the state is not a truly civil and political bond, but is instead a personal one, it is subject to the unavoidable flaws of personal attachments. Frustration with politics is experienced as internal strife. With defeat or other misfortune, "[T]he regime becomes a bad object to the individual; and the socially disintegrating effects of separation-anxiety … assert themselves at the critical moment" (ibid., p. 80). Citizens of democracies can at such times find comfort in their private world. The internal world of totalitarian subjects, on the other hand, is suffused with figures that have to do with the state that denies them this sanctuary. The undoing of dictatorship therefore involves worse distress than the difficulties experienced by democracies (pp. 284–285). Rather than subsuming the family's attachments under the political structure, dictatorships seek to supplant the family by turning themselves into households, thus destroying both the domestic and the political along with the individual well-being which requires the coexistence of several interaction plains.

While negative and critical, Fairbairn's view of dictatorship is not contrasted with the cheerful perception of democratic community that one may gain from Suttie or Winnicott. What confronts totalitarianism in Fairbairn is a multilevelled and internally conflicted democracy, whose "feel" may be gloomy and subdued, owing to the opposing demands of self, family, and state. Democracy is not exempt from war and is not destroyed by it. War obviously extracts prices, but at the same time it brings out democracy's inner strength, as it proves people's ability to add an impersonal and generalised commitment onto their primary attachments. Personal health, as defined by the ability to handle relationships on various levels, is validated rather than negated by the hard experiences of political life.

Exclusion and boundaries

Short of war, civil commitment manifests itself in obeying law and morality. Disobeying them is equivalent to evading service. Fairbairn (ibid.) openly compares the "problem of the war neuroses" to what he thinks is another form of the same phenomenon: "Similar considerations apply to those who commit unnatural sexual offences in civilian life" (p. 290).

At first, the comparison appears skewed. Aetiologically, Fairbairn admits, the two are distinct. Neurotic conscripts use illness as a defence against acknowledging that a break has occurred within themselves. Having disappointed internalised social expectations, they revert to their earliest attachments and deny the later development of the personality. They pay the price of illness for a breach that they recognise committing. By contrast, sexual deviants, as Fairbairn understands them, pay no price at all for living outside the social code. Their position involves no internal break. They enjoy their deviancy regardless of social disapproval. The overall structure of their personality does not revolt against their giving in to their drives. They are therefore psychopaths rather than neurotics (ibid., p. 291).

However, for Fairbairn, these considerations give in to another one: that of mature dependence, the recognition of one's obligation to others as separate individuals who have different interests than one's own. The sexual deviant and the neurotic soldier reach the same terminus of avoiding mature dependence by renouncing their link to society at large. The military patient evades military service, while the sexual deviant evades morality and law.

The treatment in both cases is also similar. While, as individuals, neurotic soldiers may be treated in the clinic, collectively they present a delinquent pattern that has to be addressed as such. Fairbairn (ibid.) comments: "After gaining some experience of psychoneurotic and psychotic servicemen *en masse*, I was driven to remark, 'What these people need is not a psychotherapist, but an evangelist'" (p. 81). The issue, and therefore the clinical response, has to do with the ability to attach oneself to other people and their shared ends, rather than with mending internal fractures. Group treatment, Fairbairn contends, has during the war proved more efficient in rehabilitating fatigued troops than individual therapy (p. 295). He accordingly favours a special environment for addressing such cases, a form of institutionalisation in which inmates are inculcated with collective discipline through the experience of a regulated life within a group. "Evangelism" takes on an appropriately medical form. Moreover, on the symbolic level, Fairbairn thinks that soldiers who left service because of neurosis should not be awarded a war pension. While their illness is genuine and so merits compensation, its title should be differentiated from the remuneration of other veterans: these veterans have participated fully in the life of their society, while the neurotics have not (pp. 287–288).

Similarly, Fairbairn (ibid.) suggests that sexual deviants should not be approached primarily by individual psychotherapy, as they do not repress anything that the therapist may explore. The one end of treating them is implanting in them a commitment to society. Hence, Fairbairn recommends the "establishment of special communities for offenders ... with a group life of their own, in which offenders can participate, and which is psychologically controlled with a view to its gradual approximation to the life of the community at large" (p. 294). Dysfunctional neurotic soldiers are sent to an institution which imitates army life. Sexual offenders are sent to an institution which imitates society generally. In both cases, incarceration is training in cooperating with non-intimate and differentiated others. It is an apprenticeship in citizenship for those not currently fit for citizenship itself.

Fairbairn therefore draws a boundary between normal society, with its imperfect individuals who all suffer from internal splits and are accessible to and remediable by therapy, and the cluster of outcasts of various descriptions and aetiologies. These are placed beyond the reach of individual therapy, and are instead regulated by institutionalised discipline calculated to ultimately allow them to turn into full participants. The underlying causes of each individual case are less important to Fairbairn than the visible outcome, and it is by the standard of this outcome that he proposes to determine policy.

This approach contrasts with the position taken by other object relations thinkers, for whom delinquency is fully accessible to individual therapy and does not necessarily involve a form of exclusion. Winnicott, as earlier mentioned, recommends that the directors of reformatory schools assume a psychoanalytically inspired therapeutic attitude to their inmates: far from being banished from human converse by being relegated to institutions, these delinquents could be redeemed precisely by such converse, which imitates the dynamic of the nursery and the consulting room. Rather than nudging the inmates out of infantile dependence by placing them in an environment that simulates civil society but is cut off from that society, Winnicott would follow these inmates to their internal experiences in order to amend them—just as he does with extramural, ordinary patients.

The difference in therapeutic posture between Fairbairn and Winnicott corresponds to their different background metaphysics. Winnicott's world is concentric. Home is where we start from, and whatever occurs in the home repeats elsewhere. Winnicott sees no tension between different levels of organisation. As the dynamic is fundamentally benevolent, Winnicott assumes the possibility of a largely tension-free civilisation, where violence appears only as pathology. Fairbairn, by contrast, perceives the world as multilevelled and dialectic, with civil obligation differing qualitatively from and occasionally conflicting with the parental function which is nonetheless its necessary basis. The civilisation he envisages is not a harmony marred only by the occasional illness which may be treated individually, but a society of which tension, coercion, and exclusion are essential parts.

Conclusion

In his perception of home and public life as beset by friction and struggling to define their relations with each other, Fairbairn approximates the model laid out by Hegel and his British followers. The mind is essentially unified but also universally divided. Acknowledging both features is a condition of health. Hence, both the individual's internal complexities and his links to the outside world should be taken heed of, with the second receiving a higher value. The attachment to the home, as well as the impersonal bond of civil society should be acknowledged simultaneously. As in Hegel, the home is retained but is placed beneath the social and political structures where mature dependence plays itself out.

While Fairbairn's outlook displays some of the social sensibilities shown by other object relations authors of the period, it also makes him a shade more conservative than these authors. Suttie, Winnicott, and Bowlby describe a trajectory from dependence to relative independence. Fairbairn agrees with them, but his emphasis is on independence as a goal rather than on dependence and holding as an origin. In terms of policy, this leads Fairbairn, as it led Bosanquet, to distinguish citizens from outcasts and delinquents. This outlook resists any notion of Utopia or perfectibility, and instead views strife and violence as inescapable.

Object relations theory has, in a sense, been a British response to continental inputs: an effort to retain local attitudes to family and other relationships while endorsing a terminology and a discipline that challenged these very concepts. However, this project could be undertaken in different ways that reflected different strands within the local context. Suttie, and in varying ways Bowlby and Winnicott, represented one venue, Fairbairn another. Fairbairn's project of weaning professional debate back from what he saw as the reductionist nomenclature of drives and body zones was explicit. He resented the perception that social concerns should be addressed as primarily medical. This perception, Fairbairn argues, makes us lose sight of moral issues and ethical choices. Presenting crime and deviance as *symptoms* spring from "a general modern tendency to substitute purely scientific standards for the moral standards of the past" (ibid., pp. 290–291). This, he warns, "represents an interpretation based upon an erroneous psychopathology" (p. 291). His endopsychic model and the dynamics it implied are an effort to retrieve psychology from this error and make it concur with morality again.

It is an openly conservative project as it looks back to a past in which psychology and ethics colluded.

A well-known question in the discussion of psychoanalysis's place in culture has to do with Oedipus as a trope: what happens if we substitute Antigone for Oedipus? Replies usually converge around replacing the masculine preoccupation with castration with a more feminine-sounding emphasis on kinship. However, Fairbairn's revision of Freud suggests that the move to Antigone may have a different meaning. *Oedipus Rex* is an investigation: why did plague come to Thebes? In Freud, this stands for the psychoanalytic process by which the individual delves into his emotional past for elements which disturb his present. However, for Hegel, *Antigone* is not about resolving contradiction by exposing the truth. It is about burying a partial truth to enable us to pursue a more comprehensive one. Kinship is not denied. It is subjugated. To the extent that the argument here is correct, then Fairbairn's therapy is not ultimately concerned with telling us who we are. This may be a means. The end is burying the question, letting it go, so as to make us able to engage with the world in the locations it offers us, the most developed among which is the civil arena held together by the state.

References

Birtles, E. F. (2002). Why is Fairbairn relevant today—a modernist/postmodernist view. In: F. Pereira & D. E. Scharff (Eds.), *Fairbairn and Relational Theory* (pp. 36–52). London: Karnac.

Birtles, E. F. (2005). Difference, repetition and continuity: Philosophical reflections on Fairbairn's concept of mature dependence. In: J. S. Scharff & D. E. Scharff (Eds.), *The Legacy of Fairbairn and Sutherland: Psychotherapeutic Applications* (pp. 39–49). London: Routledge.

Birtles, E. F., & Scharff, D. E. (Eds.) (1994). *From Instinct to Self: Selected Papers of W. R. D. Fairbairn, Volume II: Applications and Early Contributions*. Northvale, NJ: Jason Aronson.

Bosanquet, B. (1899). *The Philosophical Theory of the State*. Kitchener, Canada: Batoche, 2001.

Bosanquet, B. (1910). Charity organization and the Majority Report. *International Journal of Ethics*, *20*(4): 395–408.

Brooks, T. (2007). *Hegel's Political Philosophy*. Edinburgh, UK: Edinburgh University Press.

Clarke, G. S. (2006). *Personal Relations Theory: Fairbairn, Macmurray and Suttie*. London: Routledge.

Clarke, G. S. (2011). Suttie's influence on Fairbairn's object relations theory. *Journal of the American Psychoanalytic Association*, *59*(5): 939–959.

Den Otter, S. (1996). *British Idealism and Social Explanation*. Oxford: Oxford University Press.

Fairbairn, N. (1987). *A Life is Too Short*. London: Quartet.

Fairbairn, W. R. D. (1952). *Psychoanalytic Studies of the Personality*. London: Tavistock.

Gerson, G. (2004). Object relations psychoanalysis as political theory. *Political Psychology*, *25*(5): 769–794.

Gerson, G. (2009). Ian Suttie's matriarchy: A feminist utopia? *Psychoanalysis, Culture & Society*, *14*(4): 375–392.

Gomez, L. (1997). *An Introduction to Object Relations*. New York: New York University Press.

Grotstein, J. S. (1994b). Notes on Fairbairn's metapsychology. In: J. S. Grotstein & D. B. Rinsley (Eds.), *Fairbairn and the Origins of Object Relations* (pp. 112–148). New York: Guilford.

Hegel, G. W. F. (1821). *Hegel's Philosophy of Right*. T. M. Knox (Ed.), Oxford: Clarendon, 1952.

Holmes, J. (1993). *John Bowlby and Attachment Theory*. London: Routledge.

Kernberg, O. F. (2002). A contemporary exploration of the contributions of W. R. D. Fairbairn. In: F. Pereira & D. E. Scharff (Eds.), *Fairbairn and Relational Theory* (pp. 11–27). London: Karnac.

Mayhew, B. (2006). Between love and aggression: The politics of John Bowlby. *History of the Human Sciences, 19*: 19–35.

Miller, G. (2008). Scottish psychoanalysis: A rational religion. *Journal of the History of the Behavioral Sciences, 44*: 38–59.

Mitchell, S. A. (2000). The origin and nature of the "object" in the theories of Klein and Fairbairn. In: J. S. Grotstein & D. B. Rinsley (Eds.), *Fairbairn and the Origins of Object Relations* (pp. 66–87). New York: Other.

Nicholson, P. P. (1990). *The Political Philosophy of the British Idealists*. Cambridge: Cambridge University Press.

Ogden, T. H. (1992). *The Matrix of the Mind: Object Relations and the Psychoanalytic Dialogue*. London: Karnac.

Ogden, T. H. (2010). Why read Fairbairn? *International Journal of Psychoanalysis, 91*: 101–118.

Riley, D. (1983). *War in the Nursery*. London: Virago.

Scharff, D. E. (2005). The development of Fairbairn's theory. In: J. S. Scharff & D. E. Scharff (Eds.), *The Legacy of Fairbairn and Sutherland* (pp. 3–18). London: Routledge.

Scharff, D. E., & Birtles, E. F. (Eds.) (1994). *From Instinct to Self: Selected Papers of W. R. D. Fairbairn, Volume I: Clinical and Theoretical Papers*. Northvale, NJ: Jason Aronson.

Scharff, D. E., & Pereira, F. (2002). Introduction. In: F. Pereira & D. E. Scharff (Eds.), *Fairbairn and Relational Theory* (pp. 1–8). London: Karnac.

Schwartz, J. (1999). *Cassandra's Daughter*. London: Penguin.

Suttie, I. D. (1935). *The Origins of Love and Hate*. New York: Julian, 1952.

van der Horst, F. C. P., & van der Veer, R. (2010). The ontogeny of an idea: John Bowlby and his contemporaries on mother–child separation. *History of Psychology, 13*(1): 25–45.

Winnicott, D. W. (1971). *Playing and Reality*. London: Routledge.

Winnicott, D. W. (1986). *Home Is Where We Start from*. C. Winnicott, R. Shepherd, & M. Davis (Eds.). New York: W. W. Norton.

CHAPTER THREE

Making Fairbairn's psychoanalysis thinkable: Henry Drummond's natural laws of the spiritual world

Gavin Miller

The contribution of W. R. D. Fairbairn to psychoanalytic psychology has received substantial scholarly attention, whether to the merits and ramifications of the theory itself (e.g., Clarke, 2006; Scharff & Scharff, 2005a), or its historical and cultural origins (e.g., Beattie, 2003; Hoffman, 2004; Miller, 2008). In this chapter I consider further the religious culture that was part of Fairbairn's upbringing in the late Victorian and early Edwardian period. The harmony between evolutionary science and religion popularised by the evangelist Henry Drummond (1851–1897) epitomises a culture in which the laws of the living world could be seen as continuous with spiritual laws paradigmatically expressed in scriptural form, but open also to modern scientific investigation. In the worldview of Christianised evolution, Drummond was regarded as having demonstrated the Providential evolution of Christian virtues such as love, tenderness, and altruism in the phylogenesis of mammalia. Knowledge of this late Victorian evangelical context not only emphasises the "thinkability" of Fairbairn's relational psychoanalytic psychology, it also invites further questions about how one should conceive the relationship in his work between psychoanalytic and theological discourse.

One of the puzzles in Fairbairn's intellectual development is the striking, and oft-noted parallel between his critique of Freudian theory and the ideas advanced by another Scottish contemporary, Ian D. Suttie (1889–1935). Fairbairn's argument in 1940 that "The first social relationship established by the individual is that between himself and his mother; and the focus of this relationship is the suckling situation" (1952, p. 10) resembles Suttie's identification in a 1932 paper co-authored with his wife, Jane Isabel, of an instinct of "formless aimless attachment of the infant to the mother" (Suttie & Suttie, 1932, p. 209)—an idea later developed at length in Suttie's 1935 monograph, *The Origins of Love and Hate*. Fairbairn's work closely parallels that of Suttie, even to the extent that socialisation is interpreted along the lines of Suttie's "endogenous" repression, which is "due to the will of the loved and desired object itself [i.e., the mother]" (Suttie, 1935, p. 102) rather than to the Oedipal conflict. Compare what Fairbairn said in a 1934 lecture: "In the early phases of childhood it is mainly due to a desire to ensure the love of their parents, a fear of losing this love and a desire to regain it when apparently lost, that children learn to do what they are told and to restrain their wayward impulses" (Fairbairn, 1934, p. 206). But, despite these similarities, the historical record is not sufficiently complete to clarify the exact nature of the relations of independence, dependence, or interdependence between these two Scottish psychoanalytic thinkers.

In time, of course, there may yet appear evidence that provides an unequivocal account of the intellectual relationship between Fairbairn and Suttie. To focus on such quasi-personal, historical relations between the two is, however, to err towards a "great man" history of psychoanalytic psychology. Although Suttie and Fairbairn were both revolutionaries (with Suttie being the more trenchant and confrontational), one should not assume that their innovations in psychoanalytic theory were in some way "unthinkable" within the wider culture of their time and place. Both Marie Hoffman and I have argued that the contemporaneous local religious culture facilitated the British (or Scottish) object relations critique of Freud's drive-centred, solipsistic model. Hoffman argues that "The early religious narrative to which Fairbairn was exposed held that a sovereign God created humans in His image, capable of love and desire, first toward Him and then toward each other, beings who by their very nature desire to relate" (Hoffman, 2004, p. 785). For my part, I have argued that Scottish psychoanalysis borrows from late Victorian anthropology and theology, and particularly the work of William Robertson Smith (1846–1894), in order to emphasise "the importance of the primordial communion between mother and child, which replaces the transcendent communion between God and man" (Miller, 2008, p. 45).

My aim in this chapter is to further explicate the thinkability of Fairbairn's object relations theory for a Scotsman of his era, place, social class, and faith—religion again provides a key reference point for my argument. Fairbairn, as a pious youth of his time, could scarcely have escaped the evangelical narratives of Victorian culture. Indeed, the traces of such influences appear in his scientific works. For instance, when describing dissociative psychological mechanisms in his 1929 MD thesis, Fairbairn refers, as common knowledge, to "[t]he dissociations of the kind which occurred to Livingstone, when he was being mauled by a lion", describing them as "dissociations determined by the unpleasantness of events" (Fairbairn, 1929b, p. 75). The world-famous Scottish missionary and explorer David Livingstone (1813–1873) thus discovers (for the European world at any rate) not only large tracts of Africa, but also the dissociative mechanism of, in his words, "a stupor similar to that which seems to be felt by a mouse after the first shake of the cat", "a sort of dreaminess, in which there was no sense of pain nor feeling of terror" (Livingstone, 1857, p. 11). This casual allusion hints not only at Fairbairn's cultural reference points and role models, but perhaps even at a personal narrative in which psychoanalytic exploration was an inner-worldly successor to Livingstone's missionary adventures in the external world—J. D. Sutherland's 1989 biography of Fairbairn, we might note, is entitled *Fairbairn's Journey into the Interior*.

Furthermore, the *rapprochement* between evangelical Christianity and evolutionary biology in late Victorian Christian culture leads, as I have indicated, to some probable anticipations of later object relations psychology. Pre-eminent among the theologians of Christianised evolution was the Scottish evangelist, Henry Drummond, whose books, *Natural Law in the Spiritual World* (1883), and *The Lowell Lectures on the Ascent of Man* (1894), synthesised evangelical Christianity with the biology of Darwin as extrapolated, in particular, by Herbert Spencer (1820–1903). James R. Moore observes that Drummond's writings, including pamphlets such as the wildly popular *The Greatest Thing in the World* (1890), were highly successful in the late Victorian book market. *Natural Law* was selling at over 1000 copies per month a year after its publication (Moore, 1985, pp. 385–386); *The Ascent of Man* "sold 10,000 copies within a year and 30,000 by 1902" (ibid., p. 386); "*The Greatest Thing in the World* […] sold a third-of-a-million copies in seven years and is still in print today" (ibid., p. 386). Moore proposes that Drummond's success as a writer overlapped with the literary success of contemporaneous Scottish literature, including the putative sentimentalism of the so-called "Kailyard" writers: "One might go so far as to suggest that the stories of Robert Louis Stevenson, Drummond's contemporary at Edinburgh University, 'Ian Maclaren' (i.e., John Watson), a boyhood chum, J. M. Barrie and the so-called 'Kailyard School' define a literary context to which Drummond's evangelic narratives formed the theological counterpart" (ibid., p. 390).

Be that as it may, Drummond's success combined evangelical appeal with a scientific credibility built upon a modest track record as a trained and active scientist: as well as holding an academic post in natural science at Free Church College in Glasgow from 1877 onwards, Drummond also had experience as a "field geologist", and was a "Fellow of the Royal Society of Edinburgh" (ibid., p. 392). Rather than separate the world of the spirit from the world known by natural science, Drummond argued that nature was one continuous whole, and that the laws of biology, in particular, were as one with the laws of the spiritual world that had been revealed by scripture (ibid., p. 397). Because of this so-called "Law of Continuity",

> Natural Laws […] do not stop with the visible and then give place to a new set of Laws bearing a strong similitude to them. The Laws of the invisible are the same Laws, projections of the natural not supernatural. Analogous Phenomena are not the fruit of parallel Laws, but of the same Laws—Laws which at one end, as it were, may be dealing with Matter, at the other end with Spirit. (Drummond, 1884, p. 11)

Natural Law is therefore full of what, to modern eyes, is the most extraordinary—even comical—moralising of Darwinian evolution, which Drummond views as an orthogenetic ascent from least to most complex, from less to more perfect. Drummond, for instance, upbraids the hermit crab for its evolutionary backsliding: "From the physiological standpoint, there is no question that the Hermit tribe have neither discharged their responsibilities to Nature nor to themselves. If the end of life is merely to escape death, and serve themselves, possibly they have done well; but if it is to attain an ever increasing perfection, then are they backsliders indeed" (ibid., p. 324). The hermit crab, in Drummond's view, has been providentially punished as a species for abandoning the difficult path to sturdy and self-reliant complexity in favour of (semi-)parasitism. This observation confirms, in his view, the general natural-spiritual law that "Any principle which secures the safety of the individual without personal effort or the vital exercise of faculty is disastrous to moral character" (ibid., p. 326). An illustration of this law in the spiritual sphere, Drummond argues, is found in Roman Catholicism, which offers to the masses a molluscan shell. They have simply to shelter themselves within its pale, and they are "safe". But what is this "safe"? It is an external safety—the safety of an institution. It is a salvation recommended to men by all that appeals to the motives in most common use with the vulgar and the superstitious, but which has as little vital connection with the individual soul as the dead whelk's shell with the living Hermit. (ibid., p. 327)

Predictably, Drummond's views on parasitism also motivate a sententious aside about the moral parasitism of "all those individuals who have secured a hasty wealth by the chances of speculation; all children of fortune; all victims of inheritance; all social sponges; all satellites of the court; all beggars of the market-place—all these are living and unlying witnesses to the unalterable retributions of the law of parasitism" (ibid., p. 350).

Drummond's account of evolutionary progress, which draws heavily upon Herbert Spencer's work, is of a variety that has been robustly criticised in recent years. Mary Midgley for instance, identifies in such views what she calls "the Escalator Fallacy", "the idea that evolution is a steady, linear upward movement, a single inexorable process of improvement leading (as a disciple of Herbert Spencer's put it) 'from gas to genius' and beyond into some superhuman spiritual stratosphere" (Midgley, 2002, p. 7). This erroneous interpretation contrasts with Darwin's "own view of selection on the humbler model of a bush—a rich radiation of varying forms, in which human qualities cannot, any more than any others, determine a general direction for the whole" (ibid., p. 7). Nonetheless, whatever its flaws, "To educated lay people *Natural Law* furnished proof that the latest science supported their faith" (Moore, 1985, p. 399). Scripture was renewed via New Testament metaphors of organic life (vines and branches, grains of mustard seed, the body of Christ) that "served as a point of contact with evangelical audiences for insinuating the claims of continuity and the authority of nature over a province that traditionally had been the most refractory to scientific explanation" (ibid., p. 412).

In itself, *Natural Law* may seem to have little relevance to the psychoanalytic psychologies of Fairbairn or Suttie, but it nonetheless helped to erode the presumed dualism between the organic and the spiritual world, allowing both to be laid open to scientific investigation. As Roger Smith notes, "There is an argument that modern psychology becomes possible as a subject once the principle of the continuity (or uniformity) of nature brought human beings into relation with natural processes and hence brought human beings under the scope of scientific explanation" (1988, p. 154). Moreover, although *Natural Law* was strongly criticised, Drummond, as Moore explains, maintained "his grand unifying belief that natural laws are valid in the spiritual world. For ten years he illustrated this belief in essays and addresses, and in *The Ascent of Man* he made it the corner-stone of a thoroughgoing evolutionary cosmogony" (Moore, 1985, p. 404). *The Ascent of Man* not only reaffirms Drummond's fundamental stance, it also clearly contributes to the thinkability of the later object relations psychoanalysis of Fairbairn and Suttie. It does so by offering an account in which increasing evolutionary complexity leads specifically to an increase in altruism. Moore explains:

Evolution, as we see in retrospect, wrote Drummond, has resulted from two factors: a Struggle for Life and a Struggle for the Life of Others. The first, a struggle for nutrition, is competitive, individualistic, and selfish. The second, a struggle to reproduce, is cooperative, corporate, and altruistic. But, although both factors are integral to the evolutionary process, they must be seen in due proportion. Since the dawn of man's ascent the Struggle for Life has been giving way to the Struggle for the Life of Others. As body and mind have evolved, self-sacrifice and co-operation, maternal and domestic virtues, have slowly but surely prevailed. Vestiges of animal nature remain, even in civilised man, but these will finally pass away in a further evolution of altruism. (ibid., p. 405)

Evolution, Drummond argues, gradually brings about an increase in Christian virtue: "Evolution is Advolution [a rolling towards]; better, it is Revelation—the phenomenal expression of the Divine, the progressive realization of the Ideal, the Ascent of Love" (Drummond, 1894, p. 435).

The revelation of a Providential design in evolution (or advolution) becomes apparent, Drummond argues, in the phylogenesis of mammalia. Drummond reassures his readers that "In as real a sense as a factory is meant to turn out locomotives or clocks, the machinery of Nature is designed in the last resort to turn out Mothers" (ibid., p. 343). He also wrote:

Hitherto, the world belonged to the Food-seeker, the Self-seeker, the Struggler for Life, the Father. Now is the hour of the Mother. And, animal though she be, she rises to the task. And that hour, as she ministers to her young, becomes to her, and to the world, the hour of its holiest birth. (ibid., p. 22)

Drummond's anticipation of object relations psychoanalysis involves more, though, than simply a scientific repristination of ethical categories such as love and maternal tenderness (a theme, for instance, which dominates the early chapters of Suttie's *The Origins of Love and Hate*, 1935, chs 5–6). Drummond specifically identifies suckling as a relationship between mother and child that provides both nutrition and love:

No young of any Mammal can nourish itself. There is that in it therefore at this stage which compels it to seek its Mother; and there is that in the Mother which compels it even physically [...] to seek her child. On the physiological side, the name of this impelling power is lactation; on the ethical side, it is Love. And there is no escape henceforth from communion between Mother and child. (Drummond, 1894, p. 358)

The anticipation of Fairbairn's work, as of Suttie's, is clear, and needs little explication: suckling is the primal form of communion between persons, and meets biological, psychological, and spiritual needs. The religious context created by Drummond's work clearly helped to build the wider cultural foundations for a later psychological theory in which the mother–child relation was the earliest relation of social communion. Drummond's theory, for instance, bears a family resemblance to the work of the late Victorian theologian and anthropologist, William Robertson Smith, who promoted a view of communion (including between mother and child) as a central social and religious phenomenon. Robertson Smith's ideas, I have argued (Miller, 2008), were also influential upon later object relations thinkers (or "personal relations" thinkers, see Clarke, 2006), including not only Fairbairn and Suttie, but also the philosopher, John Macmurray (1891–1976).

Moreover, the continuity between natural and spiritual law promoted by Drummond invites reflection, I believe, on the wider theological significance of Fairbairn's psychoanalytic project. As Hoffman explains, Fairbairn's career path was at first clerical, before it became medical:

> Fairbairn did pursue an intermediate degree in divinity at the London University and then, at age 25, returned to Edinburgh, where he began his theological training in the Presbyterian church. These studies, however, were interrupted by World War I, Fairbairn serving in the army for three and one-half years. It was during this time that Fairbairn's vision shifted from curing souls through preaching to helping people through psychology. (Hoffman, 2004, p. 772)

One might interpret this change of heart as in some way a response to the Great War, perhaps the result of some personal crisis that led Fairbairn to pursue his philanthropic ambitions through psychology, rather than theology. Though this is plausible, it may lead to an additional inference that this change in career was accompanied by some degree of loss of faith on Fairbairn's part. Indeed, Fairbairn's own statements may even seem to hint that psychotherapy is a psychological successor to, and replacement for, ideas and practices communicated in supernaturalised form through scriptural narratives of salvation, possession, and exorcism. In a 1958 conference paper, "Psychotherapy and the Clergy", Fairbairn indicates some kind of perceived similarity between the casting out of devils and his brand of psychoanalytic psychotherapy:

> In my own personal opinion, it is something very like *salvation*, rather than medical cure, that the average patient is seeking when he embarks upon a course of psychotherapy. From a religious, or at any rate a Christian point of view, what man seeks salvation *from* is sin, estrangement from God, spiritual death, and that fear which is cast out by "Perfect Love".
>
> Correspondingly, from a psychotherapeutic point of view, what (in my opinion) the patient seeks salvation *from* is anxiety, guilt, his own aggression and the bad persecuting parental figures which haunt his inner world as the result of his experiences in childhood. What he seeks, accordingly, would appear to be something very like the forgiveness of sins and the casting out of devils. (1958b, p. 364)

However, one should note that this passage is carefully equivocal, since it depicts the religious and the psychoanalytic perspectives as competing "points of view", rather than giving greater validity to one or the other. The possibility remains that Fairbairn had continuing religious convictions which were in some way accommodated to his psychoanalytic psychology. Were Fairbairn, for instance, to hold to some "Law of Continuity", he might well think of the psychoanalytic phenomena of dissociation and the return of the repressed as psychological laws which held also, in modified form, in the spiritual realm. Salvation would thus be a real phenomenon, distinct from, but nomologically similar to, successful psychoanalytic psychotherapy; psychoanalysis might shed light on salvation (by revealing similar laws), but it would not in itself reduce salvation to a psychological phenomenon. Certainly, Fairbairn had in his 1929 MD thesis no qualms in tracing continuous laws throughout the living world. He presents psychological dissociation as a phenomenon that "comes under the category of selection, and is thus in line with a fundamental biological tendency" (1929b, p. 54)—a tendency present even in "[t]he activity of the unicellular organism" (ibid., p. 54).

Whatever one's views on the truth of Christianity (and my views are at the very least agnostic), it would be an historiographical error to neglect the enormous intellectual activity generated, particularly in the nineteenth century, by the encounter between science and religion. Thinkers such as Henry Drummond, though in many ways fundamentally mistaken about the significance of evolutionary ideas, should not be cast into the outer darkness as "merely" superstitious. At least some of Drummond's ideas seem to have been renewed in the later project of object relations psychoanalysis as developed by Fairbairn and Suttie, in which love itself was dignified as a scientific reality worthy of methodical investigation.

References

Beattie, H. J. (2003). "The repression and the return of bad objects": W. R. D. Fairbairn and the historical roots of theory. *International Journal of Psychoanalysis, 84*: 1171–1187.
Clarke, G. S. (2006). *Personal Relations Theory: Fairbairn, Macmurray and Suttie*. London: Routledge.
Drummond, H. (1883). *Natural Law in the Spiritual World*. London: Hodder & Stoughton, 1884.
Drummond, H. (1890). *The Greatest Thing in the World*. London: Hodder & Stoughton.
Drummond, H. (1894). *The Lowell Lectures on the Ascent of Man*. London: Hodder & Stoughton.
Fairbairn, W. R. D. (1929b). Dissociation and repression. In: E. F. Birtles & D. E. Scharff (Eds.), *From Instinct to Self: Selected Papers of W. R. D. Fairbairn, Volume II: Applications and Early Contributions* (pp. 13–79). Northvale, NJ: Jason Aronson, 1994.
Fairbairn, W. R. D. (1934). Imagination and child development. In: E. F. Birtles & D. E. Scharff (Eds.), *From Instinct to Self: Selected Papers of W. R. D. Fairbairn, Volume II: Applications and Early Contributions* (pp. 195–209). Northvale, NJ: Jason Aronson, 1994.
Fairbairn, W. R. D. (1940). Schizoid factors in the personality. In: *Psychoanalytic Studies of the Personality* (pp. 3–27). London: Tavistock, 1952.
Fairbairn, W. R. D. (1952). *Psychoanalytic Studies of the Personality*. London: Tavistock.
Fairbairn, W. R. D. (1958b). Psychotherapy and the clergy. In: E. F. Birtles & D. E. Scharff (Eds.), *From Instinct to Self: Selected Papers of W. R. D. Fairbairn, Volume II: Applications and Early Contributions* (pp. 363–367). Northvale, NJ: Jason Aronson, 1994.
Hoffman, M. (2004). From enemy combatant to strange bedfellow: The role of religious narratives in the work of W. R. D. Fairbairn and D. W. Winnicott. *Psychoanalytic Dialogues, 14*: 769–804.
Livingstone, D. (1857). *Missionary Travels and Researches in South Africa: including a Sketch of Sixteen Years' Residence in the Interior of Africa*. London: Ward, Lock, 1899.
Midgley, M. (2002). *Evolution as a Religion: Strange Hopes and Stranger Fears* (revised ed.). London: Routledge.
Miller, G. (2008). Scottish psychoanalysis: a rational religion. *Journal of the History of the Behavioral Sciences, 44*: 39–59.
Moore, J. R. (1985). Evangelicals and evolution: Henry Drummond, Herbert Spencer, and the naturalisation of the spiritual world. *Scottish Journal of Theology, 38*: 383–417.
Scharff, J. S., & Scharff, D. E. (Eds.) (2005a). *The Legacy of Fairbairn and Sutherland: Psychotherapeutic Applications*. New York: Routledge.
Smith, R. (1988). Does the history of psychology have a subject? *History of the Human Sciences, 1*(2): 147–177.

Sutherland, J. D. (1989). *Fairbairn's Journey into the Interior*. London: Free Association.
Suttie, I. D. (1935). *The Origins of Love and Hate*. London: Free Association, 1988.
Suttie, I. D., & Suttie, J. I. (1932). The Mother: Agent or Object? Part II. *British Journal of Medical Psychology, 12*: 199–233.

CHAPTER FOUR

Splitting in the history of psychoanalysis: from Janet and Freud to Fairbairn, passing through Ferenczi and Suttie

Gabriele Cassullo

Since his doctoral thesis in 1929, Ronald Fairbairn's contribution to psychoanalysis developed as an attempt at integrating Janet's and Freud's model of the mind (Davies, 1998). Yet, even today many psychoanalysts keep wondering why should this integrative project be so important.

The return of the dissociated

As far back as 1981, Emanuel Berman—who followed the same path as Fairbairn, dedicating in 1973 his doctoral thesis to multiple personality disorders, and thus anticipating the present renewal of interest in Janet—dealt with the general distrust of the psychoanalytic community towards Janet's concept of dissociation. Berman showed that, even if Freud's "one-sided *anti-Janet* stand" (Berman, 1981, p. 285) created a detrimental ostracism towards theories based on dissociation, the notion continued to resurface in psychoanalysis—though often in a covert form—so that in time it has been incorporated in most psychoanalytic theories.

Some few years later, Janet became "the forefather" of a new theoretical trend investigating multiple personality and post-traumatic stress disorder, and reasserting the importance of the dissociative processes of the mind (Putnam, 1989; van der Hart & Friedman, 1989). But, this time around, it was psychoanalysis and its contributions to the field that were dismissed (Gullenstad, 2005). In the same year, the psychoanalyst Jules Bemporad admitted: "We may have been a bit hasty in burying Janet, and his ghost continues to reappear in very strange guises" (1989, p. 635).

Finally, in 1995 Philip Bromberg built on Bemporad's metaphor:

> If one wished to read the contemporary psychoanalytic literature as a serialized Gothic romance, it is not hard to envision the restless ghost of Pierre Janet, banished from the castle by Sigmund Freud a century ago, returning for an overdue haunting of Freud's current descendants. With uncanny commonality, most major schools of analytic thought have become appropriately more responsive to the phenomenon of dissociation, and each in its own way is attempting actively to accommodate it within its model of the mind and its approach to clinical process. (p. 189)

Psychoanalysis is now still in the process of reintegrating the legacy of Janet. However, there are two possible ways this can be achieved. The first is to conceptualise—as Fairbairn did in 1929—Janet's and Freud's legacies as two separate, completely split-off paradigms (Loewenstein & Ross, 1992) that need to be "re-mixed together" by a sort of *theoretical synthesis*. The second is to trace back the historical roots of the divide searching for a "common ground" (Wallerstein, 1990).

A misunderstanding?

Notwithstanding Fairbairn's pioneering work on Janet and Freud—which was published only in 1994 (Scharff & Birtles, 1994)—it was not until 1970 that the mutual influence between the two was amply discussed in Henri Ellenberger's *The Discovery of the Unconscious*. Nevertheless, even Ellenberger's most accurate study leaves a key question open: why was Freud so eager to assert his originality with respect to Janet? And why did he fight so hard in order not to let psychoanalysis be "contaminated" by Janet's ideas, whose shadow hovered over Breuer's conception of *hypnoid states* (Breuer & Freud, 1895, p. 286), Bleuler's and Jung's elaboration of *schizophrenia* and *introversion* (Falzeder, 2007, p. 358; McGuire, 1974, p. 160), and Adler's insistence on the *inferiority complex*, which is "an extension" of Janet's *sentiment d'incomplétude* (Adler, 1912, p. vi)?

In 1924 Freud gave the following answer:

> According to Janet's view a hysterical woman was a wretched creature who, on account of a constitutional weakness, was unable to hold her mental acts together, and it was for that reason that she fell a victim to a splitting of her mind and to a restriction of the field of her consciousness. The outcome of psycho-analytic investigations, on the other hand, showed that these phenomena were the result of dynamic factors—of mental conflict and of repression. This distinction seems to me to be far-reaching enough to put an end to the glib repetition of the view that whatever is of value in psycho-analysis is merely borrowed from the ideas of Janet. […] I always treated Janet himself with respect, […] but […] Janet behaved ill, showed ignorance of the facts and used ugly arguments. (1925d, pp. 30–31)

In going though the chronicle of the relationship between Freud and Janet (Ellenberger, 1970; Pérez-Rincón, 2012; Prévost, 1973), one gets the impression that the previous lines honestly display the thoughts and feelings of Freud towards Janet; while Janet's had been just restated a year before, having been exposed on some previous occasions.

> A foreign physician, Dr S. Freud from Vienna, came to the Salpêtrière and was interested by these last studies [Janet's experiments with hypnotism]. He ascertained the reality of the facts and published some new observations of the same kind. In those he mainly modified the terms I used: he called psychoanalysis what I had called psychological analysis, he named complex what I had named psychological system [...], he understood as a repression what I had ascribed to a narrowing of consciousness, and he gave the name of catharsis to what I had indicated as a psychological dissociation, or moral disinfection. (Janet, 1923, p. 41)

By making one of the most careful analyses of the quarrel between Janet and Freud, Claude Prévost demonstrated that the image that Freud and Janet gave of each other was largely based on a *misunderstanding*, which "crystallized the reciprocal vision of the two men in a partial or mistaken picture" (1973, p. 65). For decades, this misunderstanding excluded the work of Janet from psychoanalysis; while today the same misunderstanding is carried on by those who declare to follow *either* the legacy of Freud *or* that of Janet, as if they were alternative.

At the court of Charcot

It all started at the Salpêtrière, in Paris, where the 29-year-old Freud arrived on October 1885 in order to study with Jean-Martin Charcot. At the time he had been engaged to Martha Bernays for over three years and, having decided to get married, had left Ernst Brücke's laboratory at the Physiological Institute since it would not have enabled him to earn a living sufficient to support a family. As Freud recalls, "The turning-point came in 1882, when [Brücke], for whom I felt the highest possible esteem, corrected my father's generous improvidence by strongly advising me, in view of my bad financial position, to abandon my theoretical career" (1925d, p. 10).

At Brücke's lab, Freud also met again his friend Joseph Breuer, a 65-year-old researcher and general practitioner who had "developed into one of the most widely sought after doctors in Vienna, physician to aristocrats and members of Vienna's elite" (Makari, 2008, p. 39).

> They first met in the 1870s and quickly developed a close and mutually gratifying relationship. On his side, Breuer saw great promise in the bright young man and more or less adopted him as a son-colleague. Breuer was someone who, far from envying the talent of others, took pleasure in nurturing it. When they were later working together on the treatment of hysterics, Breuer commented: "Freud's intellect is soaring at its highest. I gaze after him as a hen at a hawk." For his part, Freud was searching for an older male ideal and he was more than pleased with what Breuer offered him: financial help, the sharing of personal information, and scientific and professional collaborations. For over six years, beginning in 1881, Breuer gave him a monthly stipend, a "loan" of money that the impoverished Freud was not expected to repay. When the younger man from time to time expressed discomfort over accepting the money, Breuer told him he could easily afford it and that Freud, rather than losing self-respect, should take the gift as an indication of his value in the world. (Breger, 2000, p. 65)

In synthesis, Breuer represented an affectively and concretely supporting figure, someone who really "gave credit" to Freud (Borgogno, 2010–2011). Charcot was to embody, instead, an open door to an unknown scientific universe, in which Freud's intellectual aspirations and emotional interests overlapped (Breger, 2000).

However, in November 1885, a month after Freud's arrival in Paris, Paul Janet—professor of philosophy at the Sorbonne (Brady Brower, 2010)—presented under the chairmanship of Charcot the early experiments with hypnosis of his nephew Pierre—a 26-year-old lycée professor—at the *Société de psychologie physiologique*. We do not know whether Pierre Janet and Freud ever met in Paris, but it is hardly conceivable that Freud did not hear about Janet's work, as he was to declare years later (1925d, p. 13).

From 1885 to 1889 Janet carried on his researches, which were regularly published on the *Revue philosophique*, and in August 1889—having graduated in philosophy at the Sorbonne just two months earlier—he lectured at two important psychological congresses—both attended by Freud—that were held in Paris for the Universal Exposition (Ellenberger, 1970, p. 759). In the same year, Janet published his dissertation under the title *L'automatisme psychologique* (1889), and in 1890—his medical training having just started—he was appointed by Charcot as director of the *Laboratoire de psychologie expérimentale* at the Salpêtrière.

It is not difficult to imagine that, if Freud saw Charcot as his "ideal master", he soon started to see Janet as his "ideal rival", the rivalry being between an outsider and an insider with relevant connections in academic circles. For his part, Janet developed an image of Freud—especially when the latter gathered more and more followers while Janet was falling into disgrace even at the Salpêtrière (Prévost, 1973, p. 71)—as an "illegitimate brother" who had come to Paris to steal the master's and his own work.

But back in 1885 Janet was more experienced in the treatment of hysterics, he had "a good mind" (as Freud himself admitted to Jung in 1907) (McGuire, 1974, p. 25), he was a perspicacious and sensitive clinician (Breger, 2009, p. 201; Ellenberger, 1970, p. 350 ff.; Frust, 2008), and he had at his disposal the most famous hospital in Europe for research on hysteria. For many reasons Freud felt himself to be behind, and indeed he was; still, he could rely on Joseph Breuer.

Far from the cold reception Freud experienced from his professors once he returned from Paris in 1886, Breuer welcomed him back in Vienna "with a warm kiss and embrace" (Breger, 2000, p. 99). Then he started to refer patients to Freud, so that he could open his private practice and eventually get married. Furthermore, before his travel to Paris Freud had been intrigued by the strange case of a girl (Bertha Pappenheim, a.k.a. Anna O.) whom from 1880 to 1882 Breuer had treated intensively by means of what he had described—on the patient's suggestion—as a *talking cure*. Freud and Breuer had often discussed the patient, who was a friend of Martha (Breger, 2000, p. 65), and in Paris Freud had even tried to interest Charcot in the case, but without success (Makari, 2008, p. 40).

Breuer's groundbreaking treatment of Anna O. in that period, combined with the insights on the case the two reached during their discussions and the new knowledge Freud brought from Paris (and from Nancy, where he had been visiting Hippolyte Bernheim), laid down the foundations on which Freud later grounded a method for the analysis of the mind that could compete with Janet's; which, by the way, was rapidly developing into a real "psychological analysis". At the International Congress of Experimental Psychology of London, in 1892, Janet even presented a new procedure—*automatic talking*—consisting of "letting the patient talk aloud at random" (Ellenberger, 1970, p. 366).

Due to Freud's rush to catch up with Janet, in 1893 Breuer and Freud published in a journal article (titled "On the Psychic Mechanism of Hysterical Phenomena") the theoretical premise of their *Studies on Hysteria* (Breuer & Freud, 1895). In retrospect, this was a self-defeating move because the anticipatory essay lacked the case material that could prove the distinctive features of the *talking cure*, which was ahead of its time in terms of mutual affective engagement with patients, while from a theoretical point of view it could be seen—above all from Janet's perspective—as simply derived from Charcot's and Janet's discoveries.

In fact, this is what Janet commented about Breuer's and Freud's work: he acknowledged it as one of the most significant of the period, and agreed with them on the relevance of emotions arising during hysterical crises and hypnoid states (Janet, 1893a, p. 432); but then he observed that the link between hypnoid states and hysterical phenomena had already been established by several authors, himself included (Janet, 1893b, p. 19); that Breuer's and Freud's remark that hysterics are reasonable when *awaken* and alienated during their *dreamlike* hypnoid states was a well-received confirmation of what he had been describing since 1885 as *désagrégation* and *dédoublement de la personnalité* (ibid., pp. 25–26); and finally he maintained, on the strength of his clinical experience, that he did not believe "that healing occurs in such an easy way, that one has just to make the patient express his fixed ideas to remove them—cure is a terribly more delicate matter" (Janet, 1893c, p. 352).

In order to answer Janet's reasonable critiques, Freud sought to "emancipate" his theory from Janet's, and this is how the well-known creation of the Freudian *conflict-defence theory* began, along with its emphasis on sexuality and all the discussions and breaks—such as those with Breuer, Bleuler, Adler, Jung, etc.—that came with it. However, the first point of differentiation from Janet was the Theory of Degeneration (Freud, 1894a, pp. 46–48).

Throwing out the baby with the bathwater: degeneration theory

The concept of *dissociation* is historically tied to that of *hereditary degeneration*, which was a popular notion in the neurology and psychiatry of the nineteenth century.

> After 1870, biologic inheritance was widely accepted as the cause of psychic functions and the central precondition that led to a mind breaking during accidental events. [...] By borrowing his student Charles Féré's notion of a "neuropathic family" and studying genealogies, Charcot linked a number of illnesses together, attributing all to the same inherited defect. Charcot mapped out family trees that bloomed with hysteria, alcoholism, suicide, progressive paralysis, apoplexy, rheumatic and arthritic disorders. When challenged as to the common inheritance of these illnesses, Charcot pointed to the neuropathic constellation that could be found among "Israelites". (Makari, 2008, pp. 34–35)

The interested reader can delve into the topic by reading the comprehensive book by Daniel Pick, *Faces of Degeneration* (1989), where the author argues that degeneration theory "needs to be understood as [...] a complex process of conceptualizing a felt crisis of history" that started "at just the moment when liberal progressivism was so powerfully in trouble" (p. 54). Diagnoses based on degeneration were "a convenient method of explaining away the widely perceived and criticized failure of psychiatry to 'cure' very many of its patients. Incurability […] was now affirmed as an unavoidable fact of nature. The function of the asylum was re-defined not as a 'cure', but as humane segregation of the degenerate and the dangerous" (ibid., p. 55).

By demonstrating that it was possible to give credit to hysterics and do something about them (Borgogno, 1999), Charcot really shaped a new culture at the Salpêtrière that would "inflame" the future of psychiatry; nonetheless he kept on asserting that organic *dégénérescence* was a necessary *precondition* for mental illness, with environmental traumas acting as "accidental triggering factors" (Goetz, Bonduelle, & Gelfand, 1995, p. 262). Later on, it was Janet who lifted the theories of Charcot from brain-level to mental-level by transforming "organic *dégénérescence*" into "psychological *désagrégation*" (Janet, 1893c, p. 497 ff.). Janet's *désagrégation* was then translated into English as *dissociation* and, from then on, also Janet often referred to it as such. But he did not dismiss Charcot's theory about the combined action of *predisposition* and *trauma*, even if in time he added more complexity to it (Ellenberger, 1970; Prévost, 1973). After all, Freud did the same in developing the concept of *Nachträglichkeit*—that is, the *deferred action* of infantile sexual trauma—which was meant to replace degenerationism (see Freud, 1896b, pp. 163–166). Not by chance, *infancy* and *sexuality* have become the two cornerstones of psychoanalysis.

Maybe for his Jewish (Rolnik, 2012, p. 7) and humble origins, Freud was quite sensitive to the problem of degeneration (Spiegel, 1986), and Janet's ascription of the genesis of hysteria to *misère, faiblesse,* and *désagrégation psychologique* sounded to his ear as an unacceptable degenerationist statement. Additionally, if the idea of degeneration could easily be associated with the image of the "uneducated" people that filled institutions like the Salpêtrière, it clashed with the upper-class and cultured patients that consulted Breuer and Freud.

In 1887 Freud started his private practice, and as early as 1888, though still identified with the hereditarism of Charcot, he already underlined that hysterics retain "complete intellectual clarity and a capacity even for unusual achievements" (1888b, p. 53). The idea was further developed in the account of the treatment of Baroness Fanny Moser, one of the wealthiest widows in Europe (a.k.a. Emmy von N.), which exerted a major impact on the subsequent evolution of Freudian theory (Bromberg, 1996). In commenting on the personality of Emmy, Freud harshly attacked Janet for the first time:

> Emmy von N. gave us an example of how hysteria is compatible with an unblemished character and a well-governed mode of life. The woman we came to know was an admirable one. The moral seriousness with which she viewed her duties, her intelligence and energy, which were no less than a man's, and her high degree of education and love of truth impressed both of us greatly [Freud and Breuer]; while her benevolent care for the welfare of all her dependants, her humility of mind and the refinement of her manners revealed her qualities as a true lady as well. To describe such a woman as a "degenerate" would be to distort the meaning of that word out of all recognition. We should do well to distinguish between the concepts of "disposition" and "degeneracy" as applied to people; otherwise we shall find ourselves forced to admit that humanity owes a large proportion of its great achievements to the efforts of "degenerates". I must confess, too, that I can see no sign in Frau von N.'s history of the

"psychical inefficiency" to which Janet attributes the genesis of hysteria. [...] During the times of her worst states she was and remained capable of playing her part in the management of a large industrial business, of keeping a constant eye on the education of her children, of carrying on her correspondence with prominent people in the intellectual world—in short, of fulfilling her obligations well enough for the fact of her illness to remain concealed. (Breuer & Freud, 1895, pp. 103–104)

Unfortunately, as Freud would learn years later (Tögel, 1999), the personality of Emmy was "split" in the most Fairbairnian sense, so that what Freud had been dealing with was—to borrow Helene Deutsch's expression—her "as if" personality (1942), or in Winnicottian terms her *false self* (1955). In brief, Freud had been misguided by what Ferenczi (1932) would have called the portion of Emmy's personality grown out of *identification with the aggressor*. This made her, on one side of the divide, behave obediently and seductively with the doctors who tried to help her, but on the other side it impelled her to reject and abandon them as soon as some "dangerous" affective contact was emerging (Breuer & Freud, 1895, p. 105 n.).

Ferenczi, Suttie, and Fairbairn

Ferenczi made one of the boldest attempts to combine Freud's emphasis on infantile sexuality with Janet's ideas on trauma and dissociation (which he accurately quoted in his works). In his view, it is not *constitutional weakness* that allows trauma to produce a split in the personality, but the ordinary *infantile dependency*, which compels the child to subordinate to, and contemporaneously identify with, the desires of the adults, libidinal and narcissistic ones included (Ferenczi, 1932, p. 228). A *nurturing environment* may, consequently, foster "intellectual progression" and "precocious maturity" by means of identification with adults, but *at the same time* neglecting, inhibiting, or even "perverting" the child's pulsional, affective, and relational development (ibid., p. 228). This creates what Fairbairn described as *schizoid personality*:

> Over-valuation of thought is related to the difficulty which the individual with a schizoid tendency experiences in making emotional contacts with other people. [...] It would appear that, so far as conscious intention is concerned, his attempts to solve his emotional problems intellectually are meant in the first instance to pave the way for adaptive behaviour in relation to external objects; but, since emotional conflicts springing from deep sources in the unconscious defy solution in this way, he tends increasingly to substitute intellectual solutions of his emotional problems for attempts to achieve a practical solution of them within the emotional sphere in his relationships with others in the outer world. (1940a, p. 20)

Ferenczi's original "mixture" of Freud and Janet landed in Scotland through the work of the psychiatrist Ian Suttie (Cassullo, 2010). As Graham S. Clarke (2011) recently demonstrated with the discovery of a heavily underlined copy of a 1939 edition of Suttie's book *The Origins of Love and Hate* (1935) belonging to Fairbairn, Suttie had a *direct* impact on the fellow Scotsman starting from 1940. Suttie's belief that the *dissociation of sentiments connected to infantile dependence* should be seen as the *main disposition* to psychopathology and social-maladjustment was thus at the root of Fairbairn's influential study on schizoid phenomena (Fairbairn, 1940), which launched the following reformulation of Freud's instinct theory in terms of "a theory of development based essentially upon object-relations" (Fairbairn, 1941, p. 31). (Strikingly, in January 1939, probably just before reading Suttie's book, Fairbairn wrote: "At birth the child is a creature of unorganized impulse, ignorant of the nature of outer reality, and incapable of adapting his impulses to the inexorable necessities of life except at a very primitive instinctive level. His mental organization conforms to hereditary biological pattern and is thus extremely simple compared to that of the adult" (1939a, p. 290).)

This reformulation could represent a modern version of the Theory of Degeneration, which is now concerned with the *deterioration* and *dissociation*, in pathological conditions, of the primary object-seeking human drive.

> From the point of view of object-relationship psychology, explicit pleasure-seeking represents a deterioration of behaviour. I speak here of a "deterioration", rather than of a "regression", of behaviour because, if object-seeking is primary, pleasure-seeking can hardly be described as "regressive", but is more appropriately described as partaking of the nature of deterioration. Explicit pleasure-seeking has as its essential aim the relieving of the tension of libidinal need for the mere sake of relieving this tension. Such a process does, of course, occur commonly enough; but, since libidinal need is object-need, simple tension-relieving implies some failure of object-relationships. The fact is that simple tension-relieving is really a safety-valve process. It is thus, not a means of achieving libidinal aims, but a means of mitigating the failure of these aims. (Fairbairn, 1946, pp. 139–140)

In concluding

In these pages, I have traced back the quarrel between Janet and Freud in order to show how their rivalry fostered fundamental clinical and theoretical advances when the ideas of the one were included in the other's own frame of reference, whereas it produced "developmental arrests" in the field when they were excluded. Such was the case for Janet's refusal of infantile sexuality and for Freud's aversion to Degeneration Theory.

In doing so, I argued that, although Fairbairn started attempting a *theoretical synthesis* of the divergences between Janet and Freud, it was not until he read Suttie's *The Origin of Love and Hate*, in 1939–1940 (Clarke, 2011), that an effective integration was achieved, and this made his theorisation suddenly flourish. It is possible, thus, to have a measure of the quality of the working-through made by Ferenczi and Suttie of the legacies of Janet and Freud by comparing the early works of Fairbairn with the later ones.

References

Adler, A. (1912). *The Neurotic Constitution. Outlines of a Comparative Individualistic Psychology and Psychotherapy*. New York: Moffat, Yard, 1917.

Bemporad, J. R. (1989). Freud, Janet and evolution: Of statuettes and plants. *Journal of the American Academy of Psychoanalysis and Dynamic Psychiatry, 17*: 623–638.

Berman, E. (1981). Multiple personality: Psychoanalytic perspectives. *International Journal of Psychoanalysis, 62*: 283–300.

Birtles, E. F., & Scharff, D. E. (Eds.) (1994). *From Instinct to Self. Selected Papers of W. R. D. Fairbairn, Volume II: Applications and Early Contributions*. Northvale, NJ: Jason Aronson.

Borgogno, F. (1999). *Psicoanalisi come percorso*. Turin, Italy: Bollati Boringhieri. [English translation: *Psychoanalysis as a Journey*. London: Open Gate.]

Borgogno, F. (2010). Presentation for the Mary Sigourney Ceremony. www.sigourneyaward.org.

Borgogno, F. (2011). *La signorina che faceva hara-kiri e altri scritti*. Turin, Italy: Bollati Boringhieri. [English translation: *The Girl Who Committed Hara-Kiri and Other Historico-Clinical Essays*. London: Karnac, 2012.]

Brady Brower, M. (2010). *Unruly Spirits: The Science of Psychic Phenomena in Modern France*. Urbana, IL: University of Illinois Press.

Breger, L. (2000). *Freud. Darkness in the Midst of Vision*. New York: J. Wiley & Sons.

Breger, L. (2009). *A Dream of Undying Fame*. New York: Basic.

Breuer, J., & Freud, S. (1895). *Studies on Hysteria. S. E., 2* (pp. 1–335).

Bromberg, P. M. (1995). Psychoanalysis, dissociation, and personality organization. In: *Standing in the Spaces: Essays on Clinical Process, Trauma, and Dissociation* (pp. 189–204). Hillsdale, NJ: Analytic Press, 1998.

Bromberg, P. M. (1996). Hysteria, dissociation, and cure: Emmy von N revisited. *Psychoanalytic Dialogues, 6*: 55–71.

Cassullo, G. (2010). Back to the roots: The influence of Ian D. Suttie on British Psychoanalysis. *American Imago, 67*: 5–22.

Clarke, G. S. (2011). Suttie's influence on Fairbairn's object relations theory. *Journal of the American Psychoanalytic Association, 59*: 939–959.

Davies, J. (1998). Repression and dissociation—Freud and Janet: Fairbairn's new model of unconscious process. In: N. J. Skolnick & D. E. Scharff (Eds.), *Fairbairn, Then and Now* (pp. 53–69). Hillsdale, NJ: Analytic Press, 1998.

Deutsch, H. (1942). Some forms of emotional disturbance and their relationship to schizophrenia. *Psychoanalytic Quarterly, 11*: 301–321.

Ellenberger, H. F. (1970). *The Discovery of the Unconscious*. New York: Basic.

Fairbairn, W. R. D. (1929). Dissociation and repression. In: Birtles, E. F., & Scharff, D. E. (Eds.), *From Instinct to Self: Selected Papers of W. R. D. Fairbairn, Volume II: Applications and Early Contributions* (pp. 13–79). Northvale, NJ: Jason Aronson, 1994.

Fairbairn, W. R. D. (1939a). Sexual delinquency. In: Birtles, E. F., & Scharff, D. E. (Eds.), *From Instinct to Self: Selected Papers of W. R. D. Fairbairn, Volume II: Applications and Early Contributions* (pp. 284–292). Northvale, NJ: Jason Aronson, 1994.

Fairbairn, W. R. D. (1940a). Schizoid factors in the personality. In: *Psychoanalytic Studies of the Personality* (pp. 3–27). London: Tavistock, 1952.

Fairbairn, W. R. D. (1941). A revised psychopathology of the psychoses and psychoneuroses. In: *Psychoanalytic Studies of the Personality* (pp. 28–58). London: Tavistock, 1952.

Fairbairn, W. R. D. (1946). Object-relationships and dynamic structure. In: *Psychoanalytic Studies of the Personality* (pp. 137–151). London: Tavistock, 1952.

Falzeder, E. (2007). The story of an ambivalent relationship: Sigmund Freud and Eugen Bleuler. *Journal of Analytical Psychology, 52*: 343–368.

Ferenczi, S. (1932). Confusion of the tongues between the adults and the child (the language of tenderness and of passion). *International Journal of Psychoanalysis, 30*: 225–230, 1949.

Freud, S. (1888b). Hysteria. *S. E., 1* (pp. 37–59).
Freud, S. (1894a). The neuro-psychoses of defence. *S. E., 3* (pp. 41–61).
Freud, S. (1896b). Further remarks on the neuro-psychoses of defence. *S. E., 3* (pp. 157–185).
Freud, S. (1925d). An autobiographical study. *S. E., 20* (pp. 1–74).
Frust, L. R. (2008). *Before Freud: Hysteria and Hypnosis in Later Nineteenth-Century Psychiatric Cases*. New York: Bucknell University Press.
Goetz, C. G., Bonduelle, M., & Gelfand, T. (1995). *Charcot: Constructing Neurology*. New York: Oxford University Press.
Gullenstad, S. E. (2005). Who is "who" in dissociation? A plea for psychodynamics in a time of trauma. *International Journal of Psychoanalysis, 86*: 639–656.
Janet, P. (1889). *L'automatisme psychologique* [Psychological Automatism]. Paris: Felix Alcan.
Janet, P. (1893a). Quelques définitions récentes de l'hystérie (I) [Some recent definitions of hysteria]. *Archives de Neurologie, 25*(76): 417–438.
Janet, P. (1893b). Quelques définitions récentes de l'hystérie (II) [Some recent definitions of hysteria]. *Archives de Neurologie, 26*(77): 1–29.
Janet, P. (1893c). *L'état mental des hystériques*. Paris: Rueff. [English translation: *The Mental State of Hystericals*. New York: G. P. Putnam's Sons, 1901.]
Janet, P. (1923). *La médecine psychologique* [Psychological Medicine]. Paris: Flammarion.
Loewenstein, R. J., & Ross, D. R. (1992). Multiple personality and psychoanalysis: An introduction. *Psychoanalytic Inquiry, 12*: 3–48.
Makari, G. (2008). *Revolution in Mind. The Creation of Psychoanalysis*. New York: Harper Collins.
McGuire, W. (Ed.) (1974). *The Correspondence Between Sigmund Freud and C. G. Jung*. Princeton, NJ: Princeton University Press.
Pérez-Rincón, H. (2012). Pierre Janet, Sigmund Freud and Charcot's psychological and psychiatric legacy. In: J. Bogousslavsky (Ed.), *Following Charcot: A Forgotten History of Neurology and Psychiatry*. Basel, Switzerland: Karger.
Pick, D. (1989). *Faces of Degeneration*. Cambridge: Cambridge University Press.
Prévost, C. M. (1973). *Janet, Freud et la psychologie clinique* [Janet, Freud and Clinical Psychology]. Paris: Payot.
Putnam, F. W. (1989). Pierre Janet and modern views of dissociation. *Journal of Traumatic Stress, 2*(4): 413–429.
Rolnik, E. J. (2012). *Freud in Zion*. London: Karnac.
Spiegel, R. (1986). Freud's refutation of degenerationism: A contribution to humanism. *Contemporary Psychoanalysis, 22*: 4–24.
Suttie, I. D. (1935). *The Origins of Love and Hate*. London: Free Association, 1988.
Tögel, C. (1999). "My bad diagnostic error": Once more about Freud and Emmy v. N. (Fanny Moser). *International Journal of Psychoanalysis, 80*: 1165–1173.
van der Hart, O., & Friedman, B. (1989). A reader's guide to Pierre Janet on dissociation. A neglected intellectual heritage. *Dissociation, 2*: 3–16.
Wallerstein, R. S. (1990). Psychoanalysis: The common ground. *International Journal of Psychoanalysis, 71*: 3–20.
Winnicott, D. W. (1955). Metapsychological and clinical aspects of regression within the psycho-analytical set-up. *International Journal of Psychoanalysis, 36*: 16–26.

CHAPTER FIVE

Fairbairn, Suttie, and Macmurray—an essay

Neville Symington

I am going to approach these three thinkers from Scotland with a very broad brush. I am not going to consider them in detail but will give the broad outlines of their thinking and show how Fairbairn and Suttie were debating in one theatre whereas Macmurray was radically different from them in his thinking. Fairbairn and Suttie were both clinicians but Macmurray was not and this is where I want to start.

Fairbairn and Suttie were under the banner of Freud whom they both admired but, at the same time, were in debate with him and wanted to show the lacunae in his system of thinking. Therefore the circumference of their perspective was a narrow one, as is a great deal of psychoanalytic thinking. One could put as a sub-title attached to both of them that Freud was their master and, although in general agreement, yet in significantly human ways they wanted to show up what they believed were the deficiencies of their master.

So in what way did Fairbairn bow his head to the master and in what ways did he disagree? Theoretically Fairbairn accepted Freud's view that the principles of action within the human individual were the instincts. The instincts—those drives that served to preserve the lifeblood of the organism and so keep the species *homo sapiens* in survival from generation to generation. He surrendered totally to Freud's view that the instincts are the core principles of action within the personality but then he defined these not on the basis of efficient causality but of final causality. With the exception of the death instinct Freud defined the instincts according to their organic source and, as Petocz (1999, p. 221) has pointed out, that when Freud, in his later formulation, included the death drive in his catalogue of instincts he had departed from the definition which he had given to the instincts previously. This latter drive was no longer an efficient cause but a final cause. So, an instinct, according to Freud's initial formulation, had been defined as an impulse whose goal was the reduction of tension within the organism. Therefore, the state of tension defined as hunger was reduced by the consumption of food, thirst reduced by the drinking of water, or sexual starvation by sexual satisfaction. This was underpinned by the view that the reduction of tension was subjectively experienced as pleasure. Ferenczi had already pointed out that there was an inconsistency in this theory in that in sexual activity pleasure was associated with an increase and not a decrease in tension (Ferenczi, 1968, pp. 60–72). So, already within Freud's lifetime, the homeostatic principle had been questioned by one of his earliest followers. If reduction of sexual tension was the goal of the act then it made no difference if this was achieved through heterosexual intercourse, homosexual intercourse, paedophilic action, bestiality, or masturbation. So Fairbairn tried to right this by saying that the sexual impulse needed to be defined not by its source—that is, the organic state of sexual tension—but by its goal, therefore defining instincts by their final cause rather than the efficient cause. This also meant that, once the sexual instinct was defined by goal, then the possible objects that satisfied the instincts were differentiated. This, in fact, would have been consistent with Freud's view that there was a hierarchy of sexual functional activity with genital sexual intercourse at its head, with homosexual action lower down the ladder, and masturbation and then the infant sucking the nipple yet further down. So Fairbairn's redefinition of instincts according to a final cause was consistent with Freud's own view of sexual maturation. This highlighted the fact that Freud's metapsychology of the instincts was not consistent with his view of the incremental stages on the ladder leading to sexual maturity.

It is important to note that in Fairbairn's recasting of Freud's instinctual theory he discarded something to which Freud had given emphasis. Freud believed that in the developing sexual hierarchy just mentioned that heterosexual genital action was a principle unifying disparate elements in the personality. Whereas Fairbairn, relying for his metaphorical imagery, of the organic unity of the body, proposed that there existed already a mental unified whole and therefore the notion of Freud's "genital primacy" was based on the sense of their being disparate instincts requiring a unifier. I think the problem here between the two men was that they were both relying upon an organic substrate which was the source of the instincts which, for both men, was libidinal. And yet, as Marie Jahoda has pointed out (1977, p. 95), Freud did not have just one metapsychology but a whole range of metapsychologies jostling with each other and Freud's greatness consisted in his refusal to bend his clinical observations into one narrow metapsychology. If his clinical observation was in contradiction to his metapsychology then so be it. Therefore Freud thought that there was an organiser integrating different mental parts whereas, paradoxically, Fairbairn, relying on the organic model, thought there was a mental whole already existing which required no mental unifier. Therefore Fairbairn corrected Freud helpfully in one area whereas Fairbairn himself needs correcting by his master in another. I am basing this comment on the view that there are disparate separated elements that require the work of an inner unifier. This is, I believe, a very important perspective from a clinical practical point of view. Clinicians have to decide whether there are disparate elements requiring an integrating unifier or whether there is already an embodied unity but shattered into parts through inner envious attacks. Whichever of these two options they endorse will greatly alter their interpretative mode with patients.

Fairbairn, correctly in my view, stressed that the source of action lay in the ego, either in its central form or one of its "satellites". Sometimes he referred to this source of action as the ego and at other times as "psychic structure". In whichever language he was using he was emphasising that the source of action is not in blind instincts. Of course once an instinct has been defined according to a final cause then it is no longer blind and, so it seems to this writer, it is a contradiction to endorse instincts on the one hand and yet say that the source of action lies in the ego or "psychic structure". It seems that Fairbairn did not quite take the bold step of renouncing altogether Freud's instinct theory. When he spoke of either the ego or psychic structure being the source of action one might almost have wished that he had scrapped the instinctual model altogether. In one way he nearly did in that he did away with Freud's *das Es* or the *Id* in our bad translation. What he did not do was to scrap entirely the instincts as a source of action and simply say that there was an inner source of action independent of the instincts. This is, in my view, a crucial step which needs to be taken. We shall come to this when we consider Macmurray.

* * *

Ian Suttie, like Fairbairn, was in debate with Freud. He, like Fairbairn, understood Freud well and made use of some of Freud's insights. A striking example is instanced in this insightful statement that he makes:

> Psychology has revealed that the unconscious infantility of adults may be so strong as to make the mother hate her own child and see in it a supplanter ousting her from the childhood role she has never truly surrendered. (1939, p. 134)

It is a puzzle to many how a mother can hate her child. This insight of Suttie's comes from two sources: first he is confronted by the puzzling circumstance of a mother who hates her child. This was something he knew from his own clinical and social experience. It is, fortunately, an exception; it is a rarity for a mother to hate her child yet, as Suttie knew, it happens. I am stressing this because what I am going to suggest shortly may make some people believe that he was a head-in-the-clouds romantic whereas he was a down to earth man who knew the blacker side of life. The influence of Freud's thinking in this quote is easy to see. Freud formulated what he referred to as a *fixation*. By this he meant that someone can be fixed at an early developmental stage; that the woman aged thirty-five can still emotionally be stuck at the age of one, three, five, ten, or fifteen. Thus if this particular woman, who hates her child, is fixated at the age of one then her physical baby is her rival and she hates him. So Suttie found in Freud's developmental schema an understanding of the dilemma that was such a puzzle to him. So, like Fairbairn, he was indebted to Freud for enunciating a principle that was capable of solving some of the puzzling dilemmas that confront the observer of the human condition. At the same time, however, like every true thinker he was not a slave to Freud's psychological system or its unitary motivational roots. He believed that people have different, and even sometimes conflicting, motives. He stresses therefore that the baby, apart from his biological need for nurture, also wanted companionship. Here are two quotes which make it clear what he thought:

> I saw the possibility that the biological need for nurture might be psychologically presented in the infant mind, not as a bundle of practical organic necessities and potential privations, but

as a pleasure in responsive companionship and as a correlative discomfort in loneliness and isolation. The Freudian conception of self-expression as a "detensioning" process or emotional evacuation now seemed to me to be false and in its place I imagined expression as an offering or stimulus directed to the other person, designed to elicit a response while love itself was essentially a state of active harmonious interplay. (ibid., p. 4)

It differs fundamentally from psycho-analysis in introducing the conception of an innate need-for-companionship which is the infant's only way of self-preservation. This need, giving rise to parental and fellowship "love", I put in the place of the Freudian Libido, and regard it as genetically independent of genital appetite. The application of this conception seems to re-orient the whole psycho-analytic dynamics … (ibid., p. 6)

If one asks Suttie the question, why the application of this conception seems to re-orient the whole psycho-analytic dynamics?, then I think the answer is that love and the desire for companionship are, as he says, genetically independent of genital appetite. This implied a theoretical departure from Freud that is highly significant. For Freud there was a single motivational principle from which all human action is derived. This was the genital appetite rooted in the struggle for survival which is capable of explaining all of human behaviour. So, in his view, love and desire for companionship were derivative of the genital appetite or libido. So also Freud's definition of sublimation is the socially useful activity but derived from the same source. This view of Freud permeated the thinkers of the Enlightenment and had its most potent expression in the anti-vitalist pact whose signatories were Helmholtz, Du Bois-Reymond, Karl Ludwig, and Ernst Brücke. Ernest Jones describes this clearly in the first volume of his biography of Freud:

Brücke's Institute was an important part indeed of that far-reaching scientific movement best known as Helmholtz's School of Medicine. The amazing story of this scientific school started in the early forties with the friendship of Emil Du Bois-Reymond (1818–96) and Ernst Brücke (1819–92), soon joined by Hermann Helmholtz (1821–94) and Carl Ludwig (1816–95). From its very beginning this group was driven forward by a crusading spirit. In 1842 Du Bois-Reymond wrote: "Brücke and I pledged a solemn oath to put into effect this truth: 'No other forces than the common physical and chemical ones are active within the organism. In those cases which cannot at the time be explained by those forces one has either to find the specific way or form of their action by means of the physical-mathematical method or to assume new forces equal in dignity to the chemical-physical forces inherent in matter, reducible to the force of attraction and repulsion.'" (1972, p. 45)

This anti-vitalist pact, against the vitalism of Johannes Müller, does exactly what this fundamentalist oath declares: it robs life of its living principle. It reduces life to action of a purely mechanical nature. Just as rivers flowing downwards, apples falling downwards, planets circling the sun are all actions originating from some "chemical-physical force", which characterises inanimate nature so all living activity is reduced to this same principle, therefore robbing life of its essential characteristic: namely a source of action from within itself. Freud, for whom Brücke and Helmholtz were admired mentors, therefore saw the source of action within living things and within human beings as originating from blind forces—*Triebe* or drives—which therefore, in fidelity to the authors of the anti-vitalist pact, robbed life of its essential principle. It was this that Suttie repudiated and gave expression to in the two quotes just given. So, like Fairbairn, he challenged this view of Freud and all those Enlightenment thinkers, devoted followers of the *Philosophes*. What Suttie installed in his outlook was love, not as a derivative of Freud's libido but as an independent motivational principle.

However, although both Fairbairn and Suttie challenged Freud, both of them were still attempting to place their understanding within Freud's instinctual schema. Neither of them, for all their originality and confidence of outlook, was able to overthrow Freud's dedication to the view that we are all ultimately driven by blind forces—we are all billiard balls dependent ultimately upon an outer or inner force in the arms of which we are helpless creatures. To move into an entirely different order of thinking we have to turn to John Macmurray.

* * *

John Macmurray is probably the deepest thinker in the field of the human sciences of the modern era. When someone is asked to name the greatest humanist thinker in the nineteenth century they will probably say Wittgenstein, Bertrand Russell, or maybe Kafka, Dostoievsky, Polanyi, or Tolstoy. Then someone says "What about John Macmurray?" and is met with a blank stare followed by "Who is he?"

Macmurray centred his thinking on friendship, freedom, and the personal. And who was his mentor? Was it Freud? No, a philosopher, a teacher named Jesus of Nazareth who is not very well known outside those parochial organisations known as churches. However, if someone truly wants to understand what this man Jesus taught he needs to abandon religious organisations of all kinds and turn to John Macmurray. Macmurray was opposed to systems, to structures, and to organisations. In fact he believed that using organism as a model for understanding human beings was one of the greatest heresies in psychological and sociological thinking in the contemporary world, and that assumptions, based on organic metaphors, underlay most psychological and sociological thinking. In much of his writing he attempted to free himself and his readers from this erroneous model. It is so much inserted into the underpinnings of our thought processes that we do not realise that we have unconsciously subscribed to this organic model. What we need, he emphasised, is a principle that embodies the form of the personal. We need a language, a way of thinking that gives precedence to the personal. As soon as we start speaking of organisations, of structures, of constructions of social frameworks, we are already in the wrong mindset.

By contrast, Fairbairn and Suttie were introducing religious perspectives, but within and against Freud's metapsychological system, because, although contradictory to what they thought, yet its basic system of thinking was wholeheartedly accepted. This was based on the Enlightenment view, together with Darwin's evolutionary theory, that all could be understood according to the limitations of that scientific vision. This was not Macmurray's outlook at all. His foundation stone, upon which he erected a radicalism hated within social science, was his conviction that the way forward to a deeper understanding of the modern dilemma was to base the human condition upon natural theology. As this concept is so little known and even less understood it is necessary to outline the contours of its subject.

The best way to outline this is to follow the stormy trajectory of his own religious development. He was brought up within the traditional religious attitudes inherited from his parents into which he was born and reared. This, simply put, was the view that God had created the world, created the universe, and that because Adam and his descendants had violated the gift which their maker had given to them and thus thrown mankind into a state of alienation from God, so God therefore, in order to rescue mankind, had sent his very own godhead in the person of his son into the world to mend that state of alienation. This, roughly speaking, was the belief system in which John Macmurray was reared and was the very breath of his emotional and thinking processes until … an eruption occurred in which this infantile yet powerful belief was reduced to rubble like the city of Pompeii by the insensate lava from Vesuvius. This eruption in his youth might have changed Macmurray from Christian belief to radical atheism but, as with Tolstoy, it wrought a change far more profound. He repudiated this Christian idolatry; the idol being some superhuman figure who demanded worship and devotion from the idol's disciples and, again like Tolstoy, he knew that atheism and agnosticism were rebellions against an idol of human fabrication. He renounced therefore his erstwhile belief and replaced it with …? It is here that he based the human condition upon what he referred to as "natural theology". He defines it thus:

> … a theology which is based upon our common human experience of the world, and which requires no help from special experiences of a peculiarly religious kind. It must be discoverable by reason alone, without the need to have recourse to faith. (1957, p. 18)

We have to turn now to Macmurray's profound reflection, which he set out to describe in his deepest reflection upon the human condition: *The Structure of Religious Experience* (1936). In this series of essays he instances that there are three axes upon which the human condition rests and, without these, our human state cannot be adequately understood. He first looks at the scientific axis: the way in which we look at the world to see how it can benefit the living-ness of all of us in the world. It is clear, for instance, that to travel from England to Australia by plane is quicker then a five week journey by boat. It is science that has enabled human beings to construct a machine that can fly through the air. The concern of science then, which used to be called "natural philosophy", is with manipulating the material world so it can be put to use for the purposes of mankind. These purposes may be destructive or constructive. So the question to which science addresses itself is, "How can the objects of this world be used by mankind to improve the methods by which he consummates his purposes?" At root science has a utilitarian purpose; he defines it as a particular attitude of mind that is different from both art and religion.

The next axis that Macmurray investigates is art and here objects in the world are not to be used in the service of improving the accomplishment of human purposes. In art an object is not in the service of yet another objective in the world but its purpose is directly to give pleasure to the human observer. It is its own objective.

Then we come to the religious axis and this is where he examines most succinctly what religion is concerned with. Here it is not the self's relationship to the world of objects that is its concern but rather the world's evaluation of the individual self within its bosom. It is the world that subjects the individual to scrutiny. The best way of describing this is to put this question to myself at the point of my death: is the world a better or worse place for my having lived in it? This is the concern of religion. It is not concerned with those supposed interventions by God into the world of human beings which characterise Judaism, Christianity, and Islam. Natural theology does not rely upon any such revelations from a supposed superhuman power but on reason alone. Macmurray came to this through his own tempestuous inner journey of early adulthood which marked a transition from revealed religion to natural religion: the former being based upon abnormal communications from God to man and the latter being based upon the common experience of the world through rational reflection without recourse to faith. It needs to be noted though that he rejected ontology which, according to my view, is an inconsistency.

If all this is true then how is it that Jesus of Nazareth was so important a figure for Macmurray? For many philosophers, social scientists, and theologians, wisdom is the supreme human achievement and the goal to be striven after, but for Macmurray the supreme good for human beings is friendship and its wedded partner freedom, and he believed that this was the central message that Jesus gave to the world: that salvation meant to be saved from inner imprisonment through friendship and freedom. The significance and centrality of friendship was expressed on many occasions by Macmurray but I cannot do better than give you this quote:

> Friendship is the supreme value in life and the source of all other values.
>
> There is nothing we fear more than friendship, nothing that strikes more terror into us than freedom. If this seems a strange saying, it must be because you are confusing friendship with friendliness. Friendliness is not to be despised, but it is only the imitation of a friendship and a poor substitute for the real thing. It is really a refined form of service, and often rather a superficial one. But friendship knows no reservations, it gives no sympathy or comfort, or advice to help, but rather itself.
>
> To be a friend is to be yourself for another person. It means committing yourself completely and revealing yourself completely without reserve. It means putting all your cards on the table and taking the consequences. It means stark reality between persons without pretence or sentimentality. How many of us could bear to be found out completely for what we are by someone else? Most of us shrink from finding ourselves out. Even with our intimates we wear a mask and insist upon their wearing one. We have tastes and decencies and dignities that we must defend, and all of them are defences against friendship. They are the lifebelts that keep us on the surface of that sea of intimate relations, and we cling to them in terror of drowning in the limitless depths of personality.
>
> So pretence creeps in and sentimentality, the grossest sin of all against friendship. Honest hatred is better than the pretence of love. There are amongst us those who are willing to spend time and thought and strength and money in the service of others in order to retain the isolation of our own personality, to conceal as it were the fraud we are guilty of in refusing to give ourselves. All that service is of no avail. What men need from us is love, not moving acts: friendship, not friendly services ... Friendship means losing ourselves, and that is apt to be a terrifying experience. (Costello, 2002, p. 163)

No psychoanalyst can read this without thinking that when he describes "revealing yourself completely without reserve" that this is what is supposed to happen in an analysis. The patient's aim is to reveal himself without reserve and this is the recommendation that the analyst delivers to the patient when he or she first meets with him or her. If this is so then what Macmurray is defining as the essence of friendship is in essence what is hoped for when someone first comes to meet with his or her analyst. I cannot help here putting in something of my own experience. I remember well when I decided to consult an analyst. It was because I knew that I needed someone to reach right down into my inner soul—that I needed someone to reach me in a place that had never been touched before and I had the idea that a psychoanalyst was the person who could do this. Of course I was mistaken: this is not something that can occur just because someone belongs to a particular professional category and, in fact, my experience was one of disappointment with my first analyst and satisfaction with the second. This was because the second, although I paid him, was my friend whereas the first would not have known what that meant. He would not have known friendship in the way that Macmurray defines it.

So what is being implied here is that psychoanalysis, according to the way Macmurray would view it, is a "friendship encounter". Psychoanalysis is to be understood within this mental framework. For Macmurray psychoanalysis is one particular form of friendship and therefore, according to his way of viewing the three axes that determine the human condition, he would see psychoanalysis first as a religion, second as an art, and third as scientific. The reader may wonder why I bring in art and science at all. It is because, although Macmurray analyses the human condition according to these three axes, yet he knew clearly that there are within art scientific principles, within science artistic principles, and within religion both scientific and artistic principles. He is not saying that within any one of these three axes the other two are excluded. In fact he is implying, in all his thoughts about the modern mode of thinking, that there is always distortion if in any mental attitude one or two of these three axes are discarded.

* * *

It is probably clear to the reader that I think Macmurray was a genius and that both Suttie and Fairbairn were lower down on the scale of human insight. The reason for this assertion is that both Fairbairn and Suttie, although in rebellion against Freud's anti-vitalist principles, yet they bowed their heads to his system of thinking. This is most clear in Fairbairn's recasting of Freud's instinct theory. As I have already stated, Fairbairn defined instincts by final rather than efficient causality and also that the source of action lay in the ego or "psychic structure", but what he did not do was to overthrow Freud's anti-vitalism. He took the view that instincts, as blind drives, turn a living being into a mechanism. He did not challenge Freud's basic anti-vitalist principles. He was too much in the Enlightenment mode of thinking to be able to do this. In his 1957 masterpiece *The Self as Agent*, Macmurray declared that this Enlightenment thinking was essentially egotistical and he replaced it with a completely different foundation stone. Fairbairn did not see, as Macmurray did, that Freudian psychoanalysis was one exemplar of human interaction; and the implication of Macmurray's thesis is that deep communication between two human beings has a therapeutic function for both parties. Both Fairbairn and Suttie, in their deepest assumption, made psychoanalysis the absolute whereas for Macmurray it was human communication itself which was the absolute. He defined human communication as "the capacity for reciprocal relations" (1961, p. 60). This was the absolute of which psychoanalysis was one exemplar but just one of which there were others.

One of the limitations in thinking characterising nearly all psychoanalytic discourse and certainly all trainings at psychoanalytic institutes throughout the world is the almost total reliance upon thinkers who have lived and thought within within the psychoanalytic "club". So, in almost every training, candidates are nurtured upon Freud, upon Jung, upon Kohut, upon Winnicott, upon Klein, and many others. Bion was an exception; he turned to the scientist Poincaré, to Milton the poet, to the religious mystic, Meister Eckhart (science, art, religion). As no two patients arrive at the analyst's consulting room with the same problem, then a mode of investigation that is able to penetrate into the personal dilemma of each individual patient is an urgent requirement if psychoanalysis is to remain a force in our world. Macmurray is the thinker who I believe points out the direction in which we need to go to achieve this purpose. Fairbairn and Suttie can then be evaluated according to the principle which their fellow Scot was so vigorously enunciating.

References

Costello, J. E. (2002). *John Macmurray—A Biography*. Edinburgh, UK: Floris.
Ferenczi, S. (1968). *Thalassa*. New York: W. W. Norton.
Jahoda, M. (1977). *Freud and the Dilemmas of Psychology*. London: Hogarth.
Jones, E. (1972). *Sigmund Freud—Life and Work, vol 1*. London: Hogarth.
Macmurray, J. (1936). *The Structure of Religious Experience*. New Haven, CT: Yale University Press.
Macmurray, J. (1957). *The Self as Agent*. London: Faber & Faber.
Macmurray, J. (1961). *Persons in Relation*. Atlantic Highlands, NJ: Humanities Press International.
Petocz, A. (1999). *Freud, Psychoanalysis, and Symbolism*. Cambridge: Cambridge University Press.
Suttie, I. D. (1939). *The Origins of Love and Hate*. London: Kegan Paul, Trench and Trubner.

CHAPTER SIX

Religion in the life and work of W. R. D. Fairbairn

Marie T. Hoffman and Lowell W. Hoffman

Introduction[1]

Ronald Fairbairn's choice of a vocation in psychoanalysis has often been misconstrued as a *deviation* from his earlier religious vision and preparation for Christian ministry. The present authors understand Fairbairn's chosen vocation as the *fulfilment* of his earlier religious vision. For Fairbairn, unlike the psychoanalytic world in which he lived, there was no split between faith and science: his faith informed his vocation and was manifest in his dedication to redeem fractured lives. The Judaic and Christian narratives portraying a pristine, personal beginning, a shattering decline, and hope of redemption through healing love is the cadence that permeates Fairbairn's lifework.

In this chapter, we will examine the centrality of Christian belief in the life and work of W. R. D. Fairbairn. We will review formative religious influences in his culture, family, education, and professional formation. Then, we will review evidence of Fairbairn's lifelong practice of Christian faith. Finally, we will identify and explicate Fairbairn's Christian narrative embedded within his psychoanalytic theory, which together evolved across his career and contributed to the monumental paradigm shift in psychoanalytic theory and practice from instinctual drives to innate relationship-seeking.

Religious influences in the life of W. R. D. Fairbairn

British cultural influences

Christianity took root in Britannia as early as 200 C.E. Over the subsequent 1,500 years, a genre of Christianity that interwove church and academy eventually flourished in Great Britain. This interweaving became most evident during the British Enlightenment that was quite different from the "high" Continental Enlightenment. In France, the *philosophes* revolted against all that was religious, Voltaire commenting, "Religion must be destroyed among respectable people and left to the *canaille* large and small, for whom it was made" (Himmelfarb, 2001, p. 8). By contrast, the "… Enlightenment in Britain took place *within*, rather than against, Protestantism" (Porter, 2000, p. 99). This distinctively British philosophy would shape the interdisciplinary thinking of Ronald Fairbairn.

Family influences

William Ronald Dodds Fairbairn was born in Edinburgh, Scotland in 1889, only child to Thomas and Cecilia Fairbairn. Thomas's family left the Church of Scotland in the 1843 "Disruption", and were founding members of the Free Church of Scotland. Cecilia, born in Yorkshire, England was Anglican. Beattie remarks,

> Both families actually had some professional religious background, for one of Thomas Fairbairn's forebears was a minister in the evangelical Free Church and Cecilia Leefe's father was a "recognized preacher" on the Methodist (i.e. nonconformist) circuit around York. (2003, p. 1175)

According to Sutherland (1989), Ronald attended the Free Church each Sunday morning and evening with his parents. The ethos of the Free Church of Scotland was conservative evangelicalism. The Free Church was associated with revivals in England, Scotland and Wales in the late 1800s/early 1900s, which were related to the "Second Great Awakening" in the United States. The leaders of the Free Church included Andrew and Horatius Bonar, and Robert Murray McCheyne, notable names in evangelical church history. Supported by the Free Church, American evangelist D. L. Moody preached to crowds of more than 20,000 in Edinburgh in 1874. In 1895, American evangelist Gipsy Smith was invited by the Free Church to preach for six weeks in Scotland, as was the evangelical South African minister Andrew Murray. Older Puritan ideals were preserved in the Free Church of Scotland and contributed to the more austere Presbyterianism to which the Fairbairns subscribed. The rigidity, masochism, and joylessness of the Free Church were factors that influenced Fairbairn's eventual decision at mid-life to leave the Free Church and join the Anglican Church. A more thorough history of Fairbairn's religious formation and evolution is found in *Toward Mutual Recognition: Relational Psychoanalysis and the Christian Narrative* (Hoffman, 2011).

Educational influences

Merchiston Castle School

Fairbairn's education "… started in the lowest class in the Preparatory School and ended in the top class of the Upper School. So Merchiston Castle was my [Fairbairn's] only school" (Birtles & Scharff, 1994, p. 462). Merchiston, a preparatory school *par excellence* founded in 1833 by Charles Chalmers, was associated with the Free Church of Scotland. Charles's brother Thomas was a scientist, theologian, leader of the 1843 Disruption, and founder of the Free Church of Scotland. The Chalmers brothers' respect for science and faith informed the curriculum at Merchiston. Succeeding headmasters retained this curriculum including John Rogerson, headmaster when Fairbairn entered the school, whose obituary affirmed: "In educational and religious matters, he ever took a keen interest" (*Otago Witness*, issue 2562, 22 April 1903, p. 12).

Divinity school

Fairbairn's philosophy studies at Edinburgh University stoked his spiritual interests. Between 1912 and 1914, Fairbairn studied theology at the universities of Kiel, Strasbourg, and Manchester. His theological studies included Hellenistic Greek. Sutherland rendered Fairbairn's study of Hellenistic Greek as "Hellenic Studies" (1989, p. 7), and inferred Fairbairn's waning interest in religion. On the contrary, Hellenistic Greek, also called *Koine* or Biblical Greek, is a mainstay of formal theological studies. Fairbairn confirms this understanding in his "Autobiographical Note": "The result was that I devoted the next three years to the study of Divinity and Hellenistic Greek" (1963b, p. 462).

Professional influences

Andrew Seth Pringle-Pattison

Fairbairn's theological studies and his valuation of personal relations were likely inspired by Andrew Seth Pringle-Pattison, his professor of mental philosophy at Edinburgh University. According to Scharff and Birtles, the "… metaphysical content of Fairbairn's first degree was strongly influenced by the interests of Professor Andrew (Seth) Pringle-Pattison (1850–1931) in the philosophies of Kant and Hegel" (1994, p. xiv). Pringle-Pattison was deeply interested in issues of faith and advanced an emphasis on "communion as the essence of religion" (Miller, 2008, p. 41). Contiguous to Fairbairn's years at Edinburgh University (1907–1911), Pringle-Pattison delivered the Gifford Lectures (1912–1913) entitled "The Idea of God in the Light of Recent Philosophy", a lectureship which asserted that belief in God enhances modern philosophy. In his final lecture, Pringle-Pattison articulated the concept of "redemption by atoning love", the central theme of the Christian narrative:

> No deeper foundation of Idealism can be laid than the perception … of the spirit's power to transform the very meaning of the past and to transmute every loss into a gain. … This is the real omnipotence of atoning love, unweariedly creating good out of evil; and it is no far-off theological mystery but, God be thanked, the very texture of our human experience. (1920, p. 416)

Pringle-Pattison's thesis is discernable in Fairbairn's subsequent work on art as restitution.

Ernest Henry Connell

In 1915, Fairbairn's divinity studies were interrupted by his military service during World War I. Sometime after his discharge in December 1918, Fairbairn reconsidered Christian ministry, and decided upon a career as a psychotherapist. He began medical studies to prepare for psychiatric practice, studied Freud and Jung, and in 1921 began a personal analysis with Ernest Connell. Sutherland's description of Connell as a "very full-blooded Christian" (1989, p. 7) also chronicles Fairbairn's continuing engagement with his faith at the age of thirty-two.

Information about Connell is sparse. Prior to moving to Edinburgh, he lived in Melbourne, Australia, where he married Mary Lillian Oldham in April 1900. The marriage ceremony was officiated in a Catholic Apostolic Church, an early expression of Christian Pentecostalism. Sometime after 1912, the Connells moved to Edinburgh where Ernest pursued medical studies and psychoanalytic training including an analysis with Ernest Jones, and in 1921 he was appointed clinical assistant at Morningside Royal Asylum, Edinburgh.

Ian and Jane Suttie

Fairbairn's library included Ian Suttie's *Origins of Love and Hate* (1935), with almost every chapter heavily annotated. He definitively interacted favourably with Suttie's integrative work in religion and psychoanalysis. A diary entry also suggests that Ian and Jane Suttie were once dinner guests at the Fairbairn residence.

Ian Suttie worked collaboratively with his wife Jane (Robertson) in writing *Origins of Love and Hate* (Dicks, 1970, p. 50). Bacal regarded the Sutties' work "as representing an epistemological break with the traditional psychoanalytic theory of his day" (1987, p. 82), and Heard (Suttie, 1935, p. xxiii) recognised this break as anticipating the work of Fairbairn, Guntrip, Balint, and Winnicott. Suttie described his emendations to Freud as "introducing the conception of an innate need-for-companionship which is the infant's only way of self-preservation. This need, giving rise to parental and fellowship 'love,' I put in the place of the Freudian Libido, and regard it as genetically independent of genital appetite" (ibid., p. 6). Linking his psychoanalytic thinking with his religious narrative, Suttie wrote that Christianity "offers the conception of social life as based upon Love, rather than upon [the] authority [basis of Freud's system]" (ibid., p. 140), and asserted "the main concern of the Christian teachings to be the cultivation of 'love' as the basis of happiness, mental stability and social harmony" (ibid., p. 154). Hadfield recapitulated Suttie's perspective, stating, "The Christian religion has … often successfully … insist[ed] on the love of God, and upon the love and friendship of man to man as the essence of social life" (ibid., p. xlviii).

John Macmurray

Clarke (2005), Hoffman (2004), and Kirkwood (2005) have observed similarities between the work of Fairbairn, Suttie, and Macmurray. While there is no known reference to Macmurray by Fairbairn, "… we know from his daughter Ellinor Fairbairn Birtles (personal communication) that the men knew each other and may have collaborated" (Scharff & Scharff, 2005, p. 20). J. A. Harrow (2003, personal communication) also confirmed that Macmurray's works were in Fairbairn's library.

John Macmurray was among a select group of Oxford scholars, including Pringle-Pattison, who began meeting in 1924 to specifically explore the "relationship of faith and science" (Costello, 2002, p. 137). Macmurray became a pre-eminent philosopher, and in concert with Martin Buber, saw their shared philosophical project as conceptualising "the form of the personal". Costello elaborates:

> This project had two dimensions to it: first, the recovery of a recognition of the fully personal from the reductionism imposed by mechanical and organic categories of thinking on human persons and social institutions … second, to achieve a coherent and consistent articulation of the unique logic of personal existence. … Martin Buber, whom Macmurray knew even more personally, considered himself to be the poet of this project; and he saw Macmurray as its metaphysician and told him so. (ibid., pp. 14–15)

Macmurray's emphasis on "the personal" pervades Fairbairn's thinking; Clarke (2005) notes: "Fairbairn wished to call his unique development of object relations theory 'personal relations theory'" (p. 36). Macmurray's philosophy articulated a theistic origin of personal relations: "Philosophically, a belief in God is necessary, since the character of the world's unity can only be personal. Only an absolute personality can be the ground of the existence of finite persons" (1928, n.p.). Macmurray propounded: "[K]nowledge of God … [comes] through knowing a human person who is himself the image of the divine personality and who reveals God to us by revealing himself" (Costello, 2002, p. 146).

Summary of professional influences

The collective influence of Pringle-Pattison, Connell, the Sutties, and Macmurray upon Fairbairn and psychoanalysis is explicated in the pages to follow. These mentoring relationships extending into the fourth decade of Fairbairn's life contributed the following presuppositions: (1) science and religion are complementary disciplines, (2) personal human relations derive from a relational first cause, (3) the basis of social life is loving relationships, (4) humans seek relationship, not drive discharge.

Religious evidences in the life of W. R. D. Fairbairn

Christian observance

Braids Schoolboys' Meetings[2]

Fairbairn's personal appointment diaries reveal his voluntary leadership at the age of twenty-nine to thirty of combined schoolboys' chapel meetings for five preparatory academies including Merchiston Castle. Fairbairn was in the rotation of (presumably) seminarians who delivered sermons and led hymn singing. Sermons entitled "Faith Without Works", "Christ the Teacher", and "The New Birth" were noted in Fairbairn's diary; Fairbairn's sermon titles included "A Trial of Faith", "Impulsive Action", and "The Use of Light". In Fairbairn's later diaries, names from these meetings appear often, a testament to his enduring spiritual bonds.

Lifelong church attendance

Fairbairn's diary entries from 1917 through 1963 document his regular participation in Christian community and worship, even in North Africa during the war. For instance, his diary entries for 1919 list fifty-one dates of church attendance. Fairbairn's active faith was clearly more than identification with his father and apparently shaped core lifespan relationships. His relationship to the church from midlife was not severed, but became less regular as he participated often in psychoanalytic conferences, and committed much time to care for psychologically maimed war veterans—his diaries reflecting a caseload of appointments seven days a week. In 1963, prior to his August diary entry, "I become unwell," Fairbairn recorded thirteen entries of church attendance. Sutherland alludes to Fairbairn's lifelong Christian faith, noting: "One matter he never raised was his continuing religious convictions" (1989, p. 31).

After an apparently momentous appointment with E. H. Connell in June 1926, which is documented in Fairbairn's diary, his church attendance abruptly shifted from the Free Church to the Anglican Church. Fairbairn's departure from the Free Church was prompted in part by dogmatic ministers who appealed to "faith" in their own interpretations that lacked a rational basis. In the Free Church "revivals", charismatic preachers would transfix masses of people. Fairbairn's conceptions of "exciting objects" and "rejecting objects" likely derived in part from personal encounters with exciting, religious leaders that devolved into rejecting experiences.

Summary of Christian observance

Space limitations permit only cursory consideration of Fairbairn's lifelong faith practice; we anticipate publication of our more comprehensive appraisal. What is clear from archived records is: (1) church attendance was regular and continuous to the end of his life, (2) purposeful cultivation of relationships with persons of Christian faith, and particularly persons who both affiliated with the psychoanalytic community and identified with Christian faith span his professional career, (3) extant personal correspondence, while curiously quite limited, documents these relationships.

Formative experiences

1910 World Missionary Conference

The World Missionary Conference convened in Edinburgh in June 1910, and was attended by 1,200 people including William Jennings Bryan, the Archbishop of Canterbury, lords, marquises, and leaders of religious and scholastic institutions from around the world. The conference convened at the Assembly Hall of the United Free Church which recruited local university students to assist in the eight day gathering. Most certainly Ronald Fairbairn, as a University of Edinburgh undergraduate and active member of the Free Church, participated as a student assistant.

Seven weeks after the conference, on his twenty-first birthday, Ronald Fairbairn penned a diary entry that questioned a myopic view of Christian "gospel" promulgated at the conference. Fairbairn writes,

> Is the religion of the average Church of today of a nature to capture and mould the full-blown life of the healthy-minded young man and woman? Or does it only provide for one type of mind? Is it only suited for half of the individual's life? True Christianity ought to satisfy every legitimate instinct and aspiration. (Sutherland, 1989, p. 7)

Fairbairn responds to his own query,

> God give me strength to do my share, however little, to effect that unspeakably desirable consummation. … I have decided to devote my life to the cause of religion; but may it be a … healthy, whole-hearted, strong religion, appealing to the enthusiasm of youth, as well as to the quiescence of old age—in other words may it be a Christlike religion. (ibid., p. 7)

1929 International Congress of Psychoanalysis

In 1929, Fairbairn attended the International Congress of Psychoanalysis at Oxford University; his copious notes about the congress are preserved in his archived papers. Fairbairn's oscillation between psychoanalytic sensibilities and his religious experiences is evident in his observations of Freud: "[I]nstead of *working out his own salvation* [Phillipians 2:12], he is trying substitutively to *save* others." Fairbairn is concerned that psychoanalysis should avoid becoming a religious cult. He notes, "Tendency of psychoanalysis to become a cult (religious). This is shown in several ways" [that Fairbairn then enumerates]:

1. Freud's "ipse dixit" [dogmatic, unproven statement, accepted on faith in the speaker].
2. Secrecy—lack of advertising.
3. Lack of controversy on fundamental "doctrines".
4. Membership of Psycho-Analytic Association [where] Analysis is a sine qua non of membership—i.e., "Initiation".
5. Analogy between process of analysis and 'conversion', where the process leads from the old life of subjection to the tyranny of the Unconscious to the new life of freedom and control—i.e., "salvation"—where the "completely analysed person" is the saved person.

Fairbairn's concerns about Freud most likely derive from experiences with "exciting leaders" and power-based dynamics in the Free Church, and his perception of similar dynamics in the psychoanalytic movement.

Summary of formative experiences

Fairbairn's formative experiences in early to middle adulthood reveal his eschewal of arbitrary power dynamics and his insistence upon authenticity and integrity. He discerned incongruities in these formative experiences, formulated incisive impressions about leaders of these groups, and blazed his own path.

A viable faith in professional writings

A prevalent conception of Fairbairn's religious faith and belief is that his psychoanalytic training and understanding superseded and replaced his early- to mid-adulthood Christian faith. In this view, Fairbairn's copious religious references in his professional papers are understood as no more than clinical utilisation of metaphor with a predominantly Christian culture. We agree that Fairbairn utilised Christian metaphor for explanatory purposes, but we also assert that Fairbairn's use of religious references reflected his enduring embrace of the Christian narrative. We offer representative, but not exhaustive occurrences of two such categories in Fairbairn's writing: (1) his assertion that the aims of psychoanalysis are akin to an alternative "belief system", and (2) his lifelong affirmation of personal Christian faith as normative, not neurotic.

Psychoanalysis as a belief system

In "Libido Theory Re-evaluated" (1994, unpublished when written in 1930), Fairbairn asserts that Freud "is no longer concerning himself with psychological tendencies, but with cosmic forces … far into the realm in which philosophy and religion [inter-related disciplines for Fairbairn] hold sway." Fairbairn continues: "… psychoanalysis is at present tending to acquire the character of a religion—with Eros as its god, Thanatos as its devil, and analytic procedure as the means of grace …" (quoted in Birtles & Scharff, 1994, p. 128). In "Freud, the psychoanalytic method and mental health" (1994, unpublished when written in 1957) Fairbairn observes, "It is true that Freud has spoken of 'the lie of salvation' (Jones, 1955, p. 20); but it is significant that, in spite of this, he devoted his life to devising a method of psychotherapeutic treatment which is very much like a means of salvation …" (quoted in Scharff & Birtles, 1994, p. 72). In "Psychotherapy and the Clergy" (1958b) Fairbairn opines,

> From a religious, or at any rate a Christian point of view, what man seeks salvation from is sin, estrangement from God, spiritual death, and that fear which is cast out by "Perfect Love" …. Correspondingly, from a psychotherapeutic point of view, what (in my opinion) the patient seeks salvation *from* … would appear to be something very much like the forgiveness of sins and the casting out of devils. (quoted in Birtles & Scharff, 1994, p. 364) [Fairbairn's capitalisation of "Perfect Love" connotes his continuing recognition of a personal "Other".]

We infer from Fairbairn's perspective of psychoanalysis as belief system that he believed that either: (1) psychoanalysis is essentially another belief system and therefore potentially implicated as an "obsessional neurosis", or (2) both *psychoanalytic* and *Christian* belief systems can be normative human expressions of faith. Our findings endorse the latter.

Christian faith as normative, not neurotic

Fairbairn (1927) speaks of normative Christianity in "Notes on the Religious Phantasies of a Female Patient". He contrasts *"ordinary* Christian experience of union with God achieved through participation by the sinner in Christ's sacrifice …" with a schizoid patient who "[felt] herself to be the principal figure in the religious mysteries" (1952, p. 188).

In "The Repression and the Return of Bad Objects (with Special Reference to the 'War Neuroses')" (1943a), Fairbairn discussed Freud's treatment (1923d) of Christoph Haitzmann and stated,

> … if Christoph was relieved of his symptoms by a conviction of the love of God, it may well be that a conviction of the analyst's "love" (in the sense of Agape, not Eros) … on the part of the patient is no unimportant factor in promoting a successful therapeutic result. (Original version, quoted in Hazell, 1994, p. 82) [Fairbairn's references to the "love of God" and "the analyst's love" are elided by "minor amendment" in *Psychoanalytic Studies*.]

We infer from Fairbairn's descriptions that he considered (1) the "Christian experience of union with God through participation by the sinner in Christ's sacrifice" as ordinary, normative, and not neurotic. In considering Freud's treatment of Christoph, we see Fairbairn resourcing Macmurray, and implying that (2) in the experience of "the analyst's love", a patient may also experience and receive benefit from "the love of God". This understanding derives from Macmurray's philosophy of personal relations based on his premise that an absolute personality is the only possible source of finite personality: "[K]nowledge of God … [comes] through knowing a human person who is himself the image of the divine personality and who reveals God to us by revealing himself" (Costello, 2002, p. 146).

Summary

In more than twenty significant professional papers written over thirty-five years beginning in 1927, Fairbairn integrated his Christian faith with his psychoanalytic thinking. He recognised the potential of psychoanalytic perspectives to enhance, refine, and clarify his flagging Christian worldview. Retaining a Christian narrative endowed with an enduring legacy of loving relationship, Fairbairn contributed to the emancipation of a psychoanalysis fettered with a dehumanising metapsychology.

Religious themes in the work of W. R. D. Fairbairn

Overview

The Christian narrative

An examination of Christian themes in Fairbairn's work is facilitated by a summary of the Christian narrative that derives from Judaic belief in a personal God in whose image humans were created. The Christian narrative posits human failure and God's design to ultimately redeem creation in a progression from "creation", to "fall", to "redemption". This progression also occurs in Judaic narratives—Suzanne Kirschner suggests that this cadence is a "Judaeo-Christian inheritance" which emerges as a "distinctive historical narrative design … [that] is detectable in many of our most taken-for-granted ideas about history, society, and psychology" (1996, p. 96). The Christian extension of Judaism that renders it uniquely Christian is the doctrine of a Trinitarian God who exists as one, and as three in one: Father, Son, and Holy Spirit. God's "otherness" *from* and "oneness" *with* creation gives a berth for the incarnation, death, and resurrection of Jesus Christ.

Scottish Presbyterianism

Presbyterianism was birthed in Scotland by John Knox who studied with Jean Calvin in Geneva. Calvin re-established in Protestantism what he believed was lost in Catholic dogma. Calvin's correctives included:

1. The basis of doctrine is not church tradition that is at the whim of self-interest; instead, doctrine must be based on *sola scriptura*—Scripture alone. Egalitarian recognition of the viability of interpretation by educated laity as well as clergy supersedes exclusive clerical interpretations of Scripture.
2. The basis of salvation is God's grace. Renewed relationship with God is not possible through good works, but is reborn through love initiated by God.

Scottish Presbyterianism is Calvinistic and begins with the first step in the Judaeo-Christian cadence: creation. A loving God communes with humans created to love and be loved.

However, Calvinism's emphatic focus is on the second step of this cadence: fall. Human nature is in a state of fragmentation as a result of "the fall"; people have no ability to redeem themselves and hopelessly veer towards "the bad". Humans "… forfeited [God's] excellent gifts and … entailed [themselves to] blindness of mind, horrible darkness, vanity and perverseness of judgment, became wicked, rebellious and obdurate in heart and will, and impure in affections" (Hanko, Hoeksema, & Van Buren, 1976, p. 8). Calvinists believe that only God as truly "Other" can enter a closed human system and restore fragmented relationships.

We find these Calvinistic themes of creation and fall emerging in Fairbairn's conceptualisations of both the parent/infant and psychotherapeutic relationships. Fairbairn's aims and process of treatment likewise envision the final movement of the cadence: the analyst's role in redemption. We will explicate below parallel conceptions of creation, fall, and redemption in Fairbairn's work and Calvinist theology.

Creation

Fairbairn

Born to relate: In a monumental departure from Freud's drive theory, Fairbairn postulated an infant born with the innate inclination to seek the parent not simply for survival in the Darwinian sense, but for relationship. Heralding the dawn of a new era in psychoanalysis, "Fairbairn was suggesting that object-seeking, in its most radical form, is not the vehicle for satisfaction of a specific need, but the expression of our very nature, the form through which we become specifically *human* beings" (Mitchell, 1998, p. 117). The infant is deterministically hardwired to seek relationship, an endowment bequeathed by the parents. Fairbairn depicted the infant's life as one of primary identification with the parent, characterised by total dependence, but took great care to emphasise that "such total parental availability is an impossibility" (Greenberg & Mitchell, 1983, p. 181).

Calvin

Born to relate: Jean Calvin's anthropology derived from Judaic and Christian narratives that commence with humans created to desire relationship with their Creator. Jean Calvin asserted: "[Every human being] is formed to be a spectator of the created world and given eyes … [to] be led to its author by contemplating so beautiful a representation" (Lane, 2001, p. 1). Lane extrapolates, "Calvin knew that human desire [for relationship] at its best is but a mirror of God's own desire for relationship" (ibid., p. 9).

We believe that Fairbairn's presuppositions concerning an innate inclination to relate derive from Calvin. There are some who would attribute Fairbairn's theory of object-seeking to a "secular" grounding in Hegel's philosophy. This assertion belies a lacuna in understanding the comprehensive system that Hegel developed through his dual-identity as both a Christian theologian and philosopher. See, for example, Hegel (1807, 1827), Hodgson (2005), Hoffman (2011).

Fall

Fairbairn

Decline and fracture: Potential object-relatedness quickly declines towards the central dynamic of Fairbairn's theory of endopsychic structure. "For Fairbairn (1944) the establishment of the endopsychic structure, while universal and inevitable, represents a fall from grace" writes Skolnick (Skolnick & Scharff, 1998, p. 141). In keeping with his Calvinistic Christian narrative, Fairbairn's structuralisation of the psyche is a fragmentation of the self. In contrast to most developmental theories that posit psychic growth, "Fairbairn maintained that, far from being the necessary condition for psychic growth, structural differentiation is a defensive and pathological process in human development" (Rubens, 2000, p. 161).

Separation from the good: Fairbairn theorised that differentiation structures an internal world bereft of good objects. Skolnick asserts, "Fairbairn's idea [was] that the internal unconscious world of objects is devoid of good objects …" (Skolnick & Scharff, 1998, p. 139). Fairbairn poignantly portrayed the infant's accommodation of his "good" longings to relate by succumbing to corrupting exciting and rejecting tokens offered by its caregivers.

Attachment to the bad: Fairbairn deciphered the transgenerational transmission of attachment to bad objects in his paper, "The Repression and the Return of Bad Objects" (1943a). Humans become not only alienated from the good; they are attracted to the bad. Fairbairn asserted "that libidinal 'badness' should be related to the cathexis of bad objects ('sin' always being regarded, according to Hebraic conception, as seeking after strange gods and, according to the Christian conception, as yielding to the Devil)" (ibid., p. 74). Fairbairn's formulation of the cathexis to bad objects reinterpreted the compulsion to repeat as one's only option to remain connected to parental objects, and accentuated this bondage by asserting "[T]he deepest source of resistance is fear of the release of bad objects from the unconscious" (ibid., p. 69). Reiterating himself, Fairbairn (1958a) wrote during the analysis of Harry Guntrip, "[P]reserving internal reality as a closed system … constitute[s] the most formidable resistance encountered in psycho-analytic treatment" (quoted in Scharff & Birtles, 1994, p. 84). (See also Guntrip, 1975.)

Alienation from others: In his 1940 paper on "Schizoid Factors in the Personality" Fairbairn depicted "the schizoid position as far more basic and universal [than the depressive] … the position that underlay *all* of human psychopathology" (Rubens, 1998, p. 219). Fairbairn's theory has "… for contemporary relational analysts, become the all-important interface where intrapsychic and interpersonal relations meet and together construct a world vision" (Davies, 1998, p. 66). That world vision depicts the ubiquitous human condition of interior cacophonous voices of bad objects locked into a mausoleum of projected internal drama, which subvert the present recognition of and connection with another as truly other, and ravage the self with "self-deprecation and self-renunciation" (Grotstein, 1994a, p. 187). Concluding his essay on "Schizoid Factors in the Personality," Fairbairn (1940a) summarised the hopeless schizoid condition by utilising a religious metaphor: "Since the joy of loving seems hopelessly barred to him, he may as well deliver himself over to the joy of hating and obtain what satisfaction he can out of that. He thus makes a pact with the Devil and says, 'Evil be thou my good'" (p. 27). For Fairbairn, the endpoint of humanity's fall from grace is the devastation of relationship.

Calvin

Decline and fracture: For Calvin, a pristine human origin marked by internal harmony, external relationship to a loving God and fellow humans, and the Edenic spectrum of nature, devolves through human agency to a fallen and fractured world. This fall was the cataclysmic event that structured a world separated from God "… the Object of our knowledge—so that love of child or nature or whatever, is replaced by absence of the sympathy or affinity that formerly aided understanding, and the loss of harmony within ourselves in the plurality of conflicting motives and emotions" (Shortt, n.d., p. 7).

Separation from the good: Calvin's Christian narrative depicted a post-fall situation in which God is transcendent "other"—a good object out of human reach. The emphasis in Calvin is on the good object that is no more. Jonathan Edwards, an American Calvinist, echoed Calvin:

> Before, his soul was under the government of that noble principle of divine love, whereby it was enlarged to the comprehension of all his fellow-creatures and their welfare … But so soon as he had transgressed against God, these noble principles were immediately lost, and all this excellent enlargedness of man's soul was gone (Edwards, 1738, p. 158).

Attachment to the bad: Calvin's "bondage to sin" was certainly a familiar theme in sermons of Fairbairn's youth. Across years of Sunday morning and evening church attendance with his parents, Fairbairn most certainly sang at least 100 times a hymn composed by Horatius Bonar of the Free Church of Scotland that begins:

Not what my hands have done, Can save my guilty soul … and concludes:

Thy pow'r alone, O Son of God, *Can this sore bondage break*.

For Calvin, "bondage to sin", was "… iniquity of the fathers [being] visited on the children to the third and fourth generation" (Exodus 20:5), an inescapable transgenerational transmission of the "bad".

Alienation from others: Calvin asserted that the consequence of internalised badness is alienation from God that becomes *de facto* alienation from one's neighbours. Jonathan Edwards again recapitulates Calvin:

> [Each person] shrank, as it were, into a little space, circumscribed and closely shut up within itself, to the exclusion of all things else. Sin, like some powerful astringent, contracted his soul to the very small dimensions of selfishness; and God was forsaken, and fellow-creatures forsaken, and man retired within himself, and became totally governed by narrow and selfish principles and feelings. (ibid., p. 158)

Redemption

Fairbairn

The new good object: Fairbairn's writing on clinical application—the redemptive process—begins with "Eden" as metaphor for how the ego was once "pristine" and structurally whole before being fractured. Fairbairn (1958a) understood "… the primary aim of psychoanalytical treatment is to effect a synthesis of the personality by reducing that triple splitting of the pristine ego which occurs to some degree in every individual …" (quoted in Scharff & Birtles, 1994, p. 83). In language that mirrors Calvinist theology, Fairbairn attended to the (1) "fracture" of the internal world, (2) "enslavement" to bad objects, and (3) "alienation"—the schizoid condition that underlies all psychopathology.

Fairbairn understood the analyst's task as finding an entrée into the closed internal world of the patient to offer the opportunity for a redemptive relationship with a real "other". His ultimate objective in this new and real relationship was restitution to the central ego of the split-off parts cathected to bad objects. Fairbairn variously characterised the analyst's function as: "messiah", "saviour", "exorcist", and "evangelist". Recapitulating the Calvinist narrative, Fairbairn's agency for redemption is personal relationship offered by a caring "other".

In one of his clearest descriptions of psychoanalytic process, Fairbairn (1958a) writes:

> Thus, in a sense, psychoanalytic treatment resolves itself into a struggle on the part of the patient to press-gang his relationship with the analyst into the closed system of the inner world through the agency of transference, and a determination on the part of the analyst to effect a breach in this closed system and to provide conditions under which, in the setting of a therapeutic relationship, the patient may be induced to accept the open system of outer reality. (quoted in Scharff & Birtles, 1994, p. 92)

As the patient experiences the analyst as a new, good object, he or she gains hope in the possibility of something better, and in Fairbairn's words "may be induced" to relinquish the bad objects and attach to a new, good one. Fairbairn's therapeutic relationship (1) recapitulates the closed space of the fragmented ego, (2) facilitates a way for the analyst to join the patient within this space where together they travail to the death and eventually mourn what will never be, and (3) creates a new relationship wherein the patient may "accept the open system of outer reality".

Calvin

The new good object: More than a century before Fairbairn's monumental contributions, the Calvinist founder of the Free Church of Scotland, Thomas Chalmers (see above) delivered a legendary sermon entitled, "The Expulsive Power of a New Affection" that presaged Fairbairn's dynamic formulations. Chalmers propounded:

> The love of the world [bad object] cannot be expunged by a mere demonstration of the world's [bad object's] worthlessness. But may it not be supplanted by the love of that which is more worthy than itself? The heart cannot be prevailed upon to part with the world [bad object], by a simple act of resignation. But may not the heart be prevailed upon to admit into its preference another, who shall subordinate the world [bad object] and bring it down from its wonted ascendancy? If the throne which is placed there must have an occupier, and the tyrant that now resides has occupied it wrongfully, he may not leave a bosom which would rather retain him than be left in desolation …. In a word, if the way to disengage the heart from the "love" of one great and ascendant object, is to fasten it in positive love to another, then it is not by exposing the worthlessness of the former, but by addressing to the mental eye the worth and excellence of the latter, that all old things are to be done away and all things are to become new …. In fullest accordance with the mechanism of the heart, a great moral revolution may be made to take place upon it. (1855, n.p.)

Chalmers's rendering of Calvinist Christianity asserted that relationship with a new, good object can persuade the frightened person to relinquish attachment to the bad. Chalmers recognised that absence of a new good object would result in desolation and deprive a person, in Fairbairn's terms, of the very defence that provided survival. If however, the internal world of badness can be breached by one who will not perpetrate further fractures, but who instead will offer a healing relationship, attachment to the bad can be surrendered (exorcised), and the previously bound person is freed to respond to a love in external reality.

Summary

The striking parallels between Fairbairn's work and Calvinist theology are self-evident.

Conclusion

Fairbairn's youthful vision became "good news" for psychoanalysis. His abiding belief in a relational cosmos guided the revolutionary, relational shift that has reconfigured the theory and practice of psychoanalysis. Fairbairn, Macmurray, Buber, Pringle-Pattison, the Sutties, and many others revolted against a dehumanising modernity, and together re-grafted the separated branches of science and the sacred and restored a forgotten reality: humans are born to relate. Their collective interdisciplinary writings affirmed a belief in the centrality of relationship, reopened a portal for consideration of an ultimate background Object, and encouraged interdisciplinary dialogue between religion and science.

Fairbairn's emphasis on the absolute dependence of the infant upon his caregivers was another re-grafting of the sacred with science. Paul Ricoeur affirms this essential understanding: "I cannot conceive of a religious attitude that did not proceed from 'a feeling of absolute dependence.' And is this not the essential relation of humankind to the sacred, transmuted into speech and, in this way, reaffirmed at the same time it is surpassed?" (1995, p. 65). Fairbairn's Judaic/Christian narrative transmuted contemporary psychoanalytic theory; correspondingly, his psychoanalytic theory reaffirmed and suffused his sacred narrative. Together they surpass what each once was, and flourish as a "tree of life" for humanity.

Notes

1. The authors reviewed Fairbairn's personal diaries, correspondence, and annotated volumes from his personal library in Edinburgh in June 2012. They gratefully acknowledge the support of Ms Olive Geddes and the staff of the Manuscripts Collection at the National Library of Scotland, and Dr Joseph Marshall, rare books librarian, and the staff of the Centre for Research Collections at the Edinburgh University Library.
2. "Braid" refers to a dialect spoken in the lowlands of Scotland from Aberdeen to Ayrshire. Apparently, the five preparatory academies of greater Edinburgh that participated in these chapel meetings adopted the title "Braids Schoolboys' Meeting" as a unifying name for their jointly sponsored activity.

References

Bacal, H. A. (1987). British object-relations theorists and self-psychology: Some critical reflections. *International Journal of Psychoanalysis, 68*: 81–98.

Beattie, H. J. (2003). The repression and return of bad objects: W. R. D. Fairbairn and the historical roots of theory. *International Journal of Psychoanalysis, 84*: 1171–1187.

Birtles, E. F., & Scharff, D. E. (Eds.). (1994). *From Instinct to Self: Selected Papers of W. R. D. Fairbairn, Volume II: Applications and Early Contributions*. Northvale, NJ: Jason Aronson.

Chalmers, T. (1855). *The Expulsive Power of a New Affection*. Minneapolis, MN: Curiosmith, 2012.

Clarke, G. S. (2005). Personal relations theory: Suttie, Fairbairn Macmurray, and Sutherland. In: J. S. Scharff & D. E. Scharff, *The Legacy of Fairbairn and Sutherland: Psychotherapeutic Applications*. London: Routledge.

Costello, J. E. (2002). *John Macmurray: A Biography*. Edinburgh, UK: Floris.

Davies, J. (1998). Repression and dissociation—Freud and Janet: Fairbairn's new model of unconscious process. In: N. J. Skolnick & D. E. Scharff (Eds.), *Fairbairn, Then and Now* (pp. 53–69). Hilllsdale, NJ: The Analytic Press.

Dicks, H. V. (1970). *50 years of the Tavistock Clinic*. London: Routledge & Kegan Paul.

Edwards, J. (1738). *Charity and its Fruits*. Edinburgh, UK: Banner of Truth Trust, 1852.

Fairbairn, W. R. D. (1927). Notes on the religious phantasies of a female patient. In: *Psychoanalytic Studies of the Personality* (pp. 183–196). London: Tavistock, 1952.

Fairbairn, W. R. D. (1930). Libido theory re-evaluated. In: E. F. Birtles & D. E. Scharff (Eds.), *From Instinct to Self: Selected Papers of W. R. D. Fairbairn, Volume II: Applications and Early Contributions* (pp. 115–156). Northvale, NJ: Jason Aronson, 1994.

Fairbairn, W. R. D. (1940a). Schizoid factors in the personality. In: *Psychoanalytic Studies of the Personality* (pp. 3–27). London: Tavistock, 1952.

Fairbairn, W. R. D. (1943a). The repression and the return of bad objects (with special reference to the "war neuroses"). *British Journal of Medical Psychology, 19*: 327–341. In: *Psychoanalytic Studies of the Personality* (pp. 59–81). London: Tavistock, 1952.

Fairbairn, W. R. D. (1944). Endopsychic structure considered in terms of object-relationships. *International Journal of Psychoanalysis, 25*: 70–92. In: *Psychoanalytic Studies of the Personality* (pp. 82–136). London: Tavistock, 1952.

Fairbairn, W. R. D. (1952). *Psychoanalytic Studies of the Personality*. London: Tavistock.

Fairbairn, W. R. D. (1957). Freud, the psycho-analytical method and mental health. *British Journal of Medical Psychology, 30*(2): 53–61. In: D. E. Scharff & E. F. Birtles (Eds.), *From Instinct to Self: Selected Papers of W. R. D. Fairbairn, Volume I: Clinical and Theoretical Papers* (pp. 61–73). Northvale, NJ: Jason Aronson, 1994.

Fairbairn, W. R. D. (1958a). On the nature and aims of psycho-analytical treatment. *International Journal of Psychoanalysis, 39*(5): 374–385. In: D. E. Scharff & E. F. Birtles (Eds.), *From Instinct to Self: Selected Papers of W. R. D. Fairbairn, Volume I: Clinical and Theoretical Papers*. Northvale, NJ: Jason Aronson, 1994.

Fairbairn, W. R. D. (1958b). Psychotherapy and the clergy. In: E. F. Birtles & D. E. Scharff (Eds.), *From Instinct to Self: Selected Papers of W. R. D. Fairbairn, Volume II: Applications and Early Contributions* (pp. 363–367). Northvale, NJ: Jason Aronson, 1994.

Fairbairn, W. R. D. (1963b). Autobiographical note. *British Journal of Medical Psychology, 36*: 107. In: E. F. Birtles & D. E. Scharff (Eds.), *From Instinct to Self: Selected Papers of W. R. D. Fairbairn, Volume II: Applications and Early Contributions* (pp. 462–464). Northvale, NJ: Jason Aronson, 1994.

Freud, S. (1923d). A seventeenth–century demonological neurosis. *S. E., 19*. London: Hogarth.

Greenberg, J., & Mitchell, S. (1983). *Object Relations in Psychoanalytic Theory*. Cambridge, MA: Harvard University Press.

Grotstein, J. (1994a). Endopsychic structure and the cartography of the internal world: Six characters in search of an author. In: J. S. Grotstein & D. B. Rinsley (Eds.), *Fairbairn and the Origins of Object Relations* (pp. 112–150). New York: Other Press..

Guntrip, H. S. (1975). My experience of analysis with Fairbairn and Guntrip. *International Review of Psycho-Analysis, 2*: 145–156.

Hanko, H., Hoeksema, H., & Van Buren, G. (1976). *The Five Points of Calvinism*. Grandville, MI: Reformed Free Publishing.

Hazell, J. (1994). *Personal Relations Therapy: The Collected Papers of H. J. S. Guntrip*. Northvale, NJ: Jason Aronson.

Hegel, G. W. F. (1807). *Phenomenology of Spirit* (A. V. Miller, Trans.). London: Oxford University Press, 1977.

Hegel, G. W. F. (1827). *Lectures on the Philosophy of Religion, Together with a Work on Proofs of the Existence of God, by Georg Wilhelm Friedrich Hegel* (E. B. Speirs & J. Burdon Sanderson, Trans.). Oxford: Oxford University Press, 2006.

Himmelfarb, G. (2001). The idea of compassion: The British vs. the French Enlightenment. *The Public Interest, 145*: 1–12.

Hodgson, P. (2005). *Hegel and Christian Theology: A Reading on the Lectures on the Philosophy of Religion.* New York: Oxford University Press.

Hoffman, M. (2004). From enemy combatant to strange bedfellow: The role of religious narratives in the work of W. R. D. Fairbairn and D. W. Winnicott. *Psychoanalytic Dialogues, 14*(6): 769–804.

Hoffman, M. (2011). *Toward Mutual Recognition: Relational Psychoanalysis and the Christian Narrative.* New York: Routledge.

Jones, E. (1955). *Sigmund Freud: Life and Work, Volume 2: The Years of Maturity 1901–1919.* London: Hogarth.

Kirkwood, C. (2005). The persons-in-relation perspective: Sources and synthesis. In: J. S. Scharff & D. E. Scharff, *The Legacy of Fairbairn and Sutherland: Psychotherapeutic Applications.* London: Routledge.

Kirschner, S. (1996). *The Religious and Romantic Origins of Psychoanalysis.* Cambridge: Cambridge University Press.

Lane, B. (2001). Spirituality as the performance of desire: Calvin on the world as a theatre of God's glory. *Spiritus, 1*: 1–30.

Macmurray, J. (1928). What I live by. *The Student Movement, 30*(9), n.p.

Miller, G. (2008). Scottish psychoanalysis: A rational religion. *Journal of the History of the Behavioral Sciences, 44*(1): 38–58.

Mitchell, S. (1988). *Relational Concepts in Psychoanalysis: An Integration.* Cambridge, MA: Harvard University Press.

Otago Witness (1903). John Rogerson [obituary]. Issue 2562, 22 April, p. 12.

Porter, R. (2000). *The Creation of the Modern World.* New York: W. W. Norton.

Pringle-Pattison, S. (1920). *The Idea of God in the Light of Recent Philosophy.* New York: Oxford University Press.

Ricoeur, P. (1995). *Figuring the Sacred.* Minneapolis, MN: Fortress.

Rubens, R. L. (1994). Fairbairn's structural theory. In: J. S. Grotstein & D. B. Rinsley (Eds.), *Fairbairn and the Origins of Object Relations* (pp. 151–173). London: Free Association.

Rubens, R. L. (1998). Fairbairn's theory of depression. In: N. J. Skolnick & D. E. Scharff (Eds.), *Fairbairn, Then and Now.* Hillsdale, NJ: The Analytic Press.

Scharff, D. E., & Birtles, E. (Eds.) (1994). *From Instinct to Self: Selected Papers of W. R. D. Fairbairn, Volume I: Clinical and Theoretical Papers.* Northvale, NJ: Jason Aronson.

Scharff, J. S., & Scharff, D. E. (Eds.) (2005). *The Legacy of Fairbairn and Sutherland: Psychotherapeutic Applications.* London: Routledge.

Shortt, J. G. (n.d.). *Toward a Reformed Epistemology and Its Educational Significance.* [Unpublished doctoral dissertation.]

Skolnick, N. J., & Scharff, D. E. (Eds.) (1998). *Fairbairn, Then and Now.* Hillsdale, NJ: The Analytic Press.

Sutherland, J. D. (1989). *Fairbairn's Journey into the Interior.* London: Free Association.

Suttie, I. (1935). *The Origins of Love and Hate.* London: Free Association, 1988.

CHAPTER SEVEN

Fairbairn and homosexuality: sex *versus* conscience

Hilary J. Beattie

Introduction

Fairbairn's practical and theoretical interest in sexual perversion, in particular male homosexuality, has surprisingly received almost no attention amid otherwise comprehensive discussion of his ideas. Greenberg and Mitchell (1983) do not mention it in their chapter on Fairbairn, and the three scholarly collections devoted to him since then are essentially bare of references to it. Yet he published five papers dealing with it over a thirty-year span, from 1935 to 1964, and from these and the numerous references elsewhere in his work it is evident that the topic was of major concern to him.

My aim here is twofold. First, I shall outline the evolution of Fairbairn's thinking on homosexuality, of interest in part because it forced him to confront the intersection of biology with his theoretical approach, based on early object relations rather than on libidinal drive theory as the major determinants of psychological development. Indeed, it may help us understand why he was able to make this fundamental breakthrough, the precursor to all subsequent work on attachment theory. It also enables us to set him in the context of other psychoanalytic thinking on this highly contentious topic in the mid-twentieth century, especially the growing tendency to see male homosexuality as a reprehensible perversion that could (and should) be "cured" (Abelove, 1993; Lewes, 2009; Robinson, 2001).

Second, I shall examine the ways in which Fairbairn's personal conflicts may have affected his ideas about sexuality in general and homosexuality in particular. Fairbairn himself always acknowledged that the psychoanalyst was ultimately motivated by a desire, "largely unconscious perhaps, to resolve his own conflicts" (1958a, p. 76). From the mass of self-analytic notes he made starting early in World War II it appears that he was a man deeply conflicted and confused by his own sexuality as well as constrained by considerable homophobia. Moreover, from the 1950s onwards, his heavy reliance on the case of one patient to illustrate his ideas on the antecedents of homosexuality seems to have been complicated by a degree of identification with that patient.

Evidence of his thinking comes not only from Fairbairn's extensive publications but from unpublished papers, notes, drafts, and correspondence now held by the National Library of Scotland in Edinburgh, some of it, including the complete self-analytic notes, only recently donated by his family and thus made available to the public for the first time. This material is so rich that it is possible here to give only a selective outline of my findings; the rest will have to await more detailed publication elsewhere.

Theory

Fairbairn himself stressed (1949) that his initial interest in psychology had been stimulated by the usually unmentioned problems of "sex and conscience", a field in which Freud was the first to offer him enlightenment. His first two clinical papers (1927, 1931) in fact deal with sexual conflict and thwarted desire in two female patients, one of ambiguous gender. But in the mid-1930s he began to evidence an interest in male homosexuality, starting with "Child Assault" (1935a), written in response to what he considered the misguided approach of a 1926 government report on the issue. The aim, no doubt stimulated also by his own work in a child guidance clinic, was the practical one of alerting the public to the types, and degree of "pathogenicity", of sexual offences commonly aimed at children of both sexes, and the appropriate treatment for both victims and perpetrators. But Fairbairn's most emphatic (undocumented) assertion is that *"homosexual offences against boys are much commoner than offences against girls"* (his italics), something he thought the public would rather ignore. Moreover, he is very concerned with their later effects on the victim, such as the development of "bad sexual habits" and "perverse sexual practices", including exhibitionism and homosexuality. The (mostly male) offenders he deems to be "perverts", whose "sex instinct" has developed abnormally and whose character defects include impaired self-control.

This theme is further developed in his 1939 paper "Sexual Delinquency", in which Fairbairn advocates that such offenders be treated from a medical rather than a penal standpoint, since their "unnatural" sexual conduct is rooted in "arrested psychosexual development" and the persistence of sadistic and gratificatory infantile attitudes to sexual objects which prevent them from loving "whole persons". They have been unable to develop the compensatory traits of the psycho-neurotic, who is saved from outright "sexual delinquency" by repression, projection, or internalised parental prohibitions. As to homosexuality, he thinks it results not simply from a preference for the same-sex parent but also from early hate and fear of that parent, who has to be seduced by converting them into a sexual object. And the reason the "confirmed homosexual" is "proud, rather than ashamed, of his perverse tendency" is that forms of infantile sexuality have been incorporated in the ego itself. All of these are ideas that he would return to later.

Thus Fairbairn from the outset manifested a judgmental attitude to male homosexuality (which was illegal in England and Wales until 1967 and in Scotland until 1980) that probably owed more to his Presbyterian heritage than to Freud's open-minded view of it as a non-pathological variant of development. But it also had to do with fears, rooted in his own experience, of boys' vulnerability to sexual predators (see below). Further confirmation of these views is found in Fairbairn's responses to Edward Glover's 1938 questionnaire to practitioners concerning their analytic technique, where he states that the only "prohibitions" he employs "relate to sexual intercourse (*when such is abnormal*) and active homosexuality" (his italics). And among his criteria for termination are, essentially, the capacity for heterosexual relationships at the genital level or "a socially satisfactory sublimation of freed libido" (presumably if the patient were unable to switch to the correct sexual orientation or type of sexual act).

Much of this was rethought during Fairbairn's great creative period in the early 1940s, when he turned decisively away from the "hedonistic libido theory" advanced by Freud and followed by Melanie Klein (whose theory of internal objects Fairbairn found useful). Rather, he proposed that libido was inherently object-seeking and that libidinal aims were merely channelled through the various erotogenic zones during the ego's progression from "infantile" to "mature" dependence on the (now differentiated) object. This resulted in a rather narrow focus on the early relationship with the mother as the prototype of all later object relations, and also as the ultimate source of "psychosexual difficulties". Thus, in "Schizoid Factors in the Personality" (1940a) the rejected schizoid who feels his own love must be "bad" may present with "vague complaints" that include "perverse sexual tendencies … impotence and compulsive masturbation". In "A Revised Psychopathology of the Neuroses and Psychoneuroses" (1941, pp. 40–41) he goes further, to claim that phenomena such as "exhibitionism, homosexuality, sadism and masochism" occur only when relations with "real objects" (ultimately the mother) have broken down and the child has to seek substitute satisfactions representing relations with internalised part-objects. Thus the male homosexual's regressive "search for his father's penis" revives the original oral relationship with the breast, thereby representing a "search for his father's breast".

These ideas receive their greatest elaboration in "Endopsychic Structure Considered in Terms of Object-relationships" (1944), where Fairbairn recasts the entire "Oedipus situation" as deriving from the infant's original, ambivalent dependence on the mother. The subsequent relationship with the father is patterned on that with the mother (minus the feeding aspect) and both are split into internalised exciting and rejecting objects. The situation becomes complicated by the child's jealousy of each parent (now seen to have different genital organs) in relation to the other, which then leads to sadistic concepts of the "primal scene". And it is the internalised relations with exciting and rejecting aspects of both parental objects, built up through a complex, ill-explained process of "layering" and "fusion", that ultimately determine the individual's "psycho-sexual attitude". Fairbairn concludes that in practice the child simplifies the situation by identifying the internalised rejecting object with one parent and the exciting one with the other, creating an internal Oedipus situation which is then transferred to the external world, an idea that was to be useful in explaining homosexuality (ibid., pp. 122–125). But this is definitely not a "pathology-free construct of sexual orientation", as claimed by Gomez (1997, p. 73), for Fairbairn qualifies the process as being limited in some way by "biological sexual factors", and furthermore considers it "the chief determining factor in the aetiology of the sexual perversions", among which he certainly included ego-syntonic homosexuality.

In "Object-relationships and Dynamic Structure" (1946a, pp. 139–142) Fairbairn reiterates his hostility to "hedonistic libido theory", claiming that if the libidinal goal is a good emotional relationship with the object, then "explicit pleasure-seeking represents a deterioration of behaviour", a "safety-valve process" (like infantile masturbation) that merely mitigates the failure of libidinal aims. Or, as he put it in "On the Nature and Aims of Psycho-analytical Treatment" (1958a, p. 84), the "pleasure principle can only operate within a closed [internal] system" and is therefore inherently "psychopathological". The problem for human beings is that their great variety of object-seeking libidinal techniques involve the "risk of deviations from normality", and early adverse emotional experiences may result in the unavailability of the organ that is "appropriate", in biological and evolutionary terms, for the gratification of object-seeking behaviour. Thus Fairbairn emphasises the biological and socially normative as the criteria of development, and sexual desire, problematic in itself, has to be subordinated to the primary need for supportive relationships with adult partners.

These attitudes are also evident in a paper (1946b) regarding psychotherapeutic treatment in Scottish prisons for "sexual and unnatural offenses". Again, as in 1939, Fairbairn stresses the "profound difference" between the conflicted "psychoneurotic" who controls his perverse sexual tendencies "by means of repression and other defensive techniques" to prevent them ever becoming overt, and the sexual pervert: "[…] homosexuality must be regarded, not simply as a perverse expression of natural sexuality, but as the natural sexual expression of a personality which has become perverse in its essential structure." The pervert is a "psychopath" who refuses "to acknowledge allegiance to the standards of Society" and, particularly in the case of homosexuals, forms social groups whose differences are "not necessarily confined to the sexual sphere". Fairbairn considers that the only feasible "rehabilitation" of such offenders may be through group treatment, as tried with "war neurotics".

Thus Fairbairn, unlike such contemporaries as Edmund Bergler (1944), never advocated a "cure" for homosexuality and refrained from their openly contemptuous attitudes towards homosexuals. But in an undated letter to an American psychiatrist, John Frank Pave, commenting on Pave's unpublished paper, "Toward a Cure for Homosexuality", he again argues that homosexuality is an "inherently pathological" character disorder (stemming from a hatred of the child's "natural libidinal object", the heterosexual parent and his or her genitals), which results in a "profound resistance to psychotherapy". Pave's question (which had been Freud's question also) as to why "normal individuals refrain from homosexuality", Fairbairn considers "beside the point", since it is "normal not to be homosexual". It is heterosexuality that has an "instinctive basis", the penis and vagina having evolved in mutual relation to one another, and therefore it is only the intervening psychological factors, which may obstruct this otherwise "inevitable feature of adult life", that require explanation. As to the "schizoid factor in homosexuality", he wonders if the "homosexual attitude" may represent a "defence against schizoid developments [involving] an underlying uncertainty […] whether to adopt a male or female role".

This letter, with its strongly normative stance, affords a useful transition to Fairbairn's later papers, starting with "On the Nature of Hysterical States" (1954b), in which he introduces a patient who was to feature in his continuing efforts to clarify the aetiology of homosexuality. ("Morris" can be identified, from Fairbairn's appointment books and other documents, as appearing in his practice in 1945 and staying almost to the end.) At this point Morris is characterised as a "hysterical type" who developed intense anxiety on returning from the army to live with his widowed mother. As the only boy in a family of girls he had suffered from his mother's rejection of his masculinity as embodied in his penis, and at the age of five felt "castrated" by being circumcised to remedy his phimosis, something he interpreted as a punishment for forbidden masturbation. His father was quite unavailable for support. The trauma was exacerbated by the wartime loss of a limb and return to his "castrating" mother, with whom he struggled as an internalised exciting and rejecting object; she appeared in his fantasies as holding down his penis and crushing his testicles, provoking both masochistic terror and intense sexual excitement. Morris's "internal situation" had been represented by his relationship to his penis, and the loss of his cherished foreskin (representing the breast) left him with an aversion to marriage, which would only mean having his penis "interfered with" by someone else. The whole drama of his object relationships was thus constituted by genital autoeroticism, in his hysterical substitution of a "bodily state for a personal problem". It is striking that at this point Fairbairn does not mention the word "homosexuality" in connection with this case; also that Morris's relationship with his castrating mother found parallels in Fairbairn's own life (see below).

In his review of the Schreber case (1956a) Fairbairn criticises Freud's theory of innate bisexuality and his idea that Schreber's homosexual desire for his doctor (plus his fantasy of being a woman) represented a transference of an earlier, passive wish-fantasy towards his late father. Rather, everything has to go back to a rejection of the earliest object of desire, the mother, with a resulting transfer of libido to a "defensive autoerotism" (masturbation), which "in itself predisposes to a homosexual object choice". Even if the father is also a persecutor, the greater underlying aggression is always towards the faithless mother (cf. his 1939 and 1944 papers) and the male Oedipus complex is merely a displacement of hostility from the latter (who, like Hamlet's mother, is always the object of greater hatred in the "primal scene") to the father. So although Schreber barely mentions his mother, this may merely confirm her importance, as does his "obvious identification with her".

"Horror of the primal scene itself" now becomes the key element in Fairbairn's theory of homosexuality. Thus Schreber's fantasy of "parentless generation" represents a denial of the primal scene and his transformation into a woman becomes a means of cryptic participation in it. A dramatic illustration is afforded by Morris (not named, but the details fit). A propos of Morris's dream of a political meeting where naked young men with attention-getting penises are contrasted with murderous Scottish Nationalists plotting revolution, Fairbairn claims that the former represent his enjoyment of the primal scene via masturbation while the latter reveal his sadistic attitude towards his mother. And for the first time he admits Morris's "overt homosexual leanings", while stating he is "not a practising homosexual". This theory also accounts for schizoid personalities' doubts about the nature of their sex, since this is really due to "uncertainty over identifications in the primal scene", that is, rather than to any inherent bisexuality (cf. his letter to Dr Pave). But the other supporting case he adduces, a "markedly schizoid" married man subject to homosexual dreams about one of his sons, with "profound doubts about his sexual role", sounds in some respects (including "difficulty over urinating in public lavatories") uncannily like himself, as will be seen.

The primal scene theory of homosexuality goes back to the idea of the child's identifying the internalised exciting object with the same sex parent, outlined by Fairbairn in "Endopsychic Structure" (1944), though it also echoes Melanie Klein (1932), who thought that a strongly sadistic fantasy of the parents copulating could result in the boy's turning away from women as love objects or even failing to maintain any libidinal position whatsoever. Fairbairn returned to the idea in "On the Nature and Aims of Psycho-analytical Treatment" (1958a), where he again features Morris as exemplifying the desire to maintain the internal world as a "closed system" from which the analyst would have to rescue him. Here Morris's exciting, enraged sexual fantasies about preventing the parents from ever joining in intercourse (something that would be like an "atomic bomb" exploding) were projected onto a couple he hosted overnight in his flat, his "homosexual attraction" being towards the man rather than the woman in the pair.

Morris made his final appearances in two short papers in which the primal scene idea drops out entirely, to be replaced by the castration fantasy described in 1954. In the unpublished "A Short Note on Castration" (1961), Morris (not named, but again the history fits) is described as being sexually excited only by the idea of castration, inflicted first by his hated mother and then aggravated by the loss of his leg, the "punishment" for his wartime escape into "the world of men with penises". All of this is said to explain his "repressed homosexual proclivity" and fear of marrying his girlfriend.

The second paper, "A Note on the Origin of Male Homosexuality" (1964) was actually the final one of Fairbairn's life, so it is striking that his biographer, Sutherland (1989), omits all mention of it. Starting from Freud's observation that the penis "inherits something from the nipple of the mother's breast", Fairbairn now reduces his theory of homosexuality to an essential substitution of the penis for the breast, as he had earlier claimed in 1941. While he again denies that Morris was "an overt homosexual" he presents information which does suggest it (such that he took baths with a "male friend", involving "penis play" with subsequent emissions, and had "frequent homosexual dreams and masturbation phantasies"). This time the ultimate cause is reduced to maternal deprivation (rigid feeding practices and traumatic weaning), which led to self-consoling masturbation in which his own penis was substituted for the maternal breast. Furthermore, castration trauma made him fear women and take the "penises of other men as sexual objects". "It is thus that his homosexuality arose."

And thus it took Fairbairn almost two decades to acknowledge that his patient was homosexual, though the collusive aim of their work sounds as if it was to discourage "overt" expression of the fact. Presumably this had to do with his need to distinguish the "psychoneurotic" who fought against conflict-induced homosexual fantasies from the homosexual "pervert" for whom these, and the behaviour, were ego-syntonic. But it also had much to do with his own history and sexual conflicts, to which we now turn.

Self-analysis and personal life

Any account of Fairbairn's personal struggles over sexuality has to be based on the "self-analytic notes" which he started writing in 1939–1940, and took up again in the 1950s. His biographer, J. D. Sutherland, eventually decided that this intimate material was too important to ignore and published the earlier parts of it largely verbatim (1989, pp. xii–xiii, 65–82). But Sutherland (Fairbairn's former analysand, student, and friend) was writing in a different era and tended to accept his subject's own explanations, protectively refraining from drawing other conclusions or raising obvious questions. He also passed over most of the notes from the 1950s and gave only a cursory account of Fairbairn's dramatic drawings of dreams. Here I shall give an alternative, necessarily abbreviated reading of this material, especially the unpublished parts (references are to the MSS held by the National Library of Scotland, "Notes on Self Analysis", and "Dreams and Diary").

The principal aim of Fairbairn's notes seems to have been to understand his own conflicted sexuality, especially as it related to his worsening urinary phobia. His own analysis had lasted only about two years in the early 1920s, and after that he had no one he could, or would, turn to for help (Sutherland, 1989, p. 9; 1994, p. 407). Sutherland's analysis (1989, pp. 65–80) focuses mainly on the role of Fairbairn's sexually punitive mother in inhibiting his masculine development, and the early notes afford many examples, particularly her repeated warnings on the horrific dangers of touching his penis for other than utilitarian purposes, that is, to get pleasure from it "for its own sake". Thus when a girl cousin initiated sex play with him in the bath, he would allow only mutual "poking" of anuses, something which excited him to the point of orgasm however.

Most of these notes relate to Fairbairn's urinary inhibition, starting with the traumatic boyhood incident in a railway carriage when his father (who himself had a phobia of urinating with anyone else in the vicinity) was desperate to urinate but could not. Father and son were isolated from the women at one end of the compartment, the son watching with anxious horror, pity, and guilty satisfaction as his father squeezed out a dribble on to the floor, after which he too had difficulty urinating, as Father held the carriage door ajar for him. But to judge from Fairbairn's later dream-depiction of it, where the boy, with hair erect, stares at his father's enormous organ while a woman's face glares impotently through a window, the shared "performance" may also have been obscurely exciting.

Fairbairn's own urinary retention by 1939 had generalised to a point where it limited his social life, but the notes make clear that the phobia was always linked to "urinating before other men", as well as to terror over masturbation, which had left him feeling inferior to other boys who did it guilt-free. This was aggravated both by phimosis (as in Morris's case) and by adolescent struggles over tormenting nocturnal emissions and unwanted erections, which he tried to subdue by urinating but which then led to his frequently getting an erection when he went to the bathroom (which would add to his anxiety about doing it in front of other males). At times he felt it would be better to have his penis cut off or to be a woman with breasts and vagina, and enjoyed a fantasy (some of whose details Sutherland omits) of having intercourse in the female position with "legs wide apart & opening up vulva & vagina", while being penetrated by "something (presumably penis but not formulated as such) thrust into gaping vagina [to] effect a release of tension—the sort of tension I feel when my bladder is full". This erect "penis" is never described as belonging to another man, but rather conceptualised as a kind of catheter, a fantasy that once came true in hospital after an operation. And the "alien & hostile" bladder comes to represent dangerous internal forces "that threaten to destroy one" and can lead to "suicidal thoughts".

Fairbairn's father, subject to similar fears, was evidently of little help to his adolescent son. Earlier he had been seen as a "good protective but rather ineffective figure" but later was bitterly resented when he raised narrow-minded, stingy objections to young Fairbairn's narcissistic ambitions, which led him now to side with his mother, who fostered them. Yet even if, ultimately, she ("like Hamlet's mother") remained "the villain of the piece", she may have provided a defence against any longing for the kindly father who had relieved the boy's repeated constipation by administering "enemas and suppositories"—a procedure which Fairbairn elsewhere admits (1946a, p. 142) can lead to libido being "diverted" to the anus. Sutherland acknowledges (1989, p. 84) that these enemas may have suggested the fantasy of "father's good penis entering him" but evades any homoerotic implications. And when it comes to Fairbairn's "childhood trauma" of being molested by a homosexual man, Sutherland (ibid., p. 73) separates it from its original context in a highly erotic dream from August 1940, and sees its significance primarily as showing "his mother as the frightening anti-sexual super-ego".

This dream consisted of two scenes, first, "looking for rabbit in burrow" and "dog scraping at mouth of burrow"; then "the mole burrow on top of the mound". The atmosphere in the ensuing rush of associations is one of forbidden sexual pleasure and seduction, in which Fairbairn first recounts the sexual games with his cousin in the bath, then links the dog (which seems to represent his own sexuality) trying to catch the rabbit, to searching for "Mother's hidden penis" in her enormous hole, which emits rushing flows of urine. Rather than seeking to possess the woman, he repeatedly envies the freedom and pleasure of female sexuality, wishing he could tear off his penis and insert a finger to ensure freer urination. Again, recollection of his pleasure in anal stimulation by his cousin leads him back to his embarrassment over the enemas administered by his father, which in turn leads him to recall the excitingly masochistic scene in the railway carriage, in which father and son may have helped each other in turn urinate out of the open door as it threatened to castrate them both. Fairbairn notes that after their arrival he suffered five days of constipation (thereby inviting more enemas?).

From his "desire to be a woman with a secret penis" he shifts to his jealousy that his son loses interest when he himself turns to the mole burrow (representing his own penis). The son is "more interested in his mother than in me", but the place where he plays ball with another boy reminds Fairbairn of the place where he was "taken by the h/s [homosexual] man" who touched his penis under his clothes and told him it did a boy good and made him strong to play with his penis. Despite his fright, and flight, and his mother's subsequent enraged attacks as she tried to force him to confess, he did wonder if the man was right and started touching his penis "in a spirit of bravado", but soon gave it up out of guilt and fear, along with his dreams of escaping from the "world of Mother to the world of boys". Any escape had to be enacted internally and "narcissistically" (that is, auto-erotically, like Morris?), via his own penis (the mole burrow).

Thus everything comes back to the internalised, anti-libidinal mother as the only acceptable model for his sexuality. Pleasurable release is to be found only through the penis of another man (or one's own finger), but intimate relationships with other men (whether his castrated and impotent father, his homosexual seducer, or his faithless son) are doomed to frustration by female interference, as well as by his own rigid notions of normality and perversion. The

Defying the anti-libidinal object at last?

only person to sanction his sexual enjoyment seems to have been the homosexual man, who subsequently haunted Fairbairn's dreams (always wearing a cloth cap, unlike Father, who is portrayed with bald head, or top hat, and moustache). In a drawing from 1950 he and the boy are depicted together, the man holding the boy in front of him as they face the angry mother with her raised sword, in apparent defiance of her warnings (see illustration).

This brings us to the later self-analytic notes, mostly undated but apparently from the early 1950s, like the dated drawings of dreams. Why Fairbairn resumed them at this point is unknown, though they coincide with the nadir of his marriage to a neglected, by now alcoholic wife who had always resented his absorption in his work (and whose death in 1952 was "by suicide", according to Fairbairn's medical records). The fault was hardly one-sided, as their younger son Nicholas claims (1987, pp. 30, 36) that Fairbairn was "rigidly insensitive" to Mary's suffering, and hints that he avoided her sexually, so that she was in effect a "widow and a virgin". But this was also the period when Fairbairn started to write about Morris, whose "castrating" mother and abundant castration fantasies found parallels in his own life and could have stimulated further self-scrutiny.

Sutherland claims (1989, p. 81) that these later notes "add very little", and they are indeed schematic and repetitive as they circle obsessively around the problem of Fairbairn's tormenting urinary retention. But some themes do begin to emerge more clearly. Fairbairn notes that the urinary problem became a "symptom" against the background of attacks by his wife and rejection by senior male colleagues, but this echoes early traumatic attacks by his mother (especially her locking him in the parental bedroom and beating him after he saw a "pail of blood-stained diapers" in the back kitchen) as well as his father's inability either to support him against the "Bad Castrating Mother Figure" or provide "Potency with Good Mother Figure". Thus Fairbairn felt his "Oedipus situation", in which Father was "cut out", had to be displaced from the genital to the urinary sphere, substituting "Urinary Desire for Genital (Incestuous) Excitement" and "Retention for Castration". But retention was also an "Expression of Inner Preoccupation & *Refusal to Direct Libido towards Women as Outer Objects*" (my italics), as well as a sacrifice of sexuality out of guilt over aggression to Mother. Excitement could be manifested only as a compulsive need to urinate, which was checked by fear of the libidinal impulse and anger at its frustration.

This split between Bad and Good Mother figures Fairbairn describes as being enacted between his hostile, "castrating" wife, and two successive female secretaries, the departure of the first (at the time of his wife's serious illness in 1940) being associated with his urinary retention starting to occur even in private, as well as with a diminution in "potency". This improved with the development of a dependent attachment to the second (married but separated) secretary, from 1945 onwards, but fluctuated when she became the object of another man's attention, which provoked a jealous dream of "atom bombs being dropped", akin to Morris's primal scene fantasies. It is unclear whether the attachment became sexual as well as possessive, or whether such physical contact as did apparently occur was valued more as a way of attaching the woman to him.

Fairbairn had a horror of being "imprisoned by an aggressive libidinal object" and there is no indication in this material of women being positive sexual figures. His own "sado-masochistic" primal scene trauma was based on the memory of being beaten by his mother after he discovered the bloody diapers, which he related to "secret goings-on between parents", assuming, in view of his mother's aggression, that the blood was his father's. That scene was re-enacted in 1935, when his "castrating" wife bitterly attacked him after they had had intercourse and he suffered an "attack" of kidney stone, with blood in his urine. To escape her hostility he went one night to the cinema to see Hitchcock's romantic spy thriller *The 39 Steps*, but its plot so dramatised his basic conflicts that he was seized with a sudden suicidal impulse, like when he was beaten and locked up by his mother. (Its hero is on the run from London to Scotland, falsely accused of murdering a female spy who is stabbed in his flat with his knife. After a claustrophobic chase scene on a train—of all things—he attaches himself opportunistically to an attractive young woman who assumes he is the murderer and tries repeatedly to betray him when they are forced to flee, handcuffed together by the police. But at the end she is seen surreptitiously taking his hand, still in its handcuff, indicating he will be chained to her for life!)

Fairbairn, after the beating episode, contemplated committing suicide in order to rope his father in as an ally and thereby get him to reproach his mother. This desperate need for a libidinal "Father Figure" is echoed repeatedly in the notes, whereas Father is mostly depicted in the dream-drawings as sitting off to one side or turning his back on the action. It is other men who feature as objects of curiosity or excitement, including a mysterious "Indian Servant" who once gave young Fairbairn a bath and is unmistakably portrayed in a drawing of November 1950, with the boy sitting in the bathtub, his hair standing on end (like in the railway carriage with Father) in an obvious displacement upwards that could represent sexual excitement as well as fright. The homosexual man is also featured, as in the drawing reproduced above, or in another where he and the boy together head down into a pit towards a small erect penis and a large tree/hand, while on the other side of the pit the same boy is restrained with a chain by the anti-libidinal mother (one of several images of a small boy in a kilt led on a chain by Mother, just as he leads his dog).

Elsewhere in the notes Mother's "Taboo[s] on Being Sexual" are described for the first time as extending to other males: he was not to "talk sex" or play "rough games with boys", let alone the "Man" who took him "for a Walk". And the dangerous word "homosexual" now makes its appearance, but always in the abbreviation "h/s" when it refers to himself, as in Mother's ban on "Escape from Incestuous Situation into H/S Relationships" or into masturbation. Renewed speculation on the urinary retention reveals that it was initially triggered by sudden exposure to large numbers of other men, whether in public lavatories or in the male ward of a hospital, and that this went back to Fairbairn's school days, when he felt embarrassed by his own small penis and envious of other boys' larger ones, especially if they were circumcised, like Father. Once he had felt anxious and afraid when watched by two other boys as he struggled to urinate, which he now associates with "castration anxiety & *perhaps fear of h/s attack*" (my italics). And he notes that his regression to pregenital, urinary, and anal sexuality was associated with "Passive Attitude, manifested in *Need for Catheterization and Enemas*" and "*Unconscious Passive H/S Tendency* based on (1) need of Father and (2) Guilt towards Father" (my italics). Finally, he links "Urination in lavs. with erection—& with sexual desire". Thus Fairbairn's laborious associations lead gradually to the emergence of what must, given his theoretical views, have been a deeply repressed awareness that his fear of "urinating before other men" was associated with passive sexual desire visible in an erection, thereby inviting a homosexual "attack" that might be as much desired as feared.

Such repression would surely have been undermined by Fairbairn's intensive work with Morris from 1945 onwards. Links between them are evidenced by a pair of undated index cards, the first of which lists on one side the various factors relevant to his own urinary retention (such as passivity, withholding and sadomasochistic auto-erotism) and on the other, "Specific Factors—Case of X": (1) sadomasochistic relationship with a punishing mother who, as the anti-libidinal ego, attacks the libidinal ego (father); (2) exclusion of father as objective relationship, replaced by identification with father as impotent figure in relation to mother; (3) compulsive giving of self masochistically to mother. All these were as true of himself as of Morris, whose real name, abbreviated, is noted on the other card, preceded by five Xs and the statement: "*Male Homosexuality as Attempt to Escape from Incestuous Situation with Mother—Preferably into a Community of other Men who are Also Attempting to Escape from Such a Situation*" (his emphasis).

There is much more to be said about this source material, including the ways in which it suggests revisions to Fairbairn's biography. For now, one further illustration of Fairbairn's sexual dilemmas is afforded by a dream he recorded in February 1955. He is going to a wedding, dressed in formal clothes and top hat, but never gets there. After passing two other men, also wearing top hats, going the other way, he ends up at the top of some stairs looking for a bathroom so he can urinate before the wedding. He eventually finds what appears to be a washroom with low partitions, containing several objects with mackintosh covers. Lifting one of these he discovers a lavatory pan in which is "an enormous motion curled around like a snake". As he contemplates urinating in the pan he hears a man behind him muttering "Shit", and turns round to see the man, an assistant attendant who was leaning over the partition, being given a "ticking off" by the head attendant. Following Fairbairn's own notions of dream interpretation one might see all these men as aspects of the self, with the stiff, erect headgear perhaps alluding to sexual excitement socially constrained by upper-class formal apparel. Could the lower-class voyeur/assistant attendant, who is impressed by the dirty but exciting secret under its mackintosh cover, thus represent the libidinal ego, while the anti-libidinal ego is the authoritarian head attendant who scolds him, just as Fairbairn consciously felt compelled to prohibit or explain away any "perverse" sexual interests? "Mackintosh" was incidentally the surname of his second secretary, whom he eventually married, so one could speculate that compulsory heterosexual relationships served as a "cover", whether unconsciously or not, for the urinary/anal sexuality to which he felt he regressed.

Discussion

To explore Fairbairn's own sexual confusions and fears in this way might seem a trivial and even prurient undertaking, were it not for the fact that they may have reinforced his consistent stigmatisation of homosexuality as a perversion that was better repressed and/or sublimated. He apparently had to see himself as a schizoid neurotic whose "normal", biologically based heterosexuality had been "interfered with" by early maternal prohibitions and paternal weakness. Yet at the same time his "alien and hostile" bladder evidenced "dangerous & destructive" internal (sexual?) forces whose escape might destroy him or lead to suicide.

Fairbairn thus has a place in one of the most notorious controversies in twentieth-century psychoanalysis, one from which many analysts emerge with little credit. Of course, we cannot know where he himself fell on the heterosexual-bisexual-homosexual continuum, but the point is that it was extremely difficult for him to know it himself, in spite of struggling for years to understand his crippling urinary phobia without the benefit of a personal analysis (though it is unclear how far another analyst in those times would have been able to accept his tabooed sexual impulses, any more than he himself could deal openly and acceptingly with those of his patient, Morris). His own awareness of his sexual ambivalence was cruelly circumscribed not only by the moral straitjacket in which he grew up, created by his repressive parents and the respectable Scottish Presbyterian bourgeois society whose values they exemplified, but also by the climate within psychoanalysis itself, which had moved far from Freud's more tolerant view of homosexuality and even admiration for distinguished homosexuals.

In one respect, however, might Fairbairn's own repression of genital libido and downplaying of the pleasure principle have helped in his most important theoretical breakthrough, that is, to see the primary importance of attachment to early caregivers in human emotional development? If his own libido was so inhibited in its expression and enjoyment, whether to female or male objects, then perhaps it was easier to view libido as important largely in the service of a progressively differentiated attachment to biologically and socially sanctioned objects (for men always the mother or her representative) rather than as a source of appetitive pleasure in its own right. Sadly, it sounds as if Fairbairn never did really overcome his mother's proscription of getting pleasure from his penis "for its own sake", nor the obstacles his internalised bad objects posed to passionate sexual relationships with other human beings of either gender.

References

Abelove, H. (1993). Freud, male homosexuality and the Americans. In: H. Abelove, M. A. Barale, & D. M. Halperin (Eds.), *The Lesbian and Gay Studies Reader* (pp. 381–393). New York: Routledge.

Bergler, E. (1944). Eight prerequisites for the psychoanalytic treatment of homosexuality. *Psychoanalytic Review, 31*: 253–286.

Fairbairn, N. (1987). *A Life Is Too Short: Autobiography, Volume One*. Glasgow: Fontana/Collins, 1989.

Fairbairn, W. R. D. (n.d.). Dreams and diary. National Library of Scotland: Inventory, Acc. 11258/163.

Fairbairn, W. R. D. (n.d.). Letter to Dr Pave relating to his article "Toward a cure for homosexuality". National Library of Scotland: Inventory, Acc. 11258/144.

Fairbairn, W. R. D. (n.d.). Medical records. National Library of Scotland: Inventory, Acc. 13332/89.

Fairbairn, W. R. D. (n.d.). Notes on self analysis. National Library of Scotland: Inventory, Acc. 13332/77.

Fairbairn, W. R. D. (1927). Notes on the religious phantasies of a female patient. In: *Psychoanalytic Studies of the Personality* (pp. 183–196). London: Tavistock, 1952.

Fairbairn, W. R. D. (1931). Features in the analysis of a patient with a physical genital abnormality. In: *Psychoanalytic Studies of the Personality* (pp. 197–222). London: Tavistock, 1952.

Fairbairn, W. R. D. (1935a). Child assault. In: E. F. Birtles & D. E. Scharff (Eds.), *From Instinct to Self: Selected Papers of W. R. D. Fairbairn, Volume II: Applications and Early Contributions* (pp. 165–182). Northvale, NJ: Aronson, 1994.

Fairbairn, W. R. D. (1938b). Practising psycho-analysis. In: E. F. Birtles & D. E. Scharff (Eds.), *From Instinct to Self: Selected Papers of W. R. D. Fairbairn, Volume II: Applications and Early Contributions* (pp. 272–283). Northvale, NJ: Aronson, 1994.

Fairbairn, W. R. D. (1939a). Sexual delinquency. In: E. F. Birtles & D. E. Scharff (Eds.), *From Instinct to Self: Selected Papers of W. R. D. Fairbairn, Volume II: Applications and Early Contributions* (pp. 284–292). Northvale, NJ: Aronson, 1994.

Fairbairn, W. R. D. (1940a). Schizoid factors in the personality. In: *Psychoanalytic Studies of the Personality* (pp. 3–27). London: Tavistock, 1952.

Fairbairn, W. R. D. (1941). A revised psychopathology of the neuroses and psychoneuroses. In: *Psychoanalytic Studies of the Personality* (pp. 28–58). London: Tavistock, 1952.

Fairbairn, W. R. D. (1944). Endopsychic structure considered in terms of object-relationships. *International Journal of Psychoanalysis, 25*: 70–92. In: *Psychoanalytic Studies of the Personality* (pp. 82–136). London: Tavistock, 1952.

Fairbairn, W. R. D. (1946a). Object-relationships and dynamic structure. In: *Psychoanalytic Studies of the Personality* (pp. 137–151). London: Tavistock, 1952.

Fairbairn, W. R. D. (1946b). The treatment and rehabilitation of sexual offenders. In: *Psychoanalytic Studies of the Personality* (pp. 289–296). London: Tavistock, 1952.

Fairbairn, W. R. D. (1949). Steps in the development of an object-relations theory of the personality. In: *Psychoanalytic Studies of the Personality* (pp. 152–161). London: Tavistock, 1952.

Fairbairn, W. R. D. (1954b). Observations on the nature of hysterical states. In: D. E. Scharff & E. F. Birtles (Eds.), *From Instinct to Self: Selected Papers of W. R. D. Fairbairn, Volume 1* (pp. 13–40). Northvale, NJ: Aronson, 1994.

Fairbairn, W. R. D. (1956a). The Schreber case. In: D. E. Scharff & E. F. Birtles (Eds.), *From Instinct to Self: Selected Papers of W. R. D. Fairbairn, Volume 1: Clinical and Theoretical Papers* (pp. 41–60). Northvale, NJ: Aronson, 1994.

Fairbairn, W. R. D. (1958a). On the nature and aims of psycho-analytical treatment. *International Journal of Psychoanalysis, 39*(5): 374–385. In: D. E. Scharff & E. F. Birtles (Eds.), *From Instinct to Self: Selected Papers of W. R. D. Fairbairn, Volume 1* (pp. 74–92). Northvale, NJ: Aronson, 1994.

Fairbairn, W. R. D. (1961). "A short note on castration" submitted to *The International Journal of Psychoanalysis*. National Library of Scotland: Inventory, Acc. 11258/81.

Fairbairn, W. R. D. (1964). A note on the origin of male homosexuality. *British Journal of Medical Psychology, 37*: 31–32.

Gomez, L. (1997). *An Introduction to Object Relations*. New York: New York University Press.

Greenberg, J. R., & Mitchell, S. A. (1983). *Object Relations in Psychoanalytic Theory*. Cambridge, MA: Harvard University Press.

Klein, M. (1932). The effects of early anxiety-situations on the sexual development of the boy. In: *The Psychoanalysis of Children (third edition)* (pp. 326–368). London: Hogarth, 1959.

Lewes, K. (2009). *Psychoanalysis and Male Homosexuality: Twentieth Anniversary Edition*. Lanham, MD: Jason Aronson.

Robinson, P. (2001). Freud and homosexuality. In: T. Dean & C. Lane (Eds.), *Homosexuality and Psychoanalysis*. Chicago, IL: University of Chicago Press.

Sutherland, J. D. (1989). *Fairbairn's Journey into the Interior*. London: Free Association.

Sutherland, J. D. (1994). Reminiscences. In: J. S. Scharff (Ed.), *The Autonomous Self: The Work of John D. Sutherland* (pp. 392–423). Northvale, NJ: Jason Aronson.

CHAPTER EIGHT

Fairbairn in Argentina: the "Fairbairn Space" in the Argentine Psychoanalytic Association (APA)

Mercedes Campi, Adrián Besuschio, Luis Oswald, Isabel Sharpin de Basili, and Rubén M. Basili

Introduction

In 1998 Dr Basili proposed to open a "Fairbairn Space" in the APA. Dr Fainstein, the APA president at that time, and other officers asked us, "Why teach Fairbairn?" "How would you do it?" "Why Fairbairn again in the APA?" "Why a Fairbairn Space?"

Our comments on these questions form the objectives of the present chapter, which reports the results of fourteen years of arduous labour.

Why teach Fairbairn? How would you do it?

Pichon-Rivière, one of the pioneers of the APA, brought Fairbairn to Argentina and Latin America. Pichon-Rivière, a continuer of object relations theory and exponent of the psychoanalysis of the link, considered that each subject has multiple internal link structures that come into play specifically in interactions. He also underscored the importance of relations with external objects. He developed the notion of the internal group that constantly interrelates with the external world. He spoke of link models: a good link originated in gratifying experiences and a bad link as the product of frustrating experiences. He highlighted the internalisation of the environment in which the subject's life develops, and the importance of the social environment for the constitution and support of identity.

Another pioneer, Garma (1979) took up some of Fairbairn's ideas, for example, as a base for his theory on dreams.

They were followed by others:

Bleger (1967), based on Fairbairn, proposes the "glischrocaric" position prior to the paranoid-schizoid position. He also coordinated a study group on Fairbairn at the José T. Borda Psychiatric

Hospital which was attended by many outstanding psychoanalysts (for example, Dr Julio Granel).

Racker (1969) developed Fairbairn's ideas from 1948, applying them to his widely recognised ideas about countertransference.

Baranger (1976; Baranger et al., 1980) formulated interesting constructive criticism of Fairbairn in 1976. He formed study groups that produced the book *Aportaciones al Concepto de Objeto en Psicoanálisis* (Contributions to the concept of object in psychoanalysis), of which Resnicoff is co-author.

Resnicoff is a member and training analyst, member of the Fairbairn Space and of the glorious "old guard" of the APA, where he studied, taught, and published on Fairbairn with the pioneers. He also introduced the works of Fairbairn in the School of Psychology of the University of Buenos Aires.

Faimberg was trained at the APA where she taught Fairbairn. She is now a training analyst and member of the Psychoanalytic Society of Paris.

Morgan (Basili, 1990c) was the foremost teacher of Fairbairn's ideas locally, at the José T. Borda Psychiatric Hospital and the British Hospital. After taking his training in the APA, he won the Sir John O'Connor Scholarship to study psychoanalytic psychiatry in Great Britain, where he was analysed by John Sutherland and supervised by Fairbairn and Bion.

Thanks to Morgan's teaching work, psychiatrists in Argentina, and Latin American psychiatrists and psychologists, taught Fairbairn to their students. For twenty years, Morgan coordinated a study group on the works of Fairbairn and their application to severely ill patients, inpatients, and outpatients at the José T. Borda Hospital and also patients treated psychoanalytically in private practice.

Dr Basili participated in this group which included several well-known figures of Argentine psychoanalysis such as Dr Fainstein, twice president of the APA and now an official of the IPA. "Morgan thought about and taught Fairbairn a great deal, but published little" (Fainstein, 2005).

In the 1960s, Fairbairn was a widely studied author in the APA but was later forgotten, his place occupied by authors of the French School.

Why Fairbairn again in the APA?

The most important theoretical and technical topic in the works of Fairbairn (Hughes, 1990; Skolnick & Scharff, 1998; Sutherland, 1989) is splitting, studied as a function of the schizoid phenomenon (double dissociation in the ego and the object), which is universal, foundational, and structuring of the psyche and underlies all object relations (Fairbairn, 1952).

For Fairbairn, the endopsychic situation whose psychogenesis is primitive dissociation, which originates in splitting of the psychic structure of ego and object rather than in repression, is no longer simply a psychopathological schema useful to understand the schizoid condition psychoanalytically. It becomes a universal model of the psychic apparatus based on dissociation of the psychic structure (the third topic, in the sense of Morgan, Bleger, and Faimberg or, nowadays Hagelin, in the Asociación Psicoanalítica Argentina).

This step is fundamental for realising Freud's aspiration that psychoanalysis should be a general theory of the mind and not merely psychopathology.

In clinical work today the Fairbairn model is indispensable to interpret patients, especially severely ill patients. Its features are:

a. *Primitive dissociation* precedes repression and, as in repression, takes place first in the object and then in the ego. It is fundamental in normal structuring of the psychic apparatus, not only in schizoid patients (a sub-group of borderline patients, following Kernberg) but also in all borderlines, psychoses, and neuroses.

b. *The ego*: Fairbairn continues Freud's work and constantly compares his own theses to Freudian theses, even when he disagrees with them. Like Freud, Fairbairn is a moderate continuer who does not discard earlier theories but instead subsumes them in subsequent theory.

   Freud's general theory of development has two theoretical sub-moments: first, the psychosexual libido development, to which we now add aggression (Freud, 1905d), and second, the theory of narcissism with its three sub-moments (Freud, 1914c): 1) the ego cathects objects; 2) the id cathects objects (Freud, 1923b), and 3) the ego is a cathected object and a libido deposit that, together with the id, cathects objects (Freud, 1940a).

   Freud does not explain exactly how the ego appears and develops, especially in relation to the object. On the basis of "Instincts and their Vicissitudes", Fairbairn extends Freud's ideas (1915c) concerning the way the ego develops out of the ego of initial reality (pristine and originary) and the object relation.

   Unlike others (Greenberg & Mitchell, 1983; Guntrip, 1961), we consider that Fairbairn, like Freud, M. Klein, and Bion, is a relative innatist rather than a culturalist, since he starts with the existence of a pristine ego that is a neuro-biological ego, a particular and specific distribution of cathexes, an undivided neuronal mass (Freud, 1950a). There is nothing in the mind that has not first been outside the mind (Locke's "tabula rasa") except the mind itself (Leibniz).

   We consider that the original aim of Fairbairn's work was to formulate a psychoanalytic theory of the development of the ego. He is a founder of the British School of Object Relations and for this project, he needed to formulate a theory of object relations.

   M. Klein, however, basically took up Freud's "Mourning and Melancholia" (1917e) to construct a theory of object relations in the function of early anxieties and defences.

   Fairbairn's object relations theory led him to a structural psychoanalytic personality theory, also based on contemporary theories of the affects.

   Fairbairn is the most conspicuous exponent of the structural genetic method in psychoanalysis (Piaget, 1974).

c. *The object*: One of Freud´s principal contributions to philosophy, inadvertently, was that the object is always an object of drive (sexual) or object of libido.

   Fairbairn subscribes to this concept and maintains that object relations theory is indissolubly joined to libido theory.

   In Fairbairn, interest centres on the function of the object more than the object itself, and centres more on the relationship with the object (link) than the object's function. He is one of the precursors of the link theory and of attachment-detachment (Bowlby, 1969; Fonagy & Target, 2003).

In object relations theories, there are three psychopathological models: 1) M. Klein's prioritises the lack of good objects to make structures coherent; 2) Fairbairn's prioritises the importance of the excess of bad objects and the vicissitudes of relations with them, which form structure, and 3) Bion's prioritises the lack of object: no object is worse than one that is missing.

d. *Separation-abandonment anxieties*: Fairbairn (1963a) considered that the earliest and most primary form of anxiety experienced by the child is separation anxiety. He also defines the penis as the narcissistic organ that enables the boy to reconnect with his mother. Therefore, as Freud thought, the actual meaning we need to give castration anxiety is loss of the superego's love (1926d).

We emphasise interpretation of separation-abandonment contents in terms of castration, especially in severe actual pathologies.

Developmentally, we differentiate separation anxieties that first appear when the child is separated from the mother (regulated by her gaze), from abandonment anxieties that appear when the child returns to the mother, when she may say, "So you went away? Now you're on your own." Birth anxieties that arise when the umbilical cord is cut are separation anxieties. Since the contents of both are clinically the same (paranoid and hypochondriac), we consider them synonymous, although Gunderson (2001) differentiates them.

In psychopathology, separation-abandonment anxieties are fundamental to understand borderline personality organization (Gunderson, 2001).

e. *Aggression* is a reaction to frustration or deprivation (Fairbairn, 1963a). Unlike Freud, Fairbairn considers that aggression is always secondary to object loss and that it possesses unconscious intentionality, since it reaches the object without being moved by libido. Extrapolating from Freud and Fairbairn, libido is transformed into aggression by transmutation (Sharpin de Basili, 1990).

Winnicott, influenced by Guntrip (1961), was inspired by Fairbairn when he formulated his theory on aggression. For this reason among others we consider Winnicott a Fairbairnian.

f. *Dependence*: Fairbairn's normal developmental schema is based not only on regression but also on disturbances in the progression of the psychic apparatus, ahead of contemporary authors such as Mahler and Clifford Yorke: from immature dependence, scenario of the psychoses, to mature dependence, scenario of the neuroses, passing through the transitional stage, which we postulate as the borderline scenario.

g. *Ambivalence* is an indicator in the session and in the analytic process of the developmental level of object, object relation, and ego. When Fairbairn correlates these parameters, they become clinical indicators (Basili, Montero, & Sharpin de Basili, 2002). We postulate that ambivalence is the clinical indicator of a change of object relationship in the resolution of schizoid conflict (Basili & Sharpin de Basili, 2005) and Oedipal conflict.

h. *Guilt*: Fairbairn prioritises freedom from bad internalised objects and discusses Freud's interpretation that this is the most severe type of resistance. Fairbairn considers that if Freud had taken into account his own discoveries and the return of bad objects, he would not have needed to appeal to the concept of the death instinct. On this point, several eminent Argentine psychoanalysts, for example, E. Bleger and L. Rascovsky, were his followers. This position differentiates Fairbairn from M. Klein (1977) and is one of the pillars of his theory.

Individuals attribute the object's badness to themselves (guilt) in order to save the object relationship and to protect themselves from abandonment.

i. *External reality*, prioritising relationships with material "natural" objects (breast-mother). We propose that Fairbairn, unlike M. Klein, considers internal, part, or total objects and relationships with them as "ambassadors" of the relationship with the total object, which is also true for transitional objects in the Winnicottian sense (1971). Thus, in the course of development, internal, external, and transitional objects prepare the ground for the relationship with the total object (the real, external, material object: a breast-mother).

A basic aspect of actual pathologies is *conflict with external reality* (Kernberg, 1984); the usefulness of the second step of the mutative interpretation (Strachey, 1934) is based on this factor.

Extrapolating to Fonagy (Bateman & Fonagy, 2004), severe pathologies dramatise in the external, real world, the schizoid and Oedipal conflicts that should be internalised and mentalised. For these and other reasons we consider that Fairbairn contributes to psychoanalysis of the external real world.

j. *Transitional phenomena*: in a footnote, Winnicott (1958, p. 313) writes that he has observed Fairbairn's use of the word "transitional" in many passages. Transitional objects in Fairbairn are inherent to the transitional stage in which total objects that were treated as part objects in Freud-Abraham's oral II stage are treated as oral, anal, phallic-urethral contents; we postulate that this occurs in borderline patients whose transitional object is the analyst whereas in psychoses it is the outpatient facility. In the object relation in the latter two pathologies, the object is a part object.

Fairbairn's model gives us a technical, theoretical, clinical, and metapsychological instrument to understand and apply to these clinical milestones in severe actual pathologies. For this reason, we teach Fairbairn as "the analyst of borderline patients".

Extrapolating to Fairbairn, we proposed to define behaviour psychoanalytically as a bridge that joins an internal object, an external object, and the relationships with both, something we also observe in transference-countertransference. We may interpret behaviour alongside discourse which is essential for borderline and psychotic pathologies. We need to interpret the unconscious and make it conscious, not only in digital language but also in analogical language (Liberman, 1962); for example, by analysing the acting out of borderline patients. This conceptualisation of behaviour enables us to investigate, for example, why the patient has brought this acting out to the session (in it or outside it) and what it is that the patient is communicating to us.

Over the last thirty years, Kernberg has visited the APA and given courses and lectures on severe personality disorders. His works articulate four theoretical models: two based on the British theory of object relations (M. Klein and Fairbairn) and two based on ego psychology (M. Mahler's developmental model with contemporary contributions as well as others based on Jacobson's self theory). He postulates that "borderline" pathology is pathology of dissociation and aggression (although Fairbairn considers that aggression is always acquired, whereas Kernberg views it as also innate). Kernberg has become an important promoter of the ideas of Fairbairn in Argentina.

Why the Fairbairn Space?

With other colleagues we decided to found the Fairbairn Space in the APA. From the outset, we have had the support of different executive committees that have included us in workshops, round table discussions, internal congresses, symposia, and discussions with other "author spaces"; for example, panels with the "Lacan Space" in which we discussed the concept of structure and genetic and non-genetic structural methods. We also participated in all the national and Latin American psychoanalytical congresses and in some international congresses. We have published papers, for example, in the APA's *Revista de Psicoanálisis* (Basili et al., 2011).

Our initial approach was to study Fairbairn's "Synopsis of an Object-Relations Theory of the Personality", published in 1963 by the *International Journal of Psychoanalysis* at the request of his colleague, biographer, and analysand, John Sutherland, an article featuring precision, thoughtfulness, and power of synthesis. In the Fairbairn Space, with Guillermo Montero, psychologist and training analyst of the APA, we translated the "Synopsis ..." into Spanish and took the liberty of adding Freud's Oedipus complex, which we also studied on the basis of Fairbairn's model. We followed the order proposed by Fairbairn, based on theoretical moments we found in *Psychoanalytic Studies of Personality*, translated into Spanish. A good Fairbairnian at that time, Jorge Mom, former president of the APA, applied the Fairbairn model to understanding phobias, and also wrote the excellent prologue to this translation, which was in the past material studied in seminars of the APA. In regard to the points of the synopsis that we updated, we were greatly assisted by the index of this book, articles of the *Revista de Psicoanálisis*, and British journals.

We organised our study of Fairbairn into themes, based on chronological aspects and what we refer to as the two metapsychological moments of Fairbairn's works. In the first metapsychological moment (1944), the dissociation of an object from the external world, featuring ambivalence, precedes internalisation. In the second metapsychological moment (1951), internalisation of a pre-ambivalent object precedes dissociation, at which time the concept of self-object is implicit.

From the beginning, Diego Cohen, a psychiatrist and training analyst of the APA, and a founding member of the Fairbairn Space, specialised in contemporary Fairbairnian authors such as Celani (1993), who insists on theorising on the basis of the endopsychic situation, which we consider the third topic as described earlier. He also studied the contemporary importance of Fairbairn's contributions to the theory of affects (Thomä & Kächele, 1985, 1988), and went to England several times to study attachment-detachment theory in relation to Fairbairn's theory with Fonagy.

The endopsychic situation was what was most difficult for us to understand and especially difficult to apply to clinical cases, since we were accustomed to theorising with the four models of psychic apparatus and with Freud's model of repression. Adrián Ventura, a psychiatrist and psychoanalyst of the APA and a member of the Fairbairn Space, undertook to schematise the endopsychic situation.

Rubén Basili, psychiatrist and professor of seminars of the APA and the University of Buenos Aires (UBA), and Isabel Sharpin de Basili, psychologist and training analyst of the APA, studied the schizoid position which grounds and structures the human psyche in terms of a conflict:

schizoid conflict, which they proposed as a universal model of conflict that is particularly useful to understand pre-Oedipal conflict for which there was previously no universal conflict model (Basili & Sharpin de Basili, 2005). M. Klein considers "early oral conflict" universal. According to Kernberg (1992) it is pathological and is inherent to perversions, borderline patients, and psychotic patients. Brenner (1962) defines conflict as a modality and specific type of anxiety, defence, content, object, and object relation, to which we add that it is a mode of functioning, developmental level, and level of ego organisation.

For this reason, extrapolating from Fairbairn and Brenner, we consider schizoid conflict synonymous with schizoid position. In 2003 Basili and Sharpin de Basili took to the congress in Scotland a paper on schizoid conflict, "The Legacy of Fairbairn and Sutherland," that was published in 2005 in a book with the same title. Schizoid phenomenon and schizoid conflict are universal and foundational and structure another universal: the endopsychic situation based on the splitting of the psychic structure (ego-object). We use these two universals to theorise in the Fairbairn Space in order to understand the object situation and pre-Oedipal pathology. We argue the universality of schizoid conflict on the basis of the factic-social sciences, mythology (for example, Medusa's head), literature (for example, Schopenhauer's fable of the porcupine) (Freud, 1920g), and children's play (for example, the Fort-Da game [Freud, 1920g]) (Basili & Sharpin de Basili, 2003).

With metapsychological parameters (topographic, dynamic, structural, and genetic) we studied universal approach-avoidance (Basili, 1992; Basili & Echegaray, 1995; McWilliams, 1994), proposing schizoid conflict as the vector of approach-avoidance as a universal antagonism that is in constant dynamic oscillation.

We define schizoid conflict as:

- Phenomenally: fear of approach due to fear of engulfment and/or consequent abandonment.
- Psychoanalytically: a particular and specific type of:

  a. anxiety (engulfment-separation-abandonment).
  b. defence: a schizoid phenomenon whose clinical manifestation par excellence is omnipotent control of the object. Its failure is the major source of clinical symptoms of schizoid conflict.
  c. content: of engulfment anxieties, confusional; of separation-abandonment anxieties, paranoid and hypochondriac (M. Klein, 1977; Mahler, 1971); in the Freud-Abraham schema (Freud, 1905d), oral, anal, and phallic-urethral.
  d. relationship with the object: first a part object, the breast, scenario of schizophrenia, then a total object, the mother, scenario of manic-depressive psychosis, both in relation to a part object.

We postulate that for borderline patients the scenario is the transitional stage (Fairbairn, 1952) and that the total object (mother–analyst) is treated as oral, anal, or phallic-urethral contents.

- Developmentally (Basili & Sharpin de Basili, 2005) schizoid conflict is articulated with and re-signified in the Oedipus complex, in subphase four (structuring of the internal object) of

phase three of Mahler's model (Basili, 1992), thereby conditioning normality and pathology of separation-individuation and systematically distorting it in borderline patients, perversions, and psychotic patients. The Oedipal situation is also distorted.
- Metapsychologically, schizoid conflict is an intrasystemic conflict (ego versus ego), the ego as an endopsychic structure with energy of its own deriving from the object relation (field theory: Lewin, 1978) and able to dissociate from itself, repress itself, and conflict with itself.

We consider that in schizoid conflict the Freudian *a posteriori* is not indispensable for the production of symptoms. We propose that important psychological and psychopathological developmental theories in contemporary psychoanalysis could acquire metapsychological status by virtue of schizoid conflict. Since the theories of Mahler and Kohut are not based on conflict, they cannot be considered psychoanalytic (Tyson & Tyson, 1993). However, they would acquire this status with schizoid conflict, which is the vector of normal and pathological separation-individuation, the mechanism by which symbiosis leads to separation-individuation (in Mahler's model); in contemporary terms, from the pole of symbiosis of the self to the pole of separation-individuation, from undifferentiation to psychic differentiation.

The same would occur in Kohut's theory, which also lacks a foundation in conflict. We propose schizoid conflict as the vector of passage from initial self to grandiose self and the idealised parental imago, and from grandiose self to cohesive self. It would be the agent of transmutative internalisation, by virtue of which the cohesive self acquires the properties of the grandiose self and the initial self. Schizoid conflict could be the mechanism by which narcissistic transferences are established (mirroring, idealising, twinning).

We were surprised to note that Kohut, unlike Kernberg, does not refer to Fairbairn at any point in his works in spite of the similarity of many of their concepts, although Sutherland (1989, p. 175) notes many passages of Kohut's writing that seem to derive from a familiarity with Fairbairn.

Guillermo Montero (2000), former coordinator of the Kohut Space, undertook an exhaustive bibliographic review regarding this issue.

When the Fairbairn Space studied schizoid conflict and the endopsychic situation, the concept of "object situation" was discovered and later schematised by the Basilis.

We propose to conceptualise the object situation as a psychological, clinical, and psychopathological entity consisting of:

1. A number of objects:
   In the neuroses there are three total objects which derive from the primal scene, first with a part object relationship (good-bad breast-mother) and then with a total object relationship.

   In borderlines there are two total objects with a part object relationship, the object treated as contents.

   In the psychoses there is a part object with a part object relationship (good-bad breast treated as such: schizophrenia) or two total objects with a part object relationship (good and bad mother treated as good and bad breast, respectively: manic-depressive psychosis).

   In paranoia, two total objects are treated as part objects (good and bad mother treated as good and bad breast, respectively) and projection is at the service of omnipotent control of the object and maintenance of me—not me differentiation.

In schizo-affective disorders, two total objects are also treated as part objects.

In psychotic productions (positive signs of re-cathectisation) there is no object. It is restored in delusions and hallucinations in a part object relationship.

2. Quality of the object as a product of dissociation: one is a bad, libidinal, narcissistic, exciting, "older", "needed", valued, transitional part object. The other is a part, bad, anti-libidinal, frustrating, repulsive, devalued, not needed, denigrated object. These terms are comparable but not synonymous, since they derive from different referential schemes (Basili, 1990a, 1990b).

Both objects may be the analyst in transference, where we also investigate the two interchangeable poles of dissociation.

3. Object relationship (examples: part-total; omnipotent control of the object-analyst in transference).
4. Object loss (unconscious meaning).

These parameters, together with the development of ambivalence, are noteworthy milestones in the session and in analytic process as prognostic and developmental indicators, based on Fairbairn's developmental schema of the developmental evolution of dependence.

Just as Fairbairn did, we constantly compare his model to the Freudian drive model and sometimes to M. Klein's, with the guidance of Kuhn's principle of comparison of theories (all respond to the same paradigm of the Freudian unconscious) and Bohr's principle of theoretical complementarity, using as intermediary hypothesis schizoid conflict and the psychic units that originate from it: splitting (Masterson, Kernberg), object relations (Hamilton) and building blocks (Kernberg) (cf. our chapter on "Fairbairn and Emptiness Pathology", page 223). In this way, these models may be articulated without amalgamation, as in Kernberg.

We apply Fairbairn's model as well as contributions of his disciples (H. Guntrip & J. Sutherland) and of contemporary authors of Fairbairnian orientation (O. Kernberg, T. Ogden, J. Grotstein, D. & J. Scharff, G. Clarke, and others) to clinical material of interviews and patient sessions (especially psychotic patients and patients with severe personality disorders) from the private and hospital practice of members of the Fairbairn Space.

In the Fairbairn Space, like Fairbairn, we use the development of ambivalence—a marker of intrapsychic structural change—as an indicator of analytic process, adding the object situation and comparing the developmental levels of ego and object relationship in clinical material, as Freud (1915c) aspired to do.

Elda Irungaray, psychologist and psychoanalyst, associate member of the APA, who works in the Department of Family Violence and Abuse in the Pedro de Elizalde Children's Hospital, studied sexual abuse in clinical material by applying the Fairbairn model. She considered sexual abuse a special and specific type of object relationship, a manoeuvre and psychological technique inherent to the transitional stage, for abuser and abused to obtain a transitional object and to be with a bad object and defend against separation-abandonment anxieties.

This was extrapolated by Adrián Ventura, who works in the Department of Pathology of Eating Behaviour in the José T. Borda Psychiatric Hospital, to the pathologies he treats.

The same extrapolation was applied by Ernesto Aguirre, psychologist and professor of occupational psychology at the UBA, to disorders in connection with harassment, mobbing, and bullying.

Luis Oswald, psychologist and psychoanalyst, an associate member of the APA and secretary of the Fairbairn Space, who works at the National Academy of Science, found support within mythology for the topics studied; for example, the myth of Medusa provided a ground for the attribution of universality to schizoid conflict.

In collaboration with Adrián Besucchio, MD, psychiatrist, forensic and legal physician, an associate member of the APA, we studied homicide (for example, murderers and serial rapists) and arrived at the same conclusions found by our colleagues, Ventura, Irungaray, and Aguirre. At that juncture, Daniel Cichello, psychiatrist and director of the Penitentiary Service of the José T. Borda Psychiatric Hospital, joined us and provided more clinical material.

We now receive cases from the Supreme Court and the Criminal Appeals Court, which we study psychoanalytically for the purpose of providing parameters of non-imputability and imputability; we also work with material of cases of tendency to suicide and accidents and addiction to gambling.

From the above description we derive a new cluster of mental illnesses based on exclusively psychoanalytic criteria, which was the theme of a workshop presented at the 47th IPA Congress. It was praised, for example, by Antonio Santamaría, an eminent Mexican psychoanalyst. Graham Clarke and Paul Finnegan honoured us with their presence.

This cluster gathers a group of illnesses whose common denominator is the clinical expression of a distressing and failed attempt to solve schizoid conflict by recovering the object relationship or link by means of omnipotent control of the object.

We postulate that psychic units intervene in this mechanism determining the modes of restitution and therefore clinical forms in the material, assembling the quality of the lost object through restitution.

We thereby end the old debate concerning what it is that determines the clinical form in borderline personality organisation: the quality of the loss of the lost object (Gunderson, Basili) or restitution (Blum, Rolla). We find that it is both, since the quality of the lost object determines the mode of restitution.

Mercedes Campi, psychiatrist and psychoanalyst, associate member and professor of seminars of the APA, finds traces of Fairbairn in Ogden. We continue to consider whether Fairbairn is a continuer of Freud's work or whether he contributes a new psychoanalytic metapsychology, that of object relations. In Campi's view, psychoanalysis has only one metapsychology, which is the method by which mental phenomena are analysed: the topographic, the dynamic (which subsumes the economic), the structural, the genetic, and, with Fairbairn, we add the adaptive (M. Gill & D. Rapaport, 1962). This was Kernberg's opinion in the early years of his works (Greenberg & Mitchell, 1983); however, at Lisbon (1999) he maintained, as did David E. Scharff, that there are two metapsychologies: the Freudian and the Fairbairnian.

María Cristina Milite, psychologist, psychoanalyst and associate member of the APA, contributed her experience with the battered wife syndrome. She lived and worked in a refuge house in Colonna, Italy, and extrapolated her experience by founding two refuge houses in Argentina.

She studied battered women as a phenomenon of interaction; the batterer and the battered (transitional objects) exert omnipotent control over each other. When this control is in danger of being lost or is actually lost, the beating emerges in order to recover it and to defend against separation-abandonment anxieties. She also points out the importance of isolating the patient, for instance in a refuge house, from factors that might activate schizoid conflict, and the need to file an official criminal complaint, which must occur immediately, especially when minors are involved.

Basili with Susan Pedernera, psychiatrist and training psychoanalyst of the APA, studied the psychic units that originate and are originated in schizoid conflict. These are intermediate hypotheses which led to the formulation of a general metapsychological hypothesis for all borderline pathology that was presented at several congresses.

Campi proposed that in psychic units, the ego (in the manner of Glover's 1932 model) is the "globe with little globes", the "little globes" being platforms for the take-off and landing of object losses and their restitutions, respectively; in this way, the object and the relationship with the object (the link or bridge) are connected to this or that "little globe", thereby accomplishing a Fairbairnian aspiration.

Acknowledgments

We express our gratitude to all the members of the Fairbairn Space, especially Nora Frid, María Cristina Gay, Zulema Díaz, Luis Barbero, Susana Pedernera, María Cristina Milite, and Celeste Tarrio for their valuable critiques; also to Mariano Iusim for his technical assistance, and also to Joaquín Miño for his impeccable assistance in English.

References

Baranger, W. (1976). *Posición y Objeto en la Obra de Melanie Klein*. Buenos Aires, Argentina: Kargieman.

Baranger, W., Zac de Goldstein, R., Merea, E. C., Mom, J. M., Resnicoff, B., Ricón, L., Del Campo, Romano, & Schull. (1980). *Aportaciones al Concepto de Objeto en Psicoanálisis*. Buenos Aires, Argentina: Amorrortu.

Basili, R. M. (1990a). Utilidad del diagnóstico psicoanalítico en el tratamiento de las personalidades narcisistas graves. Nuestra experiencia clínica. *Revisión Psicoanalítica*, 47(1): 153–176. Céles Cárcamo Prize, Argentine Psychoanalytic Association.

Basili, R. M. (1990b). Desarrollos en las escuelas psicoanalíticas británicas sobre las personalidades narcisistas graves. Nuestra experiencia. *Revisión Psicoanalítica*, 47(5/6): 1087–1112.

Basili, R. M. (1990c). Obituario: Juan José Morgan. *Revisión Psicoanalítica*, 47(4): 820–821.

Basili, R. M. (1992). Psicopatología mahleriana contemporánea de los cuadros limítrofes y desamparo, trauma psíquico y defecto yoico. In: B. Dorfman Lerner (Ed.), *Pacientes Limítrofes. Diagnóstico y Tratamiento* (pp. 35–46). Buenos Aires, Argentina: Lugar.

Basili, R. M., & Echegaray, E. (1995). Escuela inglesa. In: G. Vidal, R. Alarcón, & F. Lolas Stepke (Eds.), *Enciclopedia Iberoamericana de Psiquiatría, Tomo III* (pp. 1249–1252). Bogota, Colombia: Médica Panamericana.

Basili, R. M., Montero, G. J., & Sharpin de Basili, I. (2002). Conceptualización y tipificación psicoanalíticas de los trastornos narcisistas (en sentido estricto). Dos tipos de idealización (primitiva). *Revisión Psicoanalítica*, 59(3): 581–613.

Basili, R. M., & Sharpin de Basili, I. (2003). Eros y Tánatos en conflicto de diambivalencia: Su trabajo y desarrollo en la relación de objeto. Aplicabilidad en pacientes graves. *Revisión Psicoanalítica, 60*(2): 395–425.

Basili, R. M., & Sharpin de Basili, I. (2005). Fairbairn's theory and borderline pathology, and schizoid conflict. In: J. S. Scharff & D. E. Scharff (Eds.), *The Legacy of Fairbairn and Sutherland: Psychotherapeutic Applications* (pp. 129–139). London: Routledge.

Basili, R. M., Sharpin de Basili, I., Besuschio, A., Campi, M., Oswald, L., & Tarrio, A. (2011). El analista como instrumento de la cura y no cura. *Revisión Psicoanalítica, 67*(4): 845–857.

Bateman, A., & Fonagy, P. (2004). *Psychotherapy for Borderline Personality Disorder. Mentalization-based Treatment*. London: Oxford University Press.

Bleger, J. (1967). *Simbiosis y ambigüedad*. Buenos Aires, Argentina: Paidós.

Bowlby, J. (1969). *Attachment and Loss: Volume I*. London: Hogarth.

Brenner, C. (1962). *The Mind in Conflict*. New York: International Universities Press. [La mente en conflicto. Madrid, Spain: Technipublicaciones, 1989.]

Celani, D. (1993). *The Treatment of the Borderline Patient: Applying Fairbairn's Object Relations Theory in the Clinical Setting*. Madison, CT: International Universities Press.

Fainstein, A. (2005). Personal communication to Dr Basili.

Fairbairn, W. R. D. (1952). *Psychoanalytic Studies of the Personality*. London: Tavistock. [Estudio Psicoanalítico de la Personalidad. Buenos Aires, Argentina: Hormé, 1970, 3rd edition.]

Fairbairn, W. R. D. (1963a). Synopsis of an object-relations theory of the personality. *International Journal of Psychoanalysis, 44*: 224–225. In: D. E. Scharff & E. F. Birtles (Eds.), *From Instinct to Self: Selected Papers of W. R. D. Fairbairn, Volume I: Clinical and Theoretical Papers* (pp. 155–156). Northvale, NJ: Jason Aronson, 1994.

Fonagy, P., & Target, M. (2003). *Psychoanalytic Theories. Perspectives from Developmental Psychopathology*. London: Whurr.

Freud, S. (1905d). *Three Essays on the Theory of Sexuality. S. E., 7*. London: Hogarth.

Freud, S. (1914c). On narcissism: an introduction. *S. E., 14*. London: Hogarth.

Freud, S. (1915c). Instincts and their vicissitudes. *S. E., 14*. London: Hogarth.

Freud, S. (1917e). Mourning and melancholia. *S. E., 14*. London: Hogarth.

Freud, S. (1920g). *Beyond the Pleasure Principle. S. E., 18*. London: Hogarth.

Freud, S. (1923b). *The Ego and the Id. S. E., 19*. London: Hogarth.

Freud, S. (1926d). *Inhibitions, Symptoms and Anxiety. S. E., 20*. London: Hogarth.

Freud, S. (1940a). *An Outline of Psychoanalysis. S. E., 23*. London: Hogarth.

Freud, S. (1950a). project for a scientific psychology. *S. E., 1*. London: Hogarth.

Garma, A. (1979). *Nuevas Aportaciones al Psicoanálisis de los Sueños*. Buenos Aires, Argentina: Paidós.

Gill, M., & Rapaport, D. (1962). *Aportaciones a la Teoría y Técnica Psicoanalítica*. Mexico: Pax-Mexico, Librería C. Cesarman, S. A. Asociación Psicoanalítica Mexicana A.C.

Glover, E. (1932). A psychoanalytic approach to the classification of mental disorders. In: *On the Early Development of Mind*. New York: International Universities Press, 1956.

Greenberg, J. R., & Mitchell, S. A. (1983). *Object Relations in Psychoanalytic Theory*. Cambridge, MA: Harvard University Press.

Gunderson, J. (2001). *Borderline Personality Disorder. A Clinical Guide*. Washington, DC: American Psychiatric Publishing.

Guntrip, H. (1961). *Personality Structure and Human Interaction: The Developing Synthesis of Psychodynamic Theory*. London: Hogarth.

Hughes, J. (1990). *Researching the Psychoanalytic Domain. The Work of Melanie Klein, W. R. D. Fairbairn and D. W. Winnicott*. Berkeley, CA: University of California Press.
Kernberg, O. F. (1984). *Severe Personality Disorders*. New Haven, CT: Yale University Press.
Kernberg, O. F. (1992). *Aggression in Personality Disorders and Perversion*. Madison, CT: International Universities Press. [La Agresión en las Perversiones y en los Desórdenes de la Personalidad. Buenos Aires, Argentina: Paidós, 1994.]
Kernberg, O. F. (1999). The relevance of Fairbairn´s formulations for contemporary object relations theory and psychoanalytical practice. Presented at the International Conference, "Fairbairn and Relational Theory Today", Lisbon, 28–31 October.
Klein, M. (1977). *The Collected Writings of Melanie Klein*. London: Hogarth. [Obras Completas. Buenos Aires, Argentina: Paidós.]
Lewin, K. (1978). *La Teoría del Campo en las Ciencias Sociales*. Buenos Aires, Argentina: Paidós.
Liberman, D. (1962). *La Comunicación en Terapéutica Psicoanalítica*. Buenos Aires, Argentina: EUdeBA.
Mahler, M. (1971). A study of separation individuation process and its possible application to the borderline phenomena. *Psychoanalytic Study of the Child, 26*: 403–424.
McWilliams, N. (1994). *Psychoanalytic Diagnosis. Understanding Personality Structure in the Clinical Process*. New York: Guilford Press.
Montero, G. J. (2000). Personal communication to Dr Basili.
Piaget, J. (1974). Le structuralisme. Paris: Presses Universitaires de France. [El estructuralismo. Barcelona, Spain: Oikos-Tau, 1974.]
Racker, H. (1948). Sobre un caso de impotencia, asma y conducta masoquística. *Revisión Psicoanalítica, 5*(3): 578–627.
Racker, H. (1969). *Estudios sobre Técnica Psicoanalítica*. Buenos Aires, Argentina: Paidós.
Sharpin de Basili, I. (1990). El concepto "mutar" en psicoanálisis: ¿Transformación en sentido estructural? [bibliographic review]. "Ángel Garma" Institute of Psychoanalysis, Argentine Psychoanalytic Association.
Skolnick, N., & Scharff, D. E. (1998). *Fairbairn, Then and Now*. Hillsdale, NJ: The Analytic Press.
Strachey, J. (1934). Naturaleza de la acción terapéutica del psicoanálisis. *Revisión Psicoanalítica, 5*(4): 1947–1948.
Sutherland, J. D. (1989). *Fairbairn´s Journey into the Interior*. London: Free Association.
Thomä, H., & Kächele, H. (1985). *Lehrbuch der psychoanalytischen Therapie, Band 1. Grundlagen*. Berlin: Springer-Verlag. [Teoría y práctica del psicoanálisis. I. Fundamentos. Barcelona, Spain: Herder, 1990.]
Thomä, H., & Kächele, H. (1988). *Lehrbuch der psychoanalytischen Therapie, Band 2. Praxis*. Berlin: Springer-Verlag. [Teoría y práctica del psicoanálisis. II. Estudios Clínicos. Barcelona, Spain: Herder, 1990.]
Tyson, P., & Tyson, R. (1993). *The Psychoanalytic Theories of Development: An Integration*. New Haven, CT: Yale University Press. [Teorías Psicoanalíticas del Desarrollo: Una Integración. Lima, Peru: Publicaciones Psicoanalíticas.]
Winnicott, D. W. (1958). *Collected Papers: Through Paediatrics to Psycho-Analysis*. London: Hogarth. [Escritos de Pediatría y Psicoanálisis. 1931–1956, 1981.]
Winnicott, D. W. (1971). *Playing and Reality*. London: Tavistock. [Realidad y Juego. Buenos Aires, Argentina: Granica.]

CHAPTER NINE

Some comments about Ronald Fairbairn's impact today

Otto F. Kernberg

Our field owes its understanding of developmental stages and characterological organisation of the personality to Fairbairn's theory of the dyadic nature of the internalisation of self and object representations, linked by an affective valence, as the basic building blocks of the psychic apparatus.

From relative isolation in Edinburgh in the 1930s and 1940s, his work nonetheless had a profound impact on the Independent Group (Middle Group) of the British Psychoanalytical Society. Preceding Edith Jacobson's (1964) contributions by many years, and from different clinical and theoretical assumptions, he and she each reached similar conclusions, Jacobson within her own developmental approach to the internalisation of object relations in the formation of psychic structures. It says something about the intensity of the mutual distrust of the British schools, Melanie Klein, Winnicott, and Fairbairn, on the one hand, and the ego psychological approaches of Anna Freud and the corresponding North American ego psychological approach, on the other (Kernberg, 1969, 2004b) that Fairbairn, within the former, and Jacobson, within the latter, never gave any evidence in their writings of acknowledging each other's work.

Elsewhere, I have summarised Fairbairn's main contributions (Kernberg, 1976). Here, I wish to highlight the most salient consequences of his basic theory of the fundamental splitting of a primary, pristine ego into three segments: the repressed segment of the "exciting object" and the "libidinal ego" (self), the "anti-libidinal object" and the corresponding "anti-libidinal ego", and the "central ego" and its relation to the "ideal object" or ego ideal. Although these structures do not correspond exactly to Freud's ego, superego, and id, they reflect Fairbairn's attempt to explain the overall structural organisation of the mind. He saw the mind as constituted by component internalised object relations, a fundamental formulation of psychoanalytic object relations theory that, together with Melanie Klein's contributions (1946, 1975) and later on, Jacobson's work, has become the organising structure of contemporary psychoanalysis.

One important aspect of Fairbairn's formulations, however, remains debatable despite wide acceptance and refinement by the American relational approach (Kernberg, 2012). His proposal that *only* libido is a source of instinctual energy and motivation, and, then, only insofar as it coincides with the inborn disposition for object seeking, rejects Freud's concept of the death drive: the inborn nature of an aggressive drive. Fairbairn saw aggression as secondary to frustrating and traumatising early experiences, and believed that such negative experiences, the aetiological roots of the development of aggression, would lead to the organisation of the anti-libidinal segment of emotional experience, which he termed the *anti-libidinal object* and the *anti-libidinal ego*. In practice, Fairbairn analysed the profound conflicts between libido and aggression at all developmental levels: in his technical approach, he was closer to Freud than in his theoretical statement.

In earlier work, I have referred to contemporary biological instinct theory and neurobiological science (Kernberg, 1992) that have provided evidence of the development of neurobiological dispositions to both attachment and erotic engagements, on the one hand, and to activation of aggression in relation to territoriality, parental defence of the young, and sexual competition, on the other. In other words, I believe that there are inborn dispositions of both positive affective, dependent, and erotic longings and specific attachment to others, but also to hostile, destructive impulses to self and others under different organismic and psychosocial conditions. But these critical considerations regarding Fairbairn's basic motivational systems theory should not detract from his original contributions in signalling the development of a libidinal, idealised, "all-good" segment of experience dissociated or split off from an aversive, punishing, "all bad" one, both of them in sharp contrast with the nature of a central self relating to an ego ideal or an ideal object.

The Fairbairnian's understanding of unconscious conflicts as always between contradictory, idealised/exciting and punishing/persecutory internalised object relations has fundamental implications for psychoanalytic and psychotherapeutic technique. It means that, in the transference, the activation of an unconscious conflict around a particular impulse emerges not as a reflection of an impersonal impulse/defence matrix, but rather as impulse and defensive operations expressed as the activation of internalised object representations relating to corresponding defensive or impulsive self and other representations. The conflict takes place *between* contradictory internalised object relations, and, at any particular point, may be expressed as the activation of a determined object relation acting as a defence against an opposite one, while, at another point, that opposite one may act as a defence against the first one. For example, a patient with a fearful, submissive attitude towards authorities enacts a defensive relationship between a self-representation that is fearful and inhibited to assure himself of maintaining the relationship with a dominating, but potentially benign object, in contrast to the opposite experience of rage and rebellion, the impulsive, aggressive self, in relating to a sadistic, punishing object.

This formulation regarding the object relations dyads of both impulse and defence becomes particularly relevant in the psychoanalytic approach to borderline personality organisation. Here, transference focused psychotherapy (TFP) (Clarkin, Yeomans, & Kernberg, 2006) has made a significant contribution in the treatment of patients with severe personality disorders. Under conditions of severe regression or primitive mental organisation characteristic of identity diffusion, there is a predominance of split-off, idealised, and persecutory internalised object relations, and a developmental failure to achieve a "central self" through integration of internalised self and object representations. In these cases, the activation of a particular object relation in the transference may rapidly alternate in the role distribution between patient and therapist: while, at one point, an object representation is projected onto the therapist, and the patient identifies with the corresponding self-representation of that dyad, ten minutes later the same relationship may be activated with role reversal, that is, the projection onto the therapist of the patient's self-representation, while the patient identifies with the corresponding object representation of this dyad.

This crucial aspect of transference developments with severe personality disorders (borderline personality organization), permits the analysis in depth of the patient's dominant internalised object relationships. The patient becomes able, as a consequence of the interpretation of this transference, to identify in sequence consciously with both the self and the object representation of a particular dyad, which facilitates the acceptance and consciousness of all the implications of that dyadic relationship. It brings about the resolution of the need to project temporarily the intolerable representation of self or other, and the possibility for interpretation and integration of opposite internalised object relationships split from each other. This fosters the development of integration of the self, and the integration of the representations of significant others, that is, normal ego identity.

The lack of communication between Fairbairn's (1954a) and Erikson's (1956) work, again related to the profound divide between British and American schools in the 1950s through the 1970s, may have precluded the psychoanalytic community from becoming aware of the significant implications of their respective contributions for each other's development of the structural model. Fairbairn advanced in the direction of relating the internalisation of object relations to the gradual development of the tripartite structure of the mind, be it with somewhat different characteristics and fundamental theoretical assumptions than Freud. Erikson, in his model of the development of introjections, leading to identifications, and, eventually to ego identity, missed the utilisation of Fairbairn's contributions to early development in the analysis. Fairbairn's dyadic structure naturally signalled their progressive advance in the establishment of ego identity and the internalised world of object relations. Fairbairn also contributed to the study of the early development of the superego in his description of the "moral defence", that is, the tendency to submit unconsciously to a punishing, sadistically perceived object while accepting blame and guilt as caused by the self, in order to maintain the relationship between an intensely needed and ambivalently loved and hated object.

Fairbairn's phrase, "It is better to be a sinner in a world ruled by God than to live in a world ruled by the Devil," points to this basic mechanism of submission to a sadistic superego as an important component of masochistic pathology, and explains a particular aspect of advanced stages of psychoanalytic treatment in which profound levels of superego pathology would emerge in the transference. In his conception of the id as not constituted by disorganised, chaotic impulses, but by deeply repressed exciting and punishing, intolerable internalised object relations, he pointed to the object related structure of the id, as well as to that of the other psychic structures. Id, ego, and superego now could be conceptualised as representing specialised build-ups of internalised object relations derived structures.

A fundamental implication of Fairbairn's view of the construction of the internal world is that all identifications are really identifications with a relationship and not with a particular object. This view has fundamental implications for the very concept of the processes of identification in health and illness, for example, in the process of mourning, as I have suggested elsewhere (Kernberg, 2010). Fairbairn's object relations theory also provided him with an original approach to the analysis of dreams, in the sense of conceptualising various characters that emerge in the dream as different representations of objects as well as of the self, and the possibility that the self, as well as any particular object, may be represented simultaneously in various characters and interactions of a dream, reflecting different aspects of their respective affective investments. Dream analysis, for Fairbairn, becomes an important investigative tool for the activation of unconscious internalised object relations.

A crucial contribution to Fairbairn's theoretical frame has been provided by John Sutherland (1994), who in 1963 was the first to spell out that, in Fairbairn's model, implicitly all the relations between self and object are characterised by a particular affective valence, and that it is the affective investment of the relationship between self and object that determines the dynamic placement, the integration, or dissociation of various object relations within the intrapsychic life. Sutherland's introduction of the role of affects in determining the valence of the internalisation of the relationship between self and object contributed fundamentally, in my view, to increasing the power of structural analysis, deriving the overall intrapsychic structures from component internalised dyadic building blocks. For Fairbairn, the investment of the self in libidinal relations with significant others constituted, in itself, the nature of libido. Sutherland pointed to the fact that this striving towards objects implied an affective investment, and that, in fact, both libidinal and "anti-libidinal" internalised relationships were dominated, respectively, by positive and negative affect states.

Contemporary affect theory was only in its beginning at the time when Fairbairn, and even Sutherland, developed their theoretical frames. Affects, until the 1920s, were considered as peripheral discharge phenomena. Only after the work of Joyce McDougall and Cannon (1927) were they recognised as central, subjective states, and in the light of later, more advanced biological science, as basic motivational systems moving the organism towards the search for gratifying objects, and away from frustrating or traumatising ones (Kernberg, 2004a). At a still later stage of development, in the 1960s, the work of Silvan Tomkins (1970) pointed to the communicative functions of affect activation, the central role that facial expression played in this communicative function throughout the entire mammalian species, including primates and the human person. The application of Tomkins's findings to human interactions by Paul Ekman (1972; Ekman & Friessen, 1978) and, in the 1980s and 1990s by Rainer Krause (1988, 1990), systematically relating psychopathology with particular affective communication disturbances, consolidated the contemporary understanding of the central role of affective communication in the development of empathy and in psychotherapeutic interactions intuitively grasped in Fairbairn's and Sutherland's earlier work.

This contemporary understanding implies that affects, in their original function, are fundamental signals of the state of the organism and the experience of the immediate sensory perceptive impact of the environment, and communicate to the caregiver the organismic needs that the individual—the infant—cannot satisfy by himself. Affects, in short, may constitute the most basic neurobiological and psychological motivational system. I have suggested in earlier work that Freud's dual drive theory of libido and aggression may be considered as the hierarchically supraordinate integration, respectively, of positive, libidinal, and negative, aggressive affects (Kernberg, 2006).

Fairbairn's theory implicitly links temperamental affective dispositions with the activation of object relations first, and the development of internalised psychic structures as a consequence, later. These internalisations, initially consisting of positive and negative dyadic object relations, eventually become more nuanced by the tolerance of triadic relations, the tolerance of the position of an "excluded third party", which, psychologically, corresponds to the development of the Oedipal situation. Finally, the organisation of superego, ego, and id as overall psychic structures complements and contrasts with the development of an integrated sense of self and an integrated view of significant others, the "central ego", or identity formation. In this regard, Erikson's contributions to the development of ego identity on the basis of early introjections and identifications fits harmoniously into Fairbairn's fundamental psychic structures, as does Jacobson's analysis of the successive layers of internalised demands and prohibitions, linked to idealised and persecutory object relations, that would constitute the superego.

As mentioned before, Fairbairn's fundamental contributions did not influence, as far as we know, the development of the theoretical formulations of Erik Erikson and Edith Jacobson, whose ego psychologically based object relations approach complemented, and would have been enriched by such an integrative endeavour. Fairbairn significantly influenced, however, the early contributors to the relational psychoanalytic school. This included the intersubjective, interpersonal, and self psychological approaches to psychoanalysis, all of which adopted his fundamental thesis that mind was object related from the start, and evinced a fundamental aspiration of the self towards integration, relationships, and attachment, and rejected Freud's dual drive theory, particularly the concept of the death drive.

In this regard, it is remarkable that Fairbairn, on the one hand, influenced the interpersonal motivation emphasis of the relational school, while, on the other, he stimulated the conceptual linkage of the internalised dyadic object relations with the activation of basic affects as a primary motivational system. Thus, the development of intrapsychic life is linked to object relations, but also to the neurobiologically determined activation of affects, and the related basic motivational systems studied in affective neuroscience, namely, attachment, separation-panic, eroticism, play-bonding, and fight-flight (Panksepp, 1998). In short, a relation between neurobiology, behavioural motivation, intrapsychic structures, and interpersonal experiences is thus established within an extremely creative and promising model of psychic development, organisation, and psychopathology.

Fairbairn applied his theoretical model to the study of significant clinical aspects of the psychoanalytic situation, particularly dream analysis, and the "moral defence". Regarding the analysis of dreams, in his clinical case studies, Fairbairn illustrated, as mentioned before, the activation of representations of the self and others in the various characters emerging in the dream content, and illustrated how split aspects of the self might be represented by different persons in the dream content, while ambivalent object relations may be represented by multiple appearances of the same object representations under contrasting affective relationships with the self. This analysis permitted him to relate manifest dream content and the corresponding latent dream material more directly within the context of the dominant transference developments.

Fairbairn's described the "moral defence" as a submission to sadistic superego demands reflecting the internalisation of persecutory, "anti-libidinal" aspects of the parental images. This submission reflected the patient's wishes to maintain a relationship with bad objects, with an effort to take over the responsibility for their badness in the form of guilt feelings and related anti-libidinal repression of the desired exciting aspects of object relations. While rejecting the theory of an inborn death drive, Fairbairn was acutely aware of the prevalent unconscious identification with internalised persecutory objects and the need to interpret them in the transference, very much influenced in this regard by Melanie Klein's observations of the nature of early object relations, and the primitive defensive operations reflecting conflictual developments in the baby's relation to mother and mother's breasts. Fairbairn's accent on the infant's earliest love for mother, and the dread of mother's rejection or indifference were an important aspect of his general stress of the earliest maternal relationship. This stress was very much in contrast to the then predominant accent in psychoanalytic studies on the relationship to father in the Oedipal situation, highlighted by Freud.

From a general technical viewpoint, Fairbairn's formulation of the nature of early internalised object relations in the constellations of dyadic relations between self and object representations has acquired particular importance in the psychoanalytic treatment and specialised psychoanalytic psychotherapies dealing with severe personality disorders, the patients with severe identity diffusion that constitute the spectrum of borderline personality organisation (Kernberg, 1975). While Melanie Klein described the characteristics of the archaic internalised object relations activated in the transferences of these patients, Fairbairn's approach specified that the activation of these relations always manifests itself in the transference as dyadic units that reflect a specific, affectively framed relation between one aspect of the self and one particular object representation.

He established the groundwork, on the basis of which, we, at the Personality Disorders Institute at Weill Cornell Medical College were able to develop a specific psychotherapeutic approach (Clarkin, Yeomans, & Kernberg, 1999). We found that, under conditions of clear predominance of splitting mechanisms and primitive transferences, the activated dyadic units of self and object representations tended to rapidly reverse or alternate in the respective enactment of self and object representations by patient and therapist. By means of projective identification, the patient alternatively projects these two polarities of the activated internalised object relation onto the therapist. Correspondent activation of these representations by complementary countertransference identifications facilitates the interpretation of these developments. In other words, under such regressive conditions, the same object relation is activated with therapist and patient interchanging the respective identification with self and object representations. Now, transference and countertransference reflect, respectively, the enactment of the corresponding affective experiences and interactional roles, facilitating the interpretation of the total object relation by utilising countertransference developments and in-depth clarification and interpretation of the nature of the transference. Henry Dicks (1967) described the manifestation of this same tendency of regression to early dyadic units in couples' long-term, intimate relationships. This regressive development emerges in all long-term couples at points of acute interpersonal conflicts and marital crises, but becomes a dominant feature in severe, chronic marital conflicts. Dicks applied Fairbairn's theoretical understanding to the psychoanalytic diagnosis and psychotherapeutic resolution of severe marital conflicts, a major application of psychoanalytic theory and technique to couple therapy, to which I shall return below.

Fairbairn also contributed to the understanding of the psychopathology of severe personality disorders in his original description of the clinical features and underlying structural characteristics of the schizoid personality disorder. He considered this disorder to be the prototype of a severe splitting off of the central ego and its ideal object from the repressed, subordinate areas of the anti-libidinal object and the anti-libidinal ego on the one hand, and from the exciting libidinal object and its corresponding libidinal ego, on the other. The Kleinian School, particularly Rosenfeld (1964, 1978) and J. Steiner (1993) and our own contributions to the understanding of the structural development of the narcissistic personality disorder and the nature of narcissistic transferences (Kernberg, 1989), further amplified the field of specific pathological structures derived from the internalisation of early object relations. Scharff and Scharff (1987) further integrated and developed various aspects of Fairbairn's theoretical contributions to the contemporary psychodynamic psychotherapy of couples, and the therapeutic and educational application of the psychodynamic of group processes.

One might summarise contemporary developments in the general field of psychoanalytic interventions, in stating the following: unconscious conflicts at the neurotic level of intrapsychic organisation—under conditions of normal identity integration—facilitate standard psychoanalytic treatment. In contrast, fixation or regression to a level of identity diffusion—with loss or failure of normal identity integration—activates the dominance of splitting mechanisms and the corresponding primitive dyadic self representation-object representation units. Clinically, rapid reversals of patients' identifications with self or object, projecting the other, complementary representation onto the therapist, actualise these dyadic units in the transference of severe psychopathologies. Here the therapist helps the patient understand and gradually integrate dyadic units with extreme, opposite affective valences. By the same token, the therapist acquires the function of an "excluded third party". By means of his/her interpretative interventions, he/she reopens the field of development towards triangulation and of the Oedipal situation for patients caught up in conflictual primitive, dyadic situations.

Perhaps the most important, secondary complication of these regressive conditions is the particular condensation of a pathological grandiose self, characteristic of narcissistic pathology. Here real and idealised representations of self and others become condensed in a pathologically condensed self-concept that implies a parallel devaluation of real and idealised representations of significant others, and a consequent impoverishment of the development of advanced ego and superego functions. The interpretative dismantling of this pathological grandiose self is the first, crucial step in the treatment of narcissistic pathology that exposes and reactivates the underlying borderline organisation and permits its interpretative exploration and resolution. In all cases the treatment is geared to facilitate the integration of the normal self, of ego identity, and, as Fairbairn stressed, the shift from infantile dependency and corresponding conflicts to a mature capacity for dependency and intimacy with significant others, together with a mature capacity for autonomy and independence.

Fairbairn explored the function of sexual intimacy both as an expression of the search for intimate relations and as a potential pathological, defensive development. In stressing the role of sexual intimacy linked to tenderness as a sublimatory integration of the exciting libidinal impulse with the capacity for normal, gratifying dependency, he implicitly pointed to the object relations implications of both attachment and the erotic drives. But he also observed the pathological replacement of intimate relations by a compulsive search for sexual gratification, and considered that such compulsive sexuality becomes observable in sexual promiscuity and the perversions, and reflects important limitations in the capacity for optimal object relations. These limitations, in the last resort, derive from the excessive splitting off of the exciting and the anti-libidinal segments of experience, with an impoverishment of the central self in its relation to an ideal object. That reflects a schizoid solution to the conflicts around the impossibility of love, rather than an excessive repression of sexual needs under the influence of the anti-libidinal segment of experience.

In applying Fairbairn's approach to the study of marital conflicts, Henry Dicks (1967) investigated the dominant unconscious conflictual relationships with the parental objects on the part of both partners, and their unconscious collusion in enacting past, unconscious conflicts in their present interaction. In chronic marital conflicts, both participants activate their corresponding, dominant unresolved object relation with a parental object, and unconsciously tend to induce, by projective identification, the corresponding behaviour in their partner. This represents an effort to reactivate and repeat a past unresolved traumatic conflict in the present, with the powerful motivation to correct it in the present marital relationship. In other words, Fairbairn referred to a couple's shared repetition compulsion, with the unconscious wish to re-encounter the good object behind the activation of the relationship with the bad one, or rather, the transformation of the bad object into a good one and thus resolving the traumatic situation. Obviously, in chronic marital conflicts, the unconscious collusion in the reciprocal activation of dominant past conflicts may fail in its objective, and repetition compulsion creates its own regressive pressures over the relationship of the couple.

In Dicks's therapeutic approach to the resolution of severe, chronic marital conflict, the analytic exploration of the unconscious meaning of the dominant conflict of the couple would lead to the understanding of the conflicts lying behind the repetition compulsion, and the possibility of the mature segments of the personality of both partners to work through and resolve this pathological regression. Henry Dicks's approach to marital conflict also benefitted from Fairbairn's exploration of the development of severe negative transference reactions in advanced stages of the analytic treatment, reflecting the activation of profound levels of the relationship between anti-libidinal object and the anti-libidinal self in their repressive function directed against the libidinal self and a good object relationship. This development demands the working through of repetition compulsion in the transference, importantly influenced at that point by the activation of the "moral defence" in advanced stages of the treatment.

I trust that I have conveyed the importance of Fairbairn's contributions to the contemporary development of psychoanalytic object relations theory, the most fundamental modification of the original metapsychology proposed by Freud. His work constitutes an enrichment of the general theory, of the psychoanalytic understanding of the psychopathology of the personality, and of psychoanalytic technique, in addition to opening up applications to derivative psychoanalytic psychotherapy approaches with severe personality disorders. Fairbairn has deepened our understanding and psychoanalytic approaches to group processes, including group analytic therapy and the psychoanalytic exploration of marital, as well as organisational dynamics, and ideological superstructures of group processes.

References

Cannon, W. B. (1927). The James-Lange theory of emotions: a critical examination and an alternative theory. *American Journal of Psychoanalysis, 39*: 106–124.

Clarkin, J. F., Yeomans, F. E., & Kernberg, O. F. (1999). *Psychotherapy for Borderline Personality*. New York: John Wiley & Sons.

Clarkin, J. F., Yeomans, F. E., & Kernberg, O. F. (2006). *Psychotherapy for Borderline Personality: Focusing on Object Relations*. Washington, DC: American Psychiatric Publishing.

Dicks, H. V. (1967). *Marital Tensions*. London: Routledge & Kegan Paul.

Ekman, P. (1972). Universal and cultural differences in facial expression of emotion. In: J. R. Cole (Ed.), *Nebraska Symposium on Motivation* (*Vol. 19*). Lincoln, NE: University of Nebraska.

Ekman, P., & Friessen, W. V. (1978). *Facial Action Coding System*. Palo Alto, CA: Consulting Psychologists Press.

Erikson, E. H. (1956). The problem of ego identity. In: *Identity and the Life Cycle* (pp. 101–164). New York, International Universities Press.

Fairbairn, W. R. D. (1954a). *An Object-relations Theory of the Personality*. New York: Basic.

Jacobson, E. (1964). *The Self and the Object World*. New York: International Universities Press.

Kernberg, O. F. (1969). A contribution to the ego-psychological critique of the Kleinian School. *International Journal of Psychoanalysis, 50*: 317–333.

Kernberg, O. F. (1975). *Borderline Conditions and Pathological Narcissism*. New York: Jason Aronson.

Kernberg, O. F. (1976). *Object Relations Theory and Clinical Psychoanalysis*. New York: Jason Aronson.

Kernberg, O. F. (1989). *Narcissistic Personality Disorder*. Guest Editor: Psychiatric Clinics of North America. Vol. 12, No. 3. Philadelphia, PA: W. B. Saunders..

Kernberg, O. F. (1992). *Aggression in Personality Disorders and Perversion*. New Haven, CT: Yale University Press.

Kernberg, O. F. (2004a). *Contemporary Controversies in Psychoanalytic Theory, Technique and Their Applications*. New Haven, CT: Yale University Press.

Kernberg, O. F. (2004b). *Aggressivity, Narcissism and Self-destructiveness in the Psychotherapeutic Relationship: New Developments in the Psychopathology and Psychotherapy of Severe Personality Disorders*. New Haven, CT: Yale University Press.

Kernberg, O. F. (2006). Psychoanalytic sffect theory in the light of contemporary neurobiological findings. In: E. Zacharacopoulou (Ed.), *Beyond the Mind-Body Dualism: Psychoanalysis and the Human Body* (pp. 106–117). Amsterdam, The Netherlands: Elsevier Health Sciences, International Congress Series 1286.

Kernberg, O. F. (2010). Some observations on the process of mourning. *International Journal of Psychoanalysis, 91*: 601–610.

Kernberg, O. F. (2012). Divergent contemporary trends in psychoanalytic theory. *Psychoanalytic Review, 98*(5): 633–664.

Klein, M. (1946). Notes on some schizoid mechanisms. In: *Envy and Gratitude and Other Works: 1946–1963* (pp. 1–24). London: Hogarth, 1975.

Klein, M. (1975). *Love, Guilt and Reparation & Other Works: 1921–1945*. London: Hogarth.

Krause, R. (1988). [A taxonomy of affect and its use in understanding "early" disorders] (in German). *Psychotherapie Psychosomatik Medizinische Psychologie, 38*: 77–86.
Krause, R. (1990). Psychodynamik der Emotionsstorungen. In: *Psychologie der Emotion* (pp. 630–690). Göttingen: Hogrefe.
Panksepp, J. (1998). *Affective Neuroscience: The Foundations of Human and Animal Emotions*. New York: Oxford University Press.
Rosenfeld, H. (1964). On the psychopathology of narcissism: A clinical approach. *International Journal of Psychoanalysis, 45*: 332–337.
Rosenfeld, H. (1978). Notes on the psychopathology and psychoanalytic treatment of some borderline patients. *International Journal of Psychoanalysis, 59*: 215–221.
Scharff, D. E., & Scharff, J. S. (1987). *Object Relations Family Therapy*. Northvale, NJ: Jason Aronson.
Steiner, J. (1993). *Psychic Retreats*. London: Routledge.
Sutherland, J. D. (1963). Personal communication.
Sutherland, J. D. (1994). *The Autonomous Self*. J. S. Scharff (Ed.). Northvale, NJ: Jason Aronson.
Tomkins, S. S. (1970). Affect as the primary motivational system. In: M. B. Arnold (Ed.), *Feelings and Emotions: The Loyola Symposium* (pp. 101–110). New York: Academic Press.

PART II

CLINICAL

INTRODUCTION TO PART II

Graham S. Clarke and David E. Scharff

We start with Ogden's masterly paper in the *International Journal of Psychoanalysis* in 2010 on the need to read Fairbairn. This has already become influential in reasserting the importance of Fairbairn's thinking for psychoanalysis. When the paper was first published, Graham S. Clarke and Paul Finnegan wrote to the journal (2010) applauding the paper and asking Ogden to comment on what they considered to be a crucial statement, delivered for Fairbairn by Edward Glover during the Controversial Discussions of the 1940s, arguing,

> … the explanatory concept of "phantasy" has now been rendered obsolete by the concepts of "psychical reality" and "internal objects" which the work of Mrs Klein and her followers has done so much to develop; and in my opinion the time is now ripe for us to replace the concept of "phantasy" by a concept of an "inner reality" peopled by the Ego and its internal objects. These internal objects should be regarded as having an organized structure, an identity of their own, an endopsychic existence and an activity as real within the inner world as those of any objects in the outer world … (King & Steiner, 1991, pp. 358–361)

Part of Ogden's response follows,

> … for Isaacs and Klein, internal objects are thoughts and impulses, not thinkers; while, for Fairbairn, internal objects are thinkers with impulses. In sum, for Fairbairn, neither the infant's experience of the unsatisfactory mother nor the infant's psychological response to that experience involves phantasy activity: thus the concept of "phantasy" has now been rendered obsolete by the concepts of "psychical reality" and "internal objects." (Clarke & Finnegan, 2010)

Taking up this thread, Bernhard Hensel looks at the origins of internal objects and the similarities and differences between Fairbairn and Klein. He also considers the therapeutic consequences associated with the activity of Fairbairn's internal objects and ego structures. Eleanore Armstrong-Perlman looks in detail at Fairbairn's unique understanding of the Oedipus situation—"important in therapy not so in theory"—and illustrates her discussion clinically. Molly Ludlam explores Henry Dicks's Fairbairn-influenced approach to couple therapy.

James Grotstein has commented that Fairbairn's theory is "the most apposite paradigm yet proffered for child abuse, child molestation, post-traumatic stress disorder and multiple personality disorder to date" (1994b, p. 123). The contributions that follow explore the application of Fairbairn's theory to some of these areas. Carlos Rodriguez-Sutil looks at Fairbairn's contribution to understanding personality disorders. Valerie Sinason considers Fairbairn's contribution to an understanding of trauma, abuse, and multiplicity. Paul Finnegan and Graham S. Clarke propose a new understanding of multiple personality disorder/dissociative identity disorder based on a development of Fairbairn's endopsychic structure. And finally, Ruben Basili and his co-authors report on developments within the Fairbairn Space in Argentina concerning a common underlying dynamic based on Fairbairn's thinking about "schizoid conflict" during the early development of the self, which they argue lies behind a wide variety of psychiatric and psychoanalytic conditions.

In 1944 Fairbairn made the then novel suggestion that dreams should be understood as a kind of short film of internal reality stemming from components of endopsychic structure, a view that lends itself to understanding of dramatic narratives. Joshua Levy looks at Fairbairn's approach to understanding dreams and the therapeutic usefulness of the approach by comparing his approach with that of Winnicott.

One of the most striking developments of the past twenty-five years has been the rise of the Relational School following the late Stephen Mitchell, who throughout his writing privileged Fairbairn's work. The relational approach has also brought changes in conceptualisation of the therapeutic relationship. Neil Skolnick explores some of these potential changes by considering the therapist as a good object based upon concepts of the Relational School that derive in part from Fairbairn.

Finally, looking to the future of psychoanalysis by taking account of developments within disciplines allied with psychoanalysis such as attachment theory, neuroscience, and developmental psychology, David E. Scharff considers the continuing influence that Fairbairn's theory will have within and between these disciplines.

Fairbairn's insistence on the importance of the relationship between the analyst and the analysand as persons and his adaptability within the therapeutic relationship (Fairbairn, 1958a) are all consonant with the idea of a postmodern psychoanalytical approach (Goldberg, 2001) where the important goal is for the analyst to gain access to the closed world of the analysand independently of any rules concerning the relationship between analyst and analysand.

This part is the heart of our volume, since clinical relevance was always Fairbairn's guiding light and guarantor of a scientific approach. The variety and richness of these contributions is a tribute to the enduring potential of Fairbairn's thought to inspire clinical work.

References

Clarke, G. S., & Finnegan, P. (2010). On: Fairbairn and dynamic structure. *International Journal of Psychoanalysis, 91*: 1001–1003. (Original letter and response from Ogden.)

Fairbairn, W. R. D. (1958a). On the nature and aims of psycho-analytical treatment. *International Journal of Psychoanalysis, 39*(5): 374–385.

Goldberg, A. (2001). Postmodern psychoanalysis. *International Journal of Psychoanalysis, 82*: 123–128.

Grotstein, J. S. (1994b). Notes on Fairbairn's metapsychology. In: *Fairbairn and the Origins of Object Relations* (pp. 112–148). London: Free Association.

King, P., & Steiner, R. (Eds.) (1991). *The Freud-Klein Controversies 1941–1945*. London: Routledge.

CHAPTER TEN

Why read Fairbairn?*

Thomas H. Ogden

I have found that Fairbairn develops a model of the mind that incorporates into its very structure a conceptualisation of early psychic development that is not found in the writing of any other major twentieth century analytic theorist.[1] Fairbairn replaces Freud's (1923b) structural model/metaphor of the mind with a model/metaphor in which the mind is conceived of as an "inner world" (Fairbairn, 1943a, p. 67) in which split-off and repressed parts of the self enter into stable, yet potentially alterable, object relationships with one another. The "cast of characters" (i.e., sub-organisations of the personality) constituting Fairbairn's internal object world is larger than the triumvirate of Freud's structural model and provides what I find to be a richer set of metaphors with which to understand (1) certain types of human dilemmas, particularly those based on the fear that one's love is destructive; and (2) the central role played by feelings of resentment, contempt, disillusionment and addictive "love" in structuring the unconscious mind.

To my mind, Fairbairn's theory of internal object relations constitutes one of the most important contributions to the development of analytic theory in its first century. Yet, judging from the scarcity of references to his work in the analytic literature, particularly in North American and Latin American writing, his theoretical ideas (for example, ideas that he introduced in his 1940a, 1941, 1943a, and 1944 papers) and his clinical thinking (which he presented in his 1957 and 1958a papers) have attracted far less interest and study than have other major twentieth-century analytic theorists such as Klein, Winnicott, and Bion. In part this is due to the fact that Fairbairn worked in isolation in Edinburgh. He had little opportunity for personal involvement or intellectual exchange with colleagues at the Institute of Psychoanalysis in London, whose

---

*Reprinted from the *International Journal of Psychoanalysis* (2010), *91*: 101–108, with kind permission.

members, in his era, included Balint, Bion, Anna Freud, Heimann, Klein, Milner, Rosenfeld, Segal, and Winnicott (Sutherland, 1989). Consequently, exposure to his work, even for his contemporaries, was almost entirely through his writing.

Fairbairn's relatively marginalised place in psychoanalysis today also derives, I believe, from the fact that the reader who undertakes the study of Fairbairn finds himself confronted by a dense prose style, a highly abstract form of theorising, and a set of unfamiliar theoretical terms (for example, dynamic structure, endopsychic structure, central ego, internal saboteur, libidinal ego, exciting object, rejecting object, and so on) that have not been adopted by subsequent analytic theorists.[2]

In this paper, it is not my intention simply to offer an explication and clarification of Fairbairn's thinking; rather, in the process of looking closely at Fairbairn's work (particularly, his papers "Schizoid Factors in the Personality" (1940a) and "Endopsychic Structure Considered in Terms of Object-relationships", 1944), I develop what I believe to be several important implications and extensions of his thinking. I attempt to make something of my own with Fairbairn's writings, in part, by means of a close reading of his texts, and, in part, by clinically illustrating how Fairbairn's ideas have shaped, and evolved in, my own analytic work.

Elements of Fairbairn's revision of psychoanalytic theory

For Fairbairn, the most difficult and most psychically formative psychological problem that the infant or child faces is the dilemma that arises when he experiences his mother (upon whom he is utterly dependent) as both loving and accepting of his love, and unloving and rejecting of his love. Fairbairn's writing contains a critical ambiguity concerning this core human dilemma. The language that Fairbairn uses repeatedly raises in the reader's mind the questions: is every infant traumatised by experiences of deficits in his mother's love for him?, or does the infant misinterpret inevitable (and necessary) frustrations as manifestations of his mother's failure to love him? There is ample evidence in Fairbairn's work to support both conclusions. For instance, in support of the idea that the infant responds to privation as if it were wilful rejection on the part of the mother, Fairbairn writes:

> Here it must be pointed out that what presents itself to him [the infant or child] from a strictly conative standpoint as *frustration* at the hands of his mother presents itself to him in a very different light from a strictly affective standpoint. From the latter standpoint, what he experiences is a sense of lack of love, and indeed emotional *rejection* on his mother's part. (Fairbairn, 1944, pp. 112–113, italics in original)

At the same time, there is a persistent logic in Fairbairn's work that supports the idea that every infant realistically perceives the limits of his mother's capacity to love him and that this realistic perception is "traumatic" (ibid., p. 110) for the infant or child. This logic goes as follows: (1) "... everybody without exception must be regarded as schizoid" (Fairbairn, 1940a, p. 7), that is, everyone evidences pathological splitting of the self; individuals differ from one another only in the severity of their schizoid pathology. (2) Schizoid psychopathology has its origins in an "unsatisfactory" (ibid., p. 13) relationship with the mother, that is, there is a "failure on the part of the mother to convince the child that she really loves him as a person" (p. 13). (3) Since everyone is schizoid, and the schizoid condition derives from maternal failure to convince the infant of her love, it follows that every infant experiences traumatising maternal failure to love. But the language used in this logical sequence leaves open an important ambiguity. Does "failure on the part of the mother to convince the child that she really loves him as a person" (ibid., p. 13) reflect the mother's failure to be convincing, or does it reflect the child's failure/inability to be convinced, that is, the child's inability to accept love? The phrase "failure on the part of the mother", to my ear, leans in the direction of the former interpretation, but, by no means rules out the latter. Overall, in Fairbairn's work, ambiguity of language in this connection serves to convey what I believe to be Fairbairn's view that every infant or child accurately perceives the limits of the mother's ability to love him; and, at the same time, every infant or child misinterprets inevitable privations as the mother's lack of love for him. From this vantage point, Fairbairn's conception of early psychic development is a trauma theory in which the infant, to varying degrees, is traumatised by his realistic perception that he is fully dependent on a mother whose capacity to love him has passed its breaking point. (To my mind, Fairbairn's and Klein's object relations theories are complementary, and this complementarity creates the opportunity for us, as analysts, to think/see with "binocular vision" (Bion, 1962, p. 86). Fairbairn believes in the primacy of external reality and the secondary role of unconscious phantasy, while Klein believes in the primary role of unconscious phantasy and the secondary effect of external reality. (Space does not allow for an elaboration of the comparison of Fairbairn's and Klein's object relations theories.)

Fairbairn (1944) believes that the infant's subjective sense that his mother, upon whom he depends utterly, is unable to love him generates "an affective experience which is singularly devastating" (p. 113). For an older child, the experience of loving the mother who is experienced as unloving and unaccepting of his love is one of "intense humiliation" (p. 113). "At a somewhat deeper level (or at an earlier stage) the experience is one of shame over the display of needs which are disregarded or belittled" (p. 113). The child "feels reduced to a state of worthlessness, destitution or beggardom" (p. 113). "At the same time his sense of badness [for demanding too much] is further complicated by the sense of utter impotence ..." (p. 113).

But the pain of the feelings of shame, worthlessness, beggardom, badness and impotence is not the most catastrophic consequence of the infant's dependence on a mother whom he experiences as unloving and unaccepting of his love. Even more devastating is the threat to the infant's very existence posed by that relationship:

> At a still deeper level (or at a still earlier stage) the child's experience is one of, so to speak, exploding ineffectively and being completely emptied of libido. It is thus an experience of disintegration and of imminent psychical death ... [In being] threatened with loss of his libido [love] (which for him constitutes his own goodness) ... [he is threatened by the loss of what] constitutes himself. (Fairbairn, 1944, p. 113)

In other words, a universal part of earliest postnatal human existence is the terrifying experience of imminent loss of one's self, loss of one's life. What's more, the infant or child

> feels that the reason for his mother's apparent lack of love towards him is that he has destroyed her affection and made it disappear. At the same time he feels that the reason for her apparent refusal to accept his love is that his own love is destructive and bad. (Fairbairn, 1940a, p. 25)

The infant persists in his love of "bad objects" (Fairbairn, 1943a, p. 67) because bad objects are better than no objects at all: "He [the infant or child] *needs* them [maternal objects] ... he cannot do without them" (p. 67, italics in original). Hence, the infant cannot abandon his attempts to re-establish a loving tie to the unloving and unaccepting mother. The infant, in clinging to the unloving mother, is attempting to undo the imagined toxic effects of his own love. But if the infant persists too long in attempting to wring love from the unloving mother, he will suffer "disintegration and ... imminent psychical death" (Fairbairn, 1944, p. 113).

From this vantage point, the most important (life-sustaining) task faced by the infant is not simply that of establishing and maintaining a loving tie with the mother who is capable of giving and receiving love. At least as important to the psychical survival of the infant is his capacity to extricate himself from his futile efforts to wring love from the external object mother who is experienced as unloving. The infant achieves this life-saving psychological manoeuvre by developing an internal object world (an aspect of mind) in which the relationship with the external unloving mother is transformed into an internal object relationship.

The infant incorporates the breast in order to control it: "*relationships with internalized objects,* [are relationships] *to which the individual is compelled to turn in default of a satisfactory relationship with objects in the outer world*" (Fairbairn, 1941, p. 40, italics in original). In replacing a real external object relationship with an internal one, the infant staunches the haemorrhaging of libido (his "nascent love" (1944, p. 113) into an emotional vacuum (the mother who, for real and imagined reasons, is experienced as unloving). By creating an internal object relationship with the unloving mother, the infant directs his nascent object love towards an internal object, an object that is a part of himself. (Every aspect of one's mind—including all the "internalized figures" constituting one's internal object world—is necessarily an aspect of oneself.)

For Fairbairn, an internal object relationship constitutes a real relationship between aspects of the ego.[3] Fairbairn (1943a, 1944) reminds the reader again and again that to conceive of internal object relationships as relationships between a pair of split-off parts of the ego is to do nothing more than to elaborate on Freud's (1917e) conception of the creation of the "critical agency" (p. 248) (later to be called the superego). In *Mourning and Melancholia*, Freud (ibid.) describes the process by which two parts of the ego are split off from the main body of the ego (the "I") and enter into an unconscious relationship with one another. In melancholia, a part of the self (that harbours feelings of impotent rage towards the abandoning object) enters into a stable internal object relationship with another split-off part of the ego (that is identified with the abandoning object). In this way, an actual unconscious object relationship between different aspects of the self is established and maintained. The upshot of this splitting of the ego, in Freud's view, is an unconscious feeling that one has not lost the object since the abandoning object has been replaced by a part of oneself. Thus, Fairbairn's theory of internal object relationships represents both an elaboration of Freud's thinking (see Ogden, 2002, for a discussion of the origins of object relations theory in *Mourning and Melancholia*) and a radical departure from it (in his understanding of endopsychic structure and the nature of internal object relationships).

Having discussed the infant's replacement of unsatisfactory external object relationships with internal ones, I will now turn to Fairbairn's conception of the internal object world ("the basic endopsychic situation" (1944, p. 106) that results from internalisation of the unsatisfactory relationship with the mother.

To understand Fairbairn's conception of the development of the psyche it is necessary to understand his notion of "endopsychic structure" (ibid., p. 120). In brief, an endopsychic structure is a sub-organisation of the self (split off from the main "body" of the ego/self).[4] Fairbairn believes that it is erroneous to separate "endopsychic structures" (parts of the self capable of thinking, feeling, remembering, and responding in their own distinctive ways) from "psychic dynamism" (our impulses, wishes, needs, and desires). Fairbairn (1943a, 1944) differs in this regard from Freud and Klein in that he believes that it is inaccurate to posit an aspect of the self (the ego/I) that is devoid of impulses, wishes, and desires: what is a self devoid of desires and impulses? Similarly, the idea of desire or impulse divorced from the self/ego/I that is desiring or feels impelled, is, for Fairbairn, "utterly meaningless" (1944, p. 95): "'Impulses' are inseparable from an ego structure with a definite pattern" (ibid., p. 90). Note that Fairbairn specifies that the "ego structure" has "a definite pattern". This idea reflects his view that each "ego structure" (i.e., each aspect of the self) has its own unique organisation that defines the way it experiences and responds to its perceptions, needs, and desires. Feeling slighted, for example, is a different experience for each ego structure (i.e., each quasi-autonomous aspect of the self) and elicits from each ego structure qualitatively different emotional responses (for example, feelings of resentment, contempt, vindictiveness, and so on).

In an effort to simplify, and thereby gain some control over the internalised relationship with the unloving mother, the infant engages in a "divide et impera" (ibid., p. 112) manoeuvre. The infant divides the unloving (internal object) mother into two parts: the tantalising mother and the rejecting mother. Fairbairn does not explain how he has arrived at the idea that the infant divides his experience of the unloving mother into tantalising and rejecting parts. (Why not postulate jealous and murderous parts, or poisonous and devouring parts?) As we do with Freud's even bolder proposal that all human motivations are derived from the sexual instinct and the ego (or survival) instinct (later replaced by the death instinct), we must suspend judgment while we examine the theoretical and clinical consequences of the author's hypothesis.

Fairbairn (1944) proposes that an aspect of the infant's personality feels powerfully, uncontrollably attached to the alluring aspect of the internal object mother, while another aspect of the infant's personality feels hopelessly attached to the rejecting aspect of the internal object mother. Both parts of the infant's psyche—the part emotionally bound to the alluring mother and the part bound to the rejecting mother—are "split off" (ibid., p. 112) from the healthy, main body of the ego (which Fairbairn terms the central ego). At the same time, aspects of the infant's personality that are thoroughly identified with the alluring and with the rejecting aspects of the mother are also split off from the central ego. Thus, two repressed internal object relationships (made up of four split-off parts of the central ego) are created: (1) the relationship of the tantalised self (termed by Fairbairn the libidinal ego) and the tantalising self-identified-with-the-object (the exciting object), and (2) the relationship of the rejected self (the internal saboteur) and the rejecting self-identified-with-the-object (the rejecting object). These two sets of internal object relationships are angrily rejected (i.e., repressed) by the central ego because the healthy aspect of the infant's personality (the central ego) feels intense anger at the unloving internal object mother.

The exciting object and the rejecting object are no less parts of the self than are the libidinal ego and the internal saboteur. The exciting and rejecting internal "objects" have a not-me feel to them because they are parts of the self that are thoroughly identified with the unloving mother in her exciting and rejecting qualities (see Ogden, 1986a, 1986b, for a discussion of the concept of internal objects and internal object relations).

Fairbairn (1944, 1963a) believes that the internalisation of the unsatisfactory object is a defensive measure carried out in an effort to control the unsatisfactory object. But, to my mind, the illusory control that the child achieves by means of this internalisation only in part accounts for the immense psychic power of the internal object world to remain a "closed system of internal reality" (Fairbairn, 1958a, p. 385), that is, to maintain its isolation from the real world. Despite the fact that split-off and repressed aspects of the ego (the internal saboteur and libidinal ego) feel intense resentment towards, and feelings of being callously spurned by, the unloving and unaccepting object, Fairbairn (1944) states that the ties between these split-off parts of the self and the internalised unloving object are libidinal in nature.

The libidinal nature of these ties suggests that aspects of the individual (the internal saboteur and the libidinal ego) have by no means given up on the potential of the unsatisfactory object to give and receive love. It seems to me that a libidinal tie to an internal object towards whom one feels anger, resentment, and the like, necessarily involves an (unconscious) wish/need to use what control one feels one has to change the unloving and unaccepting (internal) object into a loving and accepting one.

From this vantage point, I view the libidinal ego and the internal saboteur as aspects of self that are intent on transforming the exciting object and the rejecting object into loving objects. Moreover, it seems to me, by extension of Fairbairn's thinking, that *the infant's effort to transform unsatisfactory objects into satisfactory objects—thus reversing the imagined toxic effect on the mother of the infant's love—is the single most important motivation sustaining the structure of the internal object world*. And that structure, when externalised, underlies all pathological external object relationships.

The "emotional life" of Fairbairn's internal objects

Fairbairn (ibid., p. 105) provides a diagram depicting the relationships among the psychic structures that I have just described (see Figure. 1 below). It has been my experience in reading and teaching Fairbairn that a familiarity with this diagram is useful in one's efforts to grasp the nature of the internal object world as Fairbairn conceives of it. Since the diagram necessarily has a mechanical, non-human quality to it, in what follows I try to convey what I believe to be the nature of the "emotional life" of each of the internal objects constituting Fairbairn's internal object world.

Addictive love (the bond between the libidinal ego and the exciting object)

As I understand Fairbairn's theory of internal object relationships, all the love and hate that tie internal objects to one another is inherently pathological because it is derived entirely from the pathological tie of the infant to the unreachable mother, that is, to the mother who is felt to be incapable of giving and receiving love. The relationship between the libidinal ego and the exciting object is one of addictive "love" on the part of the libidinal ego, and of desperate need on the part of the exciting object to elicit desire from the libidinal ego (which desire the exciting object will never satisfy).

When I imagine the libidinal ego and the exciting object as characters in an internal drama, I often think of a patient with whom I worked many years ago in twice weekly face-to-face psychotherapy. The patient, Mr C, was a man in his early thirties with cerebral palsy, who was desperately in love with Ms Z, a "beautiful" woman friend (who did not have cerebral palsy or any other physical impairment). In the course of years of this "friendship", the patient's advances became more insistent and beseeching. This eventually led Ms Z to end the relationship altogether. Mr C, who found it difficult to articulate words under the best of circumstances, would bellow in pain during our sessions as he tried to talk about how much he loved Ms Z.

Mr C insisted that Ms Z must love him because she enjoyed his sense of humour and had invited him to two parties at her apartment. Although I only knew Ms Z from my experience with Mr C (including my transference–countertransference experience), I suspected that Ms Z was drawn to Mr C in an unconscious pathological way. I based this suspicion, in part, on the fact that, in my work with Mr C, I regularly had the wish not only to soothe him but also to "cure" him of his cerebral palsy. I came to see the latter wish as a reflection of my own inability to appreciate and accept him as he was, and, instead, to turn to magical solutions. To have acted on these feelings, for example, by speaking to Mr C in a way that implicitly promised "cure", would have been to encourage the patient to become utterly dependent on me for continued magical evasion of reality. Under such circumstances, there would have been no opportunity for Mr C to grow and to achieve genuine maturity and independence. It seems to me that the outcome of the analytic work depended upon my ability to recognise, think about, and come to terms with my own needs to keep Mr C endlessly dependent on me.

To my mind, Mr C's "love relationship" with Ms Z (and with me in the aspect of the transference–countertransference that involved my unconscious wish to "cure" him) was an expression of a pathological mutual dependence. In Fairbairn's terms, this emotional situation might be thought of as the tie between the libidinal ego and the exciting object. Such relationships involve psychic bondage in which the participants are each jailer and jailed, stalker and stalked. (I will further discuss my work with Mr C later in this paper when I address the subject of psychological growth.)

Bonds of resentment (the tie between the internal saboteur and the rejecting object)

The relationship between the internal saboteur and the rejecting object derives from the infant's love of his mother despite (and because of) her rejection of him. The nature of the pathological love that binds together the internal saboteur and the rejecting object is a bond not of hate, but of a pathological love that is experienced as bitter "resentment" (Fairbairn, 1944, p. 115). Neither the rejecting object nor the internal saboteur is willing or able to think about, much less relinquish, that tie. In fact, there is no desire on the part of either to change anything about their mutual dependence. The power of that bond is impossible to overestimate. The rejecting object and the internal saboteur are determined to nurse their feelings of having been deeply wronged, cheated, humiliated, betrayed, exploited, treated unfairly, discriminated against, and so on. The mistreatment at the hands of the other is felt to be unforgivable. An apology is forever expected by each, but never offered by either. Nothing is more important to the internal saboteur (the rejected self) than coercing the rejecting object into recognising the incalculable pain that he or she has caused.

From the point of view of the rejecting object (the split-off aspect of self thoroughly identified with the rejecting mother), the experience of this form of pathological love involves the conviction that the internal saboteur is greedy, insatiable, thin-skinned, ungrateful, unwilling to be reasonable, unable to let go of a grudge, and so on. But despite the burdensomeness of the ceaseless complaining and self-righteous outrage of the internal saboteur, the rejecting object is both unwilling and unable to give up the relationship, that is, to extricate itself from the mutual pathological dependence. The life, the determination, the very reason for being of the rejecting object (as a part of the self) is derived from its tie to the internal saboteur. The rejecting object is an empty shell, a lost and forgotten part of the past, in the absence of the obsession on the part of the internal saboteur to wring love, remorse, and magical reparation from it. This internal object relationship (like the relationship of the libidinal ego and the exciting object) is a relationship in which the jailer is a prisoner of the jailed, and the jailed, a prisoner of the jailer. Outside the terms of their pathological, mutually dependent "love"' neither would hold meaning for the other or for itself (much less for any other part of the self). In the absence of one, the other would become a mere remnant of a once powerful pair of deities that reigned in a religion no longer practised.

A particular clinical experience comes to mind in connection with the power of the bond between the internal saboteur and the rejecting object. I was asked by the chairperson of a social service agency to serve as a consultant to the psychotherapy division of the agency. The members of the staff of that part of the organisation were in constant conflict with one another and with the rest of the agency.[5] The director of the psychotherapy division, a psychiatrist in his early fifties, oversaw a staff composed of three male psychiatrists and six female psychologists and social workers, all in their thirties and forties. The director showed consistent favouritism towards the male psychiatrists, not only in his praise of their ideas, but also in appointing them to leadership positions (which paid higher salaries). The women therapists, most of whom had worked in this agency for many years, made no secret of their discontent with the director.

In the course of speaking in confidence with individual members of the staff, I was struck by the fact that, while each of the female psychotherapists expressed intense anger and bitterness about the way she was being treated by the director, they all felt that they had no choice but to remain working at the clinic. They told me that psychiatric services at the other agencies and hospitals in the area were being shut down, so they had no choice but to stay. But none had interviewed at other hospitals or social service agencies. In my conversations with the director of the division, he spoke to me as a fellow psychiatrist whom he believed would understand the inevitable difficulty involved in working with "non-medical" female psychotherapists who invariably become ensnarled in "Oedipal attachments and rivalries" with one another and with the "medical" group leader.

My consultation to the clinic was ended abruptly after three months when the city's funding for all mental health services was cut sharply and the psychotherapy division of this clinic was shut down. One of the female staff members, whom I later met by chance at a lecture, told me: "On looking back on it, I feel as if I was living as a child in a psychotic family. I couldn't imagine leaving and finding other work. It felt as if I would end up living in a cardboard box if I were to leave. My whole world had shrunk to the size of that clinic. If the clinic hadn't closed, I'm certain I would still be working there." She described the former director of the psychotherapy division as "... a very limited person who hates women and gets pleasure out of humiliating them in a way that he feels no need to hide." "But," she added, "the really frightening thing for me is that I couldn't leave. The situation was not only bad at work, I couldn't stop thinking about it at night, over the weekends, or even when I was on vacation. It was as if I was infected by the situation."

It seems to me that all the participants in this drama felt and behaved as if their lives depended on the perpetuation of the tie between the tormentor and the aggrieved. The director, the three psychiatrists (who said they felt "caught in the middle", but did nothing to address the patent unfairness), and the female staff, all felt wronged. No one seemed to recognise the ways in which he or she actively and passively provoked feelings of anger, helplessness, outrage, and resentment in the others. In retrospect, it seems to me that what I was witnessing might be thought of as a rather intense form of the bond of mutual dependence tying the internal saboteur and the rejecting object to one another.

Bonds of contempt (the relationship of the internal saboteur to the libidinal ego and the exciting object)

For me, one of Fairbairn's most original and most significant contributions to psychoanalysis is the understanding of human nature that emerges from his conception of the relationship between the internal saboteur and the libidinal ego, and between the internal saboteur and the exciting object. The internal saboteur, filled with self-hatred for its own "dependence dictated by ... [infantile] need" (Fairbairn, 1944, p. 115), turns on the libidinal ego, and, in so doing, turns on itself at one removed (since every internal object—every endopsychic structure—is a subdivision of a subject who is one person). The internal saboteur disdainfully, contemptuously attacks the libidinal ego as a pathetic wretch, a sap, a sucker for the way it continually humiliates itself in begging for the love of the exciting object: "You [the libidinal ego] never learn your lesson. You get kicked in the face [by the exciting object] and drag yourself to your feet as if nothing has happened only to get kicked and knocked down again. How can you be so stupid as not to see what is plain as day? She [the exciting object] toys with you, leads you on, and then dumps you every time. And yet you keep going back for more. You disgust me."

It seems to me that from this perspective—the perspective of the internal saboteur—we are better able to understand the sense in which Fairbairn uses the term libidinal ego to name the aspect of self that is tied by bonds of addictive love to the exciting object. Libido, in this context, and in the internal object world in general, is synonymous with narcissistic libido (narcissistic love). All internal objects (more accurately, internal subjects) are split-off parts of the central ego/self, and therefore the relationships among them are exclusively relationships with oneself. Thus, the libidinal ego is "loving", but only loving of itself (in the form of the exciting object).

Closely tied to the attack of the internal saboteur on the libidinal ego is the attack of the internal saboteur on the object of that narcissistic love, the exciting object. The internal saboteur views the exciting object as a malicious tease, a seductress, a bundle of empty promises: "You [the exciting object] don't fool me. You may be able to make a fool of him [the libidinal ego], but I know your type, I've heard your lies, I've seen your depraved imitations of love. You're a parasite; you take, but you don't know what it means to give. You prey on the gullible, on children."

At first blush, the internal saboteur deserves its name: it demeans and shames the libidinal ego for its infantile longings, and attacks the exciting object for its endless appetite for tantalising, seducing, deceiving, and humiliating. But the contempt and disdain that the internal saboteur feels towards the libidinal ego and the exciting object are born of its feelings of self-hatred, impotence, and shame concerning its own naïve, self-deluding, infantile pursuit of the love of the rejecting object (for instance, in the clinical example presented earlier, the futile pursuit of the love of the director by the female members of the therapy staff). I believe that implicit in Fairbairn's rendering of the structure of the internal object world is the idea that the fury and contempt that the internal saboteur heaps upon the libidinal ego and the exciting object stem from a glimmer of recognition of the shame and humiliation it feels about its own absolute dependence on, and loyalty to, the rejecting (internal object) mother.

Attacks by the internal saboteur on the libidinal ego and the exciting object may take a broad range of forms in the analytic situation. In my work with Ms T, an analysand I saw over a period of many years in a five-session-per-week analysis, I could do nothing right. If I spoke, I was "missing the point"; if I was quiet, I was "being a stereotypic analyst" spewing pronouncements from behind the couch. If I was punctual, I was "being obsessional"; if I was a minute late, I was "dreading" seeing her. In a session with this patient in the fourth year of analysis, an image came to my mind of a homeless man sitting on the curb near a traffic light. It seemed that he had given up on begging, and that it would not be long before he died. Profoundly disturbed by this image, I began to become aware of my own feeling that for a number of months I had given up on ever being seen by the patient for whom I was, and, in return, I had given up on trying to be an analyst to her. It was not that I had simply made mistakes. The situation felt to me to be far worse than that: I, myself, was the mistake. My very being was wrong for her.

An integral part of my effort to make therapeutic use of the feeling state that I was beginning to recognise and put into words for myself involved thinking of myself as having experienced something like the patient's feeling that her very way of being was wrong (a far worse problem than feeling that she had made a great many serious errors).[6] I eventually said to Ms T: "For a long time, you have been telling me that I simply cannot understand you and that virtually everything I say confirms that. I don't think you've been any harsher with me than you are with yourself. In fact, I think that your attacks on yourself are far more violent than your attacks on me. I think that you feel not only that everything you do is wrong, you firmly believe that your very existence is wrong and that the only thing you can do to remedy that situation is to become another person. Of course, if you were to succeed in doing so, you would be dead: worse than that, you would never have existed."

Ms T responded immediately by saying that I was being very wordy. As she said this, I felt deflated and realised that, despite years of experience with this patient, I had actually expected that this time she would at least consider what I had said. I told this to the patient and after a few moments of silence, she said: "Please don't give up on me." In Fairbairn's terms, the patient, at least for this moment, had softened her intrapsychic attack on herself (the attack of the internal saboteur on the libidinal ego for its way of loving). She allowed herself not only to accept her dependence on me, but also to ask something of me (as a separate person) that she knew she could not provide for herself.

The relationship of the central ego to internal and external objects

Before ending the discussion of the emotional life of internal objects/endopsychic structures, I will comment very briefly on Fairbairn's concept of the central ego. The central ego is the aspect of the psyche that Fairbairn least fleshes out. What Fairbairn (1944) does say is that the central ego is an endopsychic structure capable of thinking, feeling, responding, and so on. It constitutes the original healthy self of the newborn infant. From the outset, the central ego of the infant is capable of rudimentary self-object differentiation and of operating on the basis of the reality principle. But in response to a traumatising experience with a mother whom the infant experiences as both loving and accepting of his love, and unloving and rejecting of his love, the infant splits off parts of the central ego and represses them in the form of the internal object relationships that I have described. Consequently, the central ego retains its original health, but is significantly depleted by the process of splitting off and "sending into exile" (repressing) parts of itself.

The central ego is the only part of the self that is able to engage in, and learn from, experience with external objects. Change in the unconscious internal object world is always mediated by the central ego (which sometimes acts in concert with external objects such as the analyst). Internal objects interact with the external world only in the form of narcissistic object relationships, that is, externalisations of internal object relationships (which are necessarily narcissistic in nature). The central ego includes no dynamically repressed (unsatisfactory) internal object relationships; rather, the central ego consists exclusively of good enough (as opposed to idealised) object relationships such as identifications with people whom one has loved and by whom one has felt loved, recognised, and accepted. Such identifications underlie feelings that include a sense of internal security, as well as background feelings of solidity and integrity.

Psychological growth

In the final part of this paper, I will discuss some of the ways in which a person may be helped to grow psychologically. Fairbairn regards as "relatively immutable" (1944, p. 129) the "basic endopsychic situation", that is, the constellations of split-off and repressed aspects of the central ego. For Fairbairn, the psychological changes that can be achieved through psychoanalysis primarily involve diminutions of the intensity of the feelings of resentment, addictive love, contempt, primitive dependence, disillusionment, and so on that bind the split-off, repressed sub-organisations of the self to one another. Specifically, healthy psychological change can be achieved by reducing to a minimum:

(a) the attachment of the subsidiary egos [the internal saboteur and the libidinal ego] to their respective associated objects [the rejecting object and the exciting object], (b) the aggression of the central ego towards the subsidiary egos and their objects [which takes the form of repression of the two pairs of split-off parts of the self], and (c) the aggression of the internal saboteur towards the libidinal ego and its object [the exciting object]. (ibid., p. 130)

The density of the prose, the mechanical nature of the metaphors, the level of abstraction, the heavy reliance on his own technical terminology, together denude Fairbairn's statement of almost anything recognisable as human experience. I will offer an alternative way of speaking and thinking about how people grow psychologically, that relies less on Fairbairn's explicitly stated ideas and more on ideas that I find to be implicit in his work. Although Fairbairn never puts it in this way, I believe that the most fundamental psychological principle underlying his conception of psychological growth is the idea that all psychological maturation involves the patient's genuine acceptance of himself and, by extension, acceptance of others. That acceptance is achieved by means of the work of coming to terms with the full range of aspects of oneself, including one's disturbing, infantile, split-off identifications with one's unloving, unaccepting mother. Psychological change of this sort creates the possibility of discovering a world of people and experiences that exists outside oneself, a world in which it is possible to feel curious, surprised, delighted, disappointed, homesick, and so on. The world of thought, feeling, and human relatedness that is opened by such self-acceptance is a world in which one feels no compulsion to transform the realities of one's human relationships into something other than what they are, that is, to change oneself or "the object" (who is now a whole and separate subject) into other people. It is also a world in which one can learn from one's experiences with other people because those experiences are no longer dominated by projections of static internal object relationships.

A particular analytic experience comes to mind in this regard. Mr C, the patient with cerebral palsy whom I discussed earlier, had, as a child, been savaged by his mother. As I have described, in adult life he became possessed by a "love" for Ms Z. Over a period of eight years, Ms Z twice relocated to a different city; both times the patient followed. Again and again, she tried to make it clear to Mr C that she liked him as a friend, but did not want a romantic relationship with him. He became increasingly desperate, angry, and suicidal. From the outset of the analytic work, and frequently thereafter, the patient told me that he did not know why I "tolerated" him.

In our sessions, Mr C would howl in pain as he spoke of the "unfairness" of Ms Z's rejection of him. When upset, particularly when crying, the patient would lose muscular control of his mouth, which made it very difficult for him to speak. Frothy saliva gathered at the sides of his mouth and mucous dripped from his nose while tears ran down his cheeks. Being with Mr C at these times was heartbreaking. I have only rarely felt in such an immediate, physical way that I was the mother of a baby in distress. Mr C seemed to want me to help him present himself to Ms Z in a way that would not frighten her and would help her understand how much he loved her and how much she loved him (if she would only admit it to herself). It was impossible not to hear in the patient's "plan" a wish that I transform Ms Z (and, unconsciously, his mother and the aspect of me that only "tolerated" him) into people who were genuinely able to love him, accept him, and value his love.

In retrospect, I believe that it was very important to the analytic experience that Mr C experience for himself over a period of years the reality that I was not repulsed by him even when he bellowed in pain and could not control the release of tears, nasal mucous, and saliva. It must have been apparent to Mr C, though I never put it into words, that I loved him as I would one day love my own children in their infancy. For years, the patient had been too ashamed to tell me about some of the ways his mother had humiliated him as a child, for example, by repeatedly calling him "a repulsive, slobbering monster". He only gradually entrusted me with these deeply shamed aspects of himself.

I viewed Mr C's accounts of his humiliating mother as a description not only of his external object mother, but, as important, a description of an aspect of himself that viewed himself as an object of contempt and which enlisted others (most prominently, Ms Z) to humiliate him. A humiliating connection with Ms Z was unconsciously felt to be far better than no connection at all.

Several years into the work, Mr C told me a dream: "Not much happened in the dream. *I was myself, with my cerebral palsy, washing my car and enjoying listening to music on the car radio that I had turned up loud.*" The dream was striking in a number of ways. It was the first time, in telling me a dream, that Mr C specifically mentioned his cerebral palsy. Moreover, the way that he put it—"I was myself, with my cerebral palsy"—conveyed a depth of recognition and an acceptance of himself that I had never before heard from him. How better could he have expressed a particular type of change in his relationship to himself—a psychological change that involved a loving self-recognition that contributed to freeing him from the need to perpetually attempt to wring love and acceptance from those internal and external objects who were least inclined to, or incapable of, loving him? In the dream, he was able to be a mother who took pleasure in bathing her baby (his car) while listening to and enjoying the music that was coming from inside the baby. This was not a dream of triumph; it was an ordinary dream of ordinary love: "Not much happened."

I was deeply moved by the patient's telling me his dream. I said to him: "What a wonderful dream that was."

Some years later, Mr C moved to another part of the country to take a high-level job in his field. He wrote to me periodically. In the last letter that I received from him (about five years after we stopped working together), he told me that he had married a woman he loved, a woman who had cerebral palsy. They had recently had a healthy baby girl.

Mr C, in the context of the developing relationship with me, was able to extricate himself from his addictive love of Ms Z (a bond between the libidinal ego and the exciting object) while, at the same time, diminishing his compulsive engagement in forms of relatedness based on the bond between the debasing and the debased aspects of himself (the bond between the internal saboteur and the libidinal ego).

It seems to me that a key element of the therapeutic action of the work that Mr C and I did together was the real (as opposed to the transferential) relationship between the two of us (for example, in my genuinely not feeling repulsed by the mucous, tears, and saliva flowing from his nose, eyes, and mouth as he bellowed in pain, and by my experiencing love for him of a sort that, later in my life, I would feel for my infant sons). Fairbairn, I think, would agree with this understanding and go a step further: "The really decisive [therapeutic] factor is the relationship of the patient to the analyst" (1958a, p. 379) He elaborated on this idea a bit later in the same paper:

> *Psycho-analytical treatment resolves itself into a struggle on the part of the patient to press-gang his relationship with the analyst into the closed system of the inner world through the agency of transference, and a determination on the part of the analyst to effect a breach in this closed system and to provide conditions under which, in the setting of a therapeutic relationship, the patient may be induced to accept the open system of outer reality.* (ibid., p. 385, italics in the original)

Concluding comments

Psychological growth, for Fairbairn (as I read him), involves a form of acceptance of oneself that can be achieved only in the context of a real relationship with a relatively psychologically mature person. A relationship of this sort (including the analytic relationship) is the only possible exit from the solipsistic world of internal object relationships. Self-acceptance is a state of mind that marks the (never fully achieved) relinquishment of the life-consuming effort to transform unsatisfactory internal object relationships into satisfactory (i.e., loving and accepting) ones. With psychological growth, one comes to know at a depth that one's early experiences with one's unloving and unaccepting mother will never be other than what they were. It is a waste of life to devote oneself to the effort to transform oneself (and others) into the people one wishes one were (or wishes they were). In order to take part in experience in a world populated by people whom one has not invented, and from whom one may learn, the individual must first loosen the unconscious bonds of resentment, addictive love, contempt, and disillusionment that confine him to a life lived principally in his mind.

Notes

1. This discussion of papers by Fairbairn is the sixth in a series of articles in which I offer studies of seminal analytic contributions. I have previously discussed works by Freud, Winnicott, Bion, Loewald, and Searles (Ogden, 2001, 2002, 2004, 2006, 2007).
2. Although Fairbairn's terminology is little used currently, his ideas have had considerable impact on the thinking of leading analytic theorists including Greenberg and Mitchell (1983), Grotstein (1994b), Guntrip (1968), Kernberg (1980), Klein (1946), Kohut (1971), Modell (1968), Rinsley (1977), Scharff and Scharff (1994), Sutherland (1989), and Symington (1986). It is beyond the scope of this paper to explore the ways in which these authors have critiqued, modified, and extended Fairbairn's thinking.
3. The meaning of the term *ego*, as Fairbairn uses it, is better conveyed by the term *self* since all the split-off "parts" of "the ego" are sub-organisations of the self. Fairbairn (1943a) drops the term *id* from his lexicon because he views one's impulses and passions as integral parts of the ego/self. In discussing Fairbairn's ideas, I will use the term *ego* and *self* interchangeably.
4. For Fairbairn, all unconscious endopsychic structures are split-off parts of the ego/self; and yet he misleadingly uses the term *internal objects* to refer to these split-off parts of the self, which are more accurately termed *internal subjects*.

5. While Fairbairn (1944) believed that his understanding of the psyche "provides a more satisfactory basis than does any other type of psychology for the explanation of group phenomena" (p. 128), he did not develop or clinically illustrate this idea in any of his writings.
6. Fairbairn (1944) notes that in the world of unconscious internal object relationships, feeling guilty about one's failures and misdeeds is far preferable to feeling "unconditionally, that is, libidinally bad" (p. 93). To feel unconditionally bad is to feel that one's love is bad.

References

Bion, W. R. (1962). Learning from experience. In: *Seven Servants*. New York: Jason Aronson, 1975.

Fairbairn, W. R. D. (1940a). Schizoid factors in the personality. In: *Psychoanalytic Studies of the Personality* (pp. 3–27). London: Tavistock, 1952.

Fairbairn, W. R. D. (1941). A revised psychopathology of the psychoses and psychoneuroses. In: *Psychoanalytic Studies of the Personality* (pp. 28–58). London: Tavistock, 1952.

Fairbairn, W. R. D. (1943a). The repression and the return of bad objects (with special reference to the "'war neuroses"). *British Journal of Medical Psychology, 19*: 327–341. In: *Psychoanalytic Studies of the Personality* (pp. 59–81). London: Tavistock, 1952.

Fairbairn, W. R. D. (1944). Endopsychic structure considered in terms of object-relationships. *International Journal of Psychoanalysis, 25*: 70–92. In: *Psychoanalytic Studies of the Personality* (pp. 82–132). London: Tavistock, 1952.

Fairbairn, W. R. D. (1957). Freud, the psycho-analytical method and mental health. *British Journal of Medical Psychology, 30*(2): 53–61. In: D. E. Scharff & E. F. Birtles (Eds.), *From Instinct to Self: Selected Papers of W. R. D. Fairbairn, Volume I: Clinical and Theoretical Papers* (pp. 61–73). Northvale, NJ: Jason Aronson, 1994.

Fairbairn, W. R. D. (1958a). On the nature and aims of psycho-analytical treatment. *International Journal of Psychoanalysis, 39*: 374–385. In: D. E. Scharff & E. F. Birtles (Eds.), *From Instinct to Self: Selected Papers of W. R. D. Fairbairn, Volume I: Clinical and Theoretical Papers* (pp. 74–92). Northvale, NJ: Jason Aronson, 1994.

Fairbairn, W. R. D. (1963a). Synopsis of an object-relations theory of the personality. *International Journal of Psychoanalysis, 44*: 224–225. In: D. E. Scharff & E. F. Birtles (Eds.), *From Instinct to Self: Selected Papers of W. R. D. Fairbairn, Volume I: Clinical and Theoretical Papers* (pp. 155–156). Northvale, NJ: Jason Aronson, 1994.

Freud, S. (1917e). Mourning and Melancholia. *S. E., 14*: 243–258.

Freud, S. (1923b). *The Ego and the Id. S. E., 19*: 3–66.

Greenberg, J. R., & Mitchell, S. A. (1983). *Object Relations in Psychoanalytic Theory*. Cambridge, MA: Harvard University Press.

Grotstein, J. S. (1994b). Notes on Fairbairn's metapsychology. In: J. S. Grotstein & D. B. Rinsley (Eds.), *Fairbairn and the Origins of Object Relations* (pp. 112–148). London: Free Association.

Guntrip, H. (1968). *Schizoid Phenomena, Object Relations and the Self*. London: Hogarth.

Kernberg, O. F. (1980). *External World and Internal Reality*. Northvale, NJ: Jason Aronson.

Klein, M. (1946). Notes on some schizoid mechanisms. In: *Envy and Gratitude and Other Works, 1946–1963* (pp. 1–24). New York: Delacorte.

Kohut, H. (1971). *The Analysis of the Self*. New York: International Universities Press.

Modell, A. H. (1968). *Object Love and Reality: An Introduction to a Psychoanalytic Theory of Object Relations*. New York: International Universities Press.

Ogden, T. H. (1986a). The concept of internal object relations. *International Journal of Psychoanalysis*, 64: 181–198.

Ogden, T. H. (1986b). *The Matrix of the Mind: Object Relations and the Psychoanalytic Dialogue*. Northvale, NJ: Jason Aronson.

Ogden, T. H. (2001). Reading Winnicott. *Psychoanalytic Quarterly, 70*: 299–323.

Ogden, T. H. (2002). A new reading of the origins of object-relations theory. *International Journal of Psychoanalysis, 83*: 767–782.

Ogden, T. H. (2004). An introduction to the reading of Bion. *International Journal of Psychoanalysis, 85*: 285–300.

Ogden, T. H. (2006). Reading Loewald: Oedipus reconceived. *International Journal of Psychoanalysis, 87*: 651–666.

Ogden, T. H. (2007). Reading Harold Searles. *International Journal of Psychoanalysis, 88*: 353–369.

Rinsley, D. B. (1977). An object relations view of borderline personality. In: P. Hartocollis (Ed.), *Borderline Personality Disorders* (pp. 47–70). New York: International Universities Press.

Scharff, J. S., & Scharff, D. E. (1994). *Object Relations Therapy of Physical and Sexual Trauma*. Northvale, NJ: Jason Aronson.

Sutherland, J. D. (1989). *Fairbairn's Journey into the Interior*. London: Free Association.

Symington, N. (1986). Fairbairn. In: *The Analytic Experience* (pp. 236–253). London: Free Association.

CHAPTER ELEVEN

On the origin of internal objects in the works of Fairbairn and Klein and the possible therapeutic consequences

Bernhard F. Hensel

Introduction

Through our psychological and/or psychoanalytic training we have all been confronted with the notion of the internal object and, like so many other concepts, it has been used quite frequently and stretched to an extent that its meaning and clarity have been compromised. On the other hand object relations theory has become a crucial starting point for psychoanalysis and its practice. The following material will demonstrate how the various understandings of internal objects lead to diverse technical conclusions and therapeutic stances.

Each psychoanalyst and psychotherapist generates his or her own explicit and implicit theory by integrating personal experiences, different theories, and redefining definitions throughout training and a professional career. But in order to properly communicate with each other it is extremely important to clarify these definitions, to carve out the similarities and the differences, especially since this allows us to consciously comprehend our view of the world, our stance, and our implicit manner within treatment.

The dilemma regarding the clarification of definitions is a schism based upon drive and relations based approaches to psychoanalysis and it is little comfort to know that Freud's theories supported both approaches. This schism revolves around the question: does the *innocent child*—in the sense of the tragic human—encounter a traumatic surrounding, as is implicated in Fairbairn's and Kohut's dyadic model, or does the *guilty child*—in the sense of a guilty human burdened with the original sin of destructiveness—utilise his surroundings in order to vent innate libidinal and aggressive drive impulses as described in Freud's and Melanie Klein's monadic model?

Klein and Fairbairn are both original and important psychoanalytic theoreticians with an enormous influence on modern day psychoanalysis, where both are often intermingled and

Fairbairn is frequently intentionally omitted. It is often Melanie Klein who is regarded as the object relations theoretician though in actuality she represented a one-person model. For Klein the object is considered to be preformed by drives and universal inherited predispositions. Fairbairn considered the original object to be the influencing other, co-determining all parts of life, the development of structure, psychopathology, and also emotional health. Their similarities lie in the outstanding significance of internal objects in their work, although they do not share the same definition of internal objects. Mitchell (1981) and Grotstein (1994b) have done an extraordinary job defining the details of these difficulties. This chapter relates particularly to their ideas.

The internal object in the works of Melanie Klein

During the late 1920s Melanie Klein described the children she had treated as preoccupied with fantasies relating to notions of the mother's body (breast, penis, baby, uterus) and substances (milk, poison) and notions of their own body. Her thesis was, "… that from the early beginning the child has a much deeper and immediate relationship to others than had been assumed in psychoanalysis" (Klein, 1932), which was a revolutionary step that led to some hostility. To this day Melanie Klein is criticised for the repeated notion that the drives are able to generate the objects without prior experience. So, where do objects originate? She had the idea that objects were produced as universal phylogenetically based images due to the pressure of drives and independent of reality, hence decreasing internal tension. "… the child's earliest reality is wholly phantastic" (1930). Stating that the objects are generated by the drives via fantasy a priori, she seems to have been a radical representative of drive theory. It is often noted by her followers that she also stated the importance of external object relations. This controversy has only been resolved to a certain extent. Especially in her late work "Envy and Gratitude" (1957), she emphasised the external object's (also the analyst's) particular part in ameliorating destructiveness.

While Freud was initially of the opinion that the superego incorporated parental commandments and prohibitions and placed its origin within the Oedipal phase, approximately occurring at the age of six, Melanie Klein (1928) was of the opinion that the Oedipal conflict erupts within the first year of life. An extremely rigorous and punitive superego is developed as an expression of early internal object relations, which is also related to the internal aggressive and libidinal drives and the projected and re-introjected objects. The early archaic superego is defined by projected, haunting bad objects. By means of greed and envy the breast is dismembered and evolves into the bad breast. Retaliation, defined by persecution—and poisoning—anxieties, the fear of being poisoned by the addled bad breast, ensues. In some ways Freud's late notion that the manifestation of the superego is also strongly dependent on personal aggression must have been very satisfying for Klein.

In the mid-1930s Melanie Klein added a further approach to understanding the development of internal objects, while looking into the depressive position. In this case the origins of early objects generated by drives as unconscious fantasies are insignificant. At this point she argues that every external object can also be introjected as an internal object which is then again projected. She does not view this as a defence mechanism; instead she states it is a mechanism per se. "The ego is constantly absorbing into itself the whole external world" (1935). "Not just people, but all experiences and situations are internalized." Therefore the internal world of the child consists of innumerable introjected objects depending on numerous aspects—good or bad—which in turn depend on the unconscious fantasies of the child (Klein, 1940). This aspect in particular was refined by Paula Heimann (1952), who expanded the internalisation process by stating that the ego was capable of introjecting external stimuli. Although this does provoke the question: at what point does something become a memory or an introjection and why?

If and when internal objects are generated by internal images and external experiences the question remains: where do they coincide and how do they influence each other? Klein tried to solve this intricate difficulty by postulating a timeline. Initially the internal objects are determined by the child's sadism. As in the early superego these are very rigorous and punitive. During the child's development they are attenuated along with the superego by real experiences with the parents as primary good and kind "magical helpers". The more the fantasised internal objects and the external real objects coincide the more pathology converts to health. Melanie Klein's works prior to 1934 concerning the effects of the death drive and aggression gave the impression that she saw the origin of the internal bad object as an expression of the death drive's projection. During this period she had been conceptualising the early mechanisms of the depressive position. From this point of view internal objects are similar to a phylogenetic heritage, an inbred imago, and are a priori. As Klein went on to conceptualise the paranoid-schizoid position, it would not seem surprising that there were also external influences of real objects involved in generating the internal objects, hence meeting the requirements of an introjective process. This description is confusing in the sense that external factors are influential and yet it is a drive theory based concept. Like Freud she saw the origin of life's difficulties in inbred constitutional circumstances. The real object has a primarily modifying, attenuating character in charge of taming "the internal beast". Melanie Klein actually minimised the significance of the parents' pathogenic influence with their fears, ambivalences, and character pathologies. Like Freud she repeatedly revised her notions without surrendering previous notions or trying to establish an internal consistency within her system.

The internal object in Fairbairn's object psychology

Fairbairn was a revolutionary independent thinker who developed his ideas in the seclusion of Scotland's capital, Edinburgh. He studied the works of Freud and Klein very closely and revised a number of their shared opinions. He discarded the motivation theory of psychoanalysis, the drive theory in its strict sense, and expanded the perspective by postulating that the libido does not seek drive-discharge but the object itself. He reduces the satisfaction of drives to a mere channel, a mode of attaining the object. Fairbairn was of the opinion that Freud's model was influenced by the obsolete idea of energy and structure being segregated—in the spirit of Helmholtz's physics. Fairbairn on the contrary considers the endopsychical situation to be based on the unity of structure and energy. Hence every ego structure is also simultaneously energetic.

According to Freud's pleasure principle, the psychical apparatus's main function is regulating and permitting the discharge of drives by reducing tension. This is achieved by directing drive impulses towards an object or partial object and inducing the reduction of tension. From this point of view objects deliver pleasure. Fairbairn on the other hand argues that it is not primarily about a search for a pleasure-providing object but a search for the real object itself. He develops the notion that the child is born into infantile dependency upon the original object. Later the infant passes through a transitional phase and, if all goes well, progresses to mature dependency. Pleasure primarily serves to attain the object. It is not the primary goal; instead, pleasure is the effect of having attained the object and it is followed by direct reassurance. With his object relation psychology, Fairbairn during the 1940s acknowledged the real relationship between mother and child as the decisive factor for the development of the child's self. In this, he follows Sándor Ferenczi (1921), who had also accentuated the importance of the mother–child relationship. Since the infant cannot survive without the mother and is fully dependent upon her he must adapt to her during this early phase of life. Because relationships with others are also frustrating the child soon becomes frustrated. Even if the mother is in a state of "primary maternal preoccupation" (Winnicott, 1956), she can only work within the scope of her empathy and a limited channel of reciprocal verbal communication. Within the animal kingdom mothers are generally present as long as necessary while mothers within our society tend to live under enormous domestic, social, and economic pressure. Misunderstandings and panic-stricken mortal anxiety experienced on behalf of the child are inevitable. Due to his infantile dependency in matters of life and death, the child relies solely on his mother or primary caregiver. Even in the worst case scenario the infant must maintain an unsatisfactory relationship by introjecting the external relationship at the high cost of having to cope with the introjected unsatisfying situation internally. The consequences are the equivalent of an internal civil war. Later on this will become apparent in the form of an internal, unclear, contradictory state of emotions, contradictory personality traits, or of ego-alien interactions in the sense of dissociation (Wollnik, 2005). This suggests that we are dealing with an implicit, preverbal structural development, outside linguistic confinement, due to its establishment prior to the development of symbolising abilities (Hensel & Rehberger, 2006). Fairbairn's internal objects are established after the external event of overwhelming frustration and the internal experience of overwhelming frustration, hence a posteriori. The internal objects are the result of a defence mechanism and are therefore compensatory by nature. The larger the extent of deprivation is and the less real good relationships are present, the stronger internalisations including splittings of internal objects and pertaining ego-parts will be.

Fairbairn's theories change within his main works (1940a, 1941, 1943a, 1944, and 1951a), due to the development of his thinking over time. But one major point remained the same; the internalisations of object relations possess a compensatory character for unsatisfactory real object relations.

His articles on schizoid personality factors from 1940 and the revised psychopathology of psychosis and psychoneurosis from 1941 are strongly influenced by Melanie Klein's nomenclature, concentrating particularly on the oral phase of the drive development. During this phase the child assumes a physically and psychically usurping stance towards his surroundings. Fairbairn describes a primary identification during which the child does not yet experience himself as physically differentiated. At this point he follows Melanie Klein's lead in rejecting

Freud's primary narcissism (1914c). The child tries to cope with frustrating situations by internalising the good and the bad object.

By 1943 the main focus of motivation has shifted from oral incorporation to a relational and defensive level. Fairbairn describes the dilemma originating from the internalisation of a bad relationship in order to maintain the illusion of a good relationship to the primary caregiver. This unconditional internalisation of bad relationships leads to the child itself feeling equally bad and wicked. The parents are no longer the culprits: the child has taken the wickedness and badness upon himself. The parents' chaos, depression, and sadism have reached the child's internal realm. The child has paid the high price of deeply rooted internal insecurity for illusory outer security by internalising the bad object relations. A further consequence of the situation is the feeling of omnipotent control. This enables the child to outwardly display world-wisely, confident rationality and emotional frigidity by dissociation.

With the "moral defence" Fairbairn describes a subsequent second internalisation process following the internalisation of negative objects. At first, after internalising the negative objects the child feels irreversibly and unconditionally bad. He is therefore convinced that he is undeserving of the parents' love. In order to obtain internal security and the feeling of being loved by the parents the child must then identify himself with the good aspect of the relationship, the accepted or sufficiently good object. The defence process is characterised by the transformation from an unconditional and therefore hopeless situation to an entirely new one, in which the child is preoccupied with attaining the parents' love. At this point the child feels morally or partially bad, yet he is able to hope that by fulfilling the parents' expectations he will obtain their love. In our clinical practice we are often confronted with patients suffering from rigorous superegos or who set grandiose high standards for themselves. According to Fairbairn the origin of these feelings of guilt are not related to fantasised crimes and the pursuant guilty conscience as stated in the classical drive theory, but are often deeply connected to this double process of internalisation—the internalisation of the good secondary relationship succeeding the initial internalisation of the bad relationship with the parents. By these means the child is able to fend off feeling helplessly desperate, lost, and lonely in this world and at the same time perceive bad relationships as "good" ones.

Mitchell (1981) argues that Fairbairn's approach regarding his notions of internalisation is contradictory. His basic approach in 1940 and 1941, under the influence of intense research into Klein's works, leads to the assumption that during early infant development the child internalises the good and the bad objects based upon oral incorporation. The ideas of 1943 and 1944 on the other hand are under the influence of a relational level. Fairbairn is now convinced that in order to maintain the illusion of a real good relationship to mother the absolute bad object relation must be internalised first. The good object is then internalised as a defence against the unconditionally bad object in order to internally establish a conditionally bad object along with a conditionally good object carrying hope of love and affection. In 1951 he tries to integrate this idea by stating that the ego is initially undivided and the internalisation of a pre-ambivalent object is undergone in a state of frustration. Since the external object is ambivalent the undivided ego is under pressure to maintain the external object relation as good, which can only be achieved at the expense of the internal splitting of the object and the ego. Mitchell raises the question of why a child should internalise an ambivalent object when it is already capable of ambivalence itself. He asks: "What becomes of the moral defence when the ideal object has already been internalised?" I agree that Fairbairn's 1943 version of his theory seems to be the most plausible one. At first the bad object relation is internalised; afterwards the moral defence enables the internalisation of the good relation in order to weaken the unconditionally bad object relation.

Fairbairn's ego structures

In the following I shall summarise the development of the endopsychical situation according to Fairbairn, as I personally find it to be plausible. First and foremost it seems obvious that from the beginning of life itself physical contact is crucial and hence object relations are key. The physical experience with the mother is a realm of possibilities for creating object relations as tenderly acceptant, nourishingly exciting, but also as passively dismissing or actively rejecting with the option of excretion, biting, as well as pleasure and/or pain. These processes occur implicitly prior to a symbolisation process. The loving feedback the child accepts towards his own good is crucial to his development. If the child's undivided ego is subjected to an overly unsatisfactory situation, overwhelming the ego, this traumatic situation activates the internalisation of the object as a defence mechanism. This is not an expression of imagination but a necessary defence mechanism ensuring psychical survival. The bad object relation has two aspects—an exciting and a rejecting aspect—both pertaining to the bad relation and neither of which can be overcome. Both contradictory elements of the bad relation are internalised, split from the actual nucleus of the object, and repressed. This entails two separate internalised objects—the exciting (libidinal) object and the rejecting (anti-libidinal) object. The actual nucleus of the initial object is described as the ideal object or the accepted object. Since both the libidinal and the anti-libidinal object were cathected by the original ego these objects are repressed together with the cathecting parts of the ego. The result is a splitting of the original ego into the central ego connected to the ideal object, the libidinal ego connected to the exciting object, and the anti-libidinal ego, also known as the internal saboteur, connected to the rejecting object.

A sufficient and adequate real experience of tender tactile interactions between mother and child reduces the necessity of repression and splitting. The central ego internalises them into the accepted object and therefore they are accessible as pleasant tender memories later on. Mentalisation, symbolisation, concern, cross-identification, and object consistency are located within the central ego. In contrast, parts of the ego must be split and suppressed when confronted with overly strong frustrations in early interactions under the pressure of an early life situation shared with a bad object. These parts of the ego are not integrated, hence we find there to be a lack of symbolising abilities and an inclination towards direct actions "without thinking". All affects of anger and hate towards the rejecting objects are contained within the anti-libidinal ego. Here lies the future psychical entity responsible for rejection, alienation, and hate within sexual interactions (Hensel, 2002), but also for self-hatred, self-devaluation, and chronic feelings of inferiority. The libidinal ego contains all the extremely strong unfulfilled desires deriving from the bad object experience with the libidinal object. Later on this entity will be responsible for an extreme hunger for love, hyper-sexuality, paradisiacal fusion-desires, etc.

Schizoid problems are made manifest within real object relations, especially in a romantic relationship and in sexuality, due to internal conflict of contrary object relations concealed within the defensive layer being activated—the desire for love within the libidinal ego and the anger and hatred of the anti-libidinal ego towards the particular partial objects. At an early level this means, "Will love and sexuality kill me or which object defence will at the least permit sexuality" (Hensel, 2005). In a more mature sense this sets the stage for a conflict of ambivalence, which must engender a defence mechanism.

Comparing the internal objects of Ronald Fairbairn and Melanie Klein

I have demonstrated that Melanie Klein's and Fairbairn's views differ greatly and partially represent each other's opposite. This is consistent with the schism in psychoanalysis and derives from a long tradition. Melanie Klein is a representative of the drive theory, arguing for the root of psychical misery to lie in drives and their particular fate. Greed, envy, jealousy, and personal murderous intensions are the source of internal bad objects and the paranoid-schizoid situation leading to persecution anxieties and other psychopathological conditions. Real relationships with "life-helpers" are of mitigating character towards the internal archaic drive conflicts. For Fairbairn on the other hand neurosis is the expression of real parental failure. In general the child's needs are to be fulfilled, yet the parents' inadequacy intensifies the needs and the splitting of unsatisfied relational needs. At the beginning of life Fairbairn sees a pre-moral situation (Grotstein & Rinsley, 1994, p. 118), an original innocence, and the child's right to emotionally adequate resonance, heartfelt love, and affection; only afterwards can it experience guilt.

Schizoid retreat versus paranoia

Klein's paradigm stems from Freud's work on *Mourning and Melancholia* (1917e). Imaginatively, the object which has been experienced as ambivalent is destroyed, introjected, and due to the related feelings of guilt submitted to the superego. This process results from primary process fantasies, while the secondary process is important in order to attain the depressive position. In contrast, Fairbairn views external real objects to be internalised into the internal schizoid position in order to secure the external object relations. Modern infant research verifies Klein's and Fairbairn's notions that the child immediately experiences himself as separate from his surroundings. Klein has not been confirmed in her assumption of the existence of an immediate primary process of fantasies, which could only occur around the age of thirty-six months alongside language-acquisition and symbolisation abilities. On the other hand Fairbairn's notion, that the child immediately perceives his surroundings, which proves the existence of a rudimentary secondary process, has been confirmed.

Imagination in moral defence

Fairbairn's and Klein's notions pertaining to fantastic activities generally differ from each other. While Klein regards them to be immediate, Fairbairn considers them to be a secondary compensational phenomenon—a reaction to frustrating relationships. Since the child previously projected his destructiveness, Klein argues, idealisation results from a schizoid defence mechanism in order to fend off persecution anxieties. It can only be calmed by object idealisation. Feelings of guilt are an expression of prior aggressive fantasies towards the object. By contrast Fairbairn is diametrically opposed. Based on the experience with abused children, Fairbairn comes to the conclusion that the external relationship with the object is stabilised by introjection of the bad object and only afterwards can the accepted object be introjected into the superego inducing feelings of guilt. The internal advantage lies in the conditional badness, which is clearly preferable to the unconditional. Under these circumstances imagination is utilised secondarily in order to improve an internally painful situation. To this day this notion has remained essential for treatments concerning post-traumatic stress situations and coping.

Due to the fact that we are able to perceive objects in our imagination in accordance with Klein as well as realistically in accordance with Fairbairn, Grotstein (1994b) proposes a "dual track" solution for this dilemma. While Fairbairn tended to underestimate the innate factor—innate aggression—and developed a psychological model, Klein developed a model bent on innate constitutional factors—the drives. A synthesis of both movements seems unlikely yet it is often proposed. I consider the acknowledgement of implicit theoretical or verbal restrictions to be most important. It is only through candid consideration for both movements that we are enabled to uphold the process of integration within ourselves and for our patients. Since rejecting interactions are a part of life the incidental aggressions are ubiquitous. Whether or not the construction of a death drive is necessary seems superfluous to me. Although it is correct that constitutional factors influence the extent and readiness at which defence mechanisms can be mobilised. In certain ways Klein and Fairbairn are quite similar. Either bad parents are responsible for our neurotic misery or our innate drives taint us with guilt. Perhaps the tragedy lies in human cohabitation involving painful rejection and leading to an aggression for which we carry an innate apparatus.

Therapeutic aspects

After establishing a good enough relationship with the therapist a patient is able to take the risk of wandering into the realm of split object relations and the correlating parts of the ego. The surfacing memories can also be viewed under the impression of transference, yet it is equally important for the patient to feel that he is taken seriously regarding the grievous facts of his life and given the opportunity to initiate a mourning process. It is far more difficult to acknowledge one's personal defencelessness as a child, or later on, and even in analysis, than experience oneself as an active, fate-determining, "aggressive-libidinal" perpetrator generating a feeling of omnipotence. Many of our patients were in fact victimised by their relationship to their parents, especially when it comes to major disorders.

A patient treated by a Kleinian therapist will acknowledge his own culpability and hence the possibilities to actively change the here and now, if he can tolerate his own impulses through aggressive and libidinal fantasies. It is helpful if the therapist contributes to this process of coping with conflicting drives in order to attenuate archaic fantasies by means of "containment", coping with countertransference, and modification. This can support the ability to symbolise, impulse-control, and the integration of suppressed unconscious fantasies. The revision of numerous case studies for the German Psychoanalytic Association (DPV)'s colloquiums brings me to the question: why is the biographical part often abbreviated and why are real and fantasised relationships with primary caregivers reduced to a subordinate role? Perhaps it is because it is omitted in analysis itself, that countertransference has become the main focus of treatment, which might be most associated with the Kleinian orientation.

For a therapeutic process according to Fairbairn I consider it to be crucial, whether or not the therapist has dealt with his own feelings of being defenceless as well as being the perpetrator within his self-experience in his personal past history and whether he is willing to progressively deal with them beyond his self-experience and therapeutic training.

Fairbairn decisively recognised and announced the therapist's role as a real person. This is mainly based on the fact that he considered relationships to be the root of psychopathology and by the same token to possess the ability to support a maturational process. This makes him the predecessor of intersubjectivity and relational psychoanalysis. His idea of the endopsychical situation and its immanent ego structures are the expression and result of bad real relationships.

Since Fairbairn understands the pathology of object relations, the resulting structures are based on pathological relationships. Thus he views his therapeutic goals from a slightly different angle. Regarding the therapeutic process, Fairbairn (1958a) states the following: such a relationship not only presents the possibilities to correct a dysfunctional relationship dominating the internal reality of a patient and influencing his reactions towards external objects, but also presents him with the opportunity to experience a process of emotional development within a real relationship with a consistent and benevolent parent figure, giving him a chance he had been denied during his childhood. Fairbairn considers supporting a maximum synthesis of the structures into which the ego has been split within the setting of a therapeutic relationship with the therapist to be one of the most important goals of treatment in addition to (a) a maximum reduction of infantile dependency and (b) a maximum reduction of hate towards the libidinal object, which hatred is responsible for the original splitting of the ego (ibid.). The final goal of treatment is to "pry open" the patient's sealed internal system by means of a real relationship with the therapist. The notion of a transference relationship is insufficient; it is necessary to experience a different relationship with the therapist (also see Potthoff, 2005).

How can we determine Fairbairn's approach? The decisive factor is not solely interpretation but also the therapist's being concerned with the patient, being involved, and pointing out new interrelations in transference or even extra-transference through experience while at the same time authentically being a singular differentiated person. The transference does not serve the interpretation of the patient's hate depicted by greed, envy, jealousy, and perversion as an expression of destructiveness as much as it directs the attention to justifiable anger towards an early or recently overwhelmingly frustrating object, which is or has been desired and loved, but possesses rejecting traits. Negative and positive transference are also important yet the final goal is the integration and "decontamination" (Scharff & Tsigounis, 2003) of split parts of the ego which have been charged with overly strong affects especially of self-hatred. From this point of view the therapist is responsible for a "realm" in which the patient's internal structure is able to unfold in transference.

For therapists thinking with Fairbairn's nomenclature regarding internalised object relations this means that we are dealing with relationships which are the result of prior relationships and not the expression of conflicting drives. This enables us to reflect upon the relational level on which we encounter the patient.

Relationships between the central ego and the accepted or sufficiently good object

The first level can be designated as the relationship between the central ego and the accepted object. This is the level on which a patient generally tries to communicate with us upon the first encounter. He has a positive "non-offensive" transference and schedules an appointment. During the initial interview he portrays his problems. It becomes apparent how integrated or split his self is. Is he capable of self-reflecting, cross-identification in the sense of being able to empathise with others, and of symbolising, is he able to partake in an interaction or does this seem difficult? What access do his narratives grant to his affects, are they split or integrated, and to what extent is he detached from the here and now, and his relationships? Does the patient appear to accept interpretations which he emotionally cannot grasp at all, or only fractionally accept them in order to receive the therapist's attention? Does he have rationalising explanations, attesting to his cooperation and yet rejecting the intervention? There is also the risk that the patient might talk too much, prohibiting the therapist from talking, since he is not accustomed to it and he is unwilling to be brought to a different level by growing emotionally involved with the therapist, because this level is feared, fended off, and must remain sealed off.

Relationships between the anti-libidinal ego ("the internal saboteur") and the anti-libidinal object

Serious complications are to be expected if an encounter at the level of the anti-libidinal object and the anti-libidinal ego or internal saboteur takes place in the beginning of the treatment. Commonly this is provoked by an inept intervention, a pre-verbal implicit rejection by the therapist, or the patient's loosened defence. This is the level of disappointed anger—of murderous hate. This is to be kept in mind, when the therapist's intervention leaves the patient feeling misunderstood and attacked to the extent that central ego relationships can no longer be maintained. The patient is overwhelmed by aggressive feelings of the anti-libidinal ego and is under the impression of being attacked instead of helped. He feels compromised or accused, which is often caused by absolute drive interpretations lacking the acknowledgement that the defence is justified as a palliative solution. The best case scenario would be a return to central ego relationships by jointly clarifying how the therapist offended the patient and in which sense he felt attacked, offended, devalued, or humiliated. This means that the therapist permits the questioning of his entire person. Which gesture, facial or verbal expression caused the irritation, what did this trigger within the patient, and what did it remind him of? This can become a productive process.

In a less favourable scenario the patient complies in a more or less undetectable schizoid manner, splitting his anger in the relationship with the therapist for fear of object loss. On the surface he seems calm and adapted; beneath the surface scepticism and caution have been confirmed. What is left is a neutral "residual relationship" which has been drained below the surface. Affective involvement is avoided, the relationship appears to be "good" while it is actually affectively shallow, boring, and lifeless. Thoughts wander astray during countertransference; fatigue, hopelessness, and resignation run their course. Perhaps the patient can only express the importance of the relationship by excessively talking without any apparent reference to himself and by attending sessions regularly as well as punctually.

In the worst case the patient leaves the room or does not attend the following session. It is extremely important for the therapeutic process that this level of negative transference is entered with the foundation of a good relationship established during the course of treatment, in order for the central ego to access, integrate, and "decontaminate" the parts of the anti-libidinal ego. Since this level is about early implicit interaction patterns it is also the level of enactments; their symbolisation must be acquired during the proceeding treatment.

Relationships between the libidinal ego and the libidinal object

Another aspect is the common observation that patients tend to protect their libidinal ego most fiercely. What does this mean? Many patients come with apparently clear preconceptions. They desire to be delivered of certain symptoms, yet they are unwilling to deal with themselves, their history, or even the feelings they experience in relationships. They function on the level of a relationship between the central ego and the accepted object, where the central ego is mainly reduced to functionality and rationality and feelings are hardly integrated. Conflicts on the level of the anti-libidinal ego are connected to affects of hate whereas conflicts on the level of the libidinal ego are split and suppressed. The patient has mobilised his moral defence and is also trying to attain the therapist's respect and attention with moderate and rational behaviour. If we do not recognise this level of object relations and address the seemingly apparent libidinal and aggressive conflicts too rashly we run the risk that in spite of all efforts the patient will not feel accepted. Generally the level between libidinal ego and libidinal object is fended off the most. Here lie the deepest desires for unconditional love, paradisiacal situations, or sexual ecstasy as well as all the passively experienced mortifications sustained at the hands of the original object, alongside a defenceless fear of abandonment reaching as far as the fear of death. The defence of these internally dangerous conditions is executed by splitting: "I feel nothing, I am empty, everything is senseless", or "I am unable to love another (and also myself)", "I never want to experience this love and suffering again. The agony is killing me." This is a schizoid retreat. Another version is suppression with the help of the anti-libidinal ego: "I hate him and cannot understand that I loved this person", or "I hate myself for having needed and loved this person. This will never happen to me again." During the therapeutic process a mild form of the libidinal ego's integration can be defined by the patient emotionally committing to another person much stronger or immersing further into a prior relationship in extra-transference. This becomes obvious in the transference-relationship, when he reacts emotionally to treatment interruptions with grief or anger. He retreats from the "business" level and is able to show gratitude and dependency. This can only be achieved if the patient is able to commit to the therapeutic relationship with internal stability, for this enables him to take on the risks of defencelessness, humiliation, rejection, and mortification without utilizing schizoid mechanisms. This requires the therapist to establish an atmosphere of encouragement and reinforcement. Neutral silence can be regarded as rejection perpetuating the schizoid mechanism. By the means of his own conduct the therapist is able to clarify that he is "married to the setting" and that there are boundaries even if a session might have been exceeded or an additional session added in a time of crisis. Symbolisation can slowly be achieved if these enactments are tolerated and continually acknowledged as frozen processes of traumatic deprivations.

What happens when the libidinal ego breaks through abruptly? This state is often feared by the patient as well as the therapist and fended off in transference and countertransference. The libidinal ego is most likely to unveil itself through extra-transference. The patient proclaims an "undying love". In transference this erotic transference is treated as a grave resistance. This condition can not be "allowed". A frequent attempt in preventing this development is a form of seemingly abstinent behaviour in the sense of misunderstood neutrality. When every form of reinforcement is understood as a satisfaction of drives it becomes a caricature. This can lead to the staging of an unreflected vicious cycle of desire and constant rejection. The therapist actually encourages the erotic transference if he presents a crass rejection to be seemingly necessary in order to establish neutrality. This external constellation of exciting and rejecting object rejuvenates and preserves the internal object relations. The patient hopes to attain an object through sexualisation. Often enough the therapist will wash his hands of the matter, not noticing how strongly he has contributed to an erotic transference. Treatments that have progressed in such fashion are often prematurely terminated by the therapist claiming that there is no "working alliance". Sadly, the repeated occurrence of sexual assaults shows the immense influence of the therapist's enactments regarding this matter. In my opinion these cases are also a sign of the therapist's lack of integration regarding his own libidinal ego. He is overwhelmed and acts out on behalf of an ego-part, which in real life has not been integrated. Whether it is due to a crisis or even permanently disintegrated it causes extensive harm.

If we stay aware to a child's real dependency which is in accordance to that of a patient's in a regressive condition, we can clearly see how rapidly some patients adapt to our needs and desire to treat and support us. However we may carry ourselves, we, as real people, are also "participants". As described by Bieniek (2006), sometimes if the therapist is able to accept that the patient is able to give him something, a "now-moment" can be established.

Translation by Rebecca Tovar (Tovar@sigmund-freud-institute.de)

References

Bieniek, W. (2006). Masochismus—Abwehr schlechter internalisierter Objekte. In: B. F. Hensel, D. E. Scharff, & E. Vorspohl (Eds.), *W. R. D. Fairbairns Bedeutung für die moderne Objektbeziehungstheorie*. Gießen, Germany: Psychosozial Verlag.

Fairbairn, W. R. D. (1940a). Schizoide Persönlichkeitsfaktoren. In: *Das Selbst und die inneren Objektbeziehungen* (pp. 31–56). Gießen, Germany: Psychosozial Verlag, 2000.

Fairbairn, W. R. D. (1941). Eine revidierte Psychopathologie der Psychosen und Psychoneurosen. In: *Das Selbst und die inneren Objektbeziehungen* (pp. 57–88). Gießen, Germany: Psychosozial Verlag, 2000.

Fairbairn, W. R. D. (1943a). Die Verdrängung und die Wiederkehr schlechter Objekte (unter besonderer Berücksichtigung der "Kriegsneurosen"). In: *Das Selbst und die inneren Objektbeziehungen* (pp. 89–114). Gießen, Germany: Psychosozial Verlag, 2000.

Fairbairn, W. R. D. (1944). Darstellung der endopsychischen Struktur auf der Grundlage der Objektbeziehungspsychologie. In: *Das Selbst und die inneren Objektbeziehungen* (pp. 115–170). Gießen, Germany: Psychosozial Verlag, 2000.

Fairbairn, W. R. D. (1951a). Synopse: Die Entwicklung der Ansichten des Autors über die Persönlichkeitsstruktur. In: *Das Selbst und die inneren Objektbeziehungen* (pp. 185–204). Gießen, Germany: Psychosozial Verlag, 2000.

Fairbairn, W. R. D. (1958a). On the nature and aims of psycho-analytical treatment. *International Journal of Psychoanalysis, 39*(5): 374–385. In: D. E. Scharff & E. F. Birtles (Eds.), *From Instinct to Self: Selected Papers of W. R. D. Fairbairn, Volume I: Clinical and Theoretical Papers* (pp. 74–92). Northvale, NJ: Jason Aronson, 1994.

Fairbairn, W. R. D. (2000). *Das Selbst und die inneren Objektbeziehungen*. B. F. Hensel & R. Rehberger (Eds.), E. Vorspohl (Trans.). Gießen, Germany: Psychosozial Verlag.

Ferenczi, S. (1921). Beitrag zur "Tic-Diskussion". In: *Bausteine zur Psychoanalyse. Bd. III* (pp. 168–169). Berne, Switzerland: Huber, 1984.

Freud, S. (1914c). Zur Einführung des Narzissmus. *G. W., 10*: 137–170. London: Imago.

Freud, S. (1917e). *Trauer und Melancholie. G. W., 10*: 428–446. London: Imago.

Grotstein, J. S. (1994b). Notes on Fairbairn's metapsychology. In: J. S. Grotstein & D. B. Rinsley (Eds.), *Fairbairn and the Origins of Object Relations* (pp. 112–148). London: Free Association.

Heimann, P. (1952). Certain functions of introjection and projection in early infancy. In: M. Klein, P. Heimannn, S. Isaacs, & J. Rivière. *Developments in Psychoanalysis*. London: Hogarth.

Hensel, B. F., & Rehberger, R. (2006). Das Selbst bei Fairbairn und Guntrip. *Selbstpsychologie, 24*: 140–155.

Hensel, B. F. (2002). W. R. D. Fairbairn's Objektbeziehungspsychologie: Theoretische und klinische Folgerungen für die heutige Psychoanalyse. In: G. Heising, B. F. Hensel, W.-D. Rost et al. (2002). *Zur Attraktivität des bösen Objekts* (pp. 203–248). Gießen, Germany: Psychosozial Verlag).

Hensel, B. F. (2005). An object relations view of sexuality based on Fairbairn´s theory. In: J. S. Scharff & D. E. Scharff (Eds.), *The Legacy of Fairbairn and Sutherland* (pp. 68–79). London: Routledge, 2005.

Klein, M. (1928). Frühstadien des Ödipuskonfliktes. In: R. Cycon (Ed.), *Gesammelte Schriften. Bd. I, 1* (pp. 287–305). Stuttgart-Bad Cannstatt, Germany: frommann-holzboog, 1995.

Klein, M. (1930). Die Bedeutung der Symbolbildung für die Ich-Entwicklung. In: R. Cycon (Ed.), *Gesammelte Schriften. Bd. I, 1* (pp. 347–368). Stuttgart-Bad Cannstatt, Germany: frommann-holzboog, 1995.

Klein, M. (1932). Die Psychoanalyse des Kindes. In: R. Cycon (Ed.), *Gesammelte Schriften. Bd. II*. Stuttgart-Bad Cannstatt, Germany: frommann-holzboog, 1997.

Klein, M. (1935). Beitrag zur Psychogenese der manisch-depressiven Zustände. E. Vorspohl (Trans.). In: R. Cycon (Ed.), *Gesammelte Schriften. Bd. I, 2* (pp. 29–75). Stuttgart-Bad Cannstatt, Germany: frommann-holzboog, 1996.

Klein, M. (1940). Die Trauer und ihre Beziehung zu manisch-depressiven Zuständen. E. Vorspohl (Trans.). In: R. Cycon (Ed.), *Gesammelte Schriften. Bd. I, 2* (pp. 159–199). Stuttgart-Bad Cannstatt, Germany: frommann-holzboog, 1996.

Klein, M. (1957). Envy and gratitude. In: *Envy and Gratitude and Other Works 1946–1963*. M. M. R. Khan (Ed.). The International Psycho-Analytical Library, *104*: 1–346. London: Hogarth and the Institute of Psycho-Analysis, 1975.

Mitchell, S. A. (1981). The origin and the nature of the "object" in the theories of Klein and Fairbairn. *Contemporary Psychoanalysis, 17*(3): 374–398.

Potthoff, P. (2005). The real relationship with the analyst as a new object. In: J. S. Scharff & D. E. Scharff (Eds.), *The Legacy of Fairbairn and Sutherland* (pp. 105–112). London: Routledge.

Scharff, J. S., & Tsigounis, A. (2003). *Self Hatred in Psychoanalysis—Detoxifying the Persecutory Object*. Hove, UK: Brunner Routledge.

Winnicott, D. W. (1956). Primary maternal preoccupation. In: *Collected Papers, through Paediatrics to Psychoanalysis* (pp. 300–305). London: Tavistock, 1958.

Wollnik, S. (2005). Dissociation and repression in trauma. In: J. S. Scharff & D. E. Scharff (Eds.), *The Legacy of Fairbairn and Sutherland* (pp. 121–128). London: Routledge, 2005.

CHAPTER TWELVE

Fairbairn: Oedipus reconfigured by trauma

Eleanore M. Armstrong-Perlman

Introduction

In *The Structure of Scientific Revolutions* (1962), Thomas Kuhn emphasises how the prevailing paradigm influences scientific endeavour. Data is structured, processed, and given relevance within the framework of the prevailing model. When the paradigm begins to be faced with new data that confront the model, there is a phase of accommodation. The basic theory is stretched to contain the new data in an attempt to preserve the basic structure by various modifications. At this stage, there is resistance to alternative paradigms. It is safer and more comforting to readjust the existing conceptual edifice. But such readjustments create strains and tensions which can lead to the breakdown of the resistance to new paradigms. The proliferation of the epicycles needed to cope with the data within the Ptolemaic system led to the Copernican revolution in astronomy.

I believe that the recent upsurge of interest in the work of Fairbairn is arising from the current tensions and strains facing the Freudian paradigm to accommodate and adjust to new data. In this chapter I hope to clarify how Fairbairn's concept of our fundamental nature is affected by cumulative trauma arising from too misattuned maternal responsiveness. This gives rise to defensive structures necessary for psychological survival, and these are formed in the state of absolute infantile dependence. This is prior to the resolution of the Oedipus complex in the name of preserving the "affectionate current" (Freud, 1910h), with the mother before the advent of the father.

Apart from Little Hans, the Freudian account of the Oedipus complex was developed and refined in the context of the therapeutic dyad. The consistency of the transferential response would seem to confirm that the underlying psychic structure as made manifest in the transference has little to do with external reality. These phenomena, presumed to be manifestations of unconscious processes, give rise to a model of a never-ending internal conflict between the excited body-based demands of the id and the powerful strictures exercised by the punitive superego. That beleaguered structure the ego has to maintain the delicate task of functional survival in terms of psychic necessity both internal and external. Fairbairn's central ego is already a dynamic structure formed by the need to preserve a benign environment.

For Fairbairn, "It is in the setting of the child's relationship to his mother that the basic endopsychic situation is established, that the differentiation of endopsychic structure is accomplished and that repression is originated; and it is only after these developments have occurred that the child is called upon to meet the particular difficulties which attend the Oedipus situation. So far from furnishing an explanatory concept, therefore, the Oedipus situation is rather a phenomenon to be explained in terms of an endopsychic situation which has already developed" (1952, p. 121).

An infant's primary need is to maintain a satisfactory relationship with the mother combined with the need to separate from the mother. This affects the development of psychic structures. How these structures are formed and the purpose they serve affects later development. This is prior to the formation of the Oedipus complex (Armstrong-Perlman, 2000).

As the term "object" is so fundamental, I wish to clarify it as it is conceptualised in British object relations theory. "Object" does not refer to an inanimate thing. When used to refer to an actual person it is not describing them in a depersonalised manner. An object in British object relations theory is that which an individual, or some aspect or part of an individual strives to attain or get attached to for the satisfaction of a need, a drive, or an instinct. The object might be an external real other. It may also be a representational, symbolic aspect of an other which has been created, not necessarily consciously with intent, by an individual or part of an individual for some purpose or other, as in a fetish. The British Object Relations School stresses that the infant is "object" relating from birth. The mother or maternal object is of primary importance to the infant, rather than being merely a necessary adjunct to the satisfaction of the aim of the instinct. She is not just a good breast (Armstrong-Perlman, 1986).

However, there is a need to clarify the concept of the "object". The "object" to which the child is assumed to relate can be internal and therefore still part of the fantasy element, or external and therefore environment-dependent. Melanie Klein, for example, emphasised the primacy of primitive internal objects in the structuring of the inner world of the infant long before the development of the superego proper. But her emphasis on primary envy and the death instinct reduces the role of the actual caregivers to the confirmation or modification of primitive fantasy, a product of the instincts or drives per se. Other theorists such as Balint, Fairbairn, Winnicott, or Kohut may regard these drives as secondary, arising from, and exacerbated by, an environmental situation where the fit between the child and his significant others was not good enough.

Fairbairn's theory is an account of how to negotiate a developmental process of separation individuation: there is a continuum from infantile dependence which is absolute, via transitional dependence to mature dependence.

Infantile dependence

The Fairbairnian infant needs to love and be loved, initially by his mother. He is in a state of absolute unconditional dependence on the mother for the satisfaction of physical and emotional needs. She constitutes not only the infant's world but also his or her self, in as much as he or she is not as yet completely differentiated from her. Moreover, the mother also constitutes the conditions of personal survival.

In the very early stages of development, survival means adapting to the mother and getting her to adapt in an appropriate way. The actual responsiveness of the mother is of crucial importance. To survive, the infant must develop an ability to register responses and a repertoire to cope with disappointing or frustrating responses. The Fairbairnian infant is a sentient being from the start, assimilating and registering dawning perceptual awareness, in particular those aspects of the outside world on which survival depends. Initially this is the mother. There is an awareness of reality and a developing capacity for recognition. The infant is reactive and proactive ab initio. "The point of view that I am putting forward here is that at full term, there is already a human being in the womb, one that is capable of having experiences and of accumulating body memories and even of organising defensive measures to deal with traumata (such as the interruption of continuity of being by reaction to the impingements from the environment in so far as it fails to adapt)" (Winnicott, 1988). In this respect Fairbairn's position is akin to that of Winnicott who claims that a person's story and the potential hazards for that development begin before birth.

Empirical research over the past decades has confirmed that experience of external reality can have an effect on the foetus in utero. This may later shape responsiveness in a positive or negative fashion, for example, the effect of incubators contrasted with kangaroo care (Buitelaar, Huizink, Mulder, de Medina, & Visser, 2003; Fride & Weinstock, 1988; Glover & Hill, 2012; Korhonen, Luoma, Salmelin, & Tamminen, 2012).

Like Freud, Fairbairn traces back "all [the] preconditions for loving" (Freud, 1912d) to infancy. The earliest contact with the mother is sensual, an erotic, embodied relationship. This conjunction of two bodies can alternate between passionate excitement, raging frustration, withdrawal from intrusion, taking for granted, and the beatitude of the contented sleepy suckling. The mother is the gateway through which the infant enters the world (Armstrong-Perlman, 1987).

For the infant to confidently explore the frightening maze which is the world out there, the mother, like Ariadne, must provide the appropriate thread. Loose enough to give scope for exploration, strong enough to be secure that one can return to safety. Such a potential haven provides the basis of hope. The world is not an alien place, nor is the infant alienated from the world. In states of tension, the infant can conjure up the image of the responsive mother so that they have someone to turn to. This expectation preserves hope. Absence is not equivalent to the loss of the mother. He is not abandoned. Waiting is finite; there is a light at the end of the tunnel. This is the necessary matrix for the emergence of a confident, spontaneous, vigorous, embodied self that is not compromised by separation anxiety.

But if the absence is too long and if the mother is consistently not there for the infant, he or she is deserted without sight or hope of an oasis. Waiting may then constitute a black hole of despair and desolation. There is no hope of a responsive other to relieve the intolerable tension. The infant loses the image of a loving mother that can be conjured up to relieve desolation, abandonment, and the resulting fear of the out-there.

Continuous breaches of this primary need for the responsive acceptance of the mother can stifle the infant's ability to explore and begin the necessary process of separation. If that mighty instrument, the scream, is not responded to, too often, the infant can experience "primitive agonies" (Winnicott, 1974), which can stunt the emergent self. Being reality-adapted, if despair is ignored, the child will comply. The cry becomes stifled by exhaustion. This can lead to a loss of an expectation of the responsive mother. To save the infant from primitive agonies, protection is required and hence defences need to be built.

The structure of defence in the aim of survival

For Fairbairn the first step in the construction of defence is the internalisation of the whole relationship with the mother. "With a view to controlling the unsatisfying object, he employs the defensive process of internalisation to remove it from outer reality, where it eludes his control, to the sphere of inner reality, where it offers prospects of being more amenable to control in the role of internal object" (1952, p. 172).

The protective function of internalisation is to preserve the image of his mother as a safe person in external reality that he or she can love. If the mother is too frustrating, given the infant's absolute need of her, she becomes infinitely desirable but at the same time she is infinitely frustrating. As the mother constitutes the conditions of hope, a good enough representation of an acceptable mother is essential for the maintenance of the self.

However, this first method of protection does not solve the problem, as, "[B]oth the over-exciting and the over-frustrating elements in the internal (ambivalent) object are unacceptable to the original ego" (ibid., p. 135). This duality of aspects "constitutes as great a difficulty in the inner world as that formerly constituted by the ambivalence of objects in the outer world" (ibid., p. 172). The danger has merely been transferred to an internal theatre.

The next step is that the internalised whole object is shorn of the exciting and frustrating aspects which gave rise to the conditions of trauma, leaving an idealised acceptable object for the infant to safely love. The whole purpose of the defensive structure is to cope with an outside world that is experienced as intolerable. If the pristine emerging self is still attached to the internalised representations constructed by the process of splitting of the object, it would still be confronted by all the dilemmas and frustrations encountered in outer reality. The inner world would just mirror the outer and could not affect the relationships there. There would be an inner imago of the exciting, alluring siren, metaphorically enticing one to crash yet again on the rocks of maternal unresponsiveness. This splitting of the rejective and the exciting aspects can later block awareness of how a relationship with an "exciting object" is toxic until reality is inescapable.

The central ego, which mediates between the inner and outer world, is attached to the idealised object. The libidinal ego is attached to the exciting object and the anti-libidinal ego to the rejective object. These sub-selves with their respective objects then constitute separate dynamic structures of volition. They are constellations characterised by differing needs and passions. Both the anti-libidinal ego and the central ego are involved in maintaining the repression of the relationship with the exciting object.

Now that the central ego is attached to the idealised object it can externalise this idealised object onto the original mother in outer reality, converting her into an acceptable object. If this process can be maintained, then there is a successful defensive structure in place. The infant's relationship with the outside object is maintained as "good" via the mediation of the central ego's attachment to the internal "good" object. However, this structure is constantly under threat. The transference has only modified the infant's perception as the parent may continue to frustrate. Further defences are required as the frustrated excitement and rage have to be repudiated. If too frustrated, the central ego can become progressively disembodied and devoid of aliveness.

For Fairbairn repression is the mechanism used by the central ego to maintain its libidinal attachment to the ideal object and thus preserve the external object as "good". To avoid the re-emergence of the split-off "bad" objects with the "good" object, the central ego represses the split-off parts of itself, the libidinal and anti-libidinal egos, which are attached to the exciting and rejecting objects. "Repression is primarily exercised, not against impulses which have come to appear painful or 'bad' (as in Freud's final view) or even against painful memories (as in Freud's earlier view), but against internalised objects which have come to be treated as 'bad' but also as against parts of the 'ego' which seek relationships with these internal objects" (ibid., p. 89).

The emerging significance of the father

For Fairbairn, the infant encounters the father with an established history of repression. The father is an emerging but significant relational object for the infant; though initially he is handicapped. "Indeed it is chiefly as a parent without breasts that the child would appear to regard his father in the first instance" (ibid., p. 174). In the early stages, the relationship with the father "has to be made upon an almost exclusively emotional plane" (ibid., p. 174).

By arguing that the relationship with the father is experienced primarily at the emotional level, rather than the physical level, Fairbairn perhaps underestimates the alive sensuality possible in the relationship. Be that as it may, with the child's development, the father has more to offer. As the child's capacity for relatedness expands, he is confronted with two distinct parental objects and the initial lack of the breast diminishes.

The father offers an alternative source of parental emotional responsiveness, and a separate relational opportunity. The attachment literature generated by the work of J. Bowlby and M. Main provides empirical evidence for separate patterns of attachment with the father and the mother. For example, the infant can be anxious-avoidant with the mother and ambivalently attached to the father, or vice-versa. However, the pattern established with the mother tends to dominate the future relatedness of the child to both parents. This gives some corroboration for the significance of the early relationship with the mother affecting the child's later capacity for establishing secure attachments with others.

The Oedipal dilemma

The father is also a rival for the mother's love and attention as the child becomes aware of the father's claim to her body. She is no longer the infant's sole possession. The dyad is now a triad. The infant has to cope with sharing and if too excluded, this can lead to sadistic conceptions of the primal couple. The infant's importance, which is dependent on the other, is diminished and this can threaten the child's image of the mother. For Fairbairn, such envy and jealousy are determined "not only by the biological sex of the child, but also by the state of his emotional relationships with his respective parents" (ibid., p. 175). The strength of these feelings will vary with the degree of exclusion from the couple's intimacy.

Hamlet rages when confronted with his mother's excited coupling with Claudius, and for Fairbairn, Gertrude is the real villain of the piece. She is the fickle mother who has betrayed Hamlet by sharing her bed with Claudius, whom Hamlet does not love. He has ousted not only Hamlet's father but Hamlet himself from the throne of Denmark. Hamlet is so obsessed by sadistic and destructive fantasies about their coupling, that his own loses significance. The sad Ophelia, the potential object of his genital love, is urged to get herself "to a nunnery" (Shakespeare, 1603). Poor Ophelia becomes a repudiated and devalued episode, in an ambivalent life or death struggle over his disgust with the sexual activity of his mother.

In my experience some female patients, who continuously pursue married men, often have an impoverished relationship with their mother and an ambiguous but more exciting relationship with their father. The married man is the exciting object of repressed incestuous desire; the wife, the rejected rival, whose envied coupling is to be triumphed over. Repressed relationships originating from patients' own parents are continuously replayed to their own detriment.

If the relationship with the father is also too frustrating, the child again encounters the same vicissitudes of need, frustration, and rejection as in the original situation with the mother. There are similar problems of adjustment so the infant uses the same techniques as before, internalisation, splitting, and repression. The child now has to adjust to two frustrating relationships at the same time, neither offering the possibility of a secure attachment. "The child finds it intolerable enough to be called upon to deal with a single ambivalent object; but when he is called upon to deal with two, he finds it still more intolerable" (ibid., p. 124).

This confrontation with two exciting and rejecting objects is simplified by "converting it into one in which he will only be confronted with a single exciting object and a single rejecting object" (ibid., p. 124). The child achieves this aim, with varying measure of success, by concentrating upon the exciting aspect of one parent and the rejecting aspect of the other. He thus comes to equate one parent with the exciting object, and the other with the rejecting object.

For Freud, the mother is unquestionably the exciting object and the father the rejective object and it is the father's love the child craves. He is the primary object of the child's ambivalence. Although Freud acknowledges the existence of the child's tender and sadistic feelings for his mother, the role of ambivalence is not given structural significance. The need to maintain a loving relationship with the father is enabled by the construction of the superego, an internalised object affecting psychic structure. The child represses his sexual feelings for his mother on the basis of identification with the construction of the rejective father. This castrating relationship is repressed to maintain the "affectionate current" (Freud, 1912d) with the father. For Fairbairn, the too unresponsive mother can both allure and annihilate; a Medusa, whose gaze can turn the infant to stone (Armstrong-Perlman, 1994).

The Oedipus complex arises from the layering and fusion of separate representations of frustration with each parent. This polarisation is a psychic simplification that "would appear to be partly superimposed upon, and partly fused with the corresponding figures of his mother" (Fairbairn, 1952, p. 174). To quote a friend, after obtaining the help of outside authority to free herself from an influential but menacing lover, she realised that she had been seduced by a masculine version of her charming but sociopathic mother.

If the infant has experienced multiple separations or excessive frustration, tolerance of later frustration is merely controlled rather than modified. The current of fraught, unmet infantile dependence continues to persist. There is a substrate of addictive need, which has the capacity to undermine later seemingly mature development. In the journey of individuation there is still the risk of the breakdown of repression and the reactivation of relationships with early "bad" objects that can lead to intolerable tension, confusion, despair, or even annihilatory terror. Intimacy for such people can be dangerous. Repressed desire for the body of the mother lurks beneath the surface. Evidence for this can be seen in metaphor: in hymns, God may have an asexual bosom to be close to and the de-sexualised virgin with child is adored. Contact with women is dangerous and the allure is always the fault of the woman who tempts (Armstrong-Perlman, 1994).

Fairbairn's theory represents a fundamental shift from a psychology that emphasises the gratification of sexual or aggressive impulses to one that stresses the need for "primary love" (Balint, 1956). But "primary hate" lurks beneath the tranquillity of the waters. The self develops and is structured in the context of the relationship with the parents and the ever-widening circle of others.

Case study

Mr D, a client in his late sixties, needed a second analysis after rejection by his fiancée. His first analysis, with a classical Freudian male psychoanalyst, had lasted twelve years. He had sought treatment for his sexual problems, but it had ceased abruptly with the sudden death of the analyst. Though physically a good-looking man, he was unable to relate to women. He had had intercourse once, during his first analysis, but could not have an orgasm. Neither party wished to repeat the encounter. His sexuality since early adolescence had been restricted to compulsive masturbation. He would collect used condoms from the park and masturbate at home wearing his mother's brassiere with the condoms in the cups. This enacted activity with a fetishistic object failed to satisfy. He had risked exposure but had never been caught. However, though the excitement released and relieved intolerable tension, it was followed by emptiness, shame, and despair. He was only too aware it was a surrogate for genuine intercourse.

The first analysis, conducted at the Oedipal level, presumably on the basis of the resolution of his ambivalence towards the castrating father, enabled him to establish a male identity strong enough to separate from his mother. Though he had not been as fortunate as Little Hans (Freud, 1909b) with his actual father, he was more fortunate with his analyst. He was able to come to terms with his ambivalence towards his father and build on a positive identification.

The seeming resolution of the Oedipal problem had provided symptomatic relief. He had established a new life and a profession which gave him genuine satisfaction. However, his avoidance of competition meant he did not make full use of his qualifications. He developed interests and camaraderie in a masculine, sporting milieu. It was in relation to the elaboration and development of good experience with his analyst that he was capable of affectionate durable friendships with men. He also gave up masturbating dressed in his mother's clothes. This echoed a previous situation: he had been able to desist from the cross-dressing in the navy during the war. He had a good war record, but on demob, though offered a commission, he had retreated back to living with his mother. Though his first analysis had enabled him to separate, it had not enabled him to function at the genital level. He was aware that something was not being addressed.

He was referred to me by a male psychoanalyst, after a fifteen session therapy in a UK National Health Service setting, who considered him to be defending against passive homosexuality. The patient was aware of this assumption but was adamant that this was not correct. He felt that his sexuality had been perverted from its natural course, and that underneath, his "instincts were normal". In the early days of the therapy, he was convinced that if he could only conquer his impotence, and achieve adult heterosexual intercourse, he would be liberated.

His fiancée, a widow, had ended their short engagement when he postponed the marriage. He had refrained from consummating the relationship. His potential rage must have been palpable, as she had ended the relationship in the presence of her adult sons.

Initially, the Oedipal drama dominated the therapy. He consciously viewed his father's remembered admonitions on the evils of masturbation as killing. His father, an explosive man, could brook no challenge to his authority. Mr D had witnessed the early demolition of his rebellious older brother. He had been told to look after this brother who had begun to fail at school. A broken man, his brother had become a crusty, asexual old bachelor. His mother's attempts to protect his brother from his father had been ineffectual. Aware of the fate of his brother, he did not challenge. His father died of a heart attack in his bath, when the patient was a teenager. This was traumatic. He remembered the sight of his father's flaccid penis in the water. He was left ensuring the survival of his disintegrating, hysterical mother as well as his damaged brother. There was no effective help and he was deeply shamed by her. He felt that if his father, and later his analyst, had not died, he might have been able to maintain a semblance of masculinity but the underlying problem would have persisted.

For Fairbairn, behind the imago of the castrating father there lurks the spectre of a biting/castrating mother, a veritable vagina dentata. This man spontaneously produced images of a vagina dentata. He felt horror and disgust of female genitalia. It became clear that his sexuality was stuck at the infantile level. The path to adult genitality had been blocked by his underlying overexcited but rejective ambivalent attitude to his mother's body. In the therapy, his mother emerged as the figure behind the castrating father. She had not been able to respond to his excitement. She had been ashamed of her sexuality; though married, she had hidden her pregnancy. In thinking of his parents' sexual relationship he could only envisage his father as a rapist. She, not his father, was experienced as the person who blocked access to the marital bedroom. He had memories of his mother's beauty as she would leave for social occasions with his father. He had been excited by the beauty of women but he had always been denied access.

The patient's relationship with his mother was characterised by a gross lack of attunement on her part. A perfect baby who never cried, and later a perfect child, Mr D had become attuned to her fragility. Orphaned early from a violent background, my patient had born the burden of preserving her, a sad woman, not only from her unsupportive husband but also from himself. As a child he knew he would never have babies as he would murder them. His unresolved ambivalence to the body of his mother, which had marred his later relationships, became the core issue. But her actual flesh was remembered and repudiated as flaccid and flabby.

The intensity of his excitement rendered relationships with women impossible. He was aware that women actively recoiled from him. He was afraid that if he fantasised about sexuality he would "grab". It was death to express desire and death to inhibit. He had been unable to love. In the early therapy, transferentially, I was such an idealised "good object" that I found it acutely uncomfortable. Later he informed me in no uncertain terms that he found me totally unattractive. The exciting object was transferred to a woman at work. She found his attention so disturbing that she sought the assistance of the personnel officer.

Rage was diverted to irate complaints letters to newspapers about public services, but was later transferred to me. Violent and abusive messages were left on my answerphone at night. These feelings were not accessible in sessions: the strength of the rejective frustrated rage was too strong. He was afraid it could come to murder. I had become the object in his path that had to be destroyed. During his analysis he had dated a woman. His mother had later tried to access his diary and he had nearly wrestled her to the floor.

I was acutely chilled by his guilt-free wish to kill me—such an act would "ruin" his career. However, he also became aware of the level of the bitterly resented infantile dependence. Killing me was equivalent to killing himself (Armstrong-Perlman, 1987). In the session after he expressed his wish to kill me I introduced the masculine presence. I said that I took his violence seriously and informed him that I had taken the precaution of ensuring that my husband was in the house. Later, we had to explore whether this response on my part had meant in reality that I became in the transference the ineffectual, frightened mother whom he had to protect. However, he acknowledged that the risk of violence had been real. There was then a long period of his seeing me as a weak, depressed, downtrodden woman. Inner reality had almost psychotically obscured outer reality.

Clinical implications

In this case the actual father was persecutory. Mr D had watched his brother's spirit being broken in childhood. There was no benign father to help him extricate himself from the relationship with his mother and steer a course to individuation. The underlying current of addictive repressed ambivalence persisted. Oedipus after all was abandoned by both parents while Laius was a persecutor, but that is not the fate of every child. Oedipus was a traumatised child preserved by the "kindness of strangers". Oedipus left his familiar foster home to protect them from the prophecy. Mr D had no benevolent feelings for children. He, a potential Laius, could never have had children as he would have killed them. The route to mature dependence will vary with regard to whether the prior relationships have been good enough.

Metaphorically Mr D experienced his mind as a tangled mess but he could not cut the "Gordian knot". He was in a state of primary identification with his hopelessly depressed, too fragile, needy mother. Seeing her as irretrievably damaged meant that he too was irretrievably damaged. He felt that he was only "a hysteric at heart, a screaming infant" whose cry had been suppressed. He had built a wall and had never been able to occupy the empty space that lay behind it. He did not wish to encounter the distorted ghosts that resided there.

Following his reconstruction of the Oedipal situation, Fairbairn argues that clinically, "The deep analysis of a positive Oedipus situation may be regarded as taking place at three main levels. At the first level the picture is dominated by the Oedipus situation itself. At the next level the picture is dominated by ambivalence towards the heterosexual parent: and at the deepest level it is dominated by ambivalence towards the mother" (ibid., p. 124). This is because, "[T]he child does have the experience of a physical relationship with his mother's breast while also experiencing a varying degree of frustration in this relationship that his need for his mother persists so obstinately beneath his need for his father and all subsequent genital needs" (ibid., p. 122). Therefore, "The nuclei of both the internal objects are derivatives of the original ambivalent mother and her ambivalent breasts. In conformity with this fact, a sufficiently deep analysis of the Oedipus situation invariably reveals that this situation is built up around the figures of an internal exciting mother and an internal rejecting mother" (ibid., p. 124).

This view of the multi-layered structure of the Oedipal situation has important implications for clinical practice. In the classical Freudian view when one reaches the Oedipal situation in an analysis one has hit the bedrock. One can go no further. The objective is then to somehow achieve a resolution of this problem. In the Fairbairnian view, when the Oedipal situation is reached one has only accessed the topmost level of a complex subterranean structure. To stop there would be to miss the underlying causes and the underlying problems that have created the Oedipal structure.

For Fairbairn, the breakdown of repression is the release of "bad" objects from the unconscious. Inner reality can then threaten outer reality. These emerging configurations could render important relationships intolerable. For the child the parent becomes a malign persecutor but the child cannot flee. J. Bowlby said, in conversation, that no child under nine can tolerate the belief that a parent does not love him. During the transitional stage, for example in adolescence, these emerging configurations of self and other may threaten the tolerance of the parents. For the adult patient the therapeutic relationship or "working alliance" could be overwhelmed by the reactivation of these malign relationships.

Various alternatives may arise as a safety valve to regulate the arising tensions which threaten the equilibrium of the central self. Dreams of fire and flood may occur. Mr D reported uncontrollable trembling at night. The exciting and rejective objects may be transferred to persons and causes outside the therapeutic relationship. The rage may be channelled or displaced to viable alternatives, in this case irate letters to the press.

The use of the answerphone perhaps preserved a workable and safe therapeutic relationship. If the feelings expressed in the phone calls had been brought to sessions I would have had great difficulty in containing my countertransference and preserving a therapeutic stance. The rage was later expressed in sessions but coldly. The exciting object was externalised to a woman who obviously found his attention intolerable.

But sotto voce the repressed subselves were still in a locked embrace of absolute dependence, a veritable Gordian knot. There can be a risk of psychosis when inner reality overwhelms outer reality, and this was the case when I became the rejected object and the target of Mr D's rage.

The role of permission in the development of sexuality

In the process of moving from primary identification with the maternal object to a relationship with a separate other the greatest need of a child is to obtain "conclusive assurance (a) that he is genuinely loved as a person by his parents, and (b) that his parents genuinely accept his love" (ibid., p. 39). Mr D described himself with disgust as the perfect child: "mother's dolly". His mother had "never envisaged him growing up". Later he remembered how after his mother's death he had found a chocolate box he had given her as a child. Clearly she had treasured this and had loved him in her fashion. He was moved to tears. He would later be moved to tears by the kindness of others. He loved music and brought me a tape which I accepted.

The infant is not just a hungry demander of love and attention, but as important, a giver. The acceptance of what he gives is as important to his development and maturation as is the giving. "It is only in so far as such assurance is forthcoming in a form sufficiently convincing to enable him to depend safely upon his real objects that he is able gradually to renounce infantile dependence without misgiving. In the absence of such assurance his relationship with his objects is fraught by too much anxiety over separation to enable him to renounce the attitude of infantile dependence; for such a renunciation would be equivalent in his eyes to forfeiting all hope of ever obtaining the satisfaction of his unsatisfied emotional needs. Frustration of his desire to be loved as a person and to have his love accepted is the greatest trauma that a child can experience" (ibid., p. 39).

For the infant, abandonment is death. Being sent to Coventry, difficult for any adult, is intolerable for the infant because "psychologically speaking, identification with the object and infantile dependence are but two aspects of the same phenomenon" (ibid., p. 42). This constitutes the core dilemma of the transitional phase, when the child is attempting to establish his separateness and autonomy as a person, a separate source of volition. The nature of the need changes as the infant matures and becomes increasingly aware. The infant who has had a good enough experience of a physically and emotionally responsive mother slowly begins to tolerate separation.

This slow process of tolerance of physical separation of self and mother is rendered possible not only by normal maturation but by the secure base provided by a positive experience of an actually responsive mother. On the basis of establishment of the expectation of an attuned loving mother, the infant can tolerate waiting with increasing confidence. He is beginning a successful journey to individuation.

Mature dependence

For Fairbairn, mature dependence, unlike primary dependence, is conditional. The mature adult though dependent on his objects, can desert them. Mature relatedness implies the capacity to relate to differentiated others with the capacity to relate to at least one differentiated other with his or her genital organs.

"If a mature individual loses an object, however important, he still has some objects remaining. His eggs are not all in one basket. Further he has a choice of objects and can desert one for another" (ibid., p. 47).

For Fairbairn, "The real significance of the genital stage lies in a maturity of object relationships, and that a genital attitude is but an element in that maturity … The real point about the mature individual is not that the libidinal attitude is essentially genital, but that the genital attitude is essentially libidinal" (ibid., p. 32). The emotionally mature adult seeks the object through a number of channels, among which the genital channel plays an essential, but by no means exclusive, part. Therefore the achievement of mature adult genitality is dependent on the relative resolution of the problems and vicissitudes of infantile dependence. Mature adult love is therefore a transformation of infantile love, not a replica. The mature adult can relinquish the relationship with an unsatisfactory object. He or she can let the other go, but for the route to mature dependence to be open, the maintenance of personal identity must no longer rest exclusively or predominantly upon a single other as in the early infant–mother dyad.

Conclusion

Though Fairbairn was writing before much of the research on infant development, his version of object relations theory emphasises the significance of interpersonal factors in the development of psychic structure and the genesis of psychopathology. This represents a major break with the Freudian paradigm which minimised the role of such factors in repression and defence. With Fairbairn, there is a Copernican shift in the Freudian paradigm. "Good enough" parenting is essential, providing nurturing, loving warmth and acceptance. Acute separation anxiety may blight later development. Deprivation beyond his capacity to endure threatens an isolation which is akin to a psychic death. The conditions of safety and tolerable individuation are regulated by the need to maintain tolerable relatedness.

A theory which takes account of the particularity of crucial environmental deficits differs from a theory of internal conflict based on warring dualities. Eros and Thanatos are not impersonal forces; they are derivatives of the frustrated need for loving acceptance. They reflect the vicissitudes of love and hate between the self and the other. The aetiology of psychopathology can be related to early patterns of relationship initially with the primary caregiver and then later relationships. This focuses attention on the contribution of external reality to the genesis of psychopathology and psychic structure. It also focuses attention on the quality of the relationship with the therapist.

The role of acceptance by a benign parental object becomes relevant to the theory of the aetiology of psychopathology. The embodied attuned responsiveness of the mother enters the foreground of theory construction. Fairbairn's developmental theory represents a journey from primary identification to mature separation and individuation. At each stage of this process there is a phase-appropriate natural object, and relationship to this object. Moving from one phase to another involves the abandoning of an object, or a particular way of relating to the object and substituting for it the next. Each stage of this process can be rendered traumatic by frustration leading to an inability to negotiate the next steps in the process. Defensive structures are developed to cope with any such trauma.

For Freud, the emerging significance of the father is part of the human condition and enables the separation individuation process to occur. For Fairbairn, the phenomena of the Oedipus complex are based on a tripartite division of self and object already established. It is a continuation of the process which had begun with internalisation and splitting arising from the earliest encounter with the mother. The internalised splitting is externalised onto both the parents. Just as the internalised "good" object had been split into the exciting and rejecting object, when this is externalised onto the real parental couple one becomes the exciting, the other the rejecting threatening object. The relationship with the analyst hopefully provides yet another opportunity for these core conflicts to be worked through.

Mr D became more assertive at work before he was obliged to retire. Without regret he said he might have made more use of his qualifications if he had come back to therapy earlier. He deepened good relationships, such as with couples inviting him for weekends and holidays. He began to have tea regularly with a woman, even began to like a retired intelligent woman he met regularly. However, the therapy was ended by my pregnancy. He was polite and requested further therapy. I referred him on and he did not come back. I met him some years later, now frail. We politely enquired about each other's health.

References

Armstrong-Perlman, E. M. (1986). Introduction: Narcissism and object choice in Freud. *British Journal of Psychotherapy, 3*(1): 60–64.

Armstrong-Perlman, E. M. (1987). Introduction: The child's psyche and the nature of its experience. *British Journal of Psychotherapy, 4*(2): 169–172.

Armstrong-Perlman, E. M. (1994). The allure of the bad object. In: J. S. Grotstein & D. B. Rinsley (Eds.), *Fairbairn and the Origins of Object Relations* (pp. 222–233). London: Free Association Books.

Armstrong-Perlman, E. M. (2000). Three in one: Fairbairn's volatile trinity. In: B. Burgoyne (Ed.), *Drawing the Soul: Schemas and Models in Psychoanalysis* (pp. 57–76). London: Rebus Press.

Balint, M. (1956). *Primary Love and Psychoanalytic Technique*. London: Karnac.

Buitelaar, J. K., Huizink, A. C., Mulder, E. J., de Medina, P. G., & Visser, G. H. (2003). Prenatal stress and cognitive development and temperament in infants. *Neurobiology of Aging, 24*, May–June, Suppl. 1: S53–60; discussion S67–68.

Fairbairn, W. R. D. (1952). *Psychoanalytic Studies of the Personality*. London: Tavistock.

Freud, S. (1909b). Analysis of a phobia in a five-year-old boy. *S. E., 10*. London: Hogarth.

Freud, S. (1910h). A special type of choice of object made by men. *S. E., 11*. London: Hogarth.

Freud, S. (1912d). On the universal tendency to debasement in the sphere of love. *S. E., 11*. London: Hogarth.

Fride, E., & Weinstock, M. (1988). Prenatal stress increases anxiety related behavior and alters cerebral lateralization of dopamine activity. *Life Sciences, 42*(10): 1059–1065.

Glover, V., & Hill, J. (2012). Sex differences in the programming effects of prenatal stress on psychopathology and stress responses: An evolutionary perspective. *Physiology & Behavior*, February 14.

Korhonen, M., Luoma, I., Salmelin, R., & Tamminen, T. (2012). A longitudinal study of maternal prenatal, postnatal and concurrent depressive symptoms and adolescent well-being. *Journal of Affective Disorders, 136*(3): 680–692.

Kuhn, T. (1962). *The Structure of Scientific Revolutions* (3rd edition). Chicago, IL: University of Chicago Press, 1996.

Winnicott, D. W. (1974). Fear of breakdown. *International Review of Psycho-Analysis, 1*: 103–107.

Winnicott, D. W. (1988). *Human Nature*. London: Free Association.

CHAPTER THIRTEEN

Sitting with marital tensions: the work of Henry Dicks in applying Fairbairn's ideas to couple relationships

Molly Ludlam

I should like to dedicate this chapter to the memory of Dr Douglas Haldane (1926–2012), a pioneering child and family psychiatrist and member of the Scottish Institute of Human Relations. It was on his prompting that I first read *Marital Tensions*; he later encouraged me to become involved in, and to write about couple psychotherapy.

Introduction

In this chapter, I explore the first application of Fairbairn's ideas to understanding couple relationships, as set out by Henry Dicks, in his classic text *Marital Tensions* (1967). This application was further developed, most notably by Zinner (1976) and by Scharff and Scharff (1987, 1991). I shall attempt my exploration by way of examining the difficulties described by an imaginary couple during a consultation for couple psychotherapy. I shall then summarise Dicks's thinking in relation to Fairbairnian concepts. Finally, the couple's case is further explored, as if seeking consultation from Henry Dicks himself.

Meeting Donald and Deborah

I received a telephone call from a man stating that he and his wife were seeking couple therapy. They had contacted the Scottish Institute of Human Relations (SIHR) because they were interested in working with someone who had an object relations approach and had been given my name. I offered the couple—Donald and Deborah—a consultation of three meetings, to explore their concerns and to find out whether together we could find ways of understanding their difficulties.

On arrival, the couple, in their sixties, looked relatively youthful and fit. I was struck by the fact that they were both dressed in matching shades of blue. Now retired, they had worked in caring professions allied to psychotherapy, she as a general practitioner, and he as an academic psychologist. Nevertheless, they explained that they found themselves "all at sea" as to what might be amiss between them. As their busy working lives were now over, and their family nest, which had nurtured four daughters, was now empty, they were struggling to come to terms with a shocking realisation that emptiness pervaded their lives. As we talked, they both appeared disturbed to discover that the lack of companionship and intimacy in their relationship was perhaps longstanding, masked until now by their work and family preoccupations. Donald's study at home had become his study-bedroom. Deborah socialised only with a small circle of women friends.

Having revealed this picture of themselves, Donald was also keen to establish my credentials. He wanted to know how much my training had been influenced by Fairbairn, and stressed that it was Fairbairn's connection with SIHR which had led him to seek its help. "I take it that you are well versed, being trained at SIHR. You'll know your stuff!"

I felt suddenly alone and put on the spot to answer. I wanted not to appear defensive, however, and so I responded that I was aware that this consultation was very important to them; that they were puzzled about what could have gone so awry, and were anxious for an assurance that I would be well grounded and not find myself "at sea" like them, without a map or a lode star to guide me. They appeared less anxious then, and although I felt that I had correctly interpreted their anxiety, Donald's assumption that I would be "well versed" in Fairbairn left me with lingering doubts about whether working as a solo practitioner, I could meet this couple's high expectations. I recovered my footing however before they left to say that I was curious to know why Fairbairn was so important.

Donald was quick to reply, "Well, the man's a Scot! I feel he should be celebrated. He certainly deserves to be more known on his own turf than he often is. Don't you agree?"

Deborah came in quickly (in defence of her husband or of me?): "Perhaps he's 'a prophet in his own country'. Donald gets bees in his bonnet." She added, "I think, Donald, it's because your father was one of his students at university—that's why he's important to you."

Donald retorted contemptuously, "Deborah always sees things far too simplistically! It's much more complicated than that! Come on, get your coat." He smiled politely at me, mumbling that they would see me the following week. Deborah bit her lip, looking hurt at the rebuttal. She silently followed him out. In many ways it had been a full, even rich, first meeting, but they left a wasteland behind them.

I sat alone, reflecting on my feelings of loss, confusion, and inadequacy. Even though I knew my countertransference response to be a projection, and so a communication, of their own disquiet and dismay at their not-knowing, in spite of their own professional lives, about their own relationship, I could not resist enacting a swift defence against the profound anxiety they had lodged in me. I remembered that Henry Dicks had been the first to write about the application of Fairbairn's concepts to understanding couple relationships (Scharff, 2005), and so I went straight to my bookshelf to refresh my familiarity with his book *Marital Tensions*. Perhaps in response to my feeling of lonely inadequacy, I also experienced a new curiosity in Dicks himself. Who was the person behind the author of this classic text?

Re-acquaintance with Henry V. Dicks

J. D. Sutherland's obituary of Henry Dicks (1900–1977) is marked by his sense of loss at such a "great friend ... and a loyal consistent ally" and reading it made me regretful that I had never had the opportunity of meeting him. Alongside being "one of the most outstanding and admired figures of psychiatry", I learned that he was fluent in four languages, an accomplished violinist, and that he "radiated an urbane humorous joie de vivre" which earned him great affection from friends and colleagues. He appears to have exuded enormous energy and enthusiasm; it was characteristic therefore that he "took up therapeutic work with marital problems long before such work achieved its current popularity" (Sutherland, 1977). *Marital Tensions* was written from this experience in 1967.

In the introduction to his book, Dicks sets out the reason for his choice of W. R. D. Fairbairn's ideas, as the psychoanalytic theoretical basis for his study of marital relationships. He dismisses as insufficient Freud's interest in drives and sexual gratification, quoting an aphorism he himself had coined in 1947, "Nervous systems do not marry, nor are they given in marriage." Instead he is drawn to Fairbairn's concept of the ego as a "whole person" that is instinctively "object-seeking" from birth, as "the need for others and to feel needed by them is the basis of group life" (Dicks, 1967, p. 7). Dicks sees marriage as a "social relationship", and considers that the sociological concepts of "role performance" and "culture patterns" complement his object relations perspective. I found myself wondering whether his prowess as a chamber music player, together with his linguistic skills and early experience as an interpreter, had enabled him so effectively to bring together a number of concepts and apply them to the problem of increasing marital unhappiness. Rereading and rediscovering Dicks's material, I felt drawn in, as much by his straightforward and humanitarian approach as by the methodical presentation of his arguments.

Dicks states that to understand a couple's difficulties, there should be assessments both of the partners as individuals and of the sociocultural factors of their separate pasts and shared presents, and, crucially, "an attempt to identify from the clinical phenomenon the more unconscious forces which flow between [them] forming bonds of a 'positive' and 'negative' kind, a love-hate involvement". He sees this indeed as constituting "the personal, psychological core of marital life, not only in the disorders of marriage, but also as the healthy normally functioning element which binds two persons into a dyad, an integrate different from the mere sum of its parts. If this statement is considered 'mystical', I do not flinch" (ibid., p. 8). Reading this, I want to raise a cheer at finding someone so grounded in his own authority! I think he can do this, however, because he intuits a natural fit between Fairbairn's concept of the whole-person/ego as inherently object-seeking and the marital dyad envisaged as a unit made up of two instinctively object-seeking people. Indeed, Dicks here was ahead of his field. He goes on to say that to examine a couple's interpersonal relationship, "... we must regard the dyad as the 'patient', the marriage as the 'sick person'" (p. 8). So much in current couple psychotherapy flows from this!

Although Dicks clearly speaks with authority, and "knows his stuff", he presents his ideas and case examples as a study with the scientific aim of testing the validity of two hypotheses. These he sets out as follows:

"*Hypothesis* (1). Many tensions and misunderstandings between partners seem to result from the disappointment which one, or both of them, feel and resent, when the other fails to play the role of spouse after the manner of a preconceived model or figure in their fantasy world" (ibid., p. 50).

This hypothesis Dicks later elaborates, as *Hypothesis* (1A), as follows, in the light of his findings of a particular case: "Tensions between marriage partners can result from the disappointment that the partner, after all, plays the marital role like the frustrating parent figure, similarity to whom was denied during courtship. This often collusive discovery leads to modification of the subject's own role behaviour in the direction of regression towards more childish responses to the partner" (ibid., p. 62).

"*Hypothesis* (2). Subjects may persecute in their spouses tendencies which originally caused attraction, the partner having been unconsciously perceived as a symbol of 'lost' because repressed aspects of the subject's own personality" (ibid., p. 63).

Fairbairn scholars will readily identify his influence in the formulation of these hypotheses. Dicks had prepared the ground of his argument by recounting Fairbairn's theories of the infant's defensive manoeuvres to deal with unrequited love, by withdrawing part of the self into a split-off enclave—the libidinal ego. In a complementary split, the infant could internalise, and so manage, frustrating and rejecting relationships in the anti-libidinal ego. Dicks is careful to stress that the split-off parts of the self, charged as they were with psychic energy, deprived the central ego, arguing that as a result, "[I]f my split-off internal relation to a forbidden or dangerous object takes up a quota of ambivalent cathexis, and preoccupies part of me unconsciously, I have much less investment of self to offer to an adult relationship" (ibid., p. 70).

Dicks moreover feels that Fairbairn's schema particularly fits his hypotheses in helping to understand the "dynamics of idealization" on which the hypotheses are based. For Dicks, "idealization" serves as the main defence mechanism in marriage. He follows Freud in seeing idealisation as the means by which sadistic and hateful feelings are repressed to allow "only unalloyed 'pure' love to be felt"; and he follows Fairbairn in recognising that the "return of the repressed" causes such distress because "it breaches the idealizations". He sees this as a post-honeymoon dynamic, an inevitable consequence of reality testing.

I had already begun to wonder about the meaning of Donald's idealisation of Fairbairn, and so was excited to be reminded that Dicks considered idealisation to be of particular significance as a feature of troubled relationships. I read on to appreciate how Dicks supports this application of Fairbairn's thinking by describing four examples of its marital interaction:

i. a reaction of injured self-righteousness when a partner does not accept his/her obviously correct point of view, as if to say, "If only he/she could agree with me, I could be the perfect husband/wife."

ii. "'high-minded' marriages" which reflect the dynamic of idealisation in the relationship described by Fairbairn between the ideal object and a central ego which has been "purged ... by splitting off all disturbing elements" such as "sex or any quarrelling or heat" (ibid., p. 72). In this the partner becomes the scapegoat, the embodiment of the forbidden object relation.

iii. hateful love relationships which reflect the ambivalence with which partners relate to the hated, split-off part of the self. (Dicks recalls that traditionally the scapegoat was chosen for its perfection before it was cast out, heaped with the bad qualities of those making the offering.) Recalling the Kleinian concept of projective identification, "only rejected love can generate so much hate" that might lead men to "murder intensely ambivalently loved wives" (ibid., p. 72).

iv. "faithful pain-laden bondage" in which partners feel compelled to hurt and attack those they love best, in "an unconscious commitment" to "mutual collusive interlocking". In such relationships, problems arise through the arousal of irreconcilable, repressed, childhood needs for "dependence, [and] sexual impossibilities, [as well as] the resultant frustration rage". Dicks says the "collusive marriage" is itself socially idealised, presenting a "joint *false self*". Outwardly the couple may appear enviably calm and considerate, but "such brittle unions" are liable to break tragically when the repressed breaks though.

It seemed to me that Dicks had argued his case persuasively, not least because his explication appeared to fit so much of my impressions of Donald and Deborah and I felt more empowered at the prospect of meeting them again.

Second meeting with Donald and Deborah

When they arrived they smiled at me brightly, but looked away quickly. I thought they both looked rather tired.

Donald: "We've had a reasonably good week—quite busy. Hardly seen one another ... I've been writing a paper and Deborah's been doing a lot of baking and cleaning up the house. I've had to live on supermarket sandwiches."

Deborah: "We've got a big family party coming up for our fortieth wedding anniversary. Donald's speaking at an international conference here and our daughters and their partners are coming at the same time because there's to be a reception. Donald just likes to pretend that I neglect him ..."

Donald: "You do—well you've taken to your bed quite a bit lately—I hardly get a civil word out of you. You're getting depressed again, if you ask me."

Deborah: "Where are you when I want to talk to you? You are always going off into your room! Last night, when I was in tears, you shut the door in my face ..."

Donald: "You were being unreasonable, and when you are in that childish frame of mind there's no point. You know I can't cope with it. You were a GP—you should sort yourself out!"

The facade of the bright "joint false self" was indeed brittle and was crumbling to reveal two people fearful of falling apart and fearful of what they might find behind the door ... rejection, depression, abandonment, and isolation. What was it about their mutual needs and demands that was so intolerable? I attempted to offer a containing response, acknowledging that they both appeared very tired, and perhaps they were wondering whether meeting with me was going to be of any point, and whether they would get the sort of food they felt they should ideally get to help them as a couple.

They seemed to relax more at this and sat back in their chairs. I asked Deborah about Donald's concern that she might be "depressed again". She explained that she had had postnatal depression following the birth of their oldest daughter and then again after the last two daughters—twins—had arrived. She felt it had been a shock to herself because, as a medic, she had not expected somehow to be susceptible. The twins—adorable as they were—had been an afterthought—she had hoped to give Donald a son. But when she was depressed he had not known what to do. All these years after, Donald remembered it, but they had never been able to discuss it properly.

Donald said, "That's probably right, but we've rubbed along OK. I've been a good father." Deborah quickly reassured him that indeed he had.

I wondered if Donald had ever been depressed. "Only in my early twenties when my father died." I then enquired about his family history. Donald was an only child. His father had started to study medicine, but his family, having fallen on hard times, had opened a chemist's shop. Donald felt he had not known him very well—he was "something of a workaholic". Sometimes he had talked nostalgically about his university studies and Donald knew how much he had resented having to give them up. Donald's mother was a nurse. They had been regarded as pillars of the community in the small town where they lived, until it emerged that his father had become addicted to narcotic drugs. His illness and sudden death had precipitated Donald's depression, causing him to take time off from his university course. He had always been very fond of his mother; she had nursed him back to health. Soon afterwards he met Deborah who was about to complete her medical training.

Deborah was the eldest of three children, having two younger brothers, one of whom was severely disabled. Her father had been a naval officer, spending long periods at sea. He clearly felt more at home there—being morose and taciturn at home, until his next voyage approached. Her mother, who stayed at home to look after the family, was lonely without their father. She was "a nervous soul", forever anxious about her children, and what other people thought of the family, to the degree that Deborah swiftly sought refuge in managing her own life. Her father expressed high expectations of her and encouraged her to take up medicine.

I asked both of them whether they thought that their parents had been happy together. They both said that they supposed not, but that it was not something that was ever talked about in front of them. Deborah volunteered that maybe there had been disappointments for both their parents, that early dreams had not stood the test of time.

I wondered aloud whether this had meant that marriage had had to be especially good for Donald and Deborah, and whether they were afraid that their early dreams might also not withstand the test of time.

Donald said, "I'm really afraid that we won't make it. We might carry off the party alright. But after that, I really think we should separate. We should use these sessions to work out the cleanest way of doing it. There's no point going back over the past. I can't change it for you, and you certainly can't change it for me!"

I noted to myself that, as in our first meeting, Deborah had offered a partial insight which, rather than building on it, Donald had brushed aside in a personally crushing way; I wondered what this might mean and how it might be addressed.

I said that their concern might reflect that we had come to the end of our penultimate session; that they had, it seemed, both grown up in families where some things had proved too difficult to talk about, at least in their hearing. I was aware of their investment in coming to meet with me and that we could use our third meeting to explore what might be possible for them in the future.

As they left, I again felt the strong sense as if something had been offered, only to be taken away. How could I avoid repeating that with them? I knew that I was going to have to think it through in their absence before meeting them again for the final part of the consultation, and that this meeting would prove a crucial one for them. I probably would need some consultation myself … I certainly thought I should go back to Dicks … As I wrote up my notes, I fell into a kind of reverie, as if I was consulting the great Dr Dicks.

A "consultation" with Dr Dicks

ML: I really appreciate this opportunity to talk with you. I have been feeling quite alone with this couple, quite inadequate to help them.

HVD: It's a pity you can't offer them conjoint therapy, as in my day. But really your sense of isolation and inadequacy result from the projection of their own unwanted feelings.

ML: That's helpful, but I can't help feeling nonetheless that if you were there in the room with me, they would have what they are really looking for. *You* would have the answers!

HVD: Hmm … you are dealing with powerful idealisations in this couple. Are you sure that you are not idealising me too?!

ML: You are probably right—as always! But how can I use these unhelpful feelings usefully?

HVD: Think about what Fairbairn said about what underlies idealisation. I wonder whether they have one of those "high-minded" marriages that were so common in my day.

ML: Do you think that in that respect they may be unconsciously repeating the kind of marriages their parents had? Deborah seemed to intuit that.

HVD: You know, I'm wondering about whether she was hinting that their parents had both had what I call "collusive problem marriages". You'll see it on page 73 of my book, where I say that "tensions … break surface either in psycho-somatic form, or as periodic depression; or else they appear as neurotic problems in the children, whose unconscious cannot be cheated."

ML: That's really neatly put! So Deborah is expressing insight—albeit anxiously—on behalf of both of them.

HVD: Yes, but Donald has told you that he's afraid she'll not appreciate the complexity of it for him. He wants answers, but he's really ambivalent about discovering their meaning. Don't forget what ambivalence tells us about powerful feelings of longing and hurt that have to be repressed. My guess would be that he's been really hurt by his wife's emotional withdrawal after their first child was born, because it threatened to arouse what he had had to repress in infancy. And let's not overlook his first experience of unrequited love; he says he was close to mother, but they would have been distanced, sexually. And his father was a workaholic—which might have been a way of managing *his* depression. He certainly would not have been available to this little boy.

ML: I imagine he longed for a father he could be close to and admire ...

HVD: Yes, perhaps he projected those needs into intellectual life, into Fairbairn too! Both have been idealised.

ML: You are prompting me to think about ambivalence again. I wonder if, having invested so much in his intellectual life, and men of ideas, he wonders whether after all there's no real emotional or lasting salvation in it for him. But he has pursued it instead of cultivating the relationship with Deborah, so now he is truly facing what he fears most, that ultimately there may be no answers *and* no one to comfort him?

HVD: You are intuiting that he may be a very frightened man.

ML: I've been trying to understand my sense of him sitting on a powder keg of devastating anger. It's there in his contempt. I think he must know how he hurts her. I wonder whether he's afraid of his ability to destroy her ...

HVD: His father's frustrated ambition and unconscious rage could well have damaged his mother.

ML: So for Donald, rage and desire have to be repressed—to be hidden, as we think they were between his parents. He says it's better to separate and end it all "cleanly". But when he said that, it felt sadistic too to me ... part of his anti-libidinal ego?

HVD: I hope you are not forgetting her part in it, the unconscious collusion between them. He's her exciting-rejecting object, probably like her father. She has introjected high—perhaps idealised—expectations of herself. It's a lonely row to hoe. Inside, they are both very lonely.

ML: So there is a fit between them. I was wondering what it might be. But it's not a hopeful one ... as they know. They don't have a positive pattern to follow in their parents, although in terms of role performance, she was anxious to endorse him as a good father.

HVD: Idealised ambivalence perhaps. Neither of them had very good fathers ... and their mothers were caring, but intrusive.

ML: I suppose the question is what kind of parenting can they now offer one another at this new transition point in their lives? Perhaps that highlights why they have come for help now. They can foresee that as they grow older, their dependency needs of one another are likely to increase, *if* they stay together. And I suppose they will be wondering what kind of "parenting" would I be able to offer them therapeutically?

HVD: You'll need to show that you see them as a troubled *couple* and that you can really bear to be with them *as a couple*, because they know that the couple they imagined themselves to be was a false-self dyad. Show them that you can bear to listen to their marital tensions, and then maybe they won't shut the door against the awful realisations of what has been repressed. The loss of what has been idealised is really painful—*you* know that!—and they will need to be allowed to take their time to work it through.

ML: So you are saying that when I meet them again, I should say that I think that it would be helpful for us to continue to meet.

HVD: Use your authority too.

ML: I take it you think I should say that I am aware of their fears that talking will uncover irreparable hurts, but that it would be important to allow time for issues to emerge as they feel ready.

HVD: Yes, but more important, I meant that you should use your authority to say that you know that they are looking to you for answers, but that it's only between you that you'll find them; that they have told you something significant about the role of high expectations in their lives which has got in the way of managing disappointments, and that it will be vital to find a way of understanding the meaning of that.

Oh yes, and lastly, but not least, remember to tell them that you know that *you* are sure to disappoint them, because no one, least of all a psychotherapist, even if she's a Fairbairnian, is perfect! But, you could also say that you trust that disappointment will prove to be not as catastrophic as they fear.

ML: Thank you! I feel I owe you a lot, and not just for helping me to understand something more about this couple, but for allowing me to project a lot of needs and fantasies onto you, and without your permission. I feel it will enable me to go on sitting with their tensions.

In conclusion

In this way, Henry Dicks, accompanied as always by Ronald Fairbairn, allowed the work with Donald and Deborah to proceed in time to a useful conclusion. It seemed to me that as well as a consultation I had received a tutorial in some of the founding principles of couple psychotherapy. I had been reminded of the centrality of the couple/dyad in couple therapy, bound as they are by an unconscious "love-hate involvement", and especially of the power and multiple manifestations of idealisation, the principal defence mechanism in coupling. What has been repressed in the individual will emerge either in the couple or their children. Dicks had helped me to be sensitive to those points in a couple's life when the return of the repressed shatters idealisations and presents unmanageable threats to their relationship. Partners are at such times likely to feel abandoned and isolated. Having rediscovered *Marital Tensions*, it was indeed as if Henry Dicks had joined me, and when I was reminded of the loneliness in Donald and Deborah, I could reach out and find a co-therapist.

References

Dicks, H. V. (1947). *Clinical Studies in Psychopathology (2nd edition)*. London: Edward Arnold.
Dicks, H. V. (1967). *Marital Tensions, Clinical Studies towards a Psychological Theory of Interaction*. [Republished London: Karnac, 1993.]
Scharff, D. E. (2005). The development of Fairbairn's theory. In: J. S. Scharff & D. E. Scharff (Eds.), *The Legacy of Fairbairn and Sutherland* (pp. 3–18). London: Routledge.
Scharff, D. E., & Scharff, J. S. (1987). *Object Relations Family Therapy*. Northvale, NJ: Jason Aronson.
Scharff, D. E., & Scharff, J. S. (1991). *Object Relations Couple Therapy*. Northvale, NJ: Jason Aronson.
Sutherland, J. D. (1977). Henry Dicks. *Psychiatric Bulletin*, 1977, 1: 6–7.
Zinner, J. (1976). The implications of projective identification for marital interaction. In: H. Grunebaum & J. Christ (Eds.), *Contemporary Marriage, Structure, Dynamics and Therapy* (pp. 293–308). Boston, MA: Little, Brown.

CHAPTER FOURTEEN

W. R. D. Fairbairn's contribution to the study of personality disorders*

Carlos Rodríguez-Sutil

> Futility
>
> Move him into the sun—
> Gently its touch awoke him once,
> At home, whispering of fields unsown.
> Always it woke him, even in France,
> Until this morning and this snow.
> If anything might rouse him now
> The kind old sun will know.
>
> Think how it wakes the seeds,—
> Woke, once, the clays of a cold star.
> Are limbs, so dear-achieved, are sides,
> Full-nerved,—still warm,—too hard to stir?
> Was it for this the clay grew tall?
> —O what made fatuous sunbeams toil
> To break earth's sleep at all?
>
> —Wilfred Owen

---

*I would like to thank Jacqueline Britnell (Madrid) and Patricia Fernández (New York) for their generous help in preparing the English version of this paper.

Introduction

We must avoid the mistake of believing that "personality" is just another form of diagnosis—as it is suggested in the DSM classification (American Psychiatric Association, 1980, 1987, 1994)—since we all have a character or personality, understanding "personality" as our peculiar way of relating to others, which may be more or less normal or problematic, and more or less similar to the established prototypes. As Winnicott (1965) said, every analysis is at the same time a "character analysis", because it involves the person as a whole.

For Fairbairn (1952), repression is the key mechanism in the psychological development of the child and in the creation of the endopsychic structure, with the internalisation of unsatisfactory objects that is not caused by internal phantasies but rather by bad experiences with objects in the real world. However, he uses the term "repression" broadly, not in the strict Freudian way, including, of course, the process known by the name of "primary repression" (*Urverdrängung*) (Freud, 1915d), that sometimes could be confused with other mechanisms such as intojection, disavowal, and even identification.

With Fairbairn (1929b, 1954b), the clinical emphasis shifted from the horizontal repression of drives to the vertical splitting of internal objects and their related egos. In his system, repression—that is, splitting—is actively used by the mind. He finds no fundamental feature that differentiates hysterical dissociation from the ego splitting in schizoid states. This is quite striking from the point of view of current dynamic psychopathology.

In a paper published in 1941—"A Revised Psychopathology of the Psychoses and Psychoneuroses"—Fairbairn suggested that the ego is gradually built up in the course of development from a number of primitive ego-nuclei, and these ego-nuclei are themselves the product of a process of integration or crystallisation (p. 250). They are oral, anal, and genital nuclei, but also male and female, active and passive, loving and hating, giving and taking, internal persecutors and judges. Schizoid individuals are those in whom this process of integration has never been satisfactorily realised, and in whom a regressive disintegration of the ego has also occurred.

Three years later, Fairbairn asserted the existence of a unitary ego from birth, eventually fragmented into secondary egos attached to the repressed objects (1944). This new viewpoint was fairly inconsistent with his previous description of the ego-nuclei. Maybe that is the reason why the wording of the above-mentioned 1941 article finally changed in the book published in 1952 where Fairbairn's first footnote on page 59 read: "… and now republished with minor amendments". In any event, his theory is focused on early psychic organisations, previous to the Oedipal phase, and on the basic *endopsychic structure*, a new topographical model. Oedipus is merely the last layer in the psychic formation: "At the first level the picture is dominated by the Oedipus situation itself. At the next level, the picture is dominated by ambivalence towards the heterosexual parent; and at the deepest level it is dominated by ambivalence towards the mother" (1944, p. 124). Ian Suttie (1935, p. 5)—who is not quoted by Fairbairn—had already stated that the Oedipus complex depends largely on particular forms of childrearing, family structures, and ethnic character, features which can vary within very wide limits.

In the classical Greek myth, Oedipus began his life by being abandoned on a mountain by his parents who left him there to die from exposure, completely deprived of maternal care, at an age of great dependency (Fairbairn, 1954b, p. 28). Castration anxiety becomes pale in comparison to the role played by this early separation anxiety.

For Freud and Klein, parents were always good, while—as Stephen Mitchell (1981) notes in a humorous style—in the writings of Fairbairn and even more in Guntrip, parents became universal villains, placing the child as a passive victim.

Fairbairn (1941) also criticises the Freud-Abraham theory of stages of psychosexual development. The emotionally mature adult seeks the object through a number of channels, among which the genital channel plays an essential, but by no means exclusive, role. What is most important is not the channel but the nature of the personal emotional attitude: libidinal, sadistic, destructive, or inhibited.

The schizoid position and the developmental stages

The first convincing account of the schizoid disorders, according to Masud Khan (1960), and one of Fairbairn's (1940a) most original contributions, is his description of the schizoid position. This is the most basic position of the psyche, and a certain degree of dissociation is invariably present at the deepest mental level. However, the term "position" does not occupy a central place in his basic vocabulary, though of course he uses it (i.e., Fairbairn, 1940a, 1944) but mainly alluding to "states", either schizoid or manic-depressive states. Schizoid pathology derives from a fixation in the *early oral stage* (incorporative and pre-ambivalent), while manic-depressive states derive from the *late oral stage* (ambivalent), with teething and the subsequent potential to bite. The pre-ambivalent child believes that his love is rejected when he feels frustrated by his mother, which results in a feeling of *futility* (futility: lack of importance or purpose; frivolousness), deeper and more absolute than melancholic despair.

Fairbairn's schizoid position is truly schizoid (not paranoid) and shows the alienation caused by unaccepted love, whereas Melanie Klein's paranoid-schizoid position—which excludes ambivalence—is primarily paranoid and secondarily schizoid, due to hatred (Grotstein, 1994b, p. 137ff.). In the schizoid position the external object splits off into two parts, and the bad one is introjected. The accompanying feeling is that the ego has turned the object bad with its love, which results in the splitting of the ego as well. In contrast, Klein's paranoid-schizoid position is characterised by the projection of destructive phantasies onto real objects, causing in the subject persecutory anxiety and a tendency towards primitive idealisation.

Fairbairn's work with schizoid patients permitted him to define three main features: omnipotence, isolation and detachment, and preoccupation with internal life. These attitudes and phenomena are present, to a greater or lesser degree, in a variety of subjects, ranging from pure schizophrenics to those with schizotypal psychopathic personalities, those with a schizoid character (very marked schizoid traits but not psychopathic), and transient schizoid states or "schizoid islands". In all of these cases, the need for love remains hidden under a mask of detachment and emotional apathy and futility, reaching such a state of inertia that it can often be misdiagnosed as depression. Some failure in the ability to discriminate inner reality from external reality is also common in the schizoid individuals, as is a great difficulty in expressing emotions which they try to overcome through role-playing and exhibitionism. All these features are attributed today to *borderline organisations* (Basili & Sharpin de

Basili, 2005; Kernberg, 1996), but they are also similar to those related to the concept of *false self* (Winnicott, 1971) and to the *as if personality* as articulated by Helene Deutsch (cf. Khan, 1960). Schizoid individuals allow themselves to love and be loved only in the distance (as troubadours and dictators), thus trying to protect at the same time both internal and external objects.

The type of mother who is especially prone to provoke such a regression is the mother who fails to convince her child by spontaneous and genuine expressions of affection that she loves him or her as a person (Fairbairn, 1940a). They are possessive or indifferent mothers providing a relationship devoid of affection. The supposed anxiety the baby experiences by emptying the breast is interpreted as an *anxiety over destroying its libidinal object*. At a deep psychic level, there is an emotional equivalence between mental and bodily contents; accordingly, there is an overvaluation of mental contents corresponding to the overvaluation of bodily contents implied in the oral incorporative attitude of early childhood. To take is equivalent to accumulating bodily contents and to give is to lose these bodily contents. When they give, they tend to feel impoverished. On some occasions, to reduce this sensation of impoverishment, the schizoid individuals claim that what they have given or created is worthless, as does the artist who quickly sells his/her work and forgets about it, or puts it aside in a corner of his studio.

The child comes to regard his mother as a bad object in so far as she does not seem to love him, regarding outward expressions of his own love as bad, and retaining the love inside himself, in order to protect it. The child also keeps his love shut in because he feels that it is too dangerous to release it upon his objects. In short, it is said that the depressive individual fears destroying the object with his hatred, while the schizoid fears destroying it by his love (cf. Guntrip, 1961, pp. 282–283). The huge need for a good love object overlaps with an equally great fear of interpersonal relationships.

Transitional techniques in the constitution of character

In contemporary psychoanalysis we are used to the distinction between explicit and implicit thought and memory, and between ideas and memories that can be consciously retrieved and manipulated and those that are expressed through behaviour without conscious awareness (cf. House & Portuges, 2005; Lyons-Ruth, 1999). Implicit memory can be divided into two categories: declarative and procedural. Procedural memory is body incorporated, and stems in part from early developmental stages. It operates outside verbal consciousness as well as outside the dynamic unconscious, that is to say, the repressed and declarative unconscious, verbally structured, that "speaks" through the symptoms. It does not seem unreasonable to think that this procedural memory is the basis of personality or character. Therefore, the "return of bad objects" in the therapeutic process, as described by Fairbairn (1943a), cannot, strictly speaking, be reached by simply overcoming repression, but through more primitive defences, such as "primary repression" or "splitting and disavowal" (cf. Rinsley, 1987). In patients suffering from regressive conditions, repression having failed, unconscious contents split off into "all-good" and "all-bad" entities, and endopsychic structure is dominated by the ambivalence and it is impossible to reach any form of mourning.

The delinquent child becomes bad in order to turn his/her objects, the parents, into good objects. He takes upon himself the burden of badness since: "It is obviously preferable to be conditionally good than conditionally bad; but, in default of conditional goodness, it is preferable to be conditionally bad than unconditionally bad" (Fairbairn, 1943a, p. 66). This mechanism is called the "moral defence". The child keeps on in its adherence to the internal objects and hopes that, in the future, the external anti-libidinal (rejecting) object will change and become a loving object. The masochistic subjects give themselves over to the conditionally bad object in the hopes of turning it into a good object. It has been remarked that the masochistic subject may experience a feeling of deep satisfaction and justice by destroying himself, a suitable explanation for some cases of negative therapeutic reaction (Hensel, 2005; Scharff, 1998).

I consider that the inclusion by Fairbairn of a transitional developmental stage is an extremely important contribution to the psychoanalytical psychology of personality. The infantile (oral) dependency upon the object gradually gives way to the mature (genital) dependency upon the object, through a *transitional stage*. There are four *transitional defences* in this stage: paranoid, obsessive, phobic, and hysterical; these defences, or neurotic styles, are used to avoid the two great psychopathological disasters that threaten the child: 1) a schizoid state, related to a pre-ambivalent condition; and 2) a depressive state, related to an ambivalent condition. The overcoming of infantile dependency involves the abandonment of a relationship based on primary identification, replaced with a relationship with completely *differentiated* objects. Primary identification is akin to oral incorporation and retention, while differentiation is equivalent to expulsion. Retention and expulsion are mechanisms with which we can differentiate and classify neurotic styles.

The triangular situation that underlies the conflict is not constituted by three persons (child, mother, and father) but essentially by the central ego (CE), the libidinal object (LO), and the anti-libidinal object (AO). It is in the context of the child's relationships with its maternal environment where differentiation of the endopsychic structure takes place, and where repression arises. It is only afterwards that the child is called to cope with the particular difficulties involved in the classic Oedipal situation. Psychoses are manifestations of infant dependency and primitive anxieties—schizoid and depressive—while psychoneurosis are defences against these anxieties; in other words, schizoid and depressive states must not be confused with defences, on the contrary, they are conditions against which the ego needs to be defended (Fairbairn, 1941, p. 30).

The four techniques employed against primitive anxieties can also be understood as four high range behavioural patterns, or personality structures, from the viewpoint of object relations with external objects.

Technique	Accepted object	Rejected object
Obsessional	Internalised	Internalised
Paranoid	Internalised	Externalised
Hysterical	Externalised	Internalised
Phobic	Externalised	Externalised

We must not judge paranoia and obsessive neurosis as resulting from an anal fixation (early and late, respectively), but rather as special defensive techniques, as are all those used against oral conflicts, which are interchangeable during the transitional period. In summary:

- The obsessive individual retains and tries to dominate both objects (ambivalence).
- The phobic individual externalises both objects, trying to escape from the bad one and take refuge in the good object.
- The paranoid individual externalises the bad object and attacks it, maintaining the good one inside.
- The hysterical individual does the opposite: externalises the good object and attaches to it, and internalises the bad object by rejecting it into the interior.

Ute Rupprecht-Schampera (1995, 2005) proposed a novel theory about the formation of hysteria. Although she focuses on the pre-genital stages, she understands triangulation as a phenomenon that occurs right from the beginning; duality, she states, is a developmental failure. Hysteria stems from a failure in the construction of a triadic relationship, due to a failure in the auxiliary parental function: the father provides insufficient support to overcome a mother-child relationship dominated by fear, depression, or hatred. The fundamental conflict lies in the subject's attempt to utilise the Oedipal triangulation in the context of a sexualised form of relationship with the parent of the opposite sex, in order to obtain the missing early (pre-Oedipal) triangulation (in the case of female hysterics) or to secure a substitute for it (in male hysterics), and thereby to achieve the separation from the mother that could not originally be negotiated. If the sexualised approach between the girl and her father results in severe disillusionment or retraumatisation, further defensive operations will be necessary: repression, disavowal, dissociation, and infantile withdrawal (Rupprecht-Schampera, 2005, p. 98). Through all these defensive operations, a self-container-phantasy is established, which is called "pseudo-Oedipal myth", because for the hysterical patient, the Oedipal parent was "to be had", and the early state of non-separation from the mother persists. Rupprecht-Schampera (ibid.) acknowledges the concomitances between her theoretical stance and that of Fairbairn (1941, 1954); both, for example, attribute less importance to the Oedipal complex as such, but she expresses doubts about whether all the cases included in Fairbairn's paper on hysteria (1954b) were actually hysterics: "Granted they have histories of over-excitement and rejection, but no idealization of the parent of the opposite sex, and their mass of symptoms with heavy acting out are characteristic of borderline and phobic patients" (Rupprecht-Schampera, 2005, p. 102).

The aforementioned group of cases—the "not" clearly hysterical—is used by Fairbairn to refine his theory on the psychic apparatus. As we already know, his "endopsychic structure" was basically schizoid or borderline, in other words, probably unable to encompass the hysterical pathology. For instance, during Morris's therapy the following phantasy emerges—the paper reads "inner situation" (1954b, pp. 19–20), maybe with the intent to avoid Kleinian language:

> ... as if his mother was both holding down his erect penis and crushing his testicles with her hand; and he described himself as not only terrified that she would destroy his genitals if he

struggled to get free, but also afraid that she would release her grip, since, if she did, it would put an end to the sexual excitement which her handling of his genitals provoked.

Exciting (LO) and rejecting (AO) objects were combined in this image, and the subject's solution was to adopt a masochistic position. He had a possessive and sexually repressive mother, who forbade him to masturbate, and a distant and inaccessible father. In my clinical experience, such castration phantasies so close to consciousness easily manifest in individuals presenting a borderline organisation in the sense described by Kernberg (1996), that is, separation anxiety, affective confusion, identity diffusion, predominance of shame over guilt, etc. The "regression" to a dyadic mode of functioning is also a particular feature of these patients, who do not clearly rely on the aforementioned transitional techniques, although they do occasionally use the paranoid technique.

Narcissistic and borderline disorders

The psychic organisation presented by Fairbairn, the "endopsychic structure", stems from the schizoid position but is compatible with borderline personality structures, as it has often been emphasised (Modell, 1994; Rinsley, 1987; Robbins, 1980, 1992). Grotstein (1994b, p. 118) notes that internalised objects form the mould that will host the schizoid, narcissistic, borderline, and multiple personality disorders, and the general condition of "being schizoid". Fairbairn's schizoid personality—Grotstein added—is very similar to the current concept of narcissistic personality disorder, while his account of the schizoid state is very close to the contemporary definition of borderline states. In a very similar way, Symington (1994) sees a diagnostic equivalence between Fairbairn's schizoids and Frances Tustin's autistic patients.

Internal grandiosity and exhibitionism in schizoid personality overlap with the narcissistic feelings as articulated by Kohut (1971, 1984). However, Fairbairn very rarely used the terms "narcissism" and "narcissistic". He defined *primary narcissism* as a *state* of complete *identification* with the object, and *secondary narcissism* as *a state of identification with an internalised* object (1941, p. 48). He had also cited the term twice in a clinical article published in 1931. In any event, it seems evident that Fairbairn thinks of narcissism as a kind of phenomenon occurring at a given time in the development of the human being, rather than a starting point.

But, if we affirm that Fairbairn's description of schizoid disorders comprises the current general concept of "borderline and narcissistic disorders" and is especially appropriate for their comprehension, we are unavoidably led to infer the complementary idea: that the theory is not valid for less pathological patients, as some authors have suggested (Modell, 1944). On the other hand, bearing in mind the distinction between *deficit* and *conflict psychopathology*, made by Bjørn Killingmo (1989), which differentiates pre-Oedipal disorders from those mainly Oedipal, we can accept Rinsley's (1987, p. 283) idea that Fairbairn's schizoids are the result of a fundamentally developmental, and not regressive, pathogenesis, resulting from a very early deficiency of the maternal container.

However, we may raise the question: is there any pathology that is not derived ultimately from a deficit? Perhaps that is implied in Fairbairn's statement that: "… at any rate, some measure of splitting of the ego is invariably present at the deepest mental level ... *the basic position in the psyche is invariably a schizoid position*" (1940a, p. 8).

I present below a clinical vignette of a patient suffering from borderline personality disorder in order to comprehend the nature of this pathology and the applicability of this model.

> Paul initially came to see me about his doubts whether or not to marry his partner, who worked in the same company and with whom he had a son. A while after getting married, the patient reported that his wife had a private life of her own; she went out with a group of friends, and he was not allowed to join in. She even went on holiday with them regularly.
>
> Paul is a young man in his thirties. He works for a multinational company as an electronic technician. He could be showing the relational style of a moderate, borderline personality disorder (emotional lability, mental confusion, free-floating anxiety), and he has made more than one suicide attempt disguised as a traffic accident, where at least on one occasion the car was a write-off. When speaking of his mood swings, the cause of which is unknown to him, he remembers that his father, now deceased, had "peaks" of aggression, when he would break things and beat him and his brothers, as well as his mother. In the patient, however, these "peaks" were resolved through flight and consumption of alcohol.
>
> After eighteen months of face to face psychotherapy the patient's separation anxiety is a recurring subject. During a bank holiday weekend last May, he felt very upset because he had leave from work but his wife did not, and his son (seven or eight years old) went away with a classmate to his parents' country house. He felt badly because he would have liked to be with his child; the son, by contrast, was very happy. The therapist pointed out that his reaction was more childish than his son's, and he agreed. Then he described a situation at a party that he and his wife went to that same weekend. The men decided to play cards and then the women said they were going to a bingo hall. From that moment onwards he felt abandoned and stopped enjoying the party, although the women were only away for an hour and a half. He understands that his reaction is inadequate and that it prevents him from enjoying the advantages of being alone at times. He never feels at ease when he is alone. Then he recalls a painful situation: as a child, unable to pinpoint the exact age, his mother went to work and left him locked up at home under the care of a neighbour.

Abandonment anxiety emerges as the dominant feeling. The central ego (CE) appears fragile, but we also observe important deficits in those parental figures that could serve the function of ideal object (IO), that is, a father who exhibits loss of control, in his case overtly aggressive, towards the family environment. Paul's experience of his mother and his relationship with his wife, along with his personal reactions, suggest that his central ego (CE) is dominated by the anti-libidinal aspects of personality: the anti-libidinal ego (AE) and the anti-libidinal object (AO) exert a powerful pressure on the libidinal aspects, thus depriving the patient of the most minimal enjoyment. As the reader may observe, this relational constellation cannot be just directly interpreted; effective treatment entails increasing self-reflective capacity in the patient, accompanying him in the process of gradual elaboration, and helping him understand that the feelings of frustration that he experienced in his marriage do not arise independently but resulted from past and present environmental circumstances. The AO has, in part, replaced the IO: he wants to get closer to an ideal but feels confused about what that may be; he has only learnt that it involves renunciation, self-devaluation, and self-destruction in situations of extreme frustration.

Conclusion

Fairbairn's theory, especially his description of endopsychic structure, can be very helpful in the understanding of more severe disorders, such as some narcissistic and the borderlines, as well as hysterical personality disorder and other neurotic techniques. However, I think this structure hardly applies to those individuals who are in an earlier stage, as is the case of pure schizoid and antisocial disorders, including the "thick-skinned narcissistic patient" of Rosenfeld (1987). *Endopsychic structure* is not valid before the solid constitution of an *ego ideal*—"ideal object", or IO (in Fairbairn's vocabulary)—just before the completion of the superego at the depressive position. But not every subject delineates a stable *ego ideal* to which to aspire to emulate.

Keeping this in mind, the fear that one's love is destructive does not originate in the schizoid position but, rather, it is the result of its optimal evolution. Fear of being destructive is a form of depressive anxiety, since it requires at least some elaboration, however slight, of the feeling of guilt. Forensic experience offers us many examples of individuals—narcissistic, aggressive—who have no fear to destroy. Futility, on the other hand, is a common feeling in the reckless destroyer, evidently free of guilt. Perhaps here lies a mere terminological question in nosology, that is, Fairbairn classified as "schizoid"—and Kohut as "narcissistic"—many individuals now likely to be diagnosed as suffering from a "borderline personality". If this is correct, then schizoid, (psychopathologically) aggressive, and purely narcissistic patterns should be traced back to earlier stages in personality development.

While the *moral defence* is useful to understand the dynamics of the child's attachment to his/her bad objects and the mental mechanisms of masochism, we may wonder what motivates some children to display delinquent behaviours rather than assuming the evil inside with a masochistic attitude. Furthermore, by locating moral defence in the schizoid position—that is, within the most primitive organisation of the psyche—it seems that Fairbairn may be failing to include the unconditionally good psychopath: maybe he never came across one. Beyond borderline organisation, there is the individual who, because of an early lack of empathic support, never displays any form of empathy or guilt. Fairbairn (1940a), however, identifies an immoral motivation for the discharge of aggression in schizoid states: since the pleasure of love is forbidden, the pleasure of hating is allowed, to which enjoyment we can devote ourselves. Given that love involves destructiveness, it seems best to destroy through hate, in a fashion close to the narcissistic personality individual with antisocial attitudes—the "thick-skinned narcissistic patient" above-mentioned or the "malignant narcissist" of Kernberg (1996)—and the antisocial individual in its most strict sense. However, these subjects become bad not in order to protect their good objects but, in my opinion, to keep all "goodness" inside themselves.

Some years ago we postulated the existence of an intermediate position between the Kleinian paranoid-schizoid and depressive positions, which we termed "confused position" (cf. Caparrós-Sánchez, 1981; Rodríguez-Sutil, 2002). L. J. Brown (1987) also proposed a "transitional position", intermediate to the paranoid-schizoid and the depressive positions, and prior to the traditional Oedipal phase. This "confused" or "transitional" position is characterised by the use of manic defences, including magical reparation.

In our clinical experience, the most prominent feature of this position is the oscillation between expansiveness of the self—elation, momentary identification with the ego ideal, or schizoid grandiosity—and the subsequent fall into a "depressive" state, marked by a sense of inner impoverishment and lack of worth. What these individuals predominantly show is not guilt but shame, a sense of regret and self-reproach for "not having measured up" or "having made a fool of themselves", together with intense separation anxiety and a huge need to be accepted. Aside from those periods of expansiveness, they tend to take on modest, submissive, and secondary roles, while covering up the internal grandiosity that Fairbairn intuitively identified. This oscillation is the phenomenological presentation of the "phobic-counterphobic" mechanism—getting into the feared situation—which is shared by phobic, borderline, and impulsive patients—the impulsive-borderline type of the ICD-10 (WHO, 1994).

Although Fairbairn opens the door to a relational conceptualisation of the psyche, he remains excessively focused on the intrapsychic structure, on an inner world that ultimately takes precedence, never fully conceiving personality as an open system that continuously influences and is influenced by external experience (cf. Scharff, 2005, p. 10). An authentic theory of human relations would affirm that what is introjected is neither images, nor objects; what is introjected—or, rather, *learnt*—are patterns of action or interaction. The objects Fairbairn is talking about are not, strictly speaking, "representations"; they are unconscious, procedural patterns of action, activated in interpersonal, emotional, relations, in a process of dialectical adaptation to the partner's own procedural patterns.

Grotstein (1994a, p. 175) compared Fairbairn's reform in psychoanalysis with that of Martin Luther in religion. This may be true, but much still remains to be done.

References

American Psychiatric Association (1980). *Diagnostic and Statistical Manual of Mental Disorders: DSM-III*. Washington, DC.

American Psychiatric Association (1987). *Diagnostic and Statistical Manual of Mental Disorders: DSM-III-R*. Washington, DC.

American Psychiatric Association (1994). *Diagnostic and Statistical Manual of Mental Disorders: DSM-IV*. Washington, DC.

Basili, R. M., & Sharpin de Basili, I. (2005). Fairbairn's theory, borderline pathology, and schizoid conflict. In: J. S. Scharff & D. E. Scharff (Eds.), *The Legacy of Fairbairn and Sutherland: Psychotherapeutic Applications* (pp. 128–139). London: Routledge.

Brown, L. J. (1987). Borderline personality organization and the transition to the depresive position. In: J. S. Grotstein, M. F. Solomon, & J. A. Lang (Eds.), *The Borderline Patient: Emerging Concepts in Diagnosis, Psychodynamics, and Treatment, Vol. 1* (pp. 147–180). Hillsdale, NJ: Analytic Press.

Caparrós-Sánchez, N. (1981). *La construcción de la personalidad. Las psicopatías.* (*The Construction of Personality. The Psychopathy.*) Madrid, Spain: Fundamentos. Fairbairn, W. R. D. (1929b). Dissociation and repression. In: E. F. Birtles & D. E. Scharff (Eds.), *From Instinct to Self: Selected Papers of W. R. D. Fairbairn, Volume II: Applications and Early Contributions* (pp. 13–79). Northvale, NJ: Jason Aronson, 1994.

Fairbairn, W. R. D. (1931). Features in the analysis of a patient with a physical genital abnormality. In: *Psychoanalytic Studies of the Personality* (pp. 197–222). London: Tavistock, 1952.

Fairbairn, W. R. D. (1940a). Schizoid factors in the personality. In: *Psychoanalytic Studies of the Personality* (pp. 3–27). London: Tavistock, 1952.

Fairbairn, W. R. D. (1941). A revised psychopathology of the psychoses and psychoneuroses. *International Journal of Psychoanalysis, 22*(2 & 3): 250–279. In: *Psychoanalytic Studies of the Personality* (pp. 28–58). London: Tavistock, 1952.

Fairbairn, W. R. D. (1943a). The repression and the return of bad objects (with special reference to the "war neuroses"). *British Journal of Medical Psychology, 19*: 327–341. In: *Psychoanalytic Studies of the Personality* (pp. 59–81). London: Tavistock, 1952.

Fairbairn, W. R. D. (1944). Endopsychic structure considered in terms of object-relationships. *International Journal of Psychoanalysis, 25*: 70–92. In: *Psychoanalytic Studies of the Personality* (pp. 82–136). London: Tavistock, 1952.

Fairbairn, W. R. D. (1952). *Psychoanalytic Studies of the Personality*. London: Tavistock.

Fairbairn, W. R. D. (1954b). Observations on the nature of hysterical states. In: D. E. Scharff & E. F. Birtles (Eds.), *From Instinct to Self: Selected Papers of W. R. D. Fairbairn, Volume 1: Clinical and Theoretical Papers* (pp. 13–40). Northvale, NJ: Jason Aronson, 1994.

Freud, S. (1915d). Repression. *S. E., 14*: 141–158. London: Hogarth. Die Verdrängung. In: *Studienausgabe* (vol. III). Frankfurt am Main, Germany: S. Fisher, 1975.

Grotstein, J. S. (1994a). Endopsychic structure and the cartography of the internal world: Six endopsychic characters in search of an author. In: J. S. Grotstein & D. B. Rinsley (Eds.), *Fairbairn and the Origins of Object Relations* (pp. 174–194). New York: Guilford, 1994.

Grotstein, J. S. (1994b). Notes on Fairbairn's metapsychology. In: J. S. Grotstein & D. B. Rinsley (Eds.), *Fairbairn and the Origins of Object Relations* (pp. 112–148). New York: Guilford, 1994.

Guntrip, H. (1961). *Personality Structure and Human Interaction. The Developing Synthesis of Psychodynamic Theory*. London: Karnac, 1995.

Hensel, B. F. (2005). An object relations view of sexuality based on Fairbairn's theory. In: J. S. Scharff & D. E. Scharff (Eds.), *The Legacy of Fairbairn and Sutherland. Psychotherapeutic Applications* (pp. 68–79). London: Routledge.

House, J., & Portuges, S. (2005). Relational knowing, memory, symbolization, and language: Commentary on the Boston Change Process Study Group. *Journal of the American Psychoanalytic Association, 53*: 731–743.

Kernberg, O. F. (1996). A psychoanalitic theory of personality disorders. In: J. F. Clarkin & M. F. Lenzenweger (Eds.), *Major Theories of Personality Disorders*. New York: Guilford.

Khan, M. M. R. (1960). Clinical aspects of the schizoid personality: Affects and technique. *International Journal of Psychoanalysis, 41*: 430–436.

Killingmo, B. (1989). Conflict and deficit: Implications for technique. *International Journal of Psychoanalysis, 70*: 65–79.

Kohut, H. (1971). *The Analysis of the Self*. New York: International Universities Press.

Kohut, H. (1984). *How Does Analysis Cure?* Chicago, IL: Chicago University Press.

Lyons-Ruth, K. (1999). The two-person unconscious: Intersubjective dialogue, enactive relational representation, and the emergence of new forms of relational organization. *Psychoanalytic Inquiry, 19*: 576–617.

Mitchell, S. A. (1981). The origin and nature of the "object" in the theories of Klein and Fairbairn. In: J. S. Grotstein & D. B. Rinsley (Eds.), *Fairbairn and the Origins of Object Relations* (pp. 67–87). New York: Guilford, 1994.

Modell, A. H. (1994). Fairbairn's structural theory and the communication of affects. In: J. S. Grotstein & D. B. Rinsley (Eds.), *Fairbairn and the Origins of Object Relations* (pp. 195–207). New York: Guilford.

Rinsley, D. B. (1987). A reconsideration of Fairbairn's "original object" and "original ego" in relation to borderline and other self disorders. In: J. S. Grotstein & D. B. Rinsley (Eds.), *Fairbairn and the Origins of Object Relations* (pp. 275–288). New York: Guilford, 1994.

Robbins, M. (1980). Current controversy in object relations theory as outgrowth of a schism between Klein and Fairbairn. *International Journal of Psychoanalysis, 61*: 477–492.

Robbins, M. (1992). A Fairbairnian object relations perspective on self psychology. In: J. S. Grotstein & D. B. Rinsley (Eds.), *Fairbairn and the Origins of Object Relations* (pp. 302–317). New York: Guilford, 1994.

Rodríguez-Sutil, C. (2002). *Psicopatología Psicoanalítica. Un Enfoque Vincular*. Madrid, Spain: Biblioteca Nueva.

Rosenfeld, H. A. (1987). *Impasse and Interpretation*. London: Routledge.

Rupprecht-Schampera, U. (1995). The concept of "early triangulation" as a key to a unified model of hysteria. *International Journal of Psychoanalysis, 76*: 457–473.

Rupprecht-Schampera, U. (2005). How current are Fairbairn's ideas on hysteria? In: J. S. Scharff & D. E. Scharff (Eds.), *The Legacy of Fairbairn and Sutherland: Psychotherapeutic Applications* (pp. 97–104). London: Routledge.

Scharff, D. E. (1998). Fairbairn's contribution. An interview of Otto Kernberg. In: N. J. Skolnick & D. E. Scharff (Eds.), *Fairbairn, Then and Now* (pp. 17–32). Hillsdale, NJ: Analytic Press.

Scharff, D. E. (2005). The development of Fairbairn's theory. In: J. S. Scharff & D. E. Scharff (Eds.), *The Legacy of Fairbairn and Sutherland: Psychotherapeutic Applications* (pp. 3–18). London: Routledge.

Suttie, I. D. (1935). *The Origins Of Love and Hate*. London: Free Associations, 1999.

Symington, N. (1994). The tradition of Fairbairn. In: J. S. Grotstein & D. B. Rinsley (Eds.), *Fairbairn and the Origins of Object Relations* (pp. 211–221). New York: Guilford, 1994.

WHO (1994). *International Classification of Diseases ICD-10*. Geneva, Switzerland: World Health Organization.

Winnicott, D. W. (1965). Psychotherapy of character disorders. In: *The Maturational Processes and the Facilitating Environment: Studies in the Theory of Emotional Development* (pp. 203–216). New York: International Universities Press.

Winnicott, D. W. (1971). *Playing and Reality* (pp. 72–73). London: Routledge.

CHAPTER FIFTEEN

Fairbairn: abuse, trauma, and multiplicity

Valerie Sinason

W. R. D. Fairbairn is crucial theoretically and clinically in the treatment of abused children and adults. His deep pioneering understanding of attachment processes in abusive relationships clarified the psychological need for dissociation as a defence. He understood this both in the ubiquitous dissociation that develops in "ordinary" child abuse and in the extreme situations that lead to dissociative identity disorder, a subject profoundly undeveloped in the international psychoanalytic community—and particularly the UK. Indeed, in his medical dissertation of 1929 he chose to focus on dissociation.

Sadly, I was not taught his work while studying as a child psychotherapist in the 1980s. Indeed, in my being considered one of only a handful of psychoanalytic child psychotherapists who were thought to have worked with child abuse in that period at the Tavistock Clinic in London, it was salutary to later realise that, like Ferenczi, Fairbairn had always been aware of the subject. Indeed, from 1927 to 1935 he was a lecturer in psychology at Edinburgh University, specialising in adolescence, and held a post at the Clinic for Children and Juveniles where he treated the delinquent and sexually abused.

Additionally, he was not only a relational psychoanalyst in theory and practice, understanding that the infant was object related from birth, he also understood that the baby has no choice. For sheer basic survival the baby has to attach. This has enormous theoretical and clinical applications in terms of terrorised children with infanticidal attachment (Kahr, 2007).

Like that of all pioneers, his work could not be adequately accepted at the actual time he wrote it and thirty years later he is only just beginning to be part of contemporary syllabi in the UK thanks in no small measure to the work of Birtles, Clarke, Grotstein, Rinsley, Kernberg, and the Scharffs. Indeed, in the words of another pioneer (Bowlby, 1979) *knowing what you are not supposed to know* is a ubiquitous recurring problem for all humans. While psychoanalysis can provide the tools for understanding individual and societal disavowal, denial, and dissociation, the theory can only be applied to the extent that the fragile humans internalising the theory—psychoanalysts, psychotherapists, and counsellors—can bear to face it. The topics of abuse and dissociation are no easier to face in the twenty-first century. While there has been an increased awareness of the impact of trauma societally and individually it has been slow for elements of mainstream therapy and analysis to take on any understanding of dissociation and especially dissociative identity disorder (Sinason, 2012).

Indeed, an interweaving dimension to consider is the political one as to why different training groups provide selective access to particular theories and not others. Acts of omission can be as damaging as acts of commission. While the qualified practitioner has the responsibility to be widely read, the books provided during training become part of the practitioner's professional tribal identity. There is also a moral need to write about areas that have been avoided by theoreticians. Pearl King, an independent group psychoanalyst now in her nineties, and my supervisor during and after my adult psychoanalytic training at the British Society for more than ten years, regularly stated that "… if the theory is not there for people to see then people can not see what they have not been trained to see" (personal communication, 1996). Curriculum committees play a powerful role here as do publishers. The cultural "wego" is incorporated and internalised as powerfully as ideas on the ego. At a sketch in the Tavistock Clinic Pantomime in the 1980s the receptionist pointedly commented that the Anna Freud Clinic was within "spitting distance". Melanie Klein clearly was not part of the syllabus at the Anna Freud any more than Anna Freud (or even Winnicott in that period) entered the child training at the Tavistock.

This chapter is for me also a public apology. I have written so much on abuse and trauma before reading Fairbairn and can see now how his theories throw a sharper light and add a different depth to what I previously understood and provided. Indeed, in a paper on passionate lethal attachments (Sinason, 1990), I now realise I was trying to make sense of what Fairbairn calls the exciting rejecting object through the prism of the other theories available to me, and the paper remains a far more transitional work in progress. While Bowlby, Rosenfeld, and Shengold allowed key areas to be understood, there was a profound Fairbairnian deficit.

No-choice attachment/repetition compulsion/failing environment and relational work

Angela, aged thirty-six, faced me defiantly and bravely, her bruised face bearing witness to the untreated rage of her husband. No way could she lie down on the couch. It would have hurt more of her body. It would have made her feel defenceless. In no way could she tolerate me sitting behind her. That would require a trust it would be mad to have. So she sat for her assessment, scanning my face desperately.

"If I tell you the truth you won't want to see me. You people don't. Everyone gives up on me. Counsellors, social workers. The last social says she won't see me any more. Says she has wasted time on me getting me to a refuge and then I ruin it going back to him."

"Charming!" I said. "You mean the approach where someone says—'Come to us with your drug problem when you are off them! Come to us with your alcoholism when you are dry!'"

Angela burst out laughing and a deep sigh ran through her body.

"Could it be she is blaming you because she can't bear seeing you get hurt again and again?" I asked in a gentler tone.

Angela unclenched her fists.

"Could be," she said thoughtfully. "She always looked away."

A grin returned to her face.

"But you are a tough old cow because you are looking straight at me."

We both laughed.

"I am looking at you and if tough old cow means I don't run away then you are right."

"So you know I am not ready to leave him."

"My job isn't to make you leave him or make you stay."

"So you won't get me sectioned if I come bruised?"

"Does a bit of you feel you are mad putting up with this?"

"Yes. And I know it. When I saw what my Dad did to my Mum I cursed her and said I would never put up with it but look at me, and I don't have children to support and she did."

"We all think we have made such Olympic steps in improving on what our parents did but I like the native Indian proverb, 'The apple does not fall far from the tree'."

She laughed.

"I am the bad apple and I keep finding bad apples."

I said she was a loyal daughter.

There was a long pause.

I then told her about the work I had just discovered at Newcastle University where Dr John Lazarus had done some brilliant research. It was about why antelopes in Africa fed in front of their main predator, the lion.

"I know the answer to that," she laughed.

"Yes?"

"It's the safest place isn't it? Like when my dad was asleep drunk in front of me I knew I was safe. Really safe. I could nick some food from the fridge—take his fags. But if I ran out of the house to get help I could run into a whole gang of drunk pervs—and knowing my luck I would."

"You've got it," I said. "And that's animal research and we are animals. So it is only natural you go back to him."

There were many ways I could have taken this session and at a later stage, when she started to want to read analytic books about child abuse, I could tell her about Fairbairn.

However, at this point I want to express how this extract illustrates and is informed by various important clinical points that Fairbairn has made.

Angela, for survival, has had an attachment to a painfully negative aspect of endemic childhood experience, which has become part of her identity, her whole sense of who she is. There is a huge need and compulsion to repeat these bad experiences to reaffirm identity. The existence of such an endopsychic (Fairbairn, 1944) structure from childhood leads naturally to the desperate seeking and re-finding of similar pattern relationships in adulthood in the hope of healing through re-finding identity and the giving up of such attachments evokes unbearable depths of loss. As with a bereavement it involves both the loss of the internal object relationship externalised into the adult relationship but also loss of self.

When Angela, two years later, tried again, unsuccessfully to leave her husband I reminded her:

"Angela, it is having to orphan yourself. What an unfair predicament you have been landed with."

When Angela finally was able to leave her husband, after broken ribs and cuts to the head, she had to deal with a devastating level of mourning. She was mourning, as she realised, for the unavailability of her mother to her as well as the failure of her father. She was helped by me saying: "Just imagine if someone said to a happily married woman with loving parents and children—'You pathetic co-dependent human—you have gone and repeated just what your parents did and found someone just like your dad. If you don't leave home I will never talk to you again.'"

Humour was a crucial part of the therapeutic relationship. It was the way in which the most unbearable actual and psychic realities could be expressed and received. There has, in my opinion, been an abuse of Freud's brave early concept of neutrality in terms of the analyst not representing archaic transference figures, into a "neutral" face and voice. Fairbairn's early awareness of the actual relationship (Scharff & Birtles, 1994, ch. 4) as a therapeutic factor of prime importance has taken a further half-century to be realised.

Sadly, Angela's husband was not willing to come for help for himself. Following her successful departure he deteriorated, made a suicide attempt, and was hospitalised. Without Angela as a toxic container for his unworked-through childhood pain he could not continue. Angela had been able to see the way in which through her relationship with him she was trying to seek and work through the exciting and alluring bad objects of her failing early environment.

"I knew it really," said Angela, her defensive humour now not needed. "I knew that because of what he did to me, my Dad stayed alive."

The moral defence: in work with children and adults with an intellectual disability

Mary, aged ten, had a severe intellectual disability and Down's syndrome. She had been referred for inappropriate sexual behaviour by her class teacher Miss Edwards (not her real name) and GP Dr Samson. Like most of the children and adults with an intellectual disability who had been referred to me at either the Tavistock Clinic or St Georges Hospital Medical School, she had been sexually abused (Sinason, 1992, 2010).

"Dirty Mary," she said, with a huge false smile, thrusting her hand between her legs.

"Dirty?" I asked.

"Dirty Mary!" she shouted, hitting her face with her left hand.

"Ouch!" I said. "Someone has just hit poor Mary in the face and called her dirty."

"Dirty Mary," she repeated with a false smile.

I have written extensively about the "handicapped smile", which is a secondary handicap to both appease and apologise for the grief of carrying a disability and a disguised anger (Sinason, 1986).

"That does not look like a real smile," I said softly. "Looks like you are hurting and feel bad and dirty."

She took her hand out of her knickers and thrust it towards me with a pseudo-pornographic pose. "Want dirty Mary?"

I felt deeply sad and said to her she wanted to give me something because she felt so bad and lonely and she did not think I would want to talk to her or know her if she did not offer herself.

I picked up a sad looking rag doll.

"What shall we call her?" I asked.

Mary walked round to look at her.

"Susie," she said. "Sad. Sad."

"Yes," I agreed. "Hello Susie. We think you are looking rather sad and I think you know about the kind of things that make Mary sad."

"Really?" asked Mary.

"Yes. You ask her."

"Susie—are you dirty?"

"Yes," I replied, putting on a whispery child voice.

"I am Dirty Susie".

Mary lifted up the doll's dress, all smiles gone.

"Does your Daddy poo and pee on you?" she asked.

"Yes," I whispered.

"It's your Down's syndrome," she said conversationally. "That's why."

"Is that why Susie's Daddy poos and pees on her?" I asked.

"Yes," she said.

"So if she didn't have Down's syndrome he wouldn't do that?"

"No. Sad, angry she has Down's syndrome, Mongol baby girl."

"Would you pee and poo on a little girl if you had a little girl with Down's syndrome?" I asked.

"No. No," she shouted and looked at me shocked by the power of her response.

"Nor would I and nor would Dr Samson or Miss Edwards."

"No," she agreed. "No. No."

"Grown-ups aren't allowed to do that to any children, children who are dirty, children with Down's syndrome."

"Children who can't read—children in wheelchairs," added Mary.

"That's right."

There was a pause.

"Grown-ups aren't allowed to do that even if the child asks them to, wants them to, even if the child is bad."

"I am going to wash Dirty Susie," said Mary softly, and she took her to the sink and gently washed her.

"That's nice," I whispered. "I feel nice and clean now. Thank you Mary."

Mary smiled a genuine happy smile.

"I made her clean."

"That's right," I agreed.

Then she burst into tears.

"Now her Daddy will die."

She dropped the wet doll on the floor.

"Why will he die now?"

"He's got all the dirt back and Susie won't have a Daddy."

I was astounded by her understanding.

"Goodness me," I said. "You are so clever, Mary. Is that right for you too? If you were clean happy Mary would something bad happen to your Daddy too?"

She picked up a plastic mirror from the dressing-up box.

"Look," she said.

She pointed to her eyes.

"Down's syndrome eyes. Bad Mary came out wrong."

"You feel sad you were born with Down's syndrome?"

"Not like sister or Mum or Dad or you."

"We have not got Down's syndrome, that is true."

"Daddy loves Mary when she is dirty even though she is Mongol."

"So Dirty Mary pretends to smile and be happy even when she is sad because then Daddy loves her."

"Yes. And if he does it enough dirty to me then my Down's syndrome will go away. But I am so bad it takes longer."

She sat very still.

"You are good, Valerie Sinason. You are good. How can I be good like you?"

This brief extract illustrates many painful issues. Children with intellectual disabilities have feelings and fantasies about the origins of their condition and are more vulnerable to abuse and exploitation because of this. They also have the capacity to emotionally understand at the same profound level as anyone daring to seek for psychic truth. However, I am taking us backwards in time from adult Angela to see how a young child has learned Fairbairn's moral defence.

As Clarke (2012, p. 204), drawing on Fairbairn's view on the "moral defence", puts it: "The child seeks to purge his objects of their badness by taking this badness upon himself and is rewarded by the sense of security that an environment of good objects confers. However, this outer security is purchased at the price of inner security as his ego is henceforth left at the mercy of a band of internal persecutors. The bad objects the child internalizes are unconditionally bad and, since the child has internalized them, and thus identifies with them, then he is unconditionally bad. In order to be able to redress this unconditional badness the child internalizes his good objects, which assume a super-ego role."

To see herself as bad sometimes is less terrible for Mary than to see her needed father as bad. By being the one who is bad she is in control of the awful randomness of nature—the fact that she has Down's syndrome and that this has led to her being singled out for abuse within her family. She cannot control the existence of the Down's syndrome so she ascribes this godlike possibility to her co-creator—her father. By being good to him and pleasing him she keeps him alive and can have a relationship with him. At the same time her sense of badness is further complicated by the sense of utter uselessness and imminent psychical death (Fairbairn, 1944, p. 113).

From my clinical experience of children and adults who have experienced abuse, the most entrenched long-term problem is the sense of badness and Fairbairn is a crucial ingredient here.

Indeed, I have often found it helpful to take an educational line and say:

> Do you know, thanks to your hard work you have reached the hardest part of your journey and it is something that can take a lifetime to continue working on. It is the "I am bad feeling". As a baby and little child you cannot help feeling that whatever the adults do is due to you. A little one cannot conceive of the separate motivations and pains of adult life. Theory of mind has not developed enough either. Think of loving parents who divorce and say truthfully to the children that they still love their children but they are not happy together. Depending on their ages, the children can still think it is because of them. Then add on abuse. To survive, sheer primitive survival, the child has to feel their caretaker is good and so by saying you are bad you take control of it. The next time you get raped you can say "Well I wasn't good enough but next time it will be better." That keeps Mum and Dad as OK because you are the bad one. Then, when things are really bad the adult says "Yes. You are bad and that is why I did it" and to top it all society says "What a horrid thing to say about your lovely parents".

Ritual cult abuse

"It is better to be a sinner in a world ruled by God than a saint in a world ruled by the devil. A sinner in a world ruled by God may be bad, but there is always a sense of security to be derived from the fact that the world around is good" (ibid., pp. 66–67).

Since 1990 I have been working with children and adults who have experienced spiritual and ritual abuse (Sinason, 1992). Below is the working definition we use (Sinason & Aduale, 2008):

> Spiritual abuse is the use or misuse of a position of power, leadership or control in which a child or adult is made to feel that they, their families or those they love are doomed in this life and in an after-life if they do not follow unquestioningly what they are asked to say or do.
>
> Ritual abuse is the involvement of children (and adults) in physical, psychological or sexual abuse associated with repeated activities ("ritual"), which purport to relate the abuse to contexts of a religious, magical or supernatural kind. In this abuse a child or adult is made to feel that they, their families or those they love are doomed in this life and in an after-life if they do not follow unquestioningly what they are asked to say or do.

Psychoanalysis has always struggled with how to balance the impact of internal and external factors and ritual abuse represents one of the most extreme of external factors. Donald Meltzer, a pioneering post-Kleinian theoretician and clinician taught theory seminars at the Tavistock Clinic when I was training to be a child psychotherapist there in the 1980s. Like his wife, Martha (Mattie) Williams, who was one of the founders of the child psychotherapy training there, he set great store on intellectual freedom. Indeed, he resigned from the Institute of Psychoanalysis over a difference of opinion over the training and was concerned about thought control and tyranny.

One major area of his attention was the concept of a claustrum (1992). This involved a distinction between intrusive and communicative types of projective identification, not just "massive" projective identification as in previously established Kleinian theory.

He considered there was a theological parallel in the way that there could be intrusive projective identification into the three realms of mother and her body. There were three different chambers of the claustrum—breasts, genitals, and rectum. Breasts were a heaven, the vagina was a garden of sexuality and reproduction, and the rectum was a hell of perversity and sadomasochism (Meltzer & Harris, 1976, p. 408). When an intrusive identification leads to the claustrum chamber of the rectum the result is a sadomasochistic condition of enslavement accompanied by fear of being thrown out of a rigid hierarchical internal organisation. There is a fragile grandiosity in which the position of "lieutenant" to an internal Satan can be adhered to.

Having relatively recently encountered survivors of ritual abuse at that time (Sinason, 1994) I was struck by the way Meltzer's internal claustrum theory helpfully and exactly delineated the hierarchical external structure of cults. I wrote to him asking what he considered the double disturbance would be for those survivors who struggled with both an internal and external claustrum. Although, unlike several other psychoanalysts of that period, he could make room for the reality of ritual abuse, he wrote back (personal communication, 1992) that it only mattered if the claustrum was internal. Whilst I accepted that some children and adults could amazingly hold onto a sense of fairness and hope when the external world around them had lost all values, this did not help my work with cult-identified and loyal children and adults whose disorganised attachments had led them to hold onto the exciting, alluring, and rejecting other.

Indeed, in work with ritual abuse survivors, Clarke provides us with the Fairbairnian explanation for their myriad suicide attempts: "Daniels would rather die having a view of himself as a good man, however illusory, than admit his badness and try to make some restitution" (Clarke, 2012, p. 206)—this is the crucial and complex clinical area in working with the people making multiple suicide attempts. The level of guilt is unbearable.

Text message between Beatrice and Therapist. Beatrice aged twenty-six, a ritual abuse victim. (Beatrice in italics.)

I am sorry, I can't carry on like this. I am going to kill myself tonight.
It is a really awful time for you.
Please forgive me. I want to try but I can't live with it.
I am not surprised. If you did not want to die I would worry there was something wrong with you.
You know why I have to do it don't you.
I know, I think, something of why you feel you have to do it and I am sure I would feel the same.
It's—it's—please—help me—say it—
It's not what they did to you is it.
No.

It's not the torture, the terror, the endless fear although that would be enough for most luckier people to want to top themselves.
No—that is easy. No, not easy. But that is nothing to do with it ... it's ... it's ... please ... please ...
It's what they made you do.
Yes. But I did it.
You did. And it is no good me saying you were forced under threat of death.
No. I still did it. If I was a good person I would be dead.
You know—one of the worst things I think they did to you was to make you feel that being alive was a perversion.
Yes. Yes. I was so close to death. I could feel it. Reach out to it. And that is always when they bring you back. Bring you back and give you one of those choices.
Sophie's choice.
Yes.
Don't let them win. Don't. Last out another day.
Would you miss me if I died?
Yes.
How can you bear the sight of me, with what I have done?

Professionals working in this field have the painful experience of receiving text, emails, and telephone messages like this on an almost daily level. All too often, crisis teams, who do not have consistent shifts so there can be no stable attachment, precipitously bring in a psychiatrist or a social worker who can section so that the fear of being blamed and sued is removed. This adds to the helplessness of the victim who feels controlled then by professional forces rather than listened to.

Working with dissociation and dissociative identity disorder

Fairbairn, like Bromberg (1998) saw dissociation as universally present and relevant. He saw everyone as being schizoid as a result of this and defined dissociation as an active mental process, whereby unacceptable mental content or an unacceptable mental function becomes cut off from personal consciousness, without thereby ceasing to be mental—such mental content or mental function being "unacceptable". He extended this so that it covered the extreme situations. Scharff and Birtles mention that he referred (1952, p. 5) specifically to "somnambulism, the fugue, dual personality, and multiple personality" as "dissociative phenomena". In "Observations on the Nature of Hysterical States" (Scharff & Birtles, 1994, ch. 1) Fairbairn (1954b) again reasserted the fundamental importance of *dissociation*, because "... it carries with it the implication of *a split in the personality*, variable in its extent and often multiple."

At the moment the DSM-IV international psychiatric criteria (APA, 1994) see DID as the presence of two or more distinct identities or personality states (each with its own relatively enduring pattern of perceiving, relating to, and thinking about the environment and self). At least two of these identities or personality states recurrently take control of the person's behaviour: inability to recall important personal information that is too extensive to be explained by ordinary forgetfulness and not due to the direct effects of a substance (e.g., blackouts or chaotic behaviour during alcohol intoxication) or a general medical condition (e.g., complex partial seizures).

There are many international disagreements with this definition. Personally I would like it linked to developmental trauma. However, it is often not helpful to claim that the presence of alcohol or substance abuse or seizures negates the possibility of coexisting dissociation. Indeed, with the level of trauma that comes with DID it would hardly be surprising. Suicidality is also the highest within this group.

Within the UK there is an appalling lack of knowledge and training about DID (Sinason, 2010, 2012) compared to the USA and The Netherlands. Indeed, very few child or adult trainings provide any training in it. Remarkably, Fairbairn was aware of it before his 1929 dissertation on the topic. He understood dissociation as a part of splitting in terms of trauma in everyday life as well as the extreme dissociation that leads to dissociative identity disorder.

He understood that the maintenance of the internal world as a closed system was "the greatest of all sources of resistance" (1958a, p. 380). This profoundly adds to the current concepts from Ellert Nijenhuis (van der Hart, Nijenhuis, & Steele, 2009) on the phobic response against making links or Mollon's (2002) use of the concepts of destructive narcissism. Finnegan and Clarke (2012) are amongst a very small number who have explored "resistances that derive from the maintenance of ties to bad objects and the wish to preserve the inner world as a closed system".

Since starting a Clinic for Dissociative Studies in 2000 in order to provide a space for NHS patients who were despairing of having their predicament recognised, I have been even more grateful to Fairbairn and to those who have helped bring his work to new generations.

Unsurprisingly, in the small contemporary clusters of professionals working openly with DID, there is a split. Some consider that speaking to the alter-states present is collusion or can undermine integration or mature co-consciousness. There is no research to back this assumption.

However, in view of this I was particularly grateful for the way Finnegan and Clarke speak powerfully of "the need to address alter personalities directly, respectfully and analytically prior to interpretation more specifically intended to facilitate integrative functioning" (ibid., p. 64). This, to my mind, is a crucial part of attachment-based respectful relating.

Meeting with Rosie aged thirty-two

She has DID as a result of a disorganised attachment and relentless abuse from her family and multiple perpetrators from as far back as she can remember, and was only free from external abuse from the age of twenty-six when she found a partner who recognised her predicament.

ROSIE: They *really* didn't want me to get help. You know, I can't help it, but I blame them more than my family. At least my family knew what they had done to me but these— these so-called professionals who keep telling me borderline, obsession, psychopathic, schizophrenic this or that—how dare they not listen to me and not listen to the others.

VS: The referral letter said you had had over seven diagnoses before coming here.

ROSIE: And the worst thing, you know how long it took me to get Rosita [another alter] to speak. Well—not me. My partner told me about her and I wrote her messages. She was so shy and frightened of being tortured for speaking. And then in the hospital—and with therapists there too—when she came out they carried on calling her Rosie even though she said that was not her name. And to cap it all, the psychiatrist—who was an analyst too or an analytic therapist—said it was immature and attention seeking to respond to anyone who did not own the body's name.

Fairbairn (1952) realised the child with inadequate parents (whether by omission or commission) had to split the ego in order to take into his small self the unbearable aspects of the largely unavailable parents. This cushions the situation, especially in extreme abuse, where ambivalence is least bearable. The more disorganised the attachment the greater the need for splitting.

Libidinal and anti-libidinal selves have a difficult route as a result of the sad template that created them and this limits their capacity for emotional growth. A real relationship with an external object is a relationship in an open system and this is a threat unless the external object is treated as an object within the closed system of inner reality (Fairbairn, 1958a, p. 381).

Rosie: after two years of therapy Rosie: You know, my partner has started changing through our family therapy. It is really disturbing. At the beginning she was like another child personality of mine. She cried if I was going out and she needed me there all the time. That was just right for me. But now everything is different and it is scary and hopeful all at the same time.

Conclusion

At John Bowlby's eightieth birthday party I asked him what was the best thing about being eighty. He replied, with a mischievous smile, "That all your old enemies have to admit you were right!"

The impact of separation and attachment was not bearable to most of Bowlby's psychoanalytic colleagues but he lived to see his work spread around the globe despite the inevitability of denial and dissociation. Realising the wealth of knowledge available in Fairbairn's thinking, particularly for the field of trauma, is a new treasure house for the professional. It will aid the reduction of secondary traumatisation by providing a deeper structural understanding. I am very grateful to have discovered Fairbairn at this stage and wish I had encountered him at the beginning of my career. However, I now have an extra gift to pass on to all those I meet.

References

American Psychiatric Association (1994). *Diagnostic and Statistical Manual of Mental Disorders: DSM-IV*. Washington, DC.

Bowlby, J. (1979). On knowing what you are supposed not to know and feeling what you are not supposed to feel. *Canadian Journal of Psychiatry*, 24: 403–408.

Bromberg, P. (1998). *Standing between the Spaces*. Hillsdale, NJ: Analytic Press.

Clarke, G. S. (2012). Failures of the moral defence in the films Shutter Island, Inception and Memento; narcissism or schizoid person disorder? *International Journal of Psychoanalysis*, 93: 205–218.

Fairbairn, W. R. D. (1944). Endopsychic structure considered in terms of object relationships. In: *Psychoanalytic Studies of the Personality* (pp. 162–179). Boston, MA: Routledge & Kegan Paul, 1952.

Fairbairn, W. R. D. (1952). *Psychoanalytic Studies of the Personality*. London: Routledge & Kegan Paul.

Fairbairn, W. R. D. (1954b). Observations on the nature of hysterical states. In: D. E. Scharff & E. F. Birtles (Eds.), *From Instinct to Self: Selected Papers of W. R. D. Fairbairn, Volume I: Clinical and Theoretical Papers* (pp. 13–40). Northvale, NJ: Jason Aronson. 1994.

Fairbairn, W. R. D. (1958a). On the nature and aims of psycho-analytical treatment. *International Journal of Psychoanalysis, 39*(5): 374–385. In: D. E. Scharff & E. F. Birtles (Eds.), *From Instinct to Self: Selected Papers of W. R. D. Fairbairn, Volume I: Clinical and Theoretical Papers* (pp. 74–92). Northvale, NJ: Jason Aronson, 1994.

Finnegan, P., & Clarke, G. S. (2012). Evelyn's PhD in wellness—a Fairbairnian understanding of the therapeutic relationship with a woman with DID. *Attachment, 6*(1), March: 50–68.

Kahr, B. (2007). The infanticidal attachment. *Attachment, 1*(2), July: 117–132.

Meltzer, D. (1992). *The Claustrum: An Investigation of Claustrophobic Phenomena*. Perthshire: Clunie Press.

Meltzer, D., & Harris, M. (1976). A psychoanalytic model of the child-in-the-family-in-the-community. In: D. Meltzer, *Sincerity and Other Works* (A. Hahn, Ed.) (pp. 387–454). London: Karnac, 1994.

Mollon, P. (2002). The dark dimensions of multiple personality. In: V. Sinason (Ed.), *Attachment, Trauma and Multiplicity, Working with Dissociative Identity Disorder*. London: Routledge.

Sinason, V. (1990). Passionate lethal attachments. *British Journal of Psychotherapy, 7*(1): 66–76.

Sinason, V. (Ed.) (1994). *Treating Survivors of Satanist Abuse*. London: Routledge.

Sinason, V. (Ed.) (2010). *Attachment, Trauma and Multiplicity: Working with Dissociative Identity Disorder (revised edition)*. Hove, UK: Brunner-Routledge.

Sinason, V. (Ed.) (2012). *Trauma, Dissociation and Multiplicity: Working on Identity and Selves*. Hove, UK: Routledge.

Sinason, V., & Aduale A.-K. (2008). Safeguarding London Children. [Conference presentation].

van der Hart, O., Nijenhuis, E. R. S., & Steele, K. (2009). *The Haunted Self: Structural Dissociation and the Treatment of Chronic Traumatization*. New York: W. W. Norton (Norton Series on Interpersonal Neurobiology).

CHAPTER SIXTEEN

Fairbairn and multiple personality

Paul Finnegan and Graham S. Clarke

Throughout his career Fairbairn returned to multiple personality as a condition that his "intricate theoretical probing" (Hinshelwood, 1991, p. 307) might illuminate. This started with his MD thesis on "Dissociation and Repression" (1929b) and his essay written in the same year on the superego (1929a), both of which only became available after their publication in the invaluable two-volume *From Instinct to Self* (Birtles & Scharff, 1994; Scharff & Birtles, 1994). The principal development of Fairbairn's mature theory took place in a series of papers written in the early 1940s and collected in his book *Psychoanalytic Studies of the Personality* (1952). There are explicit references to multiple personality throughout this book and also to the usefulness of the object relations model he developed for the understanding and treatment of multiple personality (1929a, 1929b, 1931, 1944, 1946a, 1952, 1954b). Similar comments also appear in his paper on hysterical states (1954b). In an important statement about his mature theory Fairbairn described it as one "… obviously adapted to explain such extreme manifestations as are found in cases of multiple personality …" (1952, p. 159).

Our purpose here is to demonstrate the usefulness of Fairbairn's theory to the psychoanalytic understanding and treatment of multiple personality, and we will begin with a brief introductory summary of Fairbairn's mature theory and highlight some aspects of his earlier thinking on multiple personality that informed the subsequent development of his theoretical perspective. We will then present a summary of the recent interpretation of Fairbairn that we will apply in our subsequent discussion of clinical material from five cases of multiple personality.

A brief introduction to Fairbairn and multiple personality

Fairbairn's mature theory or "psychology of dynamic structure" is regarded by many as the most complete object relations theory developed within the so-called British School of Object

Relations (Greenberg & Mitchell, 1983; Hughes, 1989). The active object-seeking infant who is dependent upon the caregiver for almost everything—"adapted to being unadapted" (Macmurray, 1961)—has a pristine original ego, which incorporates an original preambivalent object. With experience, ambivalent splits in the object lead to splits in the ego—these splits being based upon the acceptable, over-exciting or over-rejecting object relations with the caregiver. This gives rise to the "basic endopsychic structure" comprising several dynamic structures: a conscious central ego, a preconscious ideal ego, and two unconscious subsidiary selves—a libidinal ego and object and an anti-libidinal ego and object. There are strong parallels with Freud's structural theory but reconstructed on an updated scientific understanding of the relationship between energy and structure. The central ego and its ideal ego repress the unconscious libidinal and anti-libidinal subsidiary selves in order to regulate the child's relations with the caregiver upon whom his/her life depends. Developmentally the person moves from infantile dependence through the transitional stage towards mature dependence, which involves relations with well differentiated others (Fairbairn, 1941).

Fairbairn's psychology of dynamic structure is based upon the understanding that the split-off ego and object structures can act independently as person-like entities and function in dynamic relationships with one another. Fairbairn's clearest statement of this perspective was made in 1943, during the "Controversial Discussions" (King & Steiner, 1991), when he argued that the explanatory concept of "phantasy" in the work of Melanie Klein and her followers had been rendered obsolete and that the time was ripe for the replacement of:

> … the concept of "phantasy" by a concept of an "inner reality" peopled by the Ego and its internal objects. These internal objects should be regarded as having an organised structure, an identity of their own, an endopsychic existence and an activity as real within the inner world as those of objects in the outer world. (quoted in Birtles & Scharff, 1994, p. 294)

Subsequently Fairbairn suggested that internal objects are complex composite structures characterised by both layering and fusion—the same being true of the related ego aspects of all object relationships (1944, pp. 122–123).

In an earlier paper on a clinical case with symptoms characteristic of multiple personality (1931), Fairbairn introduces the concept of "functional structural constellations", which we believe is a precursor to the "basic endopsychic structure" of his mature theory. In considering this case he argues that Freud's tripartite division of the mind must be taken to represent "a characteristic functional grouping of structural elements in the psyche … but the facts of the case also indicate the possibility of other functioning structural units arising" (p. 218). We understand these "functional structural units" to be precursors of the dynamic ego and object structures that comprise the basic endopsychic structure of the mature theory.

In this same paper Fairbairn suggested that multiple personality could be seen to result from "the invasion of the conscious field by functioning structural constellations which become differentiated in the unconscious under pressure of economic necessity" (1931, pp. 221–222) and he argued that these constellations appear as both ego-structures and internal objects, each of which can acquire "a dynamic independence" (1944, p. 132).

We offer as an illustration of "the invasion of the conscious field by functioning structural constellations" a brief summary of clinical material from the case of Evelyn, which we have presented in detail in an earlier paper (Finnegan & Clarke, 2012). In this case, during the course of many years of analysis, there emerged three, previously long repressed, distinct constellations of ideal, libidinal, and anti-libidinal egos and objects—one composed of children that developed during the latency period when the paternal sexual abuse began; one composed of adolescents that developed during the years when Evelyn was away at school and the sexual abuse resumed; and one composed of young adults that developed in the context of Evelyn having borne and independently cared for her father's child for three years. In the language of Fairbairn's mature theory the case of Evelyn illustrates the dynamic of traumatically induced replications of the basic endopsychic structure with age related personalities—child, adolescent, and young adult—arising from each of the ego and object structures of the three replications of the basic endopsychic structure. It is important to note that these three groups of age-related alter personalities emerged from the unconscious at successive stages of the course of analysis, with a long period of analytic work being done with the child group before the adolescent group presented, and then considerable time being spent with this latter group before the young adult group were to present. We will return to this point in the discussion that follows the presentation of the case vignettes.

Readers interested in a more detailed analysis of Fairbairn's interest in multiple personality disorder and the role it played in the development of his object relations theory are directed to our recent paper on this topic in the journal *Attachment* (Clarke & Finnegan, 2011).

A recent interpretation of Fairbairn

Clarke (2005, 2006) has suggested a synthesis of Fairbairn's model of endopsychic structure with Freud's topographic categories, since Fairbairn did not further develop his original use of these categories. Drawing on the work of Grotstein (1998), Padel (1985, 1991), Rubens (1984), and Scharff and Birtles (1994, 1997), Clarke suggested that each of the dynamic structures is based upon object relationships and that applying the topographic categories consistently means there are preconscious instances of libidinal and anti-libidinal dynamic structures (ego-structures and internal objects). Further, the process of psychic growth and change involves two distinct processes, one involving learning from experience in the world and thus expanding the reach and scope of the powers of the central and ideal egos (Rubens, 1984), and the second involving development of the central and ideal selves (ego-object structure) based upon the (re)integration of object relations from the repressed subsidiary libidinal and anti-libidinal selves (ego-object structure) (Padel, 1991). Clarke argues that the establishment of the "triadic preconscious ensemble" of relations between the ideal, libidinal, and anti-libidinal dynamic structures (or "functional structural units") is an important aspect of this model. This leads to a new representation of Fairbairn's proposed endopsychic structure or psychology of dynamic structure. It is this model that Finnegan (2007) argued was ideally suited to use clinically to help us understand and treat multiple personality.

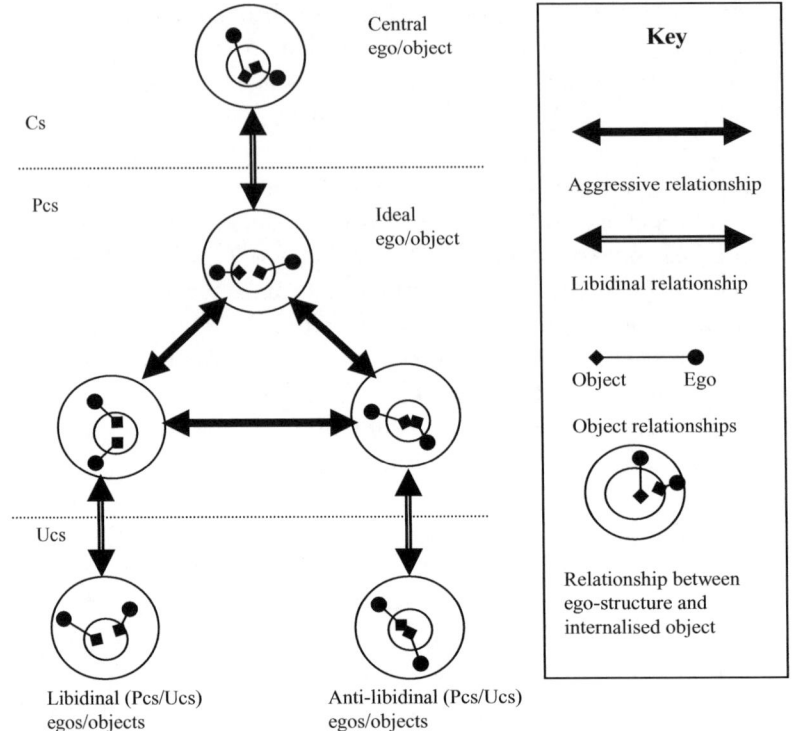

Figure 1. Endopsychic Structure and topographic categories.

The clinical application of Fairbairnian thought to multiple personality

The "paradigm of MPD" summarised by Lowenstein and Ross (1992) describes the condition as "a complex, chronic form of developmental post-traumatic dissociative disorder, primarily related to severe, repetitive childhood abuse or trauma, usually beginning before the age of five" (p. 3). In each of the cases to be discussed below, physical and sexual abuse experienced during childhood was an important aetiological factor in the development of multiple personality, although the extent of abuse varied considerably.

Research findings in the field of attachment theory suggest that disorganised attachment, and disrupted forms of parent–child communication in particular, not only generate a tendency for the development of dissociative disorder in response to trauma but may also generate dissociative symptomatology in the absence of trauma (Liotti, 1992, 1995, 1999; Lyons-Ruth, 2003, 2006). The dimensions of the parent–infant dialogue most relevant to the later development of dissociation appear to be the contradictory communications, failures to respond, withdrawing behaviours, disoriented behaviours, and role-confused behaviours that override the infant's attachment cues but are not, in and of themselves, explicitly hostile or intrusive. In such instances, the caregiver behaves in ways that have the effect of *"shutting out" the child* from the process of dialogue (Lyons-Ruth, Dutra, Schuder, & Bianchi, 2006, p. 80, emphasis added). In each of the cases discussed below, the experience of chronic recurrent maternal decathexis (CRMD)—which results in the child being *repeatedly treated as if he or she does not exist*—was an important aetiological factor in the development of multiple personality, although the extent of this experience varied considerably (Finnegan, 2007). In such circumstances, "[T]he child is faced with a lack of integrated affective, symbolic and interactive dialogue with the parent so that this lack of integration, in the form of dissociation, is eventually internalized by the child" (Lyons-Ruth, Dutra, Schuder, & Bianchi, 2006). Furman and Furman (1984), in their paper on parental "intermittent decathexis", draw attention to its many consequences for the developing child. These include the inevitable identification with the decathecting parent's use of this primitive mechanism and the ensuing compromise of integrative functioning—and, importantly, an increased vulnerability to early childhood sexual seduction. From a Fairbairnian perspective we are suggesting here that CRMD is a mother–child relational dynamic that inevitably generates and rigidifies "the basic position in the psyche ... [the] ... schizoid position" (Fairbairn, 1940a, p. 8), compromises integrative functioning, and becomes the seedbed for both decathective and dissociative responsiveness (Finnegan, 2007).

The presentation of clinical material that follows illustrates the application of Fairbairnian thought to multiple personality. Each of the analysands discussed had been in previous psychiatric or psychoanalytic treatment and each was functioning reasonably well—but not without difficulty—in both personal and working life. In each case the diagnosis of multiple personality was arrived at only after psychoanalysis had begun. Although each of the analysands was surprised to discover their multiplicity, and some initially resisted thinking of themselves in this way, in time none doubted the authenticity of the illness. Some patients immediately recognised emerging alter (alternative) personalities as "parts" or "aspects" of their selves, while others initially had no knowledge of what had happened during that portion of a session in which an alter personality had been present. For some patients, there was a near-psychotic conviction that another personality had nothing at all to do with them. In these circumstances alternative personalities are regarded, in the most literal sense, as "not me". Such latter circumstances require that the analyst be sensitively aware of the limited capacities of such patients to tolerate premature interpretations of their traumatically induced and defensively structured processes of splitting.

Roger and The Boy Underwater

Roger was a thoughtful, intelligent man who entered analysis in his early forties in the context of longstanding social isolation. Several years earlier he had withdrawn from intimate sexual relationships with men as he had repeatedly experienced being "spaced out ... without feelings, emotional or physical ... [and] not remembering much". Sexual experiences always ended in shameful failure and left Roger with angry feelings towards his partners. Unknown to Roger, whenever sexual contact began, an alter, *The Boy Underwater*, would be activated and take partial possession of consciousness, leaving Roger's capacity for integrative functioning markedly compromised. *The Boy Underwater* had developed in the context of two sexual assaults by neighbourhood adolescent boys when Roger was seven years old. These assaults precipitated dissociative defences, which resulted in the traumas being experienced in a dissociated state with an accompanying regressive loss of personal identity. Memory of these events was banished from Roger's mind as the *boy* who had experienced them was thought to have been buried *under water*. Roger was plagued for years by a terror of walking into beach water to any level past his knees.

We interpret *The Boy Underwater* to be a traumatically dissociated anti-libidinal ego alter personality. (We regard all of the alter personalities discussed below to be traumatically dissociated from dynamic structures of Fairbairn's endopsychic structure—central, ideal, libidinal, anti-libidinal ego or object—but in the interests of readability we will use the shorthand "an anti-libidinal ego alter" with the understanding that it is the longer form that we are intending.) This long "buried" alter was activated in the adult relational context of Roger exploring the possibility of intimate sexual contact with his partners. *The Boy Underwater* presented as a seven year old who thought it his duty to "be there for Roger" during sexual relations—to "protect" him by absorbing the sexual assault that was certain to come. Although *The Boy Underwater* part of Roger initially experienced the analyst as a sexually threatening anti-libidinal object, Roger as a whole person slowly developed a sense of trust. Roger then became able to communicate with *The Boy Underwater*, to express his understanding and appreciation of his protective intentions and to take on the experiences of sexual assault and their related affects as his own. *The Boy Underwater* did not feel resentment or hatred towards Roger for having initially left him to be sexually abused, for subsequently repeatedly having exposed him to danger, or for leaving him suffering with his pain for so many years. However, relations between anti-libidinal ego alters and the central ego are often far more conflicted and antagonistic.

Mary and Brenda

Mary was a talented, successful business administrator prior to the onset of anxiety and depression in her mid-forties. Maternal neglect and related sexual abuse during her childhood led to the development of several alters of whom Mary had been unaware prior to analysis, despite many years of periods of "lost time" and "voices" commenting on her thoughts, feelings, and actions. During analysis Mary collected and organised an extensive record of historical and clinical material related to herself and to the "others inside". She was shocked to discover one day that the box in which these files had been stored was empty. A year later it was revealed that *Brenda*, an alter previously unknown to Mary or the analyst, had thrown all of the files into a fire. *Brenda* was an alter who had experienced a particular period of sexual abuse during early adolescence and felt a bitter resentment towards Mary for having left her to suffer for so long without attention or concern. She wanted no part in change, because she was afraid that if Mary were to make further progress in therapy it would "be the death of me". We interpret *Brenda* to be an anti-libidinal ego alter and note that alters such as *Brenda* often feel a hateful resentment towards the central ego for having condemned them to abuse by both external and internal anti-libidinal objects. This hatred may be accompanied by such intense envy and ferocious rage that all manner of effort will be undertaken by anti-libidinal ego alters to undermine the process of analysis.

Anne and Alice-6, Alice-14 and Alice-32

In the analysis of Anne there emerged three alters of different ages, each with her name attached to an age—*Alice-6*, *Alice-14*, and *Alice-32*. Each had emerged in the context of a specific, age-related catastrophic abandonment and each presented in analysis with age-appropriate behaviour, language, and cognitive development. These alters illustrate the successive trauma-induced dissociation of a layered anti-libidinal ego. Each of these anti-libidinal ego alters had an immediate, profound distrust of the analyst. *Alice-6* was vulnerable, frightened, hurt, bitter, hopeless, and terrified of abandonment—of "being left not being". *Alice-14* was profoundly distrustful, angry, envious, vengeful, and occasionally suicidal. *Alice-32* was sensitive to slight, vicious, destructive, and vengeful, and at the same time felt vulnerable, hopeless, and despairing. *Alice-6* knew nothing of *Alice-14* or of *Alice-32*. *Alice-14* knew of the younger *Alice-6* and not of the older *Alice-32*. *Alice-32* knew of both of the younger alters. It is common in a sequence of alters such as this that their knowledge of one another follows this pattern. Further, while in this case there were no libidinal ego alters known to be associated with the three anti-libidinal ego alters, such pairings of libidinal and anti-libidinal ego alters often occur.

Marilyn *and* Edna *and* Anne

Marilyn experienced many years of emotional, and sometimes physical abuse at the hands of her mother—who was dissociative herself—and the experience of CRMD was an aspect of her everyday life. Marilyn's multiplicity developed in this context and prior to her having been raped by her uncle at the age of seven—the suddenly emerging memory of which had led her to analysis in her forties. Marilyn was constantly criticised and harassed by internal voices. These were the voices of two alters—one named *Edna*, her mother's name, an anti-libidinal object alter, and the other, *Anne*, an anti-libidinal ego alter. *Edna* spoke of Marilyn as her child and regarded her with both disappointment and contempt. She spoke of *Anne* in a similar manner. *Anne* saw herself as a part of Marilyn and, in her despair, hated Marilyn for all the pain and suffering she had brought upon her. She felt vulnerable and helpless in the face of *Edna*'s criticism of her. Over the course of the analysis each of these two alters was actively engaged with the analyst and in time both *Edna* and *Anne* agreed that their energies were being wasted in their harassment of Marilyn—and that she would be better served if they were to give over their energy to her. They each agreed to be more silent and to allow Marilyn to go about her day without criticism. Months later, Marilyn—who was very thoughtful about these two alternative personalities and frequently in collaborative communication with them, said that she had felt quite lonely on the subway while coming to her appointment. When asked why this was she spoke of missing the long familiar company of *Edna* and *Anne* she had experienced in the hearing of their voices.

We interpret *Anne* and *Edna* as anti-libidinal ego and object alters respectively and note that they constitute components of an anti-libidinal ego-object substructure. They illustrate the point that the splitting off from an ideal, libidinal, or anti-libidinal dynamic structure of an ego aspect may be accompanied by the splitting off from the related ideal, libidinal, or anti-libidinal dynamic structure of an object aspect, and that this results in the formation of a split-off ego-object substructure. The dissociation of both ego and object aspects of dynamic structures serves a similar function to the original development of unconscious libidinal and anti-libidinal ego and object dynamic structures, in that it both preserves the object relationship with the bad object(s) and removes the relationship from consciousness.

Sometimes alters develop from each of the ego and object aspects of the resultant ego-object substructure—as was the case with *Anne* and *Edna*—and sometimes an alter develops solely from the ego aspect of an ego-object substructure—as was the case with *The Boy Underwater*.

Nancy and *The Judge, Good Nan, Bad Nan, and* The Helper

Nancy sought analysis following a suicide attempt through which she had sought relief from chronic depressive moods and torturous self-doubt. After a few weeks of analysis, in the context of speaking of her suicidal feelings, she said that she frequently heard a voice saying that she had to die. She referred to this voice as *"The Judge"*.

> Sometimes I feel *The Judge* will take over the space I'm in, and I'll no longer be the confident person people think I am. *The Judge* is a very critical part of me … sometimes I feel it is right … that I should die … that it knows what's best. Sometimes it calls me by name. It is like a part of me but a little bit separate.

When Nancy had attempted suicide she had done so in the context of hearing *The Judge*'s voice telling her to kill herself, feeling "totally controlled" by this voice. When *The Judge* subsequently presented during an analytic session as an angry early adolescent she said:

> I hate Nancy. She's stupid. She's ugly and she's a fake. She fools everybody. Everybody thinks she's somebody else … that she's capable but she's not. She's needy, sad, and angry and I hate her and she should die. It would not be murder, it would be mercy killing.

The Judge went on to explain that she often takes control of Nancy and tells her what to do—sometimes to kill herself. We interpret *The Judge* to be an anti-libidinal object alter. The destructive aggression of such an anti-libidinal object alter may be life-threatening.

Nancy's multiplicity had developed in the context of her mother having been very depressed during her infancy and early childhood, and her father having repeatedly sexually abused her, beginning in the second half of her third year of life. In the context of the dissociated states to which she adaptively retreated in the context of her father's abuse—and in which there occurred the regressive loss of personal identity—Nancy developed the alter personalities of *Good Nan* and *Bad Nan*, each aged three. These two alters then developed until the age of six, which was the age at which they each presented in analysis. *Good Nan* was the innocent, loving, and excited daughter of a father to whom she looked for love and care—a libidinal ego alter. *Bad Nan* was the hateful child of the father who had caused her such terrible physical and emotional pain in his violent sexual abuse of her—an anti-libidinal ego alter. In their transferences these two alters experienced the analyst as a libidinal and anti-libidinal object respectively. While *Good Nan* knew nothing of *Bad Nan*, the latter knew and hated the former intensely. This pattern of relationship commonly exists between paired libidinal and anti-libidinal ego alters.

The Helper was an ideal ego alter and her role since childhood had been to guide Nancy and other alters through difficult times—to "help her". *The Helper* also assisted the analyst in facilitating understanding of the complex circumstances of the patient's early childhood history and in offering informed perspectives on relations between the various alters. Ideal ego alters typically serve such functions and do so in a calm, thoughtful, and emotionally detached manner. It sometimes happens, as with *The Helper*, that an ideal ego alter will originate in childhood and progressively develop and mature into the patient's adult life.

Discussion

We have illustrated the most common features of alter personalities derivative of the different dynamic structures. Dissociated ideal, libidinal, and anti-libidinal ego alters may emerge in different periods of life and fulfil different functions. Ideal ego alters are typically thoughtful, helpful, and emotionally detached and may act as a "gatekeeper" to the constellation of alternative personalities with whom they are associated. Libidinal ego alters present relational dynamics of need, idealisation, hopefulness, and excitement as well as explicit expressions of sexual excitement and the expectation of sexual responsiveness from the analyst as a related libidinal object. Anti-libidinal ego alters present relational dynamics including murderous rage, vengefulness, fury, malignant envy, and profound distrust—as well as vulnerability, helplessness, hopelessness, and despair at being abandoned in an objectless world. Ideal object alters are typically ineffectual. Libidinal object alters present as seductive and alluring and typically have no regard for the well-being of any other alter. Anti-libidinal object alters are aggressive, contemptuous, and controlling, and they present profound resistances to the process of psychic growth and integration.

Further, we have illustrated that alter personalities may take both partial and full control of consciousness, and have noted the influence of preconscious ideal, libidinal, and anti-libidinal alter dynamics on conscious affective, cognitive, and behavioural experience. We have offered examples of some of the typical relational dynamics occurring between alters derived from ideal, libidinal, and anti-libidinal dynamic structures We have also given examples of some of the typical transferences that emerge during the course of analysis and highlighted some of the resistances which derive from the maintenance of ties to bad objects and the wish to preserve the inner world as a closed system. Finally, we have given some indication of the process of analysis in these cases and of the need to address alter personalities directly, respectfully, and analytically prior to interpretation more specifically intended to facilitate integration.

As we reviewed our clinical material it became obvious that as well as being able to allocate the various alter personalities to particular ideal, libidinal, and anti-libidinal dynamic structures in Fairbairn's model, that "clusters" of such alter personalities could be readily identified. What we are suggesting here is that these clusters of alternative personalities operate as "functioning structural constellations" to provide the equivalent of alternative endopsychic structures for the person involved. These constellations manage to both preserve and obscure the traumatic object relations that have given rise to them.

As we have illustrated in our clinical material, these alternative endopsychic structures characteristically involve an ideal, a libidinal, and an anti-libidinal component. There are, however, other common patterns that are of significance: (a) the generation of paired, age-specific libidinal and anti-libidinal alternative personalities; (b) the generation of age-specific and age-appropriate alters of different ages each with an appropriate perspective, so a younger alter will know nothing of an older alter; (c) the hiving off of specific powers or skills into an alter, and (d) the development of ideal alters that know of particular clusters of alternative selves but know nothing of other ideal alters or their associated libidinal and or anti-libidinal alters. Significantly there are also some examples of individual dissociated alters related to ideal, libidinal, or anti-libidinal dynamic structures. This suggests a spectrum of dissociated alters, from individual examples related to specific dynamic structures, through multiple dissociated alters related to the same dynamic structure, to the partial or complete replication of an endopsychic structure comprising a constellation of different dynamic structures yielding a cluster of personalities—such clusters being the most common finding.

Fairbairn thought of dissociation as a defence "… directed against mental content determined ultimately by *events that happen* to the individual" (1929b, p. 77). With this in mind, we have noted the radical traumatic dissociation of alter personalities—engendered by the splitting of dynamic structures—and the resultant resistances to their becoming known. Repression for Fairbairn involves the action of one dynamic structure on another dynamic structure, for example, the *direct* repression by the central and ideal egos of the libidinal and anti-libidinal ego-objects and the *indirect* repression of the libidinal ego by the anti-libidinal ego-object. That *Good Nan*—a libidinal ego alter—knew nothing of *Bad Nan*—an anti-libidinal ego alter, while the latter knew and hated the former intensely, is an example of *indirect* repression.

In their discussion of the treatment of adult survivors of childhood sexual abuse, Davies and Frawley (1992a, 1992b) explicitly distance themselves from Fairbairn's view of the processes involved in generating the original endopsychic structure, where dynamic structures are split off and then repressed: "Unlike Fairbairn, we do not believe the dissociated ego state(s) is repressed; rather, *we stipulate that repression never occurs* and that the ego states coexist, each with its own consciousness" (1992b, p. 80, emphasis added). They argue that in circumstances of childhood sexual abuse, there is a defensive vertical splitting of the ego, which serves both to manage overwhelming affects and to protect against knowing. One of the coexisting ego states knows about and affectively reacts to the trauma while the other ego state, although somewhat depleted, is ignorant of the trauma. Davies and Frawley differentiate themselves from Fairbairn in that they see dissociation as "… a vertical split of the ego that results in two or more ego states that are more or less organized and independently functioning … [and that] … These ego states alternate in consciousness, and, under different internal and external circumstances, emerge to think, behave, remember and feel" (ibid., p. 80). In consequence of this vertical splitting, the abused child self—which exists in "the context of perpetually abusive object relations"—and the related aspect of the object are "… literally ejected from the patient's more integrated personality functioning and allowed to set up an independent existence for the sake of pursuing its separate needs" (1992a, p. 21). Under these circumstances the dissociated self is not repressed but coexists with its own consciousness. This extreme dissociation, they offer, is a form of "damage control", which "exists both to obliterate and to preserve" (1992b, p. 82). Dissociation, then, is "… a process that preserves and protects, in dissociated form, *the entire internal world* of the abused child" (1992a, p. 8, emphasis added).

In light of the clinical material we have presented this restatement of the function of dissociation for survivors of childhood sexual abuse is convincing. Some aspects of the clinical material we have offered can certainly be understood within the perspective of the "vertical split", for example, the sudden switches that occurred between *Good Nan* and *Bad Nan*. However, we also think there is a more far-reaching dissociative vertical split between "functioning structural constellations" or endopsychic structures ("the entire internal world") in many of the patients that are diagnosed with multiple personality. But we also think that there is clear clinical evidence of repression—a point to which we will return below.

Grotstein has described Fairbairn's theory of endopsychic structure as "the unsurpassed metapsychology of child abuse and of multiple personality" (1991, p. 140), and "the most apposite paradigm yet proffered for child abuse, child molestation, post-traumatic stress disorder and multiple personality disorder" (1994b, p. 123). He has stressed the autonomy of the endopsychic structures—"… each structure has its own autonomy, provenance, innocence, will (intentionality), rationale (*raison d'etre*), birthright, blessing, or curse … [and] … 'I'-ness" (1994a, p. 183)—and discussed "the dialectics of endopsychic relationships". In his discussion of psychoanalytic work with survivors of childhood sexual abuse, he noted that "… these patients experience themselves to be discontinuous; each of these apparently disconnected selves lives autonomously and independently of each other and may not even know of one another's existence, yet they seem at the same time to have some unconscious relationship with one another" (Grotstein, 1992, p. 71). Although he does not present clinical material from a case of multiple personality, Grotstein does explicitly acknowledge that "… in cases of extreme dissociation such as those occurring in multiple personality disorder, that subpersonalities can be independent of each other" (1994b, p. 182).

We greatly appreciate Grotstein's Fairbairnian approach and, at the same time, think it is insufficient to fully explain the radical traumatic dissociation of alternative personalities that we have seen. We posit the traumatic dissociation of endopsychic structures ("the entire internal world") and, informed by our clinical material, we suggest that such dissociated/split-off endopsychic structures may also be repressed for long periods of time prior to the repression being lifted and the endopsychic structure, and its related personalities, again conscious, function in a manner indicated by the concept of a vertical split. So it was in the case of Evelyn wherein the three constellations of alter personalities—child, adolescent, and young adult—emerged into consciousness in sequence and then presented clinically in states characterised by vertical splits.

Finally, regarding therapy, Davies and Frawley comment, "We believe that in making contact with the split-off, dissociated child persona within the abused adult, we free those archaic objects to work their way into the transference–countertransference paradigms through projective-introjective mechanisms and, in so doing, enable patients to work through each possible configuration within the therapeutic relationship" (1992a, p. 8). Grotstein (1992) offers a parallel description of the process of therapy in which "discrete subselves" enter into consciousness in the transference neurosis, are accepted, and then move to "integration into a unified self" (p. 72). He suggests that an "abandonment depression" follows upon the release from the ties to "persecutory objects" (p. 72)—as we illustrated in the case of Marilyn who experienced such painful loneliness upon the silencing of the ever-critical voices of *Anne* and of *Edna*. These are processes we have tried to illustrate in our clinical material.

Conclusion

Originally we both were surprised to find that Fairbairn had said that his theory was "… obviously adapted to explain such extreme manifestations as are found in cases of multiple personality …". This led us to begin to review the place of multiple personality in the development of Fairbairn's theory and to think about the application of his theory to clinical material from cases of MPD/DID. Clarke's recent interpretation of Fairbairn provided a further understanding of the complex clinical material. Once we had begun to formulate the clinical material within this theoretical context, we then moved to reconsider theoretical aspects prompted by the clinical material. We first came to ideas of the splitting of individual dynamic structures, then to the splitting off of ego-object substructures and then to the splitting off and duplication of the endopsychic structure itself—all of which are new ideas generated in response to the clinical material. These new ideas, however, are consistent with the later development of Fairbairn's own understanding of the original process of splitting, where an object is first internalised and then split into a good object (ideal) and two bad objects (libidinal and antilibidinal). Our engagement with both clinical material and Fairbairnian psychoanalytic theory has advanced our understanding in both areas. We hope that our illustration of the clinical application of Fairbairn's thought to multiple personality has suggested the usefulness of this approach in developing a structural and dynamic understanding of the disorder and has added usefully to its treatment.

References

Birtles, E. F., & Scharff, D. E. (Eds.) (1994). *From Instinct to Self: Selected Papers of W. R. D. Fairbairn, Volume II: Applications and Early Contributions*. Northvale, NJ: Jason Aronson.
Clarke, G. S. (2005). The preconscious and psychic change in Fairbairn's model of mind. *International Journal of Psychoanalysis, 86*(1): 61–77.
Clarke, G. S. (2006). *Personal Relations Theory: Fairbairn, Macmurray and Suttie*. London: Routledge.
Clarke, G. S., & Finnegan, P. (2011). Fairbairn's thinking on dissociative identity disorder and the development of his mature theory. *Attachment*, July: 131–153.
Davies, J. M., & Frawley, M. G. (1992a). Dissociative processes and transference-countertransference paradigms in the psychoanalytically oriented treatment of adult survivors of childhood sexual abuse. *Psychoanalytic Dialogues, 2*: 5–36.
Davies, J. M., & Frawley, M. G. (1992b). Reply to Gabbard, Shengold and Grotstein. *Psychoanalytic Dialogues, 2*: 77–96.
Fairbairn, W. R. D. (1929a). The superego. In: E. F. Birtles & D. E. Scharff (Eds.), *From Instinct to Self: Selected Papers of W. R. D. Fairbairn, Volume II: Applications and Theoretical Papers* (pp. 80–114). Northvale, NJ: Jason Aronson.
Fairbairn, W. R. D. (1929b). Dissociation and repression. In: E. F. Birtles & D. E. Scharff (Eds.), *From Instinct to Self: Selected Papers of W. R. D. Fairbairn, Volume II: Applications and Theoretical Papers* (pp. 13–79). Northvale, NJ: Jason Aronson.
Fairbairn, W. R. D. (1931). Features in the analysis of a patient with a physical genital abnormality. In: *Psychoanalytic Studies of the Personality* (pp. 197–222). London: Tavistock.
Fairbairn, W. R. D. (1940a). Schizoid factors in the personality. In: *Psychoanalytic Studies of the Personality* (pp. 3–27). London: Tavistock.

Fairbairn, W. R. D. (1941). A revised psychopathology of the psychoses and psychoneuroses. *International Journal of Psychoanalysis, 22*(3, 4): 250–279. In: *Psychoanalytic Studies of the Personality* (pp. 28–58). London: Tavistock.

Fairbairn, W. R. D. (1944). Endopsychic structure considered in terms of object-relationships. *International Journal of Psychoanalysis, 25*: 70–92. In: *Psychoanalytic Studies of the Personality* (pp. 82–136). London: Tavistock.

Fairbairn, W. R. D. (1946a). Object-relationships and dynamic structure. *International Journal of Psychoanalysis, 27*: 30–37. In: *Psychoanalytic Studies of the Personality* (pp. 137–151). London: Tavistock.

Fairbairn, W. R. D. (1952). *Psychoanalytic Studies of the Personality*. London: Tavistock. [Reprinted with a new introduction by Scharff, D. E. & Birtles, E. F., London: Routledge, 1994.]

Fairbairn, W. R. D. (1954b). Observations on the nature of hysterical states. *British Journal of Medical Psychology, 27*(3): 106–125. In: D. E. Scharff & E. F. Birtles (Eds.), *From Instinct to Self: Selected Papers of W. R. D. Fairbairn, Volume I: Clinical and Theoretical Papers* (pp. 13–40). Northvale, NJ: Jason Aronson.

Finnegan, P. (2007). *Towards a Fairbairnian Understanding of Multiple Personality* [master's thesis]. Sheffield, UK: School of Health and Related Research, Mental Health Section, Psychoanalytic Studies, University of Sheffield.

Finnegan, P., & Clarke, G. S. (2012). Evelyn's PhD in wellness—a Fairbairnian understanding of the therapeutic relationship with a woman with dissociative identity disorder. *Attachment, 6*(1), March: 50–68.

Furman, R. A., & Furman, E. (1984). Intermittent decathexis. *International Journal of Psychoanalysis, 65*: 423–434.

Greenberg, J. R., & Mitchell, S. A. (1983). *Object Relations in Psychoanalytic Theory*. Cambridge, MA: Harvard University Press.

Grotstein, J. S. (1991). [Review.] Hughes, J. M., *Reshaping the Psychoanalytic Domain: The Work of Melanie Klein, W. R. D. Fairbairn, and D. W. Winnicott*. *Psychoanalytic Quarterly, 60*: 136–140.

Grotstein, J. S. (1992). [Commentary.] Davies, J. M., Messler, J., & Frawley, M. G., *Dissociative Processes and Transference-Countertransference Paradigms*. *Psychoanalytic Dialogues, 2*: 61–76.

Grotstein, J. S. (1994a). Endopsychic structure and the cartography of the inner world: Six endopsychic characters in search of an author. In: J. S. Grotstein & D. B. Rinsley (Eds.), *Fairbairn and the Origins of Object Relations Theory* (pp. 174–194). New York: Guilford.

Grotstein, J. S. (1994b). Notes on Fairbairn's metapsychology. In: J. S. Grotstein & D. B. Rinsley (Eds.), *Fairbairn and the Origins of Object Relations Theory* (pp. 112–148). New York: Guilford.

Grotstein, J. S. (1998). A comparison of Fairbairn's endopsychic structure and Klein's internal world. In: N. J. Skolnick & D. E. Scharff (Eds.), *Fairbairn, Then and Now* (pp. 71–98). London: Analytic Press.

Hinshelwood, R. D. (1991). *A Dictionary of Kleinian Thought*. London: Free Association.

Hughes, J. M. (1989). *Reshaping the Psychoanalytic Domain*. London: University of California Press.

King, P., & Steiner, R. (Eds.) (1991). *The Freud-Klein Controversies 1941–1945*. London: Routledge.

Liotti, G. (1992). Disorganized/disoriented attachment in the aetiology of the dissociative disorders. *Dissociation, 5*: 196–204.

Liotti, G. (1995). Disorganized/disoriented attachment in the psychotherapy of the dissociative disorders. In: S. Goldberg, R. Muir, & J. Kerr (Eds.), *Attachment Theory: Social, Developmental and Clinical Perspectives* (pp. 343–363). Hillsdale, NJ: Analytic Press.

Liotti, G. (1999). Understanding the dissociative processes: The contribution of attachment theory. *Psychoanalytic Inquiry, 19*: 757–783.

Lowenstein, R., & Ross, D. (1992). Multiple personality and psychoanalysis: An introduction. *Psychoanalytic Inquiry, 12*(1): 3–48.

Lyons-Ruth, K. (2003). Dissociation and the parent–infant dialogue: A longitudinal perspective from attachment research. *Journal of the American Psychoanalytic Association, 51*(3): 883–911.

Lyons-Ruth, K. (2006). The interface between attachment and intersubjectivity: Perspective from the longitudinal study of disorganized attachment. *Psychoanalytic Inquiry, 26*(4): 595–616.

Lyons-Ruth, K., Dutra, L., Schuder, M., & Bianchi, I. (2006). From infant attachment disorganization to adult dissociation: Relational adaptations or traumatic experiences? *Psychiatric Clinics of North America, 29*: 63–86.

Macmurray, J. (1961). *The Form of the Personal. Vol. 2: Persons in Relation*. London: Faber and Faber, 1995.

Padel, J. (1985). Ego in current thinking. *International Review of Psycho-Analysis, 12*: 273–283.

Padel, J. (1991). Fairbairn's thought on the relationship of inner and outer worlds. *Free Associations, 2*(4): 589–615.

Rubens, R. L. (1984). The meaning of structure in Fairbairn. *International Review of Psycho-Analysis, 11*: 429–440.

Scharff, D. E., & Birtles, E. F. (Eds.) (1994). *From Instinct to Self: Selected Papers of W. R. D. Fairbairn, Volume I: Clinical and Theoretical Papers*. Northvale, NJ: Jason Aronson.

Scharff, D. E., & Birtles, E. F. (1997). From instinct to self: The evolution and implications of W. R. D. Fairbairn's theory of object relations. *International Journal of Psychoanalysis, 78*(6): 1085–1103.

CHAPTER SEVENTEEN

Fairbairn and "emptiness pathology"

Rubén M. Basili, Isabel Sharpin de Basili, Adrián Besuschio, Mercedes Campi, and Luis Oswald

Objectives

1. To define "emptiness pathology" for the first time based on Fairbairn's model. (Only a psychoanalyst is trained to diagnose borderline and "emptiness pathology" (Basili, Montero, & Sharpin de Basili, 2002).)
2. To postulate—extrapolating from Fairbairn—that "emptiness pathology" is the clinical indicator of a psychological manoeuvre, an unconscious technique inherent to Fairbairn's transitional stage of development, to recover and preserve an object relationship (link) with an object having specific qualities (narcissistic and transitional) of badness or emptiness, for example, a breast, or a mother, or the analyst in transference. Although these objects are bad and empty, they provide the patient with a defence against the experience of object loss, and from systematically increasing separation-abandonment anxieties: a bad object and the relationship with a bad object is better than no object.
3. To propose that "emptiness pathology" is a resistance to making conscious the object loss and abandonment underlying the emptiness. Clinically, the feeling of emptiness is proportionally greater when the lost object and relations with it are less frequent. For example: a) increase in the contact with the analyst tends to diminish acting out, and b) feelings of emptiness in borderline patients, or delusions and hallucinations in the psychoses, decrease when the lost object reappears. This proposes interpreting feelings of emptiness in Fairbairn's terms, as a resistance to making conscious the unconscious, whose content is abandonment by, and loss

of, the object. (This is particularly relevant in schizoid-empty depression as described by Bleger (1962).)
4. To postulate that "emptiness pathology" is the clinical expression of a painful and failed attempt to work through the schizoid position in Fairbairn's model, which we formulate as schizoid conflict (Basili & Sharpin de Basili, 2005). It is re-signified in the Oedipus conflict and in children it has no need of the Freudian "a posteriori" to produce symptoms.

Methodology

To reach these objectives, we use Fairbairn's model of object relations and, as he did, we compare it to Freud's drive model (1905d) and to M. Klein's object relations model (1977).

These three models are based on the same psychoanalytic paradigm: the Freudian unconscious (1915e). We articulate them by applying Bohr's principle of theoretical complementarity (Kuhn, 1978). The intermediate hypotheses that we use are what we refer to, extrapolating from Fairbairn, as "psychic units" (developmentally specific mutually related ego and object structures): a) "object relation units" (Hamilton, 1995); b) "splitting units" (Kernberg, 1984), and c) "building blocks", and projective identification, as described by Kernberg (Sandler, 1989), a mechanism which interrelates them in the manner of communicating vessels (Klimovsky, 1986).

"Splitting units" are "psychic units" set in motion in the face of object loss, or threat of object loss, with a narcissistic and transitional quality in order to work through affects produced by these losses, by means of splitting or primary dissociation of ego and object. Primary projection and negation derive from splitting, not repression. We postulate that these splitting and psychic units are shaped by units of object relationship.

Units of object relationship are "psychic units" set in motion in the face of threats of loss, or loss of objects, in order to work through affects they produce: first, the object and the object relation are internalised by primary dissociation, and then the object, the object relationship, and that part of the ego that intervened first in the internalisation are dissociated. After dissociation, the object and the object relationship may be repressed.

First, splitting occurs, then repression at the level of the object, and then of the ego, or rather the part of the ego involved.

Units of object relationship set in motion units of splitting.

The model of repression of the endopsychic situation and the model of psychic apparatus that we use differs from Freud's model of repression (1915e). We consider that the agent of repression is aggression rather than libido: aggression and libido are repressed by aggression.

Building blocks are "psychic units" shaped and set into motion by "units of splitting" which are constituted by:

1. mental self representations;
2. mental object representations;
3. the concomitant affect that unites them in a specific way (object relationship: the link).

We postulate a *chronological* sequence: first, units of object relationship are set in motion, then units of splitting, and then building blocks.

In this chapter, we use the model of projective identification proposed by Kernberg (1984) for adults that is "typical" of borderlines and the psychoses and "atypical" in the neuroses (found in deep regression).

Fairbairnian clinical work and the psychopathology of emptiness

"Emptiness pathology" is the psychopathological and clinical expression of the schizoid condition and borderline pathology. For the diagnosis of borderline pathology, we apply Kernberg's diagnostic criteria (ibid.) and our own (Basili, 1990a; Basili, Montero, & Sharpin de Basili, 2002). The same description applies to certain psychotic personality organisations, especially the schizophrenias and atypical psychoses (acute and chronic schizo-affective disorder) (Basili & Sharpin de Basili, 2001).

The schizoid condition is a clinical entity whose psychoanalytic substrate is de-cathexis produced by schizoid phenomenon and narcissistic object relations. It is observed particularly in the blank schizoid series described by A. Green (1993, 1994) and the narcissistic series described by Kernberg.

In clinical practice, the schizoid condition is evidenced by a specific group of symptoms; although they are not specific to these series they indicate alterations in processes of de-cathexis, cathexis, and re-cathexis (especially of de-cathexis); binding, and object relationship (link), we propose, occur through psychic units.

These symptoms are:

1. Anhedonia: maximum de-cathexis of all internal and external objects and, in the end, de-cathexis of psychic structures.
2. Omnipotence: hyper-cathexis of the ego produced by de-cathexis of the object; when omnipotence fails, other disturbances in the regulation of self-esteem appear such as depreciation and emptiness.
3. Affective isolation: de-cathexis of the external object.
4. Affective instability: instability of object cathexes, which reveals instability of the ego.
5. Feelings of emptiness: lack of cathexis of both the ego and the object. "I am empty."
6. Feelings of futility: lack of cathexis of the both the ego and the object. "Nothing is important, not even myself."
7. Feelings of abandonment with emergence of separation-abandonment anxieties. When patients feel this, they are improving and there is an object wish. In our experience, their prognosis is better.
8. Catatonia: we explain acute catatonia as de-cathexis of the drive body (libidinal or erogenous body) and the body image (mental map of drive body) and their negative "hallucination"; it is associated with "emptiness pathology". However, chronic catatonia as an expression of re-cathexis and restitution of the object relation is *not* associated with "emptiness pathology".

Negative hallucination, an economic substrate of the psychotic phenomenon, tends to accompany "emptiness pathology" (Basili & Sharpin de Basili, 2001; Donnoli & Basili, 2003).

9. Syndrome of derealisation: de-cathexis of the external world.
10. Syndrome of depersonalisation: de-cathexis of the body image.

These last three symptoms are examples of "emptiness pathology" in psychotic pathology.

In psychotic pathology, acute or chronic, the more psychotic productivity (delusion and hallucinations) there is, the less "emptiness pathology" we find. We postulate that this is because the lost object is recovered through delusion and hallucination. An exception is Cotard's nihilistic delusion in which the contents of emptiness are the essence of the delusion.

The schizoid condition and "emptiness pathology" appear linked in schizoid personalities, schizoid psychopathy, in some schizotypal personalities with preserved reality testing (subsumed in borderlines), in some acute psychoses, and in some chronic psychoses with few or no delusions or hallucinations, for example, type II schizophrenia with predominantly negative symptoms. In contrast, in type I schizophrenia with predominantly positive symptoms—delusion and hallucinations—there is no "emptiness pathology".

In other schizotypal personalities with loss of reality judgment and in chronic schizoaffective disorder with few delusions and hallucinations, the symptoms of emptiness tend to be marked.

We consider that in the psychoses, the more signs of de-cathexis and the fewer signs of re-cathexis we observe, the more "emptiness pathology" we find.

Anaclitic depression (Spitz, 1980), which is projective (Blatt & Bers, 1993), is also a tributary of "emptiness pathology". Introjective narcissistic depression, which is melancholic (ibid.), does not present "emptiness pathology" because, we postulate, the object is recovered in the ego.

There is no "emptiness pathology" in bipolar illness or in neurosis, except in the following exceptional cases: bipolar patients may have "emptiness pathology" if they are also borderline, and manic depressive psychotics may have "emptiness pathology" by virtue of a borderline or psychotic personality organisation due to schizoid and affective elements.

The hypomanic reaction (Winnicott, 1981) of borderline patients is part of hypomania and may be a borderline defence against emptiness (Singer, 1977a, 1977b).

In the neuroses there is no emptiness, except in hysteria, where there may be an experience of emptiness.

In borderline personality organisation (Kernberg, 1984), patients present "emptiness pathology", especially in schizoid personality disorder, narcissistic personality disorder, and borderline disorder *per se*. We consider the latter, in the case of psychiatrists, as the DSM-IV borderline, and for psychoanalysts "the *as if* personality" (Deutsch, 1942): both may present "emptiness pathology". In our experience, the histrionic personality also presents "emptiness pathology".

We postulate that "emptiness pathology" is a psychological manoeuvre through which a narcissistic object relation is established. In it, the ego acquires qualities of the object and the object acquires qualities of the ego; the frontiers between I and not-I and between past and present tend to be erased. This particular and specific type of object relation intervenes in the mechanisms of emptiness.

Narcissistic Object Relation (NOR)

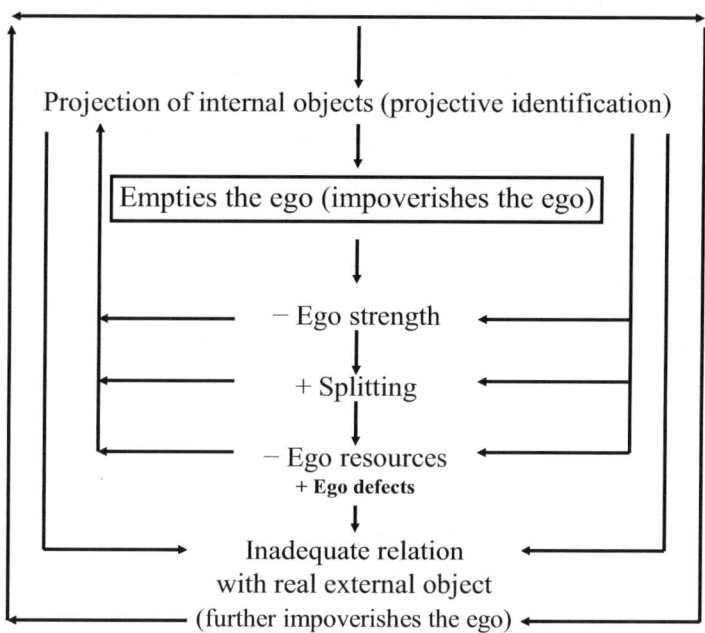

Figure 1. In the NOR, if projection is massive, delusions and hallucinations "protect" from abandonment and emptiness: an attempt to restitute the object and object relation. In the chronic psychoses, without delusions or hallucination, in which projection is not massive, there is emptiness and also feelings of abandonment. (Espacio Fairbairn: Basili, 2009)

Note: Fairbairn does not use the term 'projective identification'.

Schizoid conflict, object situation, and "emptiness pathology"

On the basis of Fairbairn's schizoid position we have proposed (Basili & Sharpin de Basili, 2005) a universal model of pre-Oedipal conflict. This is schizoid conflict, theorised with a universal model of psychic apparatus: the endopsychic situation or third topic (Fairbairn, 1952). See the chapter, "Fairbairn in Argentina", p. 101.

"Emptiness pathology" is the clinical expression of an arduous and failed attempt to resolve schizoid conflict that has systematically been inadequately worked through because of affective deprivation through a pathological object relationship in the breast-feeding link. "Emptiness pathology" is a clinical indicator of the loss of a libidinal, transitional object having the quality of an empty-emptied breast-mother. An example may be observed in the analyst's transference. Feelings of emptiness in both the patient and the analyst tend to disappear when this object appears, leading to a wish for an object.

We propose that the object situation is a universal, psychological, psychopathological, and clinical situation that it is important to understand for "emptiness pathology". The object situation and the development of ambivalence should be analysed in every session. The pre-ambivalent object or original object or pristine object is divided into three new objects: (1) the exciting libidinal object (bad object); (2) the rejecting frustrating object, anti-libidinal (bad object); and (3) the core of the object without the exciting and the frustrating parts (good object). Fairbairn took these ideas from Stekel, and these ideas were developed in Argentina by Morgan, Bleger, and Basili (Basili & Sharpin de Basili, 2003). The object situation develops in "emptiness pathology" in the following way: first the lost bad object (libidinal, valued, and transitional) is a part object (breast) with a part object relationship, and then, a total object (mother) is treated as a part object (breast).

"Emptiness pathology" occurs within the second oral phase (oral II) (Abraham, 1924). In psychotics and in "emptiness pathology", a part object relationship with an empty part-object leads to treating the breast-mother like an empty breast-mother. In borderlines in general the object is treated like contents (oral, anal, or phallic urethral). In "emptiness pathology", the breast–mother–analyst has oral contents (empty-emptied, suckle-suckling) and is treated like a part object (breast) with a great quantity of second oral phase (oral II) type aggression. The object situation and scenario are the same as in manic depressive psychosis.

In other works, we postulate that for borderlines in general the origin of their difficulties is in the transitional stage where the total object (mother–analyst) is treated like contents (oral, anal, or phallic-urethral).

The fixation points of borderlines are mainly second oral stage (oral II) (Masterson, 2000) and the first anal stage (anal I) (Blanck & Blanck, 1994), whereas those of "emptiness borderlines" are the first oral stage (oral I) and especially the second oral stage (oral II). They are considered to be multiple (as in multiple personality) throughout the course of evolutionary development (Yorke, Wiseberg, & Freeman, 1989) during which they prevent the progress of the psychic apparatus.

Regression for psychotic and borderline patients to these fixation points produces breakdowns (acting out and acute schizo-affective psychosis) with aggravation of symptoms of emptiness.

In brief, in the "emptiness borderline" the total object (mother–analyst) is treated like a part object (emptied breast) or like contents (empty—be emptied, suck—be sucked). The same occurs in the "emptiness psychotic", except in schizophrenia in which the object is an early oral phase (oral I) part object.

An infant—a future borderline—empties first the breast and then the mother when feeding. Then the baby identifies with the empty breast in order to avoid losing it and also to elude separation-abandonment anxieties. Then the infant feels empty-emptied: empty because the baby has first identified with the empty breast, a primary identification that is primary narcissism for Fairbairn, and then does the same with the emptied mother, a secondary identification that is secondary narcissism for Fairbairn. The emptier the infant feels, the more it empties the breast and the mother, subsequently feeling even emptier.

We postulate that this is one of the vicious circles of "emptiness pathology". The other is being left in phantasy without a breast as a result of the high level of aggression in feeding. In order to save the object relationship with the empty breast–mother–analyst, these subjects attribute the object's badness to themselves, feeling that they are worse, more guilty, and more devalued.

All this occurs in transference with the breast–mother–analyst who is empty–emptied, which is the essential content of the "emptiness phantasy".

Secondary identification, with differentiation between I and not-I and present and past, is fundamental for the acquisition of the quality of empty—being emptied. Other borderline symptoms such as phantasies of fusion or the oceanic experience do not require it.

Clinical case

Ian, a neurologist, is thirty-seven years old. He consulted for hypochondrias, feelings of emptiness, affective isolation, and instability and anhedonia: *lack of joy in living, with or without depression*, the latter being the major clinical feature in Ian and *the most important symptom* in "emptiness pathology". He reports, "I often feel empty in body and mind, which causes me anxiety."

When he was two years old, his three-year-old brother and only sibling drowned in a swimming pool.

He meets the criteria of Gunderson and Austin (1981), Kernberg (1984) and our own (Basili, 1990a; Basili, Montero, & Sharpin de Basili, 2002) for the psychoanalytic diagnosis of borderline, presenting clinical symptoms of the schizoid series and "emptiness pathology".

He begins analysis with three times weekly sessions. At the beginning, from the first to the fourth year of analysis, his symptoms were aggravated in situations of closeness—distance from the libidinal, exciting, valued, needed, transitional object (wife-analyst) (Basili, 1990b), at which time feelings of emptiness appeared. "After an orgasm I feel emptiness in my head and sometimes in the pit of my stomach," or "When I kiss my wife or I suck on her vagina, I feel I have no entrails, I prefer hypochondria, I feel empty and feel the world is empty." He also has feelings of futility: "Nothing matters or is important, not you, nor the analysis nor me."

We interpret the above in terms of schizoid conflict. Object losses, for example, of the analyst—a transitional object—due to vacations, weekends, or "fights" with him, separation-abandonment anxieties and schizoid phenomena with hypochondrias as a defence against abandonment anxieties and as an expression of the schizoid phenomenon in the body image, are ways to be with the analyst in transference.

Ian improved: his schizoid omnipotence decreased by virtue of the decrease in schizoid phenomena, leading to self-devaluation with unconscious feelings of abandonment that became conscious and were interpreted. Since his self-esteem was low, he did not feel abandonment as such but re-signified it as devaluation and emptiness (Basili & Sharpin de Basili, 2005). Some time later, the feeling of abandonment appeared, and consequently the syndrome of diffuse identity decreased, which we interpreted as the expression of schizoid phenomena at the level of mental representations, first with no desire of an object and then with a desire of an object: the analyst. Affective instability decreased, interpreted as a decrease in schizoid phenomena at the level of cathexes, and affective isolation improved. "Emptiness schizoid depression" appeared clearly (Bleger, 1962).

In this first stage we also worked on his affective isolation, his inadequate relation with the real external object, and his narcissistic object relations, interpreting the second step of mutative identification where internal objects were projected on to, or into, external objects such as the analyst, emptying and impoverishing the ego even further by projection. Thus he was relating more to internal, projected objects than to "real" external objects which made the relation with the real external object and *"learning from experience"* (Bion, 1962) difficult. In transference the ego was also further impoverished, thereby closing another vicious circle of "emptiness pathology".

In this first stage, the techniques used were mainly clarification, confrontation, interpretation of incompatible realities, and mutative interpretation (Strachey, 1934).

In mid-analysis, between years four and six, Ian's economic situation improved and he added one weekly session. He then brought up phantasies, dreams, and childhood memories with contents of his brother's death (affective deprivation), associated with a decrease in "emptiness pathology".

We interpreted (Basili & Sharpin de Basili, 2006) the greater capacity of his psychic apparatus to work: his better ego resources, and signs of improvement, as prognostic indicators of structural psychic change and the evolution of the analytic process, as an attempt to recover the unconscious lost object (breast–mother–analyst) with conscious feelings of emptiness and to protect against unconscious separation-abandonment anxieties.

These contents had a common denominator: the feeling that his love (libido-cathexis) destroyed the loved object (brother–analyst).

In Ian's case, the opposite was also clear. For example, in order to avoid destroying the loved object, he imagined leaving analysis, and sometimes provoked the object to reject him (infidelities to his wife, delay in paying the analyst, etc.) in order to avoid rejecting the object and thereby increase feelings of emptiness.

In an extension of previous papers (Basili, 1990a, 1990b; Basili, Montero, & Sharpin de Basili, 2002), we now propose that, in addition to the contents of the borderline's unconscious phantasy of being loved and accepted in order to avoid being abandoned by the libidinal object, we observe features inherent to the schizotypal and "emptiness pathology" borderlines: to empty and be emptied by the object that they love but not to destroy it completely and not be destroyed by it. They feel that their love is bad because it destroys the object. The schizoid kills for love, kills the object of love, and for this reason we need to "teach them" to love in transference.

In line with the theories of Guntrip and Winnicott, we propose that the appearance and working through of schizoid phantasies with these unconscious contents is an indicator of the fall of the schizoid fortress due to the failure of the false self, another indicator of improvement and of the analytic process. The *schizoid fortress* and the *false self* are universal categories (Basili, 1990b). The schizoid condition and, we add, "emptiness pathology" in borderline patients, have a poor prognosis: the inadequate relation with the real external object (lack of cathexis or link) produces further defects in the ego and weakens the strength of the ego, as well as hindering the object relation: another vicious circle of "emptiness pathology" in which cathexis, object relation, and link either never form or disappear.

This was also seen in Ian's case: when he approached the breast–mother–analyst with love libido, schizoid conflict was activated and he felt that "… with my love I destroy the object and for this reason it rejects me, may destroy me and I am left without it, abandoned." This is a vicious circle of aggression: "The more I love the object, the more I destroy it and it destroys me." He feels that he loses the object and the relation with the object: persecutory guilt in the sense of Melanie Klein.

Aggression destroys the object and produces guilt because of the ego, not because of the object. There is neither reparation nor remorse. Guilt increases aggression generated by loss of the object.

Frustration originates in 1) inadequate suckling (object relationship) from an empty breast, and 2) having an empty mother, both of which act as object losses (frustration) and further increase aggression.

Towards the end of the first half of analysis (five to six years), his depression became clinically more evident with the abandonment depression that is specific to borderlines according to Masterson. Schizoid depression is a clinical form of abandonment depression, interpreted in Ian's case as: a) decreased schizoid phenomena associated with a decrease in the diffuse identity syndrome, affective instability, and anhedonia, and b) a particular and specific form of object relation that was a defence, and a resistance to feelings of abandonment and object loss in the form of the guilt and anhedonia with which it was associated. This occurred with an increase in alcohol consumption, interpreted as an attempt to increase schizoid phenomena and return to his previous state.

In Fairbairn, depression and, we propose, emptiness, are interpreted as resistances to making object loss and abandonment conscious, but this is not so in Klein, where it is considered a distressing and failed attempt to work through the depressive position.

At the end of the analysis (nine to eleven years), Ian said, "I relate better to people and my things, I enjoy my wife, my children and my work ... I play rugby and drink alcohol because I like it, not impulsively to discharge rage ... I don't see the world or you as either so bad or so good."

Alternating and simultaneous pre-ambivalence is a state inherent to the primordial or pristine or undivided object where feelings such as love-hate coexist, according to Freud and later Fairbairn towards the same unique object without being clearly differentiated by the ego. Then, through dissociation, love and hate are felt towards the same object at different moments and later on they are felt towards two objects at the same time leading to ambivalence, another indicator of intrapsychic structural change—integration of the total object—and of analytic process (Basili & Sharpin de Basili, 2005).

Clinical and metapsychological conclusions

"Emptiness pathology" is a pathology of deprivation, de-cathexis, no object relationship (no link), loss of libido, and loss of aggression (clinical manifestation: anhedonia). In Fairbairn's model, "emptiness pathology" originates in schizoid conflict and primary and secondary identifications. In Melanie Klein, the psychogenesis of the narcissistic object relation produces the vicious circles of emptiness, the expression of an attempt to preserve an object relation with a breast-mother (unconscious material) that, although it is empty (conscious material) protects these patients from abandonment anxieties and object loss (unconscious material).

Qualities of emptiness may be attributed to the subject—"I feel empty"—and/or the object—"I feel that the world and you are empty"—by virtue of secondary identifications (differentiation between I and not-I, past and present).

Contents of emptiness are moved specifically by psychic units pre-existing in the psychic apparatus: units of object relations, splitting, and building blocks, all unconscious. They may be observed in clinical work, as phantasy contents such as emptying, empty, emptied, sucking, or sucked out, made conscious by analytic work.

We have maintained that in borderlines, phantasy contents found in schizoid conflict have diagnostic value and also differential diagnostic value among the basic personality organisations (to be loved, to be accepted, not to be abandoned by the valued, transitional object: the analyst); now we add that they have diagnostic value for clinical forms and differential diagnostic value for borderlines: for example, in schizoid and "emptiness pathology", to empty, to be emptied, to suck, to be sucked, to destroy, to be destroyed by the object they love—the analyst in transference.

We propose phantasy as the marker of structural psychic change: the fall of the schizoid fortress and the emergence of the true self are developmental and prognostic parameters in psychoanalysis.

Part objects, for example the breast, are means to relate subsequently to whole objects, for example, the mother; both objects are "real", "natural", "primary" objects whose "real" object relation the authors consider so important.

We extrapolate this concept to transitional objects whose presence in the adult is, according to Winnicott, always pathological except the mother's voice, which is repeated in transference with the analyst.

The fewer part objects and relations with part objects there are in the course of development, the more normal development will be. The same is true of transitional objects.

In "emptiness pathology", the child relates to an empty breast, which leads him to relate to an empty mother; however, although they are empty, they are still useful because they protect the child from object loss and abandonment. Since they are transitional objects, the analyst may acquire these qualities through identifications with the breast and with the mother. If this is the case, the patient treats the analyst like an empty breast-mother, repeating the infant's object relation in suckling.

The analyst may feel emptiness in countertransference or may act it out (Singer, 1977a, 1977b). For example, the analyst may leave the room frequently during the session to urinate or defecate in order to confirm that he is not empty, as occurred in Ian's case, a symptom that was resolved in the analyst's analysis.

We postulate a clinical hypothesis to explain "emptiness psychopathology", based on the Freudian drive model, which associates emptiness with unconscious object loss and abandonment.

In a child with great oral voracity produced by a high innate and acquired quantity of libido and aggression and by a borderline, psychotic, or perverse mother who opens the oral erotogenic zone too early and intensely, a pathological suction is conditioned: first the breast, then the mother and the infant are emptied. The infant feels emptied—empty through identification with the emptied-empty breast and mother.

We consider that, like the first experience of satisfaction and the oceanic experience, the experience of emptiness is universal even though Freud does not mention any of these as proto-fantasies; engulfment anxieties originate before birth when engulfment phantasies are generated by confinement in the maternal claustrum; and, during birth, in the passage through the birth canal, separation-abandonment anxieties; and in the exterior world, the experience of emptiness. When the umbilical cord is cut, anxieties of separation and abandonment intensify (Abadi, 1960). According to Fairbairn separation anxieties precede engulfment anxieties.

Based on the Fairbairn model, in which aggression is always secondary to frustration in the object relationship, we postulate that:

1. Infants feel that feeding (the object relationship) empties the breast and later the mother, thereby destroying the breast. They feel that they suck on an empty breast (part object with a partial object relationship), aggression increases because of frustration, and they identify with the breast (primary identification). Then they identify secondarily with the mother (total object with a partial object relationship), felt to be empty. They identify with the empty breast and mother in order to avoid losing them (transitional objects) because even though they are empty they protect the infant from separation-abandonment anxieties. In transference, this process is repeated first with an empty breast-analyst and then with an empty mother–analyst.

    Secondary identification, which involves I-not-I differentiation, is indispensable for the infant–mother–analyst to acquire individually the qualities of the empty breast-mother.
2. Sucking on an "empty" breast and an "empty" mother operates as an object loss that produces frustration and increases aggression. This increase of aggression tends to destroy the object. In this case, abandonment is associated with emptiness and with aggression that destroys and makes the breast-mother disappear.

In an adult faced with object loss or threats of loss of certain objects such as the analyst having a narcissistic (breast, mother) and transitional (abandonment) quality, clinical manifestations are conscious emptiness associated with unconscious abandonment.

In metapsychological terms, we propose that "emptiness pathology" is basically pathology of the preconscious (the topical level), an organiser of cathexis, de-cathexis, re-cathexis (the central ego and structural level). Emptiness is directly proportional to de-cathexis (the economic level) and inversely proportional to re-cathexis (the dynamic level), since through re-cathexis the object is recovered by delusion and hallucination. This may be seen clearly in clinical work with the psychoses: the more delusion and hallucinations (re-cathexis) there are, the less emptiness (de-cathexis) we observe.

"Emptiness pathology" involves the three egos (splits): the central ego (administrator), the libidinal ego (agent) and the anti-libidinal ego (inhibitor) of cathexis and the three objects: libidinal, anti-libidinal, and ideal.

The drive body, that is, the anatomical body cathected with libido and aggression, is the primary scenario of "emptiness pathology". In the four Freudian models of psychic apparatus, the mind considers it an object of the external world, as also in Fairbairn in the endopsychic situation. We postulate that the mental ego forms an object relation with the body ego (central ego), which is the first thing that is lost.

The body image (Schilder, 1935) is secondary and is systematically split off in this pathology. For example, in Ian this was evidenced by his hypochondrias.

Metapsychology of Emptiness

Based on the endopsychic situation, we theorize and propose a hypothesis to explain clinical work with emptiness pathology.

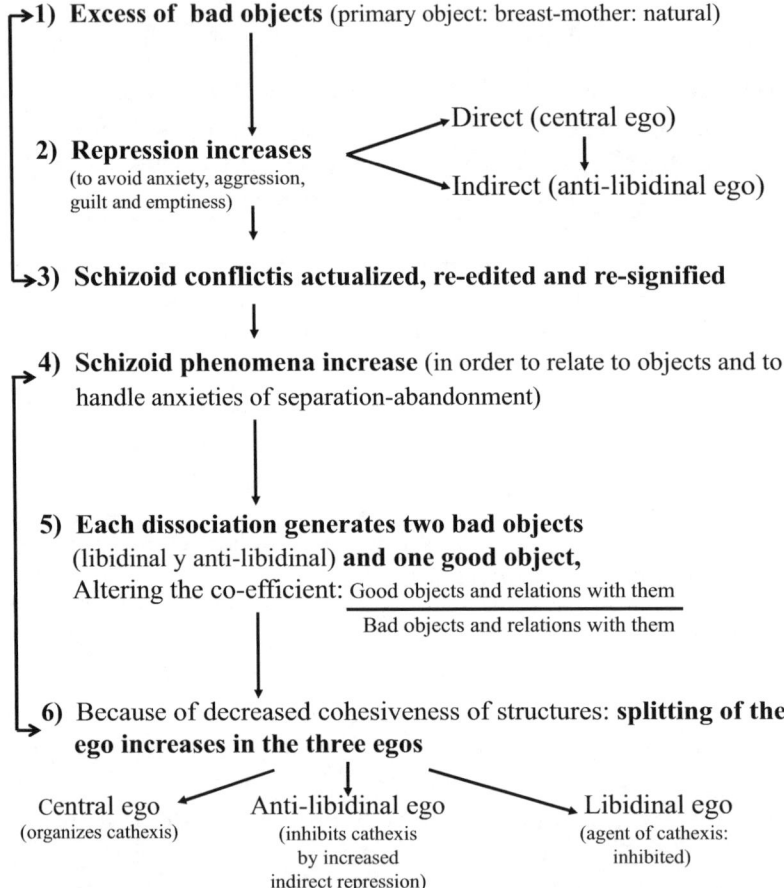

Figure 2. The three egos and their respective object relations are altered. (Espacio Fairbairn: Basili, 2012)

References

Abadi, M. (1960). Las Angustias Arquetípicas. *Acta Neuropsiquiátrica Argentina, 6* páginas 569–571.

Abraham, K. (1924). Breve estudio del desarrollo de la libido a la luz de los trastornos mentales. In: Contribuciones a la teoría de la libido. Buenos Aires, Argentina: Hormé, 1994.

Basili, R. M. (1990a). Utilidad del diagnóstico psicoanalítico en el tratamiento de las personalidades narcisistas graves. Nuestra experiencia clínica. *Revista de Psicoanálisis, 47*(1): 153–176.

Basili, R. M. (1990b). Desarrollos en las Escuelas Psicoanalíticas Británicas sobre las Personalidades Narcisistas Graves. Nuestra Experiencia. *Revista de Psicoanálisis, 47*(1): 1087–1112.

Basili, R. M., Montero, G. J., & Sharpin de Basili, I. (2002). Conceptualización y tipificación psicoanalíticas de los trastornos narcisistas (en sentido estricto). Dos tipos de idealización (primitiva). *Revista de Psicoanálisis, 59*(3): 581–613.

Basili, R. M., & Sharpin de Basili, I. (2001). Un aporte del psicoanálisis a la psiquiatría y a la medicina legal: las psicosis esquizoafectivas agudas. *Revista de Psicoanálisis*, Número Especial Internacional, *8*: 333–371.

Basili, R. M., & Sharpin de Basili, I. (2003). Eros y Tánatos en conflicto de diambivalencia: Su trabajo y desarrollo en la relación de objeto. Aplicabilidad en pacientes graves. *Revista de Psicoanálisis, 60*(2): 395–425.

Basili, R. M., & Sharpin de Basili, I. (2005). Fairbairn's theory and borderline pathology, and schizoid conflict. In: J. S. Scharff & D. E. Scharff (Eds.), *The Legacy of Fairbairn and Sutherland: Psychotherapeutic Applications* (pp. 129–139). London: Routledge.

Basili, R. M., & Sharpin de Basili, I. (2006). Los recuerdos infantiles de los borderline: implicancias teóricas, técnicas y legales. [Presented at the 2nd Encounter APA-SPP (Psychoanalytic Society of Paris), París, France, 11 & 12 February.]

Bion, W. R. (1962). Aprendiendo de la experiencia. Buenos Aires, Argentina: Paidós.

Blanck, G., & Blanck, R. (1994). *Ego Psychology. Theory and Practice*. New York: Columbia University Press.

Blatt, S. J., & Bers, S. (1993). The sense of self in depression. A psychoanalytic perspective. In: Z. Segal & S. J. Blatt (Eds.), *The Self in Emotional Distress: Cognitive and Psychodynamic Perspectives* (pp. 1717–1210). New York: Guilford Press.

Bleger, J. (1962). Modalidades de la relación objetal. *Revista de Psicoanálisis, 19*(1–2): 58–62.

Bowlby, J. (1993). El Vínculo Afectivo. Barcelona, Spain: Paidós.

Deutsch, H. (1942). Some forms of emotional disturbance and their relationship to schizophrenia. *Psychoanalytic Quarterly, 11*: 301–321.

Donnoli, V., & Basili, R. M. (2003). Borderline y catatonía. Interdisciplina. *La escucha psicoanalítica en Psiquiatría, 4*: 31–48.

Fairbairn, W. R. D. (1952). *Psychoanalytic Studies of the Personality*. London: Tavistock [Estudio psicoanalítico de la personalidad. Buenos Aires: Hormé, 1970, 3ª edición].

Freud, S. (1905d). Three essays on the theory of sexuality. *S. E., 7*. London: Hogarth.

Freud, S. (1915e). The unconscious. In: *On the History of the Psycho-Analytic Movement, Papers on Metapsychology and Other Works. S. E., 14*: 159–204. London: Hogarth.

Green, A. (1993). El trabajo de lo negativo. Buenos Aires, Argentina: Amorrortu editores, 1995.

Green, A. (1994). De locuras privadas. Buenos Aires, Argentina: Amorrortu editores, 1990.

Gunderson, J., & Austin, V. (1981). The diagnostic interview for borderline patients. *American Journal of Psychiatry, 138*: 896–903.

Guntrip, H. (1971). El Self en la Teoría y la Terapia Psicoanalítica. Buenos Aires, Argentina: Amorrortu editores.

Hamilton, N. (1995). Object relations units and the ego. *Bulletin of the Menninger Clinic, 59*(4): 416–426.

Kernberg, O. F. (1984). *Severe Personality Disorders*. New Haven, CT: Yale University Press.

Klein, M. (1977). Obras Completas. Buenos Aires, Argentina: Paidós.

Klimovsky, G. (1986). Mesa redonda: Epistemología y psicoanálisis. *Revista de Psicoanálisis, 43*(4): 837–867.

Kuhn, T. (1978). Pensamientos Sobre Paradigmas. Madrid, Spain: Tecnos.

Mahler, M. (1971). A study of separation individuation process and its possible application to the "borderline phenomena". *Psychoanalytic Study of the Child, 26*: 403–424.

Masterson, J. (2000). *Disorders of the Self: Differential Diagnosis and Treatment*. [American Psychiatric Association, 52nd Institute on Psychiatric Services, October 25–29, Philadelphia.]

Sandler, J. (Ed.) (1989). *Proyección, Identificación, Identificación Proyectiva*. Madrid, Spain: Technipublicaciones.

Schilder, P. F. (1935). *The Image and Appearance of the Human Body: Studies in the Constructive Energies of the Psyche*. New York: International Universities Press, 1951.

Singer, M. (1977a). The experience of emptiness in narcissistic and borderline states: Deficiency and ego defect versus dynamic-defensive models. *International Review of Psycho-Analysis*, 4: 459–470.

Singer, M. (1977b). The experience of emptiness in narcissistic and borderline states: The struggle for a sense of self and the potential for suicide. *International Review of Psycho-Analysis*, 4: 471–479.

Spitz, R. (1980). *El Primer Año de Vida del Niño*. Mexico: Fondo de Cultura Económica.

Strachey, J. (1934). Naturaleza de la acción terapéutica del psicoanálisis. *Revista de Psicoanálisis*, 5(4): 1947–1948.

Winnicott, D. W. (1981). *Escritos de Pediatría y Psicoanálisis. 1931–1956*. Barcelona, Spain: Editorial Laia.

Yorke, C., Wiseberg, S., & Freeman, T. (1989). *Development and Psychopathology*. New Haven, CT: Yale University Press.

CHAPTER EIGHTEEN

Fairbairn's unique contributions to dream interpretation

Joshua Levy

Purpose

As we study Fairbairn's writings, it becomes abundantly clear that his patients' dreams occupied a special place in his clinical and theoretical work. Understanding and interpreting his patients' dreams assisted him in the working through of their particular psychopathology and contributed to his building his distinctive personality theory. However, a number of distinguished analysts who have studied Fairbairn's writings in depth pointed out with surprise that his contributions to dream analysis had been "underemphasized" (Scharff, 1988, p. 31). Pereira and Scharff (2002, p. 7) commented on the "curious omission" of Fairbairn's important ideas on dreams. However, they have not presented any details of Fairbairn's own dream analysis, which would have allowed a critical discussion as to how he actually analysed his patients' dreams. In this chapter I have selected a sample of Fairbairn's published dream data to demonstrate the assets and shortcomings of his reported dream analysis with the intention of constructively criticising them. I will address the relationship between his psychological model and his processing of his patients' dream and discuss the specific function of the analysis of dreams in facilitating the working through and integration of dissociated endopsychic structures. As Fairbairn did not report the details of his working with his patients' dreams, and Winnicott—who shared with Fairbairn a common theoretical perspective—did, I shall briefly present some of Winnicott's work with dreams as they provide links that are missing in Fairbairn's reports of his analysis of dreams.

The place of the dream in Fairbairn's personality model

In a seminal article, "Schizoid Factors in the Personality" (Fairbairn, 1940a), we learned about his view regarding the exceptional position of the dream in his psychoanalytic theory of psychopathology. He strongly emphasised his conviction that schizoid psychopathology was the basic underlying structure for all mental disturbances. If the schizoid factors are not worked through, the analytic treatment would be neglecting the deepest psychological illness. Further, he also wondered whether his critics would dismiss his conviction regarding the schizoid structure as being too comprehensive and therefore meaningless. In support of his position he emphasised that both the schizoid structure and the dream are universal phenomena. The ego in both is split to various degrees and is represented in multiple facets.

In a subsequent contribution, Fairbairn (1944, p. 99) asserted that "… dreams are essentially, not wish-fulfillments, but dramatizations or 'shorts' (in the cinematographic sense) of situations existing in inner reality … [and that] … figures appearing in dreams … represent either parts of the 'ego' or internalized objects." In his "specimen dream" to be discussed later, he demonstrated that "… the situations depicted in dreams represent relationships between endopsychic structures." The phenomena of dreaming became a fertile field for the study in depth of the reciprocal influences between the patient's outer and inner worlds and the relationships between the dynamic ego and object structures.

Fairbairn clearly challenged one of Freud's basic dream hypotheses, but let us not forget how much they shared in common regarding the essential functions of dreams in the psychoanalytic process. Freud (1900a, p. 219) stated, "… that the interpretation of dreams is like a window through which we can get a glimpse of the interior of that [mental] apparatus." Freud left this profound statement unelaborated, but he returned to it in his discussion of the search for the various aspects of the dreamer's ego by the processing of the dynamics of the dreamer's identifications with the dream figures (1923c, p. 123). Thus, Freud and Fairbairn shared the common goal of reaching the internal world of their patients—their personalities. They both emphasised that the interpretation of dreams offers a unique contribution to the working through of the patient's psychopathology. However, Fairbairn left us with a detailed theory that connected the patient's dreams to his theory of dynamic structures.

How are we to extract an understanding of these endopsychic structures from the patient's manifest dream? Are they directly represented in the dream's manifest content or are they disguised and hidden and thus require the analysis of the patient's free associations? I would like to suggest that in studying Fairbairn's clinical work with his patients' dreams, we need to enquire into his perspective regarding manifest and latent dream contents—an issue that is an ongoing controversy within psychoanalysis.

Freud, in a footnote added in 1925 to his *The Interpretation of Dreams* (1900a, pp. 506–507), expressed his satisfaction that analysts, at long last, had accepted his radical distinction between the manifest and latent dream contents. For Freud, "These latent dream-thoughts contained the meaning of the dream, while its manifest content was simply a make-believe, a façade, which could serve as a starting point for the associations, but not for the interpretation" (1925d, p. 44). Freud belittled the organised narrative quality of dreams and insisted that to uncover the inner psychic life of the dreamer the analyst rely on the patient's free associations, decipher the intricacies of the dream-work, and eventually reach the unconscious significance of the dream. Little did he know how the fierce controversy surrounding the manifest and latent contents of dreams would continue in our contemporary psychoanalytic community.

Kohut (1977, p. 109) stated that for the narcissistic and vulnerable patients, asking for free associations would produce disorganising experiences and adversely affect the analytic process.

Fosshage (1987), who was affiliated with Kohut's self-psychological perspective, regarded the manifest sensory images of the dream as serving regulatory and integrative functions and advocated the complete abandonment of the process of free association.

From what is available in Fairbairn's presentation of his work with his patients' dreams, it is quite clear that he did not rely on a formal systematic method of free associations. In this he was in good company as Freud's *The Interpretation of Dreams* is replete with examples of the understanding of dreams proceeding without reference to free associations. It seems to me that both Freud and Fairbairn recognised that the dream reported in the dynamic context of the analytic process as a whole was already interlaced with embedded associations. This provided clinical data that enabled them to understand and interpret their patients' dreams without asking for further associations.

Daily events impinge on the dreamer and evoke both conscious and underlying preconscious themes that may be ascertained with few free associations. Within Fairbairn's perspective this may lead to an understanding of interpersonal object relations which can be integrated with a formulation of the dynamics of the underlying endopsychic structures. When successful, dream analysis then becomes a process of working through daily experiences, which are influenced by, and derivative of, the return of both good and bad ego and object structures.

Freud highlighted the dream-work as the "essence of dreaming" (1900a, p. 506). In this he was referring to the processes of condensation and displacement and to the means of representation. Although Fairbairn makes no explicit mention of the specific functions of dream-work, it seems clear that it was necessary for him to have understood the functions of the dream-work in order to interpret his patients' intrapsychic structural dynamics. I would like to draw attention to the common ground between Fairbairn and Freud and to how they conceived of the analysis of dream figures as the key to sound dream interpretation. To quote from Fairbairn's paper on endopsychic structure (1944, pp. 122–123), "… internal objects have already assumed the form of complex composite structures. They are built up partly on a basis of the superimposition of one object upon another, and partly on a basis of the fusion of objects." Freud, in a footnote that he added in 1914, stated that: "The fact that the meanings of dreams are arranged in superimposed layers is one of the most delicate, though also one of the most interesting, problems of dream-interpretation" (1900a, p. 219). Fairbairn and Freud understood dreams as involving both the superimposition of layers and as composite fusions of internal structures and wishes.

In my opinion, the manifest "I" within a dream, and any other dream figure, may be understood to be a condensation of various endopsychic structures, and the affects and interpersonal relations portrayed in a dream may be understood with respect to how they relate to the dynamics of these endopsychic structures.

In my opinion the processing of a patient's dreams within the context of analytic interactions leads to the most productive utilisation of Fairbairn's application of his personality theory to the analysis of dreams in clinical psychoanalysis. Regrettably, Fairbairn's references to clinical interactions between himself and his patients are relatively meagre. This may be, in part, why his model of dreams has been "underemployed" or "curiously missing" as Fairbairn scholars have lamented. If the analytic interpretation of a patient's dreams attempts to unearth the underlying dynamics of the endopsychic structures without sufficient consideration of the analytic interactions we run the risk of imposing our theory and jumping to conclusions.

Finally, Fairbairn did not inform us as to whether he examined his patients' responses to his interpretations of their dreams with respect to their possibly revealing the patient as having detected the countertransference arising from his theoretical perspective. In my opinion, we need to enquire as to how our own unconscious tendencies drive us to preclude consideration of available dream data that run counter to our cherished theoretical models.

Clinical material from Fairbairn's own work

To illustrate how Fairbairn used his theoretical understanding in interpreting dreams I shall discuss three dreams from his clinical work. I will start with the dream, which Fairbairn referred to as "a paradigm of all endopsychic situations" (1952, p. 105). This dream has already been discussed by others (e.g., Grotstein, 1998; Padel, 1991; Sutherland, 1989) who have regarded it as a major contribution to psychoanalysis, and I certainly agree with their assessment.

While others have not offered critiques of Fairbairn's presentation and discussion of this dream, I think that Fairbairn left out crucial clinical data that would have been essential to demonstrating how the dream assisted in the working through of his patient's endopsychic dynamics within the analytic process. After my discussion of this "specimen" dream I will contrast Fairbairn's presentation of dream data in this case with that to be found in his later presentation of two other dreams.

> The (manifest) dream to which I refer consisted in a brief scene in which the dreamer saw the figure of herself being viciously attacked by a well-known actress in a venerable building which had belonged to her family for generations. Her husband was looking on; but he seemed quite helpless and quite incapable of protecting her. After delivering the attack the actress turned away and resumed playing a stage part, which, as seemed to be implied, she had momentarily set aside in order to deliver the attack by way of interlude. The dreamer then found herself gazing at the figure of herself lying bleeding on the floor; but, as she gazed, she noticed that this figure turned for an instant into that of a man. Thereafter the figure alternated between herself and this man until eventually she awoke in a state of acute anxiety. (1952, p. 95)

Here is a brief summary of Fairbairn's understanding and interpreting of his "specimen" dream, which cannot do justice to the originality of his analysis.

Fairbairn derived three different levels of interpretation from the manifest dream and the patient's associations. The first level was in terms of her current marital situation. The patient, identifying with the actress dream figure, had been an actress in her relations with her husband in ignoring his extramarital affairs and in pretending to have been sexually gratified when she was actually frigid. She associated the suit of the bleeding man in the dream with her husband's suit that he had bought in the company of his lover. The patient harboured strong unconscious anger against him.

The second level of interpretation was related to her Oedipal situation. The patient had a strong libidinal attachment to her father—and transferred it to her husband—and an identification with her emotionally cold and sadistic mother who was attacking her libidinal attachment to her father.

The third level of interpretation, which was about the patient's personality structure, was based on finding evidence in her dream and associations for her schizoid position. This Fairbairn considered to be the most fruitful interpretation as it was based on the dynamic of internal relations between egos and objects. The central ego (conscious and realistic), experienced by the patient as helpless and weak, was attached to and fused with an ideal (idealised) man, the beaten and bleeding man who represented her husband. The split-off and repressed libidinal ego—beaten and lying down bleeding—was linked with a libidinal object—an exciting and frustrating man (the father). The actress in the dream represented a fusion—or condensation—of the patient's anti-libidinal ego, which was "hostile to libidinal relationships" and the patient's anti-libido object identified with the patient's sadistic mother.

Fairbairn's masterful analysis of the meanings of his patient's dream was based on his understanding of the principles of "superimposed layers", fusions, and composite dynamic structures. His analysis of the "actress" dream revealed a perplexing endopsychic situation in which his patient was entangled in complex dynamics of opposing split-off and repressed ego and object structures. He explicated three levels of interpretation aimed at ameliorating his patient's predicament. However, Fairbairn did not integrate the dream within the ongoing analytic process. In this paper, he omitted the nitty-gritty of how he actually worked with his patient in the analytic situation—the sequence of his interventions and his patient's responses, the resistances and the working through of the possible transference and countertransference entanglements. There was no clinical data that would provide us with the necessary evidence to evaluate the validity and usefulness of the levels of interpretation.

As we gather from Fairbairn's writings, he worked a good deal within the transference. Can we imagine how his patient's dreams facilitated the analysis of certain aspects of the transference? Specifically, in the case outlined above, the three levels of interpretation of the patient's dream provide us with the guidelines for imagining possible transference interpretations that would fit Fairbairn's framework. Focusing on the manifest dream figures and the patient's associations the analyst may regard them as potentially activating configurations of the transference. At any given moment the analyst would be experienced as promising to fulfil her libidinal wishes. However, some time later he would be regarded as an anti-libidinal person (husband-father) who frustrates and abandons her. Furthermore, the patient may be seeing herself not only as the victim of the attacking "actress" mother, but also, through identification with her, as the attacker and may then live this configuration in the transference. Fusions—condensations—of the patient's undifferentiated ego parts with her related object parts are multiple. They would be worked through in the process of understanding and interpreting the patient's dream. This would likely take place when the patient had moved from experiencing the dream as a "not me" dream, so characteristic of the initial phase of the analysis of the schizoid patient, to experiencing the dream as "my dream", indicating an opening of the road to the patient's psychic reality.

I would like to offer a note about the countertransference in the process of dream analysis. Fairbairn's third level of interpretation, which focuses on the complex internal ego and object relationships, is the most fruitful level for the working through of the patient's deepest psychopathology. However, this may be the most difficult phase in the analytic treatment because it may stimulate the analyst's corresponding and insufficiently worked through endopsychic structural dynamics. As Fairbairn stated, the schizoid position is a universal one. This requires that analysts be alert to its activation within themselves throughout the course of every analysis, as when this goes unrecognised and unameliorated we encounter stalemates and transference-countertransference entanglements.

Interested readers will benefit greatly from studying the full text of Fairbairn's discussion of "A Multiplicity of Egos" which is to be found in his paper on endopsychic structure considered in terms of object relationships (1944, pp. 94–105).

Jack's dream

The second dream I will discuss appears in "Observations on the nature of hysterical states" (Fairbairn, 1954b). In this paper Fairbairn's objective was to go back to hysteria, and to re-conceptualise its psychopathology within the context of his theory of endopsychic structure. I will focus on only one of the dreams presented in this paper, Jack's dream (pp. 25–26, 31–32), and I will compare Fairbairn's analysis of this dream to his analysis of the specimen dream discussed above.

The dream is reported as follows:

> I was in a room which was like the living-room of a house, but also like your waiting-room. In the room lay a leopard sprawled out sleeping on the floor. It was between me and the door. I wanted to get out of the room, but was afraid the leopard would spring at me if I made a move. So I put my hand on the leopard's head to keep it down and sidled round it to the side of it near the door. Then I quickly backed to the door and slipped out.

Fairbairn stated that: "[W]hile the patient experienced little difficulty in detecting the oral component in the symbol of the carnivorous leopard, it required interpretation on my part to bring home to him the presence of a genital component, in terms of 'keeping the leopard down' represented keeping his penis down and preventing his erecting." Fairbairn emphasised that his specific aim was to bring to light the association between the oral and the genital. Indeed, he succeeded. However, he focused on only one aspect of the intrapsychic dynamics of the dream. He left out completely the connection between the dream and the dynamics of the patient's endopsychic structures, this having been his goal in presenting a new theoretical framework for the understanding and interpretation of dreams in psychoanalysis. In my opinion, even if he did not have the chance to address these issues during the course of the session he could have discussed them in his paper as his afterthoughts. In light of what we have learned about Fairbairn's analysis of the specimen dream, I would like us to consider facets of dream analysis that might have been addressed had Fairbairn discussed this dream in a manner consistent with the innovative framework of dream analysis that he explicated in the analysis of the specimen dream.

The patient's dream took place in the analyst's waiting room and I would thus regard it as possibly being a transference dream. And why was Fairbairn absent? His absence might have suggested to Fairbairn that Jack was struggling with the multiple relational dynamics with him and thus motivated him to consider raising questions regarding Jack's endopsychic dynamic structures. Further, can we regard the leopard as a "composite figure" formed by the psychological operations of the dream-work? As such, would Jack be unconsciously experiencing Fairbairn as the leopard—as scary, devouring, and imprisoning? Were Jack's carnivorous libidinal needs directed at his analyst and did this result in a state of paralysis of him? These questions might have led Fairbairn to consider the possibility that Jack was withdrawing from him and wishing to "slip out" and to end the treatment.

Fairbairn did not let us know whether he had considered the possible transference implications of the dream—particularly as it related to the current stage of the analysis. From this perspective we could wonder why Jack might have wished to escape from the analysis. And we could wonder why Jack excluded Fairbairn from the dream given that it took place in his analyst's waiting room?

Fairbairn stressed that his interpretation of Jack's symptom of sinusitis was that: "He was dramatizing a state of imprisonment by his mother." And he noted that this interpretation resolved the symptom (ibid., p. 31). And he emphasised that the patient's genital conflicts resulted in "keeping his penis down". It seems to me that, in limiting the analytic focus of the dream analysis to a clash of personalities between the patient and his mother since early childhood (ibid., pp. 31, 35, 39) Fairbairn joined the patient in his defensiveness by not interpreting the dream as it related to *their* relationship. It seems to me that it would have been important that Fairbairn analyse Jack's intense underlying relationships with him as this would have been a clear application of his own object relations theory. For example, did Jack experience conflicts in his attempts to stand erect in the analytic situation. Regrettably there is no information provided as to whether such themes were worked through within the transference.

It may have been that this dream was presented during a difficult stage in the analysis, perhaps when the treatment was at a standstill. Were both Jack and Fairbairn consciously and unconsciously assessing whether they could move to a deeper analytic engagement? Were they both wondering about a possible ending of the analysis? From this perspective the patient's dream could be understood to be in the service of alerting Fairbairn to the challenge of working through his own countertransference issues. The irony in this was that Fairbairn, for his part, abandoned his own discoveries in his processing of Jack's dream.

The third clinical illustration

In his 1958 paper, "On the Nature and Aims of Psycho-analytical Treatment" Fairbairn stated: "Psychoanalytical treatment resolves itself into a struggle on the part of the patient to press-gang his relationship with the analyst into the closed system of the inner world through the agency of the transference, and a determination on the part of the analyst to effect a breach in this closed system and to provide conditions under which, in a setting of a therapeutic relationship, the patient may be induced to accept the open system of outer reality."

Others who have discussed this article either briefly mentioned the dreams or bypassed them altogether. Therefore it is important first to present the dreams and highlight Fairbairn's conclusions and then I will critically evaluate his manner of working with these dreams in the context of his own framework for dream analysis.

What follows are "the dreams of a recalcitrant patient of long standing", whom Fairbairn designates as Karl, and in his approach to these dreams Fairbairn demonstrated Karl's intense struggle in the process of moving from a closed psychic system to an open one.

1. I was out walking with my father; and we met you. You handed me a book or paper. My father protested that I was neglecting or forsaking him; *but I did acknowledge you*.
2. I was talking to you; but at the same time I was in bed with my mother. I felt embarrassed, because my mother was listening to what I was saying to you. Sometimes my mother leaned over me and came in contact with me. This horrified me and made me shrink away from her. *But I did not stop talking to you.* (1958a, p. 318)

Fairbairn stated that these were "not so much transference dreams" but rather dreams "… representing the impact of a realistic relationship with the analyst in the outer world upon Karl's relationships with the figures of his parents in his inner world." The analyst had become a genuinely "good object", a caring person in his patient's internal world countering the internalised "bad objects" related to his father and mother. Furthermore, there were signs of the "release of the bad object from the repressed" (1943a, p. 332), resulting from the patient having internalised the safety and trust experienced in the analytic relationship, as we can observe in the patient's manifest dream. Briefly, this represents the dynamics of an open system.

In subsequently introducing two more of Karl's dreams Fairbairn writes "… there were also *contemporary* [my italics] dreams revealing a movement in the direction of restoring the closed system …" He gave the following as examples:

1. I was with you; and, while I was talking to you, I felt a compulsive urge to masturbate. I wondered if you would notice me doing this while I kept up the flow of talk. Then I found that you were in fact *in an adjoining room*; and I felt that I could probably masturbate without your noticing.
2. *I left here and walked away. My mother was walking several yards ahead of me.* I don't know if I thought she was leaving me behind; but *I thought I might attract her attention* by throwing gravel at her. Then I found that I was terribly worked up and was pelting her with stones. (1958a, p. 381)

Fairbairn regarded these dreams as evidence for the patient having reverted to his characteristic closed psychic system by continuing his strong attachments to his bad internal objects—attachments which his relationship to the analyst did not counter.

Clearly we see evidence of the emergence of the repressed and split-off ego and object relations, indicating a breach in the patient's closed system, as we would expect at the end phase of a successful analysis. However, the only data that Fairbairn presented was the manifest dream content and thus he treated the dream figures simply on the manifest level and did not reveal whether he had analysed these dreams in terms of his framework of endopsychic structural dynamics.

Had Fairbairn detailed the working through of the dream figures as "composite figures", applying his theoretical framework to the process of analysis of these figures, he might have been able to appreciate that the transference was more complicated than "realistic and positive". In the manifest dream content there are indicators of the negative transference—the father figure feeling neglected and forsaken as Karl may have felt treated by Fairbairn. Further, the dream may express something of Karl's appreciation of the countertransference in which Fairbairn may have felt neglected and abandoned by Karl. In this manner of considering Karl's dreams after a long analytic process we would have been aware of the complexities and fluctuations of the open and closed systems as the most formidable resistances to reaching the underlying schizoid psychopathology.

Fairbairn told us that the second of two sets of dreams were "contemporary". I was wondering why the patient had reverted to his "closed" system, excluded Fairbairn as a "good object", and had struggled with masturbation in the analytic session, indulging in it when he was sure that the analyst could not see him? In the second of these two dreams Karl walks away from the analytic situation and then his mother walks away and leaves him behind and he thinks of throwing gravel at her (analyst) to get her attention. While Karl's reversion to the closed system may have been due to his formidable resistance and his imprisonment within his internalised family dynamics, it may also have been due to some awareness on Karl's part that Fairbairn's one-sided emphasis on the positive transference in his understanding and interpretation of the dreams was derivative of Fairbairn's struggle with his own schizoid dynamics. I raise this question with respect to Fairbairn's possible countertransference dynamics because Fairbairn taught us to be mindful of the universality of schizoid dynamics. This perspective on the function of dreams within the analytic situation, that the patient may be drawing the analyst's attention to potential countertransference obstacles, is a perspective that Fairbairn did not include in his framework. That Fairbairn did not discuss these essential issues left me with the impression that he was insufficiently personally involved during the process of dream analysis with Karl—which, in this paper, ironically, he instructed us to be.

The central problem I have been addressing is the process of dream analysis within the context of Fairbairn's formulation of the "aims" of psychoanalytic treatment wherein dream analysis is intended to promote the working through of the disunities and conflicts within the patient's closed internal system. My having presented examples of Fairbairn's dream analysis in three different contexts and having critically evaluated his reported approach, we may notice remarkable differences in his understandings and interpretations of his patients' dreams. In the specimen dream, he brilliantly highlighted how the dream figures embedded the conflictual dynamics of the endopsychic structures. Each dream figure contained split-off aspects of the patient's personality, dissociated and scattered, and assigned them to objects with whom the patient identified. Although Fairbairn did not apply it to the analytic relational dynamics, his comprehensive analysis is clinically powerful, as it provides us with a conceptual framework for a step-by-step analytic inquiry into the intricacies of the transference and countertransference. However, in the report of the analysis of Jack's dream Fairbairn focused on the patient's Oedipal/genital dynamics and made no mention of Jack's endopsychic structural dynamics that potentially could have been worked through by the analysis of the dream figures. Karl's dreams, from his long analysis, revealed the activation of the bad split-off and repressed egos and objects, but Fairbairn's interventions emphasised his supportive and compassionate concern for Karl. While he seemed to aim to restore Karl's trust, and to counterbalance his suffering by becoming a "good object", he ignored the central importance of signs that suggested the patient's aggression. Fairbairn warned us of the ongoing risk of becoming an omnipotent rescuer and of bypassing the patient's identifying with bad exciting and frustrating objects. Did Fairbairn himself fall into this ever-present dynamic trap?

Returning to the question of why Fairbairn's dream framework has been "curiously omitted" and "underemployed", I would like to suggest a partial answer. Fairbairn was inconsistent in his reporting of data that related to the analysis of his patients' dreams. He started off presenting a comprehensive dream analysis in the specimen dream that adhered well to his developing personality theory. However, subsequently, he left out the crucial role of analysing composite figures as derivative of the various endopsychic structures, which was the unique character of his dream analysis, and resorted to a focus on manifest dynamics and supportive measures.

Discussion and conclusion

Fairbairn helped us to listen to the many voices that were emerging from his patients' dreams, but he shut us off from knowing how he himself listened to them. He left it to others to apply his framework of dream analysis within psychoanalytic treatment (Davies & Frawley, 1992; Grotstein, 2002; Winnicott, 1971). I will briefly focus on Winnicott as: a) he himself said that he was "in the territory of Fairbairn" (1971, p. 119); b) he acknowledged Fairbairn's priority with regard to "transitional phenomena" and the "true-self/false-self" dichotomy (Grotstein, 2002, p. 167, footnote); and c) his case history (Winnicott, 1971, pp. 26–37) addresses the dreams of his schizoid patient. Further, I would suggest that Winnicott's case history may provide us with some of the missing links that we identified in Fairbairn's reported dream analysis.

Winnicott spoke of "fantasying" as being a process in which the dream is experienced as a concrete, rigid mental structure, based on dissociation, and similar to what Fairbairn referred to as futile mental activities to defend against experiencing infantile trauma. It is characteristic of the schizoid dream.

For Winnicott a "true dream" was a transitional phenomenon, within an intermediate space between reality and unconscious fantasy, with imaginative communication between primary and secondary processes and regarded by the patient as a "me" experience and as having multiple layers of meaning. I see this as being in accord with Fairbairn's aim of movement from a closed system to an open system. Winnicott paid close attention to the dynamics of the transference-countertransference during the process of understanding and interpreting his patient's dreams, an aspect that Fairbairn had neglected to report.

Here are some clinical examples of Winnicott's work with a schizoid patient's dreams. In the midst of relating her dream, the patient revealed a bit of her vivid fantasy life, but quickly, automatically, tried to dissociate from it by experiencing it as "unrealistic" and "ridiculous". Winnicott tried to help her own this fragment of her fantasy life as an emotional experience and as part of her "true-self". Winnicott used a variety of interventions—reassurance, mirroring, educational comment, and interpretation. His aim was to facilitate his patient making emotionally meaningful contacts between the manifest dream elements—images, objects, persons—that were initially experienced as a mere replica of external reality, and her internal life with its layers of symbolic significance. With Fairbairn, Winnicott warned us against premature interpretations of defences and resistances that would lead to compliance.

A figure referred to as a "slob" appeared as an element in the manifest content of the patient's dream. This figure was initially experienced by the patient as a remote figure, devoid of personal significance. In the course of the analytic session, there is evidence that the "slob" was gradually processed as a condensation and displacement, disguising intense affects of aggression—fantasies of being murdered by her mother and of wishing to kill her mother. The patient moved from experiencing the "slob" as a split-off "not me" figure to beginning to own the related distressing aggressive affects and underlying fantasies. Furthermore, in the transference were to be found aggressive feelings towards Winnicott—ridiculing him and asking, "What do you make of this stupid dream?"—and then the activation of withdrawal and the denial of Winnicott's existence. The data available provided Winnicott (and the readers) with evidence as to how the patient experienced and perceived the process of working with her dream.

Winnicott was intensely emotionally involved with his patient, and this evoked her basic internal structural dynamics, which were relived in relation to Winnicott. The murderous rage felt towards her mother may have led to her contemptuous remarks and to disconnecting from Winnicott and to withdrawal into sleep. Winnicott offered us no information as to what went through his mind during the period in which his patient slept and when she awoke he responded with reassuring and educational comments about dreams and dreaming. At this point he resorted to an intellectual approach, which he had been strenuously trying to avoid. Had he been affected by the intensity of the patient's destructive aggression during the reactivation of the maternal transference? Was Winnicott experiencing what he called "direct communication" (1971, p. 54)—a process in which his patient induced in him unbearable feelings and fantasies that he then dealt with defensively in his educational comments?

While Fairbairn and Winnicott shared common aims with respect to the analysis of dreams within the psychoanalytic process—a movement from a closed system to an open system (Fairbairn), and, where fantasying was, there dreaming shall be (Winnicott)—Winnicott provided a more detailed approach to the analysis of the dreams of a schizoid patient. However, neither Fairbairn nor Winnicott addressed the important issue of the influence of the analysts' countertransference on the process of analysis of their patients' dreams.

Acknowledgement

I am very grateful to Paul Finnegan, my friend and colleague, for his consistent support and help.

References

Davies, J. M., & Frawley, M. G. (1992). Dissociative processes and transference-countertransference paradigms in the psychoanalytically oriented treatment of adult survivors of childhood sexual abuse. *Psychoanalytic Dialogues, 2*: 5–36.
Fairbairn, W. R. D. (1940a). Schizoid factors in the personality. In: *Psychoanalytic Studies of the Personality* (pp. 3–27). London: Tavistock, 1952.

Fairbairn, W. R. D. (1941). A revised psychopathology of the psychoses and psychoneuroses. *International Journal of Psychoanalysis, 22*(3, 4): 250–279. In: *Psychoanalytic Studies of the Personality* (pp. 28–58). London: Tavistock, 1952.

Fairbairn, W. R. D. (1943a). The repression and the return of bad objects (with special reference to the "war neuroses"). *British Journal of Medical Psychology, 19*: 327–341. In: *Psychoanalytic Studies of the Personality* (pp. 59–81). London: Tavistock, 1952.

Fairbairn, W. R. D. (1944). Endopsychic structure considered in terms of object-relationships. *International Journal of Psychoanalysis, 25*: 70–92. In: *Psychoanalytic Studies of the Personality* (pp. 82–136). London: Tavistock, 1952.

Fairbairn, W. R. D. (1954b). Observations on the nature of hysterical states. *British Journal of Medical Psychology, 27*(3): 106–125. In: D. E. Scharff & E. F. Birtles (Eds.), *From Instinct to Self: Selected Papers of W. R. D. Fairbairn, Volume I: Clinical and Theoretical Papers* (pp. 13–40). Northvale, NJ: Jason Aronson.

Fairbairn, W. R. D. (1958a). On the nature and aims of psycho-analytical treatment. *International Journal of Psychoanalysis, 39*(5): 374–385. In: D. E. Scharff & E. F. Birtles (Eds.), *From Instinct to Self: Selected Papers of W. R. D. Fairbairn, Volume I: Clinical and Theoretical Papers* (pp. 74–92). Northvale, NJ: Jason Aronson, 1994.

Fosshage, J. L. (1987). A revised psychoanalytic approach. In: J. L. Fosshage & C. A. Loew (Eds.), *Dream Interpretation: A Comparative Study* (revised edition). New York: P. M. A. Publishing.

Freud, S. (1900a). *The Interpretation of Dreams. S. E., 4 & 5*. London: Hogarth.

Freud, S. (1923c). Remarks on the theory and practice of dream interpretation. *S. E., 19*: 109–121. London: Hogarth.

Freud, S. (1925d). An autobiographical study. *S. E., 20*: 7–74. London: Hogarth.

Grotstein, J. S. (1998). A comparison of Fairbairn's endopsychic structure and Klein's internal world. In: N. J. Skolnick & D. E. Scharff (Eds.), *Fairbairn, Then and Now* (pp. 71–98). Hillsdale, NJ: Analytic Press.

Grotstein, J. S. (2002). Endopsychic structures, psychic retreats, and "fantasying": the pathological "third area" of the psyche. In: F. Pereira & D. E. Scharff (Eds.), *Fairbairn and Relational Theory* (pp. 145–182). London: Karnac.

Kohut, H. (1977). *The Restoration of the Self*. New York: International Universities Press.

Padel, J. (1991). Fairbairn's thought on the relationship of inner and outer worlds. *Free Associations, 2*: 589–615.

Pereira, F., & Scharff, D. E. (2002). Introduction. In: F. Pereira & D. E. Scharff (Eds.), *Fairbairn and Relational Theory* (pp. 1–10). London: Karnac.

Scharff, D. E. (1988a). Fairbairn's contribution: an interview of Otto F. Kernberg. In: N. J. Skolnick & D. E. Scharff (Eds.), *Fairbairn, Then and Now* (pp. 17–32). Hillsdale, NJ: Analytic Press.

Sutherland, J. D. (1989). *Fairbairn's Journey into the Interior*. London: Free Association.

Winnicott, D. W. (1971). *Playing and Reality*. London: Tavistock.

CHAPTER NINETEEN

The analyst as good object: a Fairbairnian perspective*

Neil J. Skolnick

> *I think more has been written about bad internalized objects similarly disowned than about the denial of good internal forces and objects.*
>
> —D. W. Winnicott

Introduction

Psychoanalytic technique has periodically been modified to reflect historical and theoretical shifts (Lipton, 1983). Over the course of the last twenty-five years the psychoanalytic landscape has changed to reflect the mounting importance context is accorded in the structuring of our developmental and motivational selves. The relational evolution has ushered in mind-numbing changes to psychoanalytic theory and technique. Mainstays of our contemporary technique that were relegated to the heretical just a few years ago are regarded as standard fare today. Witness the debates on the efficacy of the self-revealing analyst (Burke, 1992; Davies, 1994; Greenberg, 1995; Hirsch, 1994; Tansey, 1994) or the use of enactments to further the goals of treatment (Davies, 1994). Increasingly, contemporary models of psychic functioning and organisation (Bromberg, 1998) are informing expanding emergent twists and turns of technique.

The evolutionary groove we currently traverse under the broad umbrella of relational perspectives (Skolnick & Scharff, 1992) for the most part is anchored by theorists who are reluctant to codify technical recommendations (e.g., Fairbairn, 1958a; Hoffman, 1983; Mitchell, 1988; Stolorow & Atwood, 1992). The increasing acceptance of relativistic truth in our theories has organically led to relativistic angles on technique (Skolnick, 1999). For today's analyst,

---

* A previous version of this chapter appeared as a paper in *Psychoanalytic Dialogues*, 2006, 16: 1–28.

there are many more proverbial roads than ever leading to Rome. It is my observation that while relational theories play an important role in guiding newer techniques, many of our contemporary theorists rely more on their clinical experience to expand technical possibilities. Although far from objectively reliable or valid, clinical data is the best data we have. We are at a point of hypothesis generating in our literature on technique. This chapter, as well, can be considered a heuristic, hypothesis-generating endeavour. I hold no claims to new technical theory. My clinical data is garnered from years of practice and changing theoretical contexts. It is my belief that actual clinical experience with patients (our hermeneutic data, if you will), accompanied by careful, intense circumspection and debate will lead to more reliable statements about higher levels of abstraction to accompany an evolving theory of relational technique. But we are not there yet.

For the purposes of this paper, I do not attempt to provide a comprehensive definition of the essence of a "good object". I am primarily focusing on what a good object *does* and not the essence of its nature. Others have noted that the legacy of psychoanalytic theory and technique may rest more with careful descriptions of what analysts *do* than with the explanatory validity of the theory. Moreover, psychoanalysis as a theory no longer aspires solely to the constraints of a hypothetical-deductive model of scientific inquiry. While empirical research has been considered an important contributor to the accretion of psychoanalytic knowledge, with the shift in emphasis of relational theory to studying subjective experience, and co-creating relativistic and hermeneutic truths, the cornerstones of empiricism—observation, reliability, and validity—do not always apply to the understanding of psychoanalytic phenomena. This chapter presents a description, gleaned from years of clinical practice, of what an analyst, as good object, does, not what a good object is.

Moreover, as the technique of relational psychoanalysis has increasingly disentangled itself from many of the technical dictates of drive theory, the importance of the role of the analyst has shifted from passive, neutral observer and interpreter to active participant. A relational analyst can (though not for all who consider themselves relational) insist that the analyst participate *as a good object*. To the sceptic, visions of analysts portioning out a never-ending supply of need satisfactions clouds their ability to attend to the more textured and complex nature of a good object. To the converted, objections and cautions to this relatively new technical turn can be unheeded with a cavalier acceptance of its validity. What I intend to explore in this chapter are some broad technical strokes describing how an analyst might function as a good object.

Before turning to a consideration of what actions determine a good object in treatment, I do, however, wish to provide a brief description of what I consider a good object to be. I refer to the good object as an amalgam of object imagoes as provided by the theories of Klein, Fairbairn, Winnicott, and Kohut. Whether rooted in nature or nurture or an admixture of both, the good object is mostly on the side of life. It is a mature (Fairbairn, 1952; Kohut, 1984), loving (Fairbairn, 1952; Klein, 1937; Winnicott, 1965), whole, integrated self or other (Klein, 1935; Kohut, 1984) who has acknowledged and accepted the goodness *and* badness in oneself and others. It occupies either internal or external space (Klein, 1937; Kohut, 1984). This is an integrated object who does not deny the existence of our more grandiose, idealistic strivings which pull us with endless hope through life (Kohut, 1984; Winnicott, 1965). Nor does it deny our ever-present sinister affects or destructive motivations (Klein, 1937). It has managed to accept their inevitability, to struggle with the tensions they evoke, to adapt to them, integrate them, and continue to be able to love and accept love (Fairbairn, 1952; Klein, 1937; Kohut, 1984; Winnicott, 1965).

Fairbairn and Klein differed markedly on the origins of the good object. Briefly, a good object for Klein is a part object originally rooted in the innate life instinct. Present at birth it is first projected onto the mother and later introjected along with the mother's gratifying attributes. The good object becomes a whole, integrated object if the mother loves and provides for the child's needs.

Fairbairn, on the other hand, never fully described a good object. He referred to it alternatively as the accepted object and ideal object. As opposed to Klein, who posited that we are born with internal good and bad part objects which achieve integration during development, for Fairbairn we are born as a unified whole and it is only as a consequence of the failures of the object that we split them into good and bad. The good object is an aspect of the real (not fantasised) loving mother that remains once the bad objects have been split off. The child then takes the good object into its central ego (self) in order to fend against the split-off and internalised bad objects which are aspects of the mother that have failed to love the child. Fairbairn's labelling of the good object as "ideal" is, to me, a confusing misnomer, and not to be mistaken with Klein's idealized object, which, as I noted, is a bad object. I tend to equate Fairbairn's "ideal" object with Winnicott's "good-enough" object.

It is important to distinguish a good object from both Klein's idealised and Fairbairn's exciting object. Idealised and exciting objects are bad objects. They are not loving, whole, or integrated. Klein's idealised object is an aggrandised object defensively created in fantasy in order to combat the attacks to the self by the bad objects. Fairbairn's exciting object is a split-off piece of the good object that holds out the promise of satisfaction but ultimately fails the child. These bad objects (exciting and idealised) are one-dimensional fictions, sometimes engaged with for survival, which deny the existence of complexity, ambivalence, or doubt. The achievement and acceptance of doubt and ambivalence, which is a lifetime struggle of good objects, is anathema to bad objects. Bad objects require immutable truths, truths that demand absolute adherence in order to survive. All doubt must be destroyed. If any uncertainty is entertained, the absolute truth and meaning of a bad object is in mortal jeopardy. For meaning to be maintained by bad objects, anything smacking of ambivalence, uncertainty, or doubt must be defended against, if not wiped out. In psychoanalysis we refer to this process as the deployment of primitive defence mechanisms such as splitting, projection, introjection, or denial. For Klein, the obliteration of doubt was the hallmark of a paranoid/schizoid organisation. For Fairbairn, the denial of overwhelming doubt lay at the very heart of our universally split egos.

In his seminal paper written on technique published nearly a half-century after Freud and a half-century before now, Fairbairn (1958a) demonstrated far-reaching clinical insight:

> In terms of the object-relations theory of the personality, the disabilities from which the patient suffers represent the effects of unsatisfactory and unsatisfying object relationships experienced in early life and perpetuated in an exaggerated form in inner reality; and, if this view is correct, the actual relationship existing between the patient and the analyst as persons must be regarded as in itself constituting a therapeutic factor of prime importance. The existence of such a personal relationship in outer reality not only serves the function of providing a

> means of correcting the distorted relationships which prevail in inner reality and influence the reactions of the patient to outer objects, but provides the patient with an opportunity, denied to him in childhood, to undergo a process of emotional development in the setting of an actual relationship with a reliable and beneficent parental figure. (p. 377)

By virtue of this statement, remarkable for its time, he catapulted the primary influence of the analysis out of the arena of dispassionate drive interpretations and placed it squarely in the space created by the coming together of two vital, continuously interacting people, the therapeutic dyad. Fairbairn's revolutionary idea was that the therapeutic relationship offers the provision of a good object (or more correctly, a good object relationship).

But what is a good object to do?

What does a good object look like in the analytic setting? Where are the lines between provisions of analytic goodness and provisions of exciting, taunting, or seductive false promises? How might a good object alter the therapeutic frame, including where, when, and how the boundaries are drawn or redrawn? Does the goodness of an analyst relate to the authenticity of the analyst? Or the spontaneity of the analyst? Or the behaviour of the analyst? Relational analysts struggle with these and similar questions today (Hoffman, 1998), when many of the rules of the analytic process have been thrown open for reconsideration.

In what follows I attempt to describe a sampling of characteristic actions of a good object contextualised by the therapeutic relationship. The list is not exhaustive, by any means, and it is not intended to be used formulaically. Fairbairn (1958a) for one was reluctant to spell out specific technical recommendations, fearing a slide to the rigid and mechanical, which, he bemoaned, might serve more to allay the clinician's anxieties or take care of the therapist's needs, than to help the patient.

In this chapter, I consider three categories of activity that can be provided by the analyst/ good object. The first, which I have coined "dynamic identification", is derived from Fairbairn's most seminal postulate, that of dynamic structure. I discuss here the mechanisms, not of identification with the analyst, but of the internalisation of a new object relationship provided by a relational analyst.

The second category is also rooted in Fairbairn's theory. His theory of motivation posits its bedrock in the basic nature (Mitchell, 1996) of man to establish and maintain loving connections. For Fairbairn, loving relationships, from birth, required a two-way reciprocal street. It was not news that a parent needs to love a child. What was news, and has often been ignored, is that a child, from birth, spontaneously offers his love to others. Fairbairn stressed the crucial need that the child's love be accepted and cherished. The acceptance of love provides the thematic glue for the second category of good object activity I describe.

Finally, in the third category, I expand upon Fairbairn's emphasis on the provision of a loving object relationship to a developing child. He stressed that a loving relationship was one based upon the parent empathically perceiving and providing for the child's needs, as distinct from the needs of the parent. It is this provision of loving empathy that I offer as another example of what an analyst, as good object, does. More specifically, the analytic provision of empathy is discussed as it relates to Klein's conceptualisation of positions in development. The psychological organisations of the paranoid/schizoid position are qualitatively different from the organisations of the depressive position. Likewise, the two positions generate markedly different self and other experiential modes. I will delineate the nature of the empathic response required by a good object when interacting with a patient functioning in the paranoid/schizoid experiential mode of experience.

Dynamic identification

Dynamic identification is a construct I have derived from Fairbairn's overarching principle of dynamic structure. Briefly stated, Fairbairn pronounced that psychic structure and psychic energy were equivalent: "Both structure divorced from energy and energy divorced from structure are meaningless concepts" (1952, p. 149). In an Einsteinian moment he eliminated Freud's distinction between dynamic id energy and an inert ego fuelled by the drives. Paralleling the precepts of Einstein's relativity theory, egos represent dynamic, ongoing systems, imbued with their own energy rather than discrete, singular entities. An ego (or self), for Fairbairn is what the ego *does*, and does in concert with an object, including an accompanying affect tie. Ego, object, and energy, for Fairbairn, are inseparable and inextricable and are spoken of disjointedly only for linguistic clarity. What are internalised, then, for Fairbairn, are neither good nor bad *objects*, but good or bad *object relationships* including the ego/self, the object, and the affective tie between the two. An ego cannot exist without reference to the objects, either internal or external, that structure it and perpetuate its essence. To interpret, then, becomes a useful cognitive exercise, but change itself becomes a problem of object relationships.

The provision of a good object requires a dynamic interplay between analyst and patient. No longer is the analyst a detached imparter of wise, timely mutagenic interpretations. He or she is an active engager of the patient's self in an ongoing mutually constructive process. He or she is a relational analyst resuscitated from Fairbairn's circa 1940 opus.

It follows, then, that an important aim of the good object in the therapeutic process is to provide the patient with an opportunity to relate with the analyst in multiple new configurations. The internalisation of new dynamic interactions will serve to restructure the patient's ego/self inasmuch as Fairbairn understood the self as always interacting with and being structured by an other's self. This is the process I refer to as *dynamic identification*.

The good object provides something unique. In addition to the standard activities of labelling distortions, unearthing unconscious material, and providing interpretations, the good object engages with the patient in new ways of being, repeatedly, over time. The interaction with the analyst gradually becomes coterminous with the patient's expanded self. The analyst's provision of new ways-of-being, both cognitively and affectively, become structured into a patient's expanding and expanded self. Each participant retains his/her own autonomous uniqueness while at the same time, each is being informed, stretched, and restructured by the interaction with the other. Expanded, more flexible, adaptive, and endurable selves are spun out and tried out. Over time, patients accumulate new ways of being with an other woven and textured into their existing dynamic structures.

The fomenting space for the dynamic interaction of the analyst's and patient's subjective selves, the space where new ways of being are generated, I would place in the realm of experience described by Ogden (1994) as the intersubjective third. This is a space that belongs neither exclusively to the analyst nor exclusively to the patient, but is created by the admixture of two interacting subjectivities.

Dynamic identifications between the analyst and patient are infinite in nature, and will typically though not exclusively concern themselves with the particular trouble spots that impede a patient's pursuit of satisfaction and pleasure. Of crucial importance is that the analytic process provides an intersubjective arena in which these trouble spots can emerge. They emerge in ways we alternatively, depending on theoretical preference, have labelled transference, transference/countertransference interaction, acting out, acting in, enacting, or a search for archaic and mature self-object provisions, to name a few.

Interpretations may contribute to the process but they are not sufficient, being more or less a cognitive exercise and rarely mutative. As per Fairbairn's prescription, the patient needs to actively participate in an actual, fully experienced interaction with the containing analyst who variously struggles, stumbles, survives, accepts reparations, remains calm, or loses and recovers calm, to name a few of the component activities of containing.

A dynamic identification might also, as another example, include the process participated in when the analyst makes a mistake and recovers from a mistake, without becoming defensive or inauthentic. We can extend these experiences to include most activities of the analyst such as the working-through analyst, the forgiving, integrated analyst, the modulating analyst, the analyst who struggles with conflict, the analyst who gets angry and recovers, the fallible analyst, and so forth.

For this to happen requires from the analyst concentrated devotion and unwavering commitment to venture as part of a dyad to wherever the patient leads and regardless of the disturbance of the analyst's experiences. We must be prepared to roll up our sleeves and enter the patient's inner world, as well as our own. We need to, as Pick (1985) prescribes, become greatly disturbed as we are made to experience, via dynamic identification with the patient, the object relationships inhabiting a patient's inner world. On the way, via concordant and complementary countertransference (Racker, 1968) we might be called upon to re-experience and once again work through the painful disturbances of our own inner object relationships. As we do, both consciously and unconsciously, so does the patient, who comes to identify with the struggles, failures, and successes of our own self/other dilemmas and how we negotiate them. The patient will then, through dynamic identification with the analyst, come to be able to tolerate the process of integrating new ways of being, a process that can travel through frighteningly disorienting waters before being comprehended and integrated. The more we have resolved our own issues, or are at least able to tolerate them, the further the patient can safely travel. The further we have ventured ourselves, the further the patient will feel safe to go.

Let me try to illustrate. A patient of mine, Marianna, a forty-something attorney was rather successful in her work world. By contrast her romantic life was a shambles. She was haunted by the long shadows of a mother who in many respects was loving but who was enormously anxious and would at times become impulsively and physically abusive. She remembers episodes when her mother would smash her (the patient's) head against a wall, at times drawing blood. These incidents were never spoken about or resolved.

Marianna was in a long-term relationship with a man in which she would luxuriate in comforting thoughts about the hopeful possibilities of a life together. These hopes stood in marked contrast to the couple's actual experience with each other. Inevitably, when together, their interactions would rapidly deteriorate into verbally abusive fights that were repaired, not by resolution, but rather, only by being tucked into the passage of time.

On one occasion, she entered my office following her vacation only to discover that I had replaced the old, worn patient chair with a new one. Complaining that I had not forewarned her about the change, she instantaneously entered into an enraged state, one I had not heretofore observed. She pelted me with virulent abusive language. She attacked my ability as an analyst and threatened to bring me up on ethical charges for not giving her an advanced heads-up about the change. At some point I became visibly addled, sputtering lame interpretations while feeling a fine blend of helplessness and exasperated rage. This only fuelled her sadism as she upped her attacks while simultaneously announcing that actually, she was getting great pleasure out of assaulting me. In fact, she exclaimed, she had not had this much fun in years. I was thrust into that paralysed place, familiar to most analysts at one time or another, of feeling that my understanding of her experience was hopelessly limited and any intervention would meet with utter futility.

So, what is a good object to do?

First and foremost I needed to, as I am sure most would agree, survive the attack. Whether seen as a ruthless attack by a Winnicottian, a dip into the paranoid/schizoid position by a Kleinian, or the result of empathic failure by a self psychologist, survival of the analyst is a must and a prime requisite of a good object.

Let us examine this more closely. What do we mean by survival? Allowing for nuanced differences by analysts of different theoretical orientations, we are referring to the analyst not succumbing to the patient's omnipotence, not disappearing either consciously or unconsciously in the face of the patient's conscious or unconscious fantasy of having destroyed us. We do not abandon, retaliate, or fall apart.

That we survive ensures that the patient's subjective omnipotence is challenged so that gradually he or she can tolerate the ongoing tension of surviving and tolerating an existence in which one must share the stage with others, while being allowed some measure of prime time as well. But, it is not only by virtue of the experience *that* we survive that helps our patients. As, if not more important, *how* we survive ultimately contributes to the expansion of the patient's ego or self, and by implication therapeutic change.

Surviving is not enough. To paraphrase Winnicott (1965), we can fob off a patient with a good survival. Survivals can be as staged and lifeless as a formulaic interpretation. In the face of a murderous attack, we can manage to maintain a calm veneer while internally we fume, struggle, disorganise, become massively ashamed, sadistically attack, or settle into a lifeless remove, to name a few possibilities. While technically we have visibly survived, the patient does not get to experience or identify with *how* we survived. Patients of course, can usually detect a storm raging below our best attempts to display calm.

We need to straddle an impossible line between maintaining professional control and experiencing emotional upset. While maintaining a relative professional calm, we try not to affect a false remove, an aloof, "nothing you say can affect me" attitude. Whether we are working with a more disturbed patient or a patient who is experiencing temporary paranoid/schizoid disorganisation, we need to get stuck in our own psychic mud and experience our own painful disruption, which, through our own dynamic identifications with the patient, provide us with clues about the patient's experience of us. To do otherwise (i.e., avoid, deny, etc.) we risk missing an empathic understanding of the underside of our patient's skin. We also can appear inauthentic; typically signalling to a patient it is not safe to venture further.

Then, we work through, once again, as we had in analysis or self-analysis, this place of disruption raging within ourselves, whether it resides in a more neurotic, conflict-ridden arena or a more primitive, paranoid/schizoid place. We reinstate our integrity, our wholeness, and the survival of our subjectivity, without enacting revenge on the patient whose reparations we lovingly accept and whose life we permit to continue. In the episode with Marianna I needed to allow and be disturbed by my own experiences with precipitous losses, failures of omnipotence, uncontrollable rage, and sadistic pleasures, my own experiences of paranoid/schizoid organisational states, and my own shameful disturbances. And equally as important I needed to recall my own recovery from these places.

Moreover, these disruptions and recoveries occur in active participation with the patient (either consciously or unconsciously). Through these repeated interactions, the processes of our dynamic self become available for the patient to structure into their own internal worlds. Thus through the mutual experiencing of our disruption and recovery, we both get to intimately understand the patient's object relational world while patients dynamically identify with the *how* of recovery. They gradually can internalise and incorporate our recovery processes into their own dynamic self structure. Their own dynamic self is in turn strengthened, becoming more integrated and resilient.

Let us return to Marianna whom we left enraged, in attack mode and feasting on sadistic pleasure from the experience. Without yet understanding the vehemence of the attack, my first task was to survive. I could have sat back in my chair, staying attentive, remaining calm, attempting to explore, offering interpretations, containing the rage with empathic attunement, or just remaining silent. All of the above could be considered forms of survival, which indeed they are. Unless, however, I had allowed the attack to get under my skin, to disturb me in places I would rather not be disturbed, to touch rage or sadism within my own experience, my survival would have been, in my opinion, doomed to be experienced by the patient as formulaic, inauthentic, or worse, another display of enviable perfection on my part, to be either idealised and/or destroyed. I would be saying to the patient that "I am not ready to go to that place with you. I am overly anxious or fearful, it will not be safe."

In order for the patient to internalise how we contain, organise, or negotiate such powerful overwhelming experiences, they need to likewise experience that we have gone to a place of madness and worked it through ourselves. They need to detect, either consciously or unconsciously that we have jumped into the muck like them, and despite our fears, we have reorganised and reconstituted a secure self/other vitality. This is the point of connection needed between self and other that patients observe, experience and internalise. It is not only that we survive, but how we survive, how we venture to insanity and back, that defines the process of dynamic identification.

When Marianna precipitously attacked, I was unprepared. Unwittingly I experienced and displayed a measure of stunned disturbance. She observed my discomfort, which in the moment I neither went to great lengths to express nor hide. My unsettling and shameful sadistic impulses bubbled up fueling an inner and pleasurably charged string of invectives. My internal voice gleefully, though guiltily, complained, "I can't just buy a fucking new chair without you giving me grief," and the like. Continuing to curse to myself, I pressed my imaginary eject button and pleasurably watched her fly out the window, sail uncontrollably over Central Park, and land in a strong, icy current in the East River. I was now, in an experience paralleling hers, getting pleasure from my fantasised sadistic attack.

Then, experiencing an admixture of painful guilt and shame, I caught myself, did not act on my fantasies and I recovered. I reasoned that I had identified first as a victim and then a victimiser. I had been, via projective identification, made to experience both poles of her internal object relationship. As a victim, I became precipitously shocked, ungrounded, and frightened. I had, to date, never experienced an unpredictable storm from this patient, with whom I had worked for years and with whom I had developed a mutual fondness. I was clueless as to what had just happened and frightened about what might happen next.

Moreover, through my expressions of sadism, I became identified with her precipitously assaultive mother. I inwardly cursed and took pleasure from my sadistic fantasies.

With insight rooted in experiential identification and reason I recovered and reintegrated. Had I disavowed and/or acted out my sadistic pleasure, had I denied my fear, shame, and guilt, I do not believe progress would have been made. Similarly, progress would have been truncated had I not allowed myself to react visibly to her sudden outburst.

Once recovered, I utilised my experience to formulate an intervention. I said to the patient it appeared she was more inflamed from my being visibly shaken than my having not told her about the new chair. She concurred and went on to tell me that her most terrifying experiences as a child had been when her mother appeared confused and anxious. These times typically preceded physical abuse. We began to understand that my anxiety had aroused a similar fear of abuse and her sadistic attacks were an effort to ward off my impending attack.

Through her identification with my upset and recovery, a dynamic identification started to emerge. Our minds met on a paranoid/schizoid plane and we both experienced these strange dangerous feelings of self and other. We gained some awareness of each other's struggle with powerful drive experiences, particularly sadism, as well as fear of being suddenly shamed and humiliated; as, if not more important, she began to experience how I recovered through insight, reason, and control.

Over the course of the next series of sessions, we gradually achieved a more related calm. We continued to be able to explore and resolve the episode. We had both been through hell, working our way over hot coals, and we both came through on the other side, my regaining, and she achieving, an experience of integration within our selves and with each other. Being a good object is not easy.

Relational needs require acceptance of our patients' love

Recently, psychoanalysts have turned their attention to deciphering the nature of love in a deconstructed world and by extension, in the analytic relationship. Stephen Mitchell (2001) in his last work was attempting to shine new light on love's and passion's trajectory through the lifespan, and others (Applebaum, 1999; Davies, 1994; Hoffman, 1998) have been exploring love's sexual and non-sexual presence in the analytic relationship. Freud and Klein considered love to be a derivative of our most basic instinctual inheritance and ultimately a sublimated or regressed expression of the sexual drive, at times in fusion with aggressive drive elements. Love was thought to be the ultimate mature expression of our bestial inheritance and childhood wishes. Fairbairn reversed this primal scenario, proclaiming sex to be a well-suited, though by no means exclusive, expression of mature mutual love. Speaking on a different, less drive infused level of discourse he located a person's involvement with love at birth. He located love's essence at the heart of our fundamental human nature, our need for establishing and maintaining loving connections. Mental health, for Fairbairn, was virtually ensured with parental love; pathology arose from its disruption or absence.

But Fairbairn went further than that, though little of it has carried over to today's sensibilities. As noted, he placed a need for love at the very centre of the child's psychic inheritance at birth. Love is not only a requisite of the child, needed for safe passage across developmental horizons. A child likewise enters the world with a need to *express* loving desires, desires that guide the child towards, and assure the child of, needed connections with others. In this Fairbairn was greatly influenced by Suttie (1988; Harrow, 1998), a Scottish theoretician who wrote about the deleterious psychological effects of society's taboo on intimacy.

With this in mind Fairbairn emphatically stressed the importance of parents not only being able to love their child without excessive narcissistic investment, but also, and equally as crucial, they need to accept the child's offers of love. For infants and adults alike, the acceptance of loving gestures affirms and reaffirms our secure connections and membership in a world of other like beings. Whether it be a child's offer of a smile, scrap of paper, or an actual gift, its acceptance by a parent, in neither exaggerated nor devalued manner, is a crucial signal to the child of a secure, valued connection; a connection partially contributed to by the child's loving and creative gesture.

A shortage of experience with a parent's heartfelt embrace of his offerings of love can render a child with a weakened sense of efficacy, self-worth regulation, and ability to believe in the loving intent of others. It can also lead to a devaluation of ambitions and dreams, creations and productions, whose loving offerings are also felt to be of no consequence.

The importance of analysts not retreating from their patients' loving offerings has not been emphasised nearly enough in our technical recommendations. I wholeheartedly add this wrinkle to the list of therapeutic activities engaged in by the good object. We certainly encourage our patients to express their anger and rage at us, yet we can have enormous difficulty accepting their loving gestures. These we tend to interpret or ignore, entirely missing the point.

A patient's loving gestures can take on an infinite variety of expression. It is important that we try to distinguish them from non-adaptive enactment or other collusive enticement. For example, sometimes a patient can offer an expression of sincere gratitude. Before dismissing it with interpretations of idealisation, manipulation, or sexual bidding, which they certainly might represent on occasion, I have found a simple "Thank you" to be of enormous value. An interpretation at such a time can be experienced as a devaluation, attack, or rejection. Some other, but by no means exclusive, examples I have come across have included receiving appropriate gifts, realistic compliments, constructive criticism, or real concern about real illness.

As an illustration, I think of another patient of mine. He is a thirty-something man, the son of a successful celebrity father. His father would engage in frequent contact with adoring audiences whom he likewise blessed with visible adoration. When in the presence of his son, my patient, he remained distant, aloof, and reticent. My patient reported frequent attempts to connect with his father that were shunned, ignored, or criticised. He especially recalled repeated attempts to enter his father's study, a place where his father isolated himself most of the time when at home. He craved a connection of any kind with his father, whether it was to shoot the breeze, get advice, or talk about his own endeavours. He had both athletic and artistic ability that went mostly unnoticed. When he entered the study, his father would typically regard him with a blank stare and remain eerily silent until my patient would quietly exit, nursing the sinking feeling of an unwelcome and deplorable intruder in his father's life. I remarked that while his father had rarely expressed generous feelings of love and pride towards him, what was equally, if not more unbearable, was that his father could not accept his offerings of love and friendship. My patient concurred, breaking into deep sobs. He desperately wanted his father to receive his adoration, to accept his kudos and offerings of friendship. Being the youngest by many years in a house with much older siblings and a self-centred narcissistic mother he looked to his father lovingly, as an ally. Unable to tolerate his father not accepting his offers of "sonship", he retreated to an invisible, withdrawn, and dejected place he continues to occupy as an adult.

Empathic attunement to psychic organisation

Relational analysts routinely hold up empathy or empathic attunement as a requisite provision of a good object. It is far beyond the scope of this chapter to explore the development, phenomenology, or nuanced processes of therapeutic empathy. I would like, however to note an observation on a specific use of empathy, gleaned from my work, that holds consequence for both theory and therapy.

While empathy is a concept more associated with self psychology than Fairbairn, it is my contention that when Fairbairn bases healthy development on the parent's ability to love the child *for who the child is* and not for what the narcissistic parent requires the child to be, he is appealing essentially to the parent's ability to perceive and be empathic to the needs of the particular child. By adding *for who the child is*, he is implying that the provision of love will be unique for each child and their level of development. By extension, he is implying that a key provision of the love one expresses to a child is first rooted in the capacity of a parent to be empathic to the uniqueness of each child, his or her temperament, developmental stage, and needs. The love of a parent who does not have the ability to be empathic will be compromised.

Likewise, a therapist needs to hone his loving empathy for the patient. It is my contention that a specific and crucial form of empathy involves the analyst's being aware of and empathising with the level of psychic organisation of the patient, including the accompanying powerful affects. By psychic organisation I am referring to the positional psychic organisations identified by Klein (1935) and more recently expounded upon by Ogden (1986), namely the paranoid/schizoid and the depressive. These levels of organisation each beckon for a different form of empathy as they emerge in treatment. Leaving the depressive position for another paper, I wish to describe here a variant of empathy needed by a patient operating in the paranoid/schizoid position. When a patient functions in this position, the empathic attunement is strengthened by the analyst recognising and reflecting to the patient an understanding of the patient's *experience* of their psychic level of organisation, and a diminution of attention to interpretation of psychic meaning or conflict. It also involves the analyst being responsive to the strength of the powerful accompanying affects, particularly murderous rage and fear of annihilation, which are the hallmarks of this psychic position.

The experience of the paranoid/schizoid psychic organisation, as expanded upon by Ogden (ibid.), devolves into a state of "it"-ness. Emotions, thoughts, and even behaviours do not feel to be arising from a locus within the patient. Instead, they are experienced as happening to the patient. As such, the truth of moment to moment psychic meaning is, for the patient, derived from a perceived absolute external truth. The patient has no sense that they are in any way the arbiters of meaning, the masters of their own perceptions. The contemptuous patient does not *imagine* you are a hopeless incompetent, they *know* that you are a hopeless incompetent, with no room for degrees of freedom. The adoring, idealising patient experiences the truth of his feelings similarly. Consequently, his rancour towards or adoration of you is not debatable; it is the only reasonable response from a reasonable person whose reasoning follows from the absolute truth. Furthermore, since this organisation contains split-off islands of experience, in which time has collapsed into an eternal dimensionless plane, not only do the experiences of the paranoid/schizoid organisation contain no past or future, there is also no communication with other states. The patient has no awareness he possesses alternative feelings, or could imagine the possibilities of other feeling perspectives at any point in time, past or future.

The a-historicity (ibid.) of a paranoid/schizoid organisational truth requires that the analyst address his or her empathic attunement to just this experience. For example, a patient of mine who functioned in a relatively healthy state of mutuality with me most of the time came to her session the day following her mother's death from chronic alcoholism. I greeted her with an appropriate expression of sympathy. She instantly flew into a vitriolic spewing of rage at me, declaring that my sympathy had nothing to do with her, it was rooted solely in my selfish preoccupation with my desire to be liked. I was merely a "touchy-feely leftover from the Sixties".

So once again, what is a good object to do?

I wondered, then, was she right? Have my sensibilities, honestly garnered in the Sixties, appear as immature and idealistic as they existed then? Was my expression of sympathy formulaic? Or did her rage represent a displacement of her anger towards her mother, who, being dead became a more guilt evoking target? Do I empathise with her anger? Or do I interpret? Or what?

As per what I have been arguing, I first discerned that my patient, at that moment, was ensconced in a paranoid/schizoid organisation of self and other. In that place, she lacked capability to understand an interpretation, be it transferential, interpersonal, intersubjective, or whatever. The organisation that could process the self-generative meaning of her experience was split off and unavailable to her. An interpretation at that moment would have appeared useless at best, and attacking at worst. Likewise, an empathic response to her affects would similarly fly out the window unless they had been offered with a full resonance to the extreme severity of their essence. "You're in a rage at me," would be experienced as a lame attempt at stating the obvious.

I maintain that what was needed in the situation was an empathic communication of the state of her state, the immediate experience of her paranoid/schizoid way of organising and enduring her mother's death, including a connection with the accompanying affects. It is important that we do not shy away from naming the experience of these disorganising, annihilating, and murderous affects. Focusing on the temporal discontinuity of her experience of me as a whole integrated person, I offered to my patient a statement something like, "It must be terrifying to trust me one minute, and have that trust evaporate entirely the next. Now it must seem that our relationship is permanently damaged by your rage and that hopes for it ever being re-established, futile." I made no interpretative ties to her mother, no identification of internal conflicts.

Gradually, and with the use of empathic attunement to her paranoid/schizoid states of chaos, futility, and hopelessness, she began to tolerate and internalise my calm loving offerings of holding. The process of dynamically identifying with a good (in this case surviving and integrating) object was jump-started as she returned to her previously rather high level of depressive position functioning. It also led to a greater understanding of the meanings of her original outburst following her mother's death. One of many such meanings was that she had been struggling to hold on to the internalisations of her mother by identifying with her proneness to unpredictable vitriolic outbursts. While the meanings of her outbursts were of course important, they could not be of use to her until she strengthened her ability to regain access to a more integrated and integrating depressive position organisation of self and other, a strengthening she gained in interaction with a new, loving good object.

References

Appelbaum, G. (1999). *Considering the Complexity of Analytic Love: A Relational Perspective.* [Paper presented at the Focus Series of the National Institute for the Psychotherapies Psychoanalytic Association, New York.

Bromberg, P. H. (1998). *Standing in the Spaces.* Hillsdale, NJ: Analytic Press.

Burke, W. F. (1992). Countertransference disclosure and the asymmetry/mutuality dilemma. *Psychoanalytic Dialogues,* 2: 241–271.

Davies, J. M. (1994). Love in the afternoon: A relational reconsideration of desire and dread in the countertransference. *Psychoanalytic Dialogues,* 4: 153–170.

Fairbairn, W. R. D. (1952). *Psychoanalytic Studies of the Personality.* London: Tavistock.

Fairbairn, W. R. D. (1958a). On the nature and aims of psycho-analytical treatment. *International Journal of Psychoanalysis,* 29: 374–385. In: D. E. Scharff & E. F. Birtles (Eds.), *From Instinct to Self: Selected Papers of W. R. D. Fairbairn, Volume I: Clinical and Theoretical Papers* (pp. 74–92). Northvale, NJ: Jason Aronson, 1994.

Greenberg, J. (1995). Self-disclosure: Is it psychoanalytic? *Contemporary Psychoanalysis,* 31: 193–247.

Harrow, J. A. (1998). The Scottish connection—Suttie-Fairbairn-Sutherland: A quiet revolution. In: N. J. Skolnick & D. E. Scharff (Eds.), *Fairbairn, Then and Now* (pp. 3–17). Hillsdale, NJ: Analytic Press.

Hirsch, I. (1994). Countertransference love and theoretical model. *Psychoanalytic Dialogues, 4*: 171–192.

Hoffman, I. Z. (1983). The patient as interpreter of the analyst's experience. *Contemporary Psychoanalysis, 19*: 389–442.

Hoffman, I. Z. (1998). *Ritual and Sponteneity in the Relational Process*. Hillsdale, NJ: Analytic Press.

Klein, M. (1935). A contribution to the psychogenesis of manic states. In: *Love, Guilt and Reparation, and Other Works, 1921–1945*. New York: Free Press, 1964.

Klein, M. (1937). Love, guilt and reparation. In: *Love, Guilt and Reparation, and Other Works, 1921–1945*. New York: Free Press, 1964.

Kohut. H. (1984). *How Does Analysis Cure?* Chicago, IL: University of Chicago Press.

Lipton, S. D. (1983). A critique of so-called standard psychoanalytic technique. *Contemporary Psychoanalysis, 19*: 35–45.

Mitchell, S. (1988). *Relational Concepts in Psychoanalysis*. Cambridge, MA: Harvard University Press.

Mitchell, S. (1996). Fairbairn's object seeking: Between paradigms. In: N. J. Skolnick & D. E. Scharff (Eds.), *Fairbairn, Then and Now* (pp. 115–136). Hillsdale, NJ: Analytic Press, 1998.

Mitchell, S. (2001). *From Angels to Muses: Idealization, Fantasy and the "Illusions of Romance"*. [Paper presented posthumously at the National Institute for the Psychotherapies' Annual Colloquium, New York.]

Ogden, T. H. (1986). *The Matrix of the Mind*. Northvale, NJ: Jason Aronson.

Ogden, T. H. (1994). *Subjects of Analysis*. Northvale, NJ: Jason Aronson.

Pick, I. B. (1985). Working through in the countertransference. In: E. B. Spillius (Ed.), *Melanie Klein Today, Vol. 2* (pp. 34–47). New York: Routledge, 1988.

Racker, H. (1968). *Transference and Countertransference*. New York: International Universities Press.

Skolnick, N. J. (1999). *Psychoanalysis On (and Off?) the Couch: A Relational Perspective*. [Paper presented at the Connecticut Society for Psychoanalytic Psychology, New Haven, CT.]

Skolnick, N. J., & Scharff, D. E. (1992). Introduction. In: N. J. Skolnick & S. C. Warshaw (Eds.), *Relational Perspectives in Psychoanalysis* (pp. xxiii–xxix). Hillsdale, NJ: Analytic Press.

Stolorow, R. D., & Atwood, G. E. (1992). *The Intersubjective Foundations of Psychoanalytic Life*. Hillsdale, NJ: Analytic Press.

Suttie, I. (1988). *Origins of Love and Hate*. London: Free Association.

Tansey, M. J. (1994). Sexual attraction and phobic dread in the countertransference. *Psychoanalytic Dialogues, 4*: 139–152.

Winnicott, D. W. (1965). *The Maturational Processes and the Facilitating Environment*. New York: International Universities Press.

CHAPTER TWENTY

Expanding Fairbairn's reach

David E. Scharff

Since Fairbairn first produced the basic outline of an object relations theory of mind and its applications to clinical work, his ideas have provided a sturdy framework for psychoanalysis and its applications that put relationships at the centre of development, and that place the therapeutic relationship at the heart of clinical work. This book is a testament to the depth and breadth these ideas have engendered. For me, his basic framework has continued to be the backbone of many theoretical additions that give ever more strength to an object relations approach. However, when I use the term "object relations", I include the protean developments in analytic theory, in the allied fields of family and couple therapy, in studies of human development, and in the expansion of our ideas from science that increase our understanding and reach.

In this contribution, I will summarise some of the additions that have been especially useful in augmenting my own view of the analytic universe. Fairbairn's basic contribution is summarised in the 1996 paper by Ellinor Fairbairn Birtles and myself (reprinted in Chapter One), which also gives the historical context of his core ideas. Many of these foundational concepts are explored at length in other contributions in this volume. What follows uses that paper as its foundation.

I will begin this account of recent developments with some scientific advances in neuroscience and developmental psychology. Mirror neurons were discovered about twenty years ago, by Rizzolatti and his colleagues in Parma (Rizzolatti, Fogassi, & Gallese, 2006). They are single cells found situated in the motor cortex of monkeys, adjacent to motor neurons. They fire either when a subject makes a purposeful action (like picking up a cup to drink) or when the subject sees another individual make that action. Furthermore, the same neurons fire to a sound or other sensory experience that indicates the action—for instance the sound of crumpling paper will trigger the same firing that would happen in response to seeing paper crumpled. That is to say, mirror neuron firing is cross modal, something that is important for the verbal triggering of mirror neuron response. The Parma research group realised that mirror neurons are the basis of imitative learning, and with Ferrari and colleagues' (2003) discovery of facial mirror neurons, and Gallese's (2009) extension of these to the idea of "instantiated emotional experience", mirror neurons were established as the basis for the transfer of emotional experience from one person into another. Single cell recording is possible in monkeys but not humans, but other instrumentation has allowed for measurement of mirror neuron activity in humans as well. This basis for imitative learning and the transfer of emotional experience is present at birth. It is hard-wired in us, and then is subject to modification and growing sophistication throughout development. For instance, mirror neurons that fire in response to an emotional experience signalled through facial expression or sound—like crying or a painful experience—will fire more robustly when the observation is of someone the subject is emotionally related to, than they will to observation of a stranger.

A particular aspect of developmental science that fits neatly with this series of basic neuroscience discoveries is the work by Tomkins (1995) and his colleagues on the expression of emotions in humans, especially the role of facial expression and people's ability to read emotions in other people's faces. We are able to read basic emotions more easily when faces are in movement. However, Tomkins was able to find still pictures of faces that allowed for a high degree of reliability in reading basic emotions. The face is an elaborate signalling system that lets others know what we are feeling and also—a different matter—to convey more selectively what we wish to convey to them about feelings. We carry a background affect that is visible in our faces, and we learn from birth to read others' faces. Distortions in development can impede or confuse our ability to read ambiguous facial expression, or distort what we see, and emotional development also guides what we convey to others on our faces. For instance, traumatised people may carry a facial signal of fear, and themselves may misread a neutral face as angry with regularity. In addition, we all learn to modify and falsify what we convey to others about our emotions and disguise what we signal to others. We know the difference between a real smile of delight that blooms suddenly and fades slowly, and the signal of a feigned or sarcastic smile, that might rise and fall differently. We learn to signal in these ways, and to read signals.

Both of these areas of research fit with Fairbairn's location of the introjection of experience as the basis of the organisation of mind. Fairbairn thought that experience with the mother was taken in at first only because the relationship was inevitably disappointing to some degree. There I think he was wrong: one of the several modifications that we need to make to his thinking is to understand that infants are hard-wired to take in all experience—satisfying and disappointing, matters of intense curiosity and matters of everyday business—as the building blocks of our minds, but from the correction of that idea on the initial motivation for introjection of emotional experience, his model holds. He emphasised the introjection of experience, and we need to acknowledge the equal importance of the projection of experience as first proposed by Freud and Klein. This is a necessary correlate that Fairbairn would have agreed to. In this way, the ideas on the projection of internal experience, more fully spelled out by Klein (1946) and her followers, on the actions of projective and introjective identification give analytic theory neuroscience backing both through the action of mirror neurons and through emotional signalling of facial expression and vocal intonation. Joining these differing levels of study of human mechanisms of unconscious communication, we see a process that begins with single cell firing and proceeds up the line of complexity to the inbuilt capacity to read and experience others' actions and emotions. The infant is hard-wired to reach out into the human environment to look for emotional and interpersonal experience because these are necessary ingredients for the construction of mind in the way that Fairbairn believed (Freeman, 2007).

I turn now to the work of Donald Winnicott (1960), whose close observations of mothers and infants added depth to Fairbairn's basic structure concerning the centrality of the parent–infant relationship in early development. His inspiration for his seminal work on transitional phenomena and transitional objects (1971) came from reading about Fairbairn's transitional ways of relating in the gradual move from infantile dependence to mature interdependence. Winnicott provided the first close analytic study of how emotional experience is learned in the arms of parental facilitation, passed on by the parent and taken in by the growing child. His studies fleshed out Fairbairn's more schematic and general ideas on the transmission of emotional experience from parent to child.

Bion (1970) provided another, more purely analytic building block in his study of mutual projective and introjective identification. In doing this, he transformed Klein's contribution of projective identification into a theory of the development of mind. In his construct of the container/contained he developed a model for the way a parent's mind and personality became the crucible for the development of the mind of the growing infant and child through the constant and mutual interacting cycles of projective and introjective identification. To build his mind, the child needs to be held psychologically in the emotional arms of the environment mother that Winnicott proposed; and then through a multitude of interactions across the transitional space, external interactions are taken into the mind where they become the building blocks of emotional growth. The mother, with her capacity for what Bion called her unconscious "reverie", which we can also think of as dream-work, transforms the infant's unstructured and primitive anxieties and experiences into incrementally higher levels of organisation (Ferro, 2009; Grotstein, 2000; Ogden, 2009). This process builds the infant and growing child's mind. All of this fits well with Fairbairn's conjectures about the development of the basic endopsychic situation, but these later contributions add substantially to our understanding.

Now we turn to attachment research and its extensions as another arena in which research on child development adds to Fairbairn's contribution. In a seminar for trainees at the Tavistock Clinic in 1973, John Bowlby told me that he drew from Fairbairn more than any other analytic thinker. His conception of the importance of the early treatment of infants by their caregivers, the painful impact on children when mothers threaten to leave them, the trauma of early loss, and the whole set of processes formulated in his ground-breaking *Attachment and Loss* volumes (Bowlby, 1969, 1973, 1980), add the power of ethology and observational research to a paradigm that is a direct descendent of Fairbairn's object relations theory. Bowlby drew directly from the animal studies of ethologists Robert Hinde (1970), Konrad Lorenz (1966), Harry Harlow (1961), and others in establishing a biological rationale for attachment and the vicissitudes of its rupture through loss and threats of loss. The conceptual schema he offered for the most important aspects of what analysis had heretofore thought of in the general term "pre-Oedipal development" established the early parent–infant relationship as the bedrock of development.

Bowlby's colleague, Mary Ainsworth (Ainsworth, Blehar, Waters, & Wall, 1978) operationalised attachment categories through her research in Uganda and Charlottesville. She designed the "Strange Situation" to test and categorise the infant's attachment status to her parents in a series of brief encounters in which a mother separates from her twelve-month-old infant with a stranger present, and the reunion episodes are coded. In this way, Ainsworth described secure, anxious, and distancing attachment styles (not pathologies but styles) according to the amount and pattern of expression of anxiety. These categories are now known as 1) secure, 2) insecure/avoidant, and 3) insecure/resistant. Later Mary Main (1995) described a group that had previously been uncodable, which formed the fourth attachment group: the disorganised/disoriented pattern, often seen in children with severe deprivation or trauma, or in children whose parents who had suffered deprivation or trauma.

Attachment research has led to further elaboration of Fairbairn's concepts. For instance, when Main and her colleagues described adult attachment styles, coded through linguistic analysis of the Adult Attachment Interview (Main & Solomon, 1990) using categories congruent with the infant and child attachment codings, it was possible for the first time to show that the attachment style encoded in an adult mind before the birth of her child was predictive of the attachment pattern that characterised that mother and child at twelve months. In other words, for the first time in the history of psychoanalysis and child development, research demonstrated the intergenerational transmission of psychic organisation and the behavioural aspects of that transmission. Attachment categories have also been used to inform clinical observation, and as a basis for innovation of therapeutic strategies (Holmes, 2010).

It is often unnoticed that Fairbairn's categories of acceptable and rejected internal object relations overlap considerably with the attachment schema. His category of the rejecting/persecuting internal object tied to the anti-libidinal ego or internal saboteur is virtually the same as the relationship in many insecure external attachments. The excessively exciting internal object constellation between the libidinal ego and exciting object correlates especially with the observable anxiety of insecure/avoidant attachments. When he described the hysterical personality (1954) as tolerating neither closeness nor seduction, he was in the territory of the insecure/avoidant pattern and of the disorganised/disoriented pattern. His paper on schizoid personality (1940) describes the insecure/resistant pattern. When personality is mainly characterised by a healthy relationship between the central ego and a good-enough or ideal object, this describes the internal correlate of an externally secure pattern. And finally, Fairbairn describes how the disorganising effect of trauma leads to deep splits and disorganisation of personality. This description enables us to better understand the origin of the internal organisation associated with disorganised/disoriented attachments as described in the attachment literature and the pathologies often associated with them.

In subsequent developments, Fonagy, Target, and their colleagues have transformed attachment theory, which was primarily a research tool, into something closer to clinical life. Their ground-breaking book, *Affect Regulation, Mentalization, and the Development of the Self* (Fonagy, Gergely, Jurist, & Target, 2003), proposed that the main importance of attachment was not, as Bowlby had suggested, merely survival in the wild, but the development of a mind that could thrive in social situations. For humans, this meant affect regulation, and development of reflective function by mentalisation of emotional and interpersonal experience. By growing a capacity to read both others' minds and one's own mind, and through the development of a "theory of mind", the person develops a high degree of predictive capacity in social situations. This line of research has provided an alternative way to operationalise concepts that derive from both attachment theory and child developmental research. Fairbairn's legacy can still be traced through Bowlby to these elaborations. Fonagy and his colleagues have also developed therapies based on patients' capacities for mentalisation that are operationalised forms of analytic therapies designed for populations that are deficient in mentalising capacity (Allen, Fonagy, & Bateman, 2008). In these ways and many more, attachment researchers have operationalised Fairbairn's thinking to the enormous advantage of our clinical and developmental reach.

The same can be said of Grotstein's writing on psychic mechanisms (1981) and Kernberg's (1975, 1980) work on personality disorders and their treatment, which covers overlapping clinical territory with Fonagy's, as does the relational school of psychoanalysis. However, I will not elaborate further on these, as Kernberg has written separately for this volume, and other contributions cover the relational school and the work of Stephen Mitchell (2000), its founder.

Chaos theory, the link, and the analytic field

Let us draw now on the findings analysis has begun to import from chaos or complexity theory. Chaos theory developed from mathematics and the physical sciences as a study of non-linear dynamic systems, which are characterised by continuous feedback (Gleick, 1987). It can be seen as an elaboration of open systems theory and of information processing. These systems show an extreme sensitivity to initial conditions, because small differences in the operating equations make very large and unpredictable effects downstream when the equations have been iterated thousands or millions of times. Such complex systems demonstrate complex patterns that have "fractal similarity" or similarity of pattern at differing levels of scale. In human development, for instance, there is fractal similarity between patterns of speech, action, character, and interaction with others. Clinically we rely on fractal similarity when we assume that what we learn in the small sample of a clinical session gives us a fair idea of the larger patterns in a person's overall life. We also rely on the experience that can be tracked in physical dynamic systems that changes at a small order of scale or a small sector of a dynamic system can effect change in larger dimensions. Therefore, something that changes inside a clinical hour, for instance in the transference, has the potential to affect a person's outside life, for instance the interactions with his partner, children, or colleagues. Dynamic systems can act like closed systems, with relatively fixed patterns, or like open systems in communication and mutual influence with surrounding larger systems. A system may exhibit relative sturdiness, resistance to change in the regions that are relatively far from the edges of chaos, but are more open to influence and change at the edge of chaos.

In other contributions, I have explored several interesting aspects of chaos theory that can inform clinical theory and clinical work (Scharff & Scharff, 1998, 2011). Here I only want to outline a couple of the issues that relate to Fairbairn's ideas. Fairbairn's theory of the endopsychic situation is as a dynamic system of continuously interacting subunits or operating systems. It is a system in which the central ego or self acts primarily on the subunits, but in which all aspects of personality are in interaction with others, the quality of interaction determined by affective tone, other aspects of internal experience, and on external experience. He has described the complex dynamic system of the individual mind in continual interaction with the external social world—a dynamic, non-linear system that, like dynamic systems, has emergent properties and that, in health, continues to evolve to greater levels of complexity and, at the same time, of integration. In his 1958 paper "On the Nature and Aims of Psycho-analytical Treatment", Fairbairn wrote that the patient tries to maintain his inner world as a closed system, while it is the analyst's job to breach the closed system—to open the patient's fixed ways of being to the influence of the wider world. This language, that was informed by systems theory, moves beyond it towards chaos theory and the importance of complex mutual influence in evolving, dynamic, open systems.

Fairbairn saw that the child's mind was formed by the introjection of an image of the object that derived from external interaction, and that then the individual mind modified what had been taken in. However, Fairbairn was clear that the part of the mind modelled by identification with the external object was part of the ego, and as such, was capable of agency, or of initiating action and thought alongside that part of the ego identified as "self". In his "Endopsychic" paper (1944) and "Observations on the Nature of Hysterical States" (1954b) he discussed the intrapsychic dynamics in sophisticated ways, but he did not quite see the full complexity of the situation. For instance, he described the way that, in hysterical states, the anti-libidinal object constellation attacks the libidinal one, but he did not see that this is but one dynamic—that the libidinal constellation can equally well attack (that is suppress) the anti-libidinal one. In this paper, it is implicit that in health, there is a more open dynamic among all parts of the psychic structure, but this is not fully spelled out. Furthermore, Fairbairn did not quite grasp the complexity of the simultaneous mutual resonance of the internal world with the outside world. The internal world is working to balance itself at the same time as it is involved in mutual interaction and mutual influence with the external world. Kernberg (1980, this volume, Chapter Nine) has elaborated what is implicit in Fairbairn. So have applications to family and couple therapy (Framo, 1982; Scharff & Scharff, 1987, 1991). When we add the rich thinking from chaos theory and the study of dynamic systems, we can see that the mind of the individual person represents such a dynamic system that is more or less open to the environment around, constantly in mutual influence. Sometimes a person attempts to keep his mind closed to outside influence, as in Fairbairn's description of schizoid personality (1940a). In health, people develop a variety of ways of dealing with both internal and external objects, exhibit varying degrees of openness, and maintain some degree of consistency by conserving internal structure, and some degree of capacity for change under the sway of outside influence. Another term from chaos theory—"attractor"—describes the patterns or mathematical plot of activity of complex systems. An attractor can be relatively fixed and repetitive, or complex with many different and unpredictable characteristics, never quite covering the same territory twice, always changing even though general characteristics are more or less predictable. This describes the idea of character: in health, character is complex, changeable yet more or less predictable across time. In some forms of ill health, character might be constrained, all too predictable, and repetitive. The pattern here is a limited attractor, too repetitive for a sense of vitality to be in evidence. Or in another pattern of illness, it may be wildly unpredictable, fragmented, variable, and tempestuous. However, this unpredictable and seemingly disconnected quality may be itself predictable, a kind of predictable unpredictability. In this case, the attractor is one of thinly connected sub-patterns of behaviour and mental organisation without an overall organising consistency. This could describe the characteristically changeable actions of someone with trauma, disorganised attachment, and borderline personality.

Chaos theory also shows that a complex system can have sub-units, sub-attractor patterns that have their own pattern while essentially being part of a larger pattern where these sub-patterns do not hold sway. This can be true for personality functioning, where a person can have a pattern that characterises them when angry, another when loving, and another when working. The way a complex attractor can swing from one pattern to another, under the dynamic influence of its internal workings or of external influence, helps understand how different aspects of personality emerge in differing circumstances.

In health, complex systems have emergent properties that cannot be predicted from the sum of the sub-systems. It is an inherent property of complex systems to evolve towards higher levels of complexity. This idea forms a counterpoint to Fairbairn's idea of the evolution of the self to increasing levels of integration following the initial splitting process of the simpler but relatively unsplit mind, Fairbairn's original model both of the mind and of the original introjection of a primary, unsplit object. His idea of progressive re-integration as the goal of maturation is a bit limited. The usefulness of the splitting of mind into parts is that the parts can then reconnect not in a re-synthesis towards the *original* wholeness, but in ways of evolving, emergent complexity, and richness that offers new potential, and as Sutherland has suggested, the complexity of an autonomous self (Jill Scharff, this volume, Chapter Twenty-Eight; Sutherland, 1984). There is another value of this model at a different level of conceptualisation—a fractal similarity between Fairbairn's endopsychic theory and a finding in theory itself. We can see now that aspects of analytic theory that have claimed universality may not be universally true, but may nonetheless be true or helpful in certain circumstances. This has come home to me most in understanding the place of some of Freud's foundational discoveries. His psychosocial developmental theory, the pleasure principle, death instinct, for instance, are limited truths, not universals. They have clinical usefulness, and some people act as though organised by them. But in health, development is not linear. It is full of complexities. It circles back on itself. Some people act as though organised by a death drive, which Fairbairn described as a fallback position from failures of relating through attachment to bad objects. With the aid of chaos theory, we can see that partial truths do fit into the overall complexity of the theory we need, and that we do not have to abandon the one to accept the other. They have their place as parts of complex patterns that, while not always true, do hold in certain regions of behaviour and in certain situations.

Now we come to the problem of communication between minds. Bion's extension of introjective and projective identification to the model of the container/contained gave an important thrust to analytic thinking. It is often overlooked in pure psychoanalytic circles that Henry Dicks, in his ground-breaking work *Marital Tensions*, developed a clinical picture of how mutual projective and introjective identification work clinically in the development of marital partnerships. He described detailed clinical pictures of their interaction, and further showed how the cycles of mutual projective identification build an overarching pattern between spouses, which he called the joint marital personality (1967). Jill Scharff and I have extended his work further in our investigations of family therapy, sexual development, and clinical sexual issues (D. E. Scharff, 1982; Scharff & Scharff, 1987, 1991; J. S. Scharff, 1992). We can now see that the external family world is in constant dynamic interaction with each person's internal world. Hopper's (2003) description of the social unconscious has given us a window into the constant exchange between individuals and the social world beyond the family. Aviram (2009, Chapter Thirty-Seven, this volume) refers directly to Fairbairn's model of mind in positing that we also have an internal "social object" that represents the internalisation of experience with the wider world, to which we relate with the full range of possibilities in similar ways to our other internal relations with personal objects.

While these developments were going on in the English language literature, another literature grew up in Argentina beginning in the 1950s with the work of Pichon-Rivière (English translation of Pichon-Rivière's writing in preparation, R. Losso, L. Setton, and D. E. Scharff, editors; Setton, Chapter Twenty-Nine, this volume), who developed the idea of the link (*el vinculo* in Spanish) to describe the bonds that join each person with preceding and succeeding generations in the vertical link, and that join the person with family and the social world in the horizontal link. Family and couple are at the crosshairs between generational influence and social influence. This set of ideas, developing independently in the Spanish-speaking world, certainly derived from Pichon-Rivière's knowledge of Klein, and presumably from his familiarity with Fairbairn. These ideas led Pichon-Rivière and other Latin American authors such as Berenstein (1991) to develop ideas of social psychology and family therapy, and for Kaës (2007) in France, to extend ideas about the link to his work on group and family therapy.

Madeline and Willy Baranger (1961, 2009), students of Pichon-Rivière, then described the analytic field in which mental interchange occurs. The field encompasses both patient and therapist as total personalities and minds, joined in conscious and unconscious interaction. The field is the location of action of projective and introjective identification and the container/contained as elaborated in the work of Ferro (2009), and on the mutuality of "dreaming in the field" in the work of Ogden (2005, 2009) and Grotstein (2000). For these writers, the idea of dreaming means the constant interplay of unconscious and conscious processes in the analytic situation. Unconscious processes are never off-line. They are ubiquitous; they underlie conscious processes all through the day, and have ascendency in night dreams. The analyst's reverie allows the penetration of her unconscious to her work, but in the field, there is a mutuality of unconscious process. Jill Scharff and I (Scharff & Scharff, 2011) have written that this mutuality of unconscious process is not confined to the therapeutic situation, but is present throughout life, from the beginning of life when infant and parents communicate only through affective, essentially unconscious processes, through family and social life, and in therapy as well. It was Freud who first described unconscious communication as central to analysis (Brown, 2011; Freud, 1915e), even at the same time that he described the unconscious as a property of the individual. I believe that the idea of unconscious communication as present from the beginning of life is implied by Fairbairn's conceptualisation of endopsychic structure. Clearly Fairbairn did not mean that mothers and infants communicate consciously when he described the infant's introjection of her interactions with mother, but exactly how the infant understands her mother's mental attitude was not spelled out. We need the whole panoply of ideas available to us to conceptualise the complexity of the communicative process—from Melanie Klein's projective and introjective identification, via Bion's elaboration of the container/contained model of the growth of mind, and the ideas of mentalising based on secure attachment, to ideas of the link and the field, and most recently of dreaming in the field. And so we need all these ideas to elaborate the mechanisms of mind that Fairbairn first sketched out.

Fairbairn's endopsychic structure remains, for me, the most rigorous model of mind that we have available. It has been a sturdy model, one that readily welcomes additions such as the ones I have suggested that increase the power of his thinking. Any field must move and grow, and analytic thinking must, too. But I have been impressed how Fairbairn's model welcomes a multitude of useful additions while maintaining its basic integrity, enhancing the value of such innovative ideas while improving its own usefulness through their augmentations.

References

Ainsworth, M. D., Blehar, M. C., Waters, E., & Wall, S. (1978). *Patterns of Attachment: A Psychological Study of the Strange Situation*. Hillsdale, NJ: Lawrence Erlbaum.

Allen, J. G., Fonagy, P., & Bateman, A. W. (2008). *Mentalizing in Clinical Practice*. Arlington, VA: American Psychiatric Publishing.

Aviram, R. (2009). *The Relational Origins of Prejudice*. Lanham, MD: Jason Aronson.

Baranger, M., & Baranger, W. (1961). The analytic situation as a dynamic field. *International Journal of Psychoanalysis, 89*: 795–896.

Baranger, M., & Baranger, W. (2009). *The Work of Confluence: Listening and Interpreting in the Psychoanalytic Field* (L. G. Firoini, Ed.). London: Karnac.

Berenstein, I. (1991). *Psicoanalizar una familia*. Buenos Aires, Argentina: Paidos.

Bion, W. R. (1970). *Attention and Interpretation*. London: Heinemann.

Bowlby, J. (1969, 1973, 1980). *Attachment and Loss (Three Volumes)*. London: Hogarth.

Brown, L. J. (2011). *Intersubjective Processes and the Unconscious*. Hove, UK: Routledge.

Dicks, H. V. (1967). *Marital Tensions*. London: Routledge and Kegan Paul.

Fairbairn, W. R. D. (1940a). Schizoid factors in the personality. In: *Psychoanalytic Studies of the Personality* (pp. 3–27). London: Tavistock, 1952.

Fairbairn, W. R. D. (1944). Endopsychic structure considered in terms of object-relationships. *International Journal of Psychoanalysis, 25*: 70–92. In: *Psychoanalytic Studies of the Personality* (pp. 82–135). London: Tavistock, 1952.

Fairbairn, W. R. D. (1954b). Observations on the nature of hysterical states. *British Journal of Medical Psychology, 27*(3): 106–125. In: D. E. Scharff & E. F. Birtles (Eds.), *From Instinct to Self: Selected Papers of W. R. D. Fairbairn, Volume I: Clinical and Theoretical Papers* (pp. 13–40). Northvale, NJ: Jason Aronson, 1994.

Fairbairn, W. R. D. (1958a). On the nature and aims of psycho-analytical treatment. In: D. E. Scharff & E. F. Birtles (Eds.), *From Instinct to Self: Selected Papers of W. R. D. Fairbairn, Volume I: Clinical and Theoretical Papers* (pp. 74–92). Northvale, NJ: Jason Aronson, 1994.

Ferrari, P. F., Gallese, V., Rizzolatti, G., & Fogassi, L. (2003). Mirror neurons responding to the observation of ingestive and communicative mouth actions in the monkey ventral premotor cortex. *European Journal of Neuroscience, 17*: 1703–1714.

Ferro, A. (2009). *Mind Works: Techniques and Creativity in Psychoanalysis*. London: Routledge.

Fonagy, P., Gergely, B., Jurist, F., & Target, M. (2003). *Affect Regulation, Mentalization, and the Development of the Self*. New York: Other Press.

Framo, J. L. (1982). *Explorations in Marital and Family Therapy*. New York: Springer.

Freeman, W. J. (2007). A biological theory of brain function and its relevance to psychoanalysis. In: C. Piers, J. P. Muller, & J. Brent (Eds.), *Self-Organizing Complexity in Psychological Systems* (pp. 15–36). Lanham, MD: Jason Aronson.

Freud, S. (1915e). The unconscious. *S. E., 14*: 159–215.

Gallese, V. (2009). Mirror neurons, embodied simulation, and the neural basis of social identification. *Psychoanalytic Dialogues, 19*(5): 519–536.

Gleick, J. (1987). *Chaos*. New York: Viking Penguin.

Grotstein, J. S. (1981). *Splitting and Projective Identification*. New York: Jason Aronson.

Grotstein, J. S. (2000). *Who Is the Dreamer Who Dreams the Dream?* Hillsdale, NJ: Analytic Press.

Harlow, H. F. (1961). The development of affectional patterns in infant monkeys. In: B. M. Foss (Ed.), *Determinants of Infant Behaviour, vol. 1*. London: Methuen.

Hinde, R. A. (1970). *Animal Behaviour: A Synthesis of Ethology and Comparative Psychology. Second Edition*. New York: McGraw-Hill.

Holmes, J. (2010). *Exploring in Security*. London: Routledge.

Hopper, E. (2003). *The Social Unconscious*. London: Jessica Kingsley.

Kaës, R. (2007). *Linking, Alliances, and Shared Space*. London: International Psychoanalytical Association.

Kernberg, O. F. (1975). *Borderline Conditions and Pathological Narcissism*. New York: Jason Aronson.

Kernberg, O. F. (1980). *Internal World and External Reality*. New York: Jason Aronson.

Klein, M. (1946). Notes on some schizoid mechanisms. *International Journal of Psychoanalysis, 27*: 99–110.

Lorenz, K. (1966). *On Aggression*. New York: Harcourt, Brace and World.

Main, M. (1995). Attachment: Overview with implications for clinical work. In: S. Goldberg, R. Muir, & J. Kerr (Eds.), *Attachment Theory* (pp. 407–475). Hillsdale, NJ: Analytic Press.

Main, M., & Solomon, J. (1990). Procedures for identifying infants as disorganized/disoriented during the Ainsworth Strange Situation. In: M. Greenberg, D. Cichetti, & M. Cummings (Eds.), *Attachment in Preschool Years* (pp. 95–124). Chicago, IL: University of Chicago Press.

Mitchell, S. A. (2000). *Relationality: From Attachment to Intersubjectivity*. Hillsdale, NJ: Analytic Press.

Ogden, T. H. (2005). *This Art of Psychoanalysis: Dreaming Undreamt Dreams and Interrupted Cries*. London: Routledge.

Ogden, T. H. (2009). *Rediscovering Psychoanalysis: Thinking and Dreaming, Learning and Forgetting*. London: Routledge.

Pichon-Rivière, E. (In preparation). *The Social Link and Other Papers* (tentative title). R. Losso, L. Setton, & D. E. Scharff (Eds.). Lanham, MD: Jason Aronson.

Rizzolatti, G., Fogassi, L., & Gallese, V. (2006). Mirrors in the mind. *Scientific American*, November 2006: 54–61.

Scharff, D. E. (1982). *The Sexual Relationship*. London: Routledge and Kegan Paul. [Reprinted with a new introduction, Northvale, NJ: Jason Aronson, 1998.]

Scharff, D. E., & Scharff, J. S. (1987). *Object Relations Family Therapy*. Northvale, NJ: Jason Aronson.

Scharff, D. E., & Scharff, J. S. (1991). *Object Relations Couple Therapy*. Northvale, NJ: Jason Aronson.

Scharff, D. E., & Scharff, J. S. (2011). *The Interpersonal Unconscious*. Lanham, MD: Jason Aronson.

Scharff, J. S. (1992). *Projective and Introjective Identification and the Use of the Therapist's Self*. Northvale, NJ: Jason Aronson.

Scharff, J. S., & Scharff, D. E. (1998). *Object Relations Individual Therapy*. Northvale, NJ: Jason Aronson.
Sutherland, J. D. (1984). *The Autonomous Self*. (J. S. Scharff, Ed.). Northvale, NJ: Jason Aronson.
Tomkins, S. S. (1995). *Exploring Affect: The Selected Writings of Silvan S. Tomkins*. (E. V. Demos, Ed.). Cambridge: Cambridge University Press.
Winnicott, D. W. (1960). The theory of the parent–infant relationship. *International Journal of Psychoanalysis, 41*: 585–595.
Winnicott, D. W. (1971). *Playing and Reality*. London: Tavistock.

PART III

THEORETICAL

INTRODUCTION TO PART III

Graham S. Clarke and David E. Scharff

The striking development of British object relations thinking in the UK in the 1960s and 1970s was led by John Sutherland, John Padel, and Harry Guntrip, all closely associated with Fairbairn. They continued development of Fairbairn's ideas by explicating them and by adding their own new developments. John Padel's paper (which has been difficult to access), is an early example of the influence of Fairbairn's thinking. It stands alongside Sutherland's paper on the conceptual model of psychoanalysis (1963) as one of the most penetrating explanations of Fairbairn's theory at a time that it was being marginalised after Winnicott's and Khan's critical review (1953). Graham S. Clarke discusses a number of Padel's papers on Fairbairn and his relationship with British psychoanalysis. Michael Stadter reviews Guntrip's vital work in keeping Fairbairn's ideas alive and in spreading his influence.

There are also resonances throughout the world of British object relations. The relationship between Fairbairn and Winnicott, discussed in Padel's papers, is developed here by Henri Vermorel, who points to some previously unelaborated parallels. Object relations thinking traces its origins back to Freud and then forward through Rank and Ferenczi, before its development by Klein and Fairbairn. Graham S. Clarke describes striking parallels between Fairbairn's and Ferenczi's theory of trauma, first published in the late 1920s just before the 1929 conference in Oxford where Fairbairn heard Ferenczi speak and might have met him personally.

One of the major champions of Fairbairn's work throughout his regrettably short life was Stephen Mitchell, whose ground-breaking work on object relations within psychoanalysis co-authored with Jay Greenberg ushered in the development of a new, wider relational approach to psychoanalysis. Mitchell's relationship to Fairbairn's ideas is explored by two contributors, Ariel Liberman and Aleksandar Dimitrijevic.

Graham S. Clarke raises here a proviso over one aspect of Mitchell's understanding of Fairbairn that he believes has led to a schism in the understanding of Fairbairn's theory that has echoes in this book. This concerns the "good object" that has been a bone of contention since the original publication of Fairbairn's early papers, and was a principal reason for Winnicott's and Khan's early rejection of Fairbairn's theory, a position they later modified (Padel, 1991, p. 344). The problem can be located in Mitchell's paper on the "Object" in Klein's and Fairbairn's theories (1981), in which he rejects Fairbairn's responses to criticisms from Kleinians about the place of the good object, and repeats Winnicott's and Khan's criticism about ambivalence being present from the earliest infancy. The most striking aspect of this rejection is, Clarke argues, what might be called a "semantic slippage", where Fairbairn's consistent use of the term "unsatisfying" to characterise the relations with the original object in the "pre-ambivalent" phase (Abraham's terms is the "first oral stage"), is translated by Mitchell into the term "ungratifying". The argument that something can be recognised by the child as "ungratifying" is then used to support Mitchell's view that the child can already discriminate between good and bad, and thus is already at an ambivalent stage. It is Clarke's view that "unsatisfying" has a crucially different meaning from "ungratifying", thereby nullifying Mitchell's point. This argument leads Mitchell to reject the model of endopsychic structure developed by Fairbairn in 1944, with no evidence that Mitchell ever changed his view. In *Object Relations in Psychoanalytic Theory* (1983) Greenberg and Mitchell use the term "gratifying" throughout, apparently adopting the term from Klein, whose use is quite different from Fairbairn's. By contrast, Sutherland, Padel, and Ogden all consistently use Fairbairn's term "unsatisfying". Mitchell's view that the 1944 paper on endopsychic structure and in particular the 1951 addendum to that chapter reflected "Fairbairn's characteristic tendency to become absorbed in schematic, intricate theoretical constructs which drift away from their clinical and developmental referents" (Mitchell, 1981, p. 80), is shared by others, for instance Rubens, and seems to have become part of the accepted Relational School understanding of Fairbairn. Others have, however, been happy to stay close to Fairbairn's development of his theory, including the 1951 addendum, his clarification in the 1954 paper on hysteria, and the reiteration in the 1963 summary of his object relations theory. This has enabled them to address the question of the good object and psychic growth in ways that seem to be consistent with the *whole* of Fairbairn's work (see Padel in Chapter Twenty One this volume). This continuing argument about the good object and the endopsychic structure as a system in Fairbairn's work is still in need of resolution.

Argentina has a vibrant, innovative psychoanalytic culture. One of the most influential thinkers whose writing life overlapped with Fairbairn was Pichon-Rivière, whose concept of the Link is explored by both Jill Savege Scharff and Lea de Setton, who look at the many connections there are between the two, with Pichon-Rivière's application to a wide range of thought and clinical settings. Ricardo Juan Rey, another Argentinian, makes an original contribution by linking the earliest state of the newborn's "intuitive position" to Fairbairn's thoughts on creativity, art, and science.

David Celani looks at Fairbairn's theory as a guide to day-to-day therapeutic practice and discovers, empirically, problems that lead him to suggest alternative ways of understanding or structuring the theory.

A perennial criticism of psychoanalysis is that it is not scientific. Joseph Schwartz argues that Fairbairn's work is exemplary science.

Fairbairn, as we know, took a degree in moral philosophy and did philosophically orientated postgraduate work in divinity. So it is fitting that we have two philosophical approaches to his theory, each addressing the problems with the sort of rigour that he would have appreciated. Tamas Pataki and Jim Poulton look at different aspects of Fairbairn's theory, one from the point of view of what it is we mean by multiple, separate selves and whether such a view can be sustained; and the other by looking at the resonances with intersubjectivist philosophy like that of Merleau-Ponty.

The postmodern understanding of the "decentring of the subject" finds some resonances within Fairbairn's theory since according to Fairbairn we are all to some degree or another split, but the aim of the therapeutic relationship is to heal those splits as far as we are able and to reintegrate those split-off sub-selves that inevitably follow our experience of the world into a more whole and a more realistic way of being with others in the world.

References

Greenberg, J., & Mitchell, S. A. (1983). *Object Relations in Psychoanalytic Theory*. London: Harvard University Press.

Mitchell, S. A. (1981). The origin and nature of the "object" in the theories of Klein and Fairbairn. In: *Fairbairn and the Origins of Object Relations* (pp. 88–111). London: Free Association.

Padel, J. (1991). The psychoanalytic theories of Melanie Klein and Donald Winnicott and their interaction in the British Society of Psychoanalysis. *Psychoanalytic Review, 78*: 325–345.

Sutherland, J. D. (1963). Object relations theory and the conceptual model of psychoanalysis. *British Journal of Medical Psychology, 36*: 109–124.

Winnicott, D. W., & Khan, M. M. R. (1953). Review: Psychoanalytic Studies of the Personality by W. R. D. Fairbairn. *International Journal of Psychoanalysis, 34*: 329–333.

CHAPTER TWENTY-ONE

The contribution of W. R. D. Fairbairn (1889–1965) to psychoanalytic theory and practice*

John Padel

Introduction

Ronald Fairbairn, a distinguished Scottish psychiatrist and scholar, has had a profound yet subtle influence on his fellow psychoanalysts of the English-speaking world. Some have consciously accepted from him what they needed and could use in their own ways; some have consciously rejected his theories, as being too radical, yet have shown unconscious acceptance of them. His influence has been both direct and indirect; almost all important English psychoanalytic works published after 1945 owe something to Fairbairn's thought yet not all could name the source of some of their ideas. Fairbairn applied Kretschmer's term schizoid to several groups of mental syndromes, tracing the connections between them and deepening the meaning of the term; he emphasised the importance of early splitting processes, and Mrs Melanie Klein adopted from him the use of the term to describe those processes. Dr Donald Winnicott was surprised to learn that Fairbairn had featured the term "transitional" ten years before he himself—differently indeed, yet both thinkers used it of developmental experience in the stage just after oneness-with-mother was past. *An Object Relations Theory of the Personality* was the title under which Fairbairn's most important papers were published in the USA in 1952, yet many who use the term "object relations" are unaware how pre-eminent a part he played in shaping the theory. Not that he wrote much but what he did publish is so clearly written and concisely illustrated that it has an immediate impact; his illustrations come from his experience in forensic psychiatry as well as in psychoanalysis, although his own training and reading ranged more widely.

Fairbairn was born, trained, and worked in Edinburgh. He took his degree in classics and philosophy, studying Hellenistic Greek and theology abroad and in Manchester for a

---

*Reproduced from the *Bulletin of the European Psychoanalytical Federation*, 1973, with kind permission.

higher degree. Only during the 1914–1918 war, in which he served in the Near East, did he determine to qualify in medicine and to become a psychiatric therapist. As soon as he qualified, in 1924, he began to practise psychoanalysis. His first long case paper is dated 1927, the year in which he became MD, and his second was read in January 1931 to the British Psychoanalytical Society; he then became an associate member. He first met Mrs Klein in 1934; his published papers most affected by her emphasis on destructive urges and restitution-wishes are the two papers on art and aesthetics of 1938 (they were not included in his book). But Freud was his source of inspiration and the essential Fairbairn is already apparent in his clinical papers of 1927 and 1931. Indeed his own greatest papers, four of them published in the five years 1940–1944, were obviously written in reaction against what he saw as certain weakness in Freud's and Abraham's theories and in Mrs Klein's clinical and theoretical approaches; but he confirmed the tremendous importance of Freud's studies on hysteria, on repression, and on the profound effects of the early environment of the child; he reformulated and modified slightly but significantly Freud's structural theory of the personality, and re-emphasised as crucial in the life of every individual "the origin and growth of object love", as formulated by Karl Abraham, Melanie Klein, Michael Balint, and himself in their clinical work. The positive influence of Karl Abraham is everywhere apparent, even though Fairbairn himself chose the classificatory contributions of Abraham as the chief point of his attack; he probably remained unaware how much he owed Abraham, just as many other writers have until now been unaware how much they owe Fairbairn.

Fairbairn was elected to membership of the British Psychoanalytical Society on the basis of his contributions to psychoanalytic thought and theory. His ideas have stimulated further theory, the formulation of interpretations, the notion of the psychoanalytic situation as an experimental situation, and a greater readiness among psychoanalysts to re-examine and to change their techniques.

In 1963 the editorial board of the *British Journal of Medical Psychology* paid him the tribute of devoting one of its quarterly parts to him and his ideas; its contributors both expound his ideas and describe the uses they have made of them in their own fields. Harry Guntrip has been the disciple who has warmly expounded and interpreted Fairbairn's theories in his own books and articles. Dr J. D. Sutherland has encouraged the study, use, and wider application of those theories not only clinically but in the more extended fields of the social services.

The four major theoretical advances

The book *Psychoanalytic Studies of the Personality*, published in 1952, contains all Fairbairn's psychoanalytic papers written before that year apart from the two of 1938. Three important papers were published after the book (1954b, 1956a, and 1958a); the first and the last of these are more concerned to give clinical evidence and to discuss the nature, function, and guiding principles of psychoanalytic therapy than to change substantially the theoretical position he had reached by 1951; but one important development in theory emerges in his review (1956a) of the publication in English by McAlpine and Hunter of Schreber's *Memoirs of My Nervous Illness*, which they had edited, annotated, and discussed.

Fairbairn evolved four major theories, which in their original form had some superficial inconsistencies with each other; but he noted these and in reconciling them made useful additions and amplifications to his theories in editing his book.

The first of his theories (1940a) is of the central significance of "splitting processes" in the personality; he described typical schizoid syndromes and was primarily concerned with pathology but also insisted on the normality and the universality of these processes; pathology is the outcome primarily of environmental failure and of what Freud had called "narcissistic wounds".

The second theory (1941) is psychopathological; it arranged the main psychiatric syndromes in a series partly developmental, according to the stage at which there had been the most acute failure in the parent–child relationship, and partly personal, according to the particular defence-techniques which the young child had found the most effective in coping with his parents' personalities and attitudes. He distinguished the sense of futility, characterising ego-loss and schizoid syndromes, from depression, the affect typical of unresolved ambivalence and consequent on inadequate splitting.

In his third theory (1943a) Fairbairn re-examined the chief modes of defence and particularly the concept of repression, which he came to regard as a sustained attempt to insure not only against the repetition of painful experience but more particularly against the recurrence of bad object relations, perceived unconsciously as bad object figures (in his view bad at this stage means libidinally bad—unloving, ungratifying, withholding, rejecting, denying, depriving, tantalising, retaliatory, implacable). Like Freud and Abraham, he distinguished pathological guilt-feelings from other forms of defence but he drew very different conclusions about depression and the depressive personality from those of many later workers; he insisted that the "depressive position" was not the central feature of personal development. Indeed the moral defence was to substitute a sense of guilt for a sense of helplessness; the child discovers it is slightly less unbearable to feel responsible for having damaged the object than to admit the object's inadequacy for vital needs. A pathological sense of guilt is then based on a delusion which justifies the approach to a punisher and is not the consequence of primary destructive phantasies. A negative therapeutic reaction is thus, as Freud stated, the consequence of a correct interpretation that undoes repression in a guilt-laden person: anxiety is released because bad inner objects are not held secure in old ways; it is essentially an hysterical reaction.

Fairbairn's fourth theory (1944) was to define a new image of mental structure and structures in terms of the relations between the experiencing ego and its inner objects. This theory he defined and redefined to the end of his life. It is so simple and so immediately applicable to the whole personality, to particular experiences as organised in dream or in waking life, to marital problems, and to group relationships, that he probably could not understand why it did not immediately catch on. He restated the tripartite structure of the psychic personality with one simple but crucial change. Probably psychoanalysts who have consciously rejected Fairbairn have displaced their anxiety about this change onto the idea of the multiplicity of the ego (an idea so obvious to Freud that he stated it most clearly in a casual way even with surprise that some analysts found it astonishing in dream-interpretation) and onto one addition to terminology ("anti-libidinal"), whereas Fairbairn's only essential change was to subtract the term "id" and to redistribute the notions it comprised more logically.

I shall consider Fairbairn's theories in the reverse order to the historical one described above for two reasons: first, it makes sense to begin by showing that where writers have claimed that Fairbairn was furthest from Freud he was actually closest to him; second, Fairbairn's most developed thought illumines the earlier papers, which are full of ideas important in their own right and not just because they lead up to his structural theory.

The theory of psychic structure and of psychic structures:

In his paper of 1944 Fairbairn derives two ideas from the dreams and associations of two patients: one is the notion of a dream as the representation of an inner "state of affairs" (the phrase of one of those patients) or of a situation of inner reality, often with some movement in it; this corresponds with Freud's idea of the manifest dream as a compromise, like a symptom. For Fairbairn it is a compromise between the fixation point, stated in terms of the family relationship during the traumatic period, and the dreamer's attempt to advance beyond it, a move in which libidinal experience is partially freed (the equivalent of wish-fulfilment). (A good parallel in literature would be Pirandello's play *Six Characters in Search of an Author*. In this the six unknown characters appear, take over the reality of the rehearsal for a different play, re-enact their own, unsolved family situation, and vanish; the company actors then leave one by one, looking askance at the producer; after all, they have either just witnessed a murder or else shared with him an hallucination. He could be the dreamer or madman who has imposed his inner reality on other people. It is a play about a repetition-compulsion—or rather, Fairbairn would have said, about the return of bad objects. Yet the motive for their return, as assigned to the father, is precisely the attempt to advance beyond the fixation-point.)

The second notion came from the dream of a woman patient; this dream "consisted of a brief scene in which the dreamer saw the figure of herself being viciously attacked by a well-known actress in a venerable building which had belonged to her family for generations. Her husband was looking on but he seemed quite helpless and quite incapable of protecting her. After delivering the attack the actress turned away and resumed playing a stage part, which, as seemed to be implied, she had momentarily set aside in order to deliver the attack by way of interlude. The dreamer then found herself gazing at the figure of herself lying bleeding on the floor; but, as she gazed, she noticed that this figure turned for an instant into that of a man. Thereafter the figure alternated between herself and this man until eventually she awoke in a state of acute anxiety."

From the associations Fairbairn derived three sets of interpretations: one in terms of the dreamer's current life-situation and marital relationship; a second in Oedipal terms, describing her libidinal relationship to her father as an identification with him and her relationship to her mother (the actress) as both masochistic and, by identification with her, as sadistic towards the male; and the third in structural terms, finding in the dream "a basic character which entitles it to be regarded as the paradigm of all endopsychic situations".

Briefly, Fairbairn distinguished three egos, each relating to a special kind of object: the central (observing) ego linked with an ideal or idealised object (the helpless husband of the dream), the libidinal ego (the figure of herself being attacked and then lying bleeding) linked with a libidinal object (the man with whom that figure alternates), and the anti-libidinal ego (the actress-self that conformed with her mother's pattern) linked with an anti-libidinal object (in this dream the actress-mother fused with the actress-self). (The three links of being separate-but-like, of being incompletely fused and alternating, and of being completely fused, may be seen as different stages in object relationship.)

Fairbairn represented these structures and their relationship in a diagram (1952, p. 105), which he perhaps never consciously compared with Freud's diagram of the psychic personality; I append both diagrams, changing Fairbairn's only in the shape of its outlines and in ways indicated in his own texts. The differences in Fairbairn are almost completely in accord with Freudian theory:

The superego is made up of (a) an ideal ego identified with ideal objects, (b) an observing, critical, and implacable part, (i) identified with the observing, critical parents, but (ii) often more cruel and ruthless than the real parents, a contribution from the implacable aspect of the self; (i) and (ii) are often fused, as in the actress figure of the dream; (a) and (b) are more distinguishable as a rule. "Mourning and Melancholia" (1917e) shows most explicitly Freud's awareness of the fusion between ego and bad (rejecting) object.

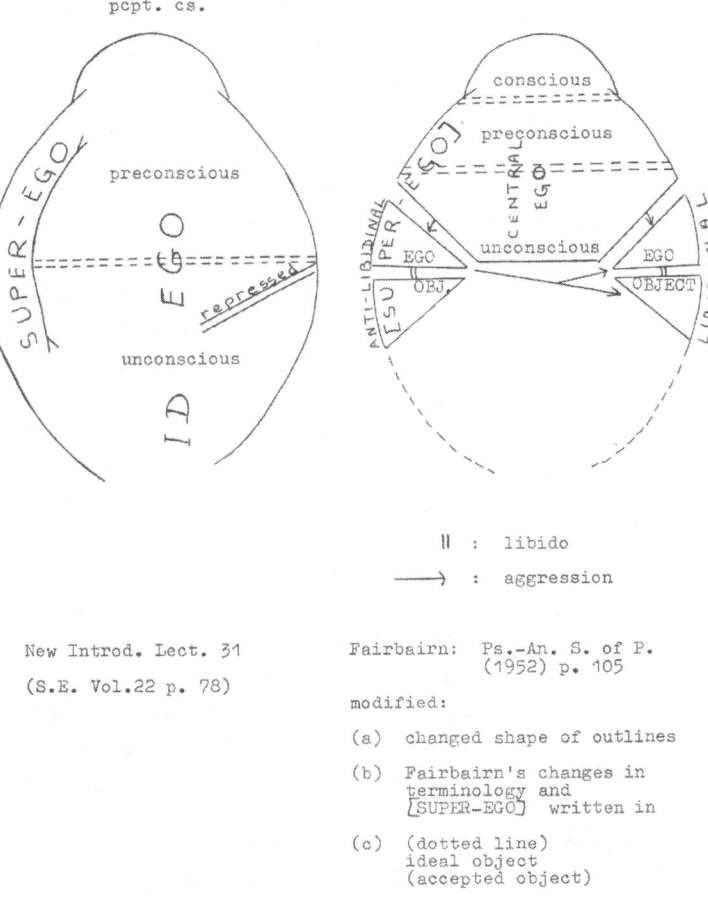

The "repressed unconscious" consists of memories, phantasies, and imagos, in which both self and objects are represented and in which an identity not of thought but of sense is experienced. Freud's change in putting "repressed" above the double line instead of below it possibly indicates an awareness that part of the ego as well as objects are repressed. Also there is a passage in "On Narcissism: an Introduction", accounting for homosexuality by the way in which the older of the pair finds a lost self-image in the younger; (each of us) "has originally two sexual objects—himself and the woman who nurses him" (1914c, p. 88).

Thus we are each left with some capacity to identify with either person of that primary couple, which can also survive as a dyad mentally or symbolically (this is the idea that underlies Winnicott's concepts "the transitional object" and "the transitional phenomenon").

The structures (ego + object) called libidinal and anti-libidinal are often represented in dreams and in other experiences as fused; but ego and object of each kind may appear separately. Fairbairn insisted that primary direct repression is effected and maintained by aggressive activity and an aggressive attitude towards the object, perceived as "bad"; secondarily a part of the ego is repressed closely associated with each repressed object, so closely that there is often a state of fusion or semi-fusion.

Perhaps Fairbairn did not emphasise enough the way in which these states of fusion, one of which we watch becoming loosened in the dream he quotes, account for the loss or recovery of parts of the self as fused with an object. (Winnicott's "true self" would be such an internal libidinal system dissociated from the central ego, which is then a "false" or "caretaker" self.) Fairbairn's 1931 case paper describes the recovery of parts of the self as personifications, a mischievous pre-adolescent boy and a vivacious young girl.

Sutherland has aptly referred to the internal structures as "systems", a primitive need-system (libidinal) and a primitive control-system (anti-libidinal). Each subsidiary ego is, in Fairbairn's sense, a structure and must have appropriate objects internal to it; so also each subsidiary object is a structure, and has been experienced as such, not only by projection but by objective perception. A child from an early age has a reality-sense that recognises in his parents greed and irrational anger directed not only towards him but towards each other.

It needs to be clearly stated that the repressed objects cannot be experienced as "bad" at the same moment. The libidinal object (and ego) is "bad" if it is over-stimulating or imperils the continuity or coherence of the central ego or of its relationships; the anti-libidinal object (and ego) is then felt to be "good" if it exercises automatic control, even if this be inhibiting to the whole personality. The anti-libidinal object is "bad" if it rejects, withholds, impedes, or attacks the libidinal experience without which life is empty and futile; libidinal experience is felt not just as "good" but as vitally necessary, whether it be shared or solitary, straight or perverse, direct or symbolic. So the anti-libidinal ego, fused with its object, maintains an aggressive opposition, even an implacable hostility, against the libidinal object, with which its portion of ego is fused; this is indirect repression (the ego has borrowed the strength of the father to repress the primary libidinal object-choices: "an energetic reaction-formation against those choices").

Then what of the id, the system unconscious? The system unconscious is represented (a) by the four repressed structures and a large area of the central ego, made, as Freud stated, out of abandoned object relationships (incidentally this allows for lines of cleavage under stress or after loss, separation, or rejection); (b) by the symbols = (libido) and (aggression); these are all that remain of the instinct theories, whether that of the component instincts, that of sexual versus ego instincts, or that of life-and-death instincts. Not that energy is absent in the structures themselves but it can be left unrepresented, since the distinction between ego and object-components that have been absorbed into the personality would be artificial. Some of the energy at the disposal of the central ego is, of course, represented by the arrows which symbolise direct repression, including what Freud called the maintenance of counter-cathexes.

By the sentence "There is no id" Fairbairn meant that he could not subscribe to the confusion of categories that Freud made when he lumped together sexual and aggressive instincts, repressing forces, and repressed imagos and experiences in a "seething cauldron". In the diagram I have represented by a dotted line the acceptable, accepted, and accepting object from which the repressed object-portions have been detached. It is only in his text (not in his diagram) because he regarded it as absorbed in the central ego and so available for forming and maintaining good object relations with figures and institutions in the outside world (cf. Helm Stierlin in *IJPA*, 1970, "The Functions of Inner Objects").

The diagram also reveals two symmetries: the symmetry about the horizontal axis indicates the relationship between self and object (it shows the self-object relationship as forming at the unconscious, not at the conscious, pole); the symmetry about the vertical axis indicates the close correspondence between the sensual need-system and the primitive control-system. The only asymmetry, the divided arrow symbolising indirect repression (aggression against the sensual need-system) comes from a structure even more tightly fused with its object than the sensual; this suggests that the mother–child bond of security, as Bowlby, using ethological findings, has argued, is even more fundamental than the bond of supply or of gratification in excitement; both bonds are represented by the sign =, because they are, as shown in *Beyond the Pleasure Principle* (Freud, 1920g), ultimately libidinal. The "aggression" of maternal rejection and of reaction to it proceeds from a self-object system for which, as Winnicott also showed, the environment is ultimately responsible. Fairbairn argued that the splitting process, the schizoid position, and the resulting structure were fundamental and normal and that they patterned all relationships, including those of the Oedipal period, when first one parent (or sibling) and then the other is identified as the exciting or libidinal object and the parent not so used is identified now as the secure base and guarantor of control, now as the rejecting or anti-libidinal object. In fact the diagram can be used to transform what Rickman and Balint called a one-body psychology into a two- and three-body psychology, into a psychology of interpersonal relations. In the process of defence the ego is split into three, but this itself makes object relationships possible—and complicated.

Although all this appears theoretical, almost mathematical, yet it is given concrete reality by the experiences, dreams, phantasies, symbols, relationships, attachments, loves, and hostilities which are the stuff of everybody's life inside analysis or out of it. As the only psychoanalyst in Edinburgh for many years Fairbairn was restricted in his publishable case material but his ideas find clinical expression and illustration in his paper "Observations on the Nature of Hysterical States" (1954b). From that paper it is easy to realise how wholeheartedly Fairbairn was identified with Freud, for example, in his paper "Constructions in Analysis" (1937d). Analysis is about the real situations that patients have actually lived through, apprehended, and (partially) assimilated, transformed, or rejected during their early development.

Before leaving this part, on endopsychic structure, readers who seize upon "the multiplicity of the ego" may refer to Freud's lucid, if casual, statement of it and his own linguistic illustration. It is in the brief, final (tenth) section of his paper "Remarks on the Theory and Practice of Dream Interpretation" (1923c, pp. 120–121). In the clause "when I think what I've done to that man" the ego appears twice and its unity seems a secondary elaboration. Fairbairn's theory is partly an amplification of that half-page of Freud's, partly a synthesis of that insight with the insights of *The Ego and the Id* (1923b).

The theory of modes of defence and their breakdown

In his 1943 paper "The Repression and the Return of Bad Objects", Fairbairn re-examines the chief forms of defence in their chronological sequence. The crucial fact is that psychological defence is an insurance against the loss or breakdown of absolutely necessary ego-object relationships, either total or libidinal and regulatory, during stages of immaturity.

a. Internalisation is the earliest defence and the one that Fairbairn had examined first in his best-known paper (1940a). It is used before ambivalence sets in, although he later recognised that the object internalised is not primarily "bad" but "in some measure unsatisfying as well as satisfying". Real, bad experience enormously amplifies the use of the defence.

b. Repression is next. Freud could never account to his own complete satisfaction for primal repression, since any act of repression needed a pull, from an unconscious structure, as well as a push from the ego at the behest of the superego, a late Oedipal ego structure. Mrs Klein tried to solve the problem by earlier dating of the Oedipus situation and earlier formation of the superego. Fairbairn's solution is to divide repression into the aggressive rejection of the "bad" (that which threatens total security) and the aggressive rejection by the parent-imagos of the child's sensuality. The disadvantage of repression as a defence is threefold:

   i. The personality is impoverished and there is a sense of futility if the libidinal system is denied or the libidinal self rejected.
   ii. External ego-object relationships go wrong because external objects are chosen (and therefore convincingly treated) on the basis of archaic, inner objects.
   iii. The repressed objects return (perhaps in delusions, in breakdowns, constructive or damaging, in self-organised failures, or in dreams). Fairbairn illustrated this from his wide experience of soldiers who had broken down in war conditions, but he accounted for "the return of the repressed" not by the hypothesis of a repetition-compulsion but by the libidinal attachment to "bad" (needed even though anti-libidinal) objects, pointing to Freud's case-paper of "A Seventeenth-Century Demonological Neurosis" (1923d) for Freud's own acknowledgement of the motive.

c. The moral defence is the latest of the three main modes. We meet it as a sense of guilt that cannot be accounted for by known acts, and which may drive people to criminality. The defence is to proclaim to oneself, and perhaps to others, that one is responsible for one's own bad experience; one denies a bit of reality-sense in doing so, in saying that the badness is one's own product and that the external object is really good (or would be if one hadn't spoilt, hurt, or provoked it). Fairbairn's official interviews with children who had been sexually assaulted and who often came from desperately bad homes led him to see this defence in operation particularly clearly.

The weakness of this defence is that it leads to profound depression or to delinquency. In either case there develops a need for punishment. Very acutely Fairbairn saw that interpretations of aggression or of guilt-feelings as due to aggressive impulses may act as the equivalent of punishment and lead to relief and symptomatic improvement but to greater repression. He had distinguished the affect of a sense of futility from the affect of depression, a distinction that is still not adequately used clinically, and he warned of the antitherapeutic consequences of interpreting aggression except in cases of true depression. Schizoid patients are ultimately made more depressed, envious, and despairing by interpretations of their aggression, envy, and hate.

The problem set by the moral defence both to patient and to therapist is how to recognise in treatment and face the environmental failure at the right time. As Winnicott later stated, "Envious mental failure is not the outcome of projection but must seem so for health." Yet the true depressive, as Fairbairn had already pointed out in 1941, is a person who has differentiated self and object but has failed to split his object adequately for normal development; his hate has never been accepted, so his inner object is constantly at risk from his ambivalence. Abraham's account of the depressive personality and of his early history is relevant here. Fairbairn's account of the negative therapeutic reaction in such a person has been given above.

The theory of the origins of clinical syndromes

The paper (1941) entitled "A Revised Psychopathology of the Psychoses and Psychoneuroses" arranged the clinical illnesses, neuroses, and personality disorders according to the following variables:

a. the degree and stage of orality and the degree of dependence on the object when the environmental failure was greatest
b. the degree of differentiation of the object
c. the degree of differentiation of the self from the object
d. the locus of disposal of the inner "bad" or "good" objects ("bad" objects have the alternative character of over-exciting and of rejection, "good" objects the alternative character of libidinally satisfying and of maintaining coherence and continuity).

There are two main disasters that can threaten the child in his first two years: loss of ego and loss of object (these are clearly not absolutely alternative). The first, the consequence of environmental failure in the pre-ambivalent stage, is experienced less as the actual rejection of himself or of his love by his mother than as the risk of destroying her by his love or of being destroyed by her love (cf. the patient's dream of being beside his mother and of having to die of hunger or of having to eat a poisoned pudding, followed by the dream of his mother in the act of eating his own heart). The second is a consequence of failure after biting and hating are established, when the narcissistic wound has occurred late enough for projective-introjective mechanisms to be used adequately; it is felt as loss or destruction of the object.

Severe schizoid states indicate early traumatic experiences or a defective relationship in the first phase; severe depressive states in the second phase, after the attainment of Winnicott's "stage of concern".

Once these two stages of absolute dependence and of predominant orality are passed, the stage of transitional dependence is reached, in which one or other disaster threatens and disposal techniques (therefore mainly excretory in imagery) are employed to avoid them:

i. For the phobic person both good and bad inner objects are located psychologically outside his ego; he is drawn to the good object and lured to a regressive identification with it but then risks total annihilation by the bad object. He flees from his bad object but, once overtaken by it, as indeed he must be in therapy, he may experience great relief (e.g., the voice of his therapist in a dream: "That's what you've been so afraid of.").

ii. The obsessional has retained both his good and his bad inner objects. He lives on the verge of expelling the bad but then, as Abraham had shown, of losing the good as well; alternatively he uses outer matter and things to symbolise his inner contamination of his good with his bad.

iii. The paranoid person has successfully split his objects, retained the good inside, and located the bad outside his ego. But he lives in constant danger of attack from any external object just because he is so identified with the good inside. Like the obsessional, he may make great use of his own body as an intermediate object (both self and not-self) to symbolise the danger; object relations are important for him to maintain the sense of his goodness and power by gaining other people's admiration, respect, and love but dangerous lest the admiration turn to envy, the respect to scorn, and the love to hatred. The bad outside can be evaded but not controlled.

iv. The hysteric, like the obsessional, keeps his good and bad internalised objects separate, but unlike the obsessional, the good outside (this makes good external relationships easy—to begin with) and the bad inside (this makes it easier to control but makes it more urgent to seek the good to remedy the feeling of inner badness, usually localised to the genitals). So the hysteric is at the mercy of his intense love relationships, in which the external object is bound to let him down; the idealised object cannot live up to the exaggerated value set upon him or adequately supply the needy, self-depreciated ego of the hysteric.

The phobic lives the dilemma: flight to or from the objects? The obsessional lives the dilemma: expel or retain. The paranoid's dilemma is: encourage or reject the object's approach, the risks being persecution or loss. The hysteric's dilemma is: surrender or not to the good object, the risks being rejection and humiliation or unending worthlessness.

Opposing Abraham, Fairbairn insisted that "The various (transitional) techniques cannot be classified in any order corresponding to presumptive levels of libidinal development. On the contrary they must be regarded as alternative techniques, all belonging to the same stage in the development of object-relationships." The choice and range of techniques "would appear to depend in large measure on the nature of the object-relationships established during the preceding stage of infantile dependence". (Fairbairn does not theoretically, though he does clinically, relate the actual techniques to the actual early environment and personalities of the parents.)

However, there are indications that Fairbairn did think of them in an ascending order of development:

i. He saw hysteria as the state nearest to maturity or normality.
ii. In treating a woman with marked phobic symptoms and generalised anxiety, who felt nausea when her libidinal tension rose during a session (her father's penis being equated with a bad breast), she advanced to the stage of "wanting to go to the lavatory" (i.e., closer to the obsessional's dilemma—reject or retain assimilated contents) and of a willingness to express libidinal feelings in front of an external object.
iii. The most reasonable explanation for the fact that the "good" and "bad" inner objects of the phobic and obsessional are always found together is that the original object has been incompletely split or dichotomised into good and bad.

Fairbairn carried through what Abraham had promised and begun—an account of "The Origins and Growth of Object Love" (1924). Abraham has fallen back on elaborating the zones and phases theory (the "one-body psychology" of John Rickman); Fairbairn portrays the two- and threebody psychology by never losing sight of the relationships between the developing ego and the actual objects encountered.

The real test of Fairbairn's classificatory system will come only when the differentiation and location of the important internal objects can be estimated by means independent of clinical assessment, perhaps by projective tests or by grid, and when changes of personality during treatment can be similarly assessed. Meanwhile there is no doubt that clinicians are immediately interested in his account of the four transitional states; they seem to have natural ways of knowing about their patients' inner objects and so find the classification highly significant.

The theory of "Schizoid Factors in the Personality"

The paper (1940a) so entitled is the most known and quoted of Fairbairn's. He called attention to splitting processes in many pathological syndromes and also in normal life (the dream) and in normal development (the formation of the superego). He described residual narcissistic states and accounted for them by various techniques and attitudes (e.g., showing instead of giving; intellectualising; rejection of, and hostility towards, the needed figures), all developed to ensure that the greatest wound of early life is never repeated, viz. such rejection of himself and of his love in his pre-ambivalent, sucking phase, as made him experience himself and his love as bad and dread another's love as well as his own. Fairbairn faced squarely something that few other analysts have tried to deal with theoretically: the basic and structural effects on the personality of bad or defective mothering, the forms taken by the psychological diseases due to environmental deficiency.

Developments after 1951

In his review (1956a) of McAlpine and Hunter's edition of Schreber's *Memoirs*, Fairbairn acknowledged the acuteness of some of their criticisms of psychoanalytic theories of the case and the perceptiveness of some of their ideas, especially their interpretation of Schreber's hypochondriac symptoms as "primitive, procreation fantasies in the form of body hallucinations". But Fairbairn points out the need to synthesise this interpretation with Freud's interpretation of the paranoid aspect of Schreber's illness; he puts forward the suggestion that both interpretations can be reconciled in terms of the enormous significance of the primal scene (we can now add, in view of the published researches into the facts of Schreber's childhood, "especially for a child who has been physically immobilised by his parents and restrained by night and by day from all spontaneous movement except such movement as is willed by them"). Fairbairn gives material from five of his current cases to illustrate the pathogenic significance of the primal scene.

In a wider sense we might speak of the primal relationship of the parents as evinced not only in the scene itself but in their whole attitude to the bodies of themselves, each other, and their children. At some point quite early in life, the primal scene, experienced or imagined, but based on the real personalities of the parents, apparently becomes the internal object of the child. The vicissitudes of that object determine his emotional and sexual future, beginning with his Oedipal experience; it is profoundly affected by the actual family life.

Perhaps the preceding paragraph takes a step that Fairbairn never explicitly took; yet it is implied both in his 1954 paper on hysterical states and in that of 1958 "On the Nature and Aims of Psycho-analytical Treatment". In the latter he gives reasons for modifying technique in some cases; for example, to have to lie on a couch with the analyst out of sight can be emotionally equivalent to being exposed to the risk of being physically excited by the presence of the sexual parents.

More important, however, is Fairbairn's way of conceptualising the importance to the patient of the analyst as a needed object, needed not only to provide him with security but to allow movement and communication between the dissociated parts of his ego. In this Fairbairn is saying in plainer words what Sterba and Strachey had said of the mode of action of psychoanalytical treatment in their separate papers of 1934 (*IJPA*). But particularly striking is Fairbairn's picture of the neurotic patient's attempt to live his life as a closed system and to press the analyst into it; the psychoanalyst's interpretations are directed towards breaching that closed system and eventually towards influencing the patient to want to turn it into an open system and establish free communication with the world.

References

Abraham, K. (1924). The origins and growth of object love. In: *Selected Papers of Karl Abraham M. D.* (pp. 480–502). London: Hogarth, 1927.

Fairbairn, W. R. D. (1927). Notes on the religious phantasies of a female patient. In: *Psychoanalytic Studies of the Personality* (pp. 183–196). London: Tavistock, 1952.

Fairbairn, W. R. D. (1931). Features in the analysis of a patient with a physical genital abnormality. In: *Psychoanalytic Studies of the Personality* (pp. 197–222). London: Tavistock, 1952.

Fairbairn, W. R. D. (1938a). Prolegomena to a psychology of art. *British Journal of Psychology, 28*: 288–303. In: E. F. Birtles & D. E. Scharff (Eds.), *From Instinct to Self: Selected Papers of W. R. D. Fairbairn, Volume II: Applications and Early Contributions* (pp. 381–396). Northvale, NJ: Jason Aronson, 1994.

Fairbairn, W. R. D. (1938b). The ultimate basis of aesthetic experience. *British Journal of Psychology, 29*: 167–181. In: E. F. Birtles & D. E. Scharff (Eds.), *From Instinct to Self: Selected Papers of W. R. D. Fairbairn, Volume II: Applications and Early Contributions* (pp. 397–409). Northvale, NJ: Jason Aronson, 1994.

Fairbairn, W. R. D. (1940a). Schizoid factors in the personality. In: *Psychoanalytic Studies of the Personality* (pp. 3–27). London: Tavistock, 1952.

Fairbairn, W. R. D. (1941). A revised psychopathology of the psychoses and the psychoneuroses. *International Journal of Psychoanalysis, 22*(3, 4): 250–279. In: *Psychoanalytic Studies of the Personality* (pp. 28–58). London: Tavistock, 1952.

Fairbairn, W. R. D. (1943a). The repression and return of bad objects (with special reference to the "war neuroses"). *British Journal of Medical Psychology, 19*: 327–341. In: *Psychoanalytic Studies of the Personality* (pp. 59–81). London: Tavistock, 1952.

Fairbairn, W. R. D. (1944). Endopsychic structure considered in terms of object-relationships. *International Journal of Psychoanalysis, 25*: 70–92. In: *Psychoanalytic Studies of the Personality* (pp. 82–136). London: Tavistock, 1952.

Fairbairn, W. R. D. (1952). *Psychoanalytic Studies of the Personality*. London: Tavistock, 1952.

Fairbairn, W. R. D. (1954b). Observations on the nature of hysterical states. *British Journal of Medical Psychology, 27*(3): 105–125. In: D. E. Scharff & E. F. Birtles (Eds.), *From Instinct to Self: Selected Papers of W. R. D. Fairbairn, Volume I: Clinical and Theoretical Papers* (pp. 13–40). Northvale, NJ: Jason Aronson, 1994.

Fairbairn, W. R. D. (1956a). The Schreber case. In: D. E. Scharff & E. F. Birtles (Eds.), *From Instinct to Self: Selected Papers of W. R. D. Fairbairn, Volume I: Clinical and Theoretical Papers* (pp. 41–60). Northvale, NJ: Jason Aronson, 1994.

Fairbairn, W. R. D. (1958a). On the nature and aims of psycho-analytical treatment. *International Journal of Psychoanalysis, 39*(5): 374–385. In: D. E. Scharff & E. F. Birtles (Eds.), *From Instinct to Self: Selected Papers of W. R. D. Fairbairn, Volume I: Clinical and Theoretical Papers* (pp. 74–92). Northvale, NJ: Jason Aronson, 1994.

Freud, S. (1914c). On narcissism: an introduction. *S. E., 14*. London: Hogarth.

Freud, S. (1917e). Mourning and melancholia. *S. E., 14*. London: Hogarth.

Freud, S. (1920g). *Beyond the Pleasure Principle. S. E., 18*. London: Hogarth.

Freud, S. (1923b). *The Ego and the Id. S. E., 19*. London: Hogarth.

Freud, S. (1923c). Remarks on the theory and practice of dream interpretation. *S. E., 19*. London: Hogarth.

Freud, S. (1923d). A seventeenth-century demonological neurosis. *S. E., 19*. London: Hogarth.

Freud, S. (1933a). *New Introductory Lectures on Psycho-Analysis. S. E., 22*. London: Hogarth.

Freud, S. (1937d). Constructions in analysis. *S. E., 13*. London: Hogarth.

Sterba, R. (1934). The fate of the ego in analytic therapy. *International Journal of Psychoanalysis, 15*: 117–126.

Stierlin, H. (1970). The functions of "inner objects". *International Journal of Psychoanalysis, 51*: 321–330.

Strachey, J. (1934). The nature of the therapeutic action of psycho-analysis. *International Journal of Psychoanalysis, 15*: 127–159.

Sutherland, J. D. (1963). Object relations theory and the conceptual model of psychoanalysis. *British Journal of Medical Psychology, 36*: 109–124.

Winnicott, D. W. (1953). Transitional objects and transitional phenomena—a study of the first not-me possession. *International Journal of Psychoanalysis, 34*: 89–97.

CHAPTER TWENTY-TWO

John Padel's contribution to an understanding of Fairbairn's object relations theory

Graham S. Clarke

Introduction

We are very fortunate to be able to reprint John Padel's paper "The Contribution of W. R. D. Fairbairn (1889–1965) to Psychoanalytic Theory and Practice", originally published in the *European Psycho-Analytic Foundation Bulletin* in 1973. I was unaware of it, and so had never read it, before this book was commissioned, but I wish that I had known it when I first read Fairbairn and tried to make sense of his thinking. It is a wonderfully concise and illuminating introduction to Fairbairn's theory that everyone interested in Fairbairn's thinking should read even if they already believe they have come to grips with the full complexity of his "psychology of dynamic structures".

For me John Padel's work on Fairbairn and his theory has been the single source most influential on my own work and understanding of Fairbairn apart from Fairbairn himself. It is for that reason that I want to both point to the work and bring out what I consider to be the many important contributions that Padel has made to Fairbairn scholarship.

Padel was not just a commentator on Fairbairn and object relations thinking in the British Psychoanalytical Society. As a former classicist he had developed his own approach to literature and psychoanalysis producing a variant ordering of Shakespeare's sonnets, which he published (1981) as *New Poems by Shakespeare*, details of which, along with details of his professional career, his other work, and interests can be found in Mary Twyman's obituary of him in *The Independent*, 24 November 1999. He remains one of the foremost interpreters of Fairbairn's work and of the history of object relations in the UK.

I have chosen five papers (1985, 1991a, 1991b, 1994, 1996) and three reviews (1970, 1990, 1995), most of which are available via the PEPWeb database, to indicate the important ideas that he developed over the thirty plus years of his writing. A penetrating understanding of

Fairbairn's "psychology of dynamic structure" is embodied in these papers, as comprehensive and convincing as any other contemporary commentator on Fairbairn's work.

It is not only Padel's deep understanding of Fairbairn's model of endopsychic structure that I value him for, but also for his knowledge and understanding of the British Psychoanalytical Society and the relationship between Fairbairn, Klein, and Winnicott and his appreciation of the relations between Fairbairn, Sutherland, and Guntrip, all based upon first-hand experience with them.

Some reviews

John Padel reviewed a number of books and papers for the *International Journal of Psychoanalysis* (*IJPA*) and other journals. I have concentrated on the points that Padel made concerning Fairbairn and the British Society, ignoring other interesting things that he had to say.

Padel's review of Object Love and Reality *by Arnold H. Modell.* IJPA, 1970, 51: 84–87

While acknowledging that "there are important and original things" in Modell's book, Padel is critical of Modell, whose book is subtitled "An Introduction to a Psychoanalytic Theory of Object Relations" for not properly considering the object relations theories of Klein, Fairbairn, and Winnicott, although Padel says that Modell's position is very close to that of Fairbairn. However, Modell dismisses Fairbairn's writings in language reminiscent of Winnicott and Khan's 1953 review of Fairbairn's book when it was first published in 1952 (more on this later). Padel presents Modell's book in some detail, arriving at his description of Chapter Eight which is designed to be the climax of the book and introduces Modell's notion of "'topographical regression' with a superimposition of structural concepts", and its development in Chapter Nine at which point Padel comments, "Surely this is exactly what Fairbairn pointed out and using exactly the same principle, the superimposition of an internal-external shift upon differentiated ego-structures subserving different functions at different times!"

Towards the end of the review Padel, using Modell's language, writes, "'The superimposition of the topographic metaphor upon the structural' is in fact exactly the principle invented and elaborated brilliantly and carefully by Fairbairn in his papers of 1941, 1943 and 1944."

Padel robustly disagrees with Modell about Fairbairn's relation to Freud. "Dr Modell's earlier statements about the relations between Fairbairn and Freud are simply untrue, both as implying that Fairbairn did not fundamentally adhere to Freud's theory and to psychoanalytic thinking and as stating that we are forced to choose between them."

He goes on to say that Fairbairn, like Modell, "… insisted there was an object-relations theory implicit in Freud from the beginning and never worked out"—something developed later by Padel (1985) and also discussed by Ogden (1983).

Padel's review of Reshaping the Psychoanalytic Domain *by Judith Hughes.* IJPA, 1990, 71: 715–717

Padel liked this book, calling it "A well researched piece of work from a professor of history, who ends her preface by thanking her analyst" (p. 715). Concerning the relations between Klein, Winnicott, and Fairbairn, Padel states that

> Fairbairn certainly influenced Klein as well as *vice versa*. She not only took over the term schizoid from him but also the concept of ego-splitting; she was aware that he was urging that severely *schizoid* patients (including schizophrenics) did form a strong transference and were treatable. Since Klein indicated in a letter (which Grosskurth quotes) that it was urgent for her to put forth her ideas because Fairbairn was making such claims about schizophrenia, it is clear that he was the first initiator of treating such patients by psychoanalysis and she did not wish him to get the public ear before she did. (p. 717)

Padel thought that knowing the history of the British Psychoanalytical Society was essential since, "… understanding Klein, Fairbairn and Winnicott, still needs historical reconstruction" (p. 717). Padel comments on the degree to which Klein's ideas were new, arguing that this could only be assessed after the investigation of themes discussed before and after she arrived. He quotes Sylvia Payne as saying that they were discussing similar ideas to Klein's, derived from Sachs and Abraham, before Klein arrived in Britain. Padel also comments on the effect that the Controversial Discussions had on the British Psychoanalytical Society, pointing out that the "middle group" (later the "Independents") came into being in 1946 at the same time "as the two groups which had formed by mutual antagonistic polarisation within the Society" (p. 717). But as far as Padel is concerned, "It [the middle group] was the original British Society, and so it only later became more tightly organised … unlike the other two which had been militant from their inception" (p. 717). This comment seemed necessary to Padel because "of a current erroneous way of speaking of the middle group as a later formation than the others" (p. 717).

Padel's review of The Autonomous Self: The Work of John D. Sutherland edited by Jill Savege Scharff. IJPA, 1995, 76: 177–179

In his review of Sutherland's collected papers, which had been "beautifully edited by Dr [Jill Savege] Scharff", Padel highlights a perceived shortcoming in Fairbairn's theory: "Sutherland apparently felt that the biggest weakness in Fairbairn's theories was his inadequate account of growth over time" (pp. 178–179). Padel's thinking on psychic growth within Fairbairn's theory will be discussed later as of great significance.

Padel comments on Sutherland's use of concepts like *processes* and *systems* instead of *structures* in his accounts of the make-up of personality.

> Fairbairn always called his structures "dynamic" and the inherent power and instinctual forces which the word implies could only be exerted in processes over time; but Sutherland is surely right that Fairbairn was feeling his way towards an "open systems theory" … "System" is a better word to convey objectively the internal relationships that compose the personality and also the long-term external relationships in which a person becomes involved. (p. 178)

Towards the end of the review there is a short section concerning the dichotomy of "object-relations theory or instinctual-drive theory" which Padel sees as misrepresenting Fairbairn's thought: "The theory of object relations does not deny the instincts, it simply insists that they are not external to the structures of the self or of subselves, but are inherent in them" (p. 179).

This might stand as a warning regarding Greenberg and Mitchell, who in their now classic *Object Relations in Psychoanalytic Theory* (1983) tend to dichotomise psychoanalytic theory on the basis of the distinction between relational and drive-based theories.

Padel's comments on The Case of Harry Guntrip. IJPA, 1996, 77: 755–761

This is a fascinating look at Guntrip's account of his analyses with Fairbairn and later Winnicott. Full of interesting detail and offering an alternative approach to Guntrip through his dreams, based upon Freud's paper of 1917 on anal eroticism, this gives an absorbing insight into three of the developers of object relations thinking in Britain. From my perspective Padel makes two far-reaching comments in this paper. One concerns the Oedipus situation and its importance within therapy: "Fairbairn had replied that it [the Oedipus complex] came first in treatment but not in theory" (p. 759). Fairbairn had already developed a view of the "Oedipus situation", as he called it, that made it of less fundamental importance for theory than Freud thought. This may be due to the influence of Suttie but depended upon there having already been a prior splitting of the self in the endopsychic structure and Fairbairn's view that "[T]he child constitutes the Oedipus situation for himself" (*Psychoanalytic Studies of the Personality*, 1952, p. 124, emphasis in original). The other concerns Guntrip's alteration of Fairbairn's theory. Guntrip ...

> "felt better" with each analyst but his improvement did not outlast his treatments ... However he was able to survive by teaching and by writing his own version of Fairbairn's theories, to which he added the one thing which he believed they lacked: this was the concept of "a split in the libidinal ego", a split that made it necessary for severely schizoid individuals to undergo regression in order to heal it. (p. 760)

Padel's response to this is telling: "I find this idea, which he actually managed to persuade Fairbairn to accept before he died, quite incompatible with Fairbairn's structural theory. A split that hampers normal functioning can only be one in the Central Ego, and indeed only the Central Ego is capable of regression. The libidinal ego is split off and cannot be healed by regression" (p. 760).

Rightly or wrongly, I have always been suspicious of Guntrip's reconstructions of Fairbairn's theory, preferring myself to go back to what is, after all, perhaps the smallest oeuvre in psychoanalysis. Because it was written in such a concentrated way, I find that it allows for new insight at every visit.

Papers by Padel

I have picked four of Padel's papers that focus most on Fairbairn and object relations. Three of these can be found on the PEPWeb database while the last of them was originally published in the *British Journal of Psychotherapy* in 1986, and was "modified and slightly amplified" for publication in *Fairbairn and the Origin of Object Relations*, edited by Grotstein and Rinsley (1994). I have chosen to present them in roughly the order they were written.

"Ego in Current Thinking" (1985), International Review of Psycho-Analysis, 12: *273–283.*

In a wide-ranging review of the psychoanalytic understanding of the term "ego", Padel starts by exploring alternative understandings of the term within Freud's work, basing his discussion on Laplanche and Pontalis (1973). The line of thought that Laplanche and Pontalis consider the most fruitful, according to Padel, is of "the ego as a formation arising from early perceptions of subject-object ("interhuman") relationships" (p. 273). Having reviewed aspects of an argument in the International Society circa 1971 between the language of egos and that of selves, Padel goes on to consider "identification" and the need for a move beyond a "one-person" psychology and in particular to "an interpersonal account by which object-cathexes are internalised and contribute to the ego's growth" (p. 274). Padel notes that this discussion takes place without reference to Freud's paper "Group Psychology and the Analysis of the Ego" (1921c), which Padel refers to as "… the most penetrating piece of thinking [on the ego] that Freud did and that *The Ego and the Id* (1923b) was a retreat from it" (p. 274). The principal reason for this judgment concerns the degree to which Freud was struggling to understand the idea of "identification" and its contribution to our understanding of the way the ego "is created and grows". Padel goes on to suggest that "If identifying is a prime ego-function … [then] … splitting must occur along with or precede the act of choosing …" (p. 275). This leads him on to consider Freud's paper "On Narcissism: An Introduction" (1914c) and to present its consequences as follows: "The outcome of the suckler-suckling relationship … [is] … the formation of a deep-rooted memory of it which is the basis of all subsequent relationships but affords the possibility of choice, flexibility and change" (p. 275).

He points out that the ability to choose between an identification with one or the other of the "nursing couple" means that a third position has been created.

> The new, observing and reflective self can identify now more with one end of the composite unity of self-and-mother, now more with the other, and re-establish a two term relationship by making either identification. Pathology would start from an inability, or a lessened ability, to take up any one of the three positions; the normal ego is able to move between them. (p. 275)

This discussion is at the heart of Fairbairn's model of endopsychic structure. In particular Padel stresses,

> Exchange in that first relationship is of far more than milk and bodily contacts: there is acknowledgement of feelings and of mutuality in feeling and there is reciprocal observation. In the infant's internalisation of the relationship, a special place is taken by the mother's eyes; if we suppose that the composite unity of lips-and-nipple, of mouth-and-breast forms the oral nucleus of the ego, the observing eyes, in so far as they are separate, form the nucleus of the later superego … (Gough, 1962, p. 275)

Padel suggests that these wider considerations of relations between egos have led to "a good beginning" for psychology through the work of Fairbairn and Winnicott. His interpretation is based on Fairbairn's understanding of endopsychic structure.

> One of Fairbairn's most important contributions to our ideas about the functioning of the ego is that what is repressed is always a relationship (though it may be symbolised or

represented as an object). On the two-person level the relation is one between self and others; on the three-person level it is between self-and-other bound in mutual control and self-and-other bound in mutual desire. The idea that what is repressed is always a relationship, simple or complex, is consonant with the idea that I have stated earlier, that what is internalised is always a relationship (or that complex of relationships which is a total situation) although it may be symbolised or represented by an object ... Fairbairn's papers are often written in one-person-psychology terms, yet the three-person relationship (not just the oedipal) are always present, with the two-person relationship either just past, threatening to return, or seen as a goal ahead. (p. 278)

Padel points out that Fairbairn, like Winnicott, believed "in the importance of the real, as well as the phantasied, relationship" (p. 278). He goes on to explain that

[Fairbairn] related all pathology to failure to maintain essential closeness at various stages of development, and saw the failures to do so as necessitating the individual's sustained attempts to divest his object of its most disturbing features, i.e. its over-exciting quality and its forbidding authority. This defensive splitting of the object was of course undertaken after internalisation and entailed an involuntary splitting of the ego, because of the profound attachment to the exciting object and no less because of the profound reliance upon the overseeing and control which the forbidding authority ensured. (p. 278)

Padel also relates the internalisation and splitting of the object relationships to Palombo's (1976, 1984) thinking on dreams. Palombo's explanation of where dream thoughts come from has strong parallels to Fairbairn's "state of affairs" account of dreaming. It goes as follows,

[I]n transferring items from the day's residue from short-term to long-term memory overnight, in one phase of that transfer we visually recall selected events of the day, and alongside of the recall engage in a search of the early-established (filed therefore under childhood memories) for matching and then for the establishing of association-points for rapid reference. (p. 280)

"'Narcissism' in Fairbairn's Theory of Personality Structure"
(originally published 1986, *British Journal of Psychotherapy*)

Padel locates Fairbairn, living in Edinburgh, and his relationship to others in the British Psychoanalytical Society in London, as one solely mediated during the 1940s and 1950s by his writings. Fairbairn's not being present at discussions of the Society meant that theorists like Klein, Winnicott, and Balint did not often relate their thought to Fairbairn's even though his theories transcended the one-person psychology that Balint and Rickman felt had long restricted classical psychoanalytic thinking. Winnicott had not recognised that the term "transitional", which he came to adopt in the early 1950s, had been used by Fairbairn a decade before and he never "overtly related the gap between what he called 'the true self' and 'the false self' to the splitting processes that Fairbairn had shown to be of central importance in human development and psychopathology" (p. 289).

Padel rehearses Fairbairn's journey from his 1940 paper that maintained that "the basic position in the psyche is invariably a schizoid position" to his development four years later of his model of "endopsychic structure considered in terms of object-relationships", in which the schizoid processes were shown to lead to and account for the structured development of the psyche, both normal and pathological.

He cites Phyllis Grosskurth's biography of Melanie Klein (1986), which argues that it was Fairbairn's 1944 paper "Endopsychic Structure Considered in Terms of Object-relationships" that initiated the last major creative period of Klein's life.

Padel then reviews Fairbairn's use of the term "narcissism", and his definition of primary narcissism as identification with an external object and secondary narcissism as identification with an internalised object. Narcissism in these terms is common to both early and late oral phases of development. However, loss of the object in the early oral phase is likely to lead to an experience of losing one's own ego, whereas loss of the object in the later oral phase is likely to lead to depression. "It is therefore justifiable to think of Fairbairn's whole exposition of object-relationships (certainly internal, and external as long as they are influenced by the internal) as a detailed account of narcissism …" (p. 291).

But Padel continues to say that Fairbairn probably thought that the term narcissism was not a useful term since it was too biased towards the pathological and too derogatory as a scientific term.

Padel next turns to an article by Rubens (1984). In introducing Rubens's paper, he agrees with Fairbairn's criticism of Freud's separation of energy and structure in his structural model and the prime importance of object seeking and relationship from the start.

> Fairbairn had maintained the inseparability of energy and structure and therefore would not accept the presence in the mind of unstructured energy (Freud's Id) in contradistinction to the structured (and relatively unenergised) Ego … he had insisted that the individual ego is object-related from the start and therefore seeks an emotionally satisfying *relationship* with another person (an "object"). (p. 293)

He points out that for Rubens, Fairbairn's account of psychic structure is one of psychopathology. Padel says that while almost all psychoanalytic theories have a metaphor for psychoanalytic growth, in Fairbairn the differentiated structures have been created by a defensive act against "intolerably bad" object relationships. Rubens argues that all internalisations cannot be structure generating and that psychic growth must depend upon "non-structuring internalisations". Padel does raise the question of the initial structuring of the endopsychic structure and argues for the internalisation of the whole situation prior to its being split into the exciting and rejecting bad objects.

> Pace Rubens, my inference is that Fairbairn came to regard any act of internalisation as preceding the splitting of the object into good and bad elements which are only then disposed of by acceptance (of "good") in the central self or by repression (of "bad") into the libidinal-antilibidinal system. (p. 295)

Padel refers back to Freud's paper "On Narcissism" (1914c) and quotes Freud, "A human being has originally two sexual objects—himself and the women who nurse him …", and he goes on to argue that this is Fairbairn's model for all forms of internalisation. He accepts that Rubens has …

> pointed to an important incompleteness in Fairbairn's theory of psychic structure: although Fairbairn insisted on "dynamic structure", he has no image for psychic growth and gives no account of the ongoing interchange which there must be between the central ego and the split-off libidinal and antilibidinal selves [for growth to occur]. (p. 296)

Padel then develops his own view of the process of psychic growth, which includes an understanding of how Fairbairn came to present a "rather static" picture of the psyche. He revisits the discussion of how the good object is internalised, which Fairbairn had initially rejected since he assumed that there was goodness inside. Fairbairn's final idea is that an unsatisfactory pre-ambivalent object is internalised, and *after* internalisation, *and* more experience of relations with the object, *and* after the arrival of ambivalence (second oral phase), there is splitting of the internalised object into acceptable (good, ideal, preconscious), over-exciting (libidinal, unconscious) and over rejecting/frustrating (anti-libidinal, unconscious) selves. Padel comments,

> … by asking about the conditions upon which a good ego-object relationship is centrally internalised or an ambivalent ego-object relationship, having been internalised, is made good enough for acceptance by the central ego, it may be possible here to remedy the incompleteness to which Rubens has pointed … [E]very meaningful encounter with another person may modify, slightly or radically, the primary nucleus with all the transformations it has undergone since it was first formed by the internalisation of the nursing couple. (p. 299)

Padel specifies two conditions for the acceptance of a newly internalised relationship into the central ego. The positive condition is that we have been able to reflect upon it and to regard each of its elements from the point of view of the other. The negative condition is the judgment that there are no obstacles to reflection upon it, no elements in conflict with the ego's established nature, and nothing to prevent regard of each element from the point of view of the other. If any unacceptable elements are found the relationship may be filed for working over or may be relegated to join repressed libidinal-antilibidinal systems. Reflection, regard, and judgment are the central activities that maintain growth of self.

"The Psychoanalytic Theories of Melanie Klein and Donald Winnicott and their interaction in the British Psychoanalytical Society" (1991)

Padel presents his reminiscences of Klein and Winnicott, who were distant from him: "[T]hey were high-ups and, anyway had their own colleagues and supporters." This is a detailed, personal account of Padel's experience of the British Society from the time of his own training beginning in 1952, to the time of its presentation in 1989. He argues that Klein and Winnicott were important because they wrote more than the others, were seen to be founders of the object relations approach, and because their charisma attracted followers.

In this paper, Padel restates his belief that Winnicott's paper entitled "Primitive Emotional Development" (1945) was an attempt to get Klein to accept his formulation of the earliest stages of an infant's development. Padel believes that Klein's "Notes on Some Schizoid Mechanisms" (1946) was a response to Winnicott's paper, but he also notes that, according to Grosskurth (1986), Klein had also been spurred to write the paper by Fairbairn's publication in 1944 of his paper on endopsychic structure. Padel notes,

> Fairbairn's paper had interested her, particularly its emphasis on schizoid (i.e., splitting) processes in the personality, which, he argued, were the factor that determined the structure of object-relationships and so psychic structure itself; the schizoid state and position were more fundamental than the depressive position. (p. 338)

According to Padel, Klein paid tribute to Fairbairn's important new ideas, but qualified her approval by combining Fairbairn's term "schizoid" with her term "paranoid". She therefore proposed to call the pre-depressive position the "paranoid-schizoid" position. Padel comments,

> The splitting that Fairbairn had described was not only a splitting of the object but a splitting of the ego. This Klein accepted but not that the splitting of the ego is bound up with the splitting of the object; what brings about ego-splitting is a process for which she invented the term projective identification. (p. 338)

Towards the end of this paper, Padel describes the situation at around the time of Fairbairn's death in 1965:

> The concept of splitting as a basic function in the human mind, which could be used to *explain development and growth as well as pathology*, was first written about in a series of papers by Fairbairn, to which both Klein and Winnicott showed an ambivalent attitude. (p. 344, emphasis added)

Padel suggests that Sutherland, who was head of the Tavistock Clinic, and editor of the *International Journal* and the *International Library of Psychoanalysis*, "did more even than the star performers to shape psychoanalytic thinking in the fifties and sixties" (p. 344). Padel comments on a scientific meeting in the year of Fairbairn's death, which Winnicott chaired and at which Sutherland gave an "illuminating account" of Fairbairn's work, saying,

> I was glad that both he (Winnicott) and Masud Khan individually recanted the joint paper they had published in 1953 as a review of Fairbairn's book. Each confessed that he had not really understood it at the time. I should think they both had a strong resistance to understanding it, because it put forward a scheme that bridged both Winnicott's and Klein's individual statements of infantile development. Winnicott did not like his paradoxes deconstructed any more than Klein liked alternative terminology to her own, still less a discussion of how pathology in the mother affected the child. (p. 344)

"Fairbairn's Thought on the Relationship of Inner and Outer Worlds",
Free Associations, Vol. 2, 24(4) (1991).

This profound paper was delivered at a conference in Edinburgh in September 1989, celebrating the centenary of Fairbairn's birth. He began with an appreciation of Dr John Sutherland, who had first recommended Fairbairn's work to him at the end of Padel's training at the Tavistock. Padel goes on to show appreciation for the "new interest, which American writers are taking in the British school of object-relations". He mentions Otto Kernberg in particular who "has been calling attention ... to Fairbairn's papers for over twenty years", and notes Sutherland's opinion that Fairbairn was strongly influential on Kohut. He also referenced both Greenberg and Mitchell's *Object Relations in Psychoanalytic Theory* (1983) and Judith Hughes's *Reshaping the Psychoanalytical Domain* (1989), repeating her judgment that "... only Fairbairn systematically scrutinised structure and only he directly challenged Freudian theory," and Greenberg and Mitchell's assertion that "only Fairbairn shows internal objects in relation to each other and that for him the internal world is a transformed version of the external world ... [but they add] that his is a psychopathological theory and not a general psychological theory" (p. 590).

Padel goes on to show his appreciation for Sutherland's recently published biography of Fairbairn—*Fairbairn's Journey into the Interior* (1989)—where he says there is a "fine balance between his account of the facts and circumstances of Fairbairn's life and his discussion of the influence which they had upon his psychological make-up" (p. 591).

Padel suggests that two of Fairbairn's later papers, "Observations on the Nature of Hysterical States" (1954b) and "On the Nature and Aims of Psycho-analytical Treatment" (1958a) would make "an excellent introduction to psychotherapy" (p. 592).

What is new in this paper is Padel's comparison between Freud and Fairbairn. He overlays Fairbairn's diagram on the classical Freudian diagram from "The Dissection of the Psychical Personality" (1933a), and then revisits Fairbairn's account and interpretation of his patient's specimen dream in 1944. (This diagram is reproduced in this book on page 285.)

Padel concedes that Rubens's criticism that Fairbairn's theory allows only "pathological structure and gives little or no account of normal growth and development" is just, but Padel is not happy with Rubens's account of growth. His search for a better solution leads him back to Freud's paper on narcissism (1914c), where he addresses the uses to which the two and three-term relationship are put in therapy:

> ... the analyst uses a split in him or herself creatively to help the patient to overcome the rigidity of a split in him or her. This is implied in the use of countertransference, recommended by Paula Heimann (1950). With one side of him or herself the therapist may experience the intense feelings which the patient's talk may from time to time evoke; from another position he notices objectively, and may interpret, what is happening in the therapeutic relationship to account for it. (p. 602)

Having discussed how a split in the ego can make a three-term relationship out of a two-person situation, Padel goes on to discuss Ogden's (1987) account of how a split in the object can have a similar effect:

> The little girl finds a father in mother before she makes her own discovery of her real father; thanks to the split in mother based on her identification with her own father, it becomes easy for the girl to establish a three-person relationship between herself and her mother. (p. 602)

After a detailed look at Fairbairn's model and its origins in a patient's dream, Padel cites Gough's (1962) observation of mother–infant feeding relations, concluding that "looking and feeding were intimately related; mothers who never looked had babies that fed interruptedly; mothers who stared at their babies quickly inhibited their feeding; those babies fed best whose mothers looked now and then" (p. 605).

Padel says that from this point on he has taken the nucleus of the superego to be the mother's eyes.

Padel goes on to ask, "What is the structure of the Central Ego, and how has it grown?" (p. 607). For Padel the central ego is an emotionally rich and complex store of available relationships and relational possibilities. The subsidiary ego-object relationships are also complex, but they cannot be "absolutely split off" from the central ego. If analytical therapy works "it does so by making more exchanges available between the Central Ego and its subsidiaries, which allows the whole personality more possibilities of exchange with other people in the outside world" (p. 608).

Referring to recent work by Palombo (1976), Padel argues that new experiences are internalised by …

> sorting and filing largely unconsciously during sleep. The already repressed attracts relational experiences that have links with it but also may be worked over and even released from repression if suitable links are found with preconscious memories and with fresh material. In that way new experiences can change one's attitude to the external world and make one re-sort one's internal files. (p. 608)

Padel then offers an account of growth in the central ego.

"The growth of the Central Ego must take place by working over and accepting elements from the repressed structures … This is the crucial importance of transference interpretations" (p. 608).

His account is along the following lines: "[F]irst the therapist shows understanding of the three-person situation presented by the patient." The repressed relationships in this situation cannot be equally bad or equally repressed at the same time. "[T]he libidinal is 'bad' when it threatens basic stability, which the anti-libidinal ensures; the anti-libidinal is 'bad' when it prevents or inhibits basic enjoyment which gives meaning to living." Based upon the therapist's assessment of the situation, "[T]he therapist [is] showing that the patient is putting him in the role now of the seducer or disturber, now the disapprover or inhibitor." "Finally the previously rejected libidinal-anti-libidinal relationship may be reviewed for its reality-based badness or desirability" (p. 609).

After discussing Guntrip's paper on his analyses with Fairbairn and Winnicott, Padel offers an interpretation of one of Guntrip's dreams and presents clinical material from his own practice. Padel summarises his view of Fairbairn's ideas, which I will quote in full.

Identification, which he assumed to be almost total initially for the infant, implies complete acceptance of the world outside: this establishes the libidinal side of the personality. Opposing barriers to such openness are soon raised, also by identification, and establish the anti-libidinal side, which serves as a control system. However, the external world is always available, even if less so than it might be. Setting free the inner world so as to bring about new internal relations takes place mostly in the two-person relationship; to do this is to promote exchanges with other people in the world outside, but perceiving and thinking are primarily in terms of relations between other people and between others and ourselves. (p. 613)

Conclusion and summary

I have listed below what I consider to be the most important topics Padel deals with in his various papers.

- The origin of object relations lie in Freud's papers "On Narcissism" and "Group Psychology and the Analysis of the Ego".
- Fairbairn took more from Abraham than he realised.
- Fairbairn influenced Klein strongly in her work after 1944.
- Winnicott and Khan both retracted their damning review of Fairbairn's book after he died.
- Guntrip tried to introduce a new aspect to Fairbairn's model with the regressed ego, the cogency of which Padel seriously challenges.
- Sutherland was a crucial supporter and interpreter of Fairbairn's work.
- Fairbairn discussed transitional processes a decade before Winnicott.
- Padel uses the work of Gough on early object relations to identify the mother's eyes as the nucleus of the early superego.
- Padel show's how Fairbairn's model of endopsychic structure and Freud's structural model can be reconciled, with significant provisos.
- Padel shows how Fairbairn's model can provide both two- and three-person models of relationships.
- Padel addresses Rubens's and Mitchell's accounts of Fairbairn's model as being based in psychopathology and therefore not accounting for psychic growth. He offers a solution.
- Padel's account of growth as the working over of object relationships in relation to libidinal and anti-libidinal selves, leading to their reintegration into the central self.
- Padel uses Palombo's account of the way in which daily experience gets stored in inner reality during sleep to illuminate the ways in which two-person relationships might become three-term relationships.
- Padel quotes Fairbairn's view of the importance of the Oedipus situation—for therapy but not for theory.

References

Fairbairn, W. R. D. (1938a). Prolegomena to a psychology of art. *British Journal of Psychology, 28*: 288–303. In: E. F. Birtles & D. E. Scharff (Eds.), *From Instinct to Self: Selected Papers of W. R. D. Fairbairn, Volume II: Applications and Early Contributions* (pp. 381–396). Northvale, NJ: Jason Aronson, 1994.

Fairbairn, W. R. D. (1938b). The ultimate basis of aesthetic experience. In: E. F. Birtles & D. E. Scharff (Eds.), *From Instinct to Self: Selected Papers of W. R. D. Fairbairn, Volume II: Applications and Early Contributions* (pp. 397–409). Northvale, NJ: Jason Aronson, 1994.

Fairbairn, W. R. D. (1940a). Schizoid factors in the personality. In: *Psychoanalytic Studies of the Personality* (pp. 3–27). London: Tavistock, 1952.

Fairbairn, W. R. D. (1941). A revised psychopathology of the psychoses and the psychoneuroses. *International Journal of Psychoanalysis, 22*(3, 4): 250–279. In: *Psychoanalytic Studies of the Personality* (pp. 28–58). London: Tavistock. 1952.

Fairbairn, W. R. D. (1943a). The repression and return of bad objects (with special reference to the "war neuroses"). *British Journal of Medical Psychology, 19*: 327–341. In: *Psychoanalytic Studies of the Personality* (pp. 59–81). London: Tavistock, 1952.

Fairbairn, W. R. D. (1944). Endopsychic structure considered in terms of object-relationships. *International Journal of Psychoanalysis, 25*: 70–92. In: *Psychoanalytic Studies of the Personality* (pp. 82–136). London: Tavistock, 1952.

Fairbairn, W. R. D. (1952). *Psychoanalytic Studies of the Personality*. London: Tavistock.

Fairbairn, W. R. D. (1954b). Observations on the nature of hysterical states. *British Journal of Medical Psychology, 27*(3): 105–125. In: D. E. Scharff & E. F. Birtles (Eds.), *From Instinct to Self: Selected Papers of W. R. D. Fairbairn, Volume I: Clinical and Theoretical Papers* (pp. 13–40). Northvale, NJ: Jason Aronson, 1994.

Fairbairn, W. R. D. (1958a). On the nature and aims of psycho-analytical treatment. *International Journal of Psychoanalysis, 39*(5): 374–385. In: D. E. Scharff & E. F. Birtles (Eds.), *From Instinct to Self: Selected Papers of W. R. D. Fairbairn, Volume I: Clinical and Theoretical Papers* (pp. 74–92). Northvale, NJ: Jason Aronson, 1994.

Freud, S. (1914c). On narcissism: an introduction. *S. E., 14*. London: Hogarth.

Freud, S. (1917c). On transformations of instinct as exemplified in anal erotism. *S. E., 17*. London: Hogarth.

Freud, S. (1921c). *Group Psychology and the Analysis of the Ego. S. E., 18*. London: Hogarth.

Freud, S. (1923b). *The Ego and the Id. S. E., 19*. London: Hogarth.

Freud, S. (1933a). *New Introductory Lectures on Psycho-Analysis. S. E., 22*. London: Hogarth.

Gough, D., (1962). The visual behaviour of the human infant in the first few weeks of life. *Proceedings of the Royal Society of Medicine, 55*: 308–310.

Greenberg, J. R., & Mitchell, S. A. (1983). *Object Relations in Psychoanalytic Theory*. Cambridge, MA: Harvard University Press.

Grosskurth, P. (1986). *Melanie Klein: Her World and Her Work*. London: Hodder.

Guntrip, H. (1996). My experience of analysis with Fairbairn and Winnicott: (How complete …). *International Journal of Psychoanalysis, 77*: 739–754.

Hughes, J. M. (1990). *Reshaping the Psychoanalytic Domain*. Berkeley, CA: University of California Press.

Klein, M. (1946). Notes on some schizoid mechanisms. In: *Envy and Gratitude and Other Works: 1921–1963* (pp. 1–24). London: Hogarth, 1975.

Laplanche, J., & Pontalis, J. B. (1973). *The Language of Psycho-Analysis*. D. Nicholson-Smith (Trans.). The International Psycho-Analytical Library, 94: 1–497. London: Hogarth and the Institute of Psycho-Analysis.

Modell, A. H. (1970). *Object Love and Reality*. London: Hogarth.

Ogden, T. H. (1983). The concept of internal object relations. *International Journal of Psychoanalysis, 64*: 227–241.

Ogden, T. H. (1987). The transitional Oedipal relationship in female development. *International Journal of Psychoanalysis, 68*: 485–498.
Padel, J. (1970). *Object Love and Reality* by Arnold H. Modell. *International Journal of Psychoanalysis, 51*: 84–87.
Padel, J. (1973). The contribution of W. R. D. Faisrbairn (1889–1965) to psychoanalytic theory and practice. *European Psycho-Analytic Foundation Bulletin.*
Padel, J. (1981). *New Poems by Shakespeare: Order and Meaning Restored to the Sonnets.* London: Herbert Press.
Padel, J. (1985). Ego in current thinking. *International Review of Psycho-Analysis, 12*: 273–283.
Padel, J. (1990). *Reshaping the Psychoanalytic Domain* by Judith Hughes. *International Journal of Psychoanalysis, 71*: 715–717.
Padel, J. (1991a). Fairbairn's thought on the relationship of inner and outer worlds. *Free Associations, 2*: 589–615.
Padel, J. (1991b). The psychoanalytic theories of Melanie Klein and Donald Winnicott and their interaction in the British Society of Psychoanalysis, *Psychoanalytic Review, 78*: 325–345.
Padel, J. (1986). "Narcissism" in Fairbairn's theory of personality structure. *British Journal of Psychotherapy, vol. 3* (pp. 256–264). In: J. S. Grotstein & D. B. Rinsley (Eds.), *Fairbairn and the Origin of Object Relations.* London: Free Association, 1994.
Padel, J. (1995). *The Autonomous Self: The Work of John D. Sutherland.* J. S. Scharff (Ed.). *International Journal of Psychoanalysis, 76*: 177–179.
Padel, J. (1996). The case of Harry Guntrip. *International Journal of Psychoanalysis, 77*: 755–761.
Palombo, S. R. (1976). The dream and the memory cycle. *International Review of Psycho-Analysis, 3*: 65–83.
Palombo, S. R. (1984). The poet as dreamer. *Journal of the American Academy of Psychoanalysis, 12*: 59–73.
Rubens, R. L. (1984). The meaning of structure in Fairbairn. *International Review of Psycho-Analysis, 11*: 429–440.
Scharff, J. S. (Ed.) (1994). *The Autonomous Self: The Work of John D. Sutherland.* London: Jason Aronson.
Sutherland, J. D. (1989). *Fairbairn's Journey to the Interior.* London: Free Association.
Winnicott, D. W. (1945). Primitive emotional development. *International Journal of Psychoanalysis, 26*: 137–143.
Winnicott, D. W. (1951). Transitional objects and transitional phenomena. In: *Through Paediatrics to Psycho-Analysis.* London: Tavistock, 1975.
Winnicott, D. W., & Khan, M. R. (1953). Psychoanalytic Studies of the Personality: By W. Ronald D. Fairbairn (London: Tavistock). *International Journal of Psychoanalysis, 34*: 329–333.

CHAPTER TWENTY-THREE

Fairbairn elaborated: Guntrip and the psychoanalytic romantic model

Michael Stadter

Harry Guntrip, a student, patient and colleague of Fairbairn, was the earliest and most effective writer and teacher in introducing the world to Fairbairn's writing. He also wrote extensively on the work of others in the British Object Relations School prompting Greenberg and Mitchell (1983) to describe him as "the foremost historian, synthesizer, and popularizer of the study of object relations within the writings of Klein, Fairbairn, and Winnicott" (p. 209). Guntrip clearly saw the revolutionary importance of Fairbairn's theories and promoted his work in a manner that was passionate, clear, clinically grounded, and much more readable than Fairbairn's. Odgen (2010) characterised Fairbairn's writing as having: "… a dense prose style, a highly abstract form of theorizing and a set of unfamiliar theoretical terms (for example, dynamic structure, endopsychic structure, central ego, internal saboteur, libidinal ego, exciting object, rejecting object, and so on) that have not been adopted by subsequent analytic theorists" (p. 103), and "The density of the prose, the mechanical nature of the metaphors, the level of abstraction, the heavy reliance on his own technical terminology, together denude Fairbairn's statement of almost anything recognizable as human experience" (p. 115).

By contrast, Guntrip very successfully presents the humanity in Fairbairn's work, further extending those elements in his own writing. A highly creative thinker and clinician in his own right, Guntrip, in my opinion, both presented Fairbairn's work in a manner true to Fairbairn's writing and also diverged from it. Guntrip became somewhat of a controversial figure, and some writers have argued that he distorts Fairbairn's work (Greenberg & Mitchell, 1983; Hughes, 1989; Kernberg, 1980; Rinsley, 1994) while others have defended him (Forbes, 1996; Hazell, 1994).

In this chapter, I suggest that the tensions between the classical and romantic trends in psychoanalysis are evidenced in Guntrip's relationship to Fairbairn's contributions. Primarily, he emphasised the romantic elements of Fairbairn's thinking and minimised or dismissed the classical elements. This has both benefits and liabilities. Guntrip's emphasis on regression, elaboration of schizoid experience, the concept of self, development of the concept of the regressed libidinal ego, and work on the nature of the therapeutic relationship, advance clinical practice. The work of many therapists has been greatly enhanced by his thinking. These concepts move his work in line with subsequent developments such as self psychology, humanistic psychology, implicit experience, and the therapeutic alliance. After describing the classical and romantic psychoanalytic visions, I present an overview of Guntrip's life and relationship with Fairbairn, highlighting his analyses with Fairbairn and Winnicott. I conclude with a summary of some of Guntrip's major contributions and situate them within the romantic psychoanalytic tradition.

The classical and romantic traditions and Guntrip's romantic emphasis

In an insightful article, Strenger (1989) wrote of two paradigms in psychoanalysis, philosophy, and life. He quotes Hulme (1924) on the two. The classical view is that humanity "… is intrinsically limited, but disciplined by order and tradition to something fairly decent," while "… the romantic vision holds that man is intrinsically good, spoilt by circumstance" (p. 117). Each vision highlights certain aspects of psychic life and while no analytic perspective on development, theory, or technique is purely one or the other, there may be more of an emphasis on the classical or the romantic. Strenger suggests Freud and Klein as representatives of a strongly classical view. In their work there is an emphasis on rationality and maturity, on identifying unconscious, negative, disavowed motivations and on not fully trusting the patient's statements. "The analyst's attitude towards the patient is a combination of respect and suspicion and the analyst takes the side of the reality principle. The ethic is stoic: maturity and mental health depend on the extent to which a person can acknowledge reality as it is and be rational and wise" (Strenger, 1989, p. 601). He identifies Kohut and Winnicott as exemplars of the romantic tradition with importance placed on freedom, subjectivity, development of a unique, cohesive self, and on liveliness and spontaneity *vs.* depletion and depression. "The patient's symptoms are [seen as] the desperate attempt to fill the vacuum in his depleted self. The analyst's attitude towards the patient is one of trust in his humanity and the analyst takes the side of joy and vitality. The ethic is romantic: maturity and mental health consist in the ability to sustain enthusiasm and a sense of meaning" (p. 601). The classical tradition favours attitudes of realism, measured pessimism, control, and unblinking attention to problems and malevolence in the human psyche. The romantic tradition tilts towards attitudes of aspiration, measured optimism, the search for meaning, and attention to the positive potentials of what the person can become. A full view of humanity requires both perspectives. Both of these approaches can and do contribute to therapeutic change. Strenger gives a technical illustration.

> Many good interpretations are combinations of the two attitudes. They confront the patient with what he does, desires, believes and how he distorts his perception of himself and others. This helps the patient to improve on his reality testing, and it opens new options to understand and experience himself and others [the classical]. But they also enable him to see that there has not been another way for him to deal with particular aspects of internal and external

reality, they help him to see the human core behind what has seemed irreducibly perverse and revolting to him [the romantic]. (ibid., p. 605)

The classical approach would highlight the mutative effect of skilful, timely, and accurate interpretations while the romantic analytic approach would emphasise the healing effect of deep empathy and attunement. As stated above, my view is that Guntrip stressed the romantic elements of Fairbairn's work and extended them in his own contributions. Certainly the influence of Winnicott is apparent in Guntrip's writing and he puts forth a therapeutic approach that integrates the two theorists. Some of Guntrip's concepts are natural extensions of the romantic aspects of Fairbairn, and Guntrip indicated that Fairbairn agreed with them. Yet, if readers were to only read his descriptions of Fairbairn, they would not fully see the classical dimension of his theory.

Harry Guntrip (1901–1975)

Unless otherwise noted, I have summarised biographical and treatment information from Guntrip's (1975) evocative article on his analyses with Fairbairn and Winnicott. His father was a minister and Guntrip initially followed in his father's footsteps by joining the ministry himself. While a connection to and conflict about religion was a key theme throughout his life, he found that psychoanalysis provided him with a deeper understanding of the human condition. He described his first seven years of life as "the grossly disturbed period for me" (p. 149). His mother had great difficulty being a caregiver and said later in life that she should never have had children. The central traumas in his life revolved around this neglectful and abusive mother and a repressed experience at the age of three and a half of seeing his one-and-a-half-year-old brother, Percy, dead on his mother's lap. He believed this generated a lifelong struggle between states of regressive collapse—both physical and psychic—and states of productive, even driven, vitality.

Guntrip became an analysand of Fairbairn (in the 1950s) and then of Winnicott (1962–1968), taking careful notes on his analytic sessions with both of them. A highly unusual aspect of his analysis with Fairbairn is that, following the analytic sessions, they had meetings in which they would discuss theory. Guntrip experienced Fairbairn quite differently in each of these contexts. "Realistically, he was my understanding good father after sessions, and in session in the transference he was my dominating bad mother imposing exact interpretations" (p. 147). Of course, his interactions with Fairbairn in both roles were infused with both transference and realistic elements.

While he wrote that he benefited from Fairbairn's orthodox analysis of his "internalized bad-object defences" (p. 152), he believed he needed something more: "To my surprise, I found him gradually falling back on the 'classical analyst' with an interpretive technique, when I felt I needed to regress to the level of that severe infancy trauma" (p. 146). Both his protest against Fairbairn's predominantly interpretative approach in sessions and his expressed need for a regression back to an early developmental stage illustrate his romantic analytic vision.

With Fairbairn's health failing, Guntrip ended treatment in 1959 and began analysis with Winnicott in 1962. He experienced Winnicott as a good mother: "Here at last I had a good mother who could value her child so that I could cope with what was to come ... Winnicott becoming the good mother, freeing me to be alive and creative, transformed the significance of Percy's death in a way that was to enable me to resolve that trauma" (p. 153). Also, here is evidence of the romantic paradigm.

Yet, Guntrip found he could not fully resolve the trauma with either of his analysts, but did so alone years later. The catalyst was retirement forced by health issues and it produced a series of dreams about a terrifying, unresponsive mother. He came to understand his regressive collapses as retreats from this mother—the regressions were necessary for survival, literally and psychically. Consistent with Fairbairn's proposition that the patient cannot give up a bad object without having something to replace it, Winnicott had become a good object in the analysis, enabling Guntrip to set free his own potential to heal and to grow. Yet, it was only on his own—and after the deaths of both analysts—that he would be able to work through the trauma. Note again the romantic vision of the inherent goodness of the self, freed by a good, generative relationship to become more fully one's self. Guntrip's Oedipal analytic work with Fairbairn opened up the possibility of pre-Oedipal exploration but he believed that Fairbairn's approach could not go to that level. He did find that Winnicott and he made very significant pre-Oedipal progress. While grateful to both analysts, Guntrip's narrative of his journey of self-development ends with the *self* being the agent of self-development. This emphasis diverges from Fairbairn's (see below).

Guntrip offered dramatically contrasting pictures of his two analysts. Fairbairn was formal, presented exacting interpretations, and was rather traditional in technique but revolutionary in his theory. The implication was that Fairbairn did not follow through on the clinical implications of how revolutionary and divergent from Freud his theory was. He may have exaggerated Fairbairn's differences from Freud (see Kernberg, 1980). By contrast, Winnicott was described as being warm and informal, presenting interpretations as "imaginative hypotheses" (p. 155), and was highly creative in technique but rather traditional in theory. Despite his view of Winnicott as being traditional theoretically, Guntrip was very influenced by Winnicott's concepts of self and development.

For more detail on Guntrip's life and work, I highly recommend Hazell (1994, 1996). Readers interested in critiques of Guntrip's article on his analyses can refer to Eigen (1981), Glatzer and Evans (1977), Greenberg and Mitchell (1983), and Hughes (1989). Much has been made by some of these writers (e.g., Hughes, 1989) about what this article says about Guntrip's personality and unresolved psychological issues. I would urge readers, though, as does Forbes (1996), to not use the critiques as ad hominem arguments against his theory and practice but, rather to evaluate them on their own analytic and applied merits. It is clear that Guntrip wrote this article, in part, to present clinical material to support his theories and he explicitly acknowledges that his personal life played an important role in their development.

Guntrip's major contributions

Schizoid phenomena

Both Fairbairn and Guntrip were fascinated by the schizoid realm and wrote evocatively about schizoid individuals and the schizoid trends in all of us. Fairbairn's (1952) landmark book,

Psychoanalytic Studies of the Personality, opens with a chapter on schizoid phenomena. In it, he described the three signature characteristics of the inner world of schizoid individuals. All three can be conscious or unconscious, overt or covert. The first is an attitude of omnipotence which may operate only in some domains of the person's personality and which may be concealed behind an appearance of inferiority. The second characteristic is an attitude of isolation and detachment which can also be hidden; the exterior can be one of sociability and/or emotionality. Third, Fairbairn described a preoccupation with inner reality which he stated was the most important of the three. The primacy of inner reality creates a closed system whereby the impact of the outer world is diminished as the inner world becomes a substitute for external reality.

Building on these three characteristics, Guntrip elaborated on the psyche and subjectivity of the schizoid person and on the experience of others relating to a person in a schizoid state. The most extensive presentation of his own views on theory and practice are in his book, *Schizoid Phenomena, Object Relations and the Self* (1969). The three themes in the title are particularly apt. The conceptualisation of *schizoid phenomena* and his treatment of schizoid patients are foundational in his work, life, and connection to Fairbairn. Guntrip's work is firmly grounded in the British Object Relations School and in the centrality of relatedness in health and illness. Finally, the forward thrust of his writing leads him to centre on the concept of *self* (see below).

Guntrip (1969) deepens our appreciation of schizoid features by enumerating nine characteristics:

Introversion

Psychic energy is directed towards the inner world and the person is cut off emotionally from the external world. Guntrip thought this was "the most general and all-embracing" (p. 41) of the nine features. The inner world may become rich while the external world may become impoverished.

Withdrawal

This is "the other side of introversion" (p. 42). Attachment is directed away from the outer world and others may experience the person as not really present.

Narcissism

Guntrip's emphasis on trends in the romantic model brings him closer to the work of some of the self psychologists (e.g., Kohut, 1971, 1977) and he explicitly lists narcissism as a schizoid characteristic with psychic energy directed towards the self. Including narcissism as a feature of the schizoid picture is very useful in alerting therapists to the narcissistic trends in schizoid experience and to the schizoid elements in narcissism. It is noteworthy that Fairbairn's theory itself bears many striking similarities to Kohut's subsequent theory, however, unacknowledged by Kohut (see Robbins, 1992).

Self-sufficiency

The person manages self experience and difficulty with dependency through an attitude of needing no one else. As an example, Guntrip described a woman who had the phantasy of not only having a baby but also of being the baby as well as the mother—and feeling in total control.

A sense of superiority

This is a state closely related to self-sufficiency and narcissism and wards off the vulnerability of the need for others and "feelings of inferiority, smallness and weakness" (1969, p. 43).

Loss of affect

Guntrip quoted a patient, "I can feel cold about all the people who are near and dear to me" (p. 44). Loss of affect is a natural consequence of the other aspects of the schizoid state. Guntrip described a particularly disturbing lack of affect in which people have no care or appreciation for their hurtful impact on others (lack of empathy). He also wrote of the "inhibition of the capacity to love" (p. 97).

Loneliness

It is significant that he includes this in his schizoid list because the foregoing characteristics describe how schizoid processes can inoculate the person against the experience of loneliness and longing for others. Yet, he emphasised that the need for others remains in schizoid individuals, painfully breaking through consciousness, at times. Guntrip's inclusion of loneliness highlights his and Fairbairn's view of the schizoid dilemma. It is not simply an escape or lack of desire for human contact. It is both a fear of and a desire for relationships—there are often states of either anxiety or longing. Guntrip describes schizoid individuals as frequently having difficulty achieving equilibrium. He termed this the "in and out programme" (p. 36) because they oscillate between states of being too closely connected with another person and states of being too distant. In attempting to find a balanced state, they try to work out a "schizoid compromise" (p. 288), which may feel comfortable but isolated or devitalised.

Depersonalisation

The schizoid processes may be so extensive—so much is split off—that a profound absence is created and the person loses a sense of identity. He described *"a schizoid problem of feeling a nobody, of never having grown an adequate feeling of a real self"* (p. 127, italics in the original). Similarly, the widespread withdrawal from external reality can cause an experience of derealisation with the external world appearing unreal. The lack of a real sense of self—a fear or experience of non-existence—was central in Guntrip's thinking on schizoid phenomena.

Regression

Guntrip saw schizoid processes as regressive phenomena. The person in a schizoid state flees from the terrifying external world into the relative safety of an internal world. Then, part of the self flees even from the internal world (the regressed libidinal ego). Regression is a central aspect of Guntrip's theories of development, pathology, treatment, and growth.

Regression and the regressed libidinal ego

His study of Fairbairn's ground-breaking work on the schizoid personality stimulated him to further explore schizoid experience and led him to the importance of regression, as just noted. Indeed, he saw the two as inextricably connected.

> Though *schizoid withdrawal and regression are fundamentally the same phenomenon*, they have different meanings for different parts of the total self. From the point of view of the central ego, i.e. the conscious self of everyday living, withdrawal means total loss. From the point of view of the part of the self that has withdrawn, it is not "loss" but "regression" or retreat backwards inside the small safe place, as represented in the extreme by the fantasy of a return to the womb. (ibid., p. 57, italics in original)

This emphasis on regression represented a divergence from Fairbairn. Guntrip noted that Fairbairn stressed the dangers of regression (Hazell, 1994, 1996) and resisted letting him regress in his analysis with him (Guntrip, 1975). While Guntrip (1969) acknowledged the risks (sometimes severe) of regression in his writing, he emphasised the benefits—perhaps even the necessity—of regression in development and in treatment (Ehrlich, 2009). This difference between Fairbairn and Guntrip was a difference between the classical and romantic analytic models. A major mechanism of change in the romantic paradigm is creating a safe enough environment so that patients become free to use their own inherent strengths for growth and revitalisation. This emphasis on regression moved Guntrip's work closer to the writing of Winnicott, Balint, and Ferenczi.

While still employing Fairbairn's concepts, Guntrip believed that they could not account for the earliest developmental processes manifested in deeply regressed states (Forbes, 1996).

> Fairbairn was the first analyst to expose the questionable logic of a developmental scheme based upon the energic concepts that Freud retained as his theoretical base. Fairbairn's scheme, however, did not account adequately for the earliest developmental stages as these were inferred from the study of regressive states. Guntrip, making full use of Winnicott's views, has sought to make good this limitation. (Sutherland, 1980, p. 858)

Fairbairn (1958a) held that the ultimate source of resistance in therapy was cathexis to internal bad objects. Guntrip (1961) found this to be valuable but incomplete and wrote that there was an even greater resistance—the regressive pull to a state of non-existence, a loss of self. Yet, he viewed regression as also crucial in recovering the self. Drawing on Winnicott's (1960) notion of the importance of regression to a level of the true self and on Balint's (1959, 1968) view that "radical" psychotherapy aims at offering a new beginning, Guntrip proposed his most important theoretical contribution, the "regressed libidinal ego" (RLE). This is the most deeply private and unconscious part of the psyche.

Guntrip situated the RLE as an addition to Fairbairn's endopsychic system. Fairbairn's paradigm, very briefly, includes three pairs of part-egos in primary relationship with part-objects: the central ego/ideal object, the libidinal ego/exciting object and the anti-libidinal ego/rejecting object. A central element of this model of personality is that the internal world is made up of ego-object pairs. Just as babies cannot exist without mothers (to paraphrase Winnicott's often quoted statement), an ego does not exist without a connection to an object. Some writers have concluded (e.g., Greenberg & Mitchell, 1983) that Guntrip argues otherwise with his concept of the RLE—that is, a self existing without an object. While Guntrip's writing on this can be somewhat confusing, my reading is that he (Guntrip, 1961, p. 435) indicates that the RLE *is* object-related. It is, though, a different type of object relationship—a relationship within a womb—unlike that described by Fairbairn which is a relationship with specific, differentiated objects.

The RLE splits off from the libidinal ego (that part of the self that wants and longs for relationship). It forms a fourth part-ego that is not in connection with a specific, differentiated Fairbairnian object. It is a retreat from the other internal psychic structures to return to the womb and so is in relationship with a phantasised intrauterine environment. As Hazell (1994) points out, the RLE is a split-off part of the libidinal ego and the term Guntrip selected is the regressed *libidinal* ego indicating that "however devitalized it may become, the regressed ego never loses its libidinal (i.e., person-seeking) quality" (p. 14). Winnicott's terms of object mother and environmental mother can be helpful here (for an application of this distinction to therapy, see also Scharff & Scharff, 1998, on focused and contextual transferences). While the Fairbairnian internal objects develop more from the object mother, the RLE is in connection with aspects of the environmental mother. It is noteworthy that Fairbairn accepted the RLE as an addendum to his theory and wrote to Guntrip, "I consider your concept of the splitting of the Libidinal Ego into two parts—an oral, needy libidinal ego, and a regressed libidinal ego—an original contribution of considerable explanatory value. It solves a problem which I had not hitherto succeeded in solving" (quoted in Hazell, 1994, p. 15).

The withdrawal into the inner world occurs because the external world is too unsafe due to either attack or neglect. However, once a person withdraws into the inner world, there is still no total safety. There are active attacks from other parts of the personality on the libidinal ego, for example, from the central ego and the anti-libidinal ego. In other words, two withdrawals are necessary—from the external world *and* from the internal world. First, there is the generally observable withdrawal from the external world of relationships because it is too unsafe. The person then becomes preoccupied with the inner world behaviourally, cognitively, and affectively. The second withdrawal is from the *inner* world because it too is unsafe and frightening. The regressed ego is disconnected from other parts of the personality. In a recent article, Ehrlich (2009) critiques the concept of the RLE as very valuable but argued that Guntrip exaggerated its importance.

I have previously written about the RLE as a useful concept in understanding dissociative phenomena and the management of intense or primitive affects, such as shame (Stadter,

2012). For instance, an individual can escape from the shaming eyes of other people when alone but still feel intense shame from the "eyes" of one's own inner world. Escape from that shame requires a second withdrawal. The concept of the RLE depicts the predicament of the shamed self—both the outer world *and* the inner world are threatening, unsafe, and shaming.

The withdrawal to the RLE can function paradoxically both to promote and to impair the person. The retreat of the person into the regressed ego state can be to a womb or it can be to a tomb.

The RLE as a womb: Donald

The regression can be towards a nurturing, life-giving, early maternal environment and it can also cause a deadening, dissociated, devitalised state since it is so split off from the other objects, internal and external. As a womb it provides a protected state of isolation and safety. The person can escape from the pain and disorganisation of intense affects and this can stabilise the self. When the process moves positively, the individual recovers and finds enough equilibrium to leave the regressed ego state. The person no longer needs this second withdrawal, can tolerate psychic integration, and can manage the attacks from the various parts of the inner world. Guntrip (1961) wrote that the RLE represents the capacity for radical psychotherapeutic change: "… whereas all the other parts of the psyche tend to the rigidities characteristic of defensive structures, the Regressed L. E. retains the primary capacity for spontaneous and vigorous growth once it has been freed from fears. There lies the ultimate hope of psychotherapy" (p. 433).

Here is a clinical vignette (adapted from Stadter, 2012). In the first session, Donald averted his eyes, blushed, and in a nervous voice said he was feeling hopelessly inadequate with women. Over time, this shame-prone lawyer of twenty-seven revealed two patterns of failure with women that had prevented him having an enduring relationship. He often would choose unattainable women and then feel rejected by them. In a less frequent pattern, he would find a woman who wanted the relationship to continue. However, soon after Donald felt secure with her he would begin to feel that she was not good enough for him and he would end the relationship. I will describe a dream he had in the second year of his three-year, twice weekly therapy, but first here is a bit of history. As a child, he was very prone to shame. When he felt embarrassed at or near his home he literally retreated into a closet. He stayed there until his shame diminished and then he came out and resumed his interactions. The closet was the external equivalent of his RLE. During therapy, he reported several dreams about closets and he was always alone in them—until this dream:

> I'm in the closet again but different than it's ever been before. Susan's in it, too! The closet's not peaceful this time. Somebody's coming to attack us. I don't know who. We're trying to clear off shelves—there are shelves in the closet—so we can move. You know, so we can maneuver when they attack us. But she's getting in the way! She's not helping at all and I'm thinking, oh God! We're going to die! All because of her! I'm furious at her and I'm scared shitless. It wakes me up.

At the time Donald had the dream, he had been dating Susan for four months. He was feeling secure and accepted by her and was at his characteristic point of thinking that she wasn't good enough for him. However, he was resisting the urge to break up with her. His dream represented the beginning of him letting the RLE part of his psyche reconnect with the object world (internal and external). However, he was terrified about this intrusion into his "womb" and feared that his RLE or true self would not survive. He did persist in the relationship with Susan and was able to be more connected with parts of himself and with other people as well. He and Susan eventually married.

The dream also represented his struggle around intimacy with me. The "Susan" in the dream also symbolised me and his fear that I and some parts of himself would shame him for relying on and being vulnerable with me. We went through many cycles of his idealisation and subsequent disappointment and states of him expecting that I would shame him as his father, women, and Donald himself had done. In the therapy he gradually came to realise that I was good enough to continue with and safe enough to bring in deeper, more private material.

The RLE as a tomb: Miguel

Alternatively, the RLE can also be a tomb, in that such a profound internal retreat leaves this part of the self inaccessible to the rest of the personality, leaving it depleted. The RLE may fear leaving this safe place and this most private part of the self may stay concealed both from the rest of the psyche and from the external world of relationships. "It is the true source of all passive and regressive phenomena, exhaustion and fatigue, compulsive sleep, agoraphobic anxieties and the claustrophobias which are a reaction from them, phantasies of a return to the womb and retirement and escapist phantasies and longings in real life" (Guntrip, 1961, p. 432).

To illustrate the RLE as a tomb, I offer a dream from a patient in therapy with a colleague (J. Poulton, personal communication, 2012). Miguel, thirty-eight, had been successful financially and professionally but suffered from unstable self-esteem and lack of future direction in life. A key part of his history was a devaluing and hyper-controlling mother who impaired his development of self by telling him what he should do, think, and feel. During the therapy, he reported the following dream:

> I'm walking down a road and I come to a pasture with a fence around it, I climb the fence and there's a bull—it's enraged and big and it charges me. I run into the middle of the pasture where there's a tree. I climb it and the tree was dead all over but it was safe although I didn't know if I'd get down. The dream ended and I was feeling sad.

This dream illustrates a central aspect of Miguel's inner world: the fearful retreat of a part of the libidinal ego under attack by the anti-libidinal ego (the bull/mother). His RLE achieved a safe base but it is a dead place (the tree)—and he does not know if he will be able to escape from it. The sadness signifies the libidinal element of the RLE and the longing for vital object relations—internal and external. Guntrip described such a retreat as a flight away from the attacks of internal bad objects. As an aside, I think that, using our contemporary analytic sensibility, we can also view it as a regression *back to* the early deadened or neglectful environmental mother.

However, I believe this would not be consistent with Guntrip's view of regressive flight *away from* bad objects.

Miguel benefited from the therapy and his progress was promoted by a new awareness that he had unconsciously curbed his self-expression to protect against expected attacks from his internalised mother.

Regression and the therapeutic relationship

Guntrip (1969) saw Fairbairn's work as unfinished, not only concerning intrapsychic structure, but also regarding the therapeutic relationship. Fairbairn (1958a) wrote of the prime therapeutic importance of the therapist's "personal", "actual", "real", "total" relationship with the patient beyond its significance in providing the matrix for transference work. To write this in the 1950s was a major contribution and introduced a perspective that has been further developed by contemporary clinicians especially from object relations and relational school perspectives. Moreover, it has been validated by research on the therapeutic alliance (Muran & Barber, 2010) and common factors in psychotherapy efficacy (Norcross, 2002, 2011). Guntrip took this romantic element in Fairbairn's work and emphasised it even further as the only way to successfully treat what he viewed as the central terror in life and the source of all or most psychopathology—the fear of non-existence and the need to become "a person in one's own right" (Guntrip, 1961, p. 427). Using Winnicott's concepts of being and doing, Guntrip argued that the being of the therapist was a more important therapeutic factor than what the therapist did.

The RLE is an internal retreat to protect against psychic non-existence. This level of the personality must be addressed in the psychotherapy of many patients for them to feel a sense of self and of vitality. "Regression is a flight backwards in search of security and a chance of a new start. But regression becomes illness in the absence of any therapeutic person to regress with and to" (Guntrip, 1969, p. 86). He did note that many patients either did not want or require an approach that addressed the deepest level of the psyche—the level of the RLE. He also thought that it might not be possible for some. However, some patients did need it (he believed he himself did) and he proposed an outline for "radical" psychotherapy that addressed three psychic levels of increasing depth. He noted that these levels are not simply addressed sequentially or progressively in therapy but often coexist and may be present in the same session. The therapist must be sensitive and responsive to the given level of regression and depth and must revisit it again and again.

Level one: *support for the ego functioning of everyday life*
Guntrip (1969) described this as involving therapeutic attention to the person's need to feel understood and to function effectively (central ego functioning) in the external world. The therapist offers realistic hope and this is the domain of supportive therapy as the patient struggles with the demands of life and the pulls of regression (both benign and malignant). Describing it as one aspect of the parent–child relationship, he used romantic model terms: "It is the child's need for a purely supportive, protective, reassuring love as a basis for existence" (p. 336). Guntrip stated that even at this level the therapy addresses the need for the person to feel

he or she—the self—exists; and, this occurs through the relationship with the therapist which creates the conditions to promote therapeutic regression. The prominence of this therapeutic level varies during the course of therapy and from patient to patient.

Level two: *analysis of the internal world of bad object relations*
This is the level of transference analysis. Patient and therapist persistently experience, reflect upon, and analyse the internalisation of past object relations and the unconscious repetitions of those relational patterns both inside and outside therapy. In Fairbairn's endopsychic system, this especially includes the analysis of the libidinal ego/exciting object and the anti-libidinal ego/rejecting object. This is also the level that Guntrip (1975) felt that he and Fairbairn successfully addressed in his own analysis. However, it left him troubled and did not touch the deepest level of his psyche. "For as frankly oedipal transference phenomena are analysed, the result may well be, not that the patient is straightway released to grow up to a mature adult love, but is rather deprived of a main defence against the ultimate problem, the profound sense of inner emptiness which shows that no very real ego got a start at all" (Guntrip, 1969, p. 337).

Level three: *creation of a safe, symbolic womb for the emergence of the RLE*
Working with this level requires a particular stance and way of being on the part of the therapist.

> Now the therapist must be the kind of person with whom the patient can find some sense of reality in his own experience of him, and who can at times see something in the patient that he cannot see for himself, because he has never before adequately experienced it. The therapist must now sense, not the patient's repressed conflicts but his unevoked potentialities for personal relationship and creative activity, and enable him to feel 'real'. (ibid., p. 337)

Developmentally, Guntrip (ibid.) held that there is a psyche at birth but not an ego—only "unevoked potentialities"—and he defined the ego as "the psyche growing toward self-realization and identity" (p. 250). Therapy aims at facilitating the emergence of the potentials so that the latent becomes the actual and the patient develops or strengthens "… an individuality of his own, a maturing sense of selfhood through which he becomes separate without feeling 'cut off'" (p. 336). This occurs through the facilitating environment of the therapeutic relationship—the therapist's authenticity, the affirmation of the patient, the support for everyday functioning and suffering (level one), the effective analysis of the internal object world (level two) and then the provision of safety for the emergence of the RLE (level three). As therapy progresses, level three becomes more predominant. Guntrip (ibid.) wrote movingly about many patients and their desire for a therapeutic regression to the level of the RLE in a safe symbolic womb as well as their powerful resistances against that regression due to shame and fear.

Closing comments

While Guntrip very effectively advanced and disseminated Fairbairn's work, he also used it to promote his own views. He emphasised Fairbairn's romantic model aspects, modifying and extending them on his own. He also minimised the classical elements of Fairbairn's work and, perhaps, underappreciated them.

Ogden (2010), in his article "Why Read Fairbairn?" noted Fairbairn's view that the endopsychic system is relatively immutable (a classical perspective). He summarised Fairbairn's perspective on change: it occurs through (1) reduction in the attachment of the libidinal ego and anti-libidinal ego to their respective objects, (2) reduction in the aggression of the central ego towards the other parts of the personality, and (3) reduction in the aggression of the anti-libidinal ego towards the libidinal ego and exciting object. While Guntrip, in my view, would not disagree with those change mechanisms, they all involve classical processes of *reducing problematic patterns and affects*. He would add and emphasise romantic processes of *evoking, enhancing, and increasing self-potential*. This is a clear classical *vs.* romantic distinction. Yet Ogden (2010) in the same article writes, as I see it, of the romantic elements in Fairbairn's perspective on change. Describing his analysis of a patient, Ogden noted the change mechanisms involved and included the following: "I believe that it was very important to the analytic experience that Mr C experience for himself over a period of years the reality that I was not repulsed by him ... It must have been apparent to Mr C, though I never put it into words, that I loved him as I would one day love my own children in their infancy" (p. 116). He concluded that Fairbairn would agree with this explanation. I am confident Guntrip would, too.

During discussions late in his life in 1972, Guntrip (Landis, 1981) stated that he had become less interested in theory and saw it used all too often as a schizoid defence. "It doesn't lead to change. This only occurs through an enduring personal relationship" (p. 114). As Guntrip (1969) stated elsewhere, "Only when the therapist finds the person behind the patient's defences, and perhaps the patient finds the person behind the therapist's defences, does true psychotherapy happen" (p. 352).

I believe that Guntrip's elaboration of schizoid phenomena, the concept of the regressed libidinal ego, the centrality and contours of the therapeutic relationship, and his efforts to integrate Fairbairn and Winnicott continue to be major contributions to psychoanalytic theory and practice. It is a stance situated strongly within the romantic psychoanalytic tradition.

References

Balint, M. (1959). *Thrills and Regressions*. New York: International Universities Press.
Balint, M. (1968). *The Basic Fault: Therapeutic Aspects of Regression*. New York: Brunner/Mazel.
Ehrlich, R. (2009). Guntrip's concept of the regressed ego. *Journal of American Academy of Psychoanalysis and Dynamic Psychiatry*, 37(4): 605–625.
Eigen, M. (1981). Guntrip's analysis with Winnicott—A critique of Glatzer and Evans. *Contemporary Psychoanalysis*, 17: 103–111.
Fairbairn, W. R. D. (1952). *Psychoanalytic Studies of the Personality*. London: Tavistock.
Fairbairn, W. R. D. (1958). On the nature and aims of psycho-analytic treatment. *International Journal of Psychoanalysis*, 39: 374–385.
Forbes, M. E. (1996). Guntrip's contribution: An analysis of his major departures from Fairbairn. *Canadian Journal of Psychoanalysis*, 4: 149–167.
Glatzer, H. T., & Evans, W. N. (1977). On Guntrip's analysis with Fairbairn and Winnicott. *International Journal of Psychoanalysis*, 6: 81–98.

Greenberg, J. R., & Mitchell, S. A. (1983). *Object Relations in Psychoanalytic Theory*. Cambridge, MA: Harvard University Press.

Guntrip, H. (1961). *Personality Structure and Human Interaction: The Developing Synthesis of Psychodynamic Theory*. New York: International Universities Press.

Guntrip, H. (1969). *Schizoid Phenomena, Object Relations and the Self*. New York: International Universities Press.

Guntrip, H. (1975). My experience of analysis with Fairbairn and Winnicott. *International Review of Psycho-Analysis, 2*: 145–156.

Hazell, J. (1994). *Personal Relations Therapy: The Collected Papers of H. J. S. Guntrip*. Northvale, NJ: Jason Aronson.

Hazell, J. (1996). *H. J. S. Guntrip: A Psychoanalytical Biography*. London: Free Association.

Hughes, J. M. (1989). *Reshaping the Psychoanalytic Domain: The Work of Melanie Klein, W. R. D. Fairbairn and D. W. Winnicott*. Berkeley, CA: University of California Press.

Hulme, T. S. (1924). *Classicism and Romanticism in Speculations*. London: Routledge & Kegan Paul.

Kernberg, O. F. (1980). Fairbairn's theory and challenge. In: J. S. Grotstein & D. B. Rinsley (Eds.), *Fairbairn and the Origins of Object Relations* (pp. 41–65). New York: Guilford, 1994.

Kohut, H. (1971). *The Analysis of the Self*. New York: International Universities Press.

Kohut, H. (1977). *The Restoration of the Self*. New York: International Universities Press.

Landis, B. (1981). Discussions with Harry Guntrip. *Contemporary Psychoanalysis, 17*: 112–117.

Muran, J. C., & Barber, J. P. (Eds.) (2010). *The Therapeutic Alliance: An Evidence-based Guide to Practice*. New York: Guilford.

Norcross, J. C. (Ed.) (2002). *Psychotherapy Relationships that Work: Therapist Contributions and Responsiveness to Patients*. New York: Oxford University Press.

Norcross, J. C. (Ed.) (2011). *Psychotherapy Relationships that Work: Evidence-based Responsiveness* (2nd ed.). New York: Oxford University Press.

Ogden, T. H. (2010). Why read Fairbairn? *International Journal of Psychoanalysis, 91*: 101–118.

Rinsley, D. B. (1994). Fairbairn's concepts and terminology. In: J. S. Grotstein & D. B. Rinsley (Eds.), *Fairbairn and the Origins of Object Relations* (pp. 335–339). New York: Guilford.

Robbins, M. (1992). A Fairbairnian object relations perspective on self-psychology. *American Journal of Psychoanalysis, 52*: 247–261.

Scharff, J. S., & Scharff, D. E. (1998). *Object Relations Individual Therapy*. Northvale, NJ: Jason Aronson.

Stadter, M. (2012). *Presence and the Present: Relationship and Time in Contemporary Psychodynamic Therapy*. Lanham, MD: Jason Aronson.

Strenger, C. (1989). The classical and the romantic vision in psychoanalysis. *International Journal of Psychoanalysis, 70*: 593–610.

Sutherland, J. D. (1980). The British object relations theorists: Balint, Winnicott, Fairbairn, Guntrip. *Journal of the American Psychoanalytic Association, 28*: 829–860.

Winnicott, D. W. (1960). The theory of the parent–infant relationship. In: *The Maturational Processes and the Facilitating Environment* (pp. 37–55). New York: International Universities Press, 1965.

CHAPTER TWENTY-FOUR

From Fairbairn to Winnicott

Henri Vermorel

Two careers contrasted

Donald W. Winnicott's ideas, which were disseminated in France around the 1960s and 1970s, contributed, along with Bion's in the aftermath of the Controversies of World War II (King & Steiner, 1991) to the renewal of French psychoanalysis which fully assimilated them. Winnicott's ideas were so extraordinarily successful that their reach extended beyond analytical circles, so much so that he lent his name to several psychiatric institutions in France. This striking fame is in sharp contrast with the lack of knowledge in France of another member of the Middle Group of the British Psychoanalytical Society, W. Ronald D. Fairbairn, who was long ignored in France until the publication by Edouard Korenfeld of most of his work in a two-volume edition (Fairbairn, 1998–1999). However, what is generally not known is that most of Winnicott's fundamental ideas, which were developed in a particularly original and personal manner, originated in Fairbairn's innovative theory.

Why then did the Scottish psychoanalyst remain unknown in France for so long? Some hypotheses can be formulated: among them, his relatively late recognition within British psychoanalysis. He led a solitary life in Edinburgh, trained himself almost entirely after a brief analysis with an Australian psychoanalyst who spent a few years in Scotland—this made the development of his original ideas possible—but lived without the support of an analytical group or regular contacts with a close circle of colleagues. This may have been one of the reasons why he was admitted only relatively late into the British Society in view of the quality of his work, but without ever having been recognised as a training analyst. It should also be noted that Fairbairn is part of an intermediary generation of British psychoanalysts, somewhat stuck as he was between pioneers such as Ernest Jones and the post-Kleinians Bion and Winnicott.

On the French side, Fairbairn's work, which strove to replace the drive theory with that of object relations, could not but shock francophone analytical sensibility, which is very attached to the notion of drives. The first commentator of Fairbairn's work, Jacques Lacan, made a trenchant criticism of Fairbairn's object relations theories in 1955 which in his view confused the imaginary dimension with the intersubjective dimension of a symbolic nature, the analyst risking to supplant the central observing ego; projecting onto it his function, the analyst thus recomposing the subject's imaginary world in accordance with the analyst's norms while neglecting the unconscious dimension. But this criticism, which was of a general nature, missed Fairbairn's essential contribution to the understanding of borderline states to which Lacan himself paid little attention (1955). The fact remains that this first approach left a negative mark on object relations theory in French psychoanalysis, reaching far beyond Lacan's circles. It is only in 1974 with Pontalis's publication of Fairbairn's article on schizoid states that the true value of the Scottish psychoanalyst's work was fully appreciated. For his part, Didier Anzieu (1996) noted that Fairbairn had been the first to describe the original mechanism of paradox, which had only been intuitively sketched in Fairbairn's work: the unloved child, unable to blame his parents for this felt deficiency, internalises the bad object to protect himself from outside insecurity, but at the price of inner insecurity. This reversal of values plays an important part in the genesis of perversions and psychoses.

Another difference between the two psychoanalysts lies in the fact that Winnicott's writings are, at first blush, easy to read even if they are often deep and complex; whereas Fairbairn, whose training was in philosophy, used an often austere style, developing an original metapsychology rigorously structured in an abstraction which often renders access to it difficult. The Scottish psychoanalyst, however, even though he never went so far as to do radio shows for mothers the way Winnicott did, expended a lot of effort in explaining his way of thinking to related professions such as psychologists, as is demonstrated by numerous articles published in the *British Journal of Medical Psychology*, where he was welcomed long before he was in analytical journals; and he often participated in conferences for educators, social workers, and even women's associations and men of the cloth. The fact remains that the reception in France of Fairbairn's work (Vermorel, 2005), which was delayed by his late recognition in his own country, preceded but was then eclipsed by the large distribution in France of translations of Winnicott's work starting in the Sixties.

Fairbairn, inspirer of Winnicott

What Fairbairn and Winnicott had in common was a connection with Freud, whom both recognised as a source of inspiration. Fairbairn possessed an in-depth knowledge of Freud's work to which he constantly referred even while suggesting a revision of some of his essential premises. For his part, Winnicott had the notion very early on (at high school) that he was locked in a struggle with Freud, and from his understanding of Freud's work he retained the idea of a method that leads to discoveries, in complete opposition to any form of dogmatism. Within the framework of their common participation in the Middle Group, both authors took a keen interest in object relations, not wanting to side with Anna Freud or Melanie Klein, while both benefited from the latter's work.

Thus Winnicott, who was supervised by Melanie Klein, after an analysis with Strachey, had a second analysis with Joan Rivière, a Kleinian psychoanalyst. Fairbairn says that he borrowed the notion of internal object from Melanie Klein to which he added his own developments—to the great displeasure of Kleinians—whereas Melanie Klein modifies the paranoid position into a paranoid-schizoid position by reference to Fairbairn. For his part, Winnicott, who was often engaged in lively debates with her, recognised at the end of his life that he had found inspiration in her work.

The study of Fairbairn and Winnicott demonstrates, despite numerous differences, that both authors converged on some essential points.

From "object-seeking" in Fairbairn to the "primary maternal preoccupation" in Winnicott

Winnicott is close to Fairbairn when he underlines the importance of the primary environment for the psychological nurture of the baby, with the necessity of a "good enough mother" capable of holding and handling the baby's emotional range and with the concept of "primary maternal preoccupation". We owe the seeking for the primary object to Fairbairn—an idea which is close to that of "attachment" which can be found in Bowlby, another member of the Middle Group—and the need for the mother to love her child while satisfying the child's needs. Indeed, it could be said that the innate drives of self-preservation must be sufficiently supported by motherly care to fully exist within the framework of what has come to be known, following the ethologists, as the "interactional epigenesis" (Cosnier, 1981). Sexual drives themselves only occur if the drives for self-preservation are sufficiently well established.

Like Melanie Klein, Fairbairn gives a prominent place to the introjection by the baby of the relation to the breast, but he calls it "internalization", to which he adds the relation of the ego (self) to these objects. This explains the importance Fairbairn gives to the reality of the maternal object—differentiated from the reality of fantasy—and to its consequences, for the development of the psyche, of the frustrations linked to non-recognition of the baby's needs. In line with Fairbairn, Winnicott sheds a light on the disturbances created by the primitive deficiency of the environment. Much like Fairbairn, Winnicott considers these pathologies are a consequence of the deficiency of *holding*, but he adds some innovations by suggesting, with the "fear of breakdown" (1963), that the analysis of an event which occurred in the past but was never fully experienced or symbolised because of the subject's immaturity, also play a part.

Winnicott adds that the success of this first period of the baby's psychological development gives the baby the "continuity of being", which is the source of primary creativity. Because even though he borrows the baby's object-seeking from Fairbairn, he emphasises the baby's creative and active role, while the infant in Fairbairn's theory seems more passive. It is true that although Fairbairn did a lot of work with children, especially delinquents, unlike Winnicott, he did not have any formal training as a paediatrician or a psychoanalyst for young children and babies.

For Winnicott, the baby creates the object, but he first needs to find it: the object found-created. This could also have been borrowed from Fairbairn (1938a), who in his theory of art, having visited a surrealist exhibition in London in 1937 on this very theme, uses the "found-object" as the basis for his theory about creativity. Fairbairn did not apparently make a direct connection between this remarkable intuition and the later elaboration of transitional objects or processes.

By demonstrating that the satisfaction of basic needs is a first step in the development of the psyche, Fairbairn rightfully contests the existence of self-eroticism and primary narcissism (see, among the work of French psychoanalysts in the same vein, "primitively secondary" narcissism by Michel Fain) (Fain & Braunschweig, 1975). But the question finds new life with Winnicott who describes a mother–baby fusion before the establishment of object relations, which for Fairbairn, as for Melanie Klein, are there from the very beginning.

Early frustrations and delinquency

As with many British psychiatrists and psychoanalysts during the Second World War, Fairbairn and Winnicott were confronted with the problems of children who had been separated from their parents during the German bombardments of English cities. Winnicott actually said that he thought it would have been better not to separate these children from their families. This experience most certainly led those who emphasised the role of the environmental deficit in pathogenesis to reflect. It is by working for many years with young delinquents in a children's psychiatric facility for social cases that Fairbairn found the clinical foundations for his theoretical work. But, later on, his work on criminals was interrupted because he did not think analysis would benefit criminals, but rather re-education or a priest (1946b). His thinking later evolved, however, when he wrote that any feeling of moral indignation should be banned from such a study to understand the factors which explain the acts of delinquents, and thought that sexual perverts could benefit from appropriate treatment in prison (1957). He was one of the first people to suggest medico-psychological assessments for these people when they were tried by the courts. Winnicott considered juvenile delinquency as acting on a deficiency in the infantile environment, lost after a time when the family circle was good enough. He interpreted certain delinquent behaviour as the desire to find the good lost environment again, without discounting in others the destructive current that can invade the entire stage and raises other metapsychological questions.

Schizoid states

As early as 1953, Winnicott had appreciated the value of Fairbairn's work on schizoid states and, at the end of his life, recognised what he owed to his predecessor for their understanding. Since the 1940s, Fairbairn had been one of the pioneers in the study of borderline states by showing that his patients, who often did not know how to clearly formulate a demand, were nevertheless analysable and, contrary to what was believed at the time, were capable of transference. The "sense of futility" which Winnicott observed in this pathology is close to Fairbairn; it is the result of a defensive over-evaluation of internal reality in reaction to an environment perceived as dangerous. To Winnicott, this sense of futility is the result of the generation of a false self, which can be a successful protection of the true self but at the cost of an attack on the sense of self. In the cure, he differentiates the classical defensive regression and the defence which consists in putting the suffering to one side to seek invulnerability: it is in line with

Fairbairn's work who had placed the split at the basis of the psyche: "At any rate, some measure of splitting of the ego is invariably present at the deepest level—or [...] *the basic position in the psyche is invariably a schizoid position*" (1952, p. 8) and especially with borderline patients.

From Fairbairn's transitional object to Winnicott's transitional space extended to the realm of culture

As early as 1941, Fairbairn made the major innovation in the psychoanalysis of transitional objects and processes when he described the transitional object and sketched out a transitional space consisting of three stages in the baby's dependence on the people surrounding him: first an absolute "infantile dependence" of the newborn baby which precedes an intermediary transitional phase or "relative dependence" that paves the way for "mature dependence" (ibid., p. 39). Winnicott takes up the same scheme but is not as pessimistic as Fairbairn is because he recognises that the third stage is a step towards independence even though it is never completely accomplished.

Winnicott largely develops the transitional phenomenon, which belongs neither to internal reality nor to external reality and is both self and non-self at the same time. More than Fairbairn, Winnicott gives an active and creative role to the baby and especially places an emphasis on the function of the game, which can be found in his conception of the cure with patients suffering from early deficiencies where the role of the psychoanalyst is closer to a game than to verbal interpretation. Later developments of Winnicott's also relate to the function of symbolising the transitional object whose defects can be studied within the framework of an adjusted cure.

The transitional phase is a space within which the baby can find a place between primary creativity—which is a source of omnipotence and supports an illusion, and gives meaning to relations with others—and the challenge of reality, which is founded on perception. If the baby has been able to experience the feeling of having created the world, then he can face the experience of disillusion and find the road to separation with his mother. Finally, the extension from the notion of the transitional to the realm of culture is an innovation taken from Fairbairn and carried very far with Winnicott's highly original mark.

Object relations and drives

Winnicott was more interested in objects than in drives which would have brought him closer to Fairbairn, but unlike Fairbairn he does not challenge the notion of drive (even though it is better not to take Fairbairn's sometimes peremptory statements at face value, as was suggested to me by one of his former analysands, James Innes-Smith). In one of his last articles, Winnicott mentions the life drive/death drive tandem much like Freud in his later years. Even though he did not spend much time tackling these issues, auto-eroticism and narcissism find their way into his work: these concepts are challenged by Fairbairn. Winnicott, like Fairbairn, emphasises the impact of the environment's deficiency on destructiveness, but, contrary to him, admits an innate drive of aggression, which could be compared to Freud's ideas that belatedly introduce the notion of "primary hostility" (1930a). In Winnicott, the idea takes the shape of "cruelty" or "ruthless love", whose origins can be found in Fairbairn when he says that the child who destroys the breast while feeding is not moved by an intention to destroy an object which does not yet exist. This ruthless love for an object, which has not yet been individualised as such, can be differentiated from hate, the flip-side of love, which includes an intentional destructiveness towards an individualised object. With Fairbairn and Winnicott, we might add that this violence, which serves life, becomes self-destructiveness when the drives of self-preservation have not been sufficiently supported by the satisfaction of needs. To establish oneself on the basis of primary aggressiveness, the life drive requires contribution from the environment, without which the attachment that supports the quest for the object falls into destructiveness. Such a perspective would make it possible to overcome the dilemma of the Freudian concepts of primary hostility/death drive, which Freud never fully explained.

We know what use Winnicott made of hate in the countertransference, especially with psychotics. We may, however, ask ourselves whether the patient's affect, perceived by the analyst by the means of a projective and introjective identification, is for the most part the manifestation of an original violence transformed into destructiveness by deprivation and therefore not yet situated within the register of hatred towards an object that has trouble realising itself in psychotics.

A metapsychology pulled downwards?

There are therefore many similarities between Winnicott's and Fairbairn's ideas, which would tend to lend support to the idea that the latter was a privileged source of inspiration for the former. This proximity extends to what could be considered as weak points or gaps in Fairbairn's system, Winnicott sometimes adopting the same views.

We know that Fairbairn stressed a "basic endopsychic situation" that was established early on—a valuable technical innovation—and even though he defended himself from this accusation, he neglected what he calls the "Oedipal situation", even though he mitigated the rigour of his views in the last years of his work. Winnicott's approach is more flexible, but the importance he placed on early maternal relations leaves the Oedipal phase slightly to one side. Fairbairn went so far as to say that the father figure could be seen as a pale copy of the mother. In Winnicott, alongside the ever-present mother, the father holds a small place in his writings; it is not that he does not take his role into consideration in the treatment of the children, but it is only in his later writings that the father figure acquires a greater presence.

More broadly, too strong an emphasis on early maternal relations runs the risk of narcissistic seduction in the sense that the Oedipal triangle of which the father is the main pillar would be absent. Such dangers may be observed in Ferenczi's early research (1932) where he did not avoid these pitfalls with patients presenting early wounds. For Winnicott also there is no escape: we know the contrasted career that his analyst and disciple Masud Khan had, a gifted psychoanalyst but whose narcissistic failings led him to regrettable transgressive behaviour with some of his patients. Winnicott's tolerance of Khan casts a dark shadow on the dangers of insufficient consideration of the narcissistic seduction in a practice, which would be too narrowly focused on relations with primary objects.

Harry Guntrip, analysand of Winnicott and Fairbairn

Guntrip, a psychoanalyst and priest, undertook a long analysis with Fairbairn in his later years (it was in fact interrupted for a few months because of Fairbairn's becoming ill), and, according to Guntrip, Fairbairn's creative capacities were diminished. On Fairbairn's advice, Guntrip underwent a second analysis with Winnicott, interrupted by Winnicott's death, both cures spanning about twenty years and ending when Guntrip himself was an elderly man.

This author describes (1975) a difference in the setting of both analysts: Fairbairn's office with old furniture was both vast and solemn looking, even aristocratic, whereas Winnicott's was small and cosy; Fairbairn was reserved with his patient, never shaking his hand, apart from the last session when he showed considerable emotion. Fairbairn, whose picture was taken sitting at his desk with his patient lying on a laterally placed couch, seems to have kept his patients at a distance. Guntrip, who admired both his analysts, describes classical sessions at Fairbairn's followed by friendly conversations spent discussing theory over a cup of tea. Guntrip recounts Fairbairn's views on the Oedipal situation, which Fairbairn considered crucial for therapy but not theory. Guntrip says that in his analysis Fairbairn underlined the Oedipal situation, thus demonstrating the evolution of his ideas in the last years of his life. He suggests that Fairbairn practised a sort of mirror-analysis, essentially based on intellectual and precise interpretations.

For Harry Guntrip, Fairbairn is revolutionary in theory, whereas Winnicott was revolutionary in practice as he possessed an exceptional capacity to enter into a genuinely personal relationship with his patients and had a penetrating intuition concerning his patients' early childhood. According to Winnicott, Guntrip's problems were characterised by his brother Percy's death at the age of three and a half, which resulted in a lasting amnesia only lifted at the end of both analyses. Guntrip was saved by a nursing aunt to whom he was sent to be looked after because his mother was grief-stricken and incapable of taking care of her surviving son. Guntrip was besieged by mysterious illnesses on several occasions during separations or at the death of friends with whom he had a close relationship. This was only brought to light during the analysis with Fairbairn, who himself was sick, thus becoming a dying friend in the transference which led Guntrip to consult with Winnicott.

Winnicott did not forego the opportunity to criticise Fairbairn by telling Guntrip that he had wasted some good work by his desire to diminish Freud. Guntrip thought that he had undertaken a radical analysis of his defences against the bad internalised object with Fairbairn. With Winnicott, he was able to link his hyperactivity to a defence against the gap of the object-relation which he felt when his mother abandoned him, and thus find in the transference a period, before Percy's death, where he had had a good relationship with his mother. Guntrip was then afforded the possibility to use an object, a concept which Winnicott was working on at the end of his life with patients such as Guntrip. With Winnicott, Harry Guntrip had been able to understand what had made him plunge into a state of apparent death: it was not only his brother's death but the fear of remaining alone with a mother who was incapable of keeping him alive. After Winnicott's death, which occurred during his analysis, Guntrip had a dream, which he interpreted as the breakdown he went through during the bereavement of his youth, and which lifted the veil of his amnesia. Guntrip died in 1975, only a few years after Winnicott.

The debt recognised

Winnicott was familiar with Fairbairn's work as is shown by the detailed analysis he performed with Masud Khan in 1952 of Fairbairn's book, which comprised most of Fairbairn's early articles (Winnicott & Khan, 1953). Winnicott and Khan list the main themes, underlining Fairbairn's "stimulating contribution" to understanding schizoid states, and also examine his other work such as his theory of the basic endopsychic situation. The overall tone of the article swings between praise, which cannot disguise a certain admiration for the originality of Fairbairn's thinking, and a certain ambivalence, almost irritation, with, for example, what they take to be Fairbairn's pretension to replace Freud's drive theory with his own: "The claim is that Fairbairn's theory supplants that of Freud. If Fairbairn is right, then we teach Fairbairn and not Freud to our students" (ibid., p. 329). Or Fairbairn's misunderstanding of the work of others than Freud, Abraham, or Klein and the huge chasm which Winnicott and Khan detected between the author's clinical intuitions and his theorisation: "Fairbairn's clinical and intuitive sense brings him all the way while his theory gets bogged down a few miles in the rear" (ibid., p. 332). On a no less critical note, Winnicott and Khan rightfully detect that Fairbairn in his recognised contribution to the primary seeking for the maternal object does not grasp the role of the child's creativity and find an explanation for this in his lack of clinical experience with babies and the mother–baby relationship. But the article ends on a laudatory note: "This is a valuable and stimulating book, giving the fruits of the life-work of a colleague; as such it will be widely read, and it cannot fall to be a stimulus to new thought" (ibid., p. 333).

In a posthumous article, Winnicott, after an original and independent analytical journey, seems to have repented the fact that he did not sufficiently talk to the colleagues he felt the closest to and those he felt indebted to: "I've realised more and more as time went on what a tremendous lot I've lost from not properly correlating my work with the work of others," seemingly attributing its cause to his self-centred nature (1967). The main thrust of the article is devoted to his relations with Melanie Klein, and, after many years of often bitter discussions, Winnicott recognises his debt to her in a more appeased atmosphere. Only one or two paragraphs are devoted to Fairbairn but they are explicit. Thus, he remembers that one of Fairbairn's conferences "goes right beyond [his] comprehension" and he did not find his ideas interesting, but he later recognised the importance of his thesis on childhood frustrations in the seeking for an unsatisfying object. He adds at the end of the article: "I now became aware that Fairbairn had made a tremendous contribution [...] One is object-seeking, which comes into the area of transitional phenomena and so on, and the other is this thing of feeling real instead of feeling unreal."

Therefore, Fairbairn's ideas, which Winnicott had studied in 1953 with Masud Khan, were for him a "stimulant for new ideas" which he developed in a particularly original and creative way.

References

Anzieu, D. (1996). *Créer, détruire*. Paris: Dunod.
Cosnier, J. (1981). Observation directe des interactions précoces, ou les bases de l'épigenèse interactionnelle. *Psychiatrie de l'enfant*, 27(1): 107–126.

Fain, M., & Braunschweig, D. (1975). *La nuit, le jour.* Paris: PUF.
Fairbairn, W. R. D. (1938b). The ultimate basis of aesthetic experience. *British Journal of Psychology, 29*: 167–181. In: E. F. Birtles & D. E. Scharff (Eds.), *From Instinct to Self: Selected Papers of W. R. D. Fairbairn, Volume II: Applications and Early Contributions* (pp. 397–409). Northvale, NJ: Jason Aronson, 1994.
Fairbairn, W. R. D. (1946b). The treatment and rehabilitation of sexual offenders. In: *Psychoanalytic Studies of tne Personality* (pp. 289–296). London: Tavistock, 1952.
Fairbairn, W. R. D. (1952). *Psychoanalytic Studies of the Personality.* London: Tavistock.
Fairbairn, W. R. D. (1957). Freud, the psycho-analytical method and mental health. *British Journal of Medical Psychology, 30*(2): 53–61. In: D. E. Scharff & E. F. Birtles (Eds.), *From Instinct to Self, Selected Papers of W. R. D. Fairbairn, Volume I: Clinical and Theoretical Papers* (pp. 61–73). Northvale, NJ: Jason Aronson, 1994.
Fairbairn, W. R. D. (1998). Vermorel Henri (préface).; Innes-Smith James (post-face); Lecointe Pierre (trad.). *Etudes Psychanalytiques de la Personnalité.* Paris, Editions du Monde Interne. (traduction de: Fairbairn W. Ronald D., *Psychoanalytic Studies of the Personality*, London, Tavistock, 1952).
Fairbairn, W. R. D. (1999). Lecointe Pierre (trad.) *Structure endopsychique et relations d'objet. Vol. I: Les fondements théoriques*, Puteaux (traduction d'un choix de chapitres par Scharff, David E. et Fairbairn-Birtles, Ellinor *From Instinct to Self*, vol. I et II) Éditions du Monde Interne.
Ferenczi, S. (1932). *Journal clinique.* Traduction française du Groupe de traduction du Coq Héron. Paris: Payot, 1982.
Freud, S. (1930a). *Das Unbehagen in der Kultur (Civilization and Its Discontents). S. E., 21*: 64–145. London: Hogarth, 1961.
Guntrip, H. (1975). My experience of analysis with Fairbairn and Winnicott (How complete a result does psychoanalytic therapy achieve?). *International Review of Psycho-Analysis, 2*: 145–156.
King, P., & Steiner, R. (Eds.) (1991). The Freud-Klein Controversies 1941–1945. London: Institute of Psychoanalysis.
Lacan, J. (1955). L'analyse objectivée. Critique de Fairbairn. *Le Séminaire, Livre II.* Paris: Seuil, 1975.
Pontalis, J.-B. (1974). A propos de Fairbairn. Le psychisme comme double métaphore du corps. *Nouvelle Revue de Psychanalyse, 10*: 56–59.
Vermorel, H. (2005). Fairbairn in France. In: J. S. Scharff & D. E. Scharff (Eds.), *The Legacy of Fairbairn and Sutherland: Psychotherapeutic Applications* (pp. 50–60). London: Routledge.
Winnicott, D. W. (1967). Postscript: D. W. W. on D. W. W. In: D. W. Winnicott, C. Winnicott, R. Shepard, & M. Davis (Eds.), *Psycho-analytic Explorations* (pp. 569–582). Cambridge, MA: Harvard University Press, 1989.
Winnicott, D. W., & Khan, M. M. R. (1953). Psychonalytic Studies of the Personality by W. Ronald D. Fairbairn. *International Journal of Psychoanalysis, 34*: 329–333.

CHAPTER TWENTY-FIVE

Fairbairn and Ferenczi

Graham S. Clarke

This will be an exploration of a series of links between Ferenczi's and Fairbairn's theories, aspects of which are already known and discussed by others, notably Jay Frankel (1998, 2002a, 2002b), and some which I suggest are important but unrecognised parallels between their theories. I think that Fairbairn's object relations theory, or "psychology of dynamic structure" as he called it, embodies many aspects of Ferenczi's thinking on trauma.

Ferenczi's most famous, or perhaps infamous, paper was the "Confusion of Tongues between the Adults and the Child" (1955, pp. 156–167), presented at the 12th IPA congress in 1932 but denied publication in English by Ernest Jones as editor of the *IJPA*. This paper developing Ferenczi's late ideas on trauma was eventually published in the *IJPA* in 1949 but was the occasion for Ferenczi's break with Freud and his effective rejection by the IPA. This long quotation from one of Jones's letters to Freud gives some insight into how Ferenczi's paper was viewed at the time.

> I thought at the time of asking you about its publication in the *ZEITSCHRIFT* and whether you would add any Anmerkung der Redaktion [trans. "editor's note"]. I hoped that Ferenczi himself would not publish it, but when I received the proofs of the *ZEITSCHRIFT* I felt he would be offended if it were not translated into English and so asked his permission for this. He seemed gratified, and we have not only translated it but set it up in type as the first paper in the July number. Since his death I have been thinking over the removal of the personal reason for publishing it. Others also have suggested that it now be withdrawn and I quote the following passage from a letter of Mrs Rivière's, … with … which I quite agree: "Now that Ferenczi has died, I wondered whether you will not reconsider publishing his last paper. It seems to me it can only be damaging to him and a discredit, while now that he is no longer to be hurt by its not being published, no good purpose could be served by it. Its scientific contentions and its statements about analytic practice are just a tissue of delusions, which can only discredit

psa and give credit to its opponents. It cannot be supposed that all *JOURNAL* readers will appreciate the mental condition of the writer and in this respect one has to think of posterity too!" I therefore think it best to withdraw the paper unless I hear from you that you have any wish to the contrary. (Jones, 1933)

I am going to look at this paper initially from the point of view of its structural implications since for me it represents a very clear set of parallels to Fairbairn's developed model. Later on I will suggest a number of other links between Fairbairn and Ferenczi, but given that Fairbairn did read German, I will work on the assumption that he could have read the original in 1933 when first published in the *Internationale Zeitschrift für Psychoanalyse*, and been influenced by it although his 1927 and 1931 papers already suggest that he had begun to develop his ideas on endopsychic structure.

The central point of Ferenczi's paper is the reality of sexual and other abuse of children as the exogenous origin of neurosis, a possibility that Freud had given up in the late 1890s. The reality of abuse and its role in generating neurosis and psychosis is something that is recognised by Fairbairn, whose theory has been describes as a "deficit" theory precisely because of the pathogenic lack of care from significant others in the family and society.

One of the most common consequences of such abuse is the splitting of the self or personality as a form of defence; "We talk a lot about the splitting of the personality, but do not seem sufficiently to appreciate the depth of these splits" (ibid., p. 160).

A problem that Ferenczi first encounters in therapy as he is trying to get his patients, who seem to be stuck in repetitive processes, to criticise him, is uncovered again in the relationship of the patient to the abuser. At the bottom of this repetition seems to be a compulsion,

> *to subordinate themselves like automata to the will of the aggressor, to divine each one of his desires and to gratify these; completely oblivious of themselves they identify themselves with the aggressor.* (ibid., p. 162, emphasis in original)

This understanding of the "introjection of the aggressor" (ibid.) finds strong parallels in Fairbairn's idea of the "moral defence" and his understanding of the "repetition compulsion" (and the "death instinct") as attachment to internalised bad objects. It is worth noting that Ferenczi's account of his relationships with his patients who are stuck in repetitive patterns and Fairbairn's own description of the way that hysterical patients idealise their analyst is another strong parallel and pointer towards a structural correlate in Fairbairn of the insights that Ferenczi had reached.

Fairbairn argued that his theory was ideally suited to understanding multiple personality disorder (now usually called DID) and its origins in repeated traumas during childhood, a point that Ferenczi seems to be already familiar with.

> If the shocks increase in number during the development of the child, the number and the various kinds of splits in the personality increase too and soon it becomes extremely difficult to maintain contact without confusion with all of the fragments, each of which behaves as a separate personality yet does not know of even the existence of the others. (ibid., p. 165)

Ferenczi's description could be taken to be a description of the endopsychic structure that Fairbairn developed.

Throughout this paper with the various splits of the personality and the introjection of the other, one can feel Ferenczi encountering the limitations of the language of classical psychoanalysis and his reaching towards a language of an endopsychic structure comprised by ego-structures and internal objects.

There is a lot more in Ferenczi's paper than I have brought out but it seems to me that the parallels between this late theory of trauma and Fairbairn's own theory are strong.

Fairbairn did not cite Ferenczi in his major work so establishing a provenance is difficult. Fairbairn did not cite many other people either but as I have argued recently (Clarke, 2011), based upon a heavily underlined copy of *The Origins of Love and Hate* (1935) that Fairbairn had in his library, Ian Suttie did have a strong influence on his thinking. Suttie was friendly with and influenced by Ferenczi, his wife Jane also having translated many of Ferenczi's papers into English, for example, *Further Contributions to the Theory and Technique of Psycho-Analysis* (1926), so one possible and significant link between Fairbairn and Ferenczi is through the work of Suttie.

Fairbairn had books by Ferenczi in his personal library that predate the development of his own object relations theory—*Contributions to Psycho-Analysis* (1916) and *The Development of Psychoanalysis* (1925), co-authored with Otto Rank. The full development of the relationship between Fairbairn and Ferenczi would require a detailed examination of Fairbairn's underlining of these texts but I do not have room to analyse these underlinings in any detail here. Otto Rank did produce a paper called "The Genesis of the Object Relation" in 1926 which appears in a section of his book *A Psychology of Difference: The American Lectures* (1996) entitled "Exploring the dark continent of maternal power: The 'bad mother' Freud has never seen". All of which is very suggestive, but the editor of the book, Robert Kramer, in his notes says that "It is almost inconceivable that Fairbairn ... could have known of Rank's object relations theory" (p. 149).

Berman (2002), commenting on Frankel's paper on identifying with the aggressor (2002b, p. 145), suggests that Ferenczi's work on "identification/introjection and transference" can be seen "as a groundbreaking potential foundation for an object-relations theory of the personality" even if this was never developed fully by Ferenczi. Berman notes parenthetically that when Fairbairn developed his own object relations theory he "never recognised Ferenczi's contribution" (p. 146). Berman then quotes the following sentence from Ferenczi's 1909 paper "Introjection and Transference":

> The neurotic is constantly seeking objects with whom he can identify himself, to whom he can transfer feelings, whom he can thus draw into his circle of interest i.e. introject. (Ferenczi, 1916, pp. 40–41)

This is *not* one of the passages Fairbairn had marked even though he had marked passages before and after it—but it was clearly a passage that he had read.

Fairbairn met Ferenczi at the 1929 International Congress of Psycho-Analysis in Oxford, UK (Birtles & Scharff, 1994, Vol. II, p. 454). Birtles and Scharff note a number of characteristics of Ferenczi's approach, which they imply are also found in Fairbairn. They refer to an historic conference on Ferenczi in London in October 1993 where Ferenczi's move from a one-person to a two-person psychology was noted, as was,

> an awareness of the participatory nature of the mother–infant relationship and ideas of "narcissistic splitting", with a potentially pathological outcome, resulting from infantile deprivation. (p. 454)

They then list a number of other areas developed by Ferenczi and reflected in the papers they include in their collection of Fairbairn's work. In particular, work on the "nature and aims" of psychoanalysis and the practical application of its "method", both of which would be consistent with the underlined copy of Ferenczi and Rank's *The Development of Psychoanalysis* (1925) in Fairbairn's library.

A few years ago I was looking in some detail at Fairbairn's model and trying to find a consistent way of recasting it to make all the implicit aspects of the overall operation of the model explicit and ordered in accordance with the Freudian topographic categories (Clarke, 2005). I suggested that the model should be modified to include preconscious libidinal and anti-libidinal object-relations–based dyads, a model that my colleague Paul Finnegan and I have used recently to discuss multiple personality disorder or dissociative identity disorder (Finnegan & Clarke, 2012).

In Fairbairn's only contribution to the "Controversial Discussions" he suggested that,

> the time is ripe for us to replace the concept of "phantasy" by a concept of an "inner reality" peopled by the Ego and its internal objects. These internal objects should be regarded as having an organised structure, an identity of their own, an endopsychic existence and an activity as real within the inner world as those of any objects in the outer world. (quoted in Birtles & Scharff, 1994, Vol. II, p. 294)

Since, for Fairbairn, all the egos and objects in the internal world are person-like agents, this explains why he argued consistently throughout his work that his model was perfectly suited to an understanding of multiple personality disorder (Clarke & Finnegan, 2011).

A couple of years before he died Fairbairn produced a synoptic seventeen-point outline of his object relations theory (1963a).

Point sixteen of the synopsis goes as follows:

What Freud described as the "superego" is really a complex structure comprising (a) the ideal object or ego-ideal, (b) the antilibidinal ego, and (c) the rejecting (or antilibidinal) object. (p. 225)

While developing the paper reconciling Fairbairn's model with Freud's topographic categories I came across a paper by Ferenczi, from 1928, called "The Elasticity of Psycho-Analytic Technique", which ends in a way that is startlingly reminiscent of point sixteen of Fairbairn's synopsis. In his closing summary Ferenczi says he needs to clarify the idea that he puts forward in the paper that "a sufficiently deep character analysis must get rid of any kind of super-ego". He suggests that people might misinterpret this as implying that he was "robbing people of all their ideals". He goes on to clarify,

In reality my objective was to destroy only that part of the super-ego, which had become unconscious and was therefore beyond the range of influence. I have no sort of objection to the retention of a number of positive and negative models in the pre-conscious of the ordinary individual. In any case he will no longer have to obey his pre-conscious super-ego so slavishly as he had previously to obey his unconscious parent imago. (1955, p. 101)

In Fairbairn's theory the ideal object/ego-ideal is in the preconscious and is effectively the repository of experiences with good objects, while the anti-libidinal dyad is in the unconscious and is equivalent to a punitive superego and repository of relations with bad objects.

Both Ferenczi and Fairbairn see significant aspects of the endopsychic structure in similar ways, and they share the therapeutic aim of reducing the power of, or removing completely, the unconscious punitive aspect of the superego and removing, or transforming, bad objects.

Fairbairn read German, so he could have read Ferenczi's paper on its publication in 1928 when he was already treating patients many of whom were schizoid and in whom he detected both splitting and personification of "functional structural units" that were like, but not reducible to, the ego, the id, and the superego (1931).

It was during this period (late 1920s) that Fairbairn was writing his MD thesis on "Dissociation and Repression" (Birtles & Scharff, 1994, Vol. II, pp. 13–79) in which he concluded that repression was a special form of:

… dissociation of the unpleasant viz. that form which occurs when the dissociated elements consist of tendencies belonging to the instinctive endowment and thus forming part of the structure of the mind itself. (p. 79)

Repression then becomes understood as,

… a process where mental tendencies are denied conscious expression, if their incongruity with the structure of the organised self is such that the conscious expression of these tendencies would cause unpleasure. (p. 79)

The libidinal and anti-libidinal dyads then, as unconscious structures, embody primitive feelings that threaten the relationship of the person with the world and are originally split off and repressed in a situation where the life of the person is dependent upon maintaining contact and succour with others and in particular with the mother.

There was another paper by Ferenczi from the late 1920s called "The Adaptation of the Family to the Child" (1927), which Fairbairn could easily have read since it was published in the *British Journal of Medical Psychology* under the editorship of John Rickman, whom Fairbairn admired (Fairbairn, 1959). In a section of this paper, which is of considerable importance in my view, Ferenczi writes,

The real traumas during the adaptation of the family to the child happen in its *transitional* stages from the earliest primitive childhood to civilization, not only from the point of view of cleanliness, but from the point of view of sexuality. (p. 68, emphasis added)

This quotation seems to me to resonate with Suttie's statement that "We put the whole social environment in the place once occupied by mother" (1935, p. 16). Furthermore this is, I think, the first use of the term "transitional" within psychoanalysis—a term that we later become familiar with from Winnicott, but which had been used earlier by Fairbairn, as Winnicott acknowledged in a footnote to his original version of his paper on transitional objects (1953, *IJPA, 34*: 89–97).

In Fairbairn's view development could be divided into three stages. An initial stage of "infantile dependence" when our object relationships are characterised by identification; and a final, but difficult to achieve, stage of "mature dependence," when all our object relationships are with properly differentiated external objects and the unconscious libidinal and anti-libidinal structures have been dissolved. Between these two situations is a "transitional stage" in which the various libidinal and anti-libidinal object relationship possibilities, that were repressed during infantile dependence in order to preserve and sustain our relationship with significant others, could be looked at again and our powers expanded and enhanced by allowing ourselves new object relations possibilities. This transitional stage is also the place where the various neuroses manifest themselves as we seek to come to terms with our objects, both internal and external as we grow and develop.

Psychic growth is a site of dispute within Fairbairn scholarship and one towards which my paper on Freud's topographic categories was, in part, directed. During ordinary growth and development, after the initial structure generating exchanges with significant others and the development of the basic endopsychic structure, there are different ways in which non-structuring internalisations (Rubens, 1984) might take place and account for growth and development to some degree. One is simply to expand one's skills and experience through normal social life and education, and to develop new powers. Another, which is of a more defensive nature, is to reinforce one's internalised good object through one's experience of relationships with external good objects. A commentator on Fairbairn, whom I have found particularly helpful in understanding the "psychology of dynamic structure", is John Padel. It is Padel who made a crucial point in understanding Fairbairn and in seeing how object relations thinking is already present in Freud as well. Padel's understanding is that it is object relationships that are the lingua franca of the self. As Freud, in his paper "On Narcissism: An Introduction" (1914c) says, our first internalisation is of the nursing couple and the affective link between them, a relationship that we can then "inhabit" from either side. As Padel puts it:

> One of Fairbairn's most important contributions to our ideas about the functioning of the ego is that what is repressed is always a relationship (though it may be symbolised or represented as an object) ... [and] ... what is internalised is always a relationship (or that complex of relationships which is a total situation) although it may be symbolised or represented by an object. ("Ego in Current Thinking", 1985, *IJPA, 12*: 278)

This is a view that Ogden developed at about the same time (1983). Berman's paper (2002b) commenting on Frankel contains a reference to Ogden's 1983 conclusion that Fairbairn's insight was "that it is object relationships and not objects that are internalised" (p. 233).

For Fairbairn the first defence in infancy against an unsatisfactory relationship is incorporation of the object relationships with the pre-ambivalent external object as a structure generating process creating the first internalised object relationship (*Psychoanalytic Studies of the Personality*, 1952, pp. 42–43). Fairbairn thought that the infant was reality orientated to some degree at birth and that a turn towards exclusive pleasure seeking was based upon a failure of that initial object relationship (ibid., p. 140). In short, it was the way that the infant had been treated and what he made of it that was important. Exclusive pleasure seeking was a product of failed relationships. It was Ferenczi's insistence upon the reality of abuse that led to Freud's animosity towards his "Confusion of Tongues" paper but Ferenczi's viewpoint is totally consistent with Fairbairn's view of an original orientation towards reality and the importance of what really happens to the child in the aetiology of psychological disturbance.

Fairbairn was a visiting psychiatrist to the Emergency Medical Service in Scotland during World War II. Jock Sutherland was an assistant physician at the same hospital dealing with soldiers "suffering from psychoneurotic states occurring during or after exposure to combatant action". Sutherland published a paper in the *British Medical Journal* titled "A Survey of One Hundred Cases of War Neuroses" in September 1941. In 1943 Fairbairn himself published "The War Neuroses: Their Nature and Significance" in the *British Medical Journal* based upon material gathered from the hundred cases of war neuroses described by Sutherland. In his chapter on the war neuroses in his book—a revised version of his *B.M.J.* paper—Fairbairn argues that it is infantile dependence and separation-anxiety that are the underlying problems, a view that had been noted in Sutherland's original paper but is developed by Fairbairn with a far greater amount of supporting clinical evidence.

In his separate 1943 paper on the repression and return of bad objects Fairbairn introduces a new form of defence, which he calls the "moral defence", that has obvious parallels with the concept of "identification with the aggressor". In his response to Berman and Bonomi (2002b), Frankel discusses in some detail Fairbairn's "moral defence" and the light that it might throw on the feelings of guilt that arise in the victims of abuse, which Ferenczi accounts for by reference to "the introjections of the guilt feelings of the adult" (1933, p. 162). Frankel suggests that Fairbairn was "closer to the mark" in explaining these guilt feelings and that "nothing in Fairbairn's explanations requires that the perpetrator feel guilty" (2002b, p. 165). Fairbairn's view of the treatment and rehabilitation of sexual offenders (1946b) is that

> … any distress which he may display, if he falls foul of the Law, consists rather in fear of the forfeiture of social and material advantages than in any genuine guilt or remorse, which, if present at all, is invariably short-lived. (p. 293)

For Fairbairn the moral defence or "the defence of the super-ego" or "the defence of guilt" involves the internalisation of the unconditionally bad object relationships and their transformation into conditionally bad object relationships. To do this the child has to internalise his good objects into the ego-ideal, which then performs a superego role.

> In so far as the child leans towards his internalised bad objects he becomes conditionally bad vis-à-vis his internalised good objects and in so far as he resists the appeal of his internalised bad objects he becomes conditionally good vis-à-vis his super-ego. (Fairbairn, 1952, p. 66)

In Fairbairn's own words the essential feature and aim of the moral defence is to convert a situation in which "the child is surrounded by bad objects into a new situation in which his objects are good and he himself is bad" (p. 68).

Fairbairn argues that this is a higher level of mental development, the level at which the superego operates and to which the interplay between the ego and the superego belongs. "It is the level at which analytic interpretations in terms of guilt and the Oedipus situation are alone applicable" (p. 68). This is also the level at which psychotherapy is often "rather exclusively conducted" (p. 68). Fairbairn thinks this is both regrettable and dangerous since he argues that, "*guilt operates as a resistance in psychotherapy*" (p. 69, emphasis in original). If the "coercive and moralising" therapist becomes a bad object to the patient, he simply leaves him but if he becomes a superego figure "… he may effect a temporary improvement in symptoms by supporting the patient's own super-ego and intensifying repression" (p. 69). The danger of this is that interpretations at the guilt or superego level may relieve guilt but they may actually have the effect of intensifying the repression of the internalised bad objects and "thus leaving the cathexis of these objects unresolved" (p. 70).

This is where the dynamics of the endopsychic structure and the question of the appropriate account of the process of psychic growth are rejoined. If the account that Rubens, Mitchell and others give of the combination of non-structuring internalisation and strengthening of the superego (ego-ideal) is adhered to, we can arrive at precisely the problem that Fairbairn describes above. It is only if, as Padel has argued, the repressed bad objects can be brought to consciousness and dissolved and the repressed powers transformed and reintegrated into the central self that Fairbairn's overall aim of healing the splitting that has led to the endopsychic structure in the first place can be achieved.

This brings us back to Ferenczi's 1928 comments on the elasticity of analytic technique where the aim of a sufficiently deep character analysis is to get rid of the unconscious punitive superego and to strengthen the preconscious ego-ideal. This is an aim that is totally consistent with Fairbairn's own: "The chief aim of psychoanalytical treatment is to promote a maximum 'synthesis' of the structures into which the original ego has been split, in the setting of a therapeutic relationship with the analyst" (quoted in Scharff & Birtles, 1994, Vol. I, p. 83). And, "It becomes still another aim of psychoanalytical treatment to effect breaches of the closed system which constitutes the patient's inner world. And thus to make this world accessible to the influence of outer reality" (ibid., p. 84).

Thus, Fairbairn's object relations theory can be seen as Ferenczi's theory of trauma transformed; generalised into a structural theory of psychopathology based upon object relationships.

In Ferenczi, trauma leads to introjection of the aggressor and to dissociation, and dissociation is of person-like sub-selves. If the trauma is sufficiently severe these split-off selves can be unknown to the rest of the person.

Fairbairn starts (developmentally) with identification leading to internalisation of the first object relationship and then introduces splitting/dissociation as the first defence against the possible breakdown of object relations between child and mother leading to the basic endopsychic structure.

For Ferenczi, therapy for such trauma is to reintegrate the split-off selves into the main self. And complete therapy involves recasting the unconscious aspects of the superego into preconscious parts of the superego (the ego-ideal).

Fairbairn's whole therapeutic is to reduce the splitting of the self and reintegrate the split-off parts into an increasingly whole person with as little split-off unconscious elements as possible, strengthening the preconscious ego-ideal by internalising relations with good objects.

For Ferenczi, during development, after the initial identification or early attachment to mother there is a period of transition in which the initial splitting of inner reality is open for renegotiation as the child accommodates to separation anxiety and to the sexual and social mores of the culture.

Fairbairn makes the transitional period that follows the establishment of the basic endopsychic structure a significant phase of development and the location of the psychoneuroses.

The basic endopsychic structure is three dyadic-relations-based internal working models of mother and self based upon the splitting of relationships with mother into the acceptable, the over-exciting and the over-rejecting. In the process of psychic growth, relationship possibilities that have been repressed become possible again and are reintegrated into the central ego/ideal object dyad.

Thus psychic growth within Fairbairn's theory represents the reconstitution of the mother and the reintegration of the self in a dialectical movement that rehearses the Kleinian idea of reparation towards mother and the Winnicottian idea of development of the self. This is also the best description of the creative process from an object relations perspective in my view (Clarke, 2004).

References

Berman, E. (2002). Identifying with the other—a conflictual, vital necessity: Commentary on paper by Jay Frankel. *Psychoanalytic Dialogues, 12*: 141–151.

Birtles, E. F., & Scharff, D. E. (Eds.) (1994). *From Instinct to Self: Selected Papers of W. R. D. Fairbairn, Volume II: Applications and Early Contributions*. Northvale, NJ: Jason Aronson.

Clarke, G. S. (2004). An object-relations theory of creativity: Fairbairn's theory of art in the light of his mature model of mind. *The Journal of the British Association of Psychotherapists, 24*(2): 142–157.

Clarke, G. S. (2005). The preconscious and psychic change in Fairbairn's model of mind. *International Journal of Psychoanalysis, 86*(1): 61–77.

Clarke, G. S. (2011). Suttie's influence on Fairbairn's object relations theory. *Journal of the American Psychoanalytic Association, 59*: 939–959.

Clarke, G. S., & Finnegan, P. (2011). Fairbairn's thinking on dissociative identity disorder and the development of his mature theory. *Attachment: New Directions in Psychotherapy and Relational Psychoanalysis, 5,* July: 131–153.

Fairbairn, W. R. D. (1927). Notes on the religious phantasies of a female patient. In: *Psychoanalytic Studies of the Personality* (pp. 183–196). London: Tavistock, 1952.

Fairbairn, W. R. D. (1931). Features in the analysis of a patient with a physical genital abnormality. In: *Psychoanalytic Studies of the Personality* (pp. 197–222). London: Tavistock, 1952.

Fairbairn, W. R. D. (1943c). The war neuroses: their nature and significance. *British Medical Journal*, February 13: 183–186.

Fairbairn, W. R. D. (1946b). The treatment and rehabilitation of sexual offenders. In: *Psychoanalytic Studies of the Personality* (pp. 289–296). London: Tavistock, 1952.

Fairbairn, W. R. D. (1952). *Psychoanalytic Studies of the Personality*. London: Tavistock.

Fairbairn, W. R. D. (1959). Selected contributions to psycho-analysis, by John Rickman. International Psycho-Analytical Library, No. 52. *International Journal of Psychoanalysis, 40*: 341–342.

Fairbairn, W. R. D. (1963a). Synopsis of an object-relations theory of the personality. *International Journal of Psychoanalysis, 44*: 224–225. In: D. E. Scharff & E. F. Birtles (Eds.), *From Instinct to Self: Selected Papers of W. R. D. Fairbairn, Volume I: Clinical and Theoretical Papers* (pp. 155–156). Northvale, NJ: Jason Aronson, 1994.

Ferenczi, S. (1916). *Contributions to Psycho-Analysis*. London: Stanley Phillips.

Ferenczi, S. (1926). *Further Contributions to the Theory and Technique of Psycho-Analysis*. London: Hogarth.

Ferenczi, S. (1927). The adaptation of the family to the child. In: *Final Contributions to the Problems and Methods of Psychoanalysis*. London: Karnac, 1980.

Ferenczi, S. (1928). The elasticity of psycho-analytic technique. In: *Final Contributions to the Problems and Methods of Psychoanalysis*. London: Karnac, 1980.

Ferenczi, S. (1933). Confusion of tongues between the adults and the child. In: *Final Contributions to the Problems and Methods of Psychoanalysis*. London: Karnac, 1980.

Ferenczi, S. (1955). *Final Contributions to the Problems and Methods of Psychoanalysis*. London: Karnac, 1980.

Ferenczi, S., & Rank, O. (1925). *The Development of Psychoanalysis*. New York: Nervous and Mental Diseases Publication Co.

Finnegan, P., & Clarke, G. S. (2012). Evelyn's PhD in wellness—A Fairbairnian understanding of the therapeutic relationship with a woman with dissociative identity disorder. *Attachment: New Directions in Psychotherapy and Relational Psychoanalysis, 6*, March: 50–68.

Frankel, J. (1998). Ferenczi's trauma theory. *The American Journal of Psychoanalysis, 58*: 41–61.

Frankel, J. (2002a). Exploring Ferenczi's concept of identification with the aggressor: its role in trauma, everyday life, and the therapeutic relationship. *Psychoanalytic Dialogues, 12*: 101–139.

Frankel, J. (2002b). Identification and "traumatic aloneness": Reply to commentaries by Berman and Bonomi. *Psychoanalytic Dialogues, 12*: 159–170.

Freud, S. (1914c). On narcissism: an introduction. *S. E., 14*: 67–102. London: Hogarth.

Jones, E. (1933). Letter from Ernest Jones to Sigmund Freud, June 3, 1933. *The Complete Correspondence of Sigmund Freud and Ernest Jones 1908–1939* (pp. 722–723). Cambridge, MA: Belknap, 1993.

Ogden, T. H. (1983). The concept of internal object relations. *International Journal of Psychoanalysis, 64*: 227–241.

Padel, J. (1985). Ego in current thinking. *International Review of Psycho-Analysis, 12*: 273–283.

Rank, O. (1996). *A Psychology of Difference: The American Lectures*. R. Kramer (Ed.). Princeton, NJ: Princeton University Press..

Rubens, R. (1984). The meaning of structure in Fairbairn. *International Review of Psycho-Analysis, 11*: 429–440.

Scharff, D. E., & Birtles, E. F. (Eds.) (1994). *From Instinct to Self: Selected Papers of W. R. D. Fairbairn. Volume I: Clinical and Theoretical Papers*. Northvale, NJ: Jason Aronson.

Sutherland, J. D. (1941). A survey of one hundred cases of war neuroses. *British Medical Journal*, September 13th: 365–370.

Suttie, I. D. (1935). *The Origins of Love and Hate*. London: Pelican, 1960.

Winnicott, D. W. (1953). Transitional objects and transitional phenomena—a study of the first not-me possession. *International Journal of Psychoanalysis, 34*: 89–97.

CHAPTER TWENTY-SIX

Mitchell reading Fairbairn

Ariel Liberman

> *We must recognize ourselves in Laius's and Oedipus's efforts to escape history, since each of us resists experiencing ourselves as spoken as well as speaking.*
>
> —T. Ogden (1994, p. 2)

An encounter

A reader, a reading; Mitchell pretends to no more in his reading of Fairbairn, constantly reminding us that he is conveying *his* experience of Fairbairn, simply suggesting one reading among others, and a *use*—to speak in Winnicottian terms. He does not suffer from what, with regard to the history of psychoanalysis, André Haynal has called "the loyalty which inhibits thinking", or what Ruben Zukerfeld described as "sacrificing creativity to filiation" (2005, p. 72), deadly filiation. On the contrary, Fairbairn's work allows Mitchell to discover his own clinical and theoretical perspective, acting as a passport towards new horizons, articulations, and realms of thought. When we speak of Mitchell's perspective in particular, we are clearly speaking of a perspective of debt which acknowledges its debt to a whole tradition of psychoanalytic thinking and to many psychoanalysts who were his contemporaries; a vertex modelled from diverse influences reappropriated in an exercise of authorship whose task is to construct oneself as clinician and psychoanalyst.

Mitchell trained as an interpersonal psychoanalyst in that heterogeneous world which characterised critical thinking during the decade stretching from the end of the Sixties through the Seventies. It is here that the bases of his formative influences are to be found. For him Fairbairn's work is a natural continuation of this training, of the not-yet-thought-out or thematised. Like a bridge, as he says, across which interpersonal thinking is able to extend to the fabric of the internal world, towards what post-Freudians are wont to call the *intrapsychic*.

He relates this in the following way:

> Having been trained at the White Institute between 1972 and 1977, I felt steeped in the interpersonal tradition. Yet, this was also the time during which British object relations theories were becoming more accessible. [...] The most exciting thing for me was that British-school object relations, in what I took to be its most essential features, was perfectly compatible with interpersonal psychoanalysis, as I understood and practiced it. Fairbairn, in particular, had provided an intrapsychic model of internal relationships that was a transformation of external, interpersonal relationships. So I regarded object relations theories as an extension of interpersonal psychoanalysis into a previously untheorized domain. (1999a, p. 356)

Fairbairn's impact becomes quickly apparent in 1981, in one of Mitchell's first works of comparative psychoanalysis: "The Origin and Nature of the 'Object' in the Theories of Klein and Fairbairn". Fairbairn's influence will be present throughout his work in different ways: as a constant source of reference, whereby, along with H. S. Sullivan, he will be considered one of the most lucid exponents of the relational model; or, as Greenberg points out in his obituary in 2001, he will count among his "intellectual heroes", whose thinking is full of enriching insights for his own clinical reflections; or as a reading focus in several of his later works (Mitchell, 1998, 1999b).

The first encounter between Mitchell and Fairbairn we know of took place in the context of the New York University Doctoral Programme at the end of the Sixties. Mitchell expressed his gratitude on several occasions to Bernard Friedland, his supervisor at that time, for having introduced him to the work of Fairbairn and Guntrip (personal communication by L. Aron and N. Altman).

Friedland is a paradigmatic reference for the theoretical dissatisfaction felt among interpersonal psychoanalysts at that time. The problem for certain psychoanalysts formed in this tradition of those years was how to reconcile what they found useful in object relations theory without renouncing certain assumptions at the basis of their own training and group allegiance. Friedland put this very clearly in 1978:

> Entry into the inner world of the patient to deal with experientially striking data immediately presents us with the need for a phenomenological guide. Such a guide must not violate our basic assumptions. (...) It is Fairbairn's schema (1952) that I find most illuminating of internal-world phenomenology as well as consistent with interpersonal basic assumptions. While not a full theory, the schema is interpersonal to the core and abjures instinct. In abandoning instinct Fairbairn did not abandon the intra-psychic. In moving away from Freudian metapsychology he, in fact, was developing a psychology of the self, interpersonal and intra-psychic. (p. 559)

The problem posed by Friedland is later opened up and enriched by Mitchell in various ways: in not abandoning the basic premises of the interpersonal tradition, that is to say, the centrality of interpersonal relations in the construction of subjectivity, and at the same time, in being able to benefit from all those aspects of other psychoanalytic theories that are useful in exploring the internal world, "the intrapsychic", a term which for a long time and for many classical interpersonal analysts signified the Freudian theory of the drives. As we have already remarked, Friedland was expressing in 1978 what we imagine was the feeling of a whole group of that generation and hitherto Mitchell's own, posed along similar lines, albeit developed over the years in the course of his work: that although they adhered to the basic premises of the interpersonal tradition they felt limited when exploring the internal or intrapsychic world, a place which for them, as for others, was not one for metapsychological abstraction, but a place that clinical practice was compelled to attend to once and again.

We will see that the problem of the nature and origin of the object was a key subject in this articulation. It was a primary mode of distinguishing oneself from Freudian ego psychology that dominated the analytic scene. To suggest, as Mitchell does in his 1981 text, that "For Fairbairn, the content of internal objects derives completely from real, external objects, fragmented and recombined, to be sure, but always deriving from the child's experiences of his actual parents" (p. 392), was a way of establishing that link; it was indeed a politically acceptable meeting point with the interpersonal tradition. This affirmation does not implicate him in a naïve or ingenuous form of environmentalism, rather it leads him to propose the necessity of integrating critical material from various sources—in this case Klein and Fairbairn. Mitchell considers this work of clarification as the "prologomena" of the task at hand, that theoretical integration which is one of the driving forces of his work.

This consideration does not prevent Mitchell from extracting primary conclusions at this point, which will be developed in later years:

> All caretakers, by virtue of their humanity, inevitably fail their children, each in their own particular way. Thus, internal object relations, concerning both "bad" and "good" objects are generated out of both the intensity of infantile passions as well as parental character pathology. An approach to both the child and the parent based on accountability without blame is necessary, making possible a more balanced view of the origins of neurosis in the interaction between the parents' difficulties in living and the child's infantile needs, immature understanding of the nature of reality, and primitive loyalties. (1981, p. 395)

In 1983 a book is published, which he has been writing with Greenberg over several years. This book, which became a fundamental reference for object relations theory in the USA, has as its central hypothesis the idea that the history of psychoanalysis is traversed by the presence of two antithetical models as far as its fundamental tenets are concerned: the relational model and the drive model. Each tries in its own way to account for the clinical centrality of relations to others (both external and internal). Many important psychoanalysts have made valiant contributions to the relational model, resorting to diverse strategies in order "to keep their feet on the ground" in psychoanalysis—or elaborating from the highly regarded model of drive theory. The interpersonal analysts of the first generation soon broke with the American Psychoanalytic Association (APA) and so with the International Psychoanalytical Association (IPA). They thereby elaborated their clinical model from outside the realm of enforced loyalty to the drive model. Within the IPA, it was Fairbairn who was the first to oppose the psychoanalytic theory of the time most clearly and consistently. His critique of the theory of the libido as pleasure-seeking, which we shall consider later, his questioning of instincts as existing *per se*, outside any psychological structure, or his understanding of the internal world in terms of a multiplicity of egos, or selves (as we say today), or of a multiplicity of internal ego-object relations, to cite only a few of his developments, were indeed visionary. Without neglecting the historical importance of the theory of the libido Fairbairn maintains the following position:

> Nevertheless, it would appear as if the point had now been reached at which, in the interests of progress, the classic libido theory would have to be transformed into a theory of development based essentially upon object-relationships. (1941, p. 31)

Greenberg and Mitchell begin their chapter on Fairbairn by affirming:

> In a series of dense and fertile papers written during the early 1940s, W. R. D. Fairbairn developed a theoretical perspective which, along with Sullivan's "interpersonal psychiatry", provides the purest and clearest expression of the shift from the drive/structure model to the relational/structure model. (1983, p. 151)

Here we reach one of the central concepts which has been a considerable object of debate and which Mitchell will pick up on now and again in Fairbairn's work, as much for its power of synthesis and centrality as for the particular turn it gives to his thinking.

The libido as object-seeking and the problem of motivation

Fairbairn maintains the argument that his mode of understanding psychoanalysis derives from the "general proposition that the libido is not primarily pleasure-seeking but object-seeking" (1946, p. 137).

We know that this proposition had a great impact on the psychoanalytic community and was in the first instance either neglected or ignored and many years later became a source of intense debate or disregard. Today, as Scharff and Birtles (1999) argue, this proposition may sometimes pass for a truism, which paradoxically lends it the same fate.

Indeed, initially a whole series of objections arose from the drive theory camp and those upholding the pleasure principle as the principal motivation of the psyche. Our point of interest is Mitchell's reading of Fairbairn's statement years after its early reception. Or in other words, what is its impact on today's debate? For some of the analytic community the objections and arguments remain the same. But in other sectors of the analytic community, open to the productive changes favoured in psychoanalysis over the last half century, the debate is no longer one between Freudian drive theory and object relations theory, but one emerging from what we consider most significant in terms of our perspective on today's understanding of emotional life and human motivation.

This is the question we think most interests Mitchell at the time of his thinking about our theoretical constructions on this subject. What is the bedrock or primary material of the life of the psyche, and of our constructions of it? No doubt, as a number of colleagues have suggested, Mitchell is involved in a constant debate with drive theory, the obstinacy of which they find hard to understand. Our hypothesis is that this obstinacy has a two-fold source: on the one hand it is no doubt part of the interpersonal inheritance of his training, which—as indicated earlier— was fundamentally anchored in a debate with classical Freudian theory and characterised by the rejection of drive theory and metapsychological speculations arising from this. Yet on the other hand we think that to clarify this question or posit it repeatedly, or to define its terms engages us in a crucial decision regarding our constructions of a theoretical model with clinical consequences which, despite the fact that the actual demands of day to day clinical practice tend to leave little scope for this kind of debate, to me seems to be of the utmost importance.

Mitchell returns again and again to this central hypothesis, deepening his understanding in the course of his works, meaning that he refers to it in different ways, and, although this fact may generate confusion, we consider that he is each time pursuing the same objective. In 1981 he affirms that "the critique and reformulation of the psychoanalytic theory of motivation—drive theory" (1981, p. 385) is at the centre of Fairbairn's contribution to psychoanalysis. The critique is clear, although the reformulation is less obvious and less subject to interpretative consensus. Fairbairn's statement on the libido inverts the means/end relationship: "Pleasure is not the end goal of the impulse, but a means to its real end, relations with others" (ibid., p. 385). This reversal is fundamental: pleasure, just as other emotional states of both a pleasurable and unpleasurable nature, becomes a mode of being with another person, of reaching them, of integrating a relationship. When we talk of object seeking, in Fairbairn's wake, we are not referring to the literal absence or presence of parental figures or early caregivers. Furthermore, as Mitchell indicates in relation to the Connie case: "… the centrality of Connie's attachment to her mother's absence […] constituted one of the major forms through which she became a self with others, became *herself*" (2000, p. 93).

In 1988, in his first individually authored book, he makes the following penetrating observation:

> This reversal of means and ends (captured in Fairbairn's slogan "Libido is not pleasure-seeking but object-seeking") is crucial. *Who* the other is, *what* the other does, and *how* the other regards what is going on become much more important. The other is not simply a vehicle for managing internal pressures and states; interactive exchanges with and ties to the other become the fundamental psychological reality itself. (1988, p. 25)

He thus presents here another perspective on emotional states, and a varied place for the other both in terms of the subject's origins (personal history), and, as we shall later see, in terms of the relationship in the present.

Such is the central hypothesis which Mitchell will defend in his reading of Fairbairn: that this author does not propose a further contribution to the relational conception of the mind, but rather a "radical relational project" (2000, p. 105). Mitchell is indeed aware that his own reading of Fairbairn is a radical one, that it goes to the root of what Mitchell understands to be Fairbairn's central project.

In 1993, confronting the criticism of his book *Relational Concepts in Psychoanalysis* (1988), he returns once again to the question, saying:

> Because they do not find Freud's drives in my perspective, Bachant and Richards feel I leave out motivational concepts. What they fail to grasp is that I regard object seeking, in Fairbairn's sense, or interpersonal integrating tendencies, in Sullivan's sense, as super ordinate

motivational principles that are powerfully active. I also believe that people seek pleasure, power, exercise of function, security, and all sorts of other things. I think it is more useful, however, to regard these other motives, although irreducible, as shaped and structured in the context of the relational matrix that provides a sense of self in relation to others. (Mitchell, 1992, p. 463)

This quotation makes it clear that Mitchell is not ignorant of the variety of motives that drive people's behaviour. What interests him and appears most useful to him in his theoretical and clinical thinking is to consider that this assembly of motives which different authors have emphasised and may be augmented or reduced according to the category pertaining, are structured, configured, and formed in the context of the relational matrices which give them meaning.

This leads him to wonder, not for the first time, but now more clearly, if it would be better to understand object-seeking as a "drive" or as the "ground" (2000, p. 104) in which human relations are embedded. This stage of his thinking, from one of his last texts on Fairbairn, is focused on a debate with his friend and co-author Jay Greenberg, who, in his excellent book *Oedipus and Beyond* (1991), argues with Mitchell's reading of Fairbairn and with the relational model in general. In Mitchell's view, Greenberg makes an intelligent reading of certain aspects of Fairbairn's work: those most linked to Freudian fields of reference and which make Mitchell speak of Fairbairn's work as standing "between paradigms". However, he still presupposes a hypothesis which for Mitchell is most problematic and which has important consequences in defining our construction of the psychical: that the concept of the drives is necessary—in a general sense—in order to understand what the subject is looking for in the other person, and that relational psychoanalysis has claimed to create a "drive-free psychoanalysis" (ibid., p. 70).

In the debate on the necessity or not of the concept of a drive leading the individual to seek out interaction, Mitchell insists that posing the question in this way, that is to say postulating the drive as pre-existent—and thereby pre-experiential—to the relation which brings the subject into interaction—presupposes that the "individual qua individual" is the most appropriate unit of study. According to Mitchell, this involves returning to the initial controversy over the Freudian model of drives and thereby to the age-old divisions over conceptions of man's relationship to society.

In the discussion with Greenberg, Mitchell affirms:

I believe that Fairbairn, like Sullivan (1953), was struggling toward a different way of understanding the nature of human beings as fundamentally social, not as *drawn* into interaction, but as *embedded* in an interactive matrix with others as his or her natural state. (1998, p. 117; 2000, p. 105)

Thus does Mitchell forever insist on demonstrating the importance of Fairbairn's extraordinary breakthrough in upholding and defending the idea that man—the libido, as he said, sticking to the Freudian terminology—is not pleasure-seeking but object-seeking. According to Mitchell, what interested Fairbairn was not to discover some hidden ulterior motivation, as Greenberg will affirm when he argues that Fairbairn's postulating oral dependency as the ultimate human motive results in drive monism, but to establish the ground for the comprehension of motives.

Although Mitchell knows that at times Fairbairn is unclear or vague (in some texts), he has no doubt that Fairbairn's intention was not to posit the existence of a particular drive, but to define the foundations of psychical life and the condition of its very possibility. He insists that Fairbairn perfectly understood that human beings seek pleasure and other emotional states but it is not the essential question. He says of Fairbairn in this respect:

> He was suggesting that Freud stopped his account, his understanding of pleasure seeking, too soon. [...] For Fairbairn [...] pleasure-seeking, like all other dynamic processes, occurs in the context of object-seeking, because pleasure is a powerful medium for the establishment and maintenance of connections with others. (1988, p. 120)

His conceptual strategy does not involve going over *a priori* motives or needs. He prefers, knowing that this is the clinically relevant, useful, and not necessarily "more authentic" choice for him, to take the relationship to others, the encounter, as the cornerstone of emotional significance. The alternative, to take predefined, predetermined drives as his point of departure would for him be tantamount to upholding "the myth of abstract man" as a natural state, to use José Bleger's expression (1973), and thereby to isolating man from his social entourage. This Platonic-Cartesian hermeneutic is questioned on different occasions from an Aristotelian-Hegelian perspective of man as a political animal (*zoon politikon*).

From a relational perspective, desires and motivations are only meaningful when understood in the context of relational, self-other configurations and the particular desire or motivation in question, or the predominant or most developed desires and motivations, depending on the personal history of the individual.

Mitchell will uphold that which motivates a human being will in each case bear the stamp of singularity contained in his relational history. The different dimensions of human existence which are central "dynamic processes" in one person or another depend, for Mitchell, as much on the particular contexts in which the subject operates as they do on the restrictions and possibilities imposed by biologically organised patterns.

Therefore, he argues:

> Man's social nature leads him to seek many different forms of connection, familiarity, security, dependency, merger, safety, pleasure, validation, mutual knowing, and so on. What dimensions of the infinite variety of human connection become dynamically central and conflictual for any particular person depends strongly on the particularities of the cultural and familial context and the specific constellation of talents, sensitivities, and rhythms the individual discovers in himself within that context. (1988, p. 62)

Any reduction to one or several motivations is arbitrary in Mitchell's view and of little interest since then we lose the complexity and specificity of what we have in our hands. We consider that Mitchell is making an interesting point here, characteristic of the suspicion with which the interpersonal tradition considers any generalisation of motivation as a supra-ordinate common basis for a mesh of human activity or of the human condition, be that with regard to reading Fairbairn as someone privileging oral dependency, or be that with regard to privileging narcissistic regulation or the cohesion of the self, and also, it goes without saying, those who privilege classical drive theory. Since then we have lost the richness of the complex relational tapestry (ibid.), a metaphor he uses on several occasions, being spun and woven in the context of each singularity. In this way Mitchell combats the reductionism implied by postulating supra-ordinate motives for behaviour as pre-existing the relational matrix; he also does not share those motivational systems developed by Joseph Lichtenberg (1989)—who differentiates five motivational systems based on innate needs. Once again, Mitchell does not see the point in isolating a series of motivational systems or of innate needs and giving them an *a priori* status since this is as problematic for him as the strategy of isolating a single motive, and we insist that although these are two "politically contradictory" strategies, they share the same fundamental basis as propositions. Postulating a more varied motivational system is no doubt more interesting from a clinical point of view, but in terms of theoretical construction, for Mitchell, this amounts to staying on the path and not exploring its conditions of possibility, that is to say those relationships, which encompass the different motivational systems, the varying options which different psychoanalytical schools of thought have foregrounded, and, of course, furthermore and thereby, the concept of pleasure as motivation.

Psychical change and the analytic cure

"Every New Beginning has to take place in an object-relation" (Balint, 1935, p. 185).

In 1943 Fairbairn defines psychopathology as "the study of the relationships of the ego to its internalised objects". We know that in his thinking the object and the ego are inseparable, and that different types of internal object correspond to fragments of the self, to which they are inevitably joined. We also know, as Thomas Ogden has demonstrated, that "Fairbairn's insight that it is object relationships and not objects that are internalized opened the way to thinking of both the self—and the object-components of the internal relationship as active agencies, 'dynamic structures'" (1983, p. 234). Furthermore, as Mitchell points out, it is necessary to remember that in Fairbairn conflict does not disappear from the psychical or the psychopathological scene, but will be understood as "split loyalties to different others and to different dimensions of one's relation with others" (1988, pp. 27–28), between different versions of the self (self-other), with each version of the self having a functional unity with a system of belief, emotional organisation, active intentionality, and a developmental history (Mitchell, 2000).

We wanted to begin this part by making reference to psychopathology, because it is in this sense that Mitchell's reading of the theory of psychical change in the analytic process in Fairbairn will be best understood. If for Fairbairn there is a tie to bad objects as a central element at the heart of psychopathology, each psychical change must be understood as an alteration of this tie or as its renouncement. We saw earlier that these ties govern the way in which the subject has constructed his world, his subjective universe; that the definition of the human subject as object-seeking supposes that this occurs in determined contexts or relational matrix in which passions and desires have taken shape and acquired meaning. In this vein, Fairbairn affirms, in relation to the importance of the relationship between analyst and analysand as the central point of articulation of an assembly of factors of change operating in the treatment, that:

> After all, it is on the basis of the relationships existing between the individual and his parents in childhood that his personality develops and assumes its particular form; and it seems logical to infer that any subsequent change in his personality that may be effected by psycho-analytical treatment (or any other form of psychotherapy) must be effected primarily on the basis of a personal relationship. (1958a, p. 379)

This, for Fairbairn, will be the decisive agent of change and one of the fundamental tasks of the analytic treatment will be "to open a breach" in the closed system of internal object relations while still perpetuating them. Now if the situation of "objectlessness" is unthinkable in terms of experience, or, furthermore, stems from "insupportable", or, "unthinkable" to use Winnicott's term, anxieties, as Fairbairn upholds, then we are faced with a problem which Fairbairn apprehended:

> […] it is only when the internalized bad objects are released from the unconscious that there is any hope of their cathexis being dissolved. The bad objects can only be safely released, however, if the analyst has become established as a sufficiently good object for the patient. Otherwise the resulting insecurity may prove insupportable. (1943a, pp. 69–70)

Now this is where Mitchell considers that Fairbairn has fallen short or not been sufficiently clear. If we cannot renounce old objects unless new ones appear, how can we know what is "established as a sufficiently good object" to use Fairbairn's words, or the possibility of an object offering the opportunity for the development of a new relationship? How does the analyst become a "good object", asks Mitchell?

This is what he says:

> In Fairbairn's (1952) system, the libidinal ego longs for the "exciting object," which is composed of features of early bad object relations. A truly "good" object is something else entirely and is encountered/developed in the analytic relationship. In my view, expressed in Fairbairn's terms, it is only through a willingness to be experienced as, and, perhaps, to enact some of the functions of, the exciting object that the patient and analyst together learn what a good object relationship for this particular patient might be like. (1994, p. 368)

Here Mitchell makes a clearer distinction between what he understands to be Fairbairn's position and his own vision in the wake of that position. It is true that Fairbairn discerns in the relationship between analyst and patient something which corresponds to the transference and which he calls "the total relationship", existing, as he says, between the analyst and patient as people (1958a, p. 379). In the 1958 text, to my knowledge, and it seems also Mitchell's, it remains unclear what precisely the link is between this "personal relationship"—which is apparently a decisive factor of change—and the transference as repetition. Mitchell upholds that this missing articulation is necessary in order to be able to think out not a generic solution to what is new for someone, but rather the singularity of that newness against the background of repetition.

"If the analyst isn't experienced through old patterns [...] the analysis isn't deeply engaged" (Mitchell & Black, 1995, p. 122).

It is in this context, and with this fundamental preoccupation, that Sullivan once made the provocative comment: "God keep me from a therapy that goes well!" (cited by Levenson, 1983, p. 84). The assumption behind Sullivan's provocation, one which also runs through Mitchell's work, is that the mistakes and missed moments of the analytic process, which Baranger, Baranger, and Mom (1982) call "the no-process" are a constitutive and inevitable part of the process; that the new does not suddenly appear, intact, beside the old, but rather occurs from within it, expanding old object relations "from inside out"—to use Bromberg's expression (1998). It is for this reason that for a large section of those involved in relational psychoanalysis, and indeed Mitchell, enactment is not something that can arrive and must be avoided thanks to the analyst's greater expertise. As Mitchell wondered on one occasion: "Is impasse the outcome of an analysis which is going well or going badly?" (1991). As he says in the above citation, it is the willingness to enact some of the functions of the bad object which make breakthrough and transformation possible.

> What I am suggesting, is that the central feature of the therapeutic action of psychoanalysis is the emergence of something new from something old. It cannot be there in the beginning, because you have to find yourself in the old to create the proper context for the emergence of something new. It cannot be the application of a standard technique or posture, because then it would not really be something new and would never strike the analysand that way. (Mitchell, 1997, p. 59)

We might conclude that in his critique of the analyst's clinical activity as scientific, in his emphasis on the "personal relationship" as a central point of articulation in the psychotherapeutic process, to name but a few of these contributions, perhaps Fairbairn was already forging the path which contemporary relational psychoanalysis is striving to articulate.

We would like to finish by quoting George Steiner: "To read well is to be read by that which we read" (1996, p. 6).

Translated from Spanish by Anne-Marie Smith-Di Biasio.

References

Baranger, M., Baranger, W., & Mom, J. (1982). Proceso y no-proceso en el trabajo analítico. *Revista de Psicoanálisis, 39*(4): 527–549.

Balint, M. (1935). The final goal of psycho-analytic treatment. In: *Primary Love and Psychoanalytic Technique*. London: Karnac, 1994.

Bleger, J. (1973). *Psicología de la Conducta*. Buenos Aires, Argentina: Paidós.

Bromberg, P. (1998). *Standing in the Spaces*. Hillsdale, NJ: Analytric Press.

Fairbairn, W. R. D. (1941). A revised psychopathology of the psychoses and psychoneuroses. *International Journal of Psychoanalysis, 22*(3, 4): 250–279. In: *Psychoanalytic Studies of the Personality* (pp. 28–58). London: Tavistock, 1952.

Fairbairn, W. R. D. (1943a). The repression and the return of bad objects (with special reference to the "war neuroses"). *British Journal of Medical Psychology, 19*: 327–341. In: *Psychoanalytic Studies of the Personality* (pp. 59–81). London: Tavistock, 1952.

Fairbairn, W. R. D. (1946a). Object-relationships and dynamic structure. *International Journal of Psychoanalysis, 27*: 30–37. In: *Psychoanalytic Studies of the Personality* (pp. 137–151). London: Tavistock, 1952.

Fairbairn, W. R. D. (1952). *Psychoanalytic Studies of the Personality*. London, Tavistock. [Reprinted London: Routledge, 1999.]

Fairbairn, W. R. D. (1958a). On the nature and aims of psycho-analytical treatment. *International Journal of Psychoanalysis, 39*(5): 374–385. In: D. E. Scharff & E. F. Birtles (Eds.), *From Instinct to Self: Selected Papers of W. R. D. Fairbairn, Volume I: Clinical and Theoretical Papers* (pp. 74–92). Northvale, NJ: Jason Aronson, 1994.

Friedland, B. (1978). Toward a psychology of the self. *Contemporary Psychoanalysis, 14*: 553–570.

Greenberg, J. (1991). *Oedipus and Beyond. A Clinical Theory*. Cambridge, MA: Harvard University Press.

Greenberg, J. (2001). Stephen A. Mitchell: 1946–2000. *Contemporary Psychoanalysis, 37*: 189–191.

Greenberg, J., & Mitchell, S. A. (1983). *Object Relations in Psychoanalytic Theory*. Cambridge, MA: Harvard University Press.

Levenson, E. (1983). *The Ambiguity of Change*. Northvale, NJ: Jason Aronson.

Lichtenberg, J. D. (1989). *Psychoanalysis and Motivation*. Hillsdale, NJ: Analytic Press.

Mitchell, S. A. (1981). The origin and nature of the "object" in the theories of Klein and Fairbairn. *Contemporary Psychoanalysis, 17*: 374.

Mitchell, S. A. (1988). *Relational Concepts in Psychoanalysis*. Cambridge, MA: Harvard University Press.

Mitchell, S. A. (1991). Discussion. *Contemporary Psychoanalysis, 27*: 518.

Mitchell, S. A. (1993). Reply to Bachant and Richards. *Psychoanalytic Dialogues, 3*: 461–480.

Mitchell, S. A. (1994). Something old, something new: Commentary on Steven Stern's "needed relationships". *Psychoanalytic Dialogues, 4*: 363–369.

Mitchell, S. A. (1997). *Influence and Autonomy in Psychoanalysis*. Hillsdale, NJ: Analytic Press.

Mitchell, S. A. (1998). Fairbairn's object seeking: Between paradigms. In: N. J. Skolnick & D. E. Scharff (Eds.), *Fairbairn, Then and Now*. Hillsdale, NJ: Analytic Press.

Mitchell, S. A. (1999a). Letter to the editor. *Contemporary Psychoanalysis, 35*: 355–359.

Mitchell, S. A. (1999b). Fairbairn and the problem of agency. In: F. Pereira & D. E. Scharff (Eds.), *Fairbairn and Relational Theory*. London: Karnac, 2002.

Mitchell, S. A. (2000). *Relationality: From Attachment to Intersubjectivity*. Hillsdale, NJ: Analytic Press.

Mitchell, S. A., & Black, M. J. (1995). *Freud and Beyond*. New York: Basic.

Ogden, T. H. (1983). The concept of internal object relations. *International Journal of Psychoanalysis, 64*: 227–241.

Ogden, T. H. (1994). *Subjects of Analysis*. London: Karnac.

Scharff, D. E., & Birtles, E. F. (1999). Introduction. In: Fairbairn, W. R. D. (1952), *Psychoanalytic Studies of the Personality*. [Revised edition.] London: Routledge, 1999.

Steiner, G. (1996). *No Passion Spent: Essays 1978–1995*. New Haven, CT: Yale University Press.

Zukerfeld, R. (2005). *Procesos Terciarios. De la vulnerabilidad a la resiliencia*. Buenos Aires, Argentina: Lugar.

CHAPTER TWENTY-SEVEN

Fairbairn's influence on Stephen Mitchell's theoretical and clinical work

Aleksandar Dimitrijevic

As relational psychoanalysis was taking form as a theory and as a movement, Charles Spezzano (1997) wrote that it could more fittingly be named the "American Middle Group", alluding to its closeness to the Middle or Independent group of British psychoanalysis. This may well be true, particularly because the influence of Donald Winnicott was very strong among different relational facets. Stephen Mitchell, who, as author, lecturer, supervisor, and organizer, was essential in the establishment of relational psychoanalysis, grew up on the interpersonal, Sullivanian tradition of the "William Alanson White" Institute, his psychoanalytic alma mater. Mitchell is, however, cited appropriately among the authors who have spelled out the ways in which Fairbairn's contribution influenced them in important ways (Scharff & Birtles, 1994, p. xi), as Fairbairn was among the psychoanalysts whom Mitchell quoted most often and to whose work he devoted one of his first papers (Mitchell, 1981). He also devoted one whole chapter in *Relationality: From Attachment to Intersubjectivity* (2000), the last book published during his lifetime, in which Mitchell described Fairbairn as the creator of a whole new world view.

In the interview he gave to Peter Rudnytsky, in 1998, shortly before his untimely death at the age of fifty-four, Mitchell singled out Fairbairn as the author who had had the greatest influence on his work (Rudnytsky, 2000, p. 130), adding a little later (p. 134) that this connection went back all the way to his graduate studies at New York University. Indeed, throughout his oeuvre, Mitchell sang the highest praises of Fairbairn: he claimed that Fairbairn's concepts have provided new generations of psychoanalysts with the most widely used terms for depicting self–other configurations (ibid., p. 103), and recognised that, in general, "Fairbairn has had an enormous, if often unacknowledged, impact" (1991b, p. 643). On an even higher note, Mitchell described Fairbairn's theory of object relations as revolutionary (2000, p. xvii) and visionary (2002, p. 103).

Mitchell also emphasised that he had a deep respect for Fairbairn's "broad and incisive critique of classical drive theory, his reformulation of motivational, developmental, structural, and clinical theory along purely object relations lines, [and] his emphasis on the primacy of the analytic relationship over interpretation proper" (1991b, p. 643). One can say that the qualities of Fairbairn's model he emphasises are at the same time the foundations of Mitchell's relational psychoanalysis. Decades after Fairbairn, Mitchell and his colleagues criticised Freudian metapsychology and offered alternative understanding of the concept of drives. Evidence coming from attachment theory, and other similar research, clearly showed that infants were relational beings from the very start. New approaches to countertransference, enactments, and disclosure had made psychoanalysts more interactive than ever before. Relational analysts became wary of the allegedly omniscient, interpretative attitude, and began to rely upon questioning, sharing, expressive behaviour, and support. And all these novel approaches had a strongly Fairbairnian cast to them.

It was as if Mitchell read Fairbairn to filter out what was most fruitful in his approach and to transplant it into new ground, fertilised by his other constant dialogues. He was, however, also willing to part company with almost all his theoretical predecessors if that was necessary for the relational model to be formulated. Mitchell noted more than once that, in their review of Fairbairn's book, Winnicott and Khan (1953) argued that Fairbairn forces us to choose between Freud's theory and his own model. As clearly as they chose Freud, Mitchell obviously and explicitly opted for Fairbairn and his "purely relational vision of human psychology" (1991b, p. 643).

As a reader and as a thinker, Mitchell has been omnivorous with a gift for synthesising and digesting every psychoanalytic alternative, mixing them with the humanities, literature, and contemporary music, to name but a few. I believe that, despite this, and despite his deep roots in American interpersonal psychoanalysis, Mitchell thought of his own work as a continuation of Fairbairn's and that this influence can most clearly be seen in four different areas, which I will discuss in more detail below.

What kind of science is psychoanalysis?

Fairbairn and Mitchell came from rather different academic backgrounds. While the former read philosophy before entering medical school, the latter got his PhD in clinical psychology devoting some time to community mental health care and Rorschach testing. Yet, it seems to me that Mitchell found Fairbairn's attitudes valuable even as he was looking for his basic orientation towards psychoanalysis as a discipline among the social and natural sciences, the humanities, and the helping professions.

In the interview quoted above, Mitchell agrees with Rudnytsky's description of Mitchell's attitude to the issue of the relationship between psychoanalysis and science in the following way: "[…] these are alternative visions of reality that are powerful and valid on their own terms, and there's no external frame of reference to which we can appeal to try to choose between one or the other" (2000, p. 117). Fairbairn, for his part, cared for the issue strongly enough to express his attitude in great detail thirty-five years earlier but in a strikingly similar vein to Mitchell: "[…] I regard psychology (psychoanalysis) as a *scientific discipline* rather than that I regard it as 'a natural science'" (1955, p. 121, emphasis in the original). "[…] whilst I attach extreme importance to scientific truth, I do not regard it as representing in any sense an ultimate value; and, within the psychotherapeutic field, I regard it as subordinate to the human and personal values which psychotherapy serves" (p. 127). "[…] My conception of science is that it is essentially an intellectual tool and nothing more. I do not regard it as in any sense providing an (even approximately) accurate picture of reality as it actually exists, still less a revelation of ultimate truth" (p. 125).

In the view of both authors, psychoanalysis was first and foremost a clinical and then, secondarily, a scientific discipline, and one can feel that they are, independently, trying to caution us against the, as it were, seductive powers of scientific discourse. So, for instance, Fairbairn wrote: "It seems to me obvious that the analyst is not primarily a scientist, but a psychotherapist" (ibid., p. 126). And when Mitchell tried to illustrate that same attitude, which was obviously important to him, he looked back to Fairbairn and contrasted his stance to that of John Bowlby. Although he held attachment research and particularly the work of Mary Main in high esteem, Mitchell's opinion was that Bowlby's "scientific-behavioral" approach to attachment was not very helpful in psychoanalytic work with patients, because his concepts were "too simplistic to be used clinically", while Fairbairn's can be utilised to develop a picture of the inner world in all its subtleties: "I thought Bowlby was *right*, but I thought that Fairbairn was much more useful" (Rudnytsky, 2000, pp. 134–135, emphasis in the original).

The contexts of Fairbairn's and Mitchell's attitudes were completely different. One may even say that the former worked in the time when psychoanalysis distanced itself from science and universities, and the latter in the time of its infatuation with natural sciences and especially the neurosciences. Both of these general attitudes may well be misleading for the development of psychoanalysis, whereas Fairbairn's and Mitchell's tolerance and flexibility, and caution at the same time, testifies that they have both remained open to scientific contributions and possible corrections, but that for them psychoanalytic clinical practice came before all. When Mitchell inspired an entire movement, it included some of the finest developmentalists of the time whose work proved inspirational for the refinement of psychoanalytic technique. I believe that this is proof of Fairbairn's and Mitchell's capacities to question their respective work and theorising, to innovate and improve upon them, and to risk critique and isolation from centres of psychoanalytic power—all of which are necessary preconditions for making the sort of contribution they gave us.

What does the world of internal objects look like?

In their groundbreaking 1983 book, *Object Relations in Psychoanalytic Theory*, which is now considered to have founded what is referred to as "relational psychoanalysis", Jay Greenberg and Stephen Mitchell have claimed that: "Accounting for the enormous clinical significance of object relations has been the central conceptual problem within the history of psychoanalytic ideas. Every major psychoanalytic author has had to address himself to this issue, and his manner of resolving it determines the basic approach and sets the foundation for subsequent theorizing" (p. 4). It turns out that in this most central issue, Mitchell's thinking was closest to Fairbairn's and inevitably influenced by it. He held that Fairbairn addressed himself to this central conceptual problem in a way that was most applicable to the clinical reality of psychoanalysis and decided to try to move Fairbairn's model another step forward.

Mitchell considered Fairbairn's model the purest and clearest expression of the shift from the drive/structure model to the relation/structure model (Greenberg & Mitchell, 1983, p. 151). It is now well known that Mitchell worked long and hard in order to articulate this model towards which Fairbairn pointed, and was ready to elaborate, promote, and improve it. With his usual clarity, Mitchell organised various psychoanalytic models of relations into four levels of the interactional hierarchy (2000, Chapter Three). Briefly, the lowest level is characterised by non-reflective, presymbolic interaction, of, to express it in a slightly more modern language, doing something to someone without any mentalisation; the second level is of intensive shared affects that cross permeable personality boundaries, like in love, seduction, fear, cheering the football team; the third level is the self-other configurations, which was the most frequent psychoanalytic topic of the second half of the twentieth century; finally, the fourth level is the ultimate form of human communication and includes the mutual recognition of two independent subjects. Mitchell claimed that major theorists addressed various levels but focused on one. He considered Fairbairn to have focused on the third level and, more important, Fairbairn was his basic source for thinking about this level.

Of all the aspects of Fairbairn's theoretical work his object relations theory stood the test of time as the most important, and not only because he was the first to coin the term "object-relationship psychology" (1944). Mitchell believed that after Fairbairn it makes no sense to think of a self except in relation to an other. He held that Fairbairn offered a model of internal personality structure connected to relational development that complemented and was pointedly missing from American interpersonal psychoanalysis (Margaret Black Mitchell, personal communication). In short, what he could not find in Sullivan and Loewald, due to their being too interpersonal for his taste, he found in Fairbairn.

Fairbairn (1955) wrote that "[…] 'an internal object' may be defined as 'an endopsychic structure other than an ego-structure, with which an ego-structure has a relationship comparable to a relationship with a person in external reality" (quoted in Birtles & Scharff, 1994, p. 112). Infants have natural objects and these are other people, especially the caregivers. When, however, this relationship is unsatisfactory, especially in the case of maternal deprivation, internal objects are formed as compensation (Fairbairn, 1952). Or, as Mitchell and Black summarised: "Because the child, in his object-seeking, cannot reach the unresponsive aspects of the parents in actuality, he internalizes them and fantasizes those features of the parents as now being inside of him, part of him" (1995, p. 117).

It is believed that Fairbairn came up with his theory of object relations after a formative clinical experience—his work with abused children, whom he understood to seek pain as a preferred form of connection (ibid., pp. 115–116). Thus, the basis of his theory of psychopathology, which he thought of as the study of the relationships of the ego to its internalised objects, was just Fairbairn's special theory of object relations. Fairbairn redefined Freud's principle of repetition compulsion in terms of patterns of relationships with bad objects, the exciting objects that seem to promise but never fulfil, and these patterns are seen to be repeated in seemingly new relationships: "For Fairbairn, relations with internal objects are inherently masochistic. Bad internal objects are persistent tempters and persecutors, while good internal objects do not offer real gratification, but merely a refuge from relations with bad objects" (Mitchell, 1981, p. 392). Furthermore, Fairbairn's conception of mental health and analytic cure does not include any sort of internal objects, as he thought that the restored ego needed no attachments to internal objects but can turn to relationships with real others in the outside world (ibid., p. 392). I hope that in the fourth segment of this chapter it will become obvious how all these aspects of Fairbairn's theory of illness and cure were constantly present in Mitchell's clinical practice.

Finally, it must also be noted that Mitchell repeatedly stressed that Fairbairn's theory of object relations had to be revised. He claimed that the greatest weakness of Fairbairn's model was his failure to account for the residues of good object relations and how the structure of the self is formed on the basis of healthy identifications, because for Fairbairn all internal object relations derive from the frustration of unavailability and are by definition pathological (ibid., p. 392, n.10). Later on, he insisted that "good and loving experiences, like bad and hateful experiences, also leave internal residues" (2000, p. 123). There is no need to stress how central this issue is for Fairbairn's theory, so it is a great pity that Mitchell did not elaborate his argument and suggest alternative solution(s).

How should we understand and treat split-off, dissociated states?

There is a direct connection between Fairbairn's theory of splitting and contemporary relational psychoanalysis's theorising about discontinuous, multiple self-organisations characterised by an illusory sense of continuity and coherence, where specific therapeutic techniques were developed for working with persons who experience these states. Indeed, Fairbairn wrote (1955) that he did not "regard the *developed* psyche as a *single* dynamic structure" (quoted in Birtles & Scharff, 1994, p. 112, emphasis in the original), and Mitchell (2000, p. 63) considered this to be one of Fairbairn's major contributions that is being developed by many contemporary relational analysts.

At a basic level, Mitchell reviewed and discussed this aspect of Fairbairn's theory in various publications across two decades. In his summary of the development of psychoanalytic thought he wrote that "Fairbairn envisioned people as actually structured into multiple, subtly discontinuous self-organizations" (Mitchell & Black, 1995, p. 121). He also touched on the topic of the interference of modern civilisation with the mother–infant bond that was very important to Fairbairn (Greenberg & Mitchell, 1983, p. 159; see also Mitchell, 1981, p. 386), devoting more space to Fairbairn's notion of splitting as the consequence of the proliferation of internal objects to which different parts of the ego become attached causing the fragmentation of the original ego (Greenberg & Mitchell, 1983, p. 163). Of course, dissociation is closely connected to the origin of internal objects, as understood by Fairbairn and mentioned above: "Part of the self remains directed toward the real parents in the external world, seeking actual responses from them; part of the self is redirected toward the illusory parents as internal objects to which it is bound" (Mitchell & Black, 1995, p. 120).

More profoundly, Mitchell brought Fairbairn's ideas into the then current psychoanalytic dialogues. He (1993, p. 115) wrote that it really looked as if "… the most interesting feature of contemporary psychoanalytic perspectives on self [was] precisely the creative tension between the portrayal of self as multiple and discontinuous and of self as integral and continuous." For his part, Mitchell (1991a, p. 139) tried to ease the tension between these perspectives claiming that they were not mutually exclusive. He thought that they referred to different aspects of self, one to "the multiple configurations of self patterned variably in different relational contexts", the other to the "subjective experience of the pattern making itself, activity that is experienced over time and across the different organizational schemes". Still, the emphasis that relational psychoanalysts put on the self as a product of interpersonal interactions makes it impossible to conceive of selves except as discontinuous and multiple, as being created in every single important relationship. It is said that one does not even have to be aware of these different selves, but can live in a state of "healthy illusion of cohesive personal identity", to use Philip Bromberg's phrasing (1998, p. 273). Mitchell claims that several of his colleagues would agree with him that "these multiplicitous organizations are much more than (cognitive) representations of self; rather, they are each versions, complete functional units with a belief system, affective organization, agentic intentionality, and developmental history" (2000, p. 63). Relational theorists take it for granted that each of the multiple selves performs all the functions originally attributed to the ego.

Naturally, these conceptual shifts produced further changes in psychoanalytic treatment and technique. In accordance with this new understanding of mental health and pathology, wherein dissociation is considered a healthy, adaptive function, therapeutic requirements and goals have changed substantially. An analyst is sometimes requested nothing less than to reject any therapeutic frame. Bromberg wrote that the purpose of this is to enable a patient to "feel free to enact new ways of being without fear of traumatically losing continuity of 'who he is'" while "exploring the way in which the self-states comprising [his/her] personal identity are linked to each other, to the external world, and to the past, present and future" (1998, p. 386). It is considered mistaken to assume that the melding of different versions of the self is preferable to the capacity to contain shifting and conflictual versions of the self (Mitchell, 1993, p. 105). Furthermore, the analyst is required to accept not only the patients' but also his/her own multiplicity, and that will, I assume, soon bring further changes to the theory of countertransference.

What are we to say to our patients?

The most obvious influence Fairbairn had on Mitchell was in the clinical domain, the one they both considered the most important, as I have already noted above. Mitchell paid special attention to Fairbairn's understanding of bad objects and the ways this can be made useful in psychoanalytic treatments. When Mitchell and Black (1995, p. 122) reviewed Fairbairn's model they described a situation where, although analysands claim that they are looking for something new, they indeed experience analysts as old, bad objects, transferentially looking for their parents' features, more likely the fantasised than the actual ones. Mitchell was thinking about that even earlier, when he wrote that in order to overcome fixation on bad objects, the patient must start experiencing the analyst as a good object (1988, pp. 150–151). It can be said that this, originally Fairbairn's, depiction of the patient's dedication to old and bad internal objects and how the analyst, in needing to engage the patient in something new and different, first needed to engage the "old", was fundamental to the clinical approach Mitchell endeavoured to articulate (Margaret Black Mitchell, personal communication).

Mitchell published a lot of clinical material, either from his own practice or from the work of his supervisees, always remarkable in its clarity of thinking and presentation. One of them I will briefly present here (for the whole account see Mitchell, 2000, pp. 116–123). That is the case of a forty-five-year-old man, "Will", haunted by feelings of guilt and responsibility. Will had left his first wife and daughter, who at that moment was two years of age, because of another woman, although he lived alone for four years before marrying her. He entered psychoanalysis late, because he believed "it" would try to alleviate his responsibility for what he had done. Despite his first wife remarrying after some time, he felt he had destroyed not only her life, but also those of their daughter and his wife's parents. He also imagined that his father, a figure of particular importance for him, who had died before Will met his second wife, would never be able to understand Will's life and choices, being a man who sacrificed much for both his parents and his children, and a devout Catholic. Because of Will's intense suffering, his second marriage, otherwise far more satisfying for him emotionally and sexually, was in difficulties, and for quite a time the treatment did not lead to any improvement regarding Will's guilt and his need to punish himself. What turned out to be important is that Mitchell did not focus on Will's drives and conflicts, and did not see Will's guilt as resulting from them, as the classical drive model would suggest. What he had previously explained in the context of Fairbairn's theory as "Pleasure is not the end goal of the impulse, but a means to its real end—relations with another" (Greenberg & Mitchell, 1983, p. 154), he attributed to the guilt feelings and saw them as a powerful source of relationships as well, and then applied both to a person of flesh and blood and his inner and interpersonal struggles. Mitchell clearly followed Fairbairn's path and understood Will's guilt as a tool for fixing old relationships in time. Through the feelings of badness and responsibility ("fierce determination not to let himself off the hook"), Will remained tied to his first wife and identified with his parents.

At one moment, Mitchell asked Will what he thought his daughter would feel one day about being deprived of the contact with his extended family (understanding only somewhat later that he came to this intervention through his own feelings of guilt due to his inability to help Will stop punishing his daughter because of his guilt). Explorations of this topic from different angles made Will feel guilty in an, as it were, productive, rather than a self-destructive, way. Gradually, Will managed to establish a more optimal distance towards his first wife, and realised how his guilt punished his second wife and their children. Will probably never realised that he would suffer far more trouble improving his life had his analyst, even as a young postgrad, not read almost forgotten papers written by a long-deceased Edinburgh analyst.

Conclusion

Reading and rereading Mitchell's papers and books I always marvelled at his capacity for synthesis: I do not think that any of Mitchell's numerous reviews of other authors' works was unjust or one-sided; on the contrary, he seems to have managed to see each approach as a whole and distil from it what was most inspirational for further theory building. Furthermore, his writing is always interdisciplinary and has deep roots in various scientific disciplines and cultural traditions. If, however, there was a special place in Mitchell's private pantheon of psychoanalytic theorists, then I believe that it was occupied by Ronald Fairbairn.

It seems to me that Mitchell never wrote about any other psychoanalyst, Loewald and Sullivan included, with such a degree of identification as he wrote about Fairbairn. It is difficult to read, "I suggest a reading of Fairbairn that portrays him as struggling to move from traditional psychoanalytical categories of thought to a radically different, relational theory of mind" (Mitchell, 2000, pp. 103–104), and not think that Mitchell sees Fairbairn as his predecessor, as someone who had started the struggle which Mitchell and other relationalists have won several decades later. There is no doubt that Mitchell was fully aware of this, for in one of his earliest papers he wrote that "… the most productive development of the work established by Klein and Fairbairn requires a dialectical synthesis of a more interactional nature. It is my hope that this explication and differentiation of Klein's and Fairbairn's views concerning the origin and nature of objects will serve as a prolegomena to such a synthesis" (1981, p. 395). Finally, he explicated this attitude without any ambiguity: "I believe Fairbairn was also after something more fundamental, which he never developed fully and clearly, and I want to try to get at that radical relational project" (2000, p. 105). Today, there can be no doubt that Mitchell succeeded in developing his project; but there can also be no doubt that he would not have been able to do that without standing on Fairbairn's shoulders. I hope that I have managed to illustrate this, by focusing on what is already there.

References

Bromberg, P. (1998). *Standing in the Spaces*. Hillsdale, NJ: Analytic Press.
Fairbairn, W. R. D. (1944). Endopsychic structure considered in terms of object-relationships. *International Journal of Psychoanalysis, 25*: 70–92. In: *Psychoanalytic Studies of the Personality* (pp. 82–136). London: Tavistock.
Fairbairn, W. R. D. (1952). *Psychoanalytic Studies of the Personality*. London: Tavistock.
Fairbairn, W. R. D. (1955). Observations in defence of object-relations theory of the personality. *British Journal of Medical Psychology, 28*(2, 3): 144–156. In: E. F. Birtles & D. E. Scharff (Eds.), *From Instinct to Self: Selected Papers of W. R. D. Fairbairn, Volume II: Applications and Early Contributions* (pp. 111–128). Northvale, NJ: Jason Aronson, 1994.
Greenberg, J. R., & Mitchell, S. A. (1983). W. R. D. Fairbairn. In: *Object Relations in Psychoanalytic Theory* (pp. 151–187). Cambridge, MA: Harvard University Press.
Mitchell, S. A. (1981). The origin and nature of the "object" in the theories of Klein and Fairbairn. *Contemporary Psychoanalysis, 17*: 374–398.
Mitchell, S. A. (1988). *Relational Concepts in Psychoanalysis. An Integration*. Cambridge, MA: Harvard University Press.
Mitchell, S. A. (1991a). Contemporary perspectives on self: Toward an integration. *Psychoanalytic Dialogues, 1*: 121–147.
Mitchell, S. A. (1991b). [Review] *Fairbairn's Journey into the Interior*. John D. Sutherland. London: Free Association, 1989, (pp. xiv + 191) *Psychoanalytic Review, 78*: 642–644.
Mitchell, S. A. (1993). *Hope and Dread in Psychoanalysis*. New York: Basic.
Mitchell, S. A. (2000). *Relationality: From Attachment to Intersubjectivity*. Hillsdale, NJ: Analytic Press.
Mitchell, S. A. (2002). *Can Love Last? The Fate of Romance over Time*. London: W. W. Norton.
Mitchell, S. A., & Black, M. J. (1995). The British object relations school: Fairbairn and Winnicott. In: *Freud and Beyond. A History of Modern Psychoanalytic Thought* (pp. 112–138). New York: Basic.

Rudnytsky, P. L. (2000). Stephen A. Mitchell. Between philosophy and politics. In: *Psychoanalytic Conversations. Interviews with Clinicians, Commentators, and Critics* (pp. 101–136). Hillsdale, NJ: Analytic Press.

Scharff, D. E., & Birtles, E. F. (1994). Editors' introduction. Fairbairn's contribution. In: D. E. Scharff & E. F. Birtles (Eds.), *From Instinct to Self: Selected Papers of W. R. D. Fairbairn, Volume I: Clinical and Theoretical Papers* (pp. xi–xxi). Northvale, NJ: Jason Aronson.

Spezzano, C. (1997). The emergence of an American middle school of psychoanalysis. *Psychoanalytic Dialogues, 7*: 603–618.

Winnicott, D. W., & Khan, M. M. R. (1953). A review of Fairbairn's "Psychoanalytic Studies of the Personality". *International Journal of Psychoanalysis, 34*: 329–333.

CHAPTER TWENTY-EIGHT

Self and society, trauma and the link

Jill Savege Scharff

I will bring together the ideas of Fairbairn on object relations, Sutherland on self and society, and Pichon-Rivière on the link, and then illustrate them in a vignette from individual psychotherapy with a young woman. Fairbairn's theory of object relations has been most useful for understanding individual patients and their significant attachments (Fairbairn, 1952, 1963; Grotstein & Rinsley, 1994; Scharff & Birtles, 1994). In the late 1960s, Fairbairn's major expositor and biographer, John D. Sutherland (1963, 1989), introduced me to object relations theory and showed me that it could be applied to working therapeutically not only with individuals (1963) but also couples, thanks to Henry Dicks's (1967) integration of Klein and Fairbairn, and even with communities (Savege, 1975; J. Scharff, 2007; Sutherland, 1966). Since then, I have continued to find object relations theory a flexible, powerful, full spectrum analytic theory for working in psychoanalysis, couple, sex, and family therapy, and psychoanalytic education (J. & D. Scharff, 2000, 2005; Setton, Varela, & D. & J. Scharff, 2005). In the last five years, I have found a valuable extension of Fairbairn's and Sutherland's ideas in link theory which stems from the social psychological approach of Argentine psychoanalyst Enrique Pichon-Rivière (1985).

Fairbairn: object relations theory, splitting and repression

Fairbairn recognised the effect of dissociation, a defence that, although ubiquitous and normal, is overused out of necessity in trauma-related mental, emotional, and behavioural disorders (Fairbairn, 1952). It is not surprising that Fairbairn was so attuned to dissociation, and chose it as the topic of his doctorate in medicine, because he had encountered it in his clinical sessions. He worked in a clinic for children who were sexually and physically abused, in a hospital for men who returned from war with war neuroses, and in private practice with adults who suffered from hysterical neuroses and schizoid personality (Birtles & Scharff, 1994). In these clinical populations, Fairbairn noticed the prevalence of dissociation in addition to repression as defences, but he did not stop there with dissociation as a pathological defence. He realised that dissociation in those cases was simply an exaggeration of normal defensive processes. From there, Fairbairn built his theory of the mind on dissociation as a normal defensive mechanism for actively protecting the mind as it traversed the course of development from infantile dependence to independence.

Fairbairn believed that the infant self is whole at birth, already competent to seek its mother. The vulnerable infant uses all his instinctual competence—rooting, clinging, sucking, crying, and gazing—to appeal to the mother for food, comfort, security, and love. Most important, the infant looks to find meaning for his existence by mattering to the mother. As she responds to his needs and attunes to his emotional states of mind, she gives meaning to his experience. He gives meaning to her existence as a mother, and together they create a mutually gratifying relationship. Nevertheless there will be expectable moments of mis-attunement that are a challenge to both of them, although not usually of sufficient degree to cause trauma. Yet these moments of frustration upset the infant and he reacts by erecting defences against the pain that threatens to overwhelm his immature mechanism for self-regulation.

The infant takes in the uncomfortable experience with the mother (the external object) to control the unsatisfactory perception (the internal object) and feeling (the affect) inside his mind. He splits the internal object into two pieces: the part that felt good enough, and the part that felt uncomfortable. What is good enough remains in the conscious part of the self. What is overwhelmingly uncomfortable is split off (dissociated) from what is felt as good, and is repressed deep in the unconscious layers of the mind. There it is sorted into two major categories of internal object according to whether the associated feeling of discomfort is one of longing for more than is given to meet the needs (the exciting object) or angrily feeling that the needs are being pushed away (the rejecting object).

Fairbairn recognised, in a moment of creative genius, that the ego, the executive aspect of the infant self, splits itself as well in relation to these internal objects, in order to release a part of itself to accompany the object and the affects associated with it into the unconscious and maintain its repression there, thus creating internal object relationships consisting of ego and object bonded by the specific affect that has been overwhelming. These get sorted into two main categories—the libidinal (exciting) and anti-libidinal (rejecting) internal object relationships. The anti-libidinal ego is connected to the rejecting object and its feelings of anger at abandonment and rejection, while the libidinal ego is connected to the exciting object and its feelings of longing and craving. This creates a mind with a conscious area consisting of a central part of the ego relating with feelings of satisfaction to the ideal object from which the uncomfortable aspects have been shorn, and an unconscious area consisting of exciting and rejecting internal object relationships. The central ego actively keeps the split-off internal object relationships in repression, aided by the rejecting internal object relationship which further represses the internal exciting object relationship. The overstimulation of an elusive external object that creates longing is even more painful than an absent one that abandons the infant to his needs or actively refuses to accept them, and that is why it is kept so thoroughly split off and repressed. But the split-off and repressed parts of the self always seek to return in various ways such as symptom, gesture, speech, and choice of partner.

In health, the libidinal constellation is not too rigidly repressed so that it can also come forward to support the central ego in feeling desire and responding to others who are expressing need. The anti-libidinal constellation comes forward to assert the will, set limits, and support the ego's need for separateness within a committed relationship. This is normal. We find pathology only when the exciting object is excessively exciting and evokes feelings of desperate craving and when the rejecting object is excessively persecutory and evokes terror of abandonment and rage at rejection, especially when these are also turned against the libidinal constellation. A pathological endopsychic situation occurs when splitting and repression are severely maintained, and the system loses its dynamic flux. We then find an adhesive tie to the bad object (whether of the rejecting or exciting variety), which leads to self-destructive organisations, dysregulated behaviour, and disorganised attachments.

In summary, splits in the self form by pulls towards and away from object relating. The central ego is the organising, executive function of the self. It splits and represses the other parts of the self, but in the light of learning from new experience it allows the return of the repressed to remodel its structure and enrich its functioning. In health, the boundary between conscious and unconscious is flexible enough to allow communication between the conscious and unconscious parts of the self, and secure enough to prevent psychotic eruptions. In neurosis, psychosis, and personality disorder, the boundary is more tightly maintained. After trauma, the boundaries are even more rigid, and occur not only on the horizontal divide between conscious and unconscious but vertically as well between all parts of the self. At the extreme, this splitting encapsulates fragments of self and object and leaves empty spaces behind in the mind. Extreme splits in the self occur in survival mode to permit going-on-being in the face of great damage from betrayal, sexual overstimulation, and aggression in the holding environment. Such a dissociative pattern serves the function of clearing the way for a resilient response. It provides for a part of the self that is able to carry on, but the resulting fragmentation causes vulnerability to flashbacks, poor sleep, somatic symptoms, learning disorders, and relationship difficulties.

Fairbairn: physical and sexual trauma in childhood

The term childhood trauma refers to any early experience such as parental divorce, loss of a parent, and life-threatening illness, which leads to psychological stress and symptoms of anxiety and depression. But because this kind of trauma is not secret there is not severe splitting. Adults can help the child put the experience into words, mourn for what might have been, and work through to an adjustment. In contrast to those types of childhood trauma, physical and sexual trauma refer to a cumulative experience, or to an egregious single shock, of an aggressive or sexual nature that overwhelms the self, because the trauma is severe, the self is weak, and because the child is dependent on the adult, and is helpless to change what is happening.

Fairbairn's theory of the endopsychic situation is particularly helpful in understanding children whose *parents* were victims of physical and sexual trauma. Instead of providing ordinary parental holding with good attunement and clear limits that provide safety and stimulating growth, these parents may intrude on and impose their will on the child, and stifle independence because of their own histories. According to Fairbairn, the child builds mental structure out of experiences primarily with the parent. When the parent breaks the physical and mental boundaries that the child uses to protect body and mind, the disturbed adult mind enters and shatters the child's mind. The self of the child has been used as the object of the parent's unmetabolised aggressive or inappropriately sexual urges.

The parent has related to the child's self not as a unique self but only as the parent's object. No autonomy is allowed the child, and so there is no healthy interplay. There is no gap between adult and child across which to relate. The transitional zone of relatedness is eliminated (Winnicott, 1951). When that interpersonal space collapses, the transitional space inside the child's mind is collapsed (J. & D. Scharff, 1994). There is no room for dream, imagination, and creativity, all of which promote growth and independent reflection.

The traumatised child splits off, buries, and seals the traumatic experience in encapsulated traumatic nuclei (Hopper, 1991). In some cases the central ego may be aware of these encapsulations and the gaps that they leave behind. In other cases when the trauma was severe or the ego weak, the ego may have totally lost contact with the encapsulations, which then operate as totally dissociated parts of the personality with separate memory banks, as seen in patients with dissociative identity disorder. If the capsule weakens, traumatic material threatens to escape, and then the person may panic, desperate to avoid stress and prevent activation of trauma.

When parts of the mind are sequestered, thinking becomes restricted, preoccupied with the mundane, and language becomes somewhat literal and concrete because creativity has been stifled (J. & D. Scharff, 1994). So, rather than communicate verbally, these parts of the self convert themselves to somatic symptoms, such as a cough, a tic, a pain, dysregulated food intake, obsessional behaviours, and self-harm by cutting or addiction to substances as the means of representing the traumatic experiences that cannot be recalled and cannot be expressed verbally but that do, in a displaced way, express the trauma without allowing it to come to mind. These bodily symptoms convert an unbearable mental structure based on an unbearable relationship into a situation that can be recognised as being in need of help.

Trauma happens to adults too. Studies of traumatic war neurosis in World War II, post-traumatic stress disorder after the Vietnam War, and sorrow and guilt among Shoah survivors show that stress can overwhelm even the mature, well-functioning person. The new trauma resonates with any pre-existing loss or trauma, aggravates any residual pain and damage left after the person coped with it reasonably well originally, and compounds the trauma.

Sutherland: self and society

Sutherland's bio-social concept of the self makes a useful contribution to understanding development in various human environments, including those in which trauma has intervened. He defines the self as "a dynamic organization of purposes and commitments whose behavior is governed by conscious and unconscious motives, and whose developments and functioning are inseparably linked to the social environment" (Harrow, Leishman, Macdonald, & Scott, 1994, p. xxv). At the centre, the person is a responsible free agent, both separate from and in connection to others. The mind at birth is an innately patterned process that drives the baby to seek others and build a self from that interaction. The self is a dynamic affect-driven matrix, an open system, its interconnecting parts being in flux in relation to other minds. For the self to fulfil its potential and grow into the shape it can become, it needs its own intention, and it needs feedback from other minds. The infant self learns to recognise the states of mind of those others and to monitor its own self states in relation to the impact on others. Above all the self needs love if it is to accommodate developmental differentiation, hold the parts together and enjoy a sense of wholeness and autonomy (Sutherland, 1979). Within the loving context, the self's urge to maintain the wholeness of its shape can be realised. Sometimes fighting fiercely for that level of integrity is essential for vitality. "The organism's life becomes the dynamic process of preserving its autonomy within the heteronomy of relatedness with its social group and the physical environment" (Sutherland, 1990, in J. Scharff, 1994, p. 376).

But what happens if the loving context is not there? The child has no good mother experience to take in at the core of the self. The bad object is installed in its place ever more securely. The child withdraws internally and is forced to appear to conform to the adult's pathology in order to maintain the necessary attachment, in this case to a bad object. In locking up his true self far from further harm, the infant cripples the object-seeking function that is so necessary for encountering other minds and experiences with potentially loving people. To make life possible under impossible conditions, "… the child develops an *adapted* self, adapted to the mother's excessive influence whether this be from intensive over-control or neglect, or unreliable, inconsistent responsiveness, rather than an *adaptive* self which good mothering fosters" (Sutherland, 2005 p. 196). In a traumatising context, the emerging potential of the self is denuded and hidden by a false self. Hatred for what has happened and identification with the hated mother locks in the adaptation and prevents new experience in case the hopeful, object-seeking part of the self if ever released should again meet with rejection and be filled with despair.

Sutherland (1980) is highly invested in the metapsychology of the self as "the essential organizing principle" (p. 10) of each unique individual, but he is also invested in thinking of the person as part of humanity undergoing the evolutionary process. He repeatedly places the self in that context. Sutherland says that, over the centuries, the self has fostered "the flexibility, resilience and persistence of human groups by maximizing the potential resources within each individual, and did not confine communities to rigid hierarchical organizations" (ibid., p. 25).

Clinical usefulness

I have found Fairbairn's and Sutherland's theory particularly helpful clinically in work with survivors of sexual and physical abuse (J. & D. Scharff, 1994). Having the endopsychic situation in mind, we can take up a therapeutic position of benign concern that does not impose our will on the patient. For instance, therapists who remember that literal thinking is a feature of the collapsed transitional space will not become impatient with the patients' preoccupations with the mundane and their inability to discuss sexual material and family history. They will value the resilience that is supported in this way of attaching to the ordinary as a relief from ongoing episodes of trauma. We work to establish a safe context in which therapy can proceed before attracting transference to ourselves.

Within that context, we will be experienced as a new version of those who helped or hurt the patient, and those who were bystanders to the abuse. The transference-countertransference exchange may be so painful and frightening that we need to respect the slow pace with which it becomes specific. The patient's defensive preoccupation with going-on-being serves to protect the therapy, just as it protected the child. We must wait until we are ready to be misperceived as abusive or neglectful, or worst of all as a void, and get ready to speak to it and work through it with the patient. Therapy proceeds along a rhythm of dipping into trauma and returning to going-on-being until gradually more of the trauma can be tolerated and put into words. From our experience with the patient, we put the images and themes together as a narrative of the patient's self, from which to continue our shared reflection, exploration, and eventual understanding. Then the spaces get filled in as we create new experiences in the therapeutic relationship, *genera* that heal the contents of the traumatic nuclei (Bollas, 1992).

Transgenerational transmission of trauma

To understand how trauma is transmitted, we need to look beyond Fairbairn's theory of dissociation. At the individual level, trauma is transmitted to children by projective identification, a mental mechanism of defence for protecting the self from its innate fear of annihilation and for protecting its good and vital functions in early life (Klein, 1946). In ordinary good enough mother–infant relationships, the infant projects rage, fear, and death wishes into the mother to get rid of these unpleasant affects and stop them from disturbing the good and lively parts of his self. The infant misidentifies them as emanating from her feelings towards him, which causes similar pain now experienced as coming from a persecutory external source. The infant copes, as Fairbairn said, by taking it in and splitting and repressing this monster aspect of the good mother. The infant also projects good feelings towards the mother and takes in a positive view of her, coloured by those feelings too. In health, good and bad internal objects are in balance. After trauma, the bad object is dominant, and that is what the infant is attached to, even if it is unhealthy.

In marriage the woman deals with her spouse as if he were the source of feelings that in fact arise in her. She has dissociated from feelings and projected them into her husband, and then re-found in him the lost part of herself from which those feelings stem. At the same time her husband has his own valency to project into her and find lost parts of himself in her. Husband and wife berate or cherish each other according to how they have dealt internally with those parts of themselves (Dicks, 1967). If the couple relationship cannot absorb and modify these mutual projective identifications, the marriage gets stuck in an unsatisfactory state or divorce may follow, in either case upsetting the children, who in turn may be at risk for divorce, or staying in an abusive marriage in order to avoid the trauma of divorce. When the couple cannot metabolise their mutual projective identifications, they may resort to identifying all the bad objects in a child, as if that child's behaviour is the cause of the relationship difficulties. The child who is the object of the projective identification and who identifies with it then develops behaviours that further justify the perception of the child as bad, and so the projective identification is cemented and not amenable to modification in the light of new experience.

Trauma happens to adults too, and even though they are already mature, they may resort to severe splitting and encapsulation of the trauma to help them carry on, manage their pain, and deny their fear of disaster striking again. The adult must find a way of coping with the bad internal object to the extent that it has not been balanced by the good internal object. She projects it into her own self, where it fills her with a sense of badness, devaluation, and destructiveness or she finds another object to project it into—friend, teacher, authority, spouse, or her own child. She then experiences the object of her projective identification as persecutory and treats him or her accordingly. Some parents identify with their own aggressor, and do to their children what was done to them. Others are determined to spare their children but if they inhibit all excitement and rage the child has no opportunity to learn the appropriate management of sexuality and aggression. Either way trauma affects the next generation.

At the societal level, trauma is transmitted to the next generation when social trauma such as war and natural disaster have created huge losses in segments of the population and left behind mass depression, post-traumatic disorder, and the desire for revenge. The mind of the whole society may dissociate from the pain and wall off the traumatic material. In the 1960s we saw this in German society when East Germany walled itself and the Eastern Bloc off from West Germany by a wall built through the middle of Berlin. East Germany wanted to keep out democratic elements that would interfere with its socialist vision and at the same time keep in unhappy citizens who might otherwise choose to emigrate to West Germany and Europe. The Berlin Wall was a rock hard boundary to keep the bad Westerners out and the good socialist people from the East in. I have thought of this splitting of good and bad as a diversion from the main example of splitting good and bad in Germany leading up to World War II. The post-war generation refused to acknowledge and take responsibility for what the previous generation had done or allowed to happen to Jews onto whom they projected all that was dirty and defiling to the nationalist ideal. In 1990 when the wall came down, the trauma could begin to be acknowledged, reconciliation and repair could occur, and healing of splits could begin, not just in Germany, but in Europe at large.

Similar trauma recurred in Argentina. In the 1930s, some of the Jews who emigrated from Europe and Russia to avoid pogroms and concentration camps sailed to the Americas looking for safety. Some of them landed at Buenos Aires. In the 1970s these Argentine immigrants lived through another period of social trauma (and some of them had to flee their country again, while others who thought they were free were secretly taken away and disappeared). The military in power in Argentina created hundreds of concentration camps to which anyone could be abducted, illegally detained without evidence, and hidden so that they were outside the protection of the law—all in the name of anti-communism. Detainees were tortured and often murdered, in which case their bodies were disposed of at sea so that they could be said to be *desaparecidos*, missing, not dead, and the government could deny any knowledge of their whereabouts or of what had happened to them.

Pichon-Rivière's link theory

In terms of link theory (*el vinculo*) developed by Pichon-Rivière in Argentina, internal and external object relations are constructed by the interaction of the twin pillars of development—individual influence and social interaction. Whereas Fairbairn described the individual infant taking in experience with the mother to construct a psychic structure consisting of a dynamic system of internal object relationships, and Sutherland had looked at the reflection of those individual object relationships in the functioning of parts of communities, Pichon-Rivière began his theory building by looking at the space between individual and society, the space into which the individual is born. Link theory looks closely at the overarching organisation of the internal and external worlds into which the infant arrives and within which he grows and develops to adulthood.

What exactly is the link? It connects the individual to previous generations and the social history of the past and to current relationships with family and social groups. The baby is born into the link. He arrives among past and present social influences. He accesses the link by expressing his need for safety, nurture, love, and knowing. He lives and grows in the network of influences and connections that constitute the link. Pichon-Rivière distinguished vertical and horizontal axes in the link. On the vertical axis, the infant connects to good, bad, and downright traumatic experiences in the previous generation, and he may be dreaded as living proof of their awfulness or welcomed as a hope for the future. On the horizontal link, the infant relates to the mother and other family members, extended family, and social groups, who carry the link within them in their conscious and unconscious minds. Through the link to social experience, the individual mind is shaped in both conscious and unconscious dimensions and reciprocally shapes the groups of which the individual is a part. The quality of the link is expressed in the adult individual in dreams, individual actions, speech, symptoms, and bodily experiences. In therapy, working with manner of speech, dreams, physical and mental symptoms, behaviour revealed in attitude to work and play, and quality of relationships, we can detect the quality of the link and its impact on the individual.

Here is a clinical illustration of Fairbairn's description of the endopsychic situation, Sutherland's emphasis on self in society, and Pichon-Riviére's theory of the link.

Clinical example from individual therapy

Orchidea, a beautiful, olive complexioned, curvaceous young woman with long dark hair enters my office for her first session of psychotherapy. She sounds thoroughly American but she looks exotic. She is a high achieving student now taking a gap year after college before medical school so that she can study for the Medical College Admission Test and volunteer in areas related to medicine. She asks for help in dealing with feeling lost, unhappy, anxious, judged, and uptight because of constantly performing to meet the standards she imagines others have for her. Her main emotional symptoms are unhappiness, anxiety, and lack of confidence in her self. She fluctuates between assessing herself as exceptional or fraudulent. Her physical symptoms include palpitations of her heart and a knot in her throat, and she is preoccupied with feeling fat even though she is of normal weight. Her speech is fluid, expressive, and anxiously obsessive. Her agreeable demeanour covers any upset or irritation.

After having been the only adored grandchild for seven years, she was very upset to lose her place in the spotlight when twin baby brothers were born. She developed temper tantrums that she felt helpless to control. As an adult she is determined to suppress her anger and will not let anyone see when she is unreasonably upset over tiny things. Her parents who are successful professionals in another town not an hour away from Washington want Orchidea to visit weekly but she often feels anxious about meeting their needs and is afraid that she will get angry at how dependent and entitled her teenage brothers are.

Orchidea explained herself to me: "I'm on a pedestal and I'm acting to please people, and it's exhausting. I tell myself that no one is judging me, things are up to me, but I don't listen to myself. I keep thinking about whether what I'm saying coincides with what another person thinks. There's no reason to think there's someone looking over me and judging me—I realised this from the last time I was here for the final session of the consultation. I am my own worst enemy. That's what I need to work on."

As an infant, Orchidea had received love, nurture, safety, and knowing her place in the world. She was her parents' first, much-wanted child and the first grandchild of both parents' families, three of whom had been forced to emigrate from Russia, and happened to land in Argentina. She knew who she was in relation to her close and adoring family. A gorgeous little girl, she was showered with compliments from passers-by.

In object relations terms, Orchidea was an exciting object for her family and their warm response filled her central ego with good feelings, and a sense of being special. Having such a special child filled her parents with pride. She represented the hope of leaving behind the cruel history in favour of life in the new land, free from the oppression suffered by her grandparents.

After her twin baby brothers were born, she felt dropped and not listened to any more. Her protest took the form of temper tantrums, which did nothing to encourage her mother's expressions of love. She went from being the perfect child on the pedestal to being a monster. She did not know who she was any more. She hated herself and the body she could not control.

When she expressed her outrage at her mother's attachment to the twin boys, the ideal child became a rejecting object to her family, and she felt rejected by them. She envied the attention given to the boys and began to hate herself for feeling less than them, and for hating them and her mother. As an adult, Orchidea attacks the feminine aspects of her body. At the vertical level of the link, she is connected to her grandparents as the proof that life goes on and families survive after trauma and loss but at the same time her connection to their history continues to be expressed in her feeling of neglect and persecution by the authority in her life, her mother.

Orchidea said, "This must have to do with my childhood—this thinking the only way to be liked is to fulfil others' expectations." But rather than tell me about her childhood, she changed the topic to that of her adolescence, reviewing her trauma when the family had to move to the United States when she was thirteen. She was traumatised by the move and its assault on her identity. "Trying to do what they expected was the only way to fit in with the kids in school when we moved from Argentina to here. I didn't know the language. I didn't have the words for what I was feeling. I was so insecure. I hated my accent, and I hated how different I was from those skinny blonde girls. Now I do express myself, and I sound like a North American but I'm still so aware of others, and I still feel insecure. If I could lift this, I'd no longer feel this knot in my throat all the time! This feeling has got me to hate myself. Whenever I'm not everything to everyone at once, someone will be disapproving, and because I'm not fitting someone else's standards, I'm not enough. I'm not unattractive but any little flaw I have I examine through other people's eyes, and it's no longer about me as I really am."

Like Orchidea, the grandparents had lost their country and their language. As an adolescent two generations after the original move, Orchidea had to move as a teenager to an unfamiliar culture. Orchidea's vertical link to past generations is expressed in her feeling lost, in feeling like a fake, and in bodily experiences of emotions that get stuck in her throat. The link is not expressed in her dreams, at least not yet, but it is expressed in her anxious speech and the knot in her throat, and in her attempts to fit in. This link has taken over her personality to the point that she seems to be reliving her grandparents' dislocation, whereas her parents who were fluent in English actually chose to relocate to the United States and did not suffer directly for it, nor did they fully sense her pain. They felt that they were getting away from a culture of fear and taking their family to a new land of opportunity, as their parents had done before them. But for Orchidea, the move involved the loss of personal and family ties and a rejection of the Argentine culture that was all she knew.

Orchidea continued, "What I hate in myself is what I hate in others. I'm self-conscious regarding my weight but I don't think other women my age who look a little heavy like me are bad. It's me feeling afraid others will hate me as they did when I was in school my first year in the United States. I'm conditioned to care what others think before I care what I think, as if the world revolves around me. Maybe people don't think of me at all! It feels like big brother is watching all the time. I'm so aware of my surroundings, new groups, that I'm trying to gauge them, and I don't have fun, and it's exhausting."

In object relations terms, Orchidea is suffering a rejecting internal object attack on her exciting object. She projects the rejecting object into her environment and feels a threat from every quarter. The exciting object was overdeveloped by excessive adoration in infancy. The rejecting object attacks the exciting object so as to keep it hidden and therefore safe inside. The rejecting object also attacks her central ego with all the hatred she felt for the new exciting objects projected by her family into her brothers.

In terms of link theory, in her vertical link, Orchidea is reliving both her parents' wish to escape the fear of the regime in Argentina and her grandparents' fear of the pogroms in Russia. She feels that the world will hurt her if she is not constantly on the look-out. She takes on the hope of being an exciting object for her parents but fears her potential to disappoint those hopes when she cannot adapt. Similarly her grandparents had carried the hopes of their parents when they escaped with their blessing fifty years ago.

Orchidea continued, "I have an interview tomorrow for a receptionist job at a free clinic, and I'm already freaking out if the job will be a place where I'm under pressure to prove something. I'm only going to be happy if I do my best, and if I do it without feeling someone is watching me. I was even thinking how are they going to accommodate this treatment for which I have to get out twice a week. I'm worried what they'll think about my needs. I'm worried if I express my need for accommodation, they won't want me any more. My mom thinks I'm crazy to worry. Work seems so easy for her and I try to do as well as she did, but really she doesn't give herself proper recognition for what she does. I don't value what I need enough, or rather I don't think of it first. Even with my friends, I think of what they want of me. I have a lifetime ahead of needs and desires, and they won't be fulfilled if I'm too preoccupied with fitting the world's standards. I'm afraid of having needs that are unfulfilled and feeling shitty all the time."

Orchidea's exciting object is constantly in a state of longing and her rejecting object makes her feel bad all the time. She has identified with hate and neglect she perceives as if they emanate from her mother, as a way of maintaining attachment to her. Her horizontal link is seen in her anxious connection to her mother with whom she shares an emphasis on professional success, to the friends that she wants to retain, and to her possible employers.

"What is most comforting to me is to feel that I'm caring for myself. Right now I am: this is why I'm doing this therapy. I wish I'd strike a balance, so at a job interview I can say this is what I want and need rather than fit to what they need. I actually think they're looking for someone like me. They want someone who can be versatile, bilingual, a multi-tasker, and someone with their interests. Objectively I'm fine for it. Yet I'm always scared of disappointing. I hadn't even considered that they could accommodate my need to leave for therapy. I don't want to feel superior and have my needs be treated as special: I just hope that there's room for me to get what I want. All I need is time to study for the MCAT, to enjoy exercise, and come to therapy. It's all preparation for striking the balance in my life as a person with a career and being a mother. It's so unnecessary to think of life as hard and horrible. But right now I'm worried about pleasing everyone on all I have to do. It's a pessimistic outlook."

I asked, "Is that operating here?"

I wondered how the transference might give me an opening to elucidate the themes.

Orchidea replied, "Your opinion should be, 'Good for you!' but I am self-conscious and uptight with myself, and so I feel I'm falling short here, even when I'm doing all I can. I hate what I do to myself with this mentally, and at the same time I feel sorry for myself. The judge inside me pushes me to do my best and also undermines me because I get more nervous at a task and I'm not at ease around people, and maybe people can pick up on that, but whether they do or not, I feel bad. I feel fake.

"I feel I'm performing. I hate that. I feel there's something wrong with me, and yet I second-guess myself, thinking I don't have enough problems to warrant therapy. It's crazy to doubt my need, when I feel so lost. I need to be able to realise what I need and give it to myself. I settle for things that aren't good enough, like one-sided relationships with charismatic, selfish men, and I think I can adapt to them, to almost anything. I think, I can take this job, be with that person, even though I don't like the job or the man."

Orchidea knows that she is needy but she does not want anyone to see that, and yet she wants her needs recognised by the world and by me. The rejecting and exciting objects are in conflict. The libidinal ego is trying to free itself. Orchidea has not expressed her horizontal link in a long-term love relationship, but in choosing men to date, she looks for men that other people admire even though she repeatedly finds them to be shallow and unreliable. There is hope that in therapy she can rehabilitate her link before making a lifetime choice. Hopefully she will then select a mate on the basis of fit with her good objects rather than one like the men into whom she projects an exciting and rejecting object.

Orchidea may be performing for me like a good patient, free associating and seeming to tell her history, her problems, and her shameful feelings but not facing deeper feelings of which she is ashamed or guilty. She fears that I will find her shallow and unworthy of my being with her, just as she feels about the men whom she dates. She worries that she cannot make reparation to her family for past damage.

"It's a scary thing to feel that a part of me was lost when I came here as a teenager. I felt so ashamed of my background, and that was so crazy. It was crazy to feel ashamed of my family. It's crazy now that I am ashamed to have forgotten how to be Argentinian. My family in Buenos

Aires doesn't know me any more. I am ashamed to be so Americanised. It's sad. I'm afraid I'm going to lose myself. I just want to be myself."

In this talk of shame, Orchidea seems not to be judging herself but expressing regret for how she handled her dislocation as a teenager, and for how she has allowed separation from her extended family and her culture to affect her. She is at the mercy of persecuting internal objects that magnify her potential to disappoint parental expectations, and there will be much work ahead to detoxify these objects. However, it seems to me that she has already begun the mourning that could not take place in childhood.

Summary

An early session of psychotherapy of a young woman with persecutory internal objects resulting in symptoms of self-accusation, lack of confidence, and anxiety with physical expressions as well, illustrates the clinical usefulness of the concepts of object relations (Fairbairn), the autonomous biopsychosocial self (Sutherland), and the link (Pichon-Riviere). The woman's trauma occurred once as a young child when she lost her adored self as her mother turned her affection to babies, and again as an adolescent when she lost her holding environment at the social level. This double trauma was not of sufficient degree to provoke splitting as severe as to cause dissociative identity disorder, but it did cause splitting into good and bad parts of the self, conversion of self hatred into bodily symptoms, and the formation of an adapted self. Concepts from Fairbairn, Sutherland, and Pichon-Rivière generate a psychoanalytic vantage point from which to assess the structure of mind and heritage, interpret the forces against self functioning, and give hope of creating an adaptive self.

References

Birtles, E. F., & Scharff, D. E. (Eds.) (1994). *From Instinct to Self: Selected Papers of W. R. D. Fairbairn, Volume II: Applications and Early Contributions*. Northvale, NJ: Jason Aronson.

Bollas, C. (1992). Psychic genera. In: *Being a Character: Psychoanalysis and Self Experience* (pp. 66–100). New York: Hill & Wang.

Dicks, H. (1967). *Marital Tensions*. London: Routledge.

Fairbairn, W. R. D. (1952). *Psychoanalytic Studies of the Personality*. London: Tavistock.

Fairbairn, W. R. D. (1963a). Synopsis of an object-relations theory of the personality. *International Journal of Psychoanalysis*, 44: 224–225. In: D. E. Scharff & E. F. Birtles (Eds.), *From Instinct to Self: Selected Papers of W. R. D. Fairbairn, Volume I: Clinical and Theoretical Papers* (pp. 155–156). Northvale, NJ: Jason Aronson, 1994.

Grotstein, J. S., & Rinsley, D. B. (Eds.) (1994). *Fairbairn and the Origin of Object Relations*. London: Free Association.

Harrow, A., Leishman, M., Macdonald, M., & Scott, D. (1994). Introduction. In: J. S. Scharff (Ed.), *The Autonomous Self: The Work of John D. Sutherland* (pp. xv–xxv). Northvale, NJ: Jason Aronson.

Hopper, E. (1991). Encapsulation as a defence against the fear of annihilation. *International Journal of Psychoanalysis*, 72(4): 607–624.

Klein, M. (1946). Notes on some schizoid mechanisms. In: *Envy and Gratitude and Other Works*: 1921–1963 (pp. 1–24). London: Hogarth, 1975.

Pichon-Rivière, E. (1985). *Teoría del Vínculo*. [A thematic selection of transcripts of lectures 1956–57 by F. Taragano.] Buenos Aires, Argentina: Nueva Visión.

Savege, J. (1975). Psychodynamic understanding in community psychiatry. *Psychotherapy and Psychosomatics, 25*: 272–278.

Scharff, D. E., & Birtles, E. F. (Eds.) (1994). *From Instinct to Self: Selected Papers of W. R. D. Fairbairn, Volume I: Clinical and Theoretical Papers*. Northvale, NJ: Jason Aronson.

Scharff, J. S. (Ed.) (1994). *The Autonomous Self. The Work of John D. Sutherland*. Northvale, NJ: Jason Aronson.

Scharff, J. S. (Ed.) (2007). *The Psychodynamic Image: John D. Sutherland on Self and Society*. London: Routledge.

Scharff, J. S., & Scharff, D. E. (1994). *Object Relations Therapy of Physical and Sexual Trauma*. Northvale, NJ: Jason Aronson.

Scharff, J. S., & Scharff, D. E. (2000). *Tuning the Therapeutic Instrument*. Northvale, NJ: Jason Aronson.

Setton, L., Varela, Y., Scharff, D. E., & Scharff, J. S. (2005). Teaching object relations theory with the Group Affective Model. In: J. S. Scharff & D. E. Scharff (Eds.), *The Legacy of Fairbairn and Sutherland: Therapeutic Applications* (pp. 271–282). London: Routledge.

Sutherland, J. D. (1963). Object relations theory and the conceptual model of psychoanalysis. *British Journal of Medical Psychology, 36*: 109–124.

Sutherland, J. D. (1966). The psychotherapeutic clinic and community psychiatry. *Bulletin of the Menninger Clinic, 30*: 338–350.

Sutherland, J. D. (1979). The psychodynamic image of man. In: J. S. Scharff (Ed.), *The Autonomous Self: The Work of John D. Sutherland* (pp. 268–282). Northvale, NJ: Jason Aronson.

Sutherland, J. D. (1980). Hate and autonomy of the self. *Bulletin of the Menninger Clinic, 57*(1): 1–32. Also in: J. S. Scharff (Ed.), *The Autonomous Self: The Work of John D. Sutherland* (pp. 303–330). Northvale, NJ: Jason Aronson.

Sutherland, J. D. (1989). *Fairbairn's Journey to the Interior*. London: Free Association.

Sutherland, J. D. (1990). On becoming and being a person. In: J. S. Scharff (Ed.), *The Autonomous Self* (pp. 372–391). Northvale, NJ: Jason Aronson.

Sutherland, J. D. (2005). The self and personal (object) relations. In: J. S. & D. E. Scharff (Eds.), *The Legacy of Fairbairn and Sutherland* (pp. 187–201). London: Routledge.

Winnicott, D. W. (1951). Transitional objects and transitional phenomena. In: *Through Paediatrics to Psycho-Analysis*. London: Tavistock, 1975.

CHAPTER TWENTY-NINE

Fairbairn and Pichon-Rivière: object relations, link, and group

Lea S. de Setton

Ronald Fairbairn (1889–1964), Scottish psychiatrist and psychoanalyst, became an associate member of the British Psychoanalytical Society in 1931 and a full member in 1939. Nevertheless, he travelled rarely and preferred to work in relative isolation in Edinburgh. His psychoanalytic work was influenced by Freud and later Melanie Klein, by his study of the philosophy of Hegel and Buber, and by his work with traumatised veterans, sexually abused children, and the treatment of schizoid adults. Fairbairn considered the need to relate to others, and not the sexual instinct, as the central driving force of human relations. A mental organisation called the *endopsychic structure* resulted from the need to manage experiences with significant others by internalising, splitting, and repressing them. The resulting internal structures, which he called *internal object relationships*, continue to be influenced by the external world and to press for a return to consciousness. The endopsychic situation is always in dynamic flux (Fairbairn 1943, 1990; Scharff & Scharff, 1998).

Enrique Pichon-Rivière (1907–1977), psychiatrist and psychoanalyst, was born in Geneva of French parents and became a naturalised Argentine working mainly in Buenos Aires. He was one of the founders of the Argentine Psychoanalytic Association in the 1950s and one of the first psychoanalysts in Argentina to introduce psychoanalysis for the understanding of psychotics, to study transference in psychotics, and to apply psychoanalytic treatment to psychotic patients, as described in many of his works and in his classes (Losso, 2002). His psychoanalytic work was influenced by Klein, Fairbairn, Lacan, and Ezriel. From social psychology he took up the concepts of George Mead in relation to the theoretical aspects and techniques of the group dynamic theory of Kurt Lewin and his followers, Leppit and Wight. He founded the first school of social psychology in Argentina and created the theory called *Grupo Operativo*, which refers to using the group to accomplish learning tasks. Like Fairbairn, Pichon-Rivière centred his studies on interpersonal relations and like Lewin he studied social psychology. From both areas of study he developed link theory in which he held that the individual is created by the interrelation of the subject's internal world of body and emotion and the external world of present family, earlier generations, and the wider society now and in the past (Videla, 1998).

I will compare and contrast the main concepts of Fairbairn and Pichon-Rivière. Their theories are similar in regarding internalised relations as the nucleus of the mind. They differ in that Fairbairn thinks that the individual personality is whole at birth and later splits to cope with experience with the mother, whereas Pichon-Rivière thinks that the infant is an "absence" at birth waiting to construct psychic structure from social experience. Both of them hold that intrapsychic structure is dynamic and is influenced by the external world. Pichon-Rivière differs in noting how the wider world is influenced by the individual in a process of mutual influence. He uses his own idiosyncratic language to describe ideas that are similar to Fairbairn's ideas of clinical analysis. Since most readers of this volume will be familiar with Fairbairn by now, let me begin by presenting the work of Pichon-Rivière and introducing some of his terminology for discussion.

Pichon-Rivière's ideas

Pichon-Rivière was influential in the development of psychoanalysis in Latin America. A multi- and interdisciplinary thinker, he moved beyond intrapsychic psychoanalytic theory to social psychiatry and complemented his individual psychoanalytic research with social research on institutions and socio-dynamics. Pichon-Rivière studied the individual as a person included in a family group and a social group, not as an isolated being, and simultaneously studied those groups within the dynamic fabric of society. Pichon-Rivière thought of individual development as a dynamic-mechanistic result of the interplay between the subject and both the internal and external objects in the social world, in a system of incessant and active mutual influence, which creates individually characteristic repetitive patterns of personality functioning and interpersonal relationships. He referred to this system as *el vinculo*, the link, defined as a dynamic structure in a continuous process of evolution, governed by, and governing, the totality of the person—his internal psychic structure, his place in his group, and the meaning of his group in society. A subject's personality communicates through the link. The internal link conditions the subject's external aspect while the totality of the person establishes the link, thus creating a gestalt in which the individual develops. Pichon-Rivière conceptualises the analysis of human behaviour as the analysis of the complexity of the link through a process of introspection in which the analyst identifies a particular link having a particular object and a particular purpose.

Psychoanalysis is the investigation of the self's connection, or link, to its unconscious internal objects. The dialogue of the analytic pair is conscious and deals at first with the manifest content of the link. The analyst observes the expression of this link in the transference situation and looks beyond to the link's latent content. Pichon-Rivière described the latent content of the link as that which is irrational. The irrational part of behaviour depends on the degree of latency or unconsciousness of the internal link that influences that behaviour at the moment.

Pichon-Rivière viewed neurosis as the predominance of irrational links operating on the subject's relation to the world. The neurotic lives in a disconnected world and wants to communicate but is unable to. When the neurotic loses communication with the group, feelings of loneliness and helplessness appear as attempts at communication, albeit in a seemingly distorted language. The analyst observes and collects the material of the communication, and returns it in words as an interpretation. Pichon-Rivière saw psychosis as the result of a constant interplay between processes of projection and introjection of internal links that are externalised and then re-introjected.

In paranoid states the link is characterised by distrust. In depressive states the link is filled with sadness, guilt, and fear of object loss. Obsessional conditions are related to control and order. In hypochondria the link is established through the invasion of the body by bad objects. Obsessional-hysteric neurosis is characterised by the dramatisation of symptoms under the control of the alter ego. In conversion hysteria, certain fantasies are expressed through the body. In perversions, there may be different types of links resulting in perverse mechanisms to control anxiety. In dissociative identity disorder, the personality has more than one link and hence separate, non-communicating guidelines of behaviour. In schizophrenia, all links may appear together or one may dominate, anxiety determining which link has the most control.

In psychosis the most characteristic aspect of the psychotic link is the distance from the object and the isolation from reality. Madness is the result of placing an internal link on an external one, with permanent passage from inside to outside, and vice versa. The psychotic has found a balance within the economy of suffering by using certain defences against his conflicts. The theory of the link helps in work with the psychotic patient through conceptualising the psychotic's link with internal objects—psychotic patients tend to establish animate links with inanimate objects. Dreaming is an intermediate state of confusion in which the subject is linked to internal objects and at the same time tries to connect with types of links.

The link is expressed in roles. The various roles fall within a hierarchy that determines the quality of the role and its quantity of status (high or low prestige). During treatment a number of situations emerge in which the analysand assigns the analyst different roles. In the paranoid-schizoid position the patient simultaneously represents two roles with two objects. In the depressive position, there is one object, even though the relation may be ambivalent. The degree of coherence of these roles indicates the subject's level of maturity. According to Pichon-Rivière, by assuming these roles, the analyst may discover internal objects that interfere with the patient's freedom to act and may identify the type of links that have given rise to various internalised objects and thereby understand her ways of being, particular to her personality and character. As the patient's personality gradually integrates and the patient assumes one role, several roles may be subsumed in different situations instead of being split—disavowed on the one hand and assumed on the other.

The analyst may also discover in his own mind internal objects that prevent him from accepting the role assigned to him by his patient. Pichon-Rivière emphasised the importance of the analyst's own treatment for analysing his fantasies and personal areas of difficulty so as to free his countertransference for work with various roles. During the process of analysis the irrational link may be transformed into rational external objects. At the same time, the patient internalises the analyst and establishes an ongoing introspection, a self-analytic relationship. The internal link continues. Pichon-Rivière held that most progress in modifications of structure is produced after analysis has terminated.

During treatment the analyst must help the patient to regress and repeat previous behaviours and elements of her history in the transference by assigning the analyst various roles. The assumption of a role enables the analyst to understand the structure of the link. The analyst evokes a repetition of conflicts and links in the transference, and this creates a breach in the psychotic structure, a chance to relearn it in the analytic situation, and a space in which to rectify the quality of the link. Character change results from establishing a certain relation with an object (animate, inanimate, or group) re-experienced within the analytic link.

The analytic observer is a participant. There is interaction between the observer and the observed. There is unity between subject and object. Analyst and patient act on each other. They communicate verbally and non-verbally constantly. The analyst modifies the field of work through interpretations that develop from his experience of the link in action at the moment. Like Fairbairn before him, Pichon-Rivière considered that the most important element of analysis is the analyst's relationship with the patient. Pichon-Rivière represented it in the shape of a *dialectic spiral in constant action*.

The link and dialectic learning

The dialectic spiral refers to transitorily closed and opened situations that repeat and block understanding and communication. For instance in having a fear of open spaces, the agoraphobic finds safety in enclosure but the confinement of the enclosure restricts growth and inhibits exploration and learning. The analytic process consists in opening this vicious circle by confrontation, clarification, and interpretation of the disturbance and the stagnation. In this way, an implicit situation is transformed into an explicit one. When the patient understands the analyst, the capacity for communication builds and the learning cycle continues to evolve.

Pichon-Rivière considered that the analytic situation is established on an existential basis: two people at a certain moment in a given space are trying to solve the situation of one of the partners. Their relationship develops in a spiral, a continuous dialectic in which one person expresses feelings and the other translates them in the form of interpretation in a continuous way. The situation involves permanent interaction in which each one's response conditions the other's response and modifies the narrative of both parties in the analytic pair.

The link and interpretation

The observer's internal object relationships condition his attitude, way of being, and capacity for interpretation by which he expresses understanding. Working together expressing, responding, interpreting, and responding, patient and analyst create the continuous dialectic spiral and establish the gestalt in which they work. In moments of silence, which Pichon-Rivière regarded as moments of self-analysis, the operational field is being constructed by the patient's self and by an internalised object constantly working to modify a specific structure. The patient establishes an internal link with the analyst and continues self-analysis when not in session. If the patient experiences intense loss or frustration in the analytic session she may feel depressed and leave the session with the feeling of having destroyed the internal analytic object with which there was a link. At such a time, self-analysis may be aimed at recreating that object by negation of its loss until the next session.

Although the analytic situation comprises a group of two, the basic objective is to discover *the third*. Analysis of the transference situation must include the third. For Pichon-Rivière the situation is bi-corporeal but tri-personal. It is triangular from its beginning in the mother's mind. The link with the mother is referred to as the intrauterine link. The foetus establishes a parasitic link with the mother which later becomes a symbiotic link and sometimes siamesic (like a Siamese twin) in which case the child may experience separation from the mother as death.

ECRO: the conceptual, referential, and operational schema

The *ECRO* is a conceptual schema of knowledge. Conceptual refers to modifiable ideas. Referential refers to the segment of the reality in which the system is embedded. Operational refers to its activation of reality towards change. Schema refers to the system of ideas that can be moved towards change. To construct an ECRO we need to define the operational field and methodology, and evaluate the operation.

The ECRO integrates Pichon-Rivière's theories: the illness, the link as bi-directional and tri-personal from its beginning in the mother's mind, the discovery and acceptance of the third, the internal group, the role, the spokesperson, the theory of learning, and introspection. Pichon-Rivière considered that all suffering is a depressive reaction to loss. All mental illnesses are reactions to loss. Each type of mental illness is determined by the specific defence mechanism in use, and is expressed in one of three areas: mind, body, or behaviour. At the individual level, Pichon-Rivière addresses the subject's *verticality* and observes the form of her interaction and the personal way in which her emotions, motivations, history, and past experiences contribute to her reading of reality. From this experience Pichon-Rivière establishes a hypothesis of the determinants of her character structure.

At the group level, Pichon-Rivière applies ECRO to studying the group as a task force. This technique makes it possible to approach any learning or therapeutic situation that may arise in a local or a hospital community. He uses the term *grupo operativo* (operative group, meaning task force, similar to what Bion called a work group) and regards its form as the reconstruction of a system of internalised relations in a social context. The operative group is based on Kurt Lewin's idea of the group as a totality. The function of the operative group is to place everything implicit (latent, hidden, or masked) on the level of the explicit (conscious). This produces a continuous spiralling movement between the two levels, the objective being to defeat epistemophilic obstacles that oppose knowledge and function as a resistance to change. The operative group questions the interplay between the psychosocial (internal world) and the socio-dynamic (external world) through observing the assignment and assumption of roles among members of the group. Deviant behaviour in the group is viewed as a disturbance of learning to face and accept reality. By overcoming stagnation in its individual members and in its process, the group moves into areas that promote knowledge of self and others at the same time. This process of group dynamics and individual learning confronts problematic areas of perception and cognition and provides the subject with instruments for operating in reality with others. The emerging dialectic is a shared creation that allows for constant rectification. In the group the entire system of ecological relations is mobilised. At the level of the ego these are internalised social relations in constant interplay between inside and outside through inter-group links. Every group establishes a theme to be resolved.

The ECRO of the operative group (the work group) is represented diagrammatically by what Pichon-Rivière called the "inverted cone" (Figure 1).

The inverted cone refers to observable modalities of group interactions such as affiliation, cooperation, and belonging which pertain to a fear of loss, and communication, learning and affinity which pertain to the fear of attack. At the point of the cone lie the group and individual resistances to change. There is constant interplay between the fear of losing familiar ways of functioning and the fear of attack if change is produced. The group coordinator needs to cushion the difficulty and to create circumstances of change by interpreting situations that are static and stereotyped, thereby making them dialectic, dynamic, and favourable to learning and change.

In community work, Pichon-Rivière suggests, we must realise that group demands are given voice through the spokesperson. He proposed that the group solve the underlying group problem rather than focus on individual problems that arise when anxieties are intensified in a learning situation. Any group or sector of a community may observe that there are techniques or strategies that are no longer useful to resolve problems and that it is necessary to find others that are more adequate in relation to the present reality. Here is an outline of Pichon-Rivière's way of proceeding to analyse a community group problem.

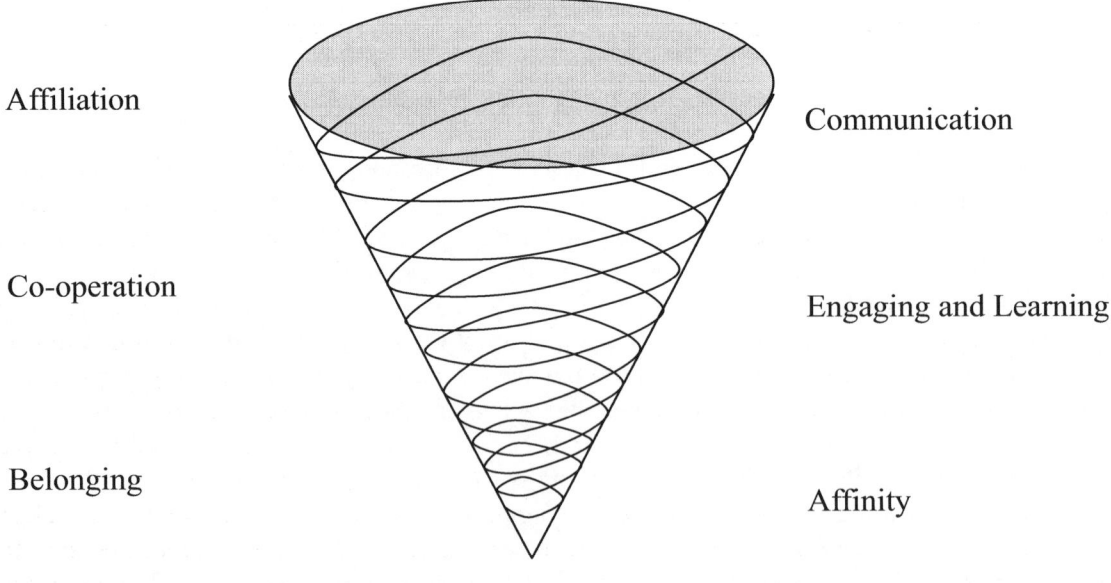

Figure 1. The Inverted Cone.

Steps for analysing interference with the group's work

- The group coordinator begins by interpreting a group situation that has been made manifest through the spokeperson at a certain point of urgency.
- Having proposed that new perspective, the coordinator tries to clarify with the group the difficulties in performing the group task.
- The relocation of the difficulty as a group event creates a change in the group's structure that enables it to resolve the difficulty and enjoy a new future.
- The goal is to decrease basic fears by breaking the stereotypes that maintain them.

When the implicit and the explicit make contact, they "click" as Pichon-Rivière liked to say. When the implicit becomes explicit, the fear of attack is minimised, and change can occur. The thesis, antithesis, and synthesis mobilise the group and create the possibility of learning without fear of loss. It is a matter of reaching a new learning of reality for the purpose of producing an active adaptation so that the group members are able to assume new roles with more responsibility, progressively abandoning previous roles inadequate to the "here and now" situation. This is accomplished through group work in which feelings of belonging, cooperation, and pertinence work harmoniously towards great productivity:

The progress of the work group

- Active adaptation to reality
- Possibility of assuming new roles
- Ability to assume more responsibility
- Leaving behind previous roles inadequate for the situation.

Pichon-Rivière stated that work with groups, institutions, or communities involves a particular type of psychological operation that involves decentralisation of the theme illness in the spokesperson and centres on a new social operator whose task is the promotion of learning, health, and active adaptation to reality.

Pichon-Rivière said that subjects are born with a fundamental lack, an absence of matter but they are in constant contact with social reality. As they relate to others, experience desire and abandonment, deal with conflict and contradiction, and develop purpose, they construct their inner world. The personality is not pre-existing: it has to be produced from interaction with individuals, groups, and classes of people in the social world. This interplay of individual and social links changes the subject's inner world and also effects change in the social world.

Psychoanalysis works on making the unconscious conscious and transforming infantile desire into a mature capacity for love, procreativity, and work. Unconscious identifications constitute a subjective referential scheme that operates as a unit of experience, knowledge, and affect that the individual uses to think, do, and operate in the world. Psychoanalysis makes it possible to understand subjective vicissitudes in processes of change. Pichon-Rivière proposed the ECRO schema as a way to proceed, constantly rectifying theory and practice, testing the operationality of the conceptual frame and methodology of psychoanalysis, and comparing them to other frames of reference. Such a systematic, semantic analysis with epistemological, methodological, and conceptual aspects presents psychoanalysis as a real philosophy of science.

The link and the theory of the three Ds: depositor, depository, and deposited: role and status

The concept of role is important in psychology and also in the operational field of analysis where it becomes a vector for integration. During treatment the analysand assigns the analyst different roles when communication fails. The patient may feel rejected or frustrated and this could reflect the repetition of an important primitive situation such as the mother–child relationship. The analyst's attitude should be to accept any role and any feeling or attitude that is *deposited* in him by the patient (the *depositor*). The patient develops trust in the analyst to become able to use him as a *depository*. If the analyst understands what has been *deposited* in him, he will interpret the transference situation in the here and now. Each pattern of behaviour, even the slightest symptom, gives access to the totality of the person, especially important in the analysis of psychotics.

Pichon-Rivière's theory of roles is based on Fairbairn's object relations theory. For Pichon-Rivière, object relations are structures that include the subject, the object, and the relation between them which is the link. In a group, aggressive individual attitudes may emerge and may trigger individual frustrations and further aggressions until the group becomes an aggressive group. The theory of the link concerns multiple relationships, including individual, group, and psychotic links, and this theory makes group life understandable. All interpersonal relations in a social group and a family are directed by the constant interplay of assumed and assigned roles. This creates coherence through links within the group. The group link may be extended to include a nation and relationships between nations.

The link and psychoanalytic therapy

For Pichon-Rivière, analysis centres on understanding the difficulties that maintain the repetitive situation of a vicious cycle in which the subject needs to face claustrophobic, agoraphobic, paranoid, and depressive anxieties. Pichon-Rivière thought it important to work with the patient to enable him to abandon previous object relations, break the internal primitive link, and dare to confront his persecutors. This analytic work should be spontaneous so that the analyst is able to build a hypothesis based on the construction of fantasies related to the patient's psychic events. The good analyst attempts to address the analytic material in a way that is unique, particular to each patient. He covers manifest and latent content situated in history and in the here and now. He aims to customise the gestalt for revealing and dealing with learning problems. He explores in what way the external link was shaped by its connection to the internal link of the patient's history and fantasy underlying manifest material.

Pichon-Rivière warns that the analyst needs to be aware of the constant presence of his own referential scheme. His personal history, store of knowledge, and fantasy life all influence his reading of the patient and the construction of his interpretations. He develops a scheme and that becomes his instrument for analysis. He will challenge his scheme continually, analyse it as a whole gestalt, and ratify or correct its tenets as the scheme interacts with the patient or group in the operational field. The analytic process may be conceptualised as a succession of spirals that establish more direct and sincere communication, progress in learning, and better adaptation to reality, as the analytic pair works to diminish anxiety.

The influence of Fairbairn's thinking on Pichon-Rivière's

Fairbairn and Pichon-Rivière were profoundly influenced by Melanie Klein's emphasis on the mother–child relationship and her concept of unconscious phantasy. Fairbairn considered the individual a result not of instincts and internalised objects but of the interrelation between the subject and the subject's internal and external objects. To that, Pichon-Rivière added the influence of the individual link on the social world. Experience with the caregiver is internalised and used to construct the psychic structure. Fairbairn stated that the infant was motivated from the beginning by a fundamental need for relationships. He thought that all development takes place and derives meaning in the context of the relation with the mother.

According to Roberto Losso, an Argentine psychoanalyst who worked with Pichon-Rivière for many years, Pichon-Rivière valued Fairbairn's work and salvaged his ideas for use as he developed his own theories (2010, personal communication). Pichon-Rivière centred his work on the study of interpersonal relations among individuals and their social groups. From this experience he developed his theory of the link. Once the style of relating to the object is fixed, we see a repetitive pattern, an enduring trait. The internal link conditions the external aspect of the subject.

Fairbairn defined the ego as an active, dynamic structure in a continuous process of evolution, as repressed and split-off parts of the ego and its objects seek reintegration to restore a whole person. Fairbairn (1943b) suggested that Klein's concept of unconscious phantasy, which she considered as the fundamental link between drives and reality, should be replaced by his own more useful concept of the internal object relationships as the inner world.

For Pichon-Rivière, in every structural link the subject and the object act, thereby nourishing each other in a dialectic relationship. This interaction, inevitably distorted by individual needs, is internalised, and in this way acquires an intra-subjective dimension. Pichon-Rivière referred to this process as the "internalised structural link". What was interpsychic becomes intrapsychic (Bolognini, 2004) and constitutes the internal group (a modification of Klein's term, internal world). The way that this internal group is integrated determines the subject's future.

Fairbairn described the process of development from infantile dependency to the achievement of mature dependency. Along the way, the infant ego inevitably meets with frustration. The ego splits and represses unpleasurable experience as an early psychic defence against pain. The ego compartmentalises experience into good and bad objects that it takes inside, some of which it retains in consciousness and some of which it represses, and out of which it creates its endopsychic structure. The degree of splitting and repression is more extreme in trauma, which Fairbairn understood well from his study of war neuroses, and in schizoid states, but the ordinary vicissitudes of early development also call for inner distortions to modify outer experience. Both aspects of the self, ego and object, are in dynamic internal relationship, and are influenced by external object relations (D. Scharff, 1996). Fairbairn described how internal relations between self and object are subject to dynamic flux in health and are frozen in pathological situations.

Pichon-Rivière conceptualised the ego as having good and bad links with the object. The good link originates from gratifying experiences and the bad link from frustrating experiences. He believed that gratifying experiences give the subject the life drive and that the death drive results from a frustrating link. Pichon-Rivière considered that bio-psychosocial needs for love, contact, protection, warmth, and nutrition are the motivational base of the link, conditioned by the initial helplessness of the human subject. Like Fairbairn who described the nature of object relations in various mental states (obsessional, paranoid, hysterical, and phobic) and the internalised or externalised location of the accepted or rejected object in each situation, Pichon-Rivière developed similar ideas concerning the functional location of the link with regard to mind, body, and external world.

Pichon-Rivière's location of the link (reminiscent of Fairbairn's transitional techniques)

- In the phobic state, the good link and the persecutory link with their two objects are located in all three areas.
- In hysteria, the persecutory link is in the body, and the persecutory object is in the mind, while in the external world there is a reassuring protector.
- In obsessive neurosis: both links are in the mind.
- In psychosis: the persecutor is in the external world in the form of a delusion and the manic defence is in the mind.

Pichon-Rivière developed Fairbairn's seminal concept of schizoid mechanisms and schizoid conditions mainly in his article, *A New Issue for Psychiatry* (1978). Pichon-Rivière's *Theory of Roles* (2002) was based on Fairbairn's theory of object relations. Pichon-Rivière believed that each of us has an internal world populated by representations of objects, each fulfilling a role that makes it possible to predict others' behaviour. He explained that the link also shapes a more integrated social structure.

Fairbairn was the first to write that the relationship with the analyst is the central element of the therapeutic process. The treatment allows working through of inner distortions and modification of external experiences. Pichon-Rivière agreed that psychoanalytic work allows modifications in the internal structure. Pichon-Rivière described the therapeutic process as *a spiral* consisting of three moments: the *existing* (what appears in the field), the *interpreted*, and the *emergent* (what emerges following interpretation). This process involves a dialectic situation established with us in the here and now, as it was before with others, and as it will be later somewhere else in a different way (Losso, 2001).

Fairbairn and Pichon-Rivière agree that the individual is not a result of instincts but of internal and external relations. Human relations are the nucleus of the human being and internalised experiences organise the mind. Internal structure is dynamically influenced by the external world. Fairbairn described the endopsychic structure as a system of internal object relationships in dynamic relationship, being repressed and seeking reunification in the whole personality. Pichon-Rivière described the link as a permanent, dynamic structure in a continuous process of evolution in the totality of the person, which includes the person's group and society. Fairbairn and Pichon-Rivière have led the development and extension of object relations theories, have been strong influences on contemporary relational theories that emphasise the intersubjective, and will be remembered as pioneers in the evolution of psychoanalytic theory as philosophy, science, and treatment modality.

References

Bolognini, S. (2004). *La empatía psicoanalítica*. Buenos Aires, Argentina: Lumen.

Fairbairn, W. R. D. (1943b). Phantasy and inner reality. In: E. F. Birtles & D. E. Scharff (Eds.), *From Instinct to Self: Selected Papers of W. R. D. Fairbairn, Volume II: Applications and Early Contributions* (pp. 293–294). Northvale, NJ: Jason Aronson, 1994.

Fairbairn, W. R. D. (1952). *Psychoanalytic Studies of the Personality*. London: Tavistock.

Losso, R. (2001). *Psicoanálisis de la Familia. Recorridos teóricos–clínicos*. Buenos Aires, Argentina: Lumen.

Pichon-Rivière, E. (1978). Una nueva problemática para la psiquiatría. *Revista de Psicoanalisis, 35*(4). In: *La Psiquiatría, una Nueva Problemática*. Buenos Aires, Argentina: Nueva Visión, 1983.

Pichon-Rivière, E. (2002). *Teoría del Vínculo*. Buenos Aires, Argentina: Nueva Visión.

Scharff, D. E. (1996). *Object Relations Theory and Practice: An Introduction*. Northvale, NJ: Jason Aronson.

Scharff, D. E., & Birtles, E. F. (Eds.) (1994). *From Instinct to Self: Selected Papers of W. R. D. Fairbairn, Volume I: Clinical and Theoretical Papers*. Northvale, NJ: Jason Aronson.

Scharff, J. S., & Scharff, D. E. (1998). *Object Relations Individual Therapy*. Northvale, NJ: Jason Aronson.

Videla, M. (1998). *Prevención: Intervención Psicológica en Salud Comunitaria*. Buenos Aires, Argentina: Ediciones Cinco.

CHAPTER THIRTY

The "intuitive position" and its relationship to creativity, science, and art in Fairbairn's work

Ricardo Juan Rey

The aim of this work is to show the connections between the concept of an intuitive position (Rey, 2005), and Fairbairn's findings about art, creativity, and science, and the conception of the psychoanalytical setting as a place where creativity may be restored.

My research about the intuitive position was motivated by the need to assign the intuitive phenomenon a role in the constitution of the psyche, by explaining how, when, and why intuition emerges. Another motivation was the need to explain how the first good object appears in our inner world, a point that was not clarified in the discussion between Fairbairn and Klein.

I will try to support the need for the existence of an intuitive position before the paranoid-schizoid position. Its conception comes together with a personal interpretation of what takes place in the mother–baby dyad from the moment of birth.

During the baby's first year, there are two periods that are separated by the mental birth trauma, which marks the appearance of the inner world.

I consider the situation in which the baby comes to the world to be tripartite (mother–baby–chaos) from the start. The irruption of the external world at birth is a traumatic and persecuting experience. Maternal care brings order to the chaos and transforms it into a cosmos.

The child recognises the continuous presence of his "extra uterine" mother in relation to the intrauterine mother. Thus, the triad baby–mother–chaotic world is formed from the beginning, and this becomes the original setting.

The mother will then provide what the baby needs at the right time. In this way, the proto-desire object the child has in mind appears embodied in a real object. Eigen (2009a, 2009b) considers that there is an environmental mother the child does not register, who supports the baby's independent life and his feeling of basic and spontaneous loneliness. This would be indispensable to develop the child's basic trust, and the belief that the external world will finally respond to our expectations (Bion's concept of faith). Thanks to it, the object tropism can be developed and maintained the way it was described by Bion (1996) in his concept of passion.

Birth mental trauma takes place when the child is faced with contradictory, frustrating aspects, different from those he usually finds in his mother.

The baby's main achievement during his postnatal life is to build an inner world. The aim of this construction is to protect him from the arbitrary changes generated by the bond with his real mother, and replace them with a good, basic trust, inner object, which is expected to remain stable over the years. Somehow, the construction of the inner world implies distorting reality to stabilise it. The first step towards building that inner world requires a universal setting, what I have called the "intuitive position".

The baby is bewildered at finding in his mother aspects that cannot be referred to the previous proto-mental setting, with the risk of reiterating irruption of the original chaos.

By means of his intuitive position, the baby can confirm that the happy mother on day A and the depressed mother on day B are the same mother (thus constructing a mental object that is independent from his vicissitudes in the real world). This mental object is built by partially denying reality and himself. A sort of denial pact is created, whereby the baby dismisses his and his mother's hostile and negative aspects to favour the continuity of a relationship that provides emotional support.

It is as if specific aspects of the object are denied (as if its superficial aspect were ignored), as if those aspects were dissolved in a chaotic magma from where—on detailed and deep examination—certain features can emerge that help recognise the continuity from mother on day A into mother on day B, with the result that a continuum is generated where there was discontinuity. It would be the acceptance of certain invariances.

This intuitive position involves:

1. An initial moment of perplexity.
2. A temporary connection with a state of mental emptiness that is related to the feeling of external chaos.
3. A projection of that mental emptiness on the mother, who would become an enigmatic object.
4. The creation of the good object through the denial of the frustrating aspects of the object and certain feelings of the baby.

It is as if the mother passed through the baby's mind, as if he were looking along a bar code that ensures her continuity. Between the proto-objective sensorial aspects and the new characteristics discovered in the object a synthetic object is created, which does not need to be introjected. It is pure mental creation.

I believe that the most appropriate way to describe it is the intuitive position, because it is universal, because unless reached it causes mental pathology, and because it is possible to regress to it in severe symptoms from the paranoid-schizoid position. I also believe that it is connected to certain erogenous areas, like breathing and smell.

The intuitive position would be a sort of depressive proto-position that synthesises new aspects of the external object with the mental proto-object from the stage supported by the environmental mother in a basic trust object.

In conclusion, my idea is that the good basic trust object is *created* by the baby to guarantee for himself a relational continuity that provides security. I believe this takes place when the baby is around three months old, and it is reflected in his social smile. I reiterate that the first good object (basic trust object) is not introjected but created.

But the result obtained by the intuitive position is ephemeral. The creative task has left a real external object damaged, mutilated, and partially repudiated. And this object is threatening retaliation. This brings to an end the bad inner object introjection and culminates in the construction of the inner world that was described by Fairbairn, with its three characteristic instances.

Once acquired, the intuitive position is used throughout life, particularly when there is a need to create or invent. This implies changing the Bionian equation PS< >D to a different equation, Intuitive Position < > (PS< >D).

This means there would be an oscillation between our conception of reality from our inner world (with good and bad objects), and our possibility of experientially reconnecting with reality to form a new and surpassing synthesis (intuition).

I believe that the intuitive position would be the earliest form of the K link described by Bion, and its final result would correspond to the thing-representation postulated by Freud. The future task will be to analyse their connections with the alpha function postulated by Bion (1996).

The analysis as a setting for creativity

In his work "On the Nature and Aims of Psycho-analytical Treatment" (1958a), Fairbairn boasts of his peculiar talent, when he marks one paradox: through creativity we protect ourselves from the vicissitudes with the real object, but remain prisoners of a closed and rigid system we cannot abandon for fear of the irruption of a dismantling and disintegrating anxiety. Fairbairn summarises it with a brilliant statement: "The ego is founded upon a basis which is essentially psychopathological" (p. 76), and he completes it with an obvious conclusion: "In so far as the inner world assumes the form of a closed system, a relationship with an external object is only possible in terms of transference" (p. 85). According to Fairbairn, this explains "the obstinate tendency of patients undergoing psychoanalytical treatment to maintain their inner worlds as closed systems, and to resist every attempt to convert these systems into open systems and so render them amenable to change through the impact of influences in outer reality" (p. 90).

The key seems to be to tolerate the impact of reality, to accept that the real world can be surprising and contradictory, which causes a state of perplexity in our minds. Buddhists talk about maintaining the mind of a beginner. Beginners find every aspect of reality surprising. Only those who approach the object with enigma and ignorance can experience the surprise of what is new.

If, as stated by Fairbairn, the role of the analyst is to mount a determined intervention to break through the patient's closed system, and thus allow him to reconnect his inner world with the external reality, the implication is that psychoanalysis is a method that rehabilitates creativity in search of reality regardless of the consequences or the capacity to accept those consequences.

But to attain that objective, the psychopathological steps that have already split the ego must be retraced, and a new synthesis must be achieved by reducing the triple splitting of the original ego. Thus, the main objective of the session is *"to promote a maximum 'synthesis' of the structures into which the original ego has been split, in the setting of a therapeutic relationship with the analyst"* (ibid., p. 83, emphasis in the original).

Creativity and science

The scientific corpus accepted by a society at a given point in time can be considered as a closed system that, like the inner world, resists changes or transformations. Fairbairn himself reminds us that: "Scientific truth … is *'simply explanatory truth'; and the picture of reality provided by science is an intellectual construct representing the fruits of an attempt to describe the various phenomena of the universe, in as coherent and systematic a manner as the limitations of human intelligence permit, by means of the formulation of general laws established by inductive inference under conditions of maximum emotional detachment and objectivity on the part of the scientific observer"* (ibid., p. 78, emphasis in original).

The creative possibility entails the capacity to leave behind that closed and conventionally accepted scheme to reconnect with reality, which will bring about an intuitive moment with a new external-inner synthesis and transform the closed system into an open system.

I believe that creative moments occur with a *controlled regression* to the intuitive position, where we make a synthesis with previous experiences and previous knowledge, together with what we are experimenting with in the reality of the here and now. Out of that meeting comes the need for a new imaginative construction, which later can be expressed in a mystic or religious idea, in a new scientific truth or an artistic object.

The creative act is a lonely act, and the creative synthesis causes a fantasised damage in reality, and the threat of retaliation. This threat is projected many times on the group (which may not understand the new ideas and persecute their bearer). That is why it is imperative that the idea is made known and supporters are attracted. The new idea must be preached. This explains why religious ideas are spread and disseminated, scientific ideas are published and exposed, and art objects are exhibited to public opinion. The purpose behind the three cases is to arouse in the receiver experiences similar to those of the creator for the group to believe in that truth and incorporate it as such.

Fairbairn and his ideas about art

Art is a lonely activity undertaken by the artist. I believe that the artistic activity starts by searching the artistic object. I believe that the artist accesses a regression to an intuitive position, and in this deficient condition he tries to repair the lost sensation of completeness. The repair is attained by means of the "found object" (Fairbairn's concept, 1938a, 1938b), which is nothing else but a creative mutilation of reality that surprises and puzzles the artist. The feeling of beauty emerges as a result of fusing together the good experience of finding again completeness and the surprising and puzzling experience.

I believe that Fairbairn's concepts about the found object support the conception of the intuitive position. According to Fairbairn, the object found by the artist always has a hidden symbolic meaning, and its disclosure uncovers the persistent union between external reality and inner world. This deep emotion aroused by the discovery would represent the feeling of beauty, since it fills the artist's emotional deficiencies. The artist then tries to perpetuate, communicate, and express that instant in the shape of a work of art. The object found is *created* by the discovery itself and perpetuated in the work of art. Actually, the found object functions as a recovered or restored object that appears to satisfy the artist's unconscious emotional needs.

Intuition in the session

Bion's proposal for the psychoanalytic session is to encounter the patient without any knowledge, memory, or wishes. I believe that this sets into motion the analyst's regression (daydreaming), which allows the intuitive detection of the patient's unsuspected aspects. The "found object" must then be put into appropriate words that render it understandable and able to be assimilated by the patient. I believe that the most fruitful moments in an analysis are when the analyst can regress to his intuitive position in the session. Mutant interpretations spring from there.

The intuitive position and psychopathology

It goes beyond the scope of this work to investigate the possibilities that are open to the interpretation of severe mental pathology with the concept of an intuitive position. I will only say that, in psychosis, regression may go beyond the paranoid-schizoid position and even further than its own intuitive position. Delusions, as restorative symptoms with their delirious conviction, could be interpreted as a pathological use of the intuitive position. It is obvious that we are convinced of our intuitions in the same way the psychotic patient is convinced of his delusions.

Conclusions

1. I believe we can find in Fairbairn's work an outline of the concept of an intuitive position in his understanding concerning scientific and artistic creativity.
2. The concept of an intuitive position explains how mutant interpretation appears in the session, and how psychoanalysis provides an opening to creativity.
3. The intuitive position is an original concept concerning the events that take place during the first year of life, with consequences on the interpretation of severe mental pathology, like psychosis.

References

Bion, W. R. (1996). *Volviendo a pensar*. Buenos Aires, Argentina: Ed Lumen Hormé.
Eigen, M. (2009a). Primary aloneness. In: *Flames from Unconscious (Trauma, Madness and Faith)* (pp. 11–17). London: Karnac.
Eigen, M. (2009b). Incommunicado core and boundless supporting unknown. In: *Flames from Unconscious (Trauma, Madness and Faith)* (pp. 19–28). London: Karnac.

Fairbairn, W. R. D. (1938a). Prolegomena to a psychology of art. *British Journal of Psychology, 28*: 288–303. In: E. F. Birtles & D. E. Scharff (Eds.), *From Instinct to Self: Selected Papers of W. R. D. Fairbairn, Volume II: Applications and Early Contributions* (pp. 381–396). Northvale, NJ: Jason Aronson, 1994.

Fairbairn, W. R. D. (1938b). The ultimate basis of aesthetic experience. *British Journal of Psychology, 29*: 167–181. In: E. F. Birtles & D. E. Scharff (Eds.), *From Instinct to Self: Selected Papers of W. R. D. Fairbairn, Volume II: Applications and Early Contributions* (pp. 397–409). Northvale, NJ: Jason Aronson, 1994.

Fairbairn, W. R. D. (1958a). On the nature and aims of psycho-analytical treatment. *International Journal of Psychoanalysis, 39*(5): 374–385. In: D. E. Scharff & E. F. Birtles (Eds.), *From Instinct to Self: Selected Papers of W. R. D. Fairbairn, Volume I: Clinical and Theoretical Papers* (pp. 74–92). Northvale, NJ: Jason Aronson, 1994.

Rey, R. J. (2005). From Fairbairn to a new systematization of psychopathology, the intuitive position, and the alienated and oscillating structures. In: J. S. Scharff & D. E. Scharff (Eds.), *The Legacy of Fairbairn and Sutherland: Psychotherapeutic Applications* (pp. 89–96). London: Routledge, 2005.

CHAPTER THIRTY-ONE

Revising Fairbairn's structural theory

David P. Celani

Fairbairn wrote his remarkable theory of the personality in the relative isolation of Edinburgh, Scotland, during the years 1940–1963. He worked alone and his lack of psychoanalytic colleagues allowed him the freedom to formulate a unique model of the mind, independent of the mainstream of analytic thought. The disadvantage of his isolation was that his theoretical mistakes went unnoticed for many years as he had no colleagues (with the exception of Harry Guntrip) who were actively applying his work and reporting back on their clinical experiences, as Symington notes in the following quote:

> The disadvantage of Fairbairn not having founded a school is that there has been little development of his theories, as there has been, for instance, among the followers of Melanie Klein. There has been no organized body of analysts working within the structure of his schemata, testing the different aspects of his theories against the phenomena thrown up by their clinical work. So there has been no Fairbairnian tradition, no recognizable development. (1994, p. 212)

Now, fifty years since Fairbairn's death, there are enough clinicians using his work to begin to sort out what parts of his model hold true in the clinical setting and more importantly, what areas of his model are in need of revision. This chapter will attempt to rectify what I see as problems with Fairbairn's structural theory: specifically I will examine and suggest modifications to those parts of his model that contain assertions that do not match clinical observations and therefore impede the application of his theory to clinical practice. All the revisions to his structural theory will be based on repeated clinical observations and they will allow his model to more accurately fit the realities and demands of treatment.

The prelude to the splitting defence

Fairbairn's ultimate discovery of the splitting defence and the structural theory began with his recognition that the child had to develop defences against bad internalised objects, objects which had to be internalised for the child to survive. Internalisation of external objects is a key factor in Fairbairn's theory as he assumed that the extreme dependency of the child was based on inner emptiness, unlike Freud's vision of the human infant who was assumed to be born with an energised and pre-programmed id, which made attachment to external objects a less pressing issue. In Fairbairn's view of the human condition, the child's innate dependency and helplessness make the parental objects supremely important, and the failure of the parents to provide the child with the necessary empathy, attention, and support is catastrophic to the child's continuing development:

> The outstanding feature of infantile dependence is its unconditional character. The infant is completely dependent upon his object not only for existence and physical well being, but for the satisfaction of his psychological needs … By contrast, the very helplessness of the child is sufficient to render him dependent in an unconditional sense … He has no alternative but to accept or to reject his object—an alternative which is liable to present itself to him as a choice between life or death. (1941, p. 47)

Fairbairn assumed that the child who was faced with parental failures was forced to internalise his objects—despite their badness—because he could not sustain a sense of aliveness within himself without them. To the deprived child, internal objects were "even as precious as life itself and their internalization of which is a measure of their importance and the extent of dependence upon them" (1940a, p. 22). Fairbairn assumed that internalisation of external objects was a defensive and purposeful act, one that led him to believe (falsely, in my view) that good objects need not be internalised. This view is not part of the current thinking today and Scharff and Scharff (1998) have addressed this issue by noting that all objects, good and bad, are internalised in a continuous process throughout childhood and adulthood;

> In Fairbairn's model, however, the introjection of good experience comes as a kind of afterthought: good objects are only introjected to compensate for bad (1952). Klein disagreed with Fairbairn's ideas that introjection of good experience was secondary. She thought that under the influence of the life instinct, good experience is also taken in from the beginning. Current infant research demonstrates that she was right, that infants, and all of us, take in good and bad experience. But we think that it happens, not because of the life and death instincts (as she thought), but simply because we are built to take in all kinds of experience as we relate in order to grow into a person. The realities of all aspects of external experience and our perceptions of them provide the building blocks for our psychic structure … They take in experience to use as material to construct an inner world, and they then actively seek to realize that inner world in the outer world, both through interaction with others and through internal modification of their selves. (Mitchell, 2000, pp. 219–220)

The fact that good objects are probably internalised does not alter the fact that children exposed to frequent interpersonal events that are characterised by rejection, abandonment, and cruelty are still at the mercy of those internalised toxic experiences as a result of the internalisation of their relationship with their parental objects.

Fairbairn saw that the child's next problem was a direct consequence of allowing the "badness" of the object to enter his internal world after he, by necessity, had internalised the bad object. One of the most graphic examples in Fairbairn's work regarding the damage done to the personality from an internalisation of a toxic object is the example of an adult patient who felt poisoned as a consequence of his internalisation of his mother (1943a). As an adult, Fairbairn's patient had a dream that he was starving and had wandered into his mother's bedroom where she was sleeping and where he saw a bowl of chocolate pudding (the patient's favourite food) next to her on the night table. The patient knew that the pudding contained poison, but if he did not eat it he would die of starvation. He ate the pudding in the dream and was sickened by it (ibid., p. 68). This patient then developed a preoccupation that his heart was damaged: "Thus is was because he had internalized his mother as a bad object that he felt his heart to be affected by a fatal disease; and he had internalized her, bad object though she was for him, because as a child he needed her" (p. 68).

Fairbairn then began to formulate defence mechanisms that had to be erected against the now internalised maternal hostility and indifference. In his 1943 paper he offered a solution with his first major defence, which he called the "moral defence". The moral defence is actually an early, simplistic version of the splitting defence, in which the child splits himself into an "all bad" person and splits the object into to an "all good" one (Mitchell, 1981, p. 79). Consequently, the child absolves his parents from being "bad", thus allowing for the hope that by pleasing them he will be loved at some time in the future:

> In becoming bad he is really taking upon himself the burden of badness which appears to reside in his objects. By this means he attempts to purge them of their badness; and in proportion as he succeeds in doing so, he is rewarded by that sense of security which an environment of good objects so characteristically confers. (Fairbairn, 1943a, p. 65)

This defence, like all defences, is only partially successful in that he unconsciously knows of his mother's malice. The basic formulation of the moral defence carries over into the splitting defence in that separate part-objects contain all the "badness" while others contain all the "goodness". Fairbairn never formally discarded the moral defence despite the fact that he replaced it with the far more complex splitting defence in 1944.

The structural model of 1944

The splitting defence itself (1944) is the absolute centrepiece of Fairbairn's metapsychology and it is the key to using his model in the clinical setting. It had, and still has, the potential to transform psychoanalysis from a one- and three-person psychology to a two-person psychology, one that is devoid of the metaphors of the last century and able to usher in a new and modern model of the development of the human psyche, as Mitchell has noted:

> First, self-formation and other-object formation are inseparable. Because libido is "object-seeking," it makes no sense psychologically to think of a self except in relation to another.

> And because others become psychically relevant only when invested by the self, it makes no sense to think of objects outside of relationships with versions of the self. The second principle inherent in Fairbairn's vision … is that we are multiplicitous, not a single self struggling with warded off impulses, but discontinuous, multiple self organizations packaged together by an illusory sense of continuity and coherence that has both conscious and unconscious features. In contemporary relational theory, the multiplicitous organizations are much more than (cognitive) representations of self; rather, they are each versions, complete functional units with a belief system, affective organization, agentic intentionality, and developmental history. (2000, p. 63)

Fairbairn's model contains three separate selves in relation to three separate aspects of the object. The child's conscious "central ego" (or self) develops in relationship to his "ideal object" (1951b), who under good circumstances involves him in a relationship saturated with empathy and age-appropriate positive relational experiences. No childhood is perfect and there will be events during which the child's needs are not understood, misinterpreted, or rejected because of external realities. These few events will be dissociated and form the child's unconscious.

Life is very different for the chronically rejected child as compared to the emotionally supported child. The deprived child's central self is structurally compromised because there are far fewer moments of support and empathy in the relationship between the child and his object. The deprived child develops two unconscious part-selves as a result of relational events with two separate but equally (in Fairbairn's view) intolerable aspects of his objects. Each of these dissociated self and object pairs includes a part-self that is linked with a specific part-object, and each part-self, part-object pair contains a specific view of the self in relation to a specific view of the object that is inimical to a loving relationship. That is, these intolerable events exceed the child's central ego's ability to integrate (them) into awareness, and if he were to accept (and consciously remember) all the events in which he was demeaned, abused, or neglected, or intolerably teased, then his central ego would see that he could no longer look to that parent for safety or love; in short, he would be faced with an abandonment crisis. Thus each pair of part-self and part-object represents an internalised version of a complex and ongoing external relationship that actually occurred. Each dissociated sub-ego or self is a functional entity with a personality that has a sense of awareness and specific strategies towards the object to whom it relates, a point Mitchell (ibid.) made in the previous quote.

Fairbairn called the dissociated self of the child that relates exclusively to the hostile/indifferent/critical aspect of the parent the "the internal saboteur" (later he changed it to the "antilibidinal ego" in his 1954 paper on hysteria), and this sub-self only interacts with the intolerably rejecting part of the parent which was appropriately called the "rejecting object" (1944). This pair of self and object structures vary in strength according to the number and intensity of events that the child has experienced (Fairbairn, 1943a, p. 65) and they are the root cause of human psychopathology in his metapsychology. The dissociative defence is an attempt by the child to create a "good object" (or in terms of the anti-libidinal ego/rejecting object pair of dissociated part-self and part-objects, a "less bad" object) for himself even if one does not exist.

The neglected/abused child experiences a desperate lack of hope because he has experienced a very limited central ego/ideal object relationship with his parent(s) and has dissociated much of his experiences with them into his anti-libidinal ego/rejecting object relationship. Fairbairn also noticed that the children in the orphanage (1943a) held completely unrealistic and illusory hopes for love from their objects, a hope that he also saw in an adult patient's dream (1944) that led to his structural theory. He proposed a second set of structures to account for this observation: a part-self in relation to an entirely love-filled aspect of the object, which acts (in my view but not in Fairbairn's view) as a counterbalance to the despair and hopelessness in the rest of their lives. This second dissociated sub-self, called the "libidinal ego", relates exclusively to the "exciting object", a part of the object that is assumed to contain unlimited love, and this fantasy sustains the child. Fairbairn assumed that this relational pair of part-self/part-object was also intolerably frustrating (a view that I will challenge), because the child's need is never actually satisfied. That is, Fairbairn believed that the child was "teased" intolerably by the prospect of love that was never fulfilled and (therefore) these part-self and part-object structures also had to be dissociated.

Problems within Fairbairn's structural model

My critique of Fairbairn's structural theory will focus on areas of his model that do not match clinical realities and therefore impede the use of his model as a clinical instrument. The overall idea encompassed within his structural theory is brilliant but a few basic misconceptions on Fairbairn's part ripple through his model and need to be rectified. Many of the problems within the structural theory are encapsulated in the following quote in which Fairbairn outlines his view of the relationship between the central ego and the subsidiary egos and internalised objects:

> As regards the relationship of the central ego to the other egos, our most important clue to its nature lies in the fact that, whereas the central ego must be regarded as compromising pre-conscious and conscious as well as unconscious, elements, the other egos must equally be regarded as essentially unconscious. From this we may infer that the libidinal ego and internal saboteur are both rejected by the central ego; and this inference is confirmed by the fact that, as we have seen, the considerable volume of libido and of aggression which has ceased to be at the disposal of the central ego is now at the disposal of the subsidiary egos. Assuming then that the subsidiary egos are rejected by the central ego, it becomes a question of the dynamic of this rejection ... So there is no alternative but to regard it as aggression. Aggression, must accordingly, be regarded as the characteristic determinant of the attitude of the central ego towards the subsidiary egos. (1944, pp. 104–105)

This rich quote contains a number of assertions that do not match clinical reality, and interfere with, if not prevent, the application of his model as a clinical tool. If a clinician was to attempt to work with Fairbairn's structural theory verbatim he/she would have no way of understanding the eruption of the sub-egos into consciousness (and the simultaneous repression of the central ego) in the borderline personality, which is the disorder that his model most perfectly explains. Clinical experience with borderline personalities (as well as with hysterics and obsessional personality disorders [Celani, 1993, 1994, 2001, 2007, 2010]) demonstrates that patients in all these diagnostic groups can function with either their libidinal or anti-libidinal ego (as well as either of their object structures) acting as the executive ego, while their central ego is repressed. The second assertion that Fairbairn makes in this quote, that energy has moved from the central ego to the subsidiary egos, contradicts the basic tenets of his theory. Finally, the last issue in this quote that cannot be validated by clinical observation is the assumption that the central ego is always more powerful than the sub-egos and has the ability to "hold" them in the unconscious with aggression.

The "unconscious sub-egos" assertion

The first assumption in this quote that does not bear up under clinical scrutiny is Fairbairn's assertion that the two sub-egos are "essentially unconscious". Clinical experience with the borderline patient demonstrates that either of the two sub-egos can become the executive ego and repress the central ego/ideal object as well as the other pair of structures. This occurs when the weak central ego collapses (another clinical reality that Fairbairn did not take into consideration) and is replaced by one of the other sub-egos or object structures. The sequential dominance of each of these sub-egos (along with the complete absence of the central ego) can be observed in the same individual during a very short period of time in many borderline patients. Despite the fact that Fairbairn was aware that his model was based on one ego structure repressing another, "It is not inconceivable that one part of the 'ego' with a dynamic charge should repress another part of the 'ego' with a dynamic charge" (Fairbairn, 1944, p. 90), he was never comfortable with the possibility that one or the other of the sub-egos could become the executive ego of the personality. In fact, Fairbairn thought that if the central ego were to collapse, due to the withdrawal of libido from the conscious part of the ego, then some form of psychosis would result (1941, p. 52). This position came three years prior to the creation of his structural model at a time when he was still using the energetic model as a psychic metaphor. However, he never modified his position that the central ego had to remain the dominant structure, one that was capable of keeping the sub-egos and their objects in the unconscious (1944, p. 105).

I have chosen an example of a past patient (Celani, 1993, 2010) to illustrate the shift in the executive function of the ego from the anti-libidinal ego, to the central ego and then to the libidinal ego;

> Susan was twenty-four years old and living at home with her parents and two older brothers while holding her first full time job as a receptionist and secretary in a law firm. When she began therapy she described her father from her antilibidinal ego position; she saw him as a monster of a human being who exploited the whole family mercilessly. In contrast, it appeared to me (from my assumedly central ego viewpoint) that my patient and her mother were caught in a traditional lower-middle-class family, and were being treated as if they were inferior to the males by the dominant husband who favored his two sons, both of whom worked with him in the family auto repair business. Susan reported that her father seldom addressed her directly, but expected her to help her mother prepare lunches for himself and her two brothers every day despite the fact that she had to ready herself for her new job. Similarly, after returning from work she was expected to help prepare dinner and clean up the dishes every evening, while her father and brothers conversed in the living room and watched

television. Her mother had developed a severe drinking problem over the years and one of Susan's unspoken tasks within the family was to help put her mother to bed most evenings when she collapsed from too much alcohol. Her description of her father was antilibidinal as it portrayed him as one of the worst villains of all time. In the past, she had tried to rescue her mother from her situation (who rejected all of her suggestions) and repeatedly complained about her treatment to relatives who she asked to intervene, but found that they were indifferent to her plight. Her life at home contrasted sharply with her ever improving relationships at work and the beginnings of a serious romantic relationship. The frustration from her long term unmet dependency needs fixated her at an earlier stage of development and she was unable to separate and live on her own during the first year of twice-weekly psychotherapy sessions informed by Fairbairn's model. During the second year she had modified her dramatic and excessive antilibidinal perceptions of her father in that she was no longer intent on reforming or defeating him, and instead, under the influence of central ego dominance decided to live a life of her own. Her increasingly powerful and realistic central ego allowed her to separate from her family and she rented an apartment of her own despite considerable guilt at leaving her hapless mother at home, without an ally. Within a week she received her first card (ever) from her father, which was filled with protestations of his love for her, saying that the home was not the same without her. She brought the card to the session and read it to me, streaming with tears, and saying that she always knew that her father loved her, and that she was going to move back to her home as soon as she could move out of her new apartment. This clever ploy on her father's part had reactivated her libidinal ego, which in turn repressed her nascent and less powerful central ego, and she now suddenly saw her father as an exciting object, filled with the potential of love. She also switched her view of me from an ideal object to a rejecting object who had somehow convinced her to leave her "loving" family. I tried to review both her antilibidinal statements and later central ego statements about her father but she became enraged and threatened to leave if I said anything negative about her family—a common situation when dealing with borderlines who split suddenly into a strong libidinal ego position. Not unexpectedly after moving back home there was a brief reunion which soon reverted to the old pattern of being ignored while serving the needs of her father and brothers. Her perception of her father split once again from a libidinal view of him as an exciting object to an even stronger antilibidinal view of him as both a tyrant and as a shameless trickster. (2010, p. 165)

This example illustrates how the executive functions of the ego can shift from the anti-libidinal ego, to the central ego, back to the libidinal ego and then to the anti-libidinal ego in a very short period of time. It appears that Fairbairn assumed that the sub-egos were kept in the unconscious by the power of the central ego. Without modifying Fairbairn's original position regarding the structural theory, the clinician trying to apply his model would have absolutely no way of understanding the shifts from one ego structure to another.

The "energetic" assumption

My second objection to this quote is based on Fairbairn's use of the energetic metaphor: that libido and aggression can move from one structure to another. This is, in my view, not only incorrect but essentially opposite to his basic thesis: that the self—or the selves—are generated from interactions with objects, and the characteristics of any specific sub-self is a response to the qualities of that specific object relationship. The anti-libidinal ego is suffused with rage, not because it has somehow taken over aggression from the central ego, but because this sub-ego has experienced mistreatment at the hands of the rejecting object. Similarly, the libidinal ego's desire for the object does not come from libidinal energy previously vested in the central ego but rather because the child's absolute need for attachment to the object forces him to create the fantasy of a loving object out of desperate hope. On the positive side, Fairbairn did see that the sub-egos are somehow stronger and more active than the central ego, but as noted, he never followed up on the possibilities inherent in this observation.

The "aggression" hypothesis

The next debatable assertion in this quote is that the central ego keeps the sub-egos in the unconscious with aggression: "Aggression must accordingly be regarded as the characteristic determinant of the attitude of the central ego towards the subsidiary egos" (1944, p. 105). In a later quote he reiterated this position: "It is this aggression that provides the dynamic of the severance of the subsidiary egos from the central ego" (ibid., p. 108). As I have already noted, the central ego cannot keep the sub-egos and their objects in the unconscious in the first place. Second, and equally important, the central ego is not only devoid of aggression, it is lacking in substance, purpose, and a sense of agency as compared to the sub-egos. Most borderline patients demonstrate that their libidinal and anti-libidinal egos are "stronger" than their attenuated central egos. I define them as "stronger" as evidenced by the fact that they often take over as the conscious executive ego for longer periods of time than does the central ego, and paradoxically, they contain a firmer identity and sense of purpose than does their central ego. That is, each sub-ego contains a meaningful (though often a self-destructive) plan for their life, one which they carry out with intensity and purpose. The anti-libidinal egos of many of my patients were in pitched battles with their rejecting object parents—they would argue and debate with their parents, and threaten them with exposure to other members of the family or even to the general public, or become embroiled in conflict with displaced objects in their workplaces (Celani, 1993, 2010). Conversely, their libidinal egos contained plans to lure or seduce the exciting object into accepting them as the worthy child that they (at times) felt themselves to be. Not only can the libidinal sub-ego guide the individual, and implement a strategy to woo back the elusive exciting object, but it can also subject the unwary therapist to a verbal thrashing (albeit with untenable logic) if he or she contradicts the patient's self-destructive plans! The anti-libidinal ego is also remarkably capable of aggression towards the therapist who tries to dissuade him from equally self-defeating plans to "destroy" or force change on his bad objects or a displaced external object who is the target of transference (Celani, 1993, 2010).

Fairbairn did not explore the possibility of variability in the strength of the central ego, despite the fact that he saw that the central ego had lost "libido and aggression" to the two sub-egos. Fortunately his model allows for this possibility, first through the process that describes how ego structures, or at least the anti-libidinal ego structure, develop, and second, through the internalisation of "part good" objects (1951b).

Fairbairn described, in the following quote on the development of psychopathology, his view on how the anti-libidinal ego strengthened:

> Whether any given individual becomes delinquent, psychoneurotic, psychotic or simply "normal" would appear to depend in the main upon the operation of three factors:
>
> 1. The extent to which bad objects have been installed in the unconscious and the degree of badness by which they are characterized. (1943a, p. 65)

The second and third factors in this same quote modify the impact of internalised bad objects including the individual's identification with the perpetrator and the level of defences the individual has against these internalised bad objects. All models must be internally consistent, thus all of the six ego structures, the conscious self and object pair of structures and the four (sometimes) unconscious structures must obey the same principles. Therefore all three ego structures and the three internalised objects must strengthen as a consequence of the number of events (either enhancing or destructive) that the child has experienced in relation to his parents and with the intensity of those events. The greater the hostility and toxicity of the rejecting object, the greater will be the growth and complexity of the anti-libidinal ego. The growth of the anti-libidinal ego/rejecting object structures will, in turn, spur on compensatory growth in the libidinal ego's fantasies of the goodness of the exciting object, which acts as a balance to the rejecting object by keeping the child's illusory hope for love alive in even the most abusive family situations. The central ego must follow the same principles, though Fairbairn was fraught with ambivalence about the internalisation of good objects in that he repeatedly stated that good objects *need not* be internalised (1944, 1954b) because they were freely available in the external world. This assumption is part of the "ripple effect" that followed from his prior assumption that internalisation of objects was a deliberate and defensive act, a position that is unlikely to be true.

Luckily for the future users of his model, Fairbairn's theory also provides for a similar pathway that allows for variability of good objects (based on actual relational events) for the internalisation of "part-good" objects in his 1951 addendum to his 1944 paper on structure:

> In accordance with my revised conception, the central ego's "accepted object" being shorn of its over-exciting and over-rejecting elements, assumes the form of a desexualized and idealized object which the central ego can safely love after divesting itself of the elements which give rise to the libidinal ego and the internal saboteur. (1951b, p. 135)

In my view of Fairbairn's model, the key to understanding relationship between the central ego and the sub-egos hinges on the ratio of loving/supportive developmental events as compared to frustrating/enraging interpersonal events. Fairbairn never discussed the impact of loving, encouraging, and tolerant parenting on the child's central ego, though he did speak of the shift in size and power of the central ego as compared to the two sub-egos as a consequence of psychoanalysis (1944, pp. 129–130). I have mentioned this point earlier in the chapter as well as having discussed it elsewhere (Celani, 2010, pp. 55–58), so I will summarise my positions here.

Children of loving and supportive families have a vastly different ratio of central ego/ideal object experiences as compared to libidinal ego/exciting object and anti-libidinal ego/rejecting object experiences, because during their developmental histories their parents supported their individuation and skills acquisition which allowed the elaboration and strengthening of their central ego. Over time, the preponderance of (and intensity of) supportive and growth inducing central ego/ideal object interactions with their parents overshadows the far fewer anti-libidinal ego/rejecting object (and libidinal ego/exciting object) interactions they had experienced. Thus, these children have anti-libidinal egos that contain relatively fewer and less intensely frustrating experiences that had to be dissociated and repressed. Similarly, these same children have little reason to develop an unrealistic libidinal ego because the goodness of their objects was real and available to them most of the time.

In contrast, the deprived/neglected/abused child has an enormous number of frustrating and enraging relational events "installed in the unconscious" (Fairbairn, 1944, p. 135), and the experiences spur the elaboration of a complex anti-libidinal self filled with self-hatred and a desire to reform or seek revenge against the rejecting object (Beattie, 2005; Celani, 2010; Ogden, 1990). Since much of the relational matrix between the rejected/abused child and parent is negative, there are far fewer positive interactions, and the child's central ego has a far smaller portion of the ideal object with which to relate. That is, more of the parent's behaviours have to be dissociated because they are excessively rejecting, and therefore the libidinal ego has to compensate with unrealistic and inflated fantasies of an exciting object, while the child's central ego is left with a mere fragment of his parent to relate to in the external world. This extreme deprivation prevents ongoing emotional development of the central ego, and the resulting stunted and immature central ego is unable to separate from his objects or stand up under age-appropriate pressures. As I have already noted, the deprived child's (mostly) unconscious structures have a clear purpose and goal (the anti-libidinal ego can become a self-righteous reformer of the rejecting object—and other similar objects in the external world), while the libidinal ego is on a quest to find love from objects who are indifferent to its needs. Fairbairn could not have accepted this view because he assumed that all the interactions between the unconscious structures remained in the inner world. His tenuous assertion that the anti-libidinal ego attacks both the libidinal ego and the exciting object (1944, p. 103) is another "ripple effect" of his assumption that the structures have to remain in the unconscious and all the activity of these structures had to be carried out intrapsychically.

The relationship between the anti-libidinal ego and the rejecting object

The last, clinically significant issue I will address regarding Fairbairn's structural model is the relationship between the anti-libidinal ego and the rejecting object, one that, in my view, Fairbairn got completely wrong (Celani, 2001, 2010). In his 1954 paper on hysteria, Fairbairn characterised the relationship between the anti-libidinal ego and the rejecting object as an "alliance" as opposed to my view based on clinical observation that the relationship is one between a defeated and dependent slave and its master:

> 12. The term "antilibidinal ego" has been adopted on the grounds that the repressed ego-structure so designated, being in alliance with the rejecting object, has aims inherently hostile to those of the libidinal ego and its alliance with the exciting object. (1954b, p. 17)

This assumption, that the anti-libidinal ego is an ally of the rejecting object and attacks the libidinal ego and its exciting object in the internal world, prevented Fairbairn from seeing aspects of his own patients that contradicted this assumption. In this same paper, Fairbairn offers the reader a very different view of the relationship between these two structures in a clinical example that is completely contrary to his assertions. The following clinical vignette from his patient "Morris" illustrates a typical battle between the anti-libidinal self and his internalised rejecting object:

> In his inner world he was constantly engaged in an argument with his mother over his right to possess a penis and to use it as he wished—a right which, in the light of his mother's reactions (to which reference has already been made), he felt that she denied to him. This imagined argument with his mother assumed the essential form of an attempt on his part to convert her to a "belief in penises", in place of the hatred of penises which he attributed to her (not without reason). More specifically, he sought to persuade her to accept his own penis, and to give him permission to use it: for, in his bondage to her, he felt that he did not dare to use his penis without her permission—except in secret masturbation, about which he felt extremely guilty. (ibid., p. 34)

This could not be a clearer example of a dialogue between the patient's anti-libidinal ego and his rejecting parental object. The patient's meek, angry, and defeated anti-libidinal self is trying to change the rejecting object into a good object that would allow him control of his own body. The anti-libidinal ego is fuelled by legitimate need coupled with the fear of losing the dependency relationship on the rejecting object, while the rejecting object can ignore the child's developmental needs without any consequences to herself. These rigid internalised structures are locked into an eternal battle and are not open to new information from the external world.

As mentioned previously, the anti-libidinal ego has a clear purpose and goals, the most pressing of which is to force the rejecting object to become a good object and therefore act as the catalyst for the child's continuing emotional development, a task in which it steadfastly refuses to participate. These two structures simply cannot leave each other alone, as Odgen has noted: "The object component may taunt, shame, threaten, lord over, or induce guilt in its object (the self component of the internal relationship) in order to maintain connectedness with the self component" (1983, p. 106). The clinician working with characterological patients will see endless variations of attachment through dependency and hate between their patients' anti-libidinal selves and their rejecting objects. If they assumed that the anti-libidinal ego is somehow in an *alliance* with the rejecting object, as Fairbairn asserted, they would misunderstand much of the reality of patient behaviour. The attachments between patients' anti-libidinal egos and their sadistic partner's rejecting aspects in the external world are the source of endless domestic violence (Celani, 1994), which today appears to be greater and more self-destructive than anything Fairbairn described in his writings. To his credit, Fairbairn did note that "The individual is extremely reluctant to abandon his original hate, no less than his original need, of his original objects in childhood" (1944, p. 117); however, he assumed once again that all the hate and aggression was all discharged in the inner world.

I will illustrate two significant disconfirmations of Fairbairn's model with a single example. The clinical material contradicts Fairbairn's assumption that the anti-libidinal ego is in an alliance with the rejecting object, and secondly, that it must carry off its attacks in the internal world. This patient had given up trying to reform his rejecting object parent and was seeking revenge. Note that the attacks that I will describe are not towards the libidinal ego/exciting object, but towards the rejecting object. I have used this example before (Celani, 1994, 2010, pp. 68–69). The patient had been singled out in a family of three children for special abuse by his father and as a teenager and in young adulthood was involved in a series of revenge-based acts against his father. He managed to "accidentally" damage his father's sports car (which he was not allowed to drive) by backing into it with the family station wagon in a parking lot, he punched a hole in his father's prized rowing shell with his foot while being instructed on how to enter it, he sank the family sailboat after his very first solo sail, and finally, several years later, he managed to "accidentally" set the sports car on fire. In therapy the patient saw himself as accident-prone and was completely unaware of his motives. However, his anti-libidinal ego, aided by preconscious awareness of reality (Clarke, 2005), had an uncanny ability to target and destroy his father's most precious objects. None of these attacks had anything to do with the patient's anti-libidinal ego attacking his libidinal ego, nor did they remain in the inner world, but rather were acted out in the external world. Not surprisingly, the despair and unmet developmental needs in his anti-libidinal ego spurred the creation of an equally potent libidinal ego, and after his father death, my patient had his father's clothing retailored to fit him (Celani, 2010). It was the only way he could remain close to the object that frustrated him throughout his developmental years.

Conclusion

I have attempted to outline the problems I have encountered in working with Fairbairn's object relations theory by focusing on assumptions within his structural theory that are not validated (and in fact are contradicted) by clinical observations. Fairbairn, despite my objections, created a wonderfully useful model of the human personality that, with the few modifications I have suggested, works flawlessly with most patients that one encounters in the clinical setting.

References

Beattie, H. J. (2005). Revenge. *Journal of the American Psychoanalytic Association, 53*: 2, 513–524.
Celani, D. P. (1993). *The Treatment of the Borderline Patient: Applying Fairbairn's Object Relations Theory in the Clinical Setting*. Madison, CT: International Universities Press.
Celani, D. P. (1994). *The Illusion of Love: Why the Battered Woman Returns to Her Abuser*. New York: Columbia University Press.
Celani, D. P. (2001). Working with Fairbairn's ego structures. *Contemporary Psychoanalysis, 37*: 391–416.
Celani, D. P. (2007). A structural analysis of the obsessional character: A Fairbairnian perspective. *American Journal of Psychoanalysis, 67*(2): 119–140.

Celani, D. P. (2010). *Fairbairn's Object Relations Theory in the Clinical Setting*. New York: Columbia University Press.

Clarke, G. (2005). The preconscious and psychic change in Fairbairn's model of mind. *International Journal of Psychoanalysis, 86*: 61–77.

Fairbairn, W. R. D. (1941). A revised psychopathology of the psychoses and psychoneuroses. *International Journal of Psychoanalysis, 22*(3, 4): 250–279. In: *Psychoanalytic Studies of the Personality* (pp. 28–58). London: Tavistock, 1952.

Fairbairn, W. R. D. (1943a). The repression and the return of bad objects (with special references to the "war neuroses"). *British Journal of Medical Psychology, 19*: 327–341. In: *Psychoanalytic Studies of the Personality* (pp. 59–81). London: Tavistock, 1952.

Fairbairn, W. R. D. (1944). Endopsychic structure considered in terms of object-relationships. *International Journal of Psychoanalysis, 25*: 70–92. In: *Psychoanalytic Studies of the Personality* (pp. 82–132). London: Tavistock, 1952.

Fairbairn, W. R. D. (1951b). Addendum. In: *Psychoanalytic Studies of the Personality* (pp. 133–136). London: Tavistock, 1952.

Fairbairn, W. R. D. (1952). *Psychoanalytic Studies of the Personality*. London. Tavistock.

Fairbairn, W. R. D. (1954b). Observations on the nature of hysterical states. *British Journal of Medical Psychology, 27*: 105–125. In: D. E. Scharff & E. F. Birtles (Eds.), *From Instinct to Self: Selected Papers of W. R. D. Fairbairn, Volume I: Clinical and Theoretical Papers* (pp. 13–40). Northvale, NJ: Jason Aronson, 1994.

Mitchell, S. A. (1981). The origins and nature of the "object" in the theories of Klein and Fairbairn. In: J. A. Grotstein & D. B. Rinsley (Eds.), *Fairbairn and the Origins of Object Relations* (pp. 66–87). New York: Guilford Press, 1994.

Mitchell, S. A. (2000). *Relationality: From Attachment to Intersubjectivity*. Hillsdale, NJ: Analytic Press.

Odgen, T. H. (1983). The concept of internal object relations. In: J. A. Grotstein & D. B. Rinsley (Eds.), *Fairbairn and the Origins of Object Relations* (pp. 88–111). New York: Guilford Press, 1994.

Odgen, T. H. (1990). *The Matrix of the Mind: Object Relations and the Psychoanalytic Dialogue*. Northvale, NJ: Jason Aronson.

Scharff, J. S., & Scharff, D. E. (1998). *Object Relations Individual Therapy*. Northvale, NJ: Jason Aronson.

Symington, N. (1994). The tradition of Fairbairn. In: J. A. Grotstein & D. B. Rinsley (Eds.), *Fairbairn and the Origins of Object Relations* (pp. 211–221). New York: Guilford Press, 1994.

CHAPTER THIRTY-TWO

Fairbairn's accomplishment is good science

Joseph Schwartz

Introduction

I do not intend to discuss the contentious subject of whether psychoanalysis is a science or not. Nor do I intend to justify Freud's characterisation of psychoanalysis as "our science". And I do not intend to explore the very real differences between the various fields of science such as those between the mathematised science of physics, the descriptive science of molecular biology, the observational science of palaeontology and the so-called gold standard of the controlled clinical trial of medical science.

Instead I ask the reader to work with me to compare Fairbairn's achievement to a classic of the scientific literature. As Feynman (1967) in his famous Messenger lectures, "The Character of Physical Law", explained it, new laws of nature are very difficult to formulate because not only must they incorporate the new, they must incorporate the old as a special case.

Feynman had in mind any number of examples familiar to every student of physics. The simplest perhaps is Einstein's special theory of relativity which replaced Newton's mechanics. The theory of relativity is now common engineering knowledge, as in the construction of the high energy particle accelerators recently in the news because of the apparent discovery of the Higgs boson.

Feynman's point is that Einstein's reformulation of Newton's laws of motion, titled "On the Electrodynamics of Moving Bodies", incorporated the new, the discovery in the nineteenth century that light was an electromagnetic signal of finite velocity, and incorporated the old by reducing to Newton's laws of motion when the velocity of the moving body was small compared to the velocity of light (Einstein, 1905; Schwartz & McGuiness, 1979).

The main point

So let us look at Fairbairn's reformulation (1946a) of Freud's theory of the human inner world—human beings are not pleasure seeking, they are object seeking:

> ... the ultimate principle from which the whole of my special views are derived may be formulated in the general proposition that libido is not primarily pleasure seeking, but object seeking. The clinical material on which this proposition is based may be summarised in the protesting cry of a patient to this effect—"You're always talking about my wanting this and that desire satisfied; but what I really want is a father." (p. 137)

If we want to be generous to Melanie Klein, we could say that Fairbairn has incorporated Klein's concept of object relations, based on her child observations, however questionable, into Freud's drive theory to make a new fundamental law of the human inner world. Fairbairn's law, that the human being (libido) is primarily relationship seeking, is a fundamental law of human psychology. Fairbairn was the first to see it clearly. Of course it is always the case that great discoveries are made years before they are inevitable (Stent, 1972). Bowlby, Suttie, Sullivan, and even Winnicott, though he would not admit it, were all looking in the same direction as Fairbairn.

But Fairbairn (1946a) did very good science in the sense of Feynman's definition. He showed that Freud's theory of pleasure seeking was a special case of object relations. In Fairbairn's reformulation, pleasure seeking is a deterioration of object relations.

> ... from the point of view of object relations psychology, explicit pleasure-seeking represents a deterioration of behaviour ... The fact is that simple tension-relieving is really a safety valve process. It is thus not a means of achieving libidinal aims, but of mitigating the failure of these aims. (pp. 139–140)

When the human connection fails, pleasure seeking becomes a solution to the fundamental need of the human being for, in Bowlby's word, attachment. No other psychoanalytic theorist has achieved the step of showing how alternative theories fit into their proposed innovation. Fairbairn was a very good scientist.

> The real position would thus appear to be that my views consist largely of a reinterpretation of Freud's views on the basis of a differing set of underlying scientific principles (ibid., p. 149).

From the basic principle that libido is primarily object seeking comes Fairbairn's formulation of the internalisation of unsatisfying experiences as a so-called bad object and its subsequent internal splitting into an exciting and rejecting object. Fairbairn's "Basic Endopsychic Situation" is well known, and there is no need to summarise it here. But the fact that his views follow from a fundamental, dare we say it?, scientific principle has been shoved under the rug.

One important consequence of the failure to recognise just how fundamental Fairbairn's achievement is is the consistent distortion of his views around so-called good and bad objects. In Fairbairn's model the internalisation process always involves the "bad", not a "good" object.

It is always the "bad" object that is internalised in the first instance, since it is difficult to find any motive for the internalisation of objects which are satisfying and "good". (Fairbairn, 1944, p. 93)

The point is that "good" experiences, that is, satisfactory experiences, simply get metabolised into the growing child's development/sense of self. Fairbairn argues that satisfactory experiences do not become internal objects. I believe this is in fact the case. We see it clinically all the time.

When I argued Fairbairn's model out with a well-known object relational colleague she finally said in exasperation, "But I want to have a good object." This is undisciplined, unfortunately a practice all too common within psychoanalysis where almost anything goes as long as it sounds good. In particular, I have in mind the excesses of Melanie Klein and Jacques Lacan (Schwartz, 1999). Marjorie Brierley (1942) wrote to Klein that her attitude to the work left something to be desired: "Various labels have been attached to this subtle something in attitude from time to time. They might be summed up in the phrase 'insufficiently scientific'."

Psychoanalysis may or may not be science according to one's definition. But with the exception of Fairbairn it certainly has lacked the discipline to insist on getting things right. What other theorist was able to create a synopsis of their views (Fairbairn, 1951a, 1963a)? Only Fairbairn has had the depth of understanding to be able to summarise his views concisely and clearly. That kind of clarity is the sign of good science.

Fine points

I would guess that we all have our own favourite Fairbairn. I particularly like his reformulation of the stages of psychological development. The human being develops from a stage of infantile dependence into a long transitional stage arriving at a final stage of adult dependence. I like his characterisation of the human adult as having adult dependency needs, that is, dependence on human relationship. This follows, of course, from his basic principle that the human being is relationship seeking. But it is also radical in our culture where the instrumental use of the human being is the rule rather than the exception and where the fundamental human need for relationship is routinely violated and exploited.

Finally, I am perhaps in a tiny minority of clinicians who are tickled pink by Fairbairn's neat recasting of obsession, hysteria, phobia, and paranoia as techniques to deal with the splitting of bad experience into exciting and rejecting objects: hysteria is the exciting object projected outwards and the rejecting object retained inwards, paranoia is the reverse, the rejecting object is projected outwards and the exciting object retained inwards, while in obsession both exciting and rejecting objects are internal, and in phobia both exciting and rejecting objects are external (Fairbairn, 1941, pp. 45–46).

An aside

Science has become totemic in our society (Lewontin, 1991). It is the great legitimator, as in the selling of patent medicines, at present by the advertising agencies hired by Big Pharma.

"Scientifically proven … It is a scientific fact that …." The scientific fact is an upmarket version of the street saying, "It's a true fact."

Physics is at the very top of the scientific totem pole because of its mathematics. A wonderful print by US artist Brian Andreas (1995) titled "Higher Maths" has two brightly coloured abstract characters saying: "We looked at the numbers of the blackboard & after awhile I finally asked if they made sense to him & he said no, I think they're there just to keep the riff-raff out." Indeed. Both Galileo and Newton used maths to keep the church out and the practice has continued since (Schwartz, 1992).

Physics is the relationship between measurable things like force, mass, and acceleration. Measurement means numbers. Numbers are arithmetic. And algebra is symbolic arithmetic as in the formulas $F = ma$ or $E = mc^2$. But it is the relationship between the numbers that is the point of physics, not the fact that the things are measurable.

But why are numbers so mystified? Or, as clinicians we can ask, why are the sciences involving numbers called hard science? What is the word "hard" doing there? The corollary, of course, is that psychology is called a soft science. Hello. One might wonder what Freud would make of this.

Conclusion

Fairbairn's accomplishment of discovering and/or naming the fundamental law of human psychology, that the human being is fundamentally relationship seeking, is even more striking because one simply does not expect there to be great generalisations in psychology. Not only is every human being different, but also every biological species is the product of 3.5 billion years of evolutionary history. As Max Delbruck (1946) famously observed about biological species: "You cannot explain so wise an old bird in a few simple words" (p. 10). Nevertheless, there are two great generalisations in biology: (almost) all organisms are composed of cells; (almost) every living organism has genetic material consisting of double stranded DNA. You can take out the "(almosts)" if you do not define a virus as an organism.

In psychology there is one great generalisation, Fairbairn's: the human being is relationship seeking. And (almost all) human psychopathology follows from the breakdown of human relationships. As Feynman (1992) puts it: "This is common to all our laws; they all turn out to be simple things, although complex in their actual actions." So it is with Fairbairn. Good stuff.

References

Brierley, M. (1942). Letter to Melanie Klein, 21 May 1942. Brierley Papers, Institute of Psychoanalysis, London.

Delbruck, M. (1946). A physicist looks at biology. In: J. Cairns, G. S. Stent, & J. D. Watson (Eds.), *Phage and the Origins of Molecular Biology* (pp. 9–24). New York: Cold Spring Harbor, 1966.

Einstein, A. (1905). *On the Electrodynamics of Moving Bodies*. New York: Dover.

Fairbairn, W. R. D. (1941). A revised psychopathology of the psychoses and neuroses. *International Journal of Psychoanalysis*, 22(3, 4): 250–279. In: *Psychoanalytic Studies of the Personality* (pp. 28–58). London: Tavistock, 1952.

Fairbairn, W. R. D. (1944). Endopsychic structure considered in terms of object-relationships. *International Journal of Psychoanalysis, 25*: 70–92. In: *Psychoanalytic Studies of the Personality* (pp. 82–136). London: Tavistock, 1952.

Fairbairn, W. R. D. (1946a). Object-relationships and dynamic structure. *International Journal of Psychoanalysis, 27*: 30–37. In: *Psychoanalytic Studies of the Personality* (pp. 137–151). London: Tavistock, 1952.

Fairbairn, W. R. D. (1951a). A synopsis of the development of the author's views regarding the structure of the personality. In: *Psychoanalytic Studies of the Personality* (pp. 162–179). London: Tavistock, 1952.

Fairbairn, W. R. D. (1963a). Synopsis of an object-relations theory of the personality. *International Journal of Psychoanalysis, 44*: 224–225. In: D. E. Scharff & E. F. Birtles (Eds.), *From Instinct to Self: Selected Papers of W. R. D. Fairbairn, Volume I: Clinical and Theoretical Papers* (pp. 155–156). Northvale, NJ: Jason Aronson, 1994.

Feynman, R. P. (1967). *The Character of Physical Law*. With an introduction by Paul Davies. London: Penguin, 1992.

Lewontin, R. C. (1991). *Biology as Ideology*. London: Penguin.

Schwartz, J., & McGuiness, M. (1979). *Einstein for Beginners*. London: Icon.

Schwartz, J. (1992). *The Creative Moment: How Science Made Itself Alien to Western Culture*. London: Cape.

Schwartz, J. (1999). *Cassandra's Daughter: A History of Psychoanalysis in Europe and America*. London: Viking/Penguin. Reissued Karnac, 2003.

Stent, G. S. (1972). Prematurity and uniqueness in scientific discovery. *Scientific American, 227*, December: 84–93.

CHAPTER THIRTY-THREE

Fairbairn and partitive conceptions of mind*

Tamas Pataki

Partitive conceptions of mind in philosophy

In the second of his *Meditations* Descartes wrote: "I am unable to distinguish any parts within myself. I understand myself to be something quite single and complete" (1642). Here Descartes identifies himself with his mind or soul, a conception akin to a pre-philosophical intuition that in each of us something inner, unified, an essential "me" is the locus of perception, deliberation, decision, and agency. That is not the only way in which to understand personal identity but some such conception underlies our everyday understanding and expectation of others, our moral attitudes to them, and our various contractual and judicial institutions. Personal unity (and continuity) seem to be ineliminable conditions of self-understanding and the understanding of others in social arrangement.

However, the conditions are strained in various circumstances. The most striking of these are multiple personality disorder and some psychoses, but there are others. Philosophers for a long time have been concerned with four sets of such circumstances: ambivalence, *akrasia* (weakness of the will), self-deception, and wishful thinking. I want to say a few words about these concepts, unfamiliar perhaps to the psychoanalytic reader.

The idea that people have two or more souls, or that their souls can undergo division or be torn in conflict were features, in different forms, of the Siberian shamanism that entered Greek thought in the seventh century BCE, home-grown Orphism, and the later Manichaean conceptions of Persian religion (Burkert, 2004; Dodds, 1951). But Plato was the first to formulate

---

*I wish to thank Agnes Petocz and Graham S. Clarke for comments on several themes in this chapter which have much improved it.

such issues in recognisably philosophical ways and provided the earliest arguments for mental partition. He was exercised by the phenomena of ambivalence and *akrasia*, and the doctrine that goes under his teacher's name: the Socratic paradox.

Socrates had maintained that nobody willingly errs. In *Protagoras* (358d) Plato has him say: "It is not in human nature to be prepared to go for what you think is bad in preference to what you think is good." Everybody acts in what they perceive to be their own interests; failure to so act is caused by defective knowledge, not by a defect in desire or motive. The trouble is that this doctrine seems manifestly false. People often do knowingly act against their best interests; they take the inferior course knowing that there is a better course. They smoke cigarettes knowing it will kill them, enter into destructive relationships knowing it will hurt them. How is that possible? The solution advanced in Plato's *Republic* is to partition the mind into three conflicting elements: reason, appetite or desire, and the third—*thumos*—rendered variously as spirit, anger, pride, or indignation. Reason seeks the Good but may be overwhelmed by the other elements: reason is not master in its own house.

But why partition and not just acknowledgement of the obvious fact that people are often riven by conflicting desires, fail to integrate their beliefs, and harmonise their dispositions? Plato has several arguments (see, e.g., *Republic*, 434 f.), none of them strong; but combined with the religious conceptions, the phenomenology of conflict and multiplicity, and the tendency of Greek thought to group mental functions with affinity into faculties, Plato's conceptual innovation offers reasonable explanation of at least some inner conflict, the phenomenology of mental dissociation and *akrasia*. Consider Medea in Euripides's play written about the middle of the fifth century BCE. Just before she is about to vengefully murder her children Medea cries: "I know what wickedness I am about to do: but the *thumos* is stronger than my purposes, *thumos*, the root of man's worst acts." Whether there is unity beneath the seeming multiplicity in Medea's conflicted mind is a question to which we will return.

But turn first to self-deception. The conceptually central cases are those modelled on interpersonal deception, though a very diverse range of phenomena have been considered under this heading in the vast literature (Rorty, 1988). In the simplest cases of deception, when A deceives B, A intentionally gets B to believe a proposition that A does not believe. Deception involves lying with the intention to deceive (inadvertent misleading is not deceiving), and lying generally involves passing off as true something the liar believes to be false. (Possibly A can lie by passing off a proposition he believes true—if for example, A tells the truth believing that B will believe the opposite of what A tells. Also, A can lie without deceiving because B may not believe him, and A can lie without intending to deceive if, for example, A knows that B is not going to believe him anyway.) Putting aside the complications, when I deceive myself I am, on this model, both A and B, so in deceiving myself I both believe some proposition and also not believe it.

Such doxastic inconsistency is a problem, and it becomes acute when belief engages with action. Suppose I believe that it is raining but also that it is not raining; will I carry an umbrella? The problem is defused if we suppose that the relevant motivational structures (of beliefs, desires, affects) are segregated, and that one or the other is deactivated. (Repression and splitting of the ego are intended to answer to such phenomena.) This kind of dissociation may not stretch common sense psychology to breaking, however, because it merely extends what we well know: that our doxastic and conative fields are not fully integrated and can be dis-integrated. But there is worse. In self-deception I am the *agent* of my deception. How do I manage to get myself to believe what I do not?

David Pears (1984, p. 79) describes a girl who "persuaded herself that her lover was not unfaithful … (but avoided) … a particular café because she believed that she might find him there with her rival …." Let us put this in a psychoanalytic frame and suppose that consciously she was persuaded of her lover's fidelity, and the troubling belief that he was unfaithful was unconscious or otherwise dissociated. Then she harbours contradictory and segregated beliefs about her lover's fidelity. But the more important point to notice is that by intentionally avoiding the café she seems to be *actively protecting* herself against discovering a belief which she (unconsciously) already has; and that unconscious belief partly motivates her protective activity. How does she manage it? One inviting way of describing this situation is that a part of her, by intentionally avoiding the café, ensures that another part, its client say, would not confront the painful reality of finding her lover with her rival. For the manoeuvre to succeed the intentions and activity of the caring part of herself must be veiled from the client. The right hand cannot know what the left hand is doing. The unconscious intentional agency involved in the girl's actively protecting her conscious self from a painful reality already unconsciously registered leads quite naturally to the supposition of a dissociation into at least two quasi-independent, person-like centres of agency: incompatible beliefs are segregated; acceptable schemas of practical reason setting out the intentions and actions of each part-agency could be articulated; self-solicitous—self-deceiving—activity is veiled from its beneficiary. Such are the gains of radical partition in accommodating self-deception.

Finally, in wishful thinking a desire manufactures a wished-for belief or belief-like representation, either directly or by manufacturing or distorting the evidence for the belief. Many philosophers find the idea of direct causation of belief by desire unproblematic (e.g., Gardner, 1993, p. 21 ff.). I do not, but even if it is granted in some cases, and warranting evidence for the wish-fulfilling belief can somehow be bypassed, there remain the more complex cases where evidence is manufactured—in phantasy, delusion, symptom—or tendentiously selected to warrant the wish-fulfilling belief. And these cases generate much the same sort of pressure for partition as the case of self-deception considered above.

However, the radical dissociation of mind into autonomous, person-like agencies has been rejected by philosophers, in the main. (Among many others, Davidson, 1982; De Sousa, 1976; Gardner, 1993; Graham, 2010; Hopkins, 1995; Johnston, 1988; Lear, 1998; Moore, 1984; Thalberg, 1974. It is endorsed, with differences, in Pataki, 1996, 2003; Pears, 1984; Rorty, 1988. Davidson has been enlisted on the side of strong partition in Clarke, 2006, but though Davidson has argued for segregating constellations of propositional attitudes, he has warned against "going so far as to demand that we speak of parts of the mind as independent agents" (1982, p. 304).)

There are persuasive reasons for rejection. I mention only a few that bear directly on psychoanalytic perspectives. Gardner (1993) argues that strong partition offends the view of persons as substantial unities embedded in ordinary psychology. He believes (as I do) that psychoanalysis is best understood as an extension of ordinary Intentional ("folk") psychology.[1] This explains, he says, "the importance of the issue of partition for the philosophy of psychoanalysis. At stake is the harmony between psychoanalysis and ordinary psychology: if psychoanalytic theory is partitive, its agreement with ordinary thought is questionable" (p. 7). Moreover, such partition seems to undermine the very concepts it is deployed to explain, for example the reflexive relation in self-deception, where one deceives *oneself*. And the subsistence of autonomous centres of agency within a person leads naturally to a budget of bedevilling questions: who is in charge?, how is sustained intentional action possible?, who is responsible?

Psychoanalysis, of course, has been much more receptive to radical partition.

Freud

By the end of the nineteenth century the idea that the mind can be partitioned into something like separate selves or sub-personalities was no novelty. The diagnosis of demonic possession was replaced by hysteria and multiple personality. Charcot and Janet had both, in their own ways, introduced the idea of split-off parts of the personality implicated in mental illness. Many researchers of the time had inclined to the view that "the human mind was rather like a matrix from which whole sets of subpersonalities could emerge and differentiate themselves" (Ellenberger, 1970, p. 139). Novels and plays about demonic possession, doppelgangers, and split personalities abounded; Dostoyevsky and Robert Louis Stevenson wrote the most enduring ones.

Freud's views evolved against this backdrop of polypsychic conceptions, including of course various conceptions of the unconscious. In the late 1890s Freud's attention shifted from the patient's nervous system and riveted on something so conspicuous that it is likely to be overlooked altogether. He noticed that the most significant objects in the patient's world were other people! This realisation—of the primacy of *object relations* in psychopathology (and, later, in normal psychological development)—was a profound event in the human sciences. However, the depth of Freud's object relational concerns are often underestimated (in the misguided attempt to drive a wedge between instinctual-drive theory and object relational approaches), a perception I would like to remedy here.

Freud's topographical account of mind is not radically partitive. The Ucs. is separated from the Pcs. by censorship, but is not conceived as a person-like agency. The innovations that concern us here, though foreshadowed some years earlier, appear definitively as the structural theory of *The Ego and the Id* (1923b). Freud there links the developmental and object relational perspectives and argues that the internalisation of objects in the course of development significantly structures or partitions the mind into the agencies id, ego, superego. Moreover, the agencies are understood to enter into relations with each other, much as people do. This was something completely new. The philosophical motives for partitioning as noted above turned on the exigencies of irrationality and conflict. Such exigencies are not of course unnoticed in Freud's account, but Freud introduced the idea that the *preconditions* for irrationality and conflict lay in developmental factors, principally the structuring of mind resulting from identification. Although we now know that other factors besides identification are involved in structural differentiation—maturational factors, false self development on the basis of compliance, parental selective attunement (Stern, 1985), and so on—the vicissitudes of identification, especially in clinical contexts, retain a pre-eminent place in psychoanalytic thought.

In Freud's account, identification is motivated principally by inability to relinquish intensely libidinised objects. "It may be", he says, "that ... identification is the sole condition under which the id can give up its objects" (1923b, p. 29). Identification preserves relationships: we make of ourselves a model of an object and enter into reflexive relationship with it. Freud puts this colourfully: "When the ego assumes the features of the object, it is forcing itself, so to speak, upon the id as a love object and is trying to make good the id's loss by saying: 'Look, you can love me too—I am so like the object'" (p. 30). In becoming like the object we adopt some of the repertoire, perspectives, characteristics, and, critically, the attitudes that the object was perceived as having towards us. We internalise and adopt roles or personae, though not necessarily public ones.

On the Freudian account the ego and superego are not merely phantasised as agents, or the Intentional objects of phantasies, or phantastic misrepresentations of the person; they *are* agents. The ego's agential character is evident in almost everything Freud says about it. As regards the superego, it "enjoys a certain degree of autonomy, follows its own intentions and is independent of the ego for its supply of energy ..." (1933a, p. 92). It is a *grade* in the ego, and when it takes the ego as object then "all the interplay between an external object and the ego as a whole, with which our study of the neuroses has made us acquainted, may possibly be repeated upon this new scene of action" (1921c, p. 62).

The recognition of these intrapsychic relationships accompanied the clinical material, particularly melancholia, paranoia, and the negative therapeutic reaction. Freud tells how forcibly he had been struck by the clinical picture of melancholia: "... the ego [is] divided, fallen apart into two pieces, one of which rages against the second" (ibid., p. 109); and "... during a melancholic attack [the] superego becomes over severe, abuses the poor ego, humiliates it and ill-treats it, threatens it with the direst punishments, reproaches it for actions in the remotest past ... as though it had spent the whole interval collecting accusations ..." (1933a, p. 61).

Delusions of self-observation in some patients also suggested partition (ibid., p. 59). In linking the unconscious sense of guilt to the need for punishment, and both to resistance (and to moral masochism) Freud presciently recognised that resistance emanated not only from the superego but also from the ego which had developed a masochistic attachment to the superego. "... the need for punishment, is an instinctual manifestation on the part of the ego, which has become masochistic under the influence of a sadistic superego; it is a portion, that is to say, of the instinct towards internal destruction present in the ego, employed for forming an erotic attachment to the superego" (1930a, p. 136).

These and many other passages describe erotic, aversive, and malevolent relations between the id, ego, and superego (e.g., 1921c, p. 62; 1923b, pp. 56, 58; 1933a, p. 58). Notice that the conflicts are not merely conflicts of desires or beliefs; they are more like a conflict of arms. The conflicts involve aggression, triumph, humiliation, and suffering.

There is one more point. The structural differentiation which creates the macro-agencies ego, superego, and id, does not, in Freud's view, necessarily impose disunity in the self. It creates only the preconditions for dissociation and conflict. Freud's insistence on unity is frequently overlooked.

> We were justified, I think, in dividing the ego from the id, for there are certain considerations which necessitate the step. On the other hand the ego is identical with the id, and is merely a specially differentiated part of it. If we think of this part by itself in contradistinction to the whole, *or if a real split has occurred between the two*, the weakness of the ego becomes evident.

> But if the ego remains bound up with the id and indistinguishable from it, then it displays its strength. The same is true of the relation between ego and superego. In many situations the two are merged; and as a rule we can only distinguish the one from the other *when there is a tension or conflict between them*. (1926d, p. 97, my italics)

Such passages cast in deep relief our uncertainty about the precise way in which Freud's conception of the agencies should be understood. However, I think that the following propositions can be supported:

i. Freud conceived of the structures or agencies as capable of entering into a broad range of mutual "personal" relations which can only be partially characterised as arising from conflict of motives and beliefs, for example, sadomasochistic relations.
ii. They are conceived as autonomous centres of agency with their own perspectives, motives, capacity for intentional action and for representing the other agencies, and a degree of mutual opacity.
iii. Despite (i) and (ii), Freud enjoined some kind of underlying unity in the mind.

I want now to turn to Fairbairn who advanced, or almost advanced, the first two, though not the third, of these propositions to their logical conclusion.

Fairbairn

Whereas Freud saw structuralisation largely as an inevitable developmental process proceeding even without conflict—the id growing up, as it were, and the ego being socialised—Fairbairn adopts a conflictual model in which structuralisation occurs because the caring (usually maternal) environment is inadequate. (A notable corollary, emphasised by Clarke (2006), is that pathological structuralisation is, in principle, avoidable; and may be undone, through therapy or other means.) The neonate's ego is unitary and is confronted with an object in some measure unsatisfactory. Attempting to improve its external circumstances the infant internalises the unsatisfactory object. (Fairbairn modified his views about the internalisation of the earliest objects, but that is not germane here.) However, the price of purchasing outer security is inner insecurity. The internalised object retains the characteristics reflecting maternal failures: specifically, an exciting, tantalising aspect and a rejecting aspect. So the internal situation now confronting the child is similar to the earlier external one and a second defensive process is set in train. The ego splits off these bad aspects, leaving it with three internal objects: the exciting object, the rejecting object, and a satisfying nucleus that becomes attached to the conscious central ego as an ideal object. The two remaining bad objects are then repressed; but since parts of the ego remain "attached" or "devoted" to them, these parts of the ego are also repressed. "We thus appear to be driven", Fairbairn concludes, "to the necessity of assuming a certain multiplicity of egos" (1952, pp. 89–90).

The endopsychic situation now consists of a central ego (CE) attached to the relatively satisfying ideal object (IO), an anti-libidinal ego (AE) attached to the rejective object (RO), and a libidinal ego (LE) attached to the exciting object (EO). At a later stage good objects are internalised as defence against internal bad objects. The Freudian superego now appears as a conglomeration of characteristics of the AE, RO, and the augmented IO. Fairbairn claims, rightly I believe, that the permutations of internal relationships afforded by this endopsychic model allows for greater explanatory resource than Freud's tripartite model. The permutations underlie many recognised clinical conditions and can be seen perspicuously to perpetuate earlier unsatisfactory interpersonal relationships. For example, the AE displays an "uncompromisingly aggressive attitude … towards the libidinal ego … based on the latter's cathexis of the exciting object and its own cathexis of the rejecting object; and it is thus a reflection of the original ambivalence of the individual towards his libidinal objects" (ibid., p. 171). The AE's attack on the EO represents persistence of the child's original resentment against the temptress, the tantalising mother who fails to satisfy the very need she excites (p. 115). But it does not appear to be Fairbairn's view that the subsidiary egos are *identified* with their objects, only that they cathect or are "devoted" to them. Then why, it may be asked, should they take on their object's attitudes? Why, for example, should the AE embody the child's hatred of his libidinal needs unless it acquired these from the RO by identification, the RO's attitudes in turn reflecting perceived parental hatred? For modification of this kind in the character of the ego(s) seems to require, as we noted above, the assimilation of a role—of the *modus operandi* of hatred, say. It would seem necessary to recognise that the roles of the subsidiary egos *are* effected through their identification with, and not just their cathexis of, internal objects. And this is a step which some theorists have taken (e.g., Grotstein, 2009; Ogden, 1993).

A further factor has to be considered at this point. Fairbairn correctly observed that Melanie Klein had failed to explain how incorporative phantasy could give rise to internal objects as endopsychic structures (1952, p. 154). They could not be "figments of phantasy" and must therefore be recognised as structures. Since they are endopsychic structures, Fairbairn reasoned, "… they must be themselves in some measure dynamic; and it should be added that they must derive their dynamic quality from their cathexis by ego structures" (p. 177).

Again, Fairbairn appears not to go so far as to identify internal objects with ego-structures; he says that they acquire their dynamism from being cathected by ego-structures. But how they do so is unclear. Ogden (1993) and others have taken the further step of attempting to explain the dynamism of internal objects as a consequence of their identification with parts of the ego (cf. Clarke, 2006, p. 76, who suggests that Fairbairn did take this step). "In brief," says Ogden, "internal objects are subdivisions of the ego that are heavily identified with an object representation while maintaining the capacities of the whole ego for thought, perception, and feeling … The fact that this structure (the internal object) is experienced as non-self is accounted for by means of its profound identification with the object" (1993, p. 150).

If we, too, take this step, we really do have a multiplicity of egos!—and a multiplicity of problems. An original unitary ego is fragmented into at least six person-like entities—three egos and three related internal objects, all of which can take over and act like egos under appropriate circumstances. The fundamental condition of personal unity that underlies our ascriptions of agency and responsibility, that enables us to understand others and ourselves as persons, seems utterly lost. Who is in charge? If different subsidiary egos or constellations of them assume "control" at different times, on what principles are these shifts in agential dominance determined?

In the "Controversial Discussions" Fairbairn stated that "… internal objects should be regarded as having an organised structure, an identity of their own, an endopsychic existence and an activity as real within the inner world as those of any objects in the outer world" (quoted in Clarke, 2006, p. 56). If internal objects are to be regarded as organised, person-like agents then Fairbairn is certainly right: they must be provided with identity conditions and specification of mental content. What is known of their identity conditions, motives, and character in general? It seems to me that sometimes there is something, but never much. In the course of therapy some re-identifiable figures with, let us say, attitudinal consistency, will regularly emerge (or be inferred) in phantasy or action. It is important also that these figures seem to know a great deal about the person's inner life, including her unconscious motivations—a feature Freud noted of the superego. But we do not attribute to the subsidiary egos the features of full personhood, most important, first person perspective in which (in Locke's phrase) they are selves to themselves; or wonder about their virtues and vices, their perspicacity, sensitivity, or serenity. These facts suggest that the independence of the subsidiary egos, if independence it is, is considerably circumscribed.

Parts of persons

How are we to understand the kind of radical partition apparently entailed by Fairbairn's account of dynamic subsidiary egos and internal objects? One response accepts partition but ignores its problematic consequences: in ordinary conscious experience, it is observed, the cracks are "smoothed over", somehow. This seems to be Stephen Mitchell's (1993) position. It is clearly inadequate. Another possible response is to interpret the endopsychic situation in the manner of Plato's division of mind. The divisions differ in their preferences, and the actions of the whole are determined by "economic" considerations, or a kind of vectorial addition or social choice. Glymour (1991) interprets Freud in this manner. One of several difficulties with this account is that it is silent on the complex intrapsychic relations, irreducible to motivational states, which, as we have seen, are features in Freud's and Fairbairn's later work.

A third response is to insist that partition is only apparent, an epiphenomenon generated by the colourful metaphorical language occasionally used by Freud and perpetuated by Klein, Fairbairn, and others. Such divisions as there are, it is claimed, are to be found in the neurological sub-stratum, in the opposition of drive structures, or other more complex sets of motivational structures. The attributions to these structures of complex Intentional properties (as in the clinical vignettes below) are merely metaphorical, clinically useful perhaps, but without ontological significance. A range of otherwise quite different views are consistent with this approach, such as Boag (2005); Hartmann (1964); Hopkins (1995, 2012); Maze (2009); Sandler and Sandler (1998).

A final response, broadly Kleinian in inspiration, denies partition by rendering passive the entities Fairbairn asserted were active or dynamic. Internal objects and subsidiary egos do not *actually* hate or attack the self; they are phantasised or experienced as hating and attacking the self. The ego is not split in reality, it is experienced *as if* it were split, a consequence perhaps of disssociative phantasies such as those underlying projective identification. This attractive proposal still leaves open the status of internal objects. On one account they are identified with more or less permanent phantasies (Segal, 1991). This view is vulnerable to Fairbairn's criticism. However, more sophisticated accounts along Kleinian lines according to which internal objects are the Intentional objects of phantasies or dispositions to phantasise, are not vulnerable (Wollheim, 1984, 1993c). I believe that despite their appeal these approaches are also problematic (Pataki, 2000, 2003). But rather than trying to disable them here I want to explore a fifth view, one that may reconcile partition with personal unity.

Let us step back. In his early work Freud used "das Ich" ambiguously to signify sometimes the whole person, sometimes a sub-personal, neural structure, and sometimes the conscious mind. After *The Ego and the Id* (1923b) he reserved the term translated as "ego" for one structure within the mind constituting together with the id and the superego the whole mind, psychical apparatus, or "psychical personality" (1933a). Neither Freud nor Fairbairn tell us precisely what structures are, but presumably they are more or less stable sets of beliefs, desires, dispositions to affectivity, skills, capacities, susceptibilities, and so on. To speak of mind, after all, is shorthand for various capacities and powers that a person can exercise. It is notable that Freud considered the id as a structure. He writes of "the structures we have assumed to exist—the ego, the superego and the id" (1923b, p. 42); the ego, however, is organised, the id is not. Fairbairn overlooks this point and that causes considerable mischief in his critique of Freud's view of drives and object relations. But the fact that both consider structures to be "person-like" has the happy consequence that the language of personal relations, including of course the Intentional or commonsense psychological idiom, can be enlisted in the description of intrapsychic relations.

Rejecting Freud's tripartite structure, "ego", for Fairbairn denotes the whole mind. But Freud was already on a slippery slope and Fairbairn and those who follow him have slipped further down. The ego, the "I", cannot be my mind because I am not my mind. My mind is not balding and cannot drink a cup of coffee. "I" does not refer to some inner thing, and is not referentially ambiguous either, referring now to my mind, now to my body: in my mouth it refers to this psycho-physical person, me.

Fairbairn, to my knowledge, always used the language of subsidiary egos, the language of mind. Most who have followed him have slipped into referring to these egos as part-selves, sub-selves or subsidiary selves (Clarke, 2006; all the other contributors in Pereira etc). They implicitly conceive of selves as *things*, things that are "in" a person, that a person "has" and "really is". On these views, selves are inner agents that can enter into relationships with other selves, threaten, sabotage, suffer, and so on. But this conception of *self* as an inner agentive entity is a confusion. My inner self is not balding and if I *have* a self, who is the "I" who mysteriously has it? *Self* understood as an inner thing, as boss-of-the-body (Dennett, 1991), is philosophical illusion exploiting a grammatical peculiarity: the fact that we can separate such terms as "myself", "yourself", and suppose that my self is something I have and your self is something you have (Bennett & Hacker, 2003, ch. 12). There are however legitimate uses of "self". It may be used synonymously with "person", as when I say "Why don't you just take your self out of here!" And it is often used (confusingly) as stand-in for "sense of self", "self-image", "self-conception", or "self-representation". We see ourselves in mirrors, are reflected in other people's attitudes towards us, sense our bodies and mental states, and form conceptions of what we are like. But selves in *that* sense are not independent agents, not subsidiary egos, though they may hugely affect how persons behave.

So let us turn to *person* and begin with Locke's famous (1706) definition: "a thinking intelligent Being, that has reason and reflection, and can consider itself as itself, the same thinking thing in different times and places …" (1968, Bk. 2, chap. 27, sec. 11).

I want to consider only one of the conditions Locke regards as necessary for personhood. Persons have reason and reflection, are rational: not, of course, in that they always use the best evidence and make the right inferences; but in being creatures that deliberate, decide, and *act for reasons*. Fully explicating that notion is difficult but it will be sufficiently clear intuitively for our purposes. I think it will be granted that if subsidiary egos and internal objects do not act for reasons they are not independent centres of agency.

Consider now this vignette. A patient of Harry Guntrip's:

> … would rave against girl children and in fantasy would describe how she would crush a girl child if she had one, and would then fall to punching herself (which perpetuated the beatings her mother gave her). One day I said to her, "You must be terrified being hit like that." She stopped and stared and said, "I'm not being hit. I'm the one that's doing the hitting." (Guntrip, 1968, p. 191)

From an external perspective we see a person wracked by internal conflict punching herself. When she speaks she does not seem to speak for the whole of her. There appear to be at least two perspectives in this person: one from the part doing the punching and one from the part being punched. They appear to be mutually alienated: the speaker says she is not being punched, she is doing the punching. This situation is obscure, but examining the patient's development and the way in which internalisation has come to structure her sheds some light on it. We know from Guntrip's observations that she has identified with and taken on (or in) the perspective of a punitive mother while retaining the aspect of the detested child she may at bottom feel herself to be. One natural way of describing the situation in Fairbairn's terms is that a part of the ego, the LE, is being maltreated by another punitive part, the AE. The LE is unconsciously perceived by the salient part under the aspect of a despicable, dependent being; while from the LE's perspective the AE part appears under the aspect of the punitive mother. Perceiving each other as alien, these parts treat each other as if they were external objects. The patient thus appears to be divided in perspective, subjectivity and agency: in all the terms of strong partition noted earlier.

Here we have a striking enactment of an internal relationship. We can observe such a relationship of even greater complexity played out largely in phantasy in a patient whose "destructive narcissistic organisation" (DNO) pretends to be a friend but is bent on destroying her. (Notice the evident inadequacy of describing these cases as instances of *akrasia*, self-deception, wishful thinking, or as mere conflicts of drive.)

> Only very gradually did she understand that the idealization of her destructiveness did not give her freedom, and that this was a trap into which she had fallen through the hypnotic power of the destructive self which posed as a saviour and friend who pretended to take care of her and give her whatever warmth and food she wanted so that she would not have to feel lonely …. In fact, however, this so-called friend attempted to spoil any contact she was trying to make in relation to work and to people. During analysis she gradually became aware that this exceedingly tyrannical and possessive friend was an omnipotent very destructive part of her self, posing as a

friend, that became very threatening if she attempted to continue cooperation in analysis or any progress in her life. For a long time she felt too frightened to challenge this aggressive force and whenever she came up against this barrier she identified herself with the aggressive narcissistic self and became aggressive and abusive towards me. (Rosenfeld, 1988, p. 117)

Let us consider the cases at an abstract level and say that a *personation* is a person engrossed in a role. The role may largely be determined by salient parental identifications but we need not exclude the influence of maturational factors and experience, or the possibility of personation in which identification plays no part. We can think of the four figures in our vignettes as personations. Personations may be activated simultaneously, as an actor may simultaneously play several roles: for example, when A plays B pretending to be C. Or near simultaneously, as when a child impersonates in play: now I am mummy, now I am daddy, now I am me. (It is instructive that in Klein (1929) and Fairbairn (1931) personifications are regarded as expressions of structural entities.)

In both vignettes the personations have reasons or *motives* for acting as they do. In Guntrip's patient the AE part despises the LE part and abuses it. The LE has perhaps become masochistically attached to the AE. In the false friend case the DNO wishes to keep its subject in submission and sabotages its attempts to escape its thrall. Each personation has a motivational set or script. But there are also reasons for the animation or activation of each personation, which are not reasons *for* the personations. For example, in the punching girl's case there appear to be reasons for activating the AE, representing the rejective aspect of her mother. Guntrip mentions several: identifying with and revivifying the parent sustains a kind of relationship with her; it represents the struggle to preserve an ego; it confers a sense of power on the girl, even if only over her self. We shall say that these are reasons for *activating* a personation. So at any one time the personations have their motives, their own reasons for acting in particular ways, but there may also be a reason why *that* personation is activated at that time. Whose reason? Well, there appear to be several abstract possibilities.

It could be a reason for any other of the personations. There are two people in the front seat and the driver, exhausted, hands over the wheel to the other. The first driver has reasons for heading in a certain direction and also for activating the second driver—he wants to rest etc. The second driver may have different motives from the first and turns the car around. Wanting to turn around was a reason for the second driver but not the first. The question of *who* is in charge at time *t* resolves into the question, who has the wheel? Perhaps there is a kind of chief personation, a backseat driver, who decides who should have the wheel. A person, on this model, is a congery of personations: an actor who is never out of a role, is fully absorbed in them, and does not have a private life. But a kind of unity is preserved because rationality reigns: there are reasons for *which* personation is activated and motives for what the personation does. There is the possibility that the behaviour of a person thus constituted may be understood, because we understand persons acting for reasons.

There are other possibilities. There may be reasons for activation of personations which are reasons for an elusive actor who is never entirely engrossed in a role (and therefore not entirely a personation) but animates them all. Such an actor will have his reasons for playing Hamlet. Hamlet has his reasons for killing Claudius. Hamlet's reasons are not the actor's reasons; the actor has no reason to kill Claudius. The actor activates the Hamlet personation and enacts

Hamlet's motives; and, if the cast is short, he may enact Claudius's role too; but this actor has a private life.

This last abstraction corresponds perhaps to what Guntrip had in mind when he wrote that the human psyche is "the kind of entity that carries on its own internal development by differentiating itself into a number of *dramatis personae* … The one person functions actually as a group of persons and that is the psychologically objective fact that theory has to represent" (1961, p. 138).

We might like to think of this person as a central ego (person) activating *as need be* the subsidiary egos but, being engrossed in the roles that constitute them, losing itself to its own interiority. One ego, then, many roles or personations, sustained as long as they are required. Personal unity, qualified, is preserved; but so, too, is a concept of the subsidiary egos as independent centres of agency satisfying the conditions set out earlier. Whether or not the abstract construction adumbrated here can answer to the complexity of psychic life it is clear that there are in general rational connections between subsidiary egos (and internal objects), and reasons that motivate them. Rosenfeld's patient has reasons for activating the DNO and clinging to it: it provides the illusion of strength, and company. The DNO has reasons (motives) for clinging to the patient while torturing her. If there were not such rational webs then psychotherapy, which may be seen partly as exploration of the reasons a person has for activating personations and partly as moderating the pathological aims which may be written into the motivations of the personations, would be a forlorn task. It is because there are discernible rational connections in persons between subsidiary egos and internal objects—between personations—that it is unnecessary to appeal to Freudian economic or energic principles or the quasi-mechanical principles of chaos theory (D. Scharff, 2002) or related non-Intentional expedients.

But another possibility cannot be excluded, if we may remain one last moment on this abstract plane, in which all rational connections simply break down. The second driver just wrenches the wheel from the first driver's hands for no intelligible reason; and these cases present the greatest difficulty for understanding and psychotherapy.

Note

1. As well as the ordinary usage in which "intentional" qualifies action as "purposeful", "meant", or "aimed at", the term is used in a technical sense which, following a common practice, I capitalise: "Intentional". Intentionality is usually explained as the property of "aboutness", possessed by the mental states ascribed in common-sense psychology to explain human behaviour. Common-sense psychology explains behaviour and relations between mental states by use of the Intentional idioms and the causal and rational connections between their denotations. It is important not to confuse Intentionality with the notion of intentional or purposeful action.

References

Bennett, M. R., & Hacker, P. M. S. (2003). *Philosophical Foundations of Neuroscience*. Malden, MA: Blackwell.

Boag, S. (2005). Addressing mental plurality: justification, objections and logical requirements of strongly partitive accounts of mind. In: N. Mackay & A. Petocz (Eds.), *Realism and Psychology*. Boston, MA: Brill, 2011.

Burkert, W. (2004). *Babylon, Memphis, Persepolis*. Cambridge, MA: Harvard University Press.
Clarke, G. S. (2006). *Personal Relations Theory: Fairbairn, Macmurray and Suttie*. London: Routledge.
Davidson, D. (1982). Paradoxes of irrationality. In: R. Wollheim & J. Hopkins (Eds.), *Freud: A Collection of Critical Essays (2nd edition)*. New York: Anchor.
De Sousa, R. (1976). Rational homunculi. In: A. Rorty (Ed.), *The Identities of Persons*. Berkeley, CA: University of California Press.
Dennett, D. C. (1991). *Consciousness Explained*. London: Penguin.
Descartes, R. (1642). *Meditations On First Philosophy*. In: E. Anscombe & P. T. Geach (Eds.), *Descartes Philosophical Writings*. London: Nelson, 1972.
Dodds, E. R. (1951). *The Greeks and the Irrational*. Berkeley, CA: University of California Press.
Ellenberger, H. F. (1970). *The Discovery of the Unconscious*. New York: Basic.
Fairbairn, W. R. D. (1931). Features in the analysis of a patient with a physical genital abnormality. In: *Psychoanalytic Studies of the Personality* (pp. 197–222). London: Tavistock, 1952.
Fairbairn, W. R. D. (1952). *Psychoanalytic Studies of the Personality*. London: Tavistock. [Reprinted Routledge & Kegan Paul, 1976.]
Freud, S. (1921c). *Group Psychology and the Analysis of the Ego. S. E., 19*. London: Hogarth.
Freud, S. (1923b). *The Ego and the Id. S. E., 19*. London: Hogarth.
Freud, S. (1926d). *Inhibitions, Symptoms and Anxiety. S. E., 20*. London: Hogarth.
Freud, S. (1930a). *Civilization and its Discontents. S. E., 21*. London: Hogarth.
Freud, S. (1933a). *New Introductory Lectures on Psycho-Analysis. S. E., 22*. London: Hogarth.
Gardner, S. (1993). *Irrationality and the Philosophy of Psychoanalysis*. Cambridge: Cambridge University Press.
Glymour, C. (1991). Freud's androids. In: J. Neu (Ed.), *The Cambridge Companion to Freud*. Cambridge: Cambridge University Press.
Graham, G. (2010). *The Disordered Mind*. London: Routledge.
Grotstein, J. S. (2009). *"But at the Same Time and on Another Level"*. London: Karnac.
Guntrip, H. (1961). *Personality Structure and Human Interaction*. London: Hogarth, 1973.
Guntrip, H. (1968). *Schizoid Phenomena, Object Relations and the Self*. London: Hogarth, 1977.
Hartmann, H. (1964). *Essays in Ego Psychology*. New York: International Universities Press.
Hopkins, J. (1995). Irrationality, interpretation and division. In: C. & G. McDonald (Eds.), *Philosophy of Psychology*. Oxford: Blackwell.
Hopkins, J. (2012). Psychoanalysis, representation, and neuroscience: The Freudian unconscious and the Bayesian brain. In: D. Pfaff, A. Fotopoulu, & M. Conway (Eds.), *Couch to the Lab*. Oxford: Oxford University Press.
Johnston, M. (1988). Self-deception and the nature of mind. In: B. P. McLaughlin & A. O. Rorty & (Eds.), *Perspectives on Self-Deception*. Berkeley, CA: University of California Press.
Klein, M. (1929). Personification in the play of children. In: *Love, Guilt and Reparation*. London: Hogarth, 1975.
Lear, J. (1998). *Open Minded*. Cambridge, MA: Harvard University Press.
Locke, J. (1706). *An Essay Concerning Human Understanding*. London: Dent and Sons, 1968.
Maze, J. (2009). *Psychologies of Mind*. R. Henry (Ed.). London: Continuum.
Mitchell, S. A. (1993). *Hope and Dread in Psychoanalysis*. New York: Basic.
Moore, M. (1984). *Law and Psychiatry*. Cambridge: Cambridge University Press.
Ogden, T. H. (1986). *The Matrix of the Mind*. Northvale, NJ: Jason Aronson, 1993.
Pataki, T. (1996). Intention in wish-fulfilment. *Australasian Journal of Philosophy, 74*(1): 17–30.
Pataki, T. (2000). Freudian wish-fulfilment and sub-intentional explanation. In: M. Levine (Ed.), *The Analytic Freud*. London: Routledge.

Pataki, T. (2003). Freud, object relations, agency and the self. In: M. C. Chung & C. Feltham (Eds.), *Psychoanalytic Knowledge*. London: Palgrave.

Pears, D. (1984). *Motivated Irrationality*. Oxford: Clarendon Press.

Pereira, F., & Scharff, D. E. (2002). *Fairbairn and Relational Theory*. London: Karnac.

Rorty, A. O. (1988). The deceptive self: liars, layers and lairs. In: B. P. McLaughlin & A. O. Rorty (Eds.), *Perspectives on Self-Deception*. Berkeley, CA: University of California Press.

Rosenfeld, H. (1987). *Impasse and Interpretation*. London: Tavistock.

Sandler, J., & Sandler, A. M. (1998). *Internal Objects Revisited*. London: Karnac.

Scharff, D. E. (2002). Fairbairn and the self as an organized system: chaos theory as a new paradigm. In: F. Pereira & D. E. Scharff (Eds.), *Fairbairn and Relational Theory*. London: Karnac.

Segal, H. (1991). *Dream, Phantasy and Art*. London: Tavistock Routledge.

Stern, D. N. (1985). *The Interpersonal World of the Infant*. New York: Basic Books.

Thalberg, I. (1974). Freud's anatomies of the self. In: R. Wollheim (Ed.), *Freud: A Collection of Critical Essays*. New York: Anchor.

Wollheim, R. (1984). *The Thread of Life*. Cambridge: Cambridge University Press.

Wollheim, R. (1993). *The Mind and its Depths*. Cambridge, MA: Harvard University Press.

CHAPTER THIRTY-FOUR

Fairbairn and the philosophy of intersubjectivity

James L. Poulton

Fairbairn's theory of the origin and nature of the mind, which posited that the individual self is structured solely and originally through its relationships with objects with which it is inseparably connected from the beginning of life, has long been regarded as one of the earliest and "purest" (Mitchell, 1988, p. 18) representatives of a *relational* model. In advancing such a model, Fairbairn drew a stark contrast with Freud's *drive* model, which viewed the individual as already structured, to a substantial degree, by such pre-relational factors as biological inheritance and instinctual endowment. In Fairbairn's view, one of the chief problems of the Freudian model was that its anachronistic atomism, dualism, and reductionism effectively condemned the mind to an irresolvable solipsistic isolation.

To counter the most problematic implications of Freud's theory, Fairbairn advanced two distinct but related metapsychological hypotheses: (1) libido, from the beginning of life, is inherently object-seeking; and (2) psychic structure and the energy that drives it are inseparable, integrated into "dynamic structures" that cannot be reduced to their component parts. With these two hypotheses, Fairbairn attempted to establish relationality, or intersubjectivity, as an inherent and formative substratum of human subjectivity—and to thereby effect a radical reformulation of the Freudian ego. Where Freud described the ego as a passive recipient of its own experience, borrowing energy from impulses emanating from instincts indifferent to their objects of gratification, the Fairbairnian ego was actively and intimately entangled with its objects, about whom it cared deeply and with whom it sought loving and protective relationships.

Fairbairn, we will discover, argued for two different versions of his two hypotheses. In one version, the ego and its objects are separate and differentiated from the beginning, and the object is regarded as an actual *external* object. In the other version, the ego and its objects are neither separate nor differentiated in the beginning, and only become separate with subsequent experience. In this version, the undifferentiated object effectively plays the role of an *internal* object. Each of these formulations created difficult problems for Fairbairn. In particular, the latter formulation constituted a foundational challenge to the very relational theory to which he was passionately committed.

The struggles Fairbairn underwent in his formulation of his two central hypotheses reflect, with a notable degree of consistency, the struggles which preceding and contemporaneous continental philosophers encountered as they grappled with similar questions of solipsism and intersubjectivity. Given that Fairbairn was himself a philosopher before he became a psychoanalyst, and retained his interest in philosophy throughout his career, the commonality between Fairbairn's and the philosophical treatment of intersubjectivity should not be surprising. What is noteworthy is the extent to which Fairbairn's views, particularly in the more radical formulation of his two hypotheses, reflected the perspectives of philosophers who were on the cutting edge of intersubjective theory in the mid and late twentieth century. The similarities between Fairbairn and these philosophers underscore the extent to which his work was not only reflective of, but also contributory to, some of the most creative solutions to the problem of intersubjectivity to be advanced in our time.

In this chapter, I will first briefly review selected philosophic approaches to intersubjectivity—beginning with Kant's and Husserl's attempts to resolve the problems raised by Descartes's sceptical solipsism, and proceeding to Merleau-Ponty's philosophy of the self as embodied in an inherently interpersonal world. I will then describe Fairbairn's two hypotheses in detail and note the strengths and weaknesses of each version. By comparing Fairbairn's contributions to those of modern philosophy, I hope to not only illuminate the broad philosophic background against which he was working, but also to provide a foundation from which to re-evaluate his two hypotheses. I will suggest such a philosophic re-examination has the potential to identify the points at which Fairbairn's theory might be revised and strengthened, thereby securing more firmly his embrace of a distinctly modern, even postmodern, vision of the foundations of being human.

Philosophic backdrop for Fairbairn's theories

Prior to his interest in psychoanalysis, Fairbairn pursued training in philosophy and theology in Edinburgh and London. His philosophic interests included Schopenhauer, Nietzsche, Kant, Hegel, Lotze, and Aristotle, and he was particularly committed to solving problems posed by the atomism and dualism that had dominated both philosophy and psychology in prior centuries. His interest in Aristotle, for example, stemmed in part from his desire to resolve the conflicts inherent in dualistic views of the mind through a holistic perspective that sees the individual as dynamic, purposeful, and essentially integrated not only with his or her own core motivations, but also with the surrounding social community (Scharff & Birtles, 1994).

Fairbairn's interest in holism and dynamism, in fact, mirrored a similar development that had been gaining influence in Europe since the eighteenth century. Spurred by the epistemological problematic introduced by Descartes in his *Meditations on First Philosophy* (published in 1641), many philosophers had attempted to solve the dual Cartesian problems of scepticism about the existence of external objects and the seemingly impenetrable solipsism following from it. Perhaps the first philosopher to attempt to systematically refute Descartes's "problematic idealism"—his insistence that the existence of other objects is neither a given nor a certainty—was Immanuel Kant in the *Critique of Pure Reason* (published in two editions, in 1781 and 1787).

Kant's argument relied on two key assertions. First, he rejected Descartes's dualistic assumption—that the substance of the mind was different from that of the body—as being inconsistent with observation and as creating a gulf between mind and body that was philosophically impossible to bridge. Second, he argued that the mind's awareness of itself as a temporal succession of representations implies it has already compared itself to a *permanent* object, that is, one that exists in the external world of objective spatiality, outside the mind's temporality. Thus, for Kant, the very nature of consciousness, and of self-consciousness in particular, presupposes access to things beyond ourselves. Although many have suggested Kant's arguments were unsuccessful because he failed to make an adequate distinction between consciousness of objects and those objects as external entities, still his intent was clear: to find a way out of Cartesian solipsism and prove we have immediate access to the things and people around us.

With Kant's and others' critiques of Descartes as a foundation, subsequent philosophers became increasingly sophisticated in their arguments against dualism and solipsism. By the early to mid twentieth century, refutations of solipsism and philosophical defences of such ideas as intersubjectivity, embodiment, and embeddedness within an "interworld" of other minds began to multiply, particularly with the rise of existentialism and existential phenomenology. An immediate precursor of the existential phenomenological movement was Edmund Husserl. In *Ideas* (1913) and *Cartesian Meditations* (1931), Husserl used his "phenomenological reduction" (an investigative method in which the philosopher suspends, or "brackets", overt or latent commitments to the existence of external objects in order to examine the means by which they are constructed or "constituted" by consciousness) to explore the foundations of our awareness of other subjectivities. One of the primary results of this bracketing was, for Husserl, his discovery of a "sphere of ownness" (ibid., p. 92), a region of pure individuality in which resides a primordial ego whose perceptive processes constitute the world and all its objects, and bears them "intentionally within" itself (p. 99).

At first glance, Husserl's idea of the sphere of ownness seems to have painted him into the same corner as Descartes, since such a sphere exhibits a similar kind of solipsistic isolation as did the Cartesian ego. Husserl, however, countered this apparent difficulty by suggesting that the sphere of ownness is found only at the most foundational level of consciousness and that, as soon as consciousness begins to develop into the mind of a particular person, it enters into a "transcendental intersubjectivity" through which both the self and other persons are coevally co-constructed. In other words, in transcendental intersubjectivity "the intersubjective community 'deposits itself (in a stratum)' uniquely *on* the 'world' of the primordial Self" (Schnell, 2010, p. 18), thereby creating both self and other at the same time.

Although some commentators have found Husserl's arguments in favour of intersubjectivity convincing (cf. Schnell, 2010; Zahavi, 2001), the general consensus is that he failed to prove the existence of other minds, and his failure could be traced to his basic concept of consciousness as a perceiving and experiencing, but not active or performative, faculty. By viewing it in this way, Husserl placed consciousness in a reduced and already removed realm of mere thought and perception, implying a transcendental idealism (too similar to Descartes's "problematic idealism") that *definitionally* isolates the mind from real interactions with other subjectivities, and replaces those interactions with only the *idea* of other persons. As Crossley has argued, under Husserl's system "otherness will always be reduced to the experience of otherness" (1996, p. 7), and any meaning the subject might generate is reduced to acts of a constituting consciousness that preclude "the possibility that meanings might be shared or communicated by subjects in an interworld or community" (p. 8).

The apparent failure of Husserl's approach to fully address the question of intersubjectivity spurred other twentieth century philosophers to attempt to correct its weaknesses. Schutz, Buber, Heidegger, Habermas, Derrida, and Foucault have all proposed modernised definitions of the subject, each from their own theoretical orientation, so that it is no longer conceptualised as the Husserlian passive perceptual subject. While there is value in each of these theorists' approaches, the writer whose work I will now review is Merleau-Ponty, in part because his approach shares many of the most convincing points made by the other theorists, and in part because it bears the most consistent similarity to some of Fairbairn's most penetrating insights.

In the early chapters of Merleau-Ponty's *The Phenomenology of Perception* (1962), the more problematic consequences of the Husserlian (and, before him, the Cartesian) subject are spelled out. Because those theories, for example, assume the ego to be a passive recipient of experience, they have concomitantly distorted our conceptualisations of the ego as an active agency. Thus, the ego's "impelling intentions" have necessarily been reduced to "objective moments", its will to "instantaneous fiat", and its execution of actions "given over to a nervous mechanism" (p. 55).

Because of these problematic implications, Merleau-Ponty explicitly denies the chief characteristics of the perceptual subject: "This phenomenal field [of experience] is not an 'inner world', the 'phenomenon' is not a 'state of consciousness', or a 'mental fact', and the experience of phenomena is not an act of introspection or an intuition" (p. 57). In the place of this failed conceptualisation, Merleau-Ponty then begins rebuilding the very concept of the subject, starting with the act of perception.

Perception, in Merleau-Ponty's view, is an act of being in the world, an active relationship between the perceiver and real objects in which the subject is "opened onto" objects by way of being purposively and actively engaged with them. "Consciousness", Merleau-Ponty says, "is in the first place not a matter of 'I think that' but of 'I can'" (1962, p. 137). This real, embodied relationship is neither intermittent nor is it the consequence of the subject's *decision* (á la Descartes) to engage with objects. Rather, it is *originary*, in the sense both that it is present from the beginning and that the subject and object do not precede it, but emerge as experiential and theoretical polarities within its dialectical process.

Merleau-Ponty and his subsequent defenders are careful to emphasise he was not talking about an *internal* process, but a relationship between the subject and the actual world that is *irreducible* to either the subject in its internality, or the object in its materiality. The primary medium of these active and purposive engagements is the body:

> … the normal subject penetrates into the object by perception, assimilating its structure into his substance, and through his body the object directly regulates his movements. This subject-object dialogue, this drawing together, by the subject, of the meaning diffused through the

object, and, by the object, of the subject's intentions … arranges round the subject a world which speaks to him of himself, and gives his own thoughts their place in the world. (ibid., p. 132)

By defining perception as an active, irreducible, and originary opening onto the world of objects, Merleau-Ponty effectively challenges the solipsism of both the Cartesian and the Husserlian world views. A subject characterised by this kind of perception cannot be isolated or disconnected from actual objects because it exists, not in terms of its passive perception of those objects, but of its active and purposive participation with them—even at levels prior to the emergence of the subject or the object itself. Moreover, once Merleau-Ponty established this view of the subject and the nature of perception, the additional step of locating the subject in a "plurality of consciousnesses" (ibid., p. 351) becomes fairly straightforward. If the body, Merleau-Ponty says, is not a detached object of perception but is rather the vehicle of the subject's intimate and irreducible (i.e., *embodied*) engagement with the world, then the body of the other is met precisely in the field of the other's own embodied consciousness. This meeting between the two embodied subjects then provides a platform for an immediacy of understanding about each other. Merleau-Ponty's description of intersubjective knowing will sound familiar to anyone who has studied the phenomenon of mirror neurons:

> A baby of fifteen months opens its mouth if I playfully take one of its fingers between my teeth and pretend to bite it. And yet it has scarcely looked at its face in a glass, and its teeth are not in any case like mine. The fact is that its own mouth and teeth, as it feels them from the inside, are immediately, for it, an apparatus to bite with, and my jaw, as the baby sees it from the outside, is immediately, for it, capable of the same intentions. "Biting" has immediately, for it, an intersubjective significance. It perceives its intentions in its body, and my body with its own, and thereby my intentions in its own body. (ibid., p. 352)

Merleau-Ponty's solution to the problem of solipsism is similar to that of other twentieth-century philosophers in that all have posited a dynamic, purposive, engaged, and performative subject in place of the mere perceptual subject with its dualistic and solipsistic implications. In the next part, we will see that Fairbairn's solution to the same problems in psychoanalysis echoed (in some cases) and presaged (in others) those of continental philosophers, but that his efforts were also undercut by his alternative versions of his two foundational hypotheses.

Object-relatedness and dynamism in Fairbairn

One of Fairbairn's central motivations for developing his metapsychology was his desire to correct the mistakes he believed Freud and Klein had made, particularly in their views of the nature and function of drives and the place of objects—both external and internal—in the formation and maintenance of psychic structure. Freud's theory, which had dominated analytic theorising for several decades, hypothesised that the fundamental aim of instincts is tension-reduction (following the pleasure principle), and that instincts are therefore directed towards an object only accidentally, "in so far as it is found to provide a means of forwarding the pleasure-seeking aim" (Fairbairn, 1956b, p. 131). In addition, Freud's theory had separated "mental structure" (i.e., the guidance the ego provides instincts in aiming them towards appropriate objects) from "mental energy" (the energy the instinct or id-impulse provides), so the two functioned independently of each other and only came together in coordinated action under pressure from the superego.

Fairbairn believed these Freudian hypotheses suffered from several fatal flaws. First, they were internally inconsistent, in that they posited conflict between the ego and the id, or between structure and energy, while at the same time asserting the ego lacks sources of energy with which to enter into that conflict. Second, they rendered the concepts of both energy and structure meaningless, since, according to Fairbairn, only structure gives form to energy, which does not exist without a particular form. Third, they implied a type of "psychological hedonism" that relegated objects—viz., other persons—to a secondary status, which in turn implied that Freud treated social behaviour as an "acquired", rather than inherent, characteristic (ibid., p. 132)—contrary to what Fairbairn believed was incontrovertible observational evidence. And fourth, they imposed an atomistic conceptualisation on a psychic structure that Fairbairn viewed as essentially and originally "organic", "integrated", and "unified" in its approach to relationships with its "natural objects" (1952, 1956b).

For Fairbairn, then, Freud's instinct theory consigned the individual to an ineluctable solipsism in which the primary determinants of experience were overly dissociated, overly intrapsychic, and far too removed from the interpersonal world (Fairbairn, 1952, 1956b; Sutherland, 1994). Similarly, Fairbairn criticised Klein's incorporation of Freud's instinct theory in her early views of the origins of internal objects because it implied those objects were, in Mitchell's terms, "phantasmagoric, solipsistic creations, with no necessary connection to the outside world" (Mitchell, 1994, p. 69).

In response to the atomism and solipsism implicit in Freud's and Klein's theories, Fairbairn advanced his two interrelated but distinct metapsychological ideas, the object-relatedness and the dynamism hypotheses. The object-relatedness hypothesis asserted that the libido is essentially object seeking ("The real libidinal aim is the establishment of satisfactory relationships with objects; and it is accordingly, the object that constitutes the true libidinal goal", 1952, p. 138). Adding to this, the dynamism hypothesis stated that mental structure is inseparable from its source of energy, and that, in contrast to the tension-reducing directionlessness of impulses in Freud's theory, libido is therefore directional and reality-oriented as it strives to attain attachments with those objects. "It seems justifiable to infer", Fairbairn said, "that man is by nature object-seeking rather than pleasure-seeking, and that his basic behavior is determined … by the reality principle rather than by the pleasure principle" (1956b, p. 132).

Before we proceed, it is important to note that with these two hypotheses—particularly if they are interpreted under the assumption that the object is indeed external and separate—Fairbairn did not just revise the atomism and solipsism of the Freudian world view, but offered an entirely different conceptualisation of the self in relationship with itself, the world, and other people. In stark contrast to the Freudian ego, this version of the Fairbairnian ego: (1) exists from the outset, and, at least in its fundamental structure, does not need to be built up out of subsequent experience; (2) is an integrated and functional whole that must be conceptualised holistically and not as a sum of its component parts; (3) is already intersubjective, in that its relationships with real others are not a developmental achievement (à la Freud, Klein and Winnicott), but are already present in the form of an original organisational factor for the self; (4) is characterised by a source of energy that is organically integrated with the short-term and long-range enterprises of the self (as Fairbairn said: "'impulse' is not, so to speak, a kick in the pants administered out of the blue to a surprised, and perhaps somewhat pained, ego, but a psychical structure in action—a psychical structure doing something to something or somebody", 1952, p. 150); and (5) is meaning-generating, in the sense that it structures experience according to its embeddedness with objects, and is thereby actively implicated in the imposition of goals, purpose, and meaning, and in the formation of a processional gestalt in here-and-now interactions with the object world at all moments of life.

In sum, under this interpretation of Fairbairn's theories, self and object are not separated by an unbridgeable metaphysical gulf, as they are in atomistic and dualistic theories. Rather, they exist in a bidirectional, dialectic relationship, in which the dynamism of being human contains, from the beginning of life onwards, the object as its designed purpose and function. From this perspective, the structure and the function of the individual can only be considered as two aspects of the same dynamic whole, operating as an indivisible process within a real world of real others.

In my view, this interpretation of Fairbairn's two hypotheses is by far the most important for the history of psychoanalysis, primarily because it offers a radical, relational revision of the nature of the self. Unfortunately, this interpretation is compromised by Fairbairn's dual conceptualisations of the object, and, secondarily, of the self, which introduced a seemingly unavoidable uncertainty regarding the basic meanings of his core hypotheses. In Fairbairn's first, and perhaps better-known, version of the object, he clearly considered it to be an actual external object. The infant's "libidinal object is really his mother as a whole," he says, but because the infant's "libidinal interest is essentially focused upon her breast … the breast itself tends to assume the role of libidinal object" (1952, p. 11), to which he added later that "impulse-tension in the ego must be regarded as inherently orientated towards objects in outer reality" (ibid., pp. 167–168). Moreover, Fairbairn's entire theory of the origin of psychopathology rests upon the infant's need to utilise internalisation to cope with dissatisfaction with actual external objects: "Internalization of the object is a defensive measure originally adopted by the child to deal with his original object (the mother and her breast) in so far as it is unsatisfying" (1963, p. 224). Following these statements by Fairbairn, a large number of theorists have interpreted him as asserting that ego and object are separate from the beginning and that the object is external (cf. Kernberg, 1994; Mitchell, 1994; Rubens, 1994; Winnicott & Khan, 1953).

In other passages, however, Fairbairn altered his view of the object—particularly the "original object" with which the infant has its first relationship. Possibly responding to criticisms from other analysts that the idea of infant and object as separate and distinct entities did not provide a foundation for him to speak of the *internal* world of the infant, from which he wanted to evolve his theory of psychopathology, Fairbairn interposed his theory of primary identification. "So far as we conceive of a mental state of the child before birth," Fairbairn wrote in a 1943 essay, "we must regard it as characterized by a degree of primary identification so absolute as to preclude his entertaining any thought of differentiation from the maternal body, which constitutes his whole environment and the whole of his experience" (1952, p. 275).

In subsequent discussion of primary identification, Fairbairn emphasises it plays a "predominant role" (ibid., p. 277) in early emotional development but its influence progressively decreases with successful emotional maturation. During the period of primary identification, however, the original ego remains in infantile dependence in which ego and object are fused: "Ego-development is characterized by a process whereby an original state of infantile dependence based upon primary identification with the object is abandoned in favour of a state of adult or mature dependence based upon differentiation of the object from the self" (p. 163). This statement is inconsistent with his more familiar statement that the ego is "inherently orientated towards objects in outer reality … from the first" (pp. 167–168), because in the one case the object is conceptualised as separate from the ego, while in the other it is distributed throughout the ego in an original state of fusion.

The inconsistency with which Fairbairn conceptualised the object is reflected in his conceptualisations of the ego. When he speaks of the object as external and differentiated, he also speaks of the ego as retaining its separate and distinct structure from the beginning. In this view, the infant is conceived of as an innocent (Grotstein, 1994b) who nevertheless exhibits a certain "pristine" (Fairbairn, 1954b, p. 15) dynamic structure whose fundamental aim is to establish relationships with (presumably external) objects. This structure is quickly divided as a consequence of unsatisfactory experiences with objects and the subsequent defensive processes of introjection, splitting, and repression (which, for Fairbairn, constitute the origins of psychopathology), but Fairbairn was clear, at least in some passages, that he considered it to be an entity that predates the ego's interactions with its objects. In a 1946 article, for example, he referred to an "original and single dynamic ego-structure present at the beginning" (1952, p. 148); while in 1954, he described a "unitary dynamic ego" (1954b, p. 15); and in 1963, he hypothesized the existence of an original ego and an "original object" (p. 224; see also Rubens, 1984, 1994). Although Fairbairn was not completely explicit in his description of the meaning of these terms, we can assume the ego is *unitary* in the sense both that it is autonomous and self-directed towards attachments with objects, and that it is originally undivided, but becomes compartmentalised by its subsequent interactions with those objects. It is *original* in the sense that it exists from the outset and is not dependent upon subsequent experience for its basic structure (Rubens, 1994; Sutherland, 1994).

The ego described in these passages, however, exhibits very different characteristics from the ego entailed by Fairbairn's theory of primary identification. That ego can be neither unitary nor original, since it is diffused between itself and its objects, and it cannot be said to be an ego at all until it has developed out of its merger with them. Moreover, Fairbairn describes this ego as something akin to a perceptual subject, in terms of which the object is treated as merely an appearance within the subject's perceptual field. Indeed, when Fairbairn speaks of primary identification, he conceptualises the ego and the object as fused together in an *internal* space, where they are each essentially comprised of mental representations. Rinsley, in his interpretation of Fairbairn's concept of the original ego and the original object, makes this implication explicit. The original object, Rinsley suggests, is "a dimly perceived proto-object associated with the infant's similarly perceived, coenaesthetic complex of self-representations that together comprise the [original ego]" (1994, p. 277). From similar considerations, Modell

(1994) makes the point that Fairbairn was never able to establish a *truly* relational model, in which the ego transacts with external objects, because his theories effectively persist in reining him back towards a model based only on internal events.

These inconsistencies in Fairbairn's views of the object and its relationship with the ego are what led some of his earliest critics to suggest his theory required significant revision. In 1953, Winnicott and Khan pointed out that Fairbairn's idea of an undifferentiated self and object embroils him in irresolvable dilemmas, pertaining to the means through which self and object *become* differentiated. Fairbairn's view of this differentiation—that the infant has unsatisfactory experiences with the object, which triggers the first internalisation and hence the first differentiation between ego and object—amounts to, according to Winnicott and Khan, circular reasoning, since the infant's capacity to even *have* unsatisfactory experiences with an object depends upon it *already* possessing an ability to differentiate self from object. Winnicott and Khan suggest this circularity forces Fairbairn into something of a *reductio ad absurdum*. "If the object is not differentiated it cannot operate as an object," they suggest (1953, p. 332), in which case the infant's libidinal needs for the object, as postulated by Fairbairn, cannot actually reach the object. This, in turn, leads to two uncomfortable conclusions: first, the infant has libidinal needs but no object to satisfy them, in which case Fairbairn's theory looks uncomfortably like Freud's impulse theory; and second, the infant is thereby locked into precisely the solipsistic isolation that Fairbairn, throughout most of his theorising, took great pains to criticise and avoid. As Winnicott and Khan state, "Fairbairn nowhere states how the infant makes the (theoretical) first object" (p. 332).

With his competing views of the object and the ego, Fairbairn has offered us two different theories of the origin and nature of the self. While he may have believed these two views were reconcilable, he did not offer, as Winnicott and Khan observed, a convincing demonstration of such a reconciliation. Rather, the reader of Fairbairn's works is left with a vertiginous feeling that both theories—one in which the ego is imagined from *inside* its perceptual apparatus, viewing the object from a primitive, fused perspective, and the other located in an "interworld" in which ego and object are separate entities—are asserted without a clear recognition they cannot be easily grafted onto one another. The stakes, however, could not be higher: as the above observations demonstrate, determining which theory is the truly Fairbairnian theory is pivotal in deciding to what extent his metapsychology can be counted as intersubjective. It is at this juncture that a comparison of Fairbairn's attempted solution to the problem of intersubjectivity with Merleau-Ponty's may be helpful.

Fairbairn and Merleau-Ponty

To fully compare Fairbairn's and Merleau-Ponty's theories of intersubjectivity would require more space than is available in this chapter, so only a brief sketch will be offered here. We can begin by noting the number of parallels between the two theories: both posit an active, purposive, and performative subject that is inherently interactive and engaged with the external world even before it is fully formed; both place the subject in an interworld of other subjects so the plurality of subjectivities is formative of each individual's experience; and both argue against prevailing atomistic and dualistic conceptualisations that isolate the subject in solipsistic directionlessness.

Where the two diverged, however, was in the extent to which they consistently defended these particular views. Fairbairn, as we have seen, clearly advanced the kind of theory that, by defining the ego as dynamic, lifted it out of its isolation and located it in actual relationships with real objects. But because he also felt it necessary to describe the internal world as the source of psychopathology, he was forced to posit two different versions of the ego: an ego of the real interpersonal world, and an ego of internality that bore uncomfortable resemblances both to the Freudian ego (as Winnicott and Khan observed) and to the perceptual subject posited by Descartes and Husserl.

It is perhaps not overstating the case to say that with his theory of primary identification (as well as subsequent theories, such as of the "pre-ambivalent object", 1952, p. 178), Fairbairn effectively performed a *retreat* to internality, and thereby undermined his own radical revision of the nature of the self. This, after all, is how some subsequent theorists have viewed his strategy: "Unlike Freud's theory, Fairbairn's is a relational theory, but one that is translated back into a one-person psychology" (Modell, 1994, p. 200). It is also how Merleau-Ponty saw similar philosophic attempts to defend the primacy of the internal self.

For Merleau-Ponty, to regard other persons as "mere" objects of my perceptual consciousness—to see them, in other words, from an *internal* perspective which is limited by the boundaries of my own subjectivity—is to deny the overarching reality of the interworld in which we all exist, and in which I, through my body, open myself onto others in the same way they open themselves onto me. "The other's gaze", Merleau-Ponty says, "transforms me into an object, and mine him, *only if both of us withdraw* into the core of our thinking nature, if we both make ourselves into an inhuman gaze, if each of us feels his actions to be not taken up and understood, but observed as if they were an insect's" (1962, p. 361, italics added).

Fairbairn himself seemed to have intuitively grasped this perspective, in that he understood that psychopathology pertains to a retreat to, and an overvaluing of, internal views of the external world, particularly the world of other persons. What he does not seem to have recognised, and what Merleau-Ponty's theory can help us to see, is that his own reliance on internality—as instantiated by his theories of pathology and of the undifferentiated ego—amounted to a retreat to a perceptual subject, as though that subject was at the centre or heart of experience. Fairbairn seems to have thus privileged the internal subject over the subject of the interworld—or, at the least, to have failed to fully elaborate his intersubjective theory so that the internal subject was accorded its appropriate place as an entity that only emerges after a necessary bracketing of the full realities of the dynamic, interactive self.

The solution, then, for the complications created by Fairbairn's two versions of his core hypotheses lies in a consistent refusal to reduce the complexities of human experience to one polarity or another. This is what Merleau-Ponty meant when he said that in performative acts of perception, the subject is never reducible to its internality, nor is the object reducible to its materiality. "Inside and outside are inseparable," Merleau-Ponty added. "The world is wholly inside and I am wholly outside myself" (1962, p. 407). In other words, the dialectic that links self, other, and things in a common language should always remain at the foundation of any philosophic or psychoanalytic theory. By following the same strategy, it is possible to revise Fairbairn's theory, so that his legacy as one of the earliest and most original contributors to the theory of intersubjectivity will have been preserved.

References

Crossley, N. (1996). *Intersubjectivity: The Fabric of Social Becoming*. London: Sage.
Descartes, R. (1641). *Meditations on First Philosophy*. D. A. Cress (Trans.). Indianapolis, IN: Hackett Publishing, 1993.
Fairbairn, W. R. D. (1952). *Psychoanalytic Studies of the Personality*. London: Tavistock.
Fairbairn, W. R. D. (1954b). Observations on the nature of hysterical states. *British Journal of Medical Psychology*, 27(3): 105–125. In: D. E. Scharff & E. F. Birtles (Eds.), *From Instinct to Self: Selected Papers of W. R. D. Fairbairn, Volume I: Clinical and Theoretical Papers* (pp. 13–40). Northvale, NJ: Jason Aronson, 1994.
Fairbairn, W. R. D. (1956b). A critical evaluation of certain psycho-analytical conceptions. *British Journal for the Philosophy of Science*, 7: 49–60. In: D. E. Scharff & E. F. Birtles (Eds.), *From Instinct to Self: Selected Papers of W. R. D. Fairbairn, Volume I: Clinical and Theoretical Papers* (as Re-evaluating some basic concepts, pp. 129–138). Northvale, NJ: Jason Aronson, 1994.
Fairbairn, W. R. D. (1963a). Synopsis of an object-relations theory of the personality. *International Journal of Psychoanalysis*, 44: 224–225. In: D. E. Scharff & E. F. Birtles (Eds.), *From Instinct to Self: Selected Papers of W. R. D. Fairbairn, Volume I: Clinical and Theoretical Papers* (pp. 155–156). Northvale, NJ: Jason Aronson, 1994.
Grotstein, J. S. (1994b). Notes on Fairbairn's metapsychology. In: J. S. Grotstein & D. B. Rinsley (Eds.), *Fairbairn and the Origins of Object Relations* (pp. 112–148). New York: Guilford Press.
Husserl, E. (1913). *Ideas: General Introduction to Pure Phenomenology*. W. R. B. Gibson (Trans.). New York: Collier, 1962.
Husserl, E. (1931). *Cartesian Meditations: An Introduction to Phenomenology*. D. Cairns (Trans.). The Hague, The Netherlands: Martinus Nijhoff, 1973.
Kant, I. (1781). *The Critique of Pure Reason*. P. Guyer & A. W. Wood (Trans.). Cambridge: Cambridge University Press, 1998.
Kernberg, O. F. (1994). Fairbairn's theory and challenge. In: J. S. Grotstein & D. B. Rinsley (Eds.), *Fairbairn and the Origins of Object Relations* (pp. 41–65). New York: Guilford Press.
Merleau-Ponty, M. (1962). *The Phenomenology of Perception*. C. Smith, (Trans.). London: Routledge & Kegan Paul.
Mitchell, S. A. (1988). *Relational Concepts in Psychoanalysis: An Integration*. Cambridge, MA: Harvard University Press.
Mitchell, S. A. (1994). The origin and nature of the "object" in the theories of Klein and Fairbairn. In: J. S. Grotstein & D. B. Rinsley (Eds.), *Fairbairn and the Origins of Object Relations* (pp. 66–87). New York: Guilford Press.
Modell, A. H. (1994). Fairbairn's structural theory and the communication of affects. In: J. S. Grotstein & D. B. Rinsley (Eds.), *Fairbairn and the Origins of Object Relations* (pp. 195–207). New York: Guilford Press. Rinsley, D. B. (1994). A reconsideration of Fairbairn's "Original Object" and "Original Ego" in relation to borderline and other self disorders. In: J. S. Grotstein & D. B. Rinsley (Eds.), *Fairbairn and the Origins of Object Relations* (pp. 275–288). New York: Guilford Press.
Rubens, R. L. (1984). The meaning of structure in Fairbairn. *International Review of Psycho-Analysis*, 11: 429–440.

Rubens, R. L. (1994). Fairbairn's structural theory. In: J. S. Grotstein & D. B. Rinsley (Eds.), *Fairbairn and the Origins of Object Relations* (pp. 151–173). New York: Guilford Press.

Scharff, D. E., & Birtles, E. F. (1994). Editors' introduction: Fairbairn's contribution. In: D. E. Scharff & E. F. Birtles (Eds.), *From Instinct to Self: Selected Papers of W. R. D. Fairbairn, Volume I: Clinical and Theoretical Papers* (pp. xi–xxi). Northvale, NJ: Jason Aronson.

Schnell, A. (2010). Intersubjectivity in Husserl's work. *META: Research in Hermeneutics, Phenomenology, and Practical Philosophy*, II(1): 9–32.

Sutherland, J. D. (1994). Fairbairn's achievement. In: J. S. Grotstein & D. B. Rinsley (Eds.), *Fairbairn and the Origins of Object Relations* (pp. 17–33). New York: Guilford Press.

Winnicott, D. W., & Khan, M. M. R. (1953). [Review.] Psychoanalytic Studies of the Personality by W. Ronald D. Fairbairn (London: Tavistock). *International Journal of Psychoanalysis*, 34: 329–333.

Zahavi, D. (2001). *Husserl and Transcendental Intersubjectivity: A Response to the Linguistic-Pragmatic Critique*. E. A. Behnke (Trans.). Athens, OH: Ohio University Press.

PART IV

APPLICATIONS

INTRODUCTION TO PART IV

Graham S. Clarke and David E. Scharff

Fairbairn's work is not as familiar to many within psychoanalysis as it should be despite the degree to which it has informed modern practice. In the world of psychoanalytic aesthetics Fairbairn's papers on art have been ignored despite being championed from the beginning by Herbert Read (1951). Steven Levine shows that Fairbairn's papers on art have unacknowledged relevance to a modern psychology of art.

Similarly, Fairbairn's development of the psychology of dynamic structure and its associated endopsychic structure offers expanded understanding of dramatic narratives. His theory of dreams and of art make it possible to see the work of art as a means of addressing problems that are both personal and universal, even while inflected with specific cultural and societal contexts. Rainer Rehrberger uses Fairbairn's theory to analyse Camus's *The Stranger*, a classical existentialist text. This points to ways in which other dramatic narratives might similarly be analysed from a Fairbairnian perspective, an approach that has been used by Graham S. Clarke to understand film narrative (Clarke, 1994, 2003, 2012).

The third section of *Psychoanalytic Studies of the Personality* has for the most part been overlooked, so we are fortunate to have two contributions in which Fairbairn's social thought is extended in exciting ways. We have already commented on Gal Gerson's contribution in the Historical part and here Ron Aviram looks in detail at Fairbairn's paper on the sociological significance of communism (1935b) to develop the idea of a social object that expands Fairbairn's ideas into the social realm.

While sadly we have no explicitly feminist contribution to this book it is worth noting that Eichenbaum and Orbach in their *Understanding Women* (1985), a revised version of their earlier book *Outside In … Inside Out* (1982), are consciously working within the tradition of British object relations thinkers and cite Fairbairn, Guntrip, and Winnicott. Their critical view of object relations and of the meaning of "object" within this theory is totally at one with our own understanding, and, we would argue, that of Fairbairn. As they write, "We acknowledge that mother is not an object, mother is a person, a social and psychological being …. What becomes internalised is … different aspects of [relations with (editor's comment)] mother … What the object relations theorists have failed to take into account is the psychology of the mother and the effect of the social position of women on the mother's psychology" (Eichenbaum & Orbach, 1985, p. 34, n. 13). It will not be difficult to see that many of the contributors to this book share this perspective.

The practical influence upon society at large is an aspect of Fairbairn's own thinking, illustrated by the many papers he delivered throughout his life to non-psychoanalytic audiences. It is also consistent with the idea of playing a full part in society—being an Aristotelian citizen—and is a crucial part of mature dependence. Our final contribution by James Raines illustrates the way in which key ideas from Fairbairn's work have driven developments in social work and child welfare in the United States and Great Britain.

References

Clarke, G. (1994). Notes towards an object-relations approach to cinema. *Free Associations, 4*: 369–390.

Clarke, G. (2003). L. A. Confidential: Object relations and psychic growth. *British Journal of Psychotherapy, 19*(3): 379–385.

Clarke, G. S. (2012). Failures of the "moral defence" in the films Shutter Island, Inception and Memento: Narcissism or schizoid personality disorder? *International Journal of Psychoanalysis, 93*: 203–218.

Eichenbaum, L.., & Orbach, S. (1985). *Understanding Women*. London: Penguin.

Fairbairn, W. R. D. (1935b). The sociological significance of communism considered in the light of psychoanalysis. *British Journal of Medical Psychology, 15*(3): 218–229. In: *Psychoanalytic Studies of the Personality* (pp. 233–246). London: Tavistock, 1952.

Read, H. (1951). Psychoanalysis and the problem of aesthetic value. *International Journal of Psychoanalysis, 32*: 73–82.

CHAPTER THIRTY-FIVE

Fair play: a restitution of Fairbairn's forgotten role in the historical drama of art and psychoanalysis

Steven Z. Levine

The art writings of Ronald Fairbairn have not found the readership they merit. "Prolegomena to a Psychology of Art" and "The Ultimate Basis of Aesthetic Experience" appeared in the *British Journal of Psychology* in 1938, were abstracted in the *International Journal of Psychoanalysis* in 1939 and 1940, and languished until their republication in 1994 by his daughter Ellinor Fairbairn Birtles and the object relations author David E. Scharff in the second volume of Fairbairn's collected papers, *From Instinct to Self*. Inspired by their editorial labour, several writers during the past decade have offered interesting interpretations of Fairbairn's theory of art (Borgegård, 2005; Brink, 2000; Clarke, 2006; Pereira, 2002).

Fairbairn proposes that "a work of art represents a restitution of objects menaced by the artist's repressed destructive impulses" and that "the aesthetic appeal of a work of art depends upon its capacity to present itself to the beholder ... as a 'restored object'" (1940b, p. 97). My chapter is offered as an act of restitution as well, whereby Fairbairn's contribution might be restored to its place among theories of art that should matter today. In an earlier essay I addressed Fairbairn's account of the surrealist art of Salvador Dalí, in whose work he saw phantasies of mutilation of the mother's body but only its incomplete artistic restoration (Levine, 1998). Here I emphasise the conversations taking place in Fairbairn's essays of 1938, in which he relies on the writings of Sigmund Freud and Melanie Klein as well as in his reviews of books on art by Joanna Field (Marion Milner's pseudonym) and Ernst Kris in 1951 and 1953.

Fairbairn was better prepared to write about aesthetics than Freud when the latter published "Leonardo da Vinci and a Memory of His Childhood" in 1910 and "The Moses of Michelangelo" in 1914. The title of Fairbairn's first paper, "Prolegomena to a Psychology of Art", echoes Immanuel Kant's *Prolegomena to Any Future Metaphysics That Will Be Able to Present Itself as a Science* (1783), whose title might serve as a motto for Fairbairn's efforts to reconcile the clinical observations of psychoanalysis with the classical philosophy of Aristotle and the modern physics of Einstein

(Scharff & Birtles, 1997). The title of Fairbairn's paper also recalls William Wallace's *Prolegomena to the Study of Hegel's Philosophy and Especially of his Logic* (1894), a presentation of the Hegelian dialectic that Fairbairn might have studied while taking his degree in mental philosophy at the University of Edinburgh between 1907 and 1911, the dynamic structure of which foreshadows Fairbairn's object relations model of the personality (1963a). Enrolling to do postgraduate work in theology at Edinburgh, between 1911 and 1914 Fairbairn also took courses in philosophy and religion at universities in England and Germany.

Fairbairn's experience with the psychotherapy of soldiers caused him to veer from the profession of divinity to the practice of medicine, undergoing his medical studies at Edinburgh from 1919 to 1923 and engaging in psychoanalytic treatment with E. H. Connell, an Australian analysand of Ernest Jones. Sponsored by Jones and Edward Glover, Fairbairn became an associate member of the British Psychoanalytical Society in 1931 and a full member in 1938. In his clinical and theoretical practice Fairbairn remained isolated in Edinburgh until his death in 1964, constrained by his urinary phobia of travel from active participation in the disputes of the analytic circles of London (Sutherland, 1989).

After completing his psychiatric training Fairbairn lectured on psychology at the University of Edinburgh, but his embrace of psychoanalysis, particularly Klein's theories of children's destructive phantasies, soon caused him to lose his position. At the university Fairbairn met one of Britain's premier critics of art, Herbert (later Sir Herbert) Read, who taught between 1931 and 1933 and whose writings on art and the unconscious he closely follows. Claiming that "psychoanalysis is also the key to most of the unsolved problems in art" (1937, p. 83), Read wrote to Fairbairn that he read "The Ultimate Basis of Aesthetic Experience" "with great interest and complete agreement", commending Fairbairn's "dialectical formulation" of a principle of "restitution" as "the right word for the essential process" (1939).

With its nuances of legal, psychoanalytic, and theological meaning, restitution lies at the heart of Fairbairn's doctrine. According to the King James Bible, Jesus Christ will remain in heaven "until the times of restitution of all things" (*Acts* 3: 21). I will argue that the restitution of divine and artistic perfection forms the ultimate basis for Fairbairn's signature concept of "moral defence" (Clarke, 2012).

In "Prolegomena to a Psychology of Art" Fairbairn quotes from Read's *Art and Society* (1937) that "art begins as a solitary activity" (Fairbairn, 1938a, p. 382), but he does not mention Read's account of creativity in the chapter "Art and the Unconscious". Fairbairn understands modern painting as the enterprise of an individual, but Read stresses both psychological and sociological factors: "The individual can, and does, create a work of art for himself; but he only reaches the full satisfaction which comes from the creation of a work of art if he can persuade the community to accept his creation" (Read, 1937, p. 83).

In support of this focus on individual and group psychology Read quotes Joan Rivière's 1922 translation of Freud's *Introductory Lectures on Psycho-analysis* of 1916–1917:

> There is, in fact, a path from phantasy back again to reality, and that is—art. The artist has also an introverted disposition and has not far to go to become neurotic. … So, like any other with an unsatisfied longing, he turns away from reality and transfers all his interest, and all his libido too, on the creation of his wishes in the life of phantasy. … A true artist has more

at his disposal. First of all he understands how to elaborate his day-dreams, so that they lose that personal note which grates upon strange ears and become enjoyable to others; he knows too how to modify them sufficiently so that their origin in prohibited sources is not easily detected. Further, he possesses the mysterious ability to mould his particular material until it expresses the ideas of his phantasy faithfully. … When he can do all this, he opens out to others the way back to the comfort and consolation of their own unconscious sources of pleasure. (quoted in Read, 1937, pp. 85–86)

Read points to Freud's inability to account for the so-called "mystery" of the artist's transformation of "forbidden and repressed desires" into a work of art capable of providing its beholder with an experience of "formal pleasure" (ibid., 87–88). Read addresses this lack by considering Freud's division of the personality into id, ego, and superego.

Quoting from Freud's *New Introductory Lectures* of 1933, Read claims "the work of art has correspondences with each region of the mind":

It derives its energy, its irrationality, and its mysterious power from the id, which is to be regarded as the source of what we usually call inspiration. It is given formal synthesis and unity by the ego; and finally it may be assimilated to those ideologies or spiritual aspirations which are the peculiar creation of the super-ego. … The ego intermediates between the primal force and the ultimate ideal; it gives form and physical harmony to what issues forceful but amorphous and perhaps terrifying from the id; and then, in the super-ego, it gives to these forms and harmonies the ideological tendencies and aspirations of religion, morality and social idealism. (ibid., 91–92, italics in original)

Read's dynamic picture of the divided mind of the artist is extremely close to Fairbairn's account in his "prolegomena" and in its abstract where he uses the relational term "endopsychic" for what may be the first time. These texts anticipate Fairbairn's development of an object relations portrayal of the interacting forces and structures of the artist's inner world (1944):

In the light of Freud's theory of mental structure, art-work is seen to be, not only a means whereby repressed phantasies are enabled to evade the censorship of the super-ego and so to be placed at the disposal of the ego for embodiment in works of art, but also a means whereby the ego is enabled to convert phantasies unacceptable to the super-ego into positive tributes to its authority. Art is thus seen to represent a creation of positive values in the service of an ideal. Within the sphere of morals the endopsychic tension created by the demands of the super-ego is experienced by the ego as "the voice of conscience"; and it is accompanied by an urge to do something by way of restitution for destructive impulses harboured. Within the sphere of art the tension created by the demands of the super-ego is experienced as an itch to make something; and the creation of a work of art thus becomes a means of restitution analogous to the moral act. (1939b, pp. 192–193)

I will return to the relation between Fairbairn's characterisation of the moral act of artistic restitution and his slightly later concept of moral defence. Here I wish to suggest that the proximity of Fairbairn's account to that of Read may conceal an anxiety of misappropriation for which restitution is due.

For Read, Freud provides a clue to the "mystery" of the artist, whose "perceptual system becomes able to grasp relations in the deeper layers of the ego and in the id which would otherwise be inaccessible to it" (Read, 1937, p. 94). Further along in Freud's text is the most famous line Freud ever wrote—"Where id was, there ego shall be" (1933a, p. 106), and indeed this axiom will inspire the motto—"regression in the service of the ego"—of Kris's *Psychoanalytic Explorations in Art* (1952) that Fairbairn will later review.

Read stresses the "wholeness or perfection" that Fairbairn makes the cornerstone of his theory of the "restored object" (Read, 1937, p. 95). At this time Fairbairn endorses the Freudian model of the mind espoused by Read, but he fleshes out the relations of ego, id, and superego with phantasies of destruction and restitution that Klein addresses in her paper of 1929, "Infantile Anxiety-Situations Reflected in a Work of Art and in the Creative Impulse".

Klein begins with Freud's "Inhibitions, Symptoms and Anxiety" (1926d), in which the deepest danger the child fears is the loss of the mother's love. Based upon her observation of young children in play treatment, Klein argues that beneath the loss of maternal love is a still deeper anxiety concerning the mother's retaliation for the child's phantasy of attacking her body. For Klein, this primary sadism is the expression of the child's destructive instinct. To illustrate the cultural relevance of her clinical observations Klein turns to examples from literature and art in which a destructive child and a depressed adult are respectively seen to make reparation for their phantasies of maternal aggression. The first example is taken from an opera libretto by Colette and the second concerns a woman without artistic training who was able to fill upon her wall "an empty space, which in some inexplicable way seemed to coincide with the empty space within her" (Klein, 1929, p. 441): "It is obvious that the desire to make reparation, to make good the injury psychologically done to the mother and also to restore herself was at the bottom of the compelling urge to paint these portraits of her relatives" (p. 443).

Fairbairn incorporates Klein's theory of art as reparation for destructive phantasies towards parental objects:

> Recent psycho-analytical research has gone to show that repression originates as a means of safeguarding the ego against the consequences of destructive id-impulses—impulses which, at the level of object-love, threaten the integrity of love-objects (thus occasioning guilt), and which, even at the narcissistic level, threaten the sources of libidinal satisfaction (thus occasioning anxiety). It follows that, since art provides a means of expression for the repressed urges of the artist, the destructive impulses must play an important part in artistic activity. In certain works of art the direct embodiment of destructive phantasies may be readily recognized. Nevertheless, the influence of the destructive impulses is usually exerted indirectly through the medium of compensatory phantasies of restitution, designed to provide some reassurance regarding the integrity of love-object; and, since artistic activity is essentially creative, we must regard it as dominated by motives of restitution. (1939b, pp. 192–193)

Fairbairn prefers "restitution" to "reparation", but in *The Psychoanalysis of Children* (1932) Klein uses the former term in a way that might have touched Fairbairn at the site of his own urinary symptomatology: "The various details of [the child's] representations showed that the sadistic significance attached to urinating and defecating was the most deeply seated cause of his sense of guilt and underlay that impulse to make restitution which found expression in his obsessional mechanisms" (p. 236). Urinating and defecating are more than "rejective" for Fairbairn, for in a note added to a 1941 paper he affirms "They are also in a sense productive and acquire for the child the additional significance of creative and giving activities" (1941, p. 36).

Fairbairn's understanding of the process of artistic creation as the reconciliation of phantasies of destruction and restitution is indebted to Freud in unacknowledged ways. Freud anticipates Fairbairn's idea that art makes manifest the reconciliation of unconscious phantasies of hate and love in "The Moses of Michelangelo":

> He does not let Moses break [the stone tablets] in his wrath, but makes him be influenced by the danger that they will be broken and makes him calm that wrath, or at any rate prevent it from becoming an act. In this way he has added something new and more than human to the figure of Moses; so that the giant frame with its tremendous physical power becomes only a concrete expression of the highest mental achievement that is possible in a man, that of struggling successfully against an inward passion for the sake of a cause to which he has devoted himself. (1914b, p. 233)

Hanna Segal later acknowledges that Freud shows in his Moses essay that "the latent meaning of this work is the overcoming of wrath" (1952, p. 207), but Fairbairn's failure to acknowledge Freud may have troubled him to such a degree that he chose not to republish these essays in *Psychoanalytical Studies of Personality* of 1952.

* * *

The first writer to respond to Fairbairn was Herbert Read, who was invited to deliver the Ernest Jones Lecture before the British Psychoanalytical Society in 1950. "Psycho-Analysis and the Problem of Aesthetic Value" challenges analysts to consider not only the unconscious psychology of the artist but also the formal characteristics of the work of art "in its presentational immediacy". Read takes this phrase from Alfred North Whitehead's 1928 book *Symbolism, Its Meaning and Effect* and in a footnote he opines that Fairbairn is "the only psycho-analyst who has given adequate recognition to the presentational immediacy of the object in aesthetic experience". Might Read have included this note in the printed article upon the urging of Fairbairn himself, whose definition of aesthetic experience he quotes: "The experience which occurs in the beholder when he discovers an object which functions for him symbolically as a means of satisfying his unconscious emotional needs" (1951, p. 75).

Read recalls Freud's proposition that the artist "softens the egotistical character of the daydream by changes and disguises, and he bribes us by the offer of a purely formal, that is aesthetic pleasure in the presentation of his phantasies" (ibid., p. 76). For Read, this thesis illuminates the creative process of the artist but fails to connect it with what truly matters to society in the work of art, its aesthetic value, a failure that Fairbairn's theory dispels. As presented by Read, Fairbairn

> ... distinguishes between over-symbolization and under-symbolization—between the true work of art and those false works of art which do not function either because (1) "the censorship of the artist's super-ego is so rigorous, and necessitates such an elaborate disguise of the urges expressed, that the work of art is deprived of almost all symbolic significance for the beholder"; or (2) the opposite case, "when the artist's super-ego is weak and his repressed urges are really 'urgent', these urgent urges express themselves in the work of art with a minimum of disguise". (ibid., p. 79)

Fairbairn further insists on the historical specificity of this differential of over- and under-symbolisation by asserting that the once moving works by the Victorian artist, Frederic Lord Leighton, had lost their capacity to move the contemporary viewer and had come to seem sterile and "over-symbolized". Conversely, the surrealists' alleged failure adequately to disguise the disruption of unconscious phantasy garners the charge of "under-symbolization" (1938b, pp. 405–406).

Read credits Fairbairn with the concept of "optimal synthesis", the process of creating an aesthetic unity of content and form "through the full development and reconciliation of the deepest and widest antagonism" (1951, p. 80). These words are not Fairbairn's but come from Edward Caird's 1901 book on Hegel in which Fairbairn finds "the central conception of Hegelian philosophy" (1938b, pp. 407–408). Fairbairn sees this Hegelian antagonism at work in Freud's psychoanalytic dualism; thus the aesthetic experience "depends upon the resolution of an antinomy created by the simultaneous operation of the libido (the life principle) and the destructive urges (the death principle)" (Read, 1951, p. 80). In a portion of the essay not quoted by Read, Fairbairn specifies that "The demands of the libido may be said to constitute the thesis, the pressure of the destructive urges, the antithesis, and the restitution the synthesis" (1938b, p. 408).

The process of artistic restitution can go awry in alternative ways: "The under-symbolized work of art fails to produce the effect of restitution, because the impression which it gives is one of more or less unmitigated destruction. ... On the other hand, restitution is meaningless apart from the presupposition of destruction; and, consequently, over-symbolization precludes the effect of restitution" (Read, 1951, p. 80). Echoing the theological language of his university training as well as the stern clergymen whose services he was required to attend twice on Sunday as a child (1963b, p. 462), Fairbairn may seem to be imploring his deceased father or widowed mother when he proclaims that "the work of art ... essentially represents a means of restitution, whereby (the artist's) ego makes atonement to his super-ego for the destruction implied in the presence of repressed destructive impulses" (Read, 1951, p. 80). Because of the internalised parental or divine authority to which restitution for sin or disobedience must be made, it is no wonder that the successful work of art for Fairbairn must be a work of beauty "able above all to produce in the beholder an impression of 'the integrity of the object'; but in order to do so, it must at the same time provide a release for the emotions which imply the destruction of the object" (1938b, p. 409).

Read admires Fairbairn's attention to the formal success or failure of works of art that he otherwise finds lacking in psychoanalytic writings on art. In a 1956 essay Fairbairn reiterates this critique on the grounds that, "Quite apart from their failure to explain why the motivations of an artist should lead him to become an artist rather than, e. g. a philosopher, and what determines the degree of an artist's greatness, such explanations, as Herbert Read has pointed out, completely fail to explain what determines the specifically aesthetic value of a work of art, and characteristically provide no clue to any scale of aesthetic values" (1956b, p. 130).

More significant than Read's acknowledgment of his friend's theory of art is the meagreness of the mention of Fairbairn, minus a first name, as the author of "The Ultimate Basis of Aesthetic Experience" in Hanna Segal's essay "A Psycho-Analytical Approach to Aesthetics", an ungenerousness of citation also characteristic of later Kleinian authors (Glover, 2009; Gosso, 2004). Repeatedly anthologised in the decades since its publication, Segal's essay updates her analyst's 1929 article on art by insisting upon Klein's later concept of the depressive position as the developmental prerequisite for the reintegration of the good and bad aspects of the mother's breast and for the child's unconscious wish to make reparation for its sadistic phantasies (Klein, 1935):

> The memory of the good situation, where the infant's ego contained the whole loved object, and the realization that it has been lost through his own attacks, give rise to an intense feeling of loss and guilt, and to the wish to restore and re-create the lost loved object outside and within the ego. This wish to restore and re-create is the basis of later sublimation and creativity. (Segal, 1952, p. 197)

As described by Segal, the depressive position is not merely a developmental phase of childhood but a permanent work of mourning the object ruined by phantasies of destruction and hate. Unlike the neurotic, whose "phantasy interferes with his relationships in which he acts it out", "the artist withdraws into a world of phantasy, but he can communicate his phantasies and share them. In that way he makes reparation, not only to his own internal objects, but to the external world as well" (ibid., p. 203). The beholder of the work of art "re-experiences his own early depressive anxieties, and through identifying with the artist he experiences a successful mourning, re-establishes his own internal objects and his own internal world, and feels, therefore, re-integrated and enriched" (p. 206).

Segal's unacknowledged echo of Fairbairn's thesis of artistic restitution is the silent reverberation of the dispute between her analytic mentor and the dissident Scotsman regarding the presumed priority of the depressive or schizoid position. In "Notes on Some Schizoid Mechanisms" Klein acknowledges Fairbairn's account of the early splitting of the ego but disagrees with his rejection of the life and death instincts and with his view that the schizoid position results from the internalisation of the bad object alone (1946, p. 100). For his part, Fairbairn repeatedly mentions Klein by name but refrains from providing specific facts of publication.

Fairbairn does not directly refer to Segal's overlooking of his work, but he indirectly responds to the views of the group around Klein in a review of a book by an analyst much influenced by her, Marion Milner. In a critical notice of *On Not Being Able to Paint*, Fairbairn commends Milner, writing under the pseudonym Joanna Field, for having been "enriched rather than compromised" by the influence of Klein, whose grandson she analysed in play therapy: "The old criticism that psychoanalysis is all analysis and no synthesis certainly does not apply here." This Hegelian witticism is accompanied by approving remarks on Milner's belief that art entails a "reconciliation of opposites":

> Pictorial composition thus resolved itself into an attempt on the painter's part to deal with all the problems involved in object-relationships, viz. problems concerned with such vital issues as separation and "ways of being together," loving and hating, having and losing, taking and withholding, innocence and guilt, freedom and slavery, security and insecurity, etc. (1951c, p. 419)

Milner's "reconciliation of differences" allows Fairbairn to surpass the summarising of her book to express his own Hegelian view:

> The essential "difference" which underlies the human predicament is that between "self and other"; but it also presents itself as a difference between, e.g. subjective and objective, internal and external, emotional and intellectual, imagination and action, dream and reality, illusion and disillusion, independence and dependence. (ibid., p. 420)

Although confined to the format of a book review, Fairbairn's critical notice of 1951 enables him to extend his aesthetic essays of 1938 into a broader philosophical discussion.

Fairbairn notes that Milner's struggles as a painter taught her what institutional psychoanalysis had not done, namely the necessity of "creative interplay between dream and external reality": "For the resulting picture is not just a dream, nor yet is it an external object independent of the artist's dream" (ibid., p. 420). Here Fairbairn articulates in object relational language what he had only been able to explain in the terminology of Freudian drive theory in his essays of 1938. Always at stake for Fairbairn is his relational portrait of the child traumatised not by unappeasable instincts of love and death but by actual parental deficiencies, a self-portrait of his own tormented experience of reproducing his father's urinary phobia and identifying his urinary retention with his mother's breasts swollen with bad milk (Sutherland, 1989, pp. 75–76):

> The essential difficulty which confronts such creative interplay has its ultimate source in the disturbing experiences of childhood through which the individual becomes so painfully aware of "the difference between what one would like and expect people to do and what they do do". The trouble is that, having once learned to differentiate these opposites, the individual is tempted to go to extremes and keep them too rigidly apart, whilst all the time never ceasing in the depths of his being to aspire to a restoration of the original situation which existed before the difference was experienced. The effect of this is not only to produce emotional difficulties for the individual in social relationships, but also to compromise creative activity on his part. (Fairbairn, 1951c, pp. 420–421)

This cry of pain is evoked in Fairbairn on the occasion of reviewing Milner's resonant prose. In the "free play" of her artistic method Fairbairn sees a mirror of his own restitutional practice, what in this essay I am calling "fair play": "I also write without fore-knowledge of where it will lead and without conscious planning, except for 'planning the gap'" (ibid., pp. 421–422). He does not notice that his use of the art of writing to fill an emotional gap uncannily recalls Klein's example of the reparative process by which the depressed painter fought to fill the empty maternal place on her wall and in her life.

In her original text Milner makes no reference to Fairbairn, but a bibliographical note in the second edition of 1957 includes his "Prolegomena" of 1938 alongside more recent essays in psychoanalytic aesthetics. Fairbairn concludes his review by professing pleasure in finding in Milner no discussion of sublimation. Fairbairn's critique of this Freudian concept of the redirection of libidinal energy into non-libidinal cultural aims is only tentatively articulated in his earlier essays on art where he suggests that "art is seen to be not only a sublimated expression of repressed urges, but also a means whereby positive values are created in the service of an ideal" (1938a, p. 394). Now he openly breaks with Freud, insisting "Sublimation is, of course, a concept which has its roots in impulse-psychology; and it is difficult to find a place for it in a psychology of object relations." What is at stake is nothing less than "the artist's relationships with his objects", and Fairbairn suggests that Milner's observations on the creative process *"from inside ...* appear to confirm some of the conclusions which I recorded in two contributions to the psychology of art in 1938 on the basis of an *objective* approach" (1951c, p. 422, italics in original).

Sublimation is the ultimate bone of contention in the Hegelian struggle for recognition between the "good" Scottish Christian Fairbairn and his "bad" German Jewish father and mother, Freud and Klein. In the 1953 critical notice of *Psychoanalytic Explorations in Art* by Freud's "good" Jewish son Ernst Kris, Fairbairn essentially repudiates his Freudo-Kleinian essays of 1938, with their references to the libidinal and destructive impulses of a pleasure-seeking and sadistic id, in favour of his picture of the good, relationship-seeking ego, tragically split by the internalisation of the rejecting libidinal parental object and its anti-libidinal punitive twin. The Freudian concept of sublimation on which Kris relies "presents considerable difficulties for those who, like the reviewer, adopt a psychology of object-relations based upon the principle of dynamic structure" (Fairbairn, 1953, p. 428).

Fairbairn distinguishes between Kris's hydraulic model, in which libido is seen as a kind of love-gasoline that powers the human genital engine, and his own Hegelian model of human relationships in which our object-seeking behaviour is energy and structure at once: "In terms of the principle of dynamic structure, the displacement of energy from a socially unacceptable to a socially acceptable goal would resolve itself, where the field of art is concerned, into a change in the relationships existing between the artist and those objects who constitute society for him" (ibid., p. 428).

Fairbairn exchanges the classical standard of Grecian marble beauty that he had earlier derived from eighteenth- and nineteenth-century philosophical aesthetics for a sociological understanding of art embedded in changing historical situations and mutating formal conventions. Citing Freud's failure to adhere to this historical premise in his book on Leonardo, Fairbairn endorses Kris's assertion that "art is not produced in an empty space" (ibid., p. 426). Fairbairn rejects the ahistorical approach of both Freudian sublimation and Kleinian reparation, the latter process said to fill an "empty space" on a wall of paintings that is also an empty space of phantasy where the internalised maternal object has been destroyed (Klein, 1929, pp. 440–442).

Fairbairn again gazes into the mirror of Narcissus, discerning both similarity and difference in the portrait painted by Kris, the art historian turned ego psychologist. In the bibliography for an article of 1946 concerning the pathological regression of a schizophrenic artist, Kris had been the first to cite Fairbairn's pre-war essays (Pappenheim & Kris, 1946), and in *Psychoanalytic Explorations in Art* Kris notes that he shares with Fairbairn an understanding of art as a form of social communication: "There is a sender, there are receivers, and there is a message" (1952, p. 16). Fairbairn agrees with this contention, but he does not endorse Kris's concept of art as regression in the service of the ego on account of the psychology of instinctual impulse, discharge, and sublimation that he is now poised to combat:

> According to the principle of dynamic structure, it is not a case of a structural ego being differentiated under the pressure of the impact of external reality out of an original id which is relatively formless, so much as the id being a structure with primitive characteristics which is differentiated from an original (and relatively primitive) ego structure under the influence of repression. … In the light of such a conception, the primary process will present itself as a characteristic feature of the activity of the repressed id-structure, and the secondary process as a characteristic feature of the activity of the conscious ego-structure; and the nature of artistic activity will then come to be described, not as an ego-controlled regression to the level of the primary process, but rather as an attempt to reconcile the primitive expression of a repressed id-structure with the requirements of a conscious ego-structure orientated towards external objects in a social milieu. (1953, p. 429)

Whereas before the war the object to which the artist makes atonement and restitution for his destructive phantasies is the superego, after the war the superego is supplanted by real others with whom the artist inhabits the shared space of history and culture. With the successive deaths of his artistic but withholding father (d. 1925), his rejecting and long-lived mother (d. 1946), and his long-ill wife who was hostile to his profession (d. 1952), had Fairbairn been freed from the unconscious need to sustain the incongruous phantasy of goodness of these intimate internal objects? Exchanging the guilt-driven principle of restitution of the twin essays of 1938 for the Hegelian reconciliation of opposites of the two book reviews of 1951 and 1953, was the fair Scottish bairn finally ready to indulge in the boyish fun of theory-building? Was it now time for "fair play"?

"Fun" has been the most contested part of Fairbairn's aesthetic legacy since 1989 when John Sutherland expressed dissatisfaction with the seemingly trivial assertion that artistic activity "consists simply in *making something for fun*" (pp. 47–56, italics in original). Assailed by the blasphemy of the surrealist exhibitions that he visited in London, Fairbairn counters the "puritanical attitude to art" of his Calvinist youth that equates art with sin with a serious plea on behalf of "fun". And he repeats that plea in his review of Kris's treatise in which there is less emphasis on "the pure joy of artistic creation" (1938a, pp. 383–384) than the cognitive flexibility of the ego:

> [Art's] specific nature can, however, be defined by the further statement that the reconciliation between the expression of the id-structure and the requirements of the conscious ego which it is the specific aim of the artist to establish is one accomplished through the specific activity of making (creating) things—and making them not primarily for utilitarian purposes, but (as the reviewer tried to establish in 1938) primarily "for fun". (1953, p. 430)

For Fairbairn, "fun" is the ratio of reconciliation between renunciation and revenge, between (self-)destructive phantasies of the anti-libidinal parental object and its affiliated ego-structure and the ego-ideal of the good object in which the conscious ego defiantly chooses to believe. This is the morality of art that defends in a joyous act of "fun" the self and its objects from ultimate ruin. This is the work of art as "moral defence".

Fairbairn's object relations theory moves psychoanalysis from the Freudo-Kleinian world of somatic instincts and their sublimated representatives to a socially constituted history where the internalisation of lustful and lethal modes of relationship constitutes an act of restitution or "moral defence" on behalf of the external possibility of a loving world, however unlikely such a world may be. In the theological language that Fairbairn often favours,

> It is better to be a sinner in a world ruled by God than to live in a world ruled by the Devil. A sinner in a world ruled by God may be bad; but there is always a certain sense of security to be derived from the fact that the world around is good—"God's in His heaven—All's right with the world!"; and in any case there is always a hope of redemption. In a world ruled by the Devil the individual may escape the badness of being a sinner; but he is bad because the world around him is bad. Further, he can have no sense of security and no hope of redemption. (1943a, pp. 66–67)

This recalls the end-of-days scenario of the King James Bible with which I opened this chapter, when all that is broken will be restored. The eschatological strain in Fairbairn's thought is opposed, however, by a more modest historical empiricism that insists on the singularity of each individual artistic case and on a sliding scale of artistic success: "What is optimal for one artist may not be optimal for another. Similarly, what is optimal for one audience may not be optimal for another audience; and what appears optimal in terms of the ethos of one age or culture may appear anything but optimal to those of a succeeding age or of a culture which is alien" (Fairbairn, 1953, p. 430). The Hegelian premise of historically particularised self-consciousness is always accompanied in Fairbairn by a countervailing Kantian universalism that impossibly hopes for communal consensus in aesthetic judgment. From the "Prolegomena" of 1938 to the final critical notice of 1953 Fairbairn alters his model of the mind while retaining his belief that works of art are valuable in so far as they "are made, not for utilitarian purposes, but for the sake of making them, viz, in so far as they are made (so to speak) for fun" (ibid., p. 432). "Above all", his daughter remembers, "he was fun, making lots of silly jokes" (Birtles, 2006).

References

Birtles, E. F. (2006). Fairbairn, W. R. D. (Ronald). In: R. Skelton (Ed.), *The Edinburgh International Encyclopaedia of Psychoanalysis*. http://www.pep-web.org/document.php?id=zbk.069.0001f#yn0003501977050

Birtles, E. F., & Scharff, D. E. (Eds.) (1994). *From Instinct to Self: Selected Papers of W. R. D. Fairbairn, Volume II: Applications and Early Contributions*. Northvale, NJ: Jason Aronson.

Borgegård, T. (2005). Theories of art and theory as art. In: J. S. Scharff & D. E. Scharff (Eds.), *The Legacy of Fairbairn and Sutherland: Psychotherapeutic Applications* (pp. 176–183). London: Routledge.

Brink, A. (2000). Ronald Fairbairn: beyond "restitution." In: *The Creative Matrix: Anxiety and the Origin of Creativity* (pp. 78–88). New York: Peter Lang.

Caird, E. (1901). *Hegel*. Edinburgh, UK: William Blackwood.

Clarke, G. S. (2006). Fairbairn's theory of art in the light of his mature model of mind. In: *Personal Relations Theory: Fairbairn, Macmurray and Suttie* (pp. 91–114). London: Routledge.

Clarke, G. S. (2012). Failures of the "moral defense" in the films *Shutter Island*, *Inception*, and *Memento*: Narcissism or schizoid personality disorder. *International Journal of Psychoanalysis*, 93: 203–218.

Fairbairn, W. R. D. (1938a). Prolegomena to a psychology of art. *British Journal of Psychology*, 28: 288–303. In: E. F. Birtles & D. E. Scharff (Eds.), *From Instinct to Self: Selected Papers of W. R. D. Fairbairn, Volume II: Applications and Early Contributions* (pp. 381–396). Northvale, NJ: Jason Aronson, 1994.

Fairbairn, W. R. D. (1938b). The ultimate basis of aesthetic experience. *British Journal of Psychology*, 29: 167–181. In: E. F. Birtles & D. E. Scharff (Eds.), *From Instinct to Self: Selected Papers of W. R. D. Fairbairn, Volume II: Applications and Early Contributions* (pp. 397–409). Northvale, NJ: Jason Aronson, 1994.

Fairbairn, W. R. D. (1939b). Author's abstract: Prolegomena to a psychology of art. *International Journal of Psychoanalysis*, 21: 192–193.

Fairbairn, W. R. D. (1940b). Author's abstract: The ultimate basis of aesthetic experience. *International Journal of Psychoanalysis*, 21: 96–97.

Fairbairn, W. R. D. (1941). A revised psychopathology of the psychoses and psychoneuroses. *International Journal of Psychoanalysis*, 22(3, 4): 250–279. In: *Psychoanalytic Studies of the Personality* (pp. 28–58). London: Tavistock, 1952.

Fairbairn, W. R. D. (1943a). The repression and the return of bad objects (with special reference to the "war neuroses"). *British Journal of Medical Psychology*, 19: 327–341. In: *Psychoanalytic Studies of the Personality* (pp. 59–81). London: Tavistock, 1952.

Fairbairn, W. R. D. (1944). Endopsychic structure considered in terms of object-relationships. *International Journal of Psychoanalysis*, 25: 70–92. In: *Psychoanalytic Studies of the Personality* (pp. 82–136). London: Tavistock, 1952.

Fairbairn, W. R. D. (1951c). Critical notice: *On Not Being Able to Paint* by Joanna Field (1950). *British Journal of Medical Psychology*, 24: 69–76. In: E. F. Birtles & D. E. Scharff (Eds.), *From Instinct to Self: Selected Papers of W. R. D. Fairbairn, Volume II: Applications and Early Contributions* (pp. 417–422). Northvale, NJ: Jason Aronson, 1994.

Fairbairn, W. R. D. (1952). *Psychoanalytic Studies of the Personality*. London: Tavistock. [Reprinted Routledge & Kegan Paul, 1972.]

Fairbairn, W. R. D. (1953). Critical notice: *Psychoanalytic Explorations in Art* by Ernst Kris (1952). *British Journal of Medical Psychology*, 26: 164–169. In: E. F. Birtles & D. E. Scharff (Eds.), *From Instinct to Self: Selected Papers of W. R. D. Fairbairn, Volume II: Applications and Early Contributions* (pp. 423–432). Northvale, NJ: Jason Aronson, 1994.

Fairbairn, W. R. D. (1956b). A critical evaluation of certain psycho-analytical conceptions. *British Journal for the Philosophy of Science*, 7: 49–60. In: D. E. Scharff & E. F. Birtles (Eds.), *From Instinct to Self: Selected Papers of W. R. D. Fairbairn, Volume I: Clinical and Theoretical Papers* (as Re-evaluating some basic concepts, pp. 129–138). Northvale, NJ: Jason Aronson, 1994.

Fairbairn, W. R. D. (1963a). Synopsis of an object-relations theory of the personality. *International Journal of Psychoanalysis*, 44: 224–225. In: D. E. Scharff & E. F. Birtles (Eds.), *From Instinct to Self: Selected Papers of W. R. D. Fairbairn, Volume I: Clinical and Theoretical Papers* (pp. 155–156). Northvale, NJ: Jason Aronson, 1994.

Fairbairn, W. R. D. (1963b). Autobiographical note. *British Journal of Medical Psychology, 36*: 107. In: E. F. Birtles & D. E. Scharff (Eds.), *From Instinct to Self: Selected Papers of W. R. D. Fairbairn, Volume II: Applications and Early Contributions* (pp. 462–464). Northvale, NJ: Jason Aronson, 1994.

Field, J. [pseud. Milner, M.] (1950). *On Not Being Able to Paint* (2nd edition). Los Angeles, CA: J. P. Tarcher, 1957.

Freud, S. (1910c). *Leonardo da Vinci and a Memory of his Childhood. S. E., 11*: 57–138. London: Hogarth.

Freud, S. (1914b). The Moses of Michelangelo. *S. E., 13*: 209–238. London: Hogarth.

Freud, S. (1926d). *Inhibitions, Symptoms and Anxiety. S. E., 20*: 75–176. London: Hogarth.

Freud, S. (1933a). *New Introductory Lectures on Psycho-Analysis. S. E., 22.* London: Hogarth.

Glover, N. (2009). *Psychoanalytic Aesthetics: An Introduction to the British School.* London: Karnac.

Gosso, S. (Ed.) (2004). *Psychoanalysis and Art: Kleinian Perspectives.* London: Karnac.

Kant, I. (1783). *Kant's Prolegomena to Any Future Metaphysics.* London: Kegan Paul, 1902.

Klein, M. (1929). Infantile anxiety-situations reflected in a work of art and in the creative impulse. *International Journal of Psychoanalysis, 10*: 436–443.

Klein, M. (1932). *The Psychoanalysis of Children.* London: Hogarth.

Klein, M. (1935). A contribution to the psychogenesis of manic-depressive states. *International Journal of Psychoanalysis, 16*: 145–174.

Klein, M. (1946). Notes on some schizoid mechanisms. *International Journal of Psychoanalysis, 27*: 99–110.

Kris, E. (1952). *Psychoanalytic Explorations in Art* (2nd edition). New York: Schocken, 1974.

Levine, S. Z. (1998). Alter egos—close encounters of the paranoid kind: W. R. D. Fairbairn, Salvador Dali, and me. In: N. J. Skolnick & D. E. Scharff (Eds.), *Fairbairn, Then and Now* (pp. 179–196). Hillsdale, NJ: Analytic Press.

Pappenheim, E., & Kris, E. (1946). The function of drawings and the meaning of the "creative spell" in a schizophrenic artist. *Psychoanalytic Quarterly, 15*: 6–31.

Pereira, F. (2002). Fairbairn, dreaming, and aesthetic experience. In: F. Pereira & D. E. Scharff (Eds.), *Fairbairn and Relational Theory* (pp. 111–125). London: Karnac.

Read, H. (1937). *Art and Society* (2nd edition). London: Pantheon, 1945.

Read, H. (1939). Letter to Fairbairn, January 1, 1939. In Fairbairn's manuscripts at the National Library of Scotland, Edinburgh (courtesy of Graham S. Clarke).

Read, H. (1951). Psycho-analysis and the problem of aesthetic value. *International Journal of Psychoanalysis, 32*: 73–82.

Scharff, D. E., & Birtles, E. F. (Eds.) (1994). *From Instinct to Self: Selected Papers of W. R. D. Fairbairn, Volume I: Clinical and Theoretical Papers.* Northvale, NJ: Jason Aronson.

Scharff, D. E., & Birtles, E. F. (1997). From instinct to self: The evolution and implications of W. R. D. Fairbairn's theory of object relations. *International Journal of Psychoanalysis, 78*(6): 1085–1103.

Segal, H. (1952). A psycho-analytical approach to aesthetics. *International Journal of Psychoanalysis, 33*: 196–207.

Sutherland, J. D. (1989). *Fairbairn's Journey into the Interior.* London: Free Association.

Wallace, W. (1894). *Prolegomena to the Study of Hegel's Philosophy and Especially of his Logic.* Oxford: Clarendon.

Whitehead, A. N. (1928). *Symbolism: Its Meaning and Effect.* New York: Macmillan.

CHAPTER THIRTY-SIX

Viewing Camus's *The Stranger* from the perspective of W. R. D. Fairbairn's object relations

Rainer Rehberger

A few years ago I encountered an analysand, who, faced with the turmoil of his own emotions was mesmerised by the lack of sorrow and the seemingly inevitable death sentence on Meursault, Camus's anti-hero of *The Stranger*. This analysand opened my eyes towards the anti-hero's dilemma, being caught between apathy and guilt. In the following I will discuss existential distress in general, and then Meursault's distress viewed from a rational psychoanalytic perspective. I will depict the basic outline of affect regulation, of grief and the consequences of alexithymia. In addition I will demonstrate how it is possible to access the experiences and behaviour as depicted in the *The Stranger* (1942) by gaining an understanding of affect regulation.

To this end I will summarise the novel's events with an emphasis on Meursault's emotional attitude towards himself and others, such as his deceased mother and other people in his life, including their emotions. Based on a few noteworthy events in Camus's biography I will argue for certain assumptions concerning the author's typical childhood experiences. I will draw out ideas on the possible internalised relationships with his father and mother, which Camus presented externally through the depiction of many interactions throughout Meursault's story. I will present these external events as reflections of internalised relationships, split into solely good or solely bad relationships. I will compare conscious grief with averted grief during depression, and portray the meaning of averting grief for Meursault, concluding with a brief depiction of the similarity with the emotional difficulties of my analysand and their immediate use for day-to-day therapeutic work. I do so from a Fairbairnian perspective.

Direct fear of death or persistent life-threatening danger, the loss of relatives and friends, and the curtailing of life's possibilities due to illness, unemployment, or delinquency equal an *existential crisis*. The greater the resulting helplessness seems, the more threatening these crises appear and the more quickly they can induce the fear of death. Infants and toddlers are overwhelmed when faced with inadequate care, neglect of their basic needs, or violence. If their cry for help is not heard, this deprivation leads them to suffer feelings of helplessness and even the fear of impending death. When they cry in need of care, comfort, safety, and help, when they are hungry or in pain and are subsequently yelled at, shaken, beat, hurt, strangled, bound, or put aside without being provided for, their despair increases exponentially. If they are forced to eat, sleep, defecate, or are painfully restricted in their quest for knowledge they will permanently feel overwhelmed and threatened by demands, reprimands, and instructions. Repeatedly sustained helplessness in combination with the fear of death is permanently stored within their emotional memory. It can be reactivated within the adult by an existential crisis and drastically worsen the subjective perception of the present—for example anxiety—and panic attacks induced by remote or non-existent danger.

Today, relational psychoanalysis and object relations theory (Fairbairn) see the origin of neurotic and psychotic disorders as well as personality disorders in painful relationship experiences. These bad experiences are internalised and frequently constitute the schizoid core of our conscious and our dynamically unconscious personality. Schizoid means that only that side of the personality revolving around unfulfilled love or that side of the personality revolving around hate become active, or that they alternate. The self-image or the image of others is then solely good or solely bad. These subconscious centres of our personality, remaining within the confines of early childhood development, are determined by emotional experiences and are acquired through emotion regulation.

Emotion or affect regulation applies to unconsciously exaggerated emotions, experiencing them as mediocre and socially compliant, or masking them. Affect regulation is characteristically firmly determined and controls the way we deal with emotions such as grief, frustration, fear, joy, or disgust. Infants learn affect regulation from the parenting person. The child is acting according to the mother's example; at the same time this kind of affect regulation ensures that the child's attachment efforts and cries for help are often ignored. Fears are suppressed and the child no longer anticipates any help. He no longer seeks intimacy in relationships. He suppresses the desire to bond, suppresses his fears and grief, even his anger, and then shuts down. This results in the typical schizoid retreat to the inner world of internalised object relations. At the same time this is experienced as severe stress, affecting the hormonal and the cardiovascular systems. This is the basis of *emotional blindness* or alexithymia—the inability to read one's own emotions. Modern imaging examination procedures of the healthy brain show that even emotions which are no longer perceived consciously are highly active and can be experienced as organ and entire organ-system dysfunctions. Suppressed relationship grief pertains to suppressed crying (dry eyes). Grief is not consciously experienced as a consequence of pain and deprivation within a relationship with others, or the feeling of loss by the means of death or divorce. Often an organ or an entire apparatus will ache—such as the stomach, the head, or the back. According to a dualistic mentality, pain is then exclusively experienced on a physical basis. This is typical for depression within the suppression of relational grief. Rubbing of dry eyes and deep sighing are fragments of crying—often clearly evident to others. The suppression of grief is a quick fix when a crying child is not consoled but beaten or ridiculed and scorned with insulting phrases such as "cry-baby", "stop whining", "stop annoying me", "boys don't cry", "wimp", or "spare me the drama". Many try to escape the grief by identifying with the bully and bashfully laughing—all the while experiencing emotional pain. They should be crying. Without the knowledge of grief and tears relationships become empty, comfort is not to be found in emphatic people, compassion with oneself and also with others is absent. Others, also experiencing grief, are often bewildered. Without experiencing conscious pain sustained through injuries—physically or morally—it becomes more difficult to sense anger towards aggressors. The hopes for empathy, respect, and comfort from others are no longer nourished. They remain desolate, desperate, and hopeless. The un-consoled and wary can only turn to themselves for help, since they mistrust others. They no longer rely on others to attain security; they shut down, pull away, and only accept superficial encounters.

Pain and coping are central elements when dealing with grief after the death of a family member. To cry is an expression of pain in almost all cultures. Mourning rituals have been established in order to ease the severe shock of the mourners and to part with the deceased (e.g., the mourners coming together at the funeral service and the burial). Close family members are isolated from other groups of society (e.g., the year of mourning). They no longer partake in festivities, parties, and other amusements. In cases of an unexpected death, family members experience shock-like pain that often evolves into a long-term chronic pain. This chronic mourning is similar to a depressive state. Separation is the common ground for everyone's grief. Hence the basic affects of grieving can be found in the affects of separation experiences, fear, the desire for solidarity, pain, helplessness, and anger.

Those who suffer early deprivation and neglect or who are strongly coerced develop a schizoid personality, as Fairbairn described. They are often incapable of sensing their own anger alongside their suppression of pain. Faced with problems in their professional life, experiencing difficulties of standing their ground, claiming to be taken advantage of on a regular basis by their superiors or spouses when assaulted, or given an impossible work load, they cannot say "No". Instead of anger they experience strong tension, muscular aches, or headaches, without noticing the connection to aggravating events or adequately distancing themselves. This proves to be immensely inhibiting in regard to their social abilities.

Being prepared for the death of a family member due to a long illness or old age facilitates grieving; an unexpected death impedes grief. When pain, helplessness, despair, and frustration with the meaning of life and death threaten to overwhelm family members left behind, grief is suppressed and averted, as is the case when there are multiple deceased, the loss of several family members within a short time span or an especially horrible cause of death. Often the reason is to be found in the suppression of grief, pain, and anger within a person with a history of neglect, coercion, or violence in their early childhood. Often they direct anger towards themselves, which is then perceived as guilt.

A psychoanalytical interpretation of The Stranger

Which of Camus's presumed own affects is it possible to find within Meursault and his friends?

Meursault is characterised as a young man, single, appreciated by his boss as a good employee. His relationships with his friends and colleagues are friendly but shallow; he has no ambitions for his professional life, no hobbies. He loves women but has not been in a committed relationship. He finds Marie's laugh especially attractive. Upon receiving the notice of his mother's death he reacts as if it was the death of a stranger. Almost unaffected, he realises, "I do not know when she died." Also he realises that he does not know her exact age. The fact that his boss does "not look delighted" after hearing the news activates a feeling of guilt, and his justification that her death is not his fault. Obviously Meursault lacks the ability to perceive his own grief and possibly even the ability to perceive empathy in others. Hence he cannot properly interpret his boss's facial expression. He thinks of him as being strict and uncooperative. Meursault reacts submissively, precisely as he does towards the director of the nursing home and his neighbour Raymond. Is Meursault, who grew up without a father (just as Camus himself—Lottman, 1979, pp. 14–19), submissive and in thrall to men, based upon an unfulfilled longing for a father? Does he confuse pity with consideration after the verdict due to the lack of consideration all through his early childhood? Does he lack tact towards Marie or Salamano because he cannot perceive empathy? Is he so captivated by the only anecdote concerning his father because the father died the same senseless death that he is bound to die? Did the execution induce the father's vomiting because in his fantasy the convict had been his son?

The most common fantasy of family members concerns the thought "the loved one is still alive", which is often witnessed after a shocking death or when the body has not actually been seen. Meursault hints at this, when stating that it was a bit as if his mother had not died. He wants the grieving process to be completed along with the burial. He reacts absent-mindedly towards the sympathy expressed by friends and acquaintances. After the burial, lack of attention and avoidance aid him in ignoring his grief. The following day he actually tries to go on as if he had not lost his only living relative, his mother. He goes for a swim, flirts, is taken out to see a Fernandel movie and makes love to a former work colleague. Camus sets up many instances of sympathy shown by others as a counterpart for Meursault's apparent numbness and indifference, be it the explicit wording, "You only have one mother", a firm handshake, or Marie's shock when she finds out that Meursault had buried his mother the day before.

Upon noticing Marie's shock that he is in mourning and yet able to go out for a swim in such a light-hearted manner, Meursault feels guilty and subsequently assumes that "one always feels a bit guilty". It appears that Camus, while writing this novel in his twenties, was experiencing a form of extensive access to the topics of grief and defence mechanisms for grief, and problems around individual and social existence. Presumably he possessed extraordinary observation and self-observation skills.

Camus presents Meursault's survival techniques when faced with grief most candidly. Meursault suppresses pain, fear, and anger. Yet at the same time he suggests that his heart was just as engulfed in these feelings as the empathy and sympathy brought forth by friends and acquaintances. The typical depressive condition caused by the suppression of emotions becomes evident in his feelings of guilt, his tendency to feel ashamed, his sleepiness, his physical aches, and his loss of appetite. Furthermore, it is likely that difficult early childhood experiences compelled him to suppress anger, hate, and rage. Due to these circumstances he often acts subserviently while he is also inclined to rebel quietly—come in late and procrastinate over cleaning his apartment.

Fairbairn (1944) describes unreasonable feelings of guilt as the "super-ego defence" or "moral defence" attributed to individuals who suffered from unbearable neglect and abuse as infants or toddlers. They compensate for their overwhelming helplessness by following the punishing parent's model and considering themselves as bad, evil, and guilty. They suppress pain and compensate for the associated helplessness with self-blame and feelings of guilt. This formulation can be applied in Meursault's case. Camus must have been very familiar with this.

Meursault does not cry for his deceased mother nor does he reminisce about the times they shared. He can only recollect a bleak memory, a state of unrelated togetherness: his old and apparently deaf mother (Camus's mother was partially deaf—Lottman, 1979, pp. 15–19) silently watches his every move in the apartment. Is she controlling him? This might have caused him to consciously send her to the nursing home. Instead of grief over his mother's death Meursault consciously experiences various ailments such as headache, exhaustion, fatigue, and sleepiness. While talking to his lawyer he explicitly verbalises that his physical condition often prevents him from experiencing relational emotions. He suppresses the reversed relation of cause and effect, and turns the perceived connections upside down. Hence his ailments are masking his grief.

The way he directly experiences the beauty and ugliness of the climate, nature, and the weather is impressively sincere. He is free in his sexual desires and vividly experiences a tender and sensual togetherness.

Camus contrasts his anti-hero's lack of grief due to the separation from his mother, with his neighbour Salamano's separation and panic at the loss of his dog. As much as he has beaten, cursed, and rejected his dog, his agony over losing the animal is intense. Meursault completely lacks any kind of empathy for Salamano's situation, and coldly advises him to acquire a new dog. Meursault is faintly bored when confronted with the old man's grief. This might be his means of protection against the realisation of fear and pain due to his own abandonment experiences, and his abandonment-induced panic and helplessness.

The moment that Meursault eagerly desires to kiss a laughing Marie coincides with the abuse and beating of a woman by the pimp. Meursault almost endorses the pimp's satisfaction at having abused the woman by considering the rest of the evening spent with the man to have been "nice".

Meursault's satisfaction during the abuse scene between the pimp and his alleged mistress can easily be understood as projection from the suppressed, hateful punishment fantasies towards woman, mother, and grandmother.

The day of the crime, sixteen days after his mother's funeral, Meursault is indisposed. This suits his depressive state of mind, which he only experiences due to the spare time he has at the weekend. He is hardly able to get up and finds his cigarette distasteful. Marie laughs at him for having such a "funeral face". After the brawl and the knife fight around noon, the sun, the heat, the drought, and the brightness have unbearably intensified Meursault's condition. The glistening sunbeams hurt him, he feels deeply wounded by the reflection of light from the glass and his victim's knife. Immediately before the crime is committed he is in a state of shock, he is blinded by sweat and salt as his mother's friend had been blinded by tears and grief during the procession. Meursault consciously thinks that this is the same sun under which he had suffered so violently during at the funeral. The shock he is experiencing through the climate is equivalent to his suppressed shock of grief accompanied by tears, grief, abandonment, despair, and hopelessness.

Until the murder is committed Raymond was the novel's bearer of hate: hate towards a disobedient woman and towards the brother wanting to avenge his sister. Meursault never expressed or experienced anger or hate. Instead he remained submissive and full of guilt. Now he has been contaminated and his own hate is touched by Raymond's bloodlust. After the bloody altercation and armed with the revolver, struck by increasing heat exhaustion, Meursault more preconsciously than intentionally taps into his own murderous rage.

When in grief, anger and rage are seldom experienced as pain and tears. Deriving from guilt, angry and hateful attacks are inverted, such as through self-mutilation. These are ritualised and performed throughout different cultures. Alternatively hate and anger are projected onto the deceased, which haunt and frighten the living as evil spirits. In suppressed grief, as in a depression, guilty anxiety and compulsive self-punishment often lead to chronic ailments. Suppressed hate in combination with suppressed hateful fantasies, including those generated in early childhood, becomes a heavy burden when grieving the loss of one's mother, father, or other close relatives. Apparently Meursault seeks out the abused woman's avenger. He shoots him in a state of shock due to the heat and the light. After quickly bracing himself he fires four more shots into the body. Are these shots symbolically meant for himself and his family?

I will continue by interpreting the events of the novel as externalised images of a single personality's various sides and depict comparable imagery in dreams, viewing the hero as an alter ego or doppelganger of the author. First a few words concerning different sides of a personality based on W. R. D. Fairbairn's object relationship psychology.

The active longing self (*the active libidinal ego*) stores unfulfilled yearnings for love and unfulfilled hunger for attention. This longing self is continuously unconscious in its origin, but is able to influence the perceptions and activity of the conscious personality, the conscious central self. Active desire is directed towards the longed for and generally inadequately obtained good, loving side of the mother, which becomes, according to Fairbairn, the exciting object.

In the novel Meursault is not consciously familiar with having any desire for another. He does not long for a fulfilling relationship or any form of recognition from others in his career. His suppressed desire for a loving woman is consciously restricted to sexual desire. His sexual pleasure is the unfulfilled puerile desire for a laughingly loving mother. Is this why he finds Marie's laughter so desirable? When Céleste takes the stand as a witness, Meursault surprisingly feels the urge to kiss his agonisingly shaken friend. Can the root of this impulse be found in an unfulfilled desire for a loving father?

The passive longing self (*the passive libidinal ego*) stores conditions of deprivation, abandonment, disappointments, helplessness, despair, meaninglessness, agony, hopelessness, and panic over abandonment in an unfulfilled desire for attention. They constitute a depressive emotional condition.

Meursault has suppressed this side. He has suppressed his relational pain and therefore is only capable of consciously feeling organ and organ-system related pain, such as heat exhaustion. When at risk of being reminded of his depressive condition he feels exhausted, tired, and becomes absent-minded, sleeps or grows bored. "I do not know", means he has repressed why the old man Salamano's desolate crying reminds him of his mother. Did he need to repress a childhood memory of remaining uncomforted by his unhappy mother when crying? Marie consciously becomes his substitute as a bearer of an unfulfilled desire for love and attention beyond sexuality. In place of himself Meursault makes her an unfulfilled woman longing for love.

In the *novel*, Salamano is haunted by abandonment-panic and breaks down when he loses his dog. He weeps bitterly at night. He is the bearer of Meursault's long-since repressed and suppressed passive unfulfilled desiring self.

In *dreams*, wishes to obtain the desired other—abandonment, unfulfilled desires, and the failure to get involved in a romantic relationship are depicted in the guise of an unfulfilled desire for a mothering object and the passive unfulfilled desiring self.

The active anti-libidinal ego (Rehberger, 2006, pp. 125–140) is the hating side of a personality. It is also continuous and compellingly unconscious in its origin. This side of the personality is the home of destructive anger and murderous hate, in other words hate's archetype, the fundamentalist's hate. This aspect is modelled in accordance with the internalised ideal of the hating and haunting object. This is the condition in which Meursault experiences the sun literally beating down on him, culminating in his headache prior to the murder, and in his suppressed anger, seen in his clenching his teeth and his fists, and tensing his entire body in order to overcome the impenetrable frenzy which the sun has cast upon him. In this condition he kills.

The hating and haunting object (*the anti-libidinal object*) is a representation of internalised strict and hateful sides of the angry and abusive mother. These bad sides are "split" from the good and desired sides, which are represented through the inner desired object. The two sides are permanently isolated and separated from each other. When hate and anger become conscious, the desired good side of the other stays completely unconscious. The inner persecution led by the hating object is consciously experienced as a guilty conscience or a feeling of guilt. The endless self-persecution accompanied by self-accusation serves as a defence against the helplessness, which is constantly threatening to surface due to the passive longing self.

To Meursault the sun is like a hating, abusive, and tormenting mother. He has learned to fend off hate and anger from consciousness by means of repression. Instead he always feels somewhat guilty, hence persecuted by the inner, hating side of his mother. His feelings of guilt and the subsequent submissiveness are the most comforting emotions he is able to experience in relationships.

In the novel his neighbour and "friend" Raymond is the bearer of hate towards man and woman alike, towards the former mistress and her avenging brother. In other words Meursault is unconsciously identified with him. Only under the pressure of suppressed grief and the consciousness of heat exhaustion does he finally express his own murderous rage. We can envision the four shots to the body as representing his murderous hate for his mother, father, grandmother, and, due to his feelings of guilt, for himself. They transform what is a conceivable act of self-defence into murder and symbolic suicide. The suicidal aspect is confirmed when, in his cell on death row, he consciously senses a venomous joy while imagining being a spectator at an execution.

In the novel the examining magistrate, the assigned counsel, and the prosecutor are the haunting objects. Enraged with hate, the prosecuting attorney demands the death sentence for a man who allegedly buried his mother with the heart of a criminal.

In dreams of murder and destruction, dreamers themselves, influenced by the hating object and the hating self, partially kill and murder. For the most part they are only spectators of implied or executed acts of violence, killing, or destruction. Dreams are fed by the hated self (*the passive anti-libidinal ego*—Rehberger, 2006, pp. 125–140) with its abundance of grief caused by physical and moral violence. The dreamer feels threatened, shamed, accused, degraded, prosecuted, raped, overrun, injured, mutilated, and killed. Within this hated self lies the representation of the pain, the violations, and the suffering caused by unjust attacks by mothers and fathers.

The bearers of this side are the abused woman and Salamano's abused dog. This side is empathically shared by various people—the dog's abuse by Céleste and Raymond, the screaming woman's suffering by Marie and the other tenants. Meursault meanwhile is untouched by the dog's whimpering and the woman's screams. At long last in his cell he is frightfully cold and his teeth chatter knowing that he will be the victim of an execution. Previously the idea of an execution had provoked venomous joy.

* * *

As I have shown Camus was able to outline the various, partially contradictory emotional experiences and emotional conditions found in a single personality, by using different characters in his novel. The affective relations are described by the conscious traits of the different characters. Meursault mainly suppresses these conditions since the admission of grief and anger would initiate an existential crisis. He is only able to detect the pathway to his murderous rage when he is "beaten by the sun" and suffers from unbearable physical shock. Meursault can only remotely experience access to the loving relationship with Marie, because of his grief, due to his feelings of abandonment, and his fear of death. His feelings of guilt, for which no explanation is given, invade every relationship. Fairbairn's concept of the "moral defence" adequately explains this inclination for guilt. The crime and the ensuing punishment finally reconcile his feelings of guilt.

In his cell Meursault undergoes a dramatic inner change. Incandescent with outrage and upheaval, he indignantly unveils his access to the blatant injustice of our individual and social existence. He racks his mind, searching for a way out, yet in the end he is forced to come to terms with the inevitable fate of a "dead man walking". Filled with rage he shocks and attacks the chaplain eager to guide him out of fear and despair. Meursault angrily hurls his philosophy of the absurd at him. At this point Camus has become one with the hero—the author has been working on *The Myth of Sisyphus*. In the end the hero is rejuvenated by the beauty of sensually experienced nature, and comes finally to understand his unhappy mother's agony. He is overcome with sympathy through understanding that a senseless war had deprived her as a young woman of a groom. Through the consciousness of his and every man's existence in his cell, his vanity, Meursault finds empathy and love for his mother. He is happy and all he yearns for is the consideration, the sympathy of others when he dies—a consideration he had not been able to provide for his deceased mother.

Years ago, my analysand provided me with a personal understanding of *The Stranger*. During analysis the patient had been struggling for years to access his suppressed pain and grief by clarifying his history of deprivation and abuse. Later on he struggled to become able to consciously experience adequate, understandable, and comprehensible, *healthy*, impotent rage and revenge fantasies, both towards his barely accessible mother, who had suffered from depression, and towards his father, who had been violently abusive throughout the patient's childhood and adolescence. The father himself apparently sought revenge for his own suffering under a strict veteran father, through the cruel treatment of his son. In the meantime I tried to convey how necessary and sensible it was to derive meaning about his dramatic everyday willingness to endure guilt and submissiveness in his marriage and in his professional life. Eventually, we agreed that he needed to understand the "soothing" fantasies he had of being executed, before falling asleep, as inverted revenge fantasies originally directed towards his parents.

Meursault's fate illustrates how far-reaching emotional blindness and the suppression of emotions can be, especially when dealing with grief, anger, and fear. On the one hand, the inner suppression serves as a protector against feeling overwhelmed, helpless, in despair, hopeless, meaningless, in pain, and anger. On the other hand, social relationships are undermined, the actual experience of a relationship degenerates, and grief is misplaced. Through Camus we recognise the revolt, the outrage, and the upheaval an infant, unequipped with the capacity for regulating affects needed for successful bonding, experiences when having to free himself from agony, fear, helplessness, and impotence.

Therapeutic work with patients suffering from dry eyes, various organ or organ-system dysfunctions and aches lacking any conventional medical cause, should take into consideration:

- the abolition of affect-suppression
- the clarification of repressed hateful fantasies in the dynamic unconscious by the active anti-libidinal self as the origin of a misplaced urge to take on blame and the compulsion for punishment
- the acknowledgement of panic and depressive conditions as an ever impending realisation of the amnesic, non-recollecting unconscious within the passive libidinal self with its experience of deprivation, abandonment, violence, and compulsion
- the clarification of bothersome characteristic traits, which the adult acquired as a quick fix and means of survival in his childhood, but which he maintains, unaware of the context and not knowing that they have become obsolete.

What are the important consequences for us as readers? We understand the shattering impact that hits us when we first acknowledge death's conclusiveness. Suddenly we are able to see that the insight of an individual living in the face of death in a prison cell with a clear perception of its inevitability, despite all inner rebellion, is the beginning of any and every cultural movement. After obtaining more knowledge and experience, we find that our ancestors, long since dead yet still living within us genetically and by their transferred knowledge, rebelled and fought against these inevitabilities. They created a variety of religions and philosophies promising a happy death. This was true even for Sartre as he called for a social revolution that was already failing. Camus's knowledge of the absurdity of religious and philosophical endeavours to avoid the individual's death, his knowledge of the futile sweet promise of individual infinity if one only strives enough, allows him to resort to the image of Sisyphus, infinitely punished for his crime in accordance with mundane ideals of justice. Within all cultural revolts, trying to evade the individual's demise, we continuously find ourselves mentally exhausted and back at the beginning of our laborious cultural endeavour. Camus's solace is a "happy death", knowing that we are closely bound to nature's beauty and ugliness, and to our kin, hence to our mothers and fathers, happy and unhappy in their mortality and vanity. *The Happy Death* had, incidentally, been the working title of *The Stranger*.

Translation by Rebecca Tovar (Tovar@sigmund-freud-institut.de)

References

Camus, A. (1942). *L'étranger*. Paris: Gallimard. English edition *The Stranger*. M. Ward (Trans.). London: Random House, Everyman's Library, 1993.

Fairbairn, W. R. D. (1944). Endopsychic structure considered in terms of object-relationships. *International Journal of Psychoanalysis*, 25: 70–92. In: *Psychoanalytic Studies of the Personality* (pp. 82–136). London: Tavistock, 1952.

Lottman, H. R. (1979). *Albert Camus. A Biography*. London: Weidenfeld and Nicholson

Rehberger, R. (2006). Libido, die das Objekt sucht, und die Bindungstheorie Bowlbys heute. In: *W. R. D. Fairbairns Bedeutung für die Moderne Objektbeziehungstheorie. Theoretische und klinische Weiterentwicklungen*. Gießen, Germany: Psychosozial.

CHAPTER THIRTY-SEVEN

The family is the first social group, followed by the clan, tribe, and nation

Ron B. Aviram

The promise of psychoanalysis to improve the lives of individuals is paralleled by its broader aspirations to contribute to a better world. Fairbairn (1939c) was a strong advocate of utilising psychoanalytic theory to this end. He wrote, "If modern psychoanalytical theory is capable of ameliorative clinical application in the case of psychological disorder, it is also capable of ameliorative clinical application in the case of sociological disorders" (1952, p. 255). Nevertheless, the field of psychoanalysis evolved as a clinical approach to treat individuals. More than a half century ago Fairbairn (1957) understood that the most significant contribution that psychoanalysis can offer in promoting mental health would be to aid in prevention. Psychoanalytic work with adult patients taught us about the lasting repercussions of early life experience. Fairbairn felt that the best education we can provide to a wider audience has to do with child rearing. He was keenly aware of the importance of the family context, especially with how it can provide emotional security to children, and protect them from the trauma of emotional deprivations. Psychoanalysis deserves credit for its part in contributing to the evolution of society by offering tangible information that assists many people in contributing to the better lives of the next generation. This is one example of how psychoanalysis does go beyond the usual one person at a time method of clinical psychoanalysis.

Unfortunately, the potential application of psychoanalytic ideas to problems in society has not been widely appreciated by psychoanalysts. Although Freud applied psychoanalytic concepts to a broad spectrum of topics, he was reluctant to comment about the use of psychoanalysis to resolve intergroup problems in society (1935b). This reluctance has persisted with the consequence of little understanding about the psychodynamic implications of large group representations in the mind. As a result, when psychoanalytic ideas are applied to large group phenomena too often the interpersonal dynamics that psychoanalysts know well are superimposed onto the conditions that manifest between nations, religious groups, ethnic groups, etc., which they are trying to explain. There may be some similarities between the dynamics that are enacted between two people and those that occur between two large groups, but they are not identical. For example, we have evidence that when people perceive themselves as members of a large group (e.g., national identity), they tend to perceive other people as large group members as well, rather than as individuals (Hogg & Abrams, 1988). People are then perceived as either members of the same group (ingroup), or members of a different group (outgroup). This helps explain why psychoanalytic theories that use projection or displacement of aggression to account for intergroup hostility have had little reliability when it comes to behaviour that is widespread in a society. Overall those kinds of formulations do not account for the ubiquitous effects of large group membership. Psychoanalytic theories have not proved to be helpful in understanding, explaining, or changing problems on a societal level. As a consequence very few significant ideas have emerged to inspire renewed efforts by psychoanalysts to tackle the large group dimension of human relations and contribute to prevention beyond one person at a time. This has limited the scope of psychoanalysis. Problems in society such as prejudice, intergroup conflict, and war have received little attention from psychoanalysts and psychoanalysis is often dismissed as unhelpful by other fields concerned with these problems.

The unconscious group

The title of this chapter comes from W. R. D. Fairbairn's paper, "The Sociological Significance of Communism Considered in the Light of Psychoanalysis" (1935b). In this paper he describes an historical evolution of national group formation which is intertwined with basic psychological functions that occur early in relationships within the family. He had an intuitive understanding about the relevance of large groups in people's lives. For example, in his paper on war neuroses he describes the psychological need that some soldiers have for their association with the Army (Fairbairn, 1943a). These individuals seem to have had a history of dependence with the family group (or mother figure in particular), which he called infantile dependence. This is a kind of dependence upon the significant people in early life which is internalised and does not mature into a more stable, well-differentiated relationship. For Fairbairn a persistence of infantile dependence into adulthood is associated with psychopathology. The Army became an important large group identification for soldiers in general, but some soldiers depended upon this affiliation for their personal well-being. The soldiers Fairbairn discussed in this paper had a psychological breakdown when the Army did not reward their enthusiasm for being soldiers. Instead, it probably gave the military authorities pause to see such eagerness to go to war, and as a soldier's over-determined zeal was thwarted the latent pathology emerged. For these soldiers the identification with the military was vital in sustaining their identity and ability to function adequately. In other words, they internalised the military as an object relationship upon which they had an infantile dependence. Fairbairn understood the quality of their dependence to be associated with a defensive process called primary identification in which there is no differentiation between self and other.

In the course of his theorising, however, Fairbairn did not pursue the implications of the role of large groups in the internal object world. This was a logical blind spot in the development of his ideas given that he considered all sociological problems to stem from individual psychology.

This suggested to him that by understanding interpersonal processes we would understand intergroup processes. He concluded that in order to learn about large group phenomena we need to study the psychology of the individual in the group. In my opinion this is an error that leads to a failure to recognise that the individual's participation in the world is at times not as an autonomous person, but as a member of a large group. We know that people experience themselves differently in an interpersonal context, as opposed to an intergroup context in which their ingroup or outgroup status is relevant. This suggests that a psychological shift has occurred in the mind. We can extrapolate from Fairbairn's ideas to recognise that large groups which end up becoming part of our self-concept are identified with in such a way that they become new and unique object relationships. This allows us to conceptualise the role of the *large group in the mind*, rather than the individual in the group.

The trajectory of psychoanalytic theory points in this direction. Historically, the emphasis was on the tension relief from internal instinctual needs and pathological adaptations of the patient in reaction to the limits of the object world in providing outlets for need gratification. Then in Fairbairn's time the importance of a satisfying interpersonal world, in and of itself, emerged as the fundamental determinant of motivation and mental health. The person in a social network was recognised but not to the extent that we were able to acknowledge the large groups in which the network gets established as an influencing entity as well. Fairbairn's paper on communism refers to the potential impact of the large group upon individuals. His focus was specifically on how the large group (in this case the nation) evolved from unconscious needs of individual psyches. By following this trajectory of ideas today we recognise the dialectical quality in interactions between individuals. Fairbairn's paper is suggestive of a dialectical influence between a person and the large groups in his or her environment which we can develop further.

Large group formation

In this early paper Fairbairn (1935b) relies on Freudian classical theory to make sense of the unavoidable attachments that begin in the family. This first group experience is then recreated with successive large groups that try to substitute for the family. He explains that libido binds members of a group together, and that the aggression of individuals is the source of disruptions in all societies. This is essentially Freud's (1921c) formulation in *Group Psychology and the Analysis of the Ego*. It is important to keep in mind that this paper was written before Fairbairn firmly developed his ideas about the natural desire for affiliation with other people. At the time he wrote this paper Fairbairn accepted aspects of the Freudian classical perspective, including natural aggression within individuals needing external sources for gratification and transformation. There are significant implications for our understanding of large group dynamics if we accept this view, or the subsequent relational perspective about aggression as a secondary reaction to threats, frustrations, and deprivations. In the following sections we will evaluate Fairbairn's contribution to our understanding of large group affiliations and offer a contemporary object relations perspective on large groups in the mind.

Fairbairn approaches the subject from a developmental perspective. He identifies the *family* as the original social group and proceeds to elaborate his view of the interplay between individual psychology and sociological conditions associated with large groups. He surmises that in the context of the family group it is necessary to retain the positive energy of libido (love), while aggression gets directed outside the family. Fairbairn relies upon the Oedipal dynamic to account for the initial experiences of rivalry that introduces aggression into the group. Out of this family drama the need to protect the cohesion and integrity of the family established the two great crimes that have allowed families, and in Fairbairn's view large groups, to persist throughout the ages. Patricide and incest continue to influence "civilised" individuals and are the taboos that protect the family from its own member's aggression. Fairbairn (1935b) writes, "The taboos of incest and patricide are undoubtedly the cultural mainstay of the family group and consequently the foundation upon which all higher forms of social organization and culture rest" (1952, p. 236).

As a result of these protective processes within a family the members are directed outside the family for marriage. The custom of exogamy led to the next evolution in social groupings. Rather than dissolving the family as a unit, this practice was a way of preserving the libidinal tie to the original family by forming bonds with other acceptable families. The *clan*, Fairbairn writes, consists of a number of families and is organised as a family itself. It is headed by a chief who is the father of the clan. However, the same practice of exogamy is necessary for the clan as it is within the family. Technically marriage within the clan constitutes incest. Therefore, just as exogamy led to the clan as a means of avoiding incest, while still trying to retain libido within the group, so too there was a need for a further evolution of social groupings. The *tribe* overshadowed the autonomous clans by organising itself as a union of clans. It too is modelled upon the family with a father-like chief, or king. At this level of social grouping, however, the threat of libido being directed outside the group was able to be avoided by the possibility of marriage between the different clans. This promoted a stable and strong social organisation. Finally, in the evolution of social grouping to date, the *nation* evolved, according to Fairbairn, out of the weakening of the clan system and its inability to influence tribal policies. Importantly, he states that this is a result of the success of the tribe to bind the libido of the individual to the tribe. Hence the clan allegiance became less relevant. Fairbairn states that when the clan system disappears the tribe becomes a nation. This is the contemporary form of social grouping that is based on the original family. Still, the demand for allegiance which the nation asks for has not been able to weaken the basic loyalty of individuals to their own families. As a result all nations have had to make concessions to the family units within the nation in order to survive as a viable social organisation. Throughout this formulation of the evolution of social groupings Fairbairn emphasises the family as the core unit at the heart of the expanding ties. Reading his account of this process we can imagine that Fairbairn's Scottish heritage with its long history of clan and tribal affiliations gave him a unique perspective on the subject.

The social structure of modern society has not diminished the relevance of the family. It seems that in Fairbairn's depiction each successive stage of social grouping has the interest and potential of eliminating the previous level's relevance. The clan and tribe erected a patriarchal order and attempted to claim the allegiance of its members to the chief as the embodiment of the clan and tribe. Similar to the original feelings of filial attachment in the basic group (the family), all subsequent group formations promote a powerful need for a strong allegiance to the social structure. Yet the family has not been able to be superseded by larger social organisations wanting the devotion of its members. This must indicate something vital about human nature. In fact, it is only pathological large group organisations like dictatorships which seek to stamp out the family as a rival for devotion of its members. That kind of large group structure instils fear that the state as a father figure will punish those who do not put the state above all other loyalties. Fairbairn is identifying the basic attachment need that individuals seem to extend to objects of identification. Fundamentally, we can say that the family and the nation wish to have the love and loyalty of its individual members. We can update this view even further. It would be more in line with Fairbairn's ideas to say that the family/nation and its individual members are interdependent.

It is possible to extrapolate further to say that the balance that emerges from a mature dependence between the nation and family promotes a healthy society. This is in parallel to Fairbairn's (1941) notion of mature dependence in personal development, which allows for a balance of attachment and separation between differentiated people. However, he did not recognise that large groups are in and of themselves necessary objects of identification. For Fairbairn, the nation is essentially a parental substitution. This is the fundamental limitation of the view he was able to articulate. If he would have recognised that the nation, or any large group identification, can become an important object representation, than he would have been in a position to describe large group phenomena as similar to, but independent of object relations that are associated with individuals of historical significance. Perhaps this was not pursued because of his view that only bad relationships are internalised. Therefore there is no accommodation for the internalisation of the large group as a positive identification that enhances one's self-concept and identity.

Fairbairn's analysis of the communist movement was that its motive was not strictly an economic one, rather it was an effort to establish a social system that would supersede the nation. In fact, he stated that it was a system that had ambitions to be supra-national by transcending national boundaries. He speculated that communism was a movement that potentially represented the next stage in the evolutionary process he described. He reasoned that the trajectory of family, clan, tribe, nation, could lead to a *world state* that would require the same loyalty that the other levels of social organisation demanded from individuals. If successful, Fairbairn states, it would wean loyalty from individual nations toward the world state that encompasses all of humanity. However, Fairbairn does not stop there. He suggests that the true aim of communism is the elimination of the family group as a competitor for loyalty, which the individual nations were unable to do. As in other nationalist systems (e.g., Nazi Germany), the communist state declares that the children belong to it rather than the family. For the communist state the only relevant loyalty is to the world state and therefore family loyalties are unconsciously regarded as obsolete. Fairbairn reminds us that he is interested in the unconscious motivation of the communist movement, rather than the stated aims of the leaders. In contrast to the aspirations of the communist world state, nations have always recognised the existence of other nations. This was a way for nations to secure internal loyalty by providing a secure space for families in a hostile world. In essence he is saying that the individual's natural affiliation to the family and nation is a basic foundation for our perceptions of ingroups and outgroups. This is an important point which will allow us to elaborate the relational motivation that underlies intergroup conditions in society (Aviram, 2009).

As an analysis of a contemporary event in his time Fairbairn was remarkably astute in his evaluation. However, the psychoanalytic explanation for his conclusions was based on the knowledge of his era. He had not developed his views on the libidinal tie to the object and therefore did not see the group as a valid object with which to establish a valid attachment. He relied on Freud's conclusions in *Group Psychology and the Analysis of the Ego* (1921c) to explain the group's existence as a by-product of the individual's need to use the group for his or her own libidinal needs. In this paper Fairbairn also relies on the Oedipal context to explain the need for a leader who represents the ego-ideal. The Oedipal situation is important in his analysis because it provides the underlying reason for the incest and patricide taboos that lead to the rules of the clan, which lead to the tribe, and then ultimately the nation. In evaluating his own conclusions Fairbairn predicts that the current system of nations is likely to change over time. He offers a possibility of a *family of nations* as part of an evolutionary process. In his time, Fairbairn could see the League of Nations as a part of that process, and the subsequent United Nations effort. We can see aspects of that in the European Union alliances and the economic alliances between nations in other parts of the world. Although Fairbairn died before the collapse of the communist experiment he would not have been surprised given the brutal assault on the family by the communist regimes. These were systems in which the state determined the possible direction individual lives would go. This must have been a fundamental threat to the basic family unit in its pursuit of its own aspirations and personally valued loyalty to important people.

The attack on the family may have contributed to the ultimate downfall of the communist system, but another factor was that the communist state was not able to eliminate the national loyalties that it would have needed to eliminate in order to survive as a world state. Erikson (1985) writes about a similar utopian ideal in which he suggests that categories like nations, religions, ethnicities, race, etc., were really pseudocategories. Erikson referred to these categories of differentiation as "pseudospeciation" to signify that these are false differences between human beings. However, like the failure of communism to abolish the personal ties to families and nations, so too are there limits for a supraordinate identification with humanity. The problem with this kind of utopian ideal is that it ignores a vital human need for identity and uniqueness. Consider recent history in the former Yugoslavian state, or in some African countries. It turned out that these nations, that supposedly made the affiliations with clans and tribes superfluous, did not eliminate the powerful historical bonds with those social groupings. During times of tension in the nation the lower level affiliations emerged to the surprise of many observers and influenced the violent behaviour of many individual members. Rather than maintain the perception of belonging to the same nation, people defined themselves according to more unique affiliations. The intergroup context had changed dramatically and individuals were willing to kill people from the re-perceived outgroup. Why did this occur after a superseding national identity had been long established? Part of the explanation is offered by Brewer (1991), who writes about the need for balancing uniqueness and belonging. In her optimal distinctiveness theory she found evidence that as assimilation increases there is a countervailing need for differentiation. Importantly, she states that too much assimilation can lead to violence in an effort to re-establish the differentiated qualities that are personally meaningful to an individual.

Can the lower level identifications ever be eliminated? If not, in what ways are large group affiliations beyond the family necessary for healthy functioning in a social world?

Mitchell (1988) writes, "The most useful way to view psychological reality is as operating within a relational matrix which encompasses both intrapsychic and interpersonal realms" (p. 9). We are in a period of knowledge in which we can include the realm of large groups as also influencing psychological reality. Let us continue to build on Fairbairn's insights. He believed that our sense of ourselves is influenced by our identifications with other people (1941). He wrote, "Identification may thus be regarded as representing the persistence into extra-uterine life of a relationship existing before birth. In so far as identification persists after birth, the individual's object constitutes not only his world, but also himself" (1952, p. 47). In other words, the degree of dependence upon the other influences more or less, but always to some extent, one's experience of self. Object relations theory tends to associate this with interpersonal relationships. As the child reaches early adulthood, however, his or her identifications have been extending beyond the family. The child and teenager have become aware of also belonging to large group categories that define who he or she is, in addition to the identifications that began to shape the sense of self much earlier in life. We can consider what happens to one's sense of self as these large group identifications become more and more important.

By bringing the large group into our consideration of object relations and self experience we are extending Fairbairn's belief that identifications with individuals contribute to our experience of ourselves. We are in a position to say that in addition to the experience of ourselves that our identifications with individuals offer, our identifications with important large groups offer an additional layer of self experience that depending on the context will have more or less influence on our self experience and behaviour. We can go one step further and suggest that the degree of emotional identification with early objects will influence the degree of identification possible with large groups. In other words, it will influence more or less differentiation as an individual within a large group. A mature dependence with our large group affiliations will feel seamless and allow us to participate in society without too much emphasis on the large group affiliation in most situations. We must remember that the context can change this dramatically, as in the examples of the former Yugoslavia and Rwanda.

Gordon Allport (1954) writes that the ingroup is primary because we establish a preference for the ingroup before we develop attitudes toward an outgroup. We can think of this as having a parallel in attachment theory which emphasises the early establishment of a secure base before the infant begins to explore. It is similar to the reality that we develop object relations with individuals before we develop psychological attachments with large groups. If we accept that society and cultural groups influence one's experience of self in new and different ways than early relationships with important individuals of historical significance, then we need to augment traditional conceptions of object representations to adequately account for identifications with large groups. This would involve recognising that large groups are incorporated and identified with as new representations in the mind. It is important to distinguish the large group in the mind from traditional object representations of relationships with individuals. I have written about the relevance of the large group in the mind in a series of articles and culminating in a book in which large groups have their unique contribution to object relations (Aviram, 2002, 2005, 2007, 2009). Large groups are consciously relevant when they become part of our self-concept and identity (collective identity). At that point they also have an unconscious role that silently contributes to the way we feel about ourselves. When we begin to discuss the large group in the mind we move beyond Fairbairn's writing. I have previously referred to the internalisation of the large group as a *social object representation* (social object: Aviram, 2009).

The large group in the mind

The social object is an internalisation of the identity group with which one is affiliated. These identity groups may be chosen, but often they are a circumstance of birth. We consciously know our large group identifications in terms of collective identity, and we can refer to the unconscious component of the large group as the social object representation. Awareness and experience of both collective identity and the social object are influenced by pre-existing object relations associated with important individuals from early life. This is simply because the infant develops relations with individuals prior to incorporating an awareness of group belonging.

If we accept that identifications with important individuals contribute to our experience of self (Fairbairn, 1941), then it is just as likely that when we establish identifications with large social groups in early adulthood that they too contribute to our experience of self. It is possible to discuss these large group identifications in the same way that we describe identifications with individuals. Our affiliation with a large group exists on a continuum from minimal identification to overidentification. In other words, the continuum of affiliation with large groups can represent the same struggle that individuals have with interpersonal relationships. They can range from difficulty in establishing any bond to being merged with the large group. Either extreme represents a pathology of affiliation and indicates a problem of self just as it would if the focus was on interpersonal relationships. The behavioural consequences, however, may be different, in that the implications of belonging to a large group involves the entire interpersonal world perceived as either ingroup or outgroup members. The range of identification between a person and a large group can be influenced by the already established psychological growth in terms of the degree of dependence with individuals of historical importance. In other words, the continuum between infantile dependence and mature dependence will influence the degree of identification with the large groups that become important for any individual at the developmentally appropriate time. However, this process can be environmentally influenced by the intergroup context so that even a person with a mature dependence can begin to overidentify with a particular large group under stressful or threatening conditions. At those times the large group can function as a source of both physical and psychological safety. That kind of overidentification is likely to be temporary and will revert back to a mature dependence as societal conditions calm down. By clarifying that a large group phenomenon has its unique intrapsychic implications we can acknowledge that intergroup behaviour is associated with different dynamics than those behaviours that reflect interpersonal dynamics. Fairbairn could see that the original identifications in the family influence group belonging. He did not recognise that these subsequent large group identifications have unique intrapsychic influence and consequences for self experience. The notion of a social object representation integrates the large group dimension into object relations theory.

The social object in action

In most of the animal world, individuals who are separated from the group face more dangers and risk their own survival (Bowlby, 1969). The same holds true for people. Almost no person can function without belonging to a number of large groups. These affiliations are not only tangible for physical survival, but they serve a psychological function as well. Large groups become part of the very core of selfhood. A psychologically whole person involves interpersonal functioning, but also includes large group affiliations. When we perceive another person as a *whole object* we are also including our perceptions of his or her large group affiliations. For example, when we see our own mother we do not automatically think, for example, "my white, Jewish mother." But that is implicit (and unconscious) in our knowledge and perception. When we see a different mother we may automatically, and to varying degrees of consciousness, note, for example, "his Asian, Buddhist mother." The implications of our awareness and use of these categories of identity depends upon the context. For example, during the Second World War these perceptions would have had potential implications and consequences depending on where these people were in the world. The challenge for psychoanalytic theory of our time is to better understand the object relational implications of large groups in the mind.

Object relations, prejudice, and war

I have alluded to the fact that events in society and large group phenomena can overwhelm individuals and influence their behaviour. The potential of psychoanalytic efforts to contribute to the positive evolution of society requires that we understand how the large group functions in the person. There is a gap in our understanding about what happens intrapsychically when we transition from interpersonal relationships to intergroup behaviour (Atkin, 1971). In fact, psychoanalytic theory discusses very little about identity groups in the mind, and therefore it is not surprising that the concept of an ingroup is missing from psychoanalysis. I will describe the effect of the social object as it may be understood in relation to the societal conditions of prejudice and war. For example, in times of war or prior to war, the individual is influenced by unconscious aspects of large group membership which can override personal values about how to treat other people. The social object concept helps us recognise that the large group in the mind influences perception, belief, and behaviour based on large group membership.

Interpersonal relationships function in a context that is encompassed by concentric social groups. This relates to Fairbairn's ideas about the family as a core group within larger social groups. By incorporating Fairbairn's premise that libido is object seeking, we are now in a better position to understand why ingroup affiliations are so important. A vital part of the process of attachment in the family involves a preference for one's own family. As associations with more identity groups develop the same need for preference ensues. This helps explain the well-established finding in social psychology known as ingroup favouritism. Brewer (2007) reports that in general ingroup favouritism is not associated with outgroup hatred. If we accept that our nature is oriented towards affiliation with a caregiver, and that it is also part of our nature to affiliate with groups, than we can understand that we develop preferences for our ingroups, without necessarily being hostile towards outgroups. We function in an interpersonal and an intergroup context simultaneously.

As a nation moves closer to war the boundary between the individual and the large group seems to dissolve. The person and the nation become one and the same. This is like Fairbairn's infantile dependence, which is based on primary identification. It implies that there is no differentiation between self and other, and in this case, self and nation. On the continuum of attachment between the person and the group this is an overidentification (Aviram, 2009). As the boundary between the individual and nation diminishes, survival of the person depends on the survival of the nation. This stems from an existential threat to physical survival of the self and nation, but it has a psychological effect as well. The existential threat is also unconsciously experienced in terms of annihilation anxiety. The extreme threat to survival, either physical or psychological, can explain the extreme behaviour of individuals in war. This same process operates within a society between ingroups and outgroups. We could say that prejudices within a society are like low level wars. It is important to acknowledge political, economic, and historical contributions to war and prejudice. The social object concept helps explain a familiar experience in which it is possible to behave far better or far worse when group membership is highlighted than we might as individuals. We are the same person, and yet we act in ways that would not have been anticipated or predicted by understanding traditional object representations associated with interpersonal relationships. The extreme behaviour of prejudice and war suggest that there is an unconscious process influencing behaviour. As anxiety increases we know that unconscious processes have a greater influence on perception and behaviour. The social object can override personal values about how to treat other people. The fact that conditions in society can influence mass behaviour suggests that there must be a common thread between unrelated individuals. At the conscious level that common influence is a national identity. Across individuals there is the common need to affiliate with other people that we can recognise as an ingroup. The unconscious part of that affiliation resides in everyone. Out of awareness the social object is more or less active assessing the risk to survival. If that risk increases in the environment or the person is developmentally vulnerable then perception of the world as friend or foe (ingroup or outgroup) will dominate.

Conclusions

The objective of this chapter is to extend our conception of object relations from the traditional understanding of internalised interpersonal relationships, to include our psychological need for belonging to a large group. People feel differently in an intergroup context than they might otherwise. Our effort to understand that shift more completely requires that we attend to the large group dimension in the mind. The important emphasis in psychoanalysis on society and culture requires that we evaluate whether current conceptions of object representations adequately account for a person's large group affiliations and intergroup relations. It seems to me that traditional conceptions of object representations may need to be augmented to account for cultural and social group affiliations. This would emphasise that large social groups become internalised as social object representations and could independently influence perception of the social world. It would clarify that affiliations with large groups, consciously experienced in terms of collective identity, can also have an intrapsychic role in addition to traditional object representations that reflect interpersonal relations. Consider a situation in which two people from different ethnic groups are talking and one says, "I like you, but why are the others so ...." This is an example of two levels of object relations in operation, one interpersonal and the other intergroup. Recognition that the large group has a place in the mind can extend psychoanalytic theorising beyond the two-person psychology to acknowledge that those two people function within a framework of large groups. The social object is a construct that helps us address sociological conditions from a psychological perspective. By acknowledging the role of large groups in the mind, and the social object, we achieve the ability to formulate a parallel to Winnicott's (1960) well-known observation that there is no baby without a mother, and say that there is no person without a large group.

References

Allport, G. W. (1954). *The Nature of Prejudice*. Cambridge, MA: Addison-Wesley.
Atkin, S. (1971). Notes on motivations for war: Toward a psychoanalytic social psychology. *Psychoanalytic Quarterly, 40*: 549–583.
Aviram, R. B. (2002). An object relations theory of prejudice: Defining pathological prejudice. *Journal for the Psychoanalysis of Culture and Society, 7*: 305–312.
Aviram, R. B. (2005). The social object and the pathology of prejudice. In: J. S. Scharff & D. E. Scharff (Eds.), *The Legacy of Fairbairn and Sutherland* (pp. 227–236). New York: Routledge.
Aviram, R. B. (2007). Object relations and prejudice: From ingroup favoritism to outgroup hatred. *International Journal of Applied Psychoanalytic Studies, 4*: 4–14.
Aviram, R. B. (2009). *The Relational Origins of Prejudice: A Convergence of Psychoanalytic and Social Cognitive Perspectives*. Latham, MD: Jason Aronson.
Bowlby, J. (1969). *Attachment and Loss*. New York: Basic.
Brewer, M. B. (1991). The social self: On being the same and different at the same time. *Personality and Social Psychology Bulletin, 17*: 475–482.
Brewer, M. B. (2007). The importance of being we: Human nature and intergroup relations. *American Psychologist, 62*: 728–738.
Erikson, E. H. (1985). Pseudospeciation in the nuclear age. *Political Psychology, 6*: 213–217.
Fairbairn, W. R. D. (1935b). The sociological significance of communism considered in the light of psychoanalysis. In: *Psychoanalytic Studies of the Personality* (pp. 233–246). London: Tavistock, 1952.
Fairbairn, W. R. D. (1939c). Psychology as a prescribed and as a proscribed subject. In: *Psychoanalytic Studies of the Personality* (pp. 247–255). London: Tavistock, 1952.
Fairbairn, W. R. D. (1941). A revised psychopathology of the psychoses and psychoneuroses. *International Journal of Psychoanalysis, 22*(3, 4): 250–279. In: *Psychoanalytic Studies of the Personality* (pp. 28–58). London: Tavistock, 1952.
Fairbairn, W. R. D. (1943a). The war neuroses: Their nature and significance. *British Journal of Medical Psychology, 19*: 327–341. In: *Psychoanalytic Studies of the Personality* (pp. 59–81). London: Tavistock, 1952.
Fairbairn, W. R. D. (1957). Freud, the psycho-analytical method and mental health. *British Journal of Medical Psychology, 30*(2): 53–61. In: D. E. Scharff & E. F. Birtles (Eds.), *From Instinct to Self: Selected Papers of W. R. D. Fairbairn, Volume I: Clinical and Theoretical Papers* (pp. 61–73). Northvale, NJ: Jason Aronson, 1994.
Freud, S. (1921c). *Group Psychology and the Analysis of the Ego. S. E., 18*. London: Hogarth.
Freud, S. (1933b). Why war? *S. E., 22*: 197–215. London: Hogarth.

Hogg, M. A., & Abrams, D. (1988). *Social Identifications: A Psychology of Intergroup Relations and Group Processes*. London: Routledge.

Mitchell, S. A. (1988). *Relational Concepts in Psychoanalysis*. Cambridge, MA: Harvard University Press.

Winnicott, D. W. (1960). The theory of the parent–infant relationship. In: *The Maturational Processes and the Facilitating Environment* (pp. 37–55). Madison, CT: International Universities Press, 1965.

CHAPTER THIRTY-EIGHT

Fairbairn's object relations theory and social work in child welfare

James C. Raines

Introduction

Fairbairn's biographer, John Sutherland (1989) wrote, "The profoundest appreciation of any thinker's ideas is surely to explore where they lead" (p. x). It is this author's sincere hope that the application of Fairbairn's thought to the field of child welfare is a tribute to the contribution he has made to social work and related fields.

Policy context

The field of child welfare has radically changed since Fairbairn's time. To put Fairbairn's ideas in historical context, we should remember that in his day, an official government report in Scotland about "Sexual Offences Against Children" recommended that victims "should be encouraged to forget as completely as possible the traumatic experience" (Sutherland, 1989, p. 32). Beginning in the 1970s, developed nations made three major policy shifts. First, they sharply decreased their tolerance of child abuse. Second, they increased the number of professionals responsible for reporting child abuse. Third, they have expanded the definition of abuse to include emotional (verbal) abuse and witnessing violence between domestic partners (Gilbert et al., 2012a).

The result was an initial explosion in the number of child abuse reports and an awareness that some forms of abuse are closely associated with poverty. The United Kingdom has a lower percentage of children living in poverty than the United States at 12.5 per cent *vs.* 21.6 per cent even though maternal participation in the workforce in the US is higher at 66.7 per cent *vs.* 61.4 per cent (ibid.). There are two primary orientations towards child welfare. The *child protection* approach focuses on protecting individual children from harm, initiating legal investigations, taking an adversarial stance to parents, and coercing more out-of-home placements. The *family service* approach focuses on helping dysfunctional families, using a therapeutic engagement, taking a partnership stance with parents, and arranging voluntary out-of-home placements (Gilbert, Parton, & Skiveness, 2011). The US works primarily from a child protection approach while the UK works from a combination of the two approaches (Gilbert et al., 2012a).

In the UK, Children's Social Care Services are responsible for both child welfare and protection. However, policy has primarily concentrated on child safety, reacting to media investigations into child deaths, and there has been less emphasis on preventive services. Inter-agency cooperation to improve identification and response to maltreatment has been a repeating theme. Since 1974, health, education, and other services have had a legal duty to refer to and cooperate with social care services, although there is no mandated reporting. A more organised approach to inter-agency cooperation developed with the 1989 Children Act and subsequent policy guidance reflected an ongoing concern that involvement of multiple services can lose sight of the child's welfare as the priority. The 1989 Children Act included a broader welfare authority by giving local social services departments the responsibility to provide services for needy children, but systemic support has been limited. In response to media pressures about the removal of children, the Act also stipulated that children should be brought up within their own families. During the 1990s, prevention was largely confined to a declining workforce of health visitors which targeted vulnerable preschool children. Systemic support to families with young children improved in the 2000s with services focused on Sure Start schemes based in Children's Centres, part of a major government investment to end child poverty (Gilbert et al., 2012b). Simultaneously, British reforms sought to promote gainful employment, to increase financial support for families with children, and to invest in child health and early childhood education (Waldfogel, 2010). These initiatives halved the proportion of children in poverty between 1999 and 2007. Throughout the 2000s, the emphasis on prevention and legal child protection measures varied. The definitions of child maltreatment were broadened in 2002 to include sexual exploitation and witnessing intimate partner violence.

The Children Act of 2004 explicitly required authorities to improve the following aspects of child well-being: (a) physical and mental health and emotional well-being; (b) protection from harm and neglect; (c) education, training, and recreation; (d) the contribution made by them to society; (e) social and economic well-being. This broad approach, however, seemed to be set back by the Working Together to Safeguard Children (2010) guide that defined "safeguarding and promoting the welfare of children" as: (a) protecting children from maltreatment; (b) preventing impairment of children's health or development; and (c) ensuring that children are growing up in circumstances consistent with the provision of safe and effective care (p. 34). This seems to place child protection rather than promotion of family welfare as the core business of children's social care services (ibid.). Of particular note, the UK has ratified (with reservations) the United Nation's (1989) Convention on the Rights of the Child.

In the US, policy operates in a complex interaction between federal, state, and local laws, and regulations. New policies generally originate in local agencies and, if viewed as successful, gradually spread to the state or federal level. Since the 1970s, states have passed mandatory reporting laws for an increasing variety of professionals who may have suspicions about child abuse. Funding streams have also had a strong effect on policy. Although child protection funding primarily comes from state sources, the federal government contributes entitlement funding to foster care and adoptions. Federal funding for child maltreatment intervention programmes has been more limited, although recently more funding has been directed to prevention, particularly targeting home visiting programmes.

During the 1980s and '90s, federal and state funding sources contributed to efforts to improve reporting infrastructure including state-wide hotlines, workforce professionalisation, actuarial risk assessment, and automated reporting systems. This period also saw increased recognition of specific forms of maltreatment, especially sexual abuse. Since 1987, improvements in state information systems have been driven by federal government outcome-based requirements to monitor and improve standards of child safety, permanency in out-of-home care, and child well-being. Economic and racial disparities are found at all points of child protection services, from an increased likelihood of referral to placement in foster care. Although US child protection agencies have limited authority for welfare support, children with welfare needs are often referred to other agencies. Since 1993, this problem has led to differential response systems in a growing number of states. Differential response systems avoid the intrusion of legal child protection investigations for children at low risk of harm. Despite these improvements, the US still has one of the highest rates of investigations, affecting around 4 per cent of all children each year (ibid.). Of particular note, the US is one of only two countries that has not ratified the United Nation's Convention on the Rights of the Child (UNICEF, 2012), but it has ratified the two Optional Protocols (2000) against (a) the involvement of children in armed conflict and (b) child sexual exploitation.

Client engagement

Abused children have widely different reactions to strangers. Some children have been so neglected for human warmth and compassion that they immediately latch on to any caregiving adult. This kind of indiscriminate attachment is actually a clue to the child's naiveté about appropriate intimacy. Other children will seem cold and indifferent to attempts to engage them in a relationship. Again, this sort of resistance is a clue to the child's deep-seated mistrust of the adult world (Perry, 1996). On both ends of the continuum, child welfare workers should not take such reactions personally (children should not be described as loving or hateful), but they should use their emotional responses to understand the mistreated child.

Foster parents must also be trained not to instinctively react to maltreated children, but to use their feelings to imagine what sort of life would lead a child to believe that such behaviour is appropriate. Perry recommends that surrogate parents: (1) nurture children while staying attuned to their sensitivities about being touched; (2) seek to understand before disciplining the children (e.g., stealing food is not "bad" if the child has experienced food deprivation); (3) be consistent even to the point of redundancy; (4) provide guidance based on the child's developmental stage rather than chronological age; (5) model and explain appropriate social behaviours; (6) practise active listening by summarising verbal and non-verbal communication; (7) teach children that feelings are okay and help them with appropriate emotional expression; (8) have realistic expectations—abuse that lasted for years will not be fixed in a few months; (9) be patient with the child's progress and expect setbacks, and finally (10) take care of oneself—mistreated children can be draining—physically, mentally, and emotionally.

It is also essential that parental perpetrators also be engaged (Gladstone et al., 2012). Case workers must learn to get beyond their visceral reactions to parental maltreatment of children. This will be most difficult in case workers who still struggle with their own history of abuse or neglect. Frost and Connolly (2004) describe four disclosure management styles with perpetrators of child abuse. The first style is *exploratory*, which aims to understand and reconsider their behaviour towards the child. The second style is *oppositional*, which views the investigation as an adversarial, even combative, process. The third style is *evasive*, an approach that uses subterfuge or excuses to deflect any perceived criticism. The final style is *placatory*, which uses the appearance of compliance to elicit the support of others while not really taking responsibility for their own actions. Alpert and Britner (2009) have piloted a scale that aims to predict how caseworkers can engage parents by focusing on client strengths, team work, active listening, respect, availability, mutual trust, and being responsive to needs. Platt (2012) places these caseworker skills into a larger framework that also includes internal parental traits (cognitive, affective, behavioural, identity, and volition) and external factors (family circumstances, resources, support, and organisational constraints), all of which affect the working alliance.

Substantiation of allegations

There are many clues to abuse. These can be categorised as environmental, physical, behavioural, and interpersonal. Environmental clues include a lack of basic necessities, such as food, clothing, and shelter. Physical clues can include signs of physical abuse (bruises, broken bones, and head trauma) as well as sexual signs (genital injury).

Behavioural signs include symptoms of post-traumatic stress disorder (PTSD), such as re-experiencing (e.g., bad dreams), avoidance (e.g., fear of specific persons, places, or objects), and hyperarousal (e.g., agitation or irritability) (Deblinger, McLeer, Atkins, Ralphe, & Foa, 1989; Livingston, 1987; Wolfe, Gentile, & Wolfe, 1989). Severe PTSD can also include psychotic symptoms (Bosson, Reuther, & Cohen, 2011; Morrison, Frame, & Larkin, 2003), including thought disorders (e.g, paranoia) and sensory hallucinations (e.g., body dissociation). While psychotic symptoms are rare in children, they do occur and are an important clue to the nature and onset of the abuse. Tremblay, Hebert, and Piche (2000) found that victims of sexual assault were more likely to have dissociative symptoms than victims of physical abuse alone. Furthermore, Faust and Stewart (2007) found that children with psychotic disorders were far more likely to be victims of early abuse and to come from families experiencing higher degrees of conflict. Children with PTSD and psychotic symptoms generally experienced their first trauma before the age of five while children with PTSD alone generally experienced their first trauma three years later. While standard deviations allow for a good deal of overlap, child welfare investigators should be sceptical of parental claims that the abuse was only physical or only recent in a child with both PTSD and psychosis.

Interpersonal clues include the child's relations with significant others (parents, siblings, teachers, and friends) and even the caseworker. Caseworkers may initially experience a child who seems to warm readily to the new relationship, sometimes developing an instantaneous "attachment" with the concerned adult. Later, however, the caseworker may experience an inexplicable distrust and distancing. Silk (2005) suggests that this is because "the survivor of abuse learns that the closer he or she becomes to someone, the more dangerous that person becomes" (p. 96). Upon closer investigation, the caseworker will establish that this behaviour has occurred before—often with a teacher or other caregiving adult. It is as if the child is simultaneously saying "I need you; I can't trust you." In Fairbairn's theory, however, the child who has split and internalised the bad object is really saying, "I need you; don't trust me." This is because the child who comes to believe that he is bad accordingly believes his love is destructive.

Case assessment

Caseworkers should approach assessment with a sense of epistemological humility. As Borden (2009) states, "What is central in understanding object relations perspectives is the realization that we experience others as we *perceive* them, not necessarily as they actually are" (p. 147, italics in the original). It is a common, but initially mystifying, experience of many child welfare investigators that abused children are often devotedly attached to the abusive parent. This is because children repress their experience of the bad object. It is important to note that Fairbairn specifically focused on abused children when he formulated his theory of repression. He noted that victims of sexual assault were always reluctant to describe their ordeal. Fairbairn says that this is not because they have repressed their memories of the event, but because they repressed their relationship with an intolerably bad object. He notes that the same process happens with victims of physical abuse. Their ambivalence leads them to split the bad object into two parts: good *vs.* bad. Then they take the bad part into themselves. Fairbairn's own explanation for this is quite simple: "The child would rather be bad himself than have bad objects" (1943a, p. 65). Why would an abused child prefer to regard himself (rather than his abusive parents) as bad? In essence, it provides the child with the hope of redemption:

> It is better to be a sinner in a world ruled by God [the good parent] than to live in a world ruled by the Devil. A sinner in a world ruled by God may be bad; but there is always a certain sense of security to be derived from the fact that the world around is good ... In a world ruled by the Devil [the abusive parent] the individual may escape the badness of being a sinner; but he is bad because the world around him is bad. (ibid., pp. 66–67)

Some of this knowledge of interpersonal patterns can only be perceived through the countertransference. As Scharff and Scharff (1994) state, therapists will feel "nauseated, anguished, frightened, guilty, and helpless" (p. xvi).

Fairbairn (1941) described three developmental stages. The first stage is one of infantile dependence, which is characterised by an attitude of taking. Children stuck in this stage seem endlessly needy; they never seem satiated by enough food, love, or attention. They always want more and we leave them feeling drained and worn out. The second stage is quasi-independence, which is characterised by "rejective" strategies, such as paranoia, obsessions, hysteria, or phobia. The paranoid child will reject others as persecutors. Accordingly, workers may feel mistreated or falsely accused. The obsessive or perfectionist child will seem open to accepting the worker, but ultimately reject them as imperfect or flawed. Workers will feel constantly controlled or never good enough for the child. The hysterical or hypochondriacal child will seem sickly (usually stomach- or headaches) or debilitated by some mysterious physical ailment. Workers may initially feel pity, but ultimately guilty and frustrated that they cannot make the phantom pain go away. Finally, the phobic or anxious child may express fears about the dark, insects, or monsters under the bed, but ultimately fears being abandoned. Unable to cope with even momentary separation, they are clingy and grasping. Workers may welcome their initial hugs, but feel strangled by them in the end. The third stage is mature dependence, which is characterized by an ability to give oneself and to receive the gift of others without a total investment in just one person.

Sometimes even minor clients can be titillating to an interviewer. For example, in one case, a young adolescent when asked to describe what her stepfather did to her, opted to describe the experience in every pornographic detail. She seemed to want the interviewer to feel sexually aroused and view her as an object of sexual desire. Upon reflection, it was concluded that she wanted to make, in Fairbairn's terms, "a desperate attempt to make an emotional contact with her object" (p. 37), but the only way she knew to achieve these ends was through sexual enticement. The difference between love and sex was blurred or unknown to her.

In Greenberg and Mitchell's (1983) reformulation of object relations theory, the primary focus of attention is not the individual client, but the interactive client-system in which all of us establish our initial connections, strive to preserve interpersonal ties, and gradually differentiate ourselves. Relations with other human beings, both real and perceived, are the core components of the human experience. It is in this early relational matrix where we gain both our identities and our schema for all future relationships.

Goal setting

The natural language of the child is drama, not speech. While "acting out" has been given a negative connotation, it is for all children their primary language. This implies that, rather than "setting limits" in sessions, it is more beneficial to help the child translate the meaning of his or her actions. What adults view as maladaptive behaviour is simply a rigid clinging to old models of relational experience. It helps investigators to remember that what is now maladaptive was once quite adaptive! Put another way, what is now dysfunctional once served a perfectly reasonable function. Thus, it behoves us to imagine what circumstances might have given rise to the originally reasonable behaviour. From there, we might also be able to imagine what circumstances might enable the child to let go of this anachronistic pattern and venture to try a new way of relating to others. We do not use the word "venture" lightly. For child victims, it means exploring an unknown country. There is nothing more frightening than the unknown so we can expect that progress will be cyclical, not linear. Two steps forward and one step back will be the norm, not the exception (Frankland, 2010).

Knight (2011) mentions three goals in working with survivors of child abuse. First, she recommends stabilisation. Survivors must be able to function in the real world and, for children, this means being able to love and be loved as well as to learn at school. Some emotional problems can create learning problems (House, 2002; Kline & Silver, 2004). For example, a child who is hypervigilant may resemble a student with ADHD in that both may be unable to focus on school-related tasks for a prolonged period. Second, she recommends focusing on the emotional problems. Survivors may express these as anxiety, depression, or conduct problems. Helping the victims give voice to their symptoms allows them to integrate split-off parts of themselves. Third, she recommends working on the survivors' memories of abuse, but here she offers the following caution, "The goal of our work with survivors shouldn't be memory recall. In fact, in many instances, we will need to assist clients in tolerating gaps in memory, and assist them in making meaning of what they do remember" (p. 190). This implies, then, that casework should be ego-supportive. Practitioners should remember that even dissociation can be a valuable and even adaptive method of coping with extreme forms of child abuse because it naturally draws upon a child's ability to fantasise (Marmar, Weiss, & Metzler, 1997; Panzer & Viljoen, 2004). Scharff and Scharff (2005) explain it as follows:

> After a major trauma, the mind may dissociate from the pain, drive the traumatic material into a sequestered place, and wall it off behind a touch capsule. It is a primitive way of dealing with overwhelming anxiety so that the person can get on with life. (p. 74)

Ultimately, however, we suggest that caseworkers enable victims to develop healthier or more mature defence mechanisms (Frankland, 2010), such as anticipation, humour, or sublimation. In addition to Knight's three goals, I recommend a fourth, helping survivors to develop a more balanced or integrated view of themselves and others. When children, for example, only refer to themselves in negative terms, it will be helpful to enable them to find some genuine strengths. When a child only idealises the worker, it will be helpful to point out some real weaknesses.

It is tempting for child welfare workers to view abusive parents as nothing more than perpetrators of heinous crimes. Éthier and Lacharité (2007), however, identify four sociocultural influences on child abuse. First, some subcultures believe that children are naturally bad and must be correctively trained. Second, some subcultures view violence as only a physical act, not one that destroys a child's soul (Shengold, 2006). Third, some subcultures see the family as a social entity where strict rules of authority and power maintain the status quo. Finally, some subcultures do not hold the needs of children as valid, only the needs of the adults. In families in which children do not meet these cultural standards, the adults believe it is not only their right, but often their duty, to enforce the rules regardless of where they eventually lead.

The first goal for working with perpetrators is to engage the parents' collaboration in the process. Fathers, especially, tend to become defensive and angry when confronted about child abuse. It helps to respect their role in the family and affirm their identity as a key problem solver. It may help, for example, to say, "As the head of the household, your presence is essential to making sure that the family works together." The importance of getting the father to agree to the initial meeting cannot be overstated. Starting each session by asking for the father's perspective and ending each session by asking the father to summarise any agreements will go a long way towards keeping him feeling important and involved. This may be difficult for feminist child protective service workers, but it will help to remember that the welfare of the child is the ultimate objective, not the "liberation" of the mother. The second goal is to contract with the parents about the goals for the family, including the child. Since most abusive parents believe in the utility of physical discipline, eliminating this technique should *not* be a goal. The goal, instead, is to increase their repertoire of parenting techniques so that each one is used thoughtfully and differentially. It may be helpful to ask parents the following questions about physical discipline:

1. Under what circumstances should a child be spanked?
2. Where on the body is it safest to spank a child?
3. How should a spanking be administered?
4. At what ages should a child be spanked?
5. How many spanks would be age-appropriate?
6. How would you know if you went too far?

It might also be helpful to list these across from a similar list for time-outs, such as:

1. Under what circumstances should a child receive a time-out?
2. Where in the household should a time-out be given?
3. How should the time-out be administered?
4. At what ages should a child receive a time-out?
5. How many minutes would be age-appropriate?
6. How would you know if you went too far?

Thinking critically about two contrasting approaches enables parents not to simply substitute one abusive method for another scheme that is potentially just as abusive, such as when parents lock children in a basement, closet, or attic all day (e.g., Rymer, 1993). As Éthier and Lacharité (2007) suggest, social workers "should reframe the abusive conduct by emphasizing the parent's intention to 'educate the child' while proposing more positive and effective methods".

Intervention planning

From an object relations perspective, the ability to develop an authentic working alliance with the child victim is essential. As Fairbairn (1958a) stated, therapy must be about "an actual relationship with a reliable and beneficent parental figure" (p. 377). Why? Fairbairn (1943a) described the healing mechanism as follows: "In the transference situation, the patient is provided in reality with an unwontedly good object, and is thereby placed in a position to risk release of his internalized bad objects" (p. 69). The therapist must be prepared for enactments of internalised relationships—empathic enough to understand their import and wise enough to provide what the earlier relationship did not. As Borden (2009) states,

> The core activities of the therapeutic process carry the potential to foster change and growth across domains of functioning, helping individuals (1) strengthen their ability to process subjective experience; (2) deepen awareness of their own and others' behavior; (3) develop problem-solving skills and coping capacities; and (4) enlarge their understandings of self, others, and life experience. (p. 160)

Good-enough social workers function as participant-observers. They welcome their own countertransference responses as necessary complements to the child's interpersonal schema.

Rather than reacting to (and inadvertently reinforcing) this complementary role, they use it for reflection and understanding how to respond in a way that elicits a willingness to try out new ways of relating to others. In Silk's (2005) terms, the practitioner aims for a "soft" attachment, in which "the patient is allowed to back off from what she experiences as too intense a session or involvement in therapy" (p. 97). This implies, of course, that the worker be both flexible and not easily offended by the apparent rejection of a close relationship. When the child denigrates the worker, agency, or the counselling process, it should be interpreted as an expression of intolerable ambivalence. Sometimes it is easier to talk around an issue than about it. For example, a child might be asked how he or she would feel if the child could talk about the abuser or the abuse. This allows the child to express ambivalence about revelations that inadvertently create more intimacy than the child can bear. Obviously, this also has implications for physical touching in the professional relationship. The worker should not initiate any touching of the child, but allow non-sexual touching by the child if it occurs spontaneously.

Outcome evaluation

Outcome evaluation should be done for both the child victim and the adult caregivers. The scales chosen will, in part, depend on whether the country takes a child protective or family service orientation (Gilbert, Parton & Skiveness, 2011). Those taking a legalistic and adversarial approach will lean towards outcome measures that meet the Daubert standards for legal admissibility. There are four requirements: rigorous testing, peer review and publication, known error rate, and general acceptance by the scientific community (Raines, 2008; Yañez & Fremouw, 2004). In any case, this review will focus on scales that can be used as outcome measures in treatment settings.

For childhood survivors, there are two types of scales. Self-report scales enable children or adolescents to report their own perceptions of their mental state. Third-party scales ask parents or adult caregivers to report their observations of the victim's behaviour.

The following self-report scales for children have been vetted for test reliability and validity. Briere's (1996) *Trauma Symptom Checklist for Children* (TSCC), for ages eight to sixteen, is a fifty-four-item questionnaire divided into six subscales, including anxiety, depression, post-traumatic stress, sexual concerns, dissociation, and anger. The TSCC is probably the most widely used self-report scale for the measurement of trauma symptoms among children and adolescents (Elhai, Gray, Kashdan, & Franklin, 2005) because it can be used as a screening or outcome measure and contains two validity measures for denial or over-reporting of problems. Furthermore, the TSCC is one of the few to be tested cross-culturally (i.e., Sweden and Iran) (Nilsson, Wadsby, & Svendin, 2008, and Mohammadkhani, Nazari, Dogaheh, Mohammadi, & Azadmehr, 2007, respectively). Gully's (2000) *Expectations Test* (for ages four to seventeen) is especially relevant to this chapter because it asks a child to look at sixteen ambiguous photos and describe (a) how the child in the picture feels (i.e., scared, sad, angry, fine, or happy) and then (b) what they expect to happen to the child. It thus enables children to use projective identification with an anonymous other.

The following third-party measures for children have been tested for reliability and validity. Putnam, Helmers, and Trickett's (1993) *Child Dissociative Checklist* (CDC) is a twenty-item scale which aims to be a screening measure for protective service workers, parents, foster parents, or teachers. Although it taps several aspects of dissociation (e.g., amnesia, shifts in demeanour, trance states, hallucinations, identity changes, and disturbances in behaviour), it has no subscales. A CDC score of twelve or higher is highly suggestive of significant dissociative psychopathology (Putnam & Peterson, 1994). Friedrich's (1997) *Child Sexual Behavior Inventory* (for ages two to twelve) is a thirty-eight-item checklist that measures both the variety and frequency of sexual behaviours. Evaluators should keep in mind that best practice demands that both child and parent/caretaker report measures should be used to assess the treatment effectiveness of traumatised victims of child abuse (Achenbach, McConaughy, & Howell, 1983; Lanktree et al., 2008).

For adult caregivers (e.g., parents), most scales are self-report measures. The *Adult Adolescent Parenting Inventory-2* (AAPI-2) is a forty-item survey specifically designed to serve as a pre-test/post-test for interventions aimed at parents or guardians suspected of child abuse. There are two forms (A for pre-test and B for post-test) and five subscales to measure the following parenting attitudes: (1) inappropriate expectations of children; (2) lack of empathy towards children's needs; (3) strong belief in the use of corporal punishment; (4) reversing parent–child roles, and (5) suppressing children's independence (Conners, Whiteside-Mansell, Deere, Ledet, & Edwards, 2006).

The following third-party measures for caregivers have been tested for reliability and validity. The *Home Visit Observation Scale* (Grietens, Geeraert, & Hellinckx, 2004) is a twenty-item scale designed for use by visiting professionals with three subscales: parental isolation, parental psychological problems, and communication problems. The *Home Observations for the Measurement of the Environment* (HOME) is a sixty-nine-item combination of observation and interview items designed to measure the quality of the home environment (Caldwell & Bradley, 2001). It has seven subscales (i.e., daily routines, childcare, toys and books, play, outings, physical environment, and interaction). According to a UNESCO report, the HOME scale has been adapted and used in more than 100 nations and has been validated in many countries including Bangladesh, Brazil, and China (Iltus, 2007).

Conclusion

Fairbairn's object relations theory has had important ramifications for child welfare workers in both the UK and the US. It enables social workers to think deeply about client engagement, substantiation of allegations, case assessment, goal setting, intervention planning, and outcome evaluation. During each stage, the caseworker must reflect before reacting and train others to do the same. With empathy and deep understanding, social workers can work effectively with abused children and their dysfunctional families.

References

Achenbach, T. M., McConaughy, S. H., & Howell, C. T. (1987). Child/adolescent behavioral and emotional problems: Implications of cross-informant correlations for situational specificity. *Psychological Bulletin*, 101(2): 213–232.

Alpert, L. T., & Britner, P. A. (2009). Measuring parent engagement in foster care. *Social Work Research*, *33*(3): 135–145.

Borden, W. (2009). *Contemporary Psychodynamic Theory and Practice*. Chicago, IL: Lyceum.

Bosson, J. V., Reuther, E. T., & Cohen, A. S. (2011). The comorbidity of psychotic symptoms and posttraumatic stress disorder: Evidence for a specifier in DSM-5. *Clinical Schizophrenia & Related Psychoses*, *5*(3): 147–154.

Bremner, J. D., Bolus, R., & Mayer, E. A. (2007). Psychometric properties of the Early Trauma Inventory—self-report. *Journal of Nervous and Mental Disease*, *195*(3): 211–218.

Briere, A. (1996). *Trauma Symptom Checklist for Children: Professional Manual*. Odessa, FL: Psychological Assessment Resources.

Caldwell, B. M., & Bradley, R. H. (2001). *Home Observations for the Measurement of the Environment HOME Inventory Administration Manual* (3rd ed.). Little Rock, AR: University of Arkansas.

Conners, N. A., Whiteside-Mansell, L., Deere, D., Ledet, T., & Edwards, M. C. (2006). Measuring the potential for child maltreatment: The reliability and validity of the Adult Adolescent Parenting Inventory-2. *Child Abuse & Neglect*, *30*(1): 39–53.

Deblinger, E., McLeer, S., Atkins, M., Ralphe, D., & Foa, E. (1989). Post-traumatic stress in sexually abused, physically abused, and nonabused children. *Child Abuse and Neglect*, *13*(3): 403–408.

Elhai, J. D., Gray, M. J., Kashdan, T. B., & Franklin, L. C. (2005). Which instruments are most commonly used to assess traumatic event exposure and posttraumatic effects? A survey of traumatic stress professionals. *Journal of Traumatic Stress*, *18*(5): 541–545.

Éthier, L S., & Lacharité, C. (2007). Physical abusers in the family. In: M. Hersen & J. C. Thomas (Eds.), *Handbook of Clinical Interviewing with Adults* (pp. 427–445). Los Angeles, CA: Sage.

Fairbairn, W. R. D. (1941). A revised psychopathology of the psychoses and psychoneuroses. *International Journal of Psychoanalysis*, *22*(3, 4): 250–279. In: *Psychoanalytic Studies of the Personality* (pp. 28–58). London: Tavistock, 1952.

Fairbairn, W. R. D. (1943a). The repression and the return of bad objects (with special reference to the "war neuroses"). *British Journal of Medical Psychology*, *19*: 327–341. In: *Psychoanalytic Studies of the Personality* (pp. 59–81). London: Tavistock, 1952.

Fairbairn, W. R. D. (1958a). On the nature and aims of psycho-analytical treatment. *International Journal of Psychoanalysis*, *34*: 374–383. In: D. E. Scharff & E. F. Birtles (Eds.), *From Instinct to Self: Selected Papers of W. R. D. Fairbairn, Volume I: Clinical and Theoretical Papers* (pp. 74–92). Northvale, NJ: Jason Aronson, 1994.

Faust, J., & Stewart, L. M. (2007). Impact of child abuse timing and family environment on psychosis. *Journal of Psychological Trauma*, *6*(2–3): 65–85.

Frankland, A. G. (2010). *The Little Psychotherapy Book: Object Relations in Practice*. New York: Oxford University Press.

Friedrich, W. N. (1997). *Child Sexual Behavior Inventory: Professional Manual*. Odessa, FL: Psychological Assessment Resources.

Friedrich, W. N., Fisher, J. L., Dittner, C. A., Acton, R., Berliner, L., Butler, J., Damon, L., Davies, W. H., Gray, A., & Wright, J. (2001). Child sexual behavior inventory: Normative, psychiatric and sexual abuse comparisons. *Child Maltreatment*, *6*(1): 37–49.

Frost, A., & Connolly, M. (2004). Reflexivity, reflection, and the change process in offender work. *Sexual Abuse*, *16*(4): 365–380.

Gilbert, N., Parton, N., & Skiveness, M. (2011). *Child Protection Systems: International Trends and Orientations*. New York: Oxford University Press.

Gilbert, R., Fluke, J., O'Donnell, M., Gonzalez-Izquierdo, A., Brownell, M., Gulliver, P., Janson, S., & Sidebotham, P. (2012a). Child maltreatment: Variation in trends and policies in six developed countries. *Lancet, 379*(9817): 758–772.

Gilbert, R., Fluke, J., O'Donnell, M., Gonzalez-Izquierdo, A., Brownell, M., Gulliver, P., Janson, S., & Sidebotham, P. (2012b). Child maltreatment: Supplementary webappendix. *Lancet, 379*, published online. DOI: 10.1016/S0140–6736(11)61087–8.

Gladstone, J., Dumbrill, G., Leslie, B., Koster, A., Young, M., & Ismaila, A. (2012). Looking at engagement and outcome from the perspectives of child protection workers and parents. *Children & Youth Services Review, 34*(1): 112–118.

Greenberg, J. R., & Mitchell, S. A. (1983). *Object Relations in Psychoanalytic Theory*. Cambridge, MA: Harvard University Press.

Grietens, H., Geeraert, L., & Hellinckx, W. (2004). A scale for home visiting nurses to identify risks of physical abuse and neglect among mothers with newborn infants. *Child Abuse & Neglect, 28*(3): 321–337.

Gully, K. J. (2000). Initial development of the Expectations Test for children: A tool to investigate social information processing. *Journal of Clinical Psychology, 56*(12): 1551–1563.

HM Government (2004). *Children Act 2004, Chapter 31*. London: HMSO.

HM Government (2010). *Working Together to Safeguard Children*: A guide to inter-agency working to safeguard and promote the welfare of children. London: HMSO.

House, A. E. (2002). *DSM-IV Diagnosis in the Schools*. New York: Guilford Press.

Iltus, S. (2007). *Significance of Home Environments as Proxy Indicators for Early Childhood Care and Education*. [Background paper prepared for the Education for All Global Monitoring Report 2007 Strong foundations: Early childhood care and education.] Paris: United Nations Educational, Scientific, and Cultural Organization. Retrieved May 19, 2012 from: http://unesdoc.unesco.org/images/0014/001474/147465e.pdf

Kantor, G. K., Holt, M. K., Mebert, C. J., Straus, M. A., Drach, K. M., Ricci, L. R., MacAllum, C. A., & Brown, W. (2004). Development and preliminary psychometric properties of the Multidimensional Neglectful Behavior Scale–Child Report. *Child Maltreatment, 9*(5): 409–428.

Kline, F. M., & Silver, L. B. (2004). *The Educator's Guide to Mental Health Issues in the Classroom*. London: Paul H. Brookes.

Knight, C. (2011). Child maltreatment and its effects. In: N. R. Heller & A. Gitterman (Eds.), *Mental Health and Social Problems: A Social Work Perspective* (pp. 174–201). New York: Routledge/Taylor & Francis.

Lanktree, C. B., Gilbert, A. M., Briere, J., Taylor, N., Chen, K., Maida, C. A., & Saltzman, W. R. (2008). Multi-informant assessment of maltreated children: Convergent and discriminant validity of the TSCC and TSCYC. *Child Abuse & Neglect, 32*(6): 621–625.

Livingston, R. (1987). Sexually and physically abused children. *Journal of the American Academy of Child and Adolescent Psychiatry, 26*: 413–415.

Marmar, C., Weiss, D., & Metzler, T. (1997). Peritraumatic dissociation and posttraumatic stress disorder. In: J. Bremner & C. Marmar (Eds.), *Trauma, Memory, and Dissociation* (pp. 229–247). Washington, DC: American Psychiatric Press.

Mohammadkhani, P., Nazari, M. A., Dogaheh, E. R., Mohammadi, M. R., & Azadmehr, H. (2007). Standardization of trauma symptoms checklist for children. *Psicologia: Teoria e Prática, 9*(1): 75–85.

Morrison, A. P., Frame, L., & Larkin, W. (2003). Relationships between trauma and psychosis: A review and integration. *British Journal of Clinical Psychology, 42*(4): 331–353.

Nilsson, D., Wadsby, M., & Svendin, C. G. (2008). The psychometric properties of the Trauma Symptom Checklist for Children (TSCC) in a sample of Swedish children. *Child Abuse & Neglect, 32*(6): 627–636.

Panzer, A., & Viljoen, M. (2004). Dissociation: A developmental psychoneurobiological perspective. *South African Psychiatry Review, 7*(3): 11–14.

Perry, B. D. (1996). *Maltreated Children: Experience, Brain Development and the Next Generation*. New York: W. W. Norton.

Platt, D. (2012). Understanding parental engagement with child welfare services: An integrated model. *Child & Family Social Work, 17*(2); 138–148.

Putnam, F. W., & Peterson, G. (1994). Further validation of the Child Dissociative Checklist. *Dissociation, 3*(4): 204–211.

Putnam, F. W., Helmers, K., & Trickett, P. K. (1993). Development, reliability, and validity of a child dissociation scale. *Child Abuse & Neglect, 17*(6): 731–741.

Raines, J. C. (2008). *Evidence-based Practice in School Mental Health*. New York: Oxford University Press.

Rymer, R. (1993). *Genie: An Abused Child's Flight from Silence*. New York: HarperCollins.

Scharff, J. S., & Scharff, D. E. (1994). *Object Relations Therapy of Physical and Sexual Trauma*. Northvale, NJ: Jason Aronson.

Scharff, J. S., & Scharff, D. E. (2005). *The Primer of Object Relations* (2nd ed.). Latham, MD: Jason Aronson.

Shengold, L. (2006). A view of severely traumatized patients—soul murder victims. In: M. I. Good (Ed.), *The Seduction Theory: In Its Second Century* (pp. 213–225). Madison, CT: International Universities Press.

Silk, K. R. (2005). Object relations and the nature of therapeutic interventions. *Journal of Psychotherapy Integration, 15*(1): 94–100.

Sutherland, J. D. (1989). *Fairbairn's Journey into the Interior*. London: Free Association.

Tremblay, C., Hebert, M., & Piche, C. (2000). Type I and type II posttraumatic stress disorder in sexually abused children. *Journal of Child Sexual Abuse, 9*(1): 65–90.

Waldfogel, J. (2010). *Britain's War on Poverty*. New York: Russell Sage Foundation.

Wolfe, V., Gentile, C., & Wolfe, D. (1989). The impact of sexual abuse on children: A PTSD formulation. *Behavior Therapy, 20*(2): 215–228.

Yañez, Y. T., & Fremouw, W. (2004). The application of the Daubert standard to parental capacity measures. *American Journal of Forensic Psychology, 22*(3): 5–28.

ENVOI

Assembling this book, working with colleagues from around the world who value Fairbairn's contribution to psychoanalysis as we do, has been a labour of love. It has given the two of us a chance to discuss what we value most, and to probe ideas when we were critical or felt that Fairbairn's thought needed revision in the light of modern developments. It has deepened our own thinking and put us in close touch with many of the ramifications of thought that stem from Fairbairn's seminal work.

Fairbairn, like his analytic forebears, with his close study of Freud uppermost, and like his contemporary Melanie Klein, did not get everything right. But, as they did, he forged new territory and got essential things right. He has been proved largely right, at least in the eyes of our contemporary perspective that considers relationships to be at the centre of human motivation. He was right to highlight the complex systemic functions of psychic organisation with the organising function of splitting and repression. His model has been the most useful one we have for an evolving understanding of trauma and the relationship between the more benign aspects of repression compared to the devastation of pathological trauma-induced dissociation—witness his 1929 MD thesis on the differentiation of repression and dissociation.

Perhaps it was his familiarity and deep interest in philosophy and religion that enabled him to step outside the confines of pure analytic thinking, steeped as it was in Freud's understanding gathered largely from nineteenth-century philosophy and science. Born a generation later than Freud, Fairbairn could take advantage of the scientific revolution offered by Einstein's theory of relativity, and could see that just as matter and energy were mutually inextricable, so were the content and structure of the mind. Experience blends with constitution to form an ever-evolving organism in open systems exchange with the environment, which means psychologically with the people with whom the individual is in contact. This fundamental shift, from drive as motivation, to relationship as offering meaning, set up further steps in analytic evolution.

Bion's container/contained, although formulated in Klein's tradition, adapts her genius to a full relational model in the wake of Fairbairn's contribution. The role of the real parents in development, never fully appreciated until the second half of the twentieth century, comes to make sense through Fairbairn's model that gives equal weight to intrapsychic and interpersonal influence. Out of this come the contributions of Bowlby's attachment theory and a whole line of development that is still being richly mined. Out of this come the Argentine contributions of the link theory of Pichon-Rivière and the field theory of Madeline and Willy Baranger. And out of this come the contributions of Guntrip on the schizoid self and of Sutherland on the autonomous self. With the recent discovery of mirror neurons by Rizzolatti and his colleagues in Italy, we have confirmation of the way primates, including we humans, are built to take in experience from the beginning of life—even in the womb. This further strengthens our conviction that the need for relationships is so fundamental to psychic life that the infant is primed to reach out for others from the first moments of life. David E. Scharff's work on couple and family therapy comes from these developments via the groundbreaking work of Henry Dicks that combined contributions of Fairbairn and Klein and has continued into ideas of the interpersonal unconscious as an overarching organisation. Graham S. Clarke continues to develop Fairbairn's model towards a fuller development of the object relations paradigm. A theoretical integration of internal and external worlds by multiple agentative selves towards mature reintegration into a unified whole remains practically, and perhaps politically difficult in an era of duelling models.

Beyond this, Fairbairn was a wonderful writer—dense but logical and internally consistent. He had tremendous range, offering ideas about sexual abuse and sex offenders, applications to dentistry, education, and social and political issues like groups and communism. And finally we might cite his usually unnoticed, but groundbreaking ideas on art and aesthetics that are explored so well in this volume.

But we have also learned some completely new personal aspects of Fairbairn's life in this book. We know more, thanks to the new documents and diaries now in the Scottish National Library, about his abiding interest in religion, and we know much more about the demons that haunted his dreams and his relationships. Much as with Freud, to know this is not to diminish the enormity of his contribution, but to steep us in the struggles that accompanied Fairbairn's unending passion for telling new truths about human organisation and human suffering.

Working with colleagues who value Fairbairn as we do has been the fulfilment of a dream for the two of us. The relationship of our own transatlantic partnership has been a singular source of pleasure in the shared pursuit of this task. We hope these contributions will continue to stimulate the pursuit of knowledge in psychoanalysis and improvement in our common human condition.

David E. Scharff
Graham S. Clarke

INDEX

Abadi, M. 233
Abelove, H. 87
Abraham, Karl 228, 282, 289–291, 306
Abrams, D. 472
abuse. *See* child abuse; ritual cult abuse; sexual abuse
Achenbach, T. M. 492
active libidinal ego/active longing self 466–467
adapted self 369
adaptive self 369
Adler, Alfred 50
Aduale, A.-K. 203
affect 118–119, 264–267
    Guntrip on loss of 314
affect regulation 461–462, 469. *See also Stranger Affect Regulation, Mentalization, and the Development of the Self* (Fonagy et al.) 266–267
aggression 104, 116, 287, 327–328
    frustration and 231, 233
    Kernberg on 105, 119
    Klein on 91–92, 148–149, 154, 250, 282, 448, 450, 453
    vicious circle of 230–231
"aggression" hypothesis 404–406
aggressor, identification with the 55, 334, 339

Ainsworth, Mary D. S. 266
alexithymia 462
Allen, J. G. 267
Allport, Gordon W. 477
Alpert, L. T. 486
Altman, Neil 344
ambivalence 104, 151–153, 164, 190, 207, 278, 417–418
    achievement of 109, 187, 189, 227–228, 231, 251, 302
    Oedipus situation and 165–170, 186
analytic field 270
analytic relationship 81–82, 157–158, 200, 351–352, 382
    Guntrip on 319–320
Andreas, Brian 414
Anna O., case of 52
anti-libidinal ego (AE) 15, 116, 192
    passive 468
    relationships between anti-libidinal object and 156–157
    See also internal saboteur
anti-libidinal object (AO) 15, 116, 189, 192–193, 467
    relationship between rejecting object and 406–408

relationships between anti-libidinal ego and 156–157
Antigone (Sophocles) 28, 38
Anzieu, Didier 9, 324
Appelbaum, G. 257
Argentina, Jews in 371
Argentine Psychoanalytic Association (APA)
    Fairbairn Space in 101, 106–109
    teaching Fairbairn in 101–102
Aristotle 8–9
Armstrong-Perlman, Eleanore M. 162–163, 166–167
Army 472
Aron, Lewis 344
art
    as reparation for destructive phantasies 450
    Fairbairn's forgotten role in the historical drama of psychoanalysis and 447–457
    Fairbairn's ideas about 394–395
    Klein on 453
"as-if" personality 55, 188, 226
Atkin, S. 479
Atkins, M. 486
attachment
    no-choice 198–200
    See also bonds
attachment theory 265–267
    trauma, dissociation, and 212–213
attractors and sub-attractor patterns (chaos theory) 268–269
Atwood, George E. 249
Austin, V. 229
automatic talking 53
autonomous self 269
Autonomous Self, The (Sutherland) 21
    Padel's review of 297–298
Aviram, Ron B. 270, 476–478, 480
Azadmehr, H. 491

Bacal, Howard A. xxiii
bad object relations, analysis of internal world of 320
bad objects
    cathexis to 315
    release of 79–80

badness, unconditional 15
Balint, Michael 167, 300, 316, 350
Baranger, Madeline 270, 352
Baranger, Willy 102, 352
Barber, J. P. 319
Basili, Isabel Sharpin de 101–102
Basili, Rubén Mario 101–103, 106–111, 128, 187–188, 223–231
Bateman, A. 105, 267
Beattie, Hilary J. 41, 70, 406
Bemporad, Jules 49–50
Bennett, M. R. 425
Berenstein, I. 270
Bergler, Edmund 90
Berman, Emanuel 49, 335, 338–339
Bers, S. 226
Besucchio, Adrián César 110
Bianchi, Ilaria 212–213
Bieniek, W. 155
Bion, Wilfred R. 133, 230, 265, 392
Birtles, Ellinor Fairbairn xxiii, 3, 12, 15, 20, 27, 32, 50, 70, 76, 80–81, 200, 205, 209–211, 335–336, 340, 346, 358–359, 365, 432, 448, 457
bisexuality, Freud's theory of innate 91
Black, Margaret J. 352, 358–359. *See also* Mitchell, Margaret Black
Blackburn, S. 11
Blanck, Gertrude 228
Blanck, Rubin 228
Blatt, Sidney J. 226
Bleger, E. 224, 229
Bleger, José 101, 349
Blehar, M. C. 266
Boag, S. 424
Bollas, Christopher J. 370
Bolognini, S. 387
bonds
    of contempt 139–141
    of resentment 137–139
    See also attachment
Bonduelle, M. 54
Bonomi, Carlo 339
Borden, W. 487, 490
borderline pathology 105, 107–108, 110–111, 228, 230
    endopsychic structure and 190–191

Kernberg on 105, 107, 120, 187–188, 191, 225–226, 229
borderline patients
   clinical vignette 192
   "emptiness borderlines" 228 (*see also* emptiness pathology)
   emptiness pathology 225–226, 228–232
   fixation points 104–105, 107–108, 228
   schizoid pathology in 103, 111, 187, 191, 193, 225–226, 229–232
   splitting 327
   sub-egos and ego functioning 401–404
   transference 326
borderline personality organisation 104, 110, 116–117, 120–121, 187, 191, 225–226
borderline states, Fairbairn's contribution to understanding of 324, 326
Borgegård, T. 447
Borgogno, F. 52, 54
Bosanquett, B. 29
Bosson, J. V. 486
boundaries and exclusion 35–37
Bowlby, John 21, 103, 197, 265, 357, 479
Bradley, R. H. 492
Braunschweig, D. 326
Breger, L. 51–52
Brenner, Charles 107
Brentano, F. 11
Breuer, Josef 50–55
Brewer, M. B. 476, 479
Briere, A. 491
Briere, J. 492
Brierley, Marjorie 413
Brink, A. 447
British cultural influences on Fairbairn 69–70
British Independent Group ("Independents")/ Middle Group xxiii, 6, 115, 297, 323–325, 355
British Journal of Medical Psychology 282, 324
British Psychoanalytical Society 7, 282. *See also* Controversial Discussions
Britner, P. A. 486
Bromberg, Philip M. 50, 54, 205, 249, 352, 360
Brooks, T. 28
Brown, L. J. 193–194, 270
Brownell, M. 483–484
building blocks 224–225

Buitelaar, J. K. 163
Burke, W. F. 249
Burkert, W. 417

Caird, Edward 452
Caldwell, B. M. 492
Calvin, Jean 79
Calvinism 78, 82
Campi, Mercedes 110–111
Campo, Emiliano del 102
Camus, Albert 461, 463–470
Caparrós-Sánchez, N. 193
Cassullo, Gabriele 55
castration anxiety 104
Celani, David P. 106, 401–408
central ego (CE) 15–16, 189, 192, 305
   John Padel on 298, 302, 305
   relationship to internal and external objects 141
   relationships with accepted or sufficiently good object 156
Chalmers, Charles 70–71, 82
chaos theory 267–269, 428
character, transitional techniques and the development of 15, 188–191
Charcot, Jean-Martin xxxii–xxxiii, 51–54, 420
Chen, K. 492
child abuse
   goals in working with survivors of 488–490
   perpetrators of
      goals in working with 489–490
      management styles in dealing with 486
   sociocultural influences on 489
   substantiation of allegations 486–487
      case assessment 487–488
   See also ritual cult abuse; sexual abuse
Child Dissociative Checklist (CDC) 491–492
child protection approach to child welfare 483–484
child welfare, social work, and Fairbairn's object relations theory 483, 492
   client engagement 485–486
   goal setting 488–490
   intervention planning 490–491
   outcome evaluation 491–492
   policy context 483–485
   See also child abuse

Children Act of 1989 (UK) 484
Children Act of 2004 (UK) 484
Christian faith as normative, not neurotic 76–77
Christianity 42–47. *See also* Jesus of Nazareth; religion
chronic recurrent maternal decathexis (CRMD) 212–213, 215
clans 474
Clarke, Graham S. xxiii, 28, 41, 45, 56, 72–73, 127, 202, 206, 211, 335–336, 341, 419, 422–425, 445, 447
Clarkin, J. F. 116, 120
claustrum 204
Cohen, A. S. 486
Cohen, Diego 106
communication, human 66
    "direct communication" 247
    unconscious communication in analysis 270
communion between people 46
communism 33, 472–473, 475–476
community group problem, analysis of a 384
    progress of the work group 385–386
    steps for analysing interference with the group's work 385
conflict
    psychoanalytic theories not based on 108
    with external reality 105
conflict-defence theory
    creation of Freudian 53
    vs. deficit psychopathology 191, 334
Connell, Ernest Henry 7, 71–72, 74
Connelly, M. 486
Conners, N. A. 492
continuity
    of being 325
    principle/law of 43–46
Controversial Discussions 6, 127, 210, 297, 323, 336, 424
Convention on the Rights of the Child 484–485
Costello, J. E. 65, 73, 77
countertransference, Winnicott on 6, 246–247, 328
couple therapy. *See* Dicks, Henry V.; marital conflict
creativity 343, 368, 448, 450–451, 453–455
    analysis as a setting for 391, 393–394
    psychic growth and 341, 368

    science and 394
    Winnicott on 30, 325–327, 330
    See also art
Crossley, N. 434

Davidson, D. 419
Davies, Jody Messler 49, 80, 218–219, 246, 249, 257
De Dousa, R. 419
de Medina, P. G. 163
death and grief 463
Deblinger, E. 486
decontamination 155, 157
Deere, D. 492
defence, structure of
    and the aim of survival 164–165
deficit *vs.* conflict psychopathology 191, 334
degeneration theory 53–56
Delbruck, Max 414
delinquency 326
democracy, Fairbairn's support for 34
Den Otter, S. 29
Dennett, D. C. 425
dependence 104
    relative (*see* transitional phase)
    See also infantile dependence; mature dependence
depersonalization, Guntrip on 314
depositor, depository, and deposited (three Ds) 386
depressive position 259, 453
Descartes, René 417, 432–434
destructive narcissistic organisation (DNO) 426–428
Deutsch, Helene 226
developmental disabilities. *See* intellectual disability
Devil/devils 46, 76, 79–80, 117, 203, 457, 487. *See also* exorcism
dialectic 8
    society and 28–29
dialectic spiral 382
Dicks, Henry V. 21, 72, 120–122, 175–179, 370
    "consultation" with 181–183
    David Scharff and 498
    integration of Klein and Fairbairn 365

Marital Tensions 175–179, 183, 269
   on joint marital personality 269–270
   on projective and introjective identification 269
   re-acquaintance with 177–179
   Sutherland's obituary of 177
dictatorships 33–35
dissociated self of the child 400
dissociation
   and return of the dissociated 49–50
   attachment theory, trauma, and 212–213, 218
   degeneration theory and 53–56
   endopsychic structures and 210–211, 214, 217–220, 237–238
   nature of 218
   primitive 103
   working with 205–206
"Dissociation and Repression" (Fairbairn's MD thesis) xxxiv, 14, 42, 46, 209, 337
dissociative identity disorder (DID)/multiple personality disorder (MPD) 205–206
   clinical application of Fairbairnian thought to 212–213, 217–220
      clinical material 213–220
   clinical material 206–207
   Fairbairn and 209–211, 334
   paradigm of 212
Dodds, E. R. 417
Dogaheh, E. R. 491
Donnoli, V. 226
dreams 119–120, 246–247, 467–468
   as dramatisations *vs.* wish-fulfillments 238
   clinical material from Fairbairn's work 240–246
      Jack's dream 242–243
   endopsychic structures and 238–246, 284
   Freud on 238–239, 288
   of Fairbairn 96–98
   place in Fairbairn's personality model 237–240
drive theory 346–350, 420, 435–436. *See also* drives; libido theory; partitive conceptions of mind; structural model
drives 17–18, 59–63, 66, 350
   Kernberg on 116, 119
   See also libido; structural model: Freud's
Drummond, Henry 41, 43–47
dualism(s) 8, 12, 14. *See also* structural model
Dumbrill, G. 485

Dutra, Lissa 212–213
dynamic identification 252–257
   clinical illustration 254–256
   defined 253
dynamic structure 302, 350, 359, 431, 438
   dissociative identity disorder and 214–215, 217–218
   dreams and 238, 241–243
   "Object-Relationships and Dynamic Structure" 89–90
   principle of 455–456
   psychology of 209–211, 295–296, 333, 338, 445
   See also dynamic identification
dynamism and object-relatedness in Fairbairn 435–439
dynamism hypothesis 436

Echegaray, E. 107
ECRO 383
   conceptual, referential, and operational schema 383–386
Edwards, Jonathan 80–81
Edwards, M. C. 492
ego 103, 438–439
   definitions of 320, 387, 425
   multiplicity of 242, 283, 288, 346, 422–423
   original 152, 164, 210, 340, 359, 394, 438
   See also central ego
ego functioning in everyday life, support for 319–320
ego ideal 193
"Ego in Current Thinking" (Padel) 299–300
ego states 218
ego structures, Fairbairn's 152–153. *See also specific structures*
Ehrlich, R. 315
Eichenbaum, L. 445–446
Eigen, Michael 312, 391
Einstein, Albert 12, 407
Ekman, Paul 118
Elhai, J. D. 491
Ellenberger, Henri F. 9, 50, 52–54, 420
emergent (moment of therapeutic process) 388
Emmy von N., case of 54
emotion. *See* affect
emotional blindness 462

empathic attunement to psychic organisation
    259–261
emptiness pathology 223–224
    clinical case 229–231
    etiology 227–229
    Fairbairnian clinical work and 225–227
    metapsychology 231–233, 234f
    nature of 224–225
    overview 231–233
    schizoid conflict, object situation, and 227–229
    symptoms and examples of 225–226
    vicious circles of 228
emptiness phantasy 220
"endopsychic", Fairbairn's first use of the term 449
endopsychic model 37
endopsychic relationships, dialectics of 219
endopsychic situation 102, 106–108, 149, 152, 155, 233, 234f, 267, 367
    as immutable 141, 321
    basic 134–135, 328, 412
        defined 141
        origin and development of 162, 265, 328
    clinical illustration 372–376
    is always in dynamic flux 379
    Plato's division of mind and 424
    repression and 224, 367
    schizoid conflict and 227
    trauma and 367
endopsychic structure xxi, 79, 144, 193, 219, 271, 278, 299–301, 341, 445
    basic 186
        origin and development of 210, 338, 340–341, 379
        precursors to 210
        traumatically induced replications of 211, 218
    borderline pathology and 190–191
    components 16, 128, 422–423
    definition and overview 135, 388
    differentiation of 162, 189
    Ferenczi, Fairbairn, and 334–338
    Freud's topographic categories and 211, 212f
    Oedipus situation and 298
    regressive conditions, ambivalence, mourning, and 188

repression and the creation of 186, 379, 387
schizoid position and 190–191
unconscious communication and 270
"Endopsychic Structure Considered in Terms of Object-relationships" (Fairbairn) 15, 17, 89, 91, 132, 239, 268, 301, 303
endopsychic structures
    alternative 217
    autonomy 219
    dissociation and 210–211, 214, 217–220, 237–238
    dreams and 238–246, 284
    phantasy and 423
"energetic" assumption 403–404
energy (physics) 11–12
energy, psychic 253
environment, failing 198–200
environmental mother 316
Erikson, Erik H. 117, 119, 476
erotic transference 158
Éthier, L. S. 489–490
Euripides 418
"evangelism" 36
Evans, W. N. 312
exciting object 15, 74
    vs. good object 251
excluded third party 119, 121
existential crisis 461–462, 468. *See also* Stranger
existing (moment of therapeutic process) 388
exorcism, theme of 46, 76. *See also* bad objects, release of; Devil/devils

Fain, Michael 326
Fairbairn, Nicholas 31
Fairbairn, William Ronald Dodds
    analytic theorists influenced by 144n2
    a recent interpretation of 211
    as writer xxxi–xxxiv
    current impact 115–123
    early studies 13–14
    marriage 95–96
    object relations tradition originated by xxiv–xxvi
    on psychical change and analytic cure 350–351
    overview of xxi–xxiv, 5–6, 281, 379, 497–498

biographical 281–282, 379, 448
personal life of
    dreams of 96–98
    early life and family of origin 70, 93–94
personality and psychopathology of 93–97
    schizoid features 98, 193
    sexuality 93–98
    suicidality 96
    urinary inhibition/retention 93–98
philosophic backdrop for the theories of 432–435
philosophical origins of the thought of 7–11
religious evidences in the life of
    a viable faith in professional writings 76–77
    Christian observance 73–74
    formative experiences 74–76
religious influences in the life of
    British cultural influences 69–70
    educational influences 70–71
    family influences 70
    professional influences 71–73
religious themes in the work of
    Christian narrative 77–78
    creation 78–79
    fall (from grace) 79–81
    redemption 81–82
    Scottish Presbyterianism 78
teaching 101–102
theoretical advances 282–284
    developments after 1951 292
    elements of his revision of psychoanalytic theory 132–136
    his reform (in psychoanalysis) compared with that of Martin Luther 194
    model of endopsychic structure 16–17, 16f, 284–288, 299–300
    object relations theory 14–22, 115–116, 431–432
    six-part structure of personality 16–17, 16f
    theory of modes of defence and their breakdown 288–289
    theory of the origins of clinical syndromes 289–291
therapeutic approach 155
transitional techniques 388
work of, as standing "between paradigms" 348
writings
    "A Revised Psychopathology of the Psychoses and Psychoneuroses" 10–11, 14–15, 19, 56, 89, 134, 150, 186–187, 191, 283, 289, 327, 346, 398, 402, 413, 451, 475, 487–488
    "Dissociation and Repression" (MD thesis) xxxiv, 14, 42, 46, 209, 337
    "Object-Relationships and Dynamic Structure" 89–90
    "Observations on the Nature of Hysterical States" xxxii–xxxiii, 17, 90, 205, 242, 268, 287, 304
    "On the Nature and Aims of Psycho-analytical Treatment" 90, 92, 243, 251–252, 268, 292, 304, 393
    "Psychotherapy and the Clergy" 46
    "Repression and the Return of Bad Objects (with Special Reference to 'War Neuroses')" 15, 77, 79, 288
    "The Sociological Significance of Communism Considered in the Light of Psychoanalysis" 472–473, 475
    "The Ultimate Basis of Aesthetic Experience" 447–448, 453
    See also Psychoanalytic Studies of the Personality
    See also specific topics
"Fairbairn's Thought on the Relationship of Inner and Outer Worlds" (Padel) 304–306
fall (from grace), theme of
    alienation from others 80–81
    attachment to the bad 79–81
    decline and fracture 79–80
    separation from the good 79–80
false *vs.* true self 55, 188, 230, 246, 286, 300, 315–316, 326
Falzeder, Ernst 50
family and polity 32–35
family service approach to child welfare 484
fantasy 246. *See also* phantasy
father, emerging significance of the 165
Faust, J. 486
Fawcett, Joseph xxxiii
Feldman, Michael 20
Ferenczi, Sándor 328, 333

"Confusion of Tongues Between the Adults and the Child" 333–334, 339
Fairbairn and 333–337, 339–340
Fairbairn's first meeting with 335
Freud and 55, 333
"Introjection and Transference" 335
Janet and 55
move from one-person to two-person psychology 336
on identification with the aggressor 55
on mother–infant relationship 150
on repetition compulsion 334
on sexual abuse 334, 339
on sexuality 55, 60
on technique 336–337, 340
on trauma and dissociation 55, 333–335, 340–341
"The Adaptation of the Family to the Child" 337–338
The Development of Psychoanalysis 335–336
"The Elasticity of Psycho-Analytic Technique" 336–337, 340
Ferrari, P. F. 264
Ferro, A. 265, 270
Feynman, Richard P. 407, 414
Field, Joanna. *See* Milner, Marion
Finnegan, Paul 127, 206, 211, 213, 336
fixation 61
Fluke, J. 483–484
Foa, E. 486
Fogassi, L. 263–264
Fonagy, Peter 103, 105, 266
Forbes, M. E. 309, 312, 315
Fosshage, James L. 239
foster parents 485–486
Frame, L. 486
Framo, J. L. 268
Frankel, Jay 333, 335
Frankland, A. G. 488–489
Franklin, L. C. 491
Frawley, Mary Gail 218–219, 246
free association 238–239
Freeman, Thomas 228
Freeman, W. J. 265
Fremouw, W. 491

Freud, Sigmund 88, 107, 109, 163, 166, 224, 288
Charcot, Breuer, and 51–55
degeneration theory and 53–56
dissociation and 49, 51
"Group Psychology and the Analysis of the Ego" 299, 473, 476
libido theory 14
Mourning and Melancholia 103, 134, 153, 285
on art and artists 448–451
on dreams 238–239, 288
on ego 288, 425 (*see also* structural model)
on group psychology and intergroup problems in society 471, 473
"On Narcissism" 286, 299, 301–302, 304, 338
on repression 186, 224
on splitting 50, 134
on superego 134
on unconscious communication in analysis 270
realisation of the primacy of object relations 420
structural model 12–14, 61, 131, 420–422, 425, 436
vs. Janet 50–56
Friedland, B. 344–345
Friedman, B. 49
Friedrich, W. N. 492
friendship 65
friendship encounter 66
Friessen, W. V. 118
From Instinct to Self: Selected Papers of W. R. D. Fairbairn (Scharff & Birtles) xxix, 3, 209, 447
Frost, A. 486
Frust, L. R. 52
frustration 132, 231, 326, 387
and aggression 231, 233
functional structural constellations 210–211
functional structural units 211
Furman, E. 213
Furman, R. A. 213

Gallese, V. 263–264
Gardner, S. 419–420
Garma, A. 101
Geeraert, L. 492
Gelfand, T. 54
Gentile, C. 486

Gergely, B. 266
Germany, division of 371
Gerson, Gal 27, 30
Gilbert, A. M. 492
Gilbert, N. 484, 491
Gilbert, R. 483–484
Gill, Merton M. 20, 110
Gladstone, J. 485
Glatzer, H. T. 312
Gleick, J. 267
Glover, Edward 89, 111, 127, 448, 453
Glymour, C. 424
Goetz, C. G. 54
Goldberg, Arnold 128
Gomez, L. 27, 89
Gonzalez-Izquierdo, A. 483–484
good enough mother 325
good object 250, 278
    analyst as 250
        categories of activity that can be provided by 252–261
        See also dynamic identification
    Klein *vs*. Fairbairn on 250–251
    origins 251
Gosso, S. 453
Gough, D. 305
Graham, G. 419
"gratifying" *vs*. "satisfying" 278
Gray, M. J. 491
Green, André 225
Greenberg, Jay R. 5, 103, 110, 210, 249, 298, 312, 316, 348
    characterisation of Fairbairn 309
    Fairbairn's influence on 144n2
    obituary of Fairbairn 344
    Object Relations in Psychoanalytic Theory 79, 87, 277–278, 298, 304, 345–346, 357–359, 361, 488
grief 462–463. *See also Mourning and Melancholia*
Grietens, H. 492
Grosskurth, Phyllis 301, 303
Grotstein, James S. 22, 31, 80, 128, 144n2, 148, 153–154, 194, 211, 265, 270, 298, 348, 357–359, 365, 423, 438
    on abandonment depression after release from ties to persecutory objects 219
    on child abuse 128, 219

    on dreams 240, 246
    on integration of discrete subselves into unified self 219
    on multiple personality disorder 128, 191, 219
    on paranoid-schizoid position 187
    on personality disorders 191
    on psychic mechanisms 267
    on sexual abuse survivors 219
    Splitting and Projective Identification 22
group as a whole. *See* operative group
"Group Psychology and Analysis of the Ego" (Freud) 299, 473, 476
groups
    Freud on 299, 471, 473, 476
    ingroup/outgroup 472–473, 475–480
    large 473–481
    the unconscious group 472–473
    See also community group problem
grupo operativo (operative group) 379, 383–384
guilt 104–105
    moral defence and 117, 120, 283, 288, 339, 464–465, 468
guilty child 147
Gullenstad, S. E. 49
Gulliver, P. 483–484
Gully, K. J. 491
Gunderson, John G. 103–104, 229
Guntrip, Harry J. S. 14, 21, 80, 103–104, 144n2, 188, 230, 282, 321, 329, 426–428
    alteration of Fairbairn's theory 298
    analyses by Fairbairn and Winnicott 20, 80, 298, 311–312, 329
    biographical overview 309–312
    death 329
    emphasis on romantic aspects of Fairbairn's work 310–311, 313, 320–321
    on regressed libidinal ego 21, 315–319
    on schizoid phenomena 312–315, 321
    on therapeutic relationship 319–320
    regression and 315–320
    relationship with Fairbairn 20–21, 80, 312, 329
    Schizoid Phenomena, Object Relations and the Self 313
    self psychology and 313
    Stephen Mitchell and 309, 312, 316, 344
    Winnicott and 104, 298, 311–312, 329

Hacker, P. M. S. 425
Haitzmann, Christoph 77
Hall, Stanley 12
Hamilton, N. 224
Hamlet (Shakespeare) 166, 427–428
Hanko, H. 78
Harlow, Harry F. 265
Harris, M. 204
Harrow, A. 368
Harrow, J. A. 72, 258
Hartmann, Heinz 424
hate 467. *See also* aggression; anti-libidinal ego; anti-libidinal object
Hazell, J. 309, 312, 315–316
Hazlitt, William xxxiii
Hebert, M. 486
Hegel, Georg Wilhelm Friedrich 8–11, 38, 453–454
    dialectic, society, and 8, 27–29
    Fairbairn and 8–11, 27–28, 30, 37, 71, 79, 448, 452, 455, 457
    object relations and 29–30
    on self-consciousness 10, 457
Heimann, Paula 6, 149
Hellinckx, W. 492
Helmers, K. 491
Helmholtz, Hermann. von 11, 14
Hensel, Bernhard F. 150, 152–153, 189
Himmelfarb, B. 70
Hinde, Robert 265
Hinshelwood, Robert D. 209
Hirsch, I. 249
Hodgson, P. 79
Hoeksema, H. 78
Hoffman, Irwin Z. 20, 249, 252, 257
Hoffman, Marie T. 41–42, 46, 70, 72, 79
Hogg, M. A. 472
holding 325
Holmes, J. 27, 266
homosexuality. *See* sex, conscience, and homosexuality
Hopkins, J. 419, 424
Hopper, E. 270
hostility
    primary 327–328
    See also aggression
House, J. 188, 488

Howell, C. T. 492
Hughes, Judith M. 102, 210, 296–297, 304, 309, 312
Huizink, A. C. 163
Hulme, T. S. 310
Husserl, Edmund 433
Huxley, Aldous 32
hypnoid states 50, 53
hysteria xxxii–xxxiii, 242, 268, 290–291, 381, 388, 413
    Charcot and 53–54
    emptiness and 226
    Freud (and Breuer) on xxxii, 51, 53–55, 282
    idealizing transference 334
    Janet and xxxii, 50, 52–55
    "Observations on the Nature of Hysterical States" (Fairbairn) xxxii–xxxiii, 17, 90, 205, 242, 268, 287, 304
    Rupprecht-Schampera's theory of 190
    See also hysterical personality
hysterical personality 90–91, 266. *See also* hysteria

ideal ego (IE) 210–211, 216–218, 285
ideal object (IO) 16, 192–193
    vs. good object 251
idealised objects 251
idealism, problematic (Descartes) 432–434
idealization, dynamics of 178
identification 306
    introjective 264–265, 269–270
    primary 150, 189, 233, 437–438, 440
        and primary and secondary narcissism 228
        case material 169
        infantile dependence and 33, 78–79, 170–172, 189, 472, 480 (*see also under* infantile dependence: identification and)
    with the aggressor 55, 334, 339
    See also dynamic identification; projective identification
Iltus, S. 492
incest taboo and clans 474
independence. *See* dependence; self-sufficiency
Independent Group ("Independents")/Middle Group xxiii, 6, 115, 297, 323–325, 355
infantile dependence 8, 150, 169, 291
    dissociation of sentiments connected to 55–56

fixation in 30, 33–34, 55, 167, 339, 472, 487 (*see also* mature dependence: failure to achieve)
frustration and 387
groups and 478
identification and xxv, 10, 55, 171, 189, 338, 438, 478, 480
overcoming 15, 36, 121, 150, 155, 171–172, 189, 210, 265, 327, 366, 387, 413, 438
overview and description of xxv, 10, 14–15, 161–164, 327, 338, 438, 472, 480, 487
soldiers, war neuroses, and 30, 34, 339, 472
transitional ways of relating and 265
unconditional character of 398
inferiority complex 50
ingroup/outgroup 472–473, 475–480
innocent child 147
instantiated emotional experience 264
instincts. *See* drives
intellectual disability, moral defence in work with persons with 200–203
internal object relationships 379. *See also specific topics*
internal object(s) 325
defined 358
"emotional life" of Fairbairn's 136
Klein and 103–104, 120, 127–128, 148–153, 325
of Fairbairn *vs.* Klein 153
terminology 144n4
therapeutic aspects 154–158
Thomas Ogden on 32, 338, 350, 423
the world of 357–359
internal saboteur
central ego and 401, 405
relationship to libidinal ego and exciting object 135–136, 139–143
tie between rejecting object and 15–16, 135–139, 152, 266, 400
See also anti-libidinal ego
internalisation 288, 302, 325
John Padel on 300–302, 305, 338
See also internal object(s)
International Congress of Psychoanalysis (1929) 7, 75
International Psychoanalytical Association (IPA) 345
interpreted (moment of therapeutic process) 388

intersubjective third 253–254
intersubjectivity 19, 431–433
ego and 436–437
Fairbairn and Merleau-Ponty's theories of 279, 435, 439–441
Husserl and 433–434
transcendental 433
"intrapsychic" 344–345
introjection 264
"Introjection and Transference" (Ferenczi) 335
introjective identification 264–265, 269–270
introversion
Bleuler and Jung on 50
Guntrip on 313
intuition in the analytic session 395
intuitive position 391–395
components of 392
psychopathology and 395
inverted cone (Pichon-Rivière) 384, 384f
Irungaray, Elda 109
Ismaila, A. 485

Jacobs, Theodore J. 20
Jacobson, Edith 115
Jahoda, Marie 60
Janet, Paul 52
Janet, Pierre xxxii–xxxiii, 49–56, 420
Janson, S. 483–484
Jesus of Nazareth 63, 65
Johnston, M. 419
joint marital personality 269–270
Jones, Ernest xxxi, 5, 62, 72, 76, 333–334
Jurist, F. 266
juvenile delinquency 326

Kächele, H. 106
Kaës, R. 270
Kahr, B. 197
Kant, Immanuel 433, 447
Kashdan, T. B. 491
Kernberg, Otto F. 21
on affect 118
on aggression 105, 119
on borderline pathology 105, 107, 120, 187–188, 191, 225–226, 229
on conflict with external reality 105

on Fairbairn 22, 28, 105, 110, 115–116, 118, 144n2, 268, 304, 309, 312, 437
on narcissistic pathology 121, 193, 225
on oral conflict 107
on personality disorders 267
on projective identification 225
on splitting units 224
on treatment 116, 120
theoretical models 105, 109–110
Khan, Masud M. R. 187, 277, 303, 328, 330, 356, 437, 439
Killingmo, Bjørn 191
King, Pearl 6, 127, 198, 210, 323
Kirkwood, C. 72
Kirschner, Suzanne 77
Klein, Melanie 6, 107, 115, 144n2, 147–151, 153, 224, 231, 278, 325, 412–413, 435, 450, 455
contrasted with Fairbairn 104–105
Fairbairn's criticism of 423, 436
Fairbairn's influence on xxiv, 281, 297, 301, 325
internal objects in the works of 103–104, 120, 127–128, 148–153
John Padel on 296–297, 302–303
"Notes on Some Schizoid Mechanisms" 303, 453
on aggression 91–92, 148–149, 154, 250, 282, 448, 450, 453
on depressive position 259, 453
on good objects 250–251
on idealised objects 251
on introjection of good experience 398
on Oedipus complex and superego formation 148, 288
on paranoid-schizoid position xxiv, 153–154, 187, 251–252, 259, 297, 303, 325
on phantasy 91–92, 127, 133, 149, 153–154, 210, 387, 448, 450, 453
on projective identification 264–265, 303, 370
on reparation 282, 341, 450–451, 453–455
on splitting 281, 297, 303
Stephen Mitchell on 344, 362
Winnicott and 296–297, 302–303, 330
Klimovsky, G. 224
Kline, F. M. 488
Knight, C. 488

Kohut, Heinz 144n2, 238–239, 250–251, 310
failure to refer to Fairbairn 108
Fairbairn compared with 191, 313
Fairbairn's influence on 22, 108, 304
Guntrip and 313
narcissism and 191, 193, 238–239, 313
theory not based on conflict 108
Koster, A. 485
Kramer, Robert 335
Krause, Rainer 118
Kris, Ernst 447, 450, 455–456
Kuhn, Thomas S. 161, 224

Lacan, Jacques 324
Lacharité, C. 489–490
Landis, B. 321
Lane, B. 79
Lanktree, C. B. 492
Laplanche, Jean 299
large group(s)
and the social object in action 479
formation 473–478
in the mind 478
object relations, prejudice, and war 479–480
Larkin, W. 486
Lear, Jonathan 419
learning from experience 230
Ledet, T. 492
Leishman, M. 368
Leslie, B. 485
Levenson, E. A. 352
Levine, Steven Z. 445, 447
Lewes, Kenneth 87
Lewin, Kurt 108
Lewontin, R. C. 413
Liberman, D. 105
libidinal ego (LE) 16–17
active vs. passive 466–467
bond between exciting object and 136–137
defined 139
relationships between libidinal object and 157–158
libidinal object (LO) 157–158, 189
anxiety over destroying 188
See also exciting object

libido 139
    as object seeking, and the problem of motivation 346–350
    as only source of instinctual energy and motivation 116
libido theory 14, 89, 345–346. *See also* drive theory
Lichtenberg, Joseph D. 350
link theory 270–271, 371–376, 380, 386–389
    the link and dialectic learning 382
    the link and interpretation 382–383
    the link and psychoanalytic therapy 386–387
    the link and theory of three Ds 386
    location of the link 388–389
Liotti, G. 212
Lipton, S. D. 249
Livingstone, David 42
loneliness and schizoid processes, Guntrip on 314
longing self 466. *See also* libidinal ego
Lorenz, Konrad 265
loss 265. *See also* Mourning and Melancholia
Losso, Roberto 379, 387
Lottman, H. R. 464–465
love
    addictive 136–137
    relational needs require acceptance of our patients' 257–259
Lowenstein, R. J. 50, 212
Lyons-Ruth, Karlen 188, 212–213

Macdonald, M. 368
Macmurray, John xxv, 45, 63–67, 72–73, 210
Mahler, Margaret S. 107–108
Maida, C. A. 492
Makari, G. 51–53
Mann, Thomas 11
marital conflict 122
    clinical vignette 175–176, 179–183
    See also Dicks, Henry V.
Marital Tensions (Dicks) 175–179, 183, 269
Marmar, C. 489
marriage, exogamy, and the incest taboo 474
Marxism 33
masochism 189
Masterson, James F. 228
mature dependence 104
    as always-incomplete process 32
    development of 14–15, 89, 150, 162, 169, 210, 327, 338, 387, 438
    failure to achieve 34–36, 167 (*see also* infantile dependence: fixation in)
    groups and 478, 488
    nature of 15, 33, 35, 338, 488
    overview 171–172
    society and 3, 34, 446, 475, 478
maturity 33
Mayhew, B. 27
Maze, J. 424
McConaughy, S. H. 492
McGuiness, M. 407
McGuire, W. 50, 52
McLeer, S. 486
McWilliams, Nancy 107
Meltzer, Donald W. 203–204
Merchiston Castle School 70–71
Merea, E. César 102
Merleau-Ponty, Maurice M. 434–435
    Fairbairn and 439–441
Metzler, T. 489
Middle Group/Independent Group xxiii, 6, 115, 297, 323–325, 355
Midgley, Mary 44
military 472. *See also* war neuroses
Milite, María Cristina 110
Miller, Gavin 28, 41–42, 45
Milner, Marion 453–455
mind/body dualism 12
Mitchell, Margaret Black 358, 360. *See also* Black, Margaret J.
Mitchell, Stephen A. 5, 22, 28, 78, 103, 110, 128, 148, 187, 210, 249, 252, 267, 298, 340, 343–352, 355–361, 399–400, 424, 431, 436–437
    case of Will 361
    characterisation of Fairbairn 309
    contrasted with Fairbairn 356
    Fairbairn's influence on the theoretical and clinical work of 144n2, 355–362
    first encounter with Fairbairn 344
    Guntrip and 309, 312, 316, 344
    identification with Fairbairn 361–362
    Object Relations in Psychoanalytic Theory 79, 87, 277–278, 298, 304, 345–346, 357–359, 361, 488
    on drives and drive theory 346–350

    on Fairbairn's approach to internalisation 151–152
    on good and bad objects 345, 351, 360
    on Klein 344, 362
    on love and passion 257–258
    on psychical change and analytic cure 350–352
    on relational matrix 477
    on splitting 31, 399
    reformulation of object relations theory 488
    viewed Fairbairn as his predecessor 355–357, 362
Modell, Arnold H. 144n2, 191, 296, 438–439
Mohammadi, M. R. 491
Mohammadkhani, P. 491
Mollon, P. 206
Mom, Jorge M. 102, 106, 352
Montero, Guillermo J. 104, 106, 108, 223, 229–230
Moore, James R. 43–45
Moore, M. 419
moral defence 122, 151–152, 157, 193, 339, 457
    basis of Fairbairn's concept of 448
    essential feature and aim of 340
    guilt and 117, 120, 283, 288, 339, 464–465, 468
    identification with aggressor and 334, 339
    imagination in 153–154
    in work with persons with intellectual disability 200–203
    overview and nature of 117, 120, 151, 189, 283, 288–289, 399
    schizoid position and 193
    splitting and 399
Morris, Fairbairn's case of 90–98, 190–191, 407
Morrison, Andrew P. 486
motivational systems 350. *See also* drives
Mourning and Melancholia (Freud) 103, 134, 153, 285
Mulder, E. J. 163
multiple personality disorder. *See* dissociative identity disorder (DID)/multiple personality disorder (MPD)
multiplicity of ego(s) 242, 283, 288, 346, 422–423. *See also* self: multiple configurations of
Muran, J. C. 319

narcissism
    as schizoid characteristic 313

    "On Narcissism" (Freud) 286, 299, 301–302, 304, 338
    primary and secondary 326
        defined 191
    terminology used by Fairbairn for 191
"'Narcissism' in Fairbairn's Theory of Personality Structure" (Padel) 300–302
narcissistic libido 139
narcissistic object relation (NOR) 225–226, 227f 229–231
narcissistic organisation, destructive 426–428
narcissistic pathology 121, 191
    Kernberg on 121, 193, 225
    Kohut on 191, 193, 238–239, 313
narcissistic wounds 283
nationalism 475, 480
Natural Law in the Spiritual World (Drummond) 43–44
natural philosophy 64
natural theology 64
Nazari, M. A. 491
neuroscience 263–265
neurosis 380–381
Nicholson, P. P. 29
Nijenhuis, Ellert R. S. 206
Nilsson, D. 491
nirvana 11
Norcross, John C. 319

"object" 278
    Freud and Fairbairn on 103
    in British object relations theory 162
Object Love and Reality (Modell) 296
object mother 316
object-relatedness
    and dynamism in Fairbairn 435–439
    See also relatedness
object relation units 224–225
Object Relations in Psychoanalytic Theory (Greenberg & Mitchell) 79, 87, 277–278, 298, 304, 345–346, 357–359, 361, 488
object relations theory 104, 263
    origins of 277, 335
    revision of 19f
    See also specific topics

Object Relations Theory of Personality, An (Fairbairn) 281. *See also Psychoanalytic Studies of the Personality*
"object-relationship psychology" 358
"Object-Relationships and Dynamic Structure" (Fairbairn) 89–90
obsessional neurosis 290–291
O'Donnell, M. 483–484
Oedipal dilemma 165–167
    reconfigured by trauma, case study of 167–169
        clinical implications of 169–170
Oedipus complex 161–162, 172, 190, 298
    Klein on 148, 288
Oedipus myth 169, 187. *See also* Oedipus Rex
Oedipus Rex (Sophocles) 38. *See also* Oedipus myth
Oedipus situation 189
    analysis of positive 169–170
        Fairbairn on 17, 32, 89, 95–96, 128, 162, 169–170, 186, 240, 298, 328–329, 476
        Guntrip and 329
        Klein on 288
Ogden, Thomas H. 22, 29, 127, 134, 136, 144n1, 265, 270, 278, 296, 343, 406
    on internal objects 32, 338, 350, 423
    on intersubjective third 253
    on paranoid-schizoid position 259–260
    on splitting 304–305
    "Why Read Fairbairn?" 321
operative group (*grupo operativo*) 379, 383–384
opposing forces. *See* dualism(s)
optimal synthesis 452
Orbach, S. 445–446
original ego 152, 164, 210, 340, 359, 394, 438
original object 148, 228, 407, 437–438
    infantile dependency on 150
    internalisation 437
    pre-ambivalent phase and 278
    splitting of 291 (*see also* splitting)
    See also pre-ambivalent object
Oswald, Luis 110

Padel, John 22, 211, 277–278, 295–296, 298–299, 303–306
    on central ego 298, 302, 305
    on dreams 240
    on Fairbairn's model of endopsychic structure 299–300
    on Freud 296, 299
    on Guntrip 298
    on internalisation 300–302, 305, 338
    on Klein and Fairbairn 296–297, 302–303
    on mother–infant relationship 305
    on narcissism 299, 301
    on Oedipus complex 298
    on psychic growth 302, 304
    on repression 338
    on schizoid states 300–301
    on splitting 298–301, 303–305, 338
    on Winnicott 302–303
    papers 277, 295–296, 298–306
    reviews 296–298
Palombo, S. R. 300, 305
Panksepp, J. 119
Panzer, A. 489
Pappenheim, E. 456
paranoia 108, 290
paranoid position xxiv, 325
paranoid-schizoid position 193, 255–256, 260
    clinical material 256–257, 260–261
    empathy and 252–253
    Grotstein on 187
    Klein on xxiv, 153–154, 187, 251–252, 259, 297, 303, 325
    obliteration of doubt as hallmark of 251
    Ogden on 259–260
parasitism 43–44, 140
partitive conceptions of mind
    Fairbairn and 422–424
    Freud and 420–422
    in philosophy 417–420
    See also parts of persons; structural model
Parton, N. 484, 491
parts of persons 424–428
passive anti-libidinal ego 468
passive libidinal ego/passive longing self 466
Pataki, Tamas 419, 425
Pave, John Frank 90
Pears, David 419
Pedernera, Susan 111
penis as narcissistic organ 104
Pereira, F. 27, 237, 447

Pérez-Rincón, H. 50
Perry, B. D. 485
personality disorders 186–187, 193–194. *See also specific disorders*
personation 427–428
perversion 36, 88, 90
Peterson, G. 492
Petocz, A. 59
phantasy 210, 387, 425–426
    endopsychic structures and 423
    Klein on 91–92, 127, 133, 149, 153–154, 210, 387, 448, 450, 453
    See also emptiness phantasy
philosophy 64
    partitive conceptions of mind in 417–420
    of science 11–12
    See also under Fairbairn
phobias 290–291
Piaget, Jean 103
Piche, C. 486
Pichon-Rivière, Enrique 101, 365, 379–380, 382–383
    Fairbairn's influence on 387–388
    ideas of 380–382
        ECRO 383–386
        inverted cone 384
        theory of roles 386
        See also link theory
    on ego 388
    on neurosis 380–381
    on object relations 386
    on therapeutic process 388
Pick, Daniel 53–54
Pick, I. B. 254
Plato 417–418
Platonic philosophy and psychology 7–8
Platt, D. 486
pleasure principle 14, 149–150, 436
Pontalis, J.-B. 299
Porter, R. 70
Portuges, S. 188
post-traumatic stress disorder (PTSD) 486
Potthoff, P. 155
Poulton, James L. 318
pre-ambivalent object 106, 151, 210, 228, 302, 338–339, 440. *See also* original object
pre-ambivalent phase 187, 189, 231, 278, 289, 291

preconscious 211, 233, 336, 401, 408
preconscious ego-ideal 210, 337, 340–341
prejudice, war, and object relations 479–480
Prévost, Claude M. 50–52, 54
primal scene 89, 91–92, 96, 108, 292
primary maternal occupation 150, 325
Pringle-Pattison, Andrew Seth 8, 71, 73
problematic idealism (Descartes) 432–434
projective identification 22, 204
    Bion on 265
    Kernberg on 225
    Klein on 264–265, 303, 370
    mutual 269–270, 370
"Prolegomena to a Psychology of Art" (Fairbairn) 447–449, 455, 457
Proust, Marcel xxxi–xxxii
psychic growth 79, 211, 217, 278, 297, 301–302, 338, 340–341. *See also* creativity
psychic organisation
    defined 259
    levels of 259–260
    See also specific topics
psychic structure. *See* structure
psychic units 224–225
psychoanalysis
    as art 66
    as belief system/religion 66, 76
    as science 66, 356–357, 411
    See also specific topics
Psychoanalytic Studies of the Personality (Fairbairn) xxv, 14, 28, 209, 282, 312–313
    Ernest Jones's introduction to 5
    Winnicott and Khan's review of 277–278, 296, 303, 330, 356, 439
    See also Object Relations Theory of Personality
"Psychoanalytic Theories of Melanie Klein and Donald Winnicott and their Interaction in the British Psychoanalytic Society, The" (Padel) 302–303
psychoanalytic treatment, aims of 18, 76, 78, 81, 245, 279, 320, 337, 340
    "On the Nature and Aims of Psycho-analytical Treatment" (Fairbairn) 90, 92, 243, 251–252, 268, 292, 304, 393
psychological growth 141–144
psychopathology, defined 350

psychoses 108–109, 381
"Psychotherapy and the Clergy" (Fairbairn) 46
Putnam, F. W. 49, 491–492

quasi-independence 419, 487–488

Racker, H. 102, 254
Raines, James C. 491
Ralphe, D. 486
Rank, Otto
    The Development of Psychoanalysis 335–336
    "Genesis of the Object Relation" 335
Rapaport, David 110
reactive tendencies and drives 17
Read, Herbert 445, 448–453
reality, external 105
redemption, theme of 81–82
    and the new good object 81
regressed libidinal ego (RLE) 21, 315–317
    as a tomb 318–319
    as a womb 317–318, 320
    case material 317–319
    creation of safe, symbolic womb for
        emergence of 320
    Guntrip on 21, 315–319
regression
    and the regressed libidinal ego 315–317
    Guntrip and 315–320
    in service of ego 450
    schizoid processes and 315
    therapeutic relationship and 319–320
Rehberger, Rainer 150, 467–468
rejecting object 15, 74, 405, 413
    relationship between anti-libidinal object and
        406–408
    tie between internal saboteur and 15–16,
        135–139, 152, 266, 400
rejection 132
relatedness
    as inborn 78–79
    See also object-relatedness
relation/structure model, shift from drive/
    structure model to 358
relational model 344–345, 348, 356, 431, 439, 498
relational project, radical 347, 362
relational work 198–200

religion 64–65. *See also* Christianity
religious evidences in the life of Fairbairn
    a viable faith in professional writings 76–77
    Christian observance
        Braids Schoolboys' Meetings 73–74
        lifelong church attendance 74
    formative experiences 74–76
religious influences in the life of Fairbairn
    British cultural influences 69–70
    educational influences 70–71
        divinity school/theological studies 71
    family influences 70
    professional influences 71–73
religious themes in the work of Fairbairn 69, 82–83
    Christian narrative 77–78
    creation 78–79
    fall (from grace) 79–81
    redemption and the new good object 81–82
    Scottish Presbyterianism 78
reparation
    Klein on 282, 341, 450–451, 453–455
    See also restitution
repetition compulsion 198–200, 284, 334
repetition, transference as 351
repressed unconscious 286
repression 186, 288
    and the creation of endopsychic structure 186,
        379, 387
    and the endopsychic situation 224, 367
    Fairbairn's object relations theory, splitting,
        and 365–367
    vs. dissociation 218
"Repression and the Return of Bad Objects
    (with Special Reference to 'War Neuroses')"
    (Fairbairn) 15, 77, 79, 288
Reshaping the Psychoanalytic Domain (Hughes)
    296–297
resistance, ultimate source of 315
Resnicoff, Benjamín 102
restitution 110–111, 447–454, 456–457. *See also*
    reparation
return of bad objects 188, 284. *See also* "Repression
    and the Return of Bad Objects (with Special
    Reference to 'War Neuroses')"
return of the dissociated 49–50
Reuther, E. T. 486

reverie 265, 270
Rey, Ricardo Juan 391
Rickman, John 337
Ricoeur, Paul 83
Ricón, Lía 102
Riley, D. 27
Rinsley, Donald B. 22, 144n2, 153, 188, 191, 298, 309, 365, 438
ritual cult abuse 203–205
Rizzolatti, G. 263–264
Robbins, M. 191, 313
Robertson Smith, William 45
Robinson, P. 87
Rodríguez-Sutil, Carlos 193
Rolnik, E. J. 54
Romano, Esther 102
romantic and classical traditions and Guntrip's romantic emphasis 310–311, 313, 320–321
Rorty, A. O. 418–419
Rosenfeld, Herbert 121, 426–428
Ross, D. R. 50, 212
Rubens, R. L. 79–80, 211, 301, 304, 437–438
Rudnytsky, P. L. 355–357
Rupprecht-Schampera, U. 190
Rymer, R. 492

saboteur, internal. *See* anti-libidinal ego
Saltzman, W. R. 492
Sandler, Anne-Marie 424
Sandler, Joseph 224, 424
"satisfying" *vs.* "gratifying" 278
Schacht, R. L. 9
Scharff, David E. xxiii, 3, 6, 12, 15, 16f, 19–22, 28, 31–32, 41, 50, 70, 72, 76, 79–81, 102, 121, 144n2, 175–176, 189, 194, 200, 205, 209–210, 237, 249, 267–268, 270, 340, 346, 358–359, 365, 368–369, 379, 387, 432, 448, 487
    on chaos theory 428
    on Fairbairn's link to Hegel 27
    on Ferenczi 335–336
    on internalisation of objects 398
    on trauma and dissociation 489
    See also specific topics
Scharff, Jill Savege 3, 21–22, 41, 72, 121, 144n2, 155, 175, 267–268, 270, 297, 365, 368–369, 379, 398, 487, 489

Schilder, P. F. 233
schizoid conditions 80–81, 102, 133, 230, 388
    symptoms 225–226
    See also emptiness pathology
schizoid conflict 108–110
    defined 107
    See also emptiness pathology
schizoid disorders and pathology 132–133, 191–192
"Schizoid Factors in the Personality" (Fairbairn) 14, 80, 89, 132, 237, 291
schizoid fortress 230
schizoid pathology in borderline patients 103, 111, 187, 191, 193, 225–226, 229–232
schizoid personality, Fairbairn on 55
schizoid phenomena, Guntrip on 312–315, 321
schizoid position 213, 303
    and the developmental stages 187–188
    endopsychic structure and 190–191
    universality of 192
    See also paranoid-schizoid position
schizoid retreat *vs.* paranoia 153
schizoid states 186–187, 189–191, 193, 290, 324
    characteristics 313–315
    Guntrip on 313–315
    Winnicott on 230, 246–247, 326–327
    See also paranoid-schizoid position
schizoid structure 238
schizophrenia 50
Schnell, A. 433
Schnitzler, Arthur xxxi
Schopenhauer, Arthur 11
Schore, Allan N. 21
Schreber, Daniel Paul 91, 292
Schuder, Michelle R. 212–213
Schull, Bernardo 102
Schwartz, Joseph 27, 407, 413–414
science 161
    creativity and 394
    Fairbairn and the philosophy of 11–12
    Fairbairn's accomplishment as good 411–414
    psychoanalysis as 66, 356–357, 411
Scott, D. 368
Segal, Hanna 425, 453
self 425
    definitions 368, 425

ego and 21, 144n3, 425
    multiple configurations of 359–360
    Sutherland on 368–369
    See also central ego; false *vs.* true self
self-analysis 382–383
self-consciousness 10, 457
self psychology 313. *See also* Kohut, Heinz
self-sufficiency, Guntrip on 314
sentiment formation 13
separation-abandonment anxieties 104
Setton, Lea S. de 365
sex, conscience, and homosexuality 60, 87–88, 98
    and Fairbairn's self-analysis and personal life 92–98
    theory 88–92
sexual abuse 109, 219
    and dissociation *vs.* repression 218
    Ferenczi on 334, 339
    See also ritual cult abuse
"Sexual Delinquency" (Fairbairn) 88
sexual deviants, Fairbairn on 36, 88
sexual intimacy 122
sexual trauma, childhood 367–368
sexuality 60, 122, 158
    role of permission in the development of 170–171
Shakespeare, William 166, 295, 427–428
Sharpin de Basili, Isabel 103–104, 106–107, 187–188, 223–231
Shengold, Leonard 489
Shortt, J. G. 80
Sidebotham, P. 483–484
Silk, K. R. 487, 491
Silver, L. B. 488
sin 117, 203, 457, 487
    bondage to 79–81
    original 147
    salvation from 46, 76
    See also fall (from grace)
Sinason, Valerie 198, 200, 203, 206
Singer, M. 226, 232
Singer, P. 9
Skiveness, M. 484, 491
Skolnick, Neil J. 79, 102, 249
Smith, Roger 44

social objects 270, 445, 478–481
    in action 479
social work. *See* child welfare, social work, and Fairbairn's object relations theory
Socratic paradox 418
solipsism
    Cartesian 432–433, 435
    implicit in Freud and Klein's theories 436
    infantile 31–32
    Merleau-Ponty and 435
solipsistic isolation 431, 433, 439
Solomon, J. 266
Sophocles 28, 38
Soviet leadership cult 33
Spezzano, Charles 355
Spiegel, R. 54
Spillius, E. B. 20
spiral
    dialectic 382
    therapeutic process as 388
spiritual abuse 203–204
Spitz, René A. 226
split-off, dissociated states 359–360
    treatment 359–360
splitting 327
    Fairbairn's object relations theory, repression, and 365–367
    Freud on 50, 134
    John Padel on 298–301, 303–305, 338
    Klein on 281, 297, 303
    sexual abuse, dissociation, and 218–219
    Stephen Mitchell on 31, 399
    wholes and splits 10–12
    See also paranoid-schizoid position; pre-ambivalent phase
Splitting and Projective Identification (Grotstein) 22
splitting defence, prelude to Fairbairn's discovery of 398–399
splitting units 224–225
Stadter, Michael 316–317
Steele, K. 206
Steiner, George 352
Steiner, John 121
Steiner, R. 6, 127, 210, 323
Stent, G. S. 412
Stern, Daniel N. 9, 19, 420

Stewart, L. M. 486
Stierlin, Helm 287
Stolorow, Robert D. 249
Stout, G. F. 9
Strachey, James 105, 230
Strange Situation 266
Stranger, The (Camus) 461
    psychoanalytic interpretation 463–470
Strenger, C. 310–311
structural model
    Fairbairn's xxviii, 286–287, 399–402
        problems with 401–402
        revising 397–408
    Freud's 12–14, 61, 131, 420–422, 425, 436
    shift from drive/structure to relation/ structure model 358
    See also partitive conceptions of mind
structure 61, 253. *See also* dynamic structure; endopsychic structure
sublimation 455
suicidality 206
Sullivan, Harry Stack 352
superego 134, 285
superego defence. *See* moral defence
superego formation, Klein on Oedipus complex and 148, 288
superego functioning 13, 117
superiority, sense of 314
Sutherland, John D. ("Jock") xxiii, 5–7, 14, 18, 21, 71, 102, 106, 132, 144n2, 240, 269, 277–278, 286, 297, 303, 315, 365, 371–372, 436, 438, 448, 454, 456, 483
    The Autonomous Self 21, 297–298
    child abuse and 15, 369
    Fairbairn's Journey into the Interior 4, 21, 42, 89, 92, 304
    Henry Dicks obituary 177
    John Padel on 297, 303–304
    on affect 118
    on autonomous self 369, 498
    on Christian faith 70, 72, 75
    on conceptual model of psychoanalysis 277
    on Ernest Connell 72
    on Fairbairn's Christian faith 74
    on Fairbairn's influence on Kohut 22, 108, 304
    on Fairbairn's self-analysis, personal life, and sexuality 92–95
    on self, society, and trauma 368–369, 372–376
    on war neuroses 339
    relationship with Fairbairn 20–21, 106
Suttie, Ian D. 29–31, 41–42, 45, 55–56, 61–62, 72, 186, 258
Suttie, Jane I. (Robertson) 41, 72
Svendin, C. G. 491
Symington, Neville 144n2, 191

Tansey, M. J. 249
Target, Mary 103, 266
Taylor, N. 492
Thalberg, I. 419
theology 64, 71. *See also* religion
therapeutic process
    Fairbairn on 81, 155
    moments of the 388
    third 383
        intersubjective 253–254
Thomä, H. 106
Tomkins, Silvan S. 118, 264
topographical model 211, 212f, 420
totalitarianism 33–35
transference 326, 334
    Fairbairnian approach to 155, 157–158, 351
transference focused psychotherapy (TFP) 116
transitional defences 189
transitional objects and transitional phenomena 105, 232, 246, 286
    from Fairbairn's transitional object to Winnicott's transitional space extended to the realm of culture 327
    Winnicott on 105, 232, 246, 281, 286, 300, 327, 338, 368
transitional phase 150, 171, 189, 327
transitional stage 104–105, 107–109, 170, 189, 210, 223, 228, 337–338, 413
transitional techniques 15, 188–191
trauma 211–213, 218, 367, 486
    Charcot and 54
    childhood 367–368 (*see also* dissociative identity disorder (DID)/multiple personality disorder (MPD))

Ferenczi on dissociation and 55, 333–335, 340–341
in adults 370–371
object relations theory, splitting and repression 365–367
transgenerational transmission of 370–371
usefulness of Fairbairn and Sutherland's theory in work with survivors of 369–370
Trauma Symptom Checklist Children (TSCC) 491
Tremblay, C. 486
Trickett, P. K. 491
true self. *See* false *vs.* true self
Tsigounis, A. 155

unconscious
    repressed 286
    system 286–287
unconscious communication in analysis 270
"unconscious sub-egos" assertion 402–403
United Kingdom (UK) 484
United Nations Convention on the Rights of the Child 484–485
urinary inhibition/retention of Fairbairn 93–98

Van Buren, G. 78
van der Hart, Onno 49, 206
van der Horst, F. C. P. 27
van der Veer, R. 27
Varela, Y. 365
Ventura, Adrián 106
Vermorel, Henri 324
Videla, M. 380
Viljoen, M. 489
Visser, G. H. 163
vitalism and anti-vitalist pact 62–63, 66

Wadsby, M. 491
Waldfogel, J. 484
Wall, S. 266
Wallace, William 448
Wallerstein, Robert S. 50
war, prejudice, and object relations 479–480
war neuroses 7, 15, 30, 34–36, 90, 339, 368, 472. *See also* "Repression and the Return of Bad Objects (with Special Reference to 'War Neuroses')"

Waters, E. 266
Weiss, D. 489
Whitehead, Alfred North 451
Whiteside-Mansell, L. 492
Winnicott, Donald W. 30, 36–37, 186, 250, 255, 289
    contrasted with Fairbairn 37, 328–329, 423–424
    death 329
    debt to Fairbairn 246, 330
    Fairbairn as inspirer of 246, 324–325, 330
    from "object-seeking" in Fairbairn to "primary maternal preoccupation" in 325–326
    Guntrip's analysis with 298, 311–312, 329
    Klein and 296–297, 302–303, 330
    Masud Khan and 328
    metapsychology of Fairbairn and 328
    moral defence and 289
    object relations, drives, and 327–328
    on aggression 104, 287, 327–328
    on countertransference 6, 246–247, 328
    on creativity 30, 325–327, 330
    on dependence 37, 327
    on "direct communication" 247
    on dreams 237, 246–247
    on early frustrations and delinquency 326
    on false and true self 55, 188, 246, 286, 300, 315–316, 326
    on good and bad objects 249
    on good enough mother 251
    on holding environment 325
    on hypomanic reaction 226
    on mother–infant relationship 30, 163–164, 265, 316, 330, 481
    on primary maternal preoccupation 150
    on regression 315–316
    on schizoid states 230, 246–247, 326–327
    on self-object differentiation 326, 437, 439
    on transitional objects and transitional phenomena 105, 232, 246, 281, 286, 300, 327, 338, 368
    "Primitive Emotional Development" 303
    review of *Psychoanalytic Studies of the Personality* 277–278, 296, 303, 330, 356, 439
Wiseberg, Stanley 228
withdrawnness, Guntrip on 313
Wolfe, D. 486
Wolfe, V. 486

Wollheim, R. 425
Wollnik, S. 150
World Missionary Conference
    of 1910 74–75

Yañez, Y. T. 491
Yeomans, F. E. 116, 120

Yorke, Clifford 228
Young, M. 485

Zac de Goldstein, Raquel 102
Zahavi, D. 433
Zinner, J. 175
Zukerfeld, Ruben 343